FROM JERUSALEM
TO
IRIAN JAYA

WORLD CHRISTIAN SERIES*

*(Missionary Education Movement, Frontier Fellowship, Inc.
    1605 Elizabeth St., Pasadena, CA 91104,   213-797-1111)

FROM JERUSALEM

TO

IRIAN JAYA

A BIOGRAPHICAL
HISTORY OF
CHRISTIAN MISSIONS

RUTH A. TUCKER

Academie
Books Grand Rapids, Michigan
Zondervan Publishing House

From Jerusalem to Irian Jaya
Copyright © 1983 by The Zondervan Corporation
Grand Rapids, Michigan

Academie Books are published by Zondervan Publishing House,
1415 Lake Drive, S.E., Grand Rapids, Michigan 49506

Library of Congress Cataloging in Publication Data

Tucker, Ruth, 1945–
   From Jerusalem to Irian Jaya.

   Bibliography: p.
   Includes index.
    1. Missionaries—Biography.
    2. Missions—History.
    I. Title.

BV3700.T83   1983   266'.0092'2 [B]   83-6906
ISBN 0-310-45931-1

Edited by Mark Hunt

Designed by Stanley N. Gundry

Printed in the United States of America

84 85 86 87 88 — 10 9 8 7 6 5 4 3

For
Randy

CONTENTS

PART III: THE EXPANDING INVOLVEMENT

PART IV: THE CALL FOR SPECIALIZATION

MAPS AND CHARTS

MAPS

CHARTS

PICTURES AND CREDITS

PREFACE

How does one write a history of Christian missions—a history that entails tens of thousands of noteworthy professionals sent out by hundreds of mission societies to every country in the world over a period of some two thousand years? It is an enormous subject that has unfortunately been almost destroyed by historians who have attempted to squeeze too many dates, events, organizations, and names into one volume. But the history of missions is not a compilation of arid facts. It is a fascinating story of human struggles and emotions, intertwined with tragedy, adventure, romance, intrigue, and sorrow.

It was only through the tireless efforts of its missionaries that Christianity became the world's largest religion, a factor that has changed the face of the globe. "World Christianity," writes Lesslie Newbigin, "is the result of the great missionary expansion of the last two centuries. That expansion, whatever one's attitude to Christianity may be, is one of the most remarkable facts of human history. One of the oddities of current affairs ... is the way in which the event is so constantly ignored or undervalued."

But if the remarkable expansion of Christianity has been ignored and undervalued, so have the men and women who have been responsible for its expansion. They were single-minded men and women, wholly equal to the task they accomplished, driven by a sense of urgency that is rarely seen even within the most patriotic and militant of causes. "The early missionaries were born warriors and very great men," wrote Pearl Buck (who could hardly be termed a missionary enthusiast). "No weak or timid soul could sail the seas to foreign lands and defy death and danger unless he did carry religion as his banner, under which even death itself would be a glorious end. To go forth, to cry out, to warn, to save others, these were frightful urgencies upon the soul already saved. There was a very madness of necessity—an agony of salvation."

Who were these missionaries who sacrificed so much to carry the gospel to the ends of the earth? Were they spiritual giants who gloriously overcame the obstacles they confronted? No. They were ordinary individuals, plagued by human frailties and failures. Supersaints they were not. Like the colorful cast of biblical characters beginning with the Book of Genesis and continuing on through the New Testament, they were often marked by personality flaws and eccentricities. Yet, they were willing to be used by God despite their human weaknesses, and it was in that sense that they were able to make such an indelible imprint on the world.

When thinking of the great missionary force that spread out over the world during the past centuries, the names that generally come to mind first are those of great men—David Brainerd, William Carey, Adoniram Judson, David Livingstone, or Hudson Taylor. But women—single and married—constituted almost two thirds of the North American missionary force. Family life and children had a significant bearing on missionary work. "Family problems," writes Harold J. Westing, "are the number one cause on the missionary casualty list." Thus, a strong emphasis on family life is fully warranted in a historical account of Christian missions.

The most difficult challenge in developing a biographical history of the Christian missionary movement has been to limit the number of individuals to be dealt with. In the final analysis, the choice of the individuals covered and the issues and incidents in their lives that are emphasized is a subjective decision of the author. A number of great missionaries and mission societies have been left out; others with fewer credits to their names have been included. Hopefully, this account covers a representative and significant cross section of those who so valiantly served in the front lines of the Christian advance.

That biography should be the element that binds a history of Christian missions together is only fitting. Emerson once said there is "properly no history, only biography," an insight that is essentially true of any field of history. But biography is especially suitable for portraying the history of missions. The Christian missionary movement through the centuries has been perpetuated by missionary biography. In fact, writes Geoffrey Moorhouse, it "became the most fruitful ... stimuli" to the vocation during the nineteenth century. It is hoped, then, that this book will not only inform and instruct but also inspire readers to be willing to be used of God in this, the greatest cause in all human history.

ACKNOWLEDGMENTS

To all the people who have given me advice and encouragement over the course of my research and writing, I extend my heartfelt appreciation.

I am especially grateful for my denominational heritage, the Christian and Missionary Alliance, and for that little Green Grove Alliance Church in northern Wisconsin where a deep concern for foreign missions began developing from my earliest childhood.

Special thanks go to several individuals who have helped along the way. To Pastor David Lott, whose invitation to me to present the heritage of Christian missions in his church was the catalyst I needed to begin the book. To Stan Gundry, Executive Editor, Academic Books, at Zondervan, for his enthusiastic support for this project from the very beginning. To Hal Olsen, friend, colleague, and long-time missionary to Africa, for his continual input and advice. To Don Richardson and Olive Fleming Liefeld for personal interviews relating to their own missionary experience. To two very helpful librarians, Galen Wilson at the Billy Graham Center and Vonita Enneper at the Grand Rapids School of the Bible and Music. And to Ralph and Roberta Winter for their invaluable help and encouragement when it was most needed.

I also extend my gratitude to my students at Grand Rapids School of the Bible and Music and Trinity Evangelical Divinity School, who plodded their way through the manuscript in rough form, giving honest and forthright constructive criticism all along the way.

Most of all I thank my husband, Randy Tucker, for spending endless hours typing, editing, and indexing, and for his fervent support of missions in general and this project in particular.

PART I

THE IRRESISTIBLE ADVANCE

The Irresistible Advance

The urgent meaning of the Great Commission that Jesus gave to his disciples was probably not well understood by many New Testament believers, nor was it as such even the primary impetus for the rapid church growth during the early centuries. Persecution scattered believers throughout the Mediterranean world and Christianity quickly took root, at first mainly where Gentile seekers had gotten a head start in synagogues. Gentiles were amazed and pleased by a gospel that did not require them to become Jews but spoke of a "heart set free." By the end of the first century the church was in this way established to some extent in Europe, Africa, and Asia. But by the middle of the fourth century the Christian movement, especially in the eastern part of the empire, had become so powerful that even the emperors had to bow to its presence. What this proves is that the New Testament statement of the Great Commission did not so much inspire missionary outreach as it described the automatic outreach of a vital dynamic faith. Jesus had said the gates of hell would not prevail against it, and neither could the power of Rome, with repeated periods of persecution, stem the tide of its irresistible advance.

While evangelism and church planting took priority in the New Testament church, theological issues soon came to the fore in the sudden freedom of the fourth century, and Christian leaders found themselves consumed not only with heretical influences from without, but also with doctrinal controversies from within. Theologians hammered out creeds, and church councils argued about everything from the deity of Christ to whether or not women had souls. But the true meaning of salvation and the need for spreading the gospel was virtually ignored.

The invasion of the barbarians and the subsequent fall of the Roman Empire, however, had put a temporary halt to such squabbling. Western Europe was in chaos, and it required the talent and ability of a man like Gregory the Great, bishop of Rome 590–

604, to stabilize the church and re-vitalize its missionary activity. He saw the necessity of political alliances, and he established a pattern of church-state cooperation that continued for centuries. He felt the church simply could not maintain its presence among hostile peoples without the military support of these temporal rulers.

Charlemagne (742–814), the great king of the Franks, ranks above all other kings as a military supporter of Christianity. No other ruler before or after gave as much stress to the copying and transmission of the Bible. Charlemagne brought nominal Christianity to vast portions of Europe and was the prime mover in the Carolingian Renaissance that fostered learning and a wide variety of Christian activity.

While the Christian movement, in alliance with such leaders, seemed to be making headway with the barbarians in middle Europe, it was rapidly losing ground to the mighty force of Islam as that newer religion spread out from east to west through Palestine, across Africa, and on into Spain. The Muslims were stopped by military might at the Battle of Tours in 732, and in these centuries force was seen by most leaders as the only viable response to this all-encompassing threat. The Crusades (1095–1291), described by Ralph Winter as "the most massive, tragic misconstrual of Christian mission in all history,"[1] were launched to reclaim lost territories. They eventually failed in that effort, while at the same time diverting vast resources of Christendom from any true missionary endeavor.

This is not to suggest that there were no sincere missionary enterprises during the Middle Ages. Celtic and Arian missionaries conducted noteworthy evangelistic ventures, bringing vast numbers of barbarians into the church. In many cases, the Roman Catholic monks later played a significant role in the evangelism of the barbarians. The Benedictines were particularly influential through their founding of mission compounds in remote areas; but gradual accumulation of wealth eventually brought about their downfall, not only by diverting the monks' attention from spiritual matters, but also by making their monasteries prime targets for Viking raids.

The attacks of the Goths, the Visigoths, and the Vandals that brought down the Roman Empire were mild in comparison to the later raids by the Vikings. These seafaring warriors "were the scourge of England and the continent," according to Herbert Kane. "So devastating were their raids on the monasteries and churches that for a time they threatened to terminate the missionary outreach of the English Church."[2] "The Irish volcano which had poured forth a passionate fire of evangelism for three centuries," writes Winter, "cooled almost to extinction." The destruction of the monasteries, though, did not erase the gospel witness. "The phenomenal power of Christianity," as Winter points out, could not be destroyed: "the conquerors became conquered by the faith of the captives. Usually it was the monks sold as slaves or the Christian girls forced to be their wives and mistresses which eventually won these savages of the north."[3] Nevertheless, the Viking attacks were a devastating blow to the stability of both the Celtic and Roman traditions in the British

Isles and in central Europe.

The destruction of biblical manuscripts along with monasteries and churches had a negative effect on missions, but there were other factors that were no doubt an even greater deterrent to evangelism during the Middle Ages. Church leadership during much of the Medieval period was in a sad state of affairs. The power of the papacy had long invited abuses, and in the tenth century the decadence representing that office had reached an all-time low. Some of the popes were among the worst scoundrels in society. Pope Stephen IV (d. 772) brought his deceased predecessor to trial (propping his corpse up in a chair to face the synod), and he himself was thrown in prison, where, after serving less than a year, he was murdered at the orders of a Catholic opponent. Other popes openly committed immoral and criminal acts while in office. The Great Schism of the fourteenth and fifteenth centuries that resulted in two popes, and for a time three, did nothing to improve the image of the office or spirituality of the church leadership.

But if this political form of Christianity was too preoccupied with other matters to be concerned about missions, so was the academic tradition. The speculative and philosophically-oriented theology of the Middle Ages known as Scholasticism occupied the best minds of the church. Education turned away from practical pursuits and instead was concentrated on reconciling dogma with reason. "With intrepid confidence," writes Philip Schaff, "these busy thinkers ventured upon the loftiest speculations, raised and answered all sorts of doubts and ran every accepted dogma through a fiery ordeal to show its invulnerable nature. They were knights of theology.... Philosophy ... was their handmaid ... dialectics their sword and lance."[4]

On the positive side, there were at almost all points movements to purify the church. A number of efforts were aimed at reforming the papacy, some more successful than others, and there were significant monastic reforms—ones that usually resulted in a greater evangelistic outreach. The Cluny reform that began in 910 at the monastery of Cluny in central France was the beginning of a spiritual renewal in monasticism. It was followed by the inspirational ministry of Bernard of Clairvaux (1090–1153) and the founding of the Cistercians that brought an even greater resurgence of evangelistic activity in Europe. The greatest development in Roman Catholic religious orders, however, came with the rise of the friars—the preaching monks who in the late Medieval period had a profound effect on church missions. The Franciscans (founded 1209) and Dominicans (founded 1216) and later the Jesuits (founded 1534) planted churches and monasteries in Europe and all over the world.

For many Christians these reform efforts were not carried far enough, and throughout the Middle Ages there were movements to purify the body of Christ that were in direct opposition to the Roman Catholic Church. The Waldensians are a prime example. Though they were branded as heretics, they were much closer to New Testament Christianity than were most Roman Catholics. They laid great stress on evangelism, Bible study, and a personal commitment to Christ, and from the twelfth through the fifteenth centuries they made their presence known in central and eastern Europe. Beginning in the fourteenth century, the followers of Wycliffe and Hus instituted similar reforms, paving the way for the Protestant Reformation.

The sixteenth-century Reformation that brought new life to Christianity unfortunately contributed little to the evangelism of previously unreached peoples. The spiritual renewal in Europe brought a meaningful faith to large segments of the population, but the urgency to reach out to others was not seen as a top priority. The Protestants were kept busy just fighting for their own survival (and regrettably among themselves), and the Great Commission was all but forgotten.

The Protestant Reformation, as with all other reform movements throughout church history, had difficulty maintaining its spiritual vitality. The enthusiasm generated by Luther, Calvin, Melanchthon, and Zwingli in many instances did not lead past the dead formalism of the Roman tradition, and Protestant churches in many areas merely became renamed appendages of the state. But as had been the case in centuries past, no matter how low the established church sank, there were always those who sought a deeper spiritual meaning in life. The Anabaptist movement that spawned the Brethren and Mennonite churches brought warmth into the religious environment of Europe, and flowed into the even more important evangelical revival that affected the entire Western church during the seventeenth and eighteenth centuries. Pietism on the continent and the evangelical movements in Britain and America led to a revitalization of Christianity from which a passion for missions arose. Pietists and their Moravian successors fanned out all over the world, and Christians in Britain and America were moved to action by a spiritual concern for the native American Indians.

Such recommitment to missions was an encouraging sign. There was a new impulse to fulfill the Great Commission. The dawning of the Protestant modern missionary movement was in some ways at hand, but only after centuries of uncertainty. Though irresistible, it had been basically a slow and unsteady course—one of advance and retreat with little reason to believe that Christianity would ever gain prominence as the largest and most diverse world religion.

Chapter 1

The Early Centuries:
Evangelizing the Roman Empire

Christianity and missions. The two are inseparably linked. It is thought-provoking to speculate where Christianity might be today without the vibrant missionary outreach that sprang forth after Pentecost and continued for the next few centuries. Perhaps, as Zoroastrianism, it would be an obscure religion of the ancients, studied by scholars but known little beyond the borders of its homeland. But from its very inception Christianity was different from all other religions. The command to go forth with the good news was the very heart of the faith.

It was the post-Pentecost generation that turned the world upside down—spreading Christianity beyond the borders of Palestine as far west as Rome and into virtually every major urban center in the entire eastern empire. "What began as a Jewish sect in A.D. 30," writes J. Herbert Kane, "had grown into a world religion by A.D. 60."[1] Inspired by the leadership of such great Christians as Peter and Paul, and driven abroad by persecution (and the destruction of the temple

in Jerusalem in A.D. 70), many trained and lay evangelists spread out, bringing the message of Christ with them. "Every Christian," writes Stephen Neill, "was a witness," and "nothing is more notable than the anonymity of these early missionaries."[2] Their names cannot be found inscribed on the ledgers of missionary annals. Yet they were some of the most effective missionaries of all time.

Fortunately for these early missionaries, circumstances were almost ideal for spreading the faith. In comparison to later missionaries who would often face almost impossible odds, these early evangelists worked within a system that often paved the way for their ministry. There was great opportunity for mobility within the Roman Empire in the centuries following Christ. The amazingly well-structured Roman roads were an open invitation for people to move about, and the relative peace that prevailed made travel even more appealing. Moreover, unlike most missionaries of later centuries, the early evangelists were not forced to

25

endure years of grueling language study. Greek was the universal language of the empire, and Christians could communicate the gospel freely wherever they went.

Another factor paving the way for a public Christian witness was the availability of synagogues. The Book of Acts over and over again mentions the preaching that occurred in Jewish synagogues—public forums that allowed Christian ideas to be disseminated throughout the empire for more than a generation following the death of Christ. Though persecution was an ever-present reality, there was room for public debate in Roman society. There was a spirit of openness to new ideas, and people were craving for something more than the impersonal and impotent mythical religion of the pagan gods.

Christianity penetrated the Roman world through five main avenues: the preaching and teaching of evangelists, the personal witness of believers, acts of kindness and charity, the faith shown in persecution and death, and the intellectual reasoning of the early apologists.

From contemporary accounts, the Christians of the early centuries were very eager to share their faith with others. When the synagogues closed their doors to them, teaching and preaching was done in private homes, usually by itinerant lay ministers. Eusebius of Caesarea, the early church historian, tells of the dedication of some of these traveling evangelists in the early second century:

At that time many Christians felt their souls inspired by the holy word with a passionate desire for perfection. Their first action, in obedience to the instructions of the Saviour, was to sell their goods and to distribute them to the poor. Then, leaving their homes, they set out to fulfill the work of an evangelist, making it their ambition to preach the word of the faith to those who as yet had heard nothing of it, and to commit to them the book of the divine Gospels. They were content simply to lay the foundations of the faith among these foreign peoples: they then appointed other pastors, and committed to them the responsibility for building up those whom they had merely brought to the faith. Then they passed on to other countries and nations with the grace and help of God.[3]

RUSSIA

Andrew

Bartholomew

PERSIA

John

Phrygia

Peter

Rome

Ephesus

Philip

Simon the Zealot

Thomas

SPAIN

Matthew

INDIA

Jerusalem

James the Greater

Mark

EGYPT

James the Just

0   500 mi
0   500   1000 km

MISSIONARY TRADITION OF THE APOSTLES

Perhaps even more significant than the evangelism conducted by the traveling lay preachers was the informal testimony that went out through the everyday lives of the believers. "In that age every Christian was a missionary," wrote John Foxe in his classic *Book of Martyrs.* "The soldier tried to win recruits for the heavenly host; the prisoner sought to bring his jailer to Christ; the slave girl whispered the gospel in the ears of her mistress; the young wife begged her husband to be baptized that their souls might not be parted after death; every one who had experienced the joys of believing tried to bring others to the faith."[4] Even the Christians' harshest critics recognized their fervent evangelistic zeal. One of them was Celsus, from whose pen came some of the most virulent diatribes against Christianity during this period. His description of Christians, though not wholly accurate, is telling: "their aim is to convince only worthless and contemptible people, idiots, slaves, poor women, and children. They behave like mountebanks and beggars; they would not dare to address an audience of intelligent men . . . but if they see a group of young people or slaves or rough folk, there they push themselves in and seek to win the admiration of the crowd. It is the same in private houses. We see wool-carders, cobblers, washermen, people of the utmost ignorance and lack of education."[5]

As important as such witnessing was, the nonverbal testimony of Christian charity may have had an even greater impact for evangelism. Christians were known by their love and concern for others, and again some of the most telling evidence of this comes not from the mouths of Christians themselves but from the critics of Christianity. Emperor Julian, a Hellenist, was concerned that members of his own religion not be outshone by Christians whom he referred to as "atheists": "Atheism has been specially advanced through the loving service rendered to strangers, and through their care for the burial of the dead. It is a scandal that there is not a single Jew who is a beggar, and that the godless Galileans care not only for their own poor but for ours as well; while those who belong to us look in vain for the help that we should render them."[6]

The testimony that the early Christians displayed in life was also visibly evident in death. Until the fourth century, when Emperor Constantine publicly professed Christianity, persecution was a real threat for believers who openly confessed their faith. Though the total number of martyrs was not as great as some historians have claimed, and though outbreaks of persecution occurred only sporadically and even then were generally local in nature, no Christian could ever feel entirely safe from official retribution. Beginning with the stoning of Stephen, they faced the grim reality that such might also be their fate—a sobering thought that excluded nominal Christians from their numbers. The fire of persecution purified the church, and the courage displayed by the innocent victims was a spectacle unbelievers could not fail to notice. There are many "well-authenticated cases of conversion of pagans," writes Neill, "in the very moment of witnessing the condemnation and death of Christians,"[7] a factor that supports the contention of the second-century apologist, Tertullian, that "the blood of the martyrs is the seed of the church."

While persecution and martyrdom drew many unbelievers to Christianity through their emotions, the reasoned and well-developed arguments of the early apologists won still others through their intellects. Christianity, unlike so many of the other religions of the Roman world, was not born out of myths and magic. It was based on reality and historic fact, and many of the early Christians, beginning with the apostle Paul in Athens, realized that this factor alone could be a drawing card in witnessing to the learned pagan philosophers. These defenders of the faith, including Origen, Tertullian, and Justin Martyr, had a powerful influence in making Christianity more reasonable to the intelligencia, a number of whom were converted.

But the vibrant evangelism that was conducted during the first two centuries of the church began to wane in the early fourth century during the reign of Emperor Constantine. Christianity became a state religion, and as a result the churches were flooded with nominal Christians who had less concern for spiritual matters than for political and social prestige. Christianity became the fashion. Elaborate structures replaced the simple house-churches, and creeds replaced the spontaneous testimonies and prayers. The need for aggressive evangelism seemed superfluous—at least within the civilized Roman world.

On the outskirts of the empire, untamed barbarians threatened the very stability of the Roman state. The prospect of converting them to Christianity became a much sought-after goal of government officials who strongly supported the work of aggressive evangelists such as Martin, Bishop of Tours. He was a fourth-century soldier who entered a monastery and went out from there spreading the gospel throughout the French countryside. Some of the earliest and most effective "foreign" missionaries, though, were not aligned in any way with the state or the church at Rome. Ulfilas (an Arian) and Patrick and Columba (both Celtics) had no direct ties with the Roman church or state (though their evangelistic efforts made certain areas of Europe more amenable to the Roman system). Their primary objective was evangelism, accompanied by spiritual growth—an objective that would often become secondary during the succeeding centuries.

Paul the Apostle

The starting point of Christian missions is, of course, the New Testament church. The frightened and doubting disciples who had fled during their master's anguishing hours on the cross were empowered with the Holy Spirit on the Day of Pentecost, and the Christian missionary movement was born. The most detailed and accurate record of this new missionary outreach is contained in the Book of Acts, where the apostle Paul stands out above all others, while Peter, Barnabas, Silas, John Mark, Philip, Apollos, and others also play an important role. Apart from Scripture, little is known of these first generation Christians, except for accounts that have been passed along through tradition, some of which declared that Jesus' own disciples carried the gospel abroad. Matthew is said to have gone to Ethiopia, Andrew to Scythia, Bartholomew to Arabia and India, and Thomas also to India.

The most plausible of these early

traditions seems to be the one surrounding the apostle Thomas. As the story goes, Thomas disregarded the Lord's call for him to take the gospel to the East—a defiance that resulted in his being carried off as a slave to India, where he was placed in charge of building a palace for King Gundaphorus. The tradition continues that while under the king's service Thomas spent his time spreading the gospel rather than building the palace—an offense that quickly brought him a prison term. In the end Thomas had the opportunity to share his faith with the king, who then became a believer himself and was baptized. Though many of the details of the story seem fanciful, the basic outline may have an element of truth. A group of "Thomas Christians" in southwest India still worships in an ancient church said to be founded by Thomas, and archaeological digs have now established that there actually was a King Gundobar who reigned in India during the first century.

The apostle Paul unquestionably ranks as the greatest missionary of the early church. He, in the words of Kenneth Scott Latourette, "has been at once the prototype, the model, and the inspiration of thousands of successors."[8] He is viewed by many as the greatest missionary of all times—a man who conducted an extraordinary ministry of establishing Christianity on a grassroots level that insured its growth and stability in the centuries that followed. From a strictly human standpoint, however, Paul is a less awesome figure than some adulatory devotees would have him be. In many ways he was a very ordinary man facing ordinary problems that have confronted missionaries ever since.

The biblical record of Paul's life and ministry are well known. Born into a Jewish family in Tarsus, he grew up a strict Pharisee, violently opposed to the latest threat menacing Judaism, namely, the new "cult" of Jesus. He witnessed the martyrdom of Stephen and was empowered by the high priest to arrest other such heretics. He was on his way to Damascus to carry out this very commission when he was suddenly and miraculously converted. From this point on he became first-century Christianity's most energetic evangelist. His missionary journeys took him to cities throughout the Mediterranean world, where he effectively established indigenous churches.

Paul's extraordinary accomplishments in the field of missions have prompted a number of missiologists to argue that his methods should be closely, if not precisely, emulated today. Roland Allen in his book *Missionary Methods: St. Paul's or Ours?*, makes a strong case for this—if for no other reason than the fact that Paul's methods worked:

> In little more than ten years St. Paul established the Church in four provinces of the Empire, Galatia, Macedonia, Achaia and Asia. Before A.D. 47 there were no Churches in these provinces; in A.D. 57 St. Paul could speak as if his work there was done.... This is truly an astonishing fact. That Churches should be founded so rapidly, so securely, seems to us today, accustomed to the difficulties, the uncertainties, the failures, the disastrous relapses of our own missionary work, almost incredible. Many missionaries in later days have received a larger number of converts than St. Paul; many have preached over a wider area than he; but none have so established Churches. We have long forgotten

PAUL'S MISSIONARY JOURNEYS

that such things could be. ... To-day if a man ventures to suggest that there may be something in the methods by which St. Paul attained such wonderful results worthy of our careful attention, and perhaps of our imitation, he is in danger of being accused of revolutionary tendencies.[9]

Allen points out that Paul, unlike so many missionaries since his day, concentrated his work in strategic population centers—centers of trade and political influence from which the gospel would quickly be carried to outlying areas. Moreover, he reached people from all levels of society, providing the church with a broad base. And above all, he established independent churches, not mission stations. He "did not gather congregations, he planted churches,"

avoiding an "elaborate" and "foreign system of church organization."[10] In other areas as well, missiologists have seen Paul's methods as particularly applicable for today. J. Christy Wilson, in his book *Today's Tentmakers*, argues that missionaries should consider the advantages of going abroad with secular careers, supporting themselves while conducting evangelism and establishing churches even as Paul did.

Besides looking to Paul for methodology, modern day missionaries can derive inspiration from the trials he endured and can gain insight through his reaction to some perplexing missiological problems. Besides imprisonments and floggings, Paul endured almost every type of persecution and hardship that has ever been meted out. ("Three times I was beaten with rods, once I was stoned, three times I was shipwrecked, I spent a night and a day in the open sea, I have been constantly on the move. I have been in danger from rivers, in danger from bandits, in danger from my own countrymen, in danger from Gentiles, in danger in the city, in danger in the country, in danger at sea; and in danger from false brothers. I have labored and toiled and have often gone without sleep; I have known hunger and thirst and have often gone without food; I have been cold and naked. Besides everything else, I face daily the pressure of my concern for all the churches"; 2 Cor. 11:25–28). If that was not enough, Paul also suffered rejection, not only by the disciples who accepted him only after Barnabas came to his defense, but also by the Jewish leaders with whom he had once been associated. And surely he must have endured loneliness without the intimate ties of a wife and family.

Likewise, Paul confronted interpersonal conflicts, as in the dispute with Barnabas over the worthiness of John Mark as a missionary companion. The sharp disagreement that ensued resulted in a split between Paul and Barnabas, while at the same time launching an additional missionary team; Barnabas went out with his nephew John Mark, and Paul went with Silas. Dealing with cultural and religious traditions also posed dilemmas for Paul. Eating meat offered to idols, the advisability of circumcision, and the proper day for worship were among the knotty issues he faced forthrightly, and in doing so he established a precedent of liberty rather than law that would be applied for all future generations.

It is difficult to overemphasize the significance of the apostle Paul in laying a pattern for effectively reaching the lost, and to a degree the successes or failures of missionary work since can be attributed in part to the adherence to or deviation from his own personal example and the general guidelines that he set forth.

Like so many of the courageous Christian evangelists who followed him, Paul met a violent end. According to tradition, he was martyred along with Peter and many other Christians during the odious persecution under Emperor Nero in A.D. 64. Even in the example he set in death, Paul inspired future generations to count not their lives dear unto themselves, for if they suffered they would also reign with Christ.

Polycarp

The unbending faith of the Christians during the first centuries of the church stood out as a shining example to the pagan world. How could anyone stand unflinching in the face of death, and claim the crucified Jesus to be God, if it was all a myth or forgery? Such absolute trust in an unseen God was a phenomenon never seen before. What was the source of such courage? Many people began their journey of faith asking those very questions.

One of the first widely publicized martyrs in the years following the New Testament period was Polycarp, the much loved bishop of Smyrna. "He was a venerable figure," writes F. F. Bruce, "forming the last link with those who had seen Christ in the flesh, for he had sat at the feet of John, the beloved disciple."[11] How or when he became a Christian is unknown, but by the early second century he had a thriving ministry in Smyrna. "Slaves, local aristocrats and . . . members of the Proconsul's staff," according to W. H. C. Frend, were counted among his "tightly knit and well-organized" congregation.[12]

So forceful was his ministry against paganism that he was denounced throughout all Asia Minor as the "atheist"—"the teacher of Asia, the destroyer of our gods."[13] In the eyes of the pagans he was glorifying a dead man, and his stirring sermons on the teachings and miracles of Jesus, of which he had been told firsthand by John, were particularly upsetting. His writings, too, were a source of irritation. The only extant document written by him is a letter to the Philippian church, a letter that shows christology as the pivotal point of his message. "Of Christ it speaks in high terms as the Lord, who sits at the right hand of God to whom everything in heaven and earth is subject."[14]

For some fifty years Polycarp wielded powerful influence in his position as bishop. Yet, in the words of Elliott Wright, "he was the gentlest . . . of men . . . a case study in humility."[15] He was not of the apostolic age, and despite his relationship with John he never equated himself with the apostles, as is evident in his own epistle: "I write these things, brethren, not in arrogance, but because ye have requested me. For neither I, nor any other like me, can attain the wisdom of the blessed and glorious Paul, who was among you . . . and firmly taught the word of truth."[16]

It was in A.D. 156 that anti-Christian persecution broke out in the province of Asia. A letter from the Smyrnaean church bears the record. Civil au-

thorities, for reasons not fully clear, decided to kill a few Christians. Polycarp was immediately feared to be a likely target, so local believers insisted that he take refuge in a secluded area. His period of hiding was short-lived. After torturing a servant, the soldiers learned his whereabouts and found him hiding in a hayloft.

But execution, it was learned, was not what the authorities wanted. After all, Polycarp was eighty-six, and what could be gained by putting him to death? What they really wanted was a denial of his faith. What a victory that would be for paganism and what a blow to the "cult" of Jesus. "Why, what harm is there in saying, 'Caesar is Lord' and offering incense and saving yourself," the officials pleaded after they had taken him into custody. "Have respect for your age," the proconsul begged; "swear by the divinity of Caesar; repent and say, 'Away with the atheists.' . . . Take the oath, and I will let you go."[17]

What followed has been emotionally recorded by the early church historian Eusebius:

Polycarp being burned at the stake in Smyrna.

But Polycarp, with his face set, looked at all the crowd in the stadium and waved his hand towards them, sighed, looked up to heaven, and cried: "Away with the godless!" The governor pressed him further: "Swear, and I will set you free; execrate Christ." "For eighty-six years," replied Polycarp, "I have been his servant, and he has never done me wrong, how can I blaspheme my king who saved me?" "I have wild beasts," said the proconsul. . . . "If you make light of the beasts, I'll have you destroyed by fire. . . ." Polycarp answered: "The fire you threaten burns for a time and is soon extinguished; there is a fire you know nothing about—the fire of the judgement to come and of eternal punishment, the fire reserved for the ungodly. But why do you hesitate? Do what you want." . . . The proconsul was amazed, and sent the crier to stand in the middle of the arena and announce three times: "Polycarp has confessed that he is a Christian." . . . Then a shout went up from every throat that Polycarp must be burnt alive. . . . The rest followed in less time than it takes to describe: the crowds rushed to collect logs and faggots from workshops and public baths. . . . When the pyre was ready . . . Polycarp prayed. . . . When he had offered up the Amen and completed his prayer, the men in charge lit the fire, and a great flame shot up.[18]

Although the execution of Polycarp had been instigated and carried out by pagan officials, spurred on by anti-Christian mobs, the end result was a victory for the Christians. The believers in Smyrna were, of course, devastated by the loss of their dear pastor, but many nonbelievers were also horrified by what happened. Polycarp's death ended the outbreak of persecution in Asia, paving the way for those not as courageous as he to openly declare their faith in Christ.

Perpetua

The cessation of persecution in Asia Minor following the death of Polycarp did not apply to the whole Roman Empire. Persecution continued elsewhere, and during the early years of the third century it became widespread and well coordinated, especially in North Africa where Perpetua and her slave girl Felicitas were executed. Before this period of intense persecution, however, there were isolated instances that were highly publicized—one in Rome just one decade following the death of Polycarp. This time it was Justin, who since his death has been referred to as Justin Martyr.

Schooled in the philosophy of Plato, Justin was converted to Christianity as a young man and soon became one of the faith's ablest defenders. He was a forceful writer who intelligently presented Christianity to his pagan readers and openly denounced the persecution of his fellow-believers. In Rome he gave instruction to believers and inquirers in private homes, and it was this crime, apparently more than any other, that led to his martyrdom. After a trial, the death sentence was pronounced by the judge, and Justin, along with five other men and one woman, was beheaded.

It was under the rule of Emperor Septimus Severus some decades later that the first widespread intense persecution of Christians occurred. In 202 he issued an edict that forbade conversion to either Christianity or Judaism. The emperor himself worshiped Serapis, an Egyptian god of the dead, and he feared Christianity was a threat to his own religion. Although the edict was aimed mainly at prospective converts, its consequences were felt by new believers as well as mature leaders in the church.

It was in Carthage that the Emperor's persecution was most bitterly felt. Here in this great Roman city of North Africa, the growth of Christianity was alarming officials, and the emperor's edict extended to anyone "teaching or making converts."[19] Among the Christians of Carthage was Saturus, a deacon who conducted catechism classes for a group of converts. Vibia Perpetua, a twenty-two-year-old mother of an infant son and her personal slave, Felicitas (who was eight months pregnant), had joined the class and were among those affected by the Emperor's edict. Nothing is known of Perpetua's husband, but historians have speculated that either he was dead or he had abandoned her because of her new-found faith. The others condemned to die were Saturus, their teacher, and three other men.

Perpetua's own personal plight has been preserved in a third-century document, *The Passion of Perpetua and Felicitas*, believed to be based on diaries and records of Perpetua and Saturus. "Some part of the story may be legendary," notes Elliott Wright, "but compared with most hagiography of third-century martyrs the account is filled with convincing human touches."[20] In this account, Perpetua tells of the distress and humiliation her father, a respected nobleman, endured when he was informed that his only daughter had been arrested and imprisoned as a common criminal. He came immediately and pleaded with her to renounce this new faith about which she had been learning. When she refused, he became so incensed

that he threatened to beat her, but she remained unmoved.

Perpetua's stolid demeanor, however, was soon broken. What her adamant father could not accomplish, her helpless infant could. She was "racked with anxiety," almost to the breaking point, when two Christians managed to have her baby brought to the prison. "I nursed my baby, who was faint from hunger. In my anxiety I spoke to my mother about the child, I tried to comfort my brother, and I gave the child in their charge. I was in pain because I saw them suffering out of pity for me. These were the trials I had to endure for many days. Then I got permission for my baby to stay with me in prison. At once I recovered my health, relieved as I was of my worry and anxiety over the child."[21]

As the time of her execution approached, the family crisis became more acute. Her father came to the prison, and again he pleaded with her to put family considerations above her creed. "Do not cut us off entirely; for not one of us will ever hold up his head again if anything happens to you." But the stoical young woman would not bend: "This will be done on the scaffold which God has willed; for I know that we have not been placed in our own power but in God."[22] The next day when her father heard the news that she was to be thrown into the arena with wild beasts, he sought to rescue her. Though it was a heroic act of compassion, authorities ordered that the aged man be beaten. It was a pathetic sight. "I grieved for my father's plight," wrote Perpetua, "as if I had been struck myself."[23]

Once the so-called trial was over, the fate of the prisoners was sealed and the remaining days before the execution were spent in personal reflection, "more concerned about their worthiness, their loyalty to Christ," according to Wright, "than about the suffering ahead of them."[24] They met for prayer, shared their last meal—their agape love feast—and witnessed their faith to the crowd outside.

On the day of the execution the prisoners were brought to the arena, where, according to Roman custom, the men were taken first to be tortured for the entertainment of the crowd before their execution. Saturus stopped at the gate for one last word of testimony with Pudens, the prison governor, who later turned to Christ and became a martyr himself. The men then were sent into the arena with a bear, a leopard, and a wild boar. Saturus was so mangled and bloody after the ordeal that spectators ridiculed him, shouting, "He is well baptized!" Perpetua and Felicitas (who had given birth to her baby in prison) were stripped and sent into the arena to face a "mad heifer." The gory torture soon became too much for the crowd and the people began shouting, "Enough!"[25]

When this preliminary exhibition was ended, the young women were brought to the executioner, at which time Perpetua called out to some grieving Christian friends, "Give out the Word to the brothers and sisters; stand fast in the faith, love one another, and don't let our suffering become a stumbling block to you."[26] She was then taken to the gladiator to be beheaded. Whether due to hesitancy or lack of skill, his first blow was not sufficient. Perpetua cried out in pain, and took the gladiator's trembling hand and directed the sword to her throat and it was over.

After this wave of persecution, there followed fifty years of relative peace during which time the church grew steadily. Many people who themselves may have never been able to pass such a test of faith that Perpetua and her comrades endured were, nevertheless, attracted by their example to a faith that demonstrated such serenity and courage.

Ulfilas

Following the much-publicized conversion of Emperor Constantine in 312, the Roman Empire became nominally Christianized, and the vibrant testimony of the Christians seemed to decline. No longer did they suffer for their faith, for it was in vogue to be a Christian, and as a result there was a weakening in spiritual fervor. Martyrdom, resulting from official persecution, had become a terror of the past. The church and the state became closely allied, and Christianity was being used more and more as a means of fostering imperial expansion. Missionaries were viewed in a political light in the hope that their evangelistic efforts could bring outlying areas within the scope of Roman control. Ulfilas was one such missionary. Though he himself was motivated by his desire to spread the gospel, his mission was, in the eyes of Roman policy, well suited to territorial expansion.

Ulfilas was one of the greatest foreign missionaries of the early church. His ministry was to the Goths, a barbarian tribe outside the Roman Empire living in the area of present-day Romania. He was born in 311 and was raised in the pagan environment of the Goths. His mother is believed to

THE ROMAN EMPIRE

have been Gothic and his father a Cappadocian Christian who was taken captive by Gothic raiders. When he was in his early twenties, Ulfilas was sent to Constantinople for diplomatic service. Here he spent several years and came under the influence of Bishop Eusebius of Nicomedia, who taught him the Scriptures in Greek and Latin. Under Eusebius he served as a "reader," ministering possibly to Gothic soldiers in the Roman army.

Eusebius, like most Byzantine bishops of his day, was Arian, or at least semi-Arian, and this heretical teaching was passed on to Ulfilas. Arius, a contemporary of Ulfilas, was a popular and persuasive Christian preacher who is most remembered for his theological struggles relating to the divinity of Christ. From Scripture passages that speak of Christ as the "be-

gotten of the Father" and the "firstborn of all creation" he concluded that, though Christ was sinless and unchangeable and the Savior of mankind, he was essentially different from the Father and was therefore not God. Although this doctrine was overruled at the Council of Nicaea, many of the churchmen, particularly in the eastern portion of the empire, continued to hold the view—Ulfilas being one. But according to Latourette, "it was a mild form of Arianism, which he professed."[27]

At the age of thirty, after spending nearly ten years in Constantinople, Ulfilas was consecrated Bishop to the Goths—those living north of the Danube outside the borders of the empire. Apparently there were already Christians there or he would not have been sent as a bishop. Nevertheless, it was evangelism that was seen as his primary task. His ministry was to a people considered barbarians—"wild and undisciplined," a "rude and crude sort, with a relatively low standard of living, dwelling often in 'wagons' because they had no fixed abodes."[28] To such "simple people," Stephen Neill suggests, Arianism "may have presented itself as a rather attractive simplification, since it set them free from the knotty controversies about the nature and person of Christ, to follow him as a leader and to concentrate on the already sufficiently difficult task of learning to live a sober, righteous, and godly life."[29]

For forty years Ulfilas conducted evangelistic work among the Goths, a work that was highly successful, but one that was hampered by persecution. At one point in 348, opposition from the Gothic chieftain Athanaric (who believed Ulfilas's mission was an effort to bring the Goths under Roman domination) became so bloody and resulted in the death of so many Christians that Ulfilas, with the permission of the Arian emperor Constantius, moved his Gothic Christian community across the Danube into safer Roman territory. Later some of these Christians returned to their people to serve as missionaries themselves.

The most enduring labor of love that Ulfilas bestowed on the Goths was his translation of the Bible into their native tongue, an unwritten language for which he had to devise an alphabet. This was "probably the first or second instance," according to Latourette, "of what has since happened for hundreds of tongues—their reduction to writing by Christian missionaries and the translation into them by that medium of a part or all of the Scrip-

tures."[30] Ulfilas was scrupulously accurate in rendering an almost word for word translation from the Greek without losing the Gothic idiom, and the Goths and Vandals alike carried it with them as they moved from place to place in Europe.

Though Ulfilas's translation was a monumental contribution to missions of the early centuries, even this area of his ministry has come under fire. He purposely omitted the books of Samuel and Kings from his translation because, in the words of an early church historian, "they are merely an account of military exploits, and the Gothic tribes were particularly devoted to war. They were in more need of checks on their warlike natures than spurs to urge them on to acts of war."[31]

Ulfilas died at the age of seventy while on a mission to Constantinople for the Gothic king. The long-time military rivalry between the Goths and the Roman Empire continued after his death. There were devastating attacks by the Visigoths against the Empire, and the plunder continued for decades, climaxing on the night of August 24, 410, when Alaric and his army stormed Rome. But despite the military campaigns, the gospel continued to be preached to the Goths by Ulfilas's faithful successors. They accompanied the wandering Gothic tribesmen to the battlefield and wherever else their caravans took them, prompting a sarcastic comment from the anti-Arian Ambrose of Milan, "Those who had formerly used wagons for dwellings, now use a wagon for a church." But sarcasm aside, that "caustic comment," writes V. Raymond Edman, "becomes a compliment for the men of faith who, like Paul, were 'all things to all men, that they might by all means save some.' Their doctrine, perhaps, was defective; their hearts were not. They sought service, not security; comradeship in Christ, not a cathedral; discipleship, not domination."[32]

Patrick

Shrouded in legend and glorified by sainthood, Ireland's great fifth-century missionary is one of the most misrepresented figures in church history. Popular opinion notwithstanding, Patrick was neither a Roman Catholic nor an Irishman, and his promotion to sainthood was bestowed at the Council of Whitby (some two centuries after his death) as an incentive for bringing the Celtic church under Roman Catholic domination. Yet today his name has become almost synonymous with Irish Catholicism, and his true ministry has been obscured beyond recognition.

Patrick was born into a Christian family in the Roman province of Britain about A.D. 389. His father was a "deacon" and his grandfather was a priest in the Celtic church. It was during the period before Roman domination when most clergy were married. Little is known of Patrick's early childhood, but when he was in his midteens his town near the west coast of Britain was invaded by a band of Irish plunderers, and many of the young boys, including Patrick, were carried away to be sold as slaves. Patrick was sold to a farmer of Slemish, where for the next six years he herded swine.

Although he had been raised in a Christian home, Patrick himself did not have a personal faith in God. During his years of captivity he began reflecting on his spiritual condition, and his life changed: "The Lord opened the understanding of my unbelief, that, late as it was, I might remember my faults and turn to the Lord my God with all my heart; and He had regard to my low estate, and pitied my youth and ignorance, and kept guard over me even before I knew Him, and before I attained wisdom to distinguish good from evil; and He strengthened and comforted me as a father does his son."[33] From that time on, writes F. F. Bruce, "Patrick's life was marked by intense and persistent prayer, and from time to time he was conscious of an inner monition in which he recognized the divine response to his prayers. It was a monition of this kind at the end of his six years of servitude which incited him to escape from his master and make his way to the sea-coast, to a port where he would find a ship to take him away from Ireland. Sure enough he found the ship of which the inner voice had forewarned him...."[34]

As a free man, Patrick went to the island of St. Honorat off the coast of the French Riviera. Secluding himself at a monastery there for a time, he later returned to his home, where he was taken in by relatives who had survived the raid in which he had been captured. It was during this time back in Britain, Patrick relates in his *Confession*, that God called him "in the depth of the night." It was his Macedonian call: "I saw a man named Victoricus, coming as if from Ireland, with innumerable letters; and he gave me one of these, and ... while I was reading out the beginning of the letter, I thought that at that very moment I heard the voice of those who were beside the wood of Focluth, near the western sea; and this is what they called out: 'Please, holy boy, come and walk among us again.' Their cry pierced to my very heart, and I could read no more; and so I awoke."[35]

Patrick's mission to Ireland did not take place immediately after his call. He first went to study at the church of Auxerre in Gaul. But even after his period of study and his ordination as a deacon, his superiors were wary of his ability for such a mission, and Palladius was chosen to go instead. Palladius, however, died in less than a year after he arrived in Ireland, and that opened the way for Patrick. He was past the age of forty, but seemingly more eager than ever to fulfill his calling.

When Patrick arrived in Ireland in 432, there were isolated enclaves of Christians, but the vast majority of the people were still entrenched in paganism. They worshiped the sun, moon, wind, water, fire, and rocks, and believed in good and evil spirits of all kinds inhabiting the trees and hills. Magic and sacrifice—including human sacrifice—were part of the religious rites performed by the druids or priests.

It is not surprising that Patrick immediately encountered stiff opposition from the druids, but he accepted their social and political order, and eventually some of the powerful druid chieftains were converted to Christianity. It was not long before the druids as a class began to lose their power, but their magical beliefs endured through Patrick's apparent compromise with paganism. He sought to diminish their prestige, according to F. F. Bruce, "not by the power of the Christian message, but by proving himself to be a mightier druid than the pagan druids,"[36] a phenom-

ena modern missiologists recognize as "power encounter." This type of superstitious magic continued for centuries in Celtic Christianity.

Soon after he arrived in Ireland, Patrick secured an important victory when he convinced King Loigaire to grant religious toleration for Christians. Not long afterward the king's brother became a convert and granted Patrick land for a church in his domain. After establishing the church, Patrick moved on to new areas where the gospel had never been preached; and by 447, after fifteen years of preaching, much of Ireland had been evangelized. Though by this time Patrick was recognized all over Ireland as a great man of God, his popularity and prestige had not come easily. In his *Confession* he recounted the perilous life that he lived. Twelve times he faced life-threatening situations, including a harrowing kidnapping and a two-week captivity. Nevertheless, he continued on for more than thirty years, motivated by fear as much as anything else. "I fear to lose the labor which I began" lest God "would note me as guilty."[37]

Patrick's methods of evangelism in some ways were similar to those of so many missionaries before and after him. His first step in evangelizing a new area was to win the political leader in hopes that his subjects would fall in behind him, and he was not averse to lavishing gifts on these local rulers. Unlike so many of the Roman Catholic missionaries, however, Patrick and the Celtic missionaries who followed him placed great emphasis on spiritual growth. Converts were given intensive training in the Scriptures and encouraged to become involved in the ministry themselves. Women played a significant role in the Celtic churches, though as a single missionary Patrick was cautious in his relationship with them, "refusing the gifts of devout women lest any breath of scandel should arise."[38]

Patrick's tremendous success as a missionary evangelist was evident in the some two hundred churches he planted and the estimated one hundred thousand converts he baptized. Yet he was ever aware of his own shortcomings and credited God with all his accomplishments. What he lacked in his own strength, God graciously provided, and he concluded his *Confession* with that testimony: "But I pray those who believe and fear God, whosoever has deigned to scan or accept this document, composed in Ireland by Patrick the sinner, an unlearned man to be sure, that none should ever say that it was my ignorance that accomplished any small thing which I did or showed in accordance with God's will; but judge ye, and let it be most truly believed, that it was the gift of God. And this is my confession before I die."[39]

Columba

The evangelism of Ireland by Patrick and others resulted in one of the most extraordinary missionary accomplishments of the Middle Ages. It was a missionary venture conducted largely by the Celtic church as compared to the Western Roman church. "There was a passion for foreign missions in the impetuous eagerness of the Irish believers," writes Edman, "a zeal not common in their day. Burning with love for Christ, fearing no peril, shunning no hardship, they went everywhere with the Gospel."[40] But though they spread out all over central Europe and as far north as Iceland, it was Britain, the homeland of the first great missionary to Ireland, that became their first "foreign" field. Although the church there would later become enmeshed in the Roman Catholic system, it would be that land that centuries later would provide the impetus for the global evangelism of the nineteenth century.

Celtic missionary monks, according to E. H. Broadbent, conducted "a purer form of missionary work ... than that which went out from Rome."

Their method was to visit a country and, where it seemed suitable, found a missionary village. In the centre they built a simple wooden church, around which were clustered school-rooms and huts for the monks, who were the builders, preachers, and teachers. Outside this circle, as required, dwellings were built for the students and their families, who gradually gathered around them. The whole was enclosed by a wall, but the colony often spread beyond the original enclosure. Groups of twelve monks would go out, each under the leadership of an abbot, to open up fresh fields for the Gospel. Those who remained taught in the school, and, as soon as they had sufficiently learned the language of the people among whom they were, translated and wrote out portions of Scripture, and also hymns, which they taught to their scholars. They were free to marry or to remain single; many remained single so that they might have greater liberty for the work. When some converts were made, the missionaries chose from among them small groups of young men who had ability, trained them specially in some handicraft and in languages, and taught them the Bible and how to explain it to others, so that they might be able to work among their own people. They delayed baptism until those professing faith had received a certain amount of instruction and had given some proof of steadfastness. They avoided attacking the religions of the people, counting it more profitable to preach the truth to them than to expose their errors. They accepted the Holy Scriptures as the source of faith and life and preached justification by faith. They did not take part in politics or appeal to the State for aid. All this work, in its origin and progress, though it had developed some features alien to New Testament teaching and Apostolic example, was independent of Rome and different in important respects from the Roman Catholic system.[44]

One of the most famous of these Celtic abbot-missionaries was Columba, who was born into a noble Irish family in 521 and brought up in the Christian faith. As a young man he entered a monastery, where he was ordained a deacon and later a priest. His evangelistic zeal was evident early in his ministry, and he is credited with establishing many churches and monasteries in Ireland, including those famous ones at Derry, Durrow, and Kells.

Columba's switch from "home" missions to "foreign" missions at the age of forty-two was, according to his seventh-century biographer, motivated "for the love of Christ," but there were apparently other factors involved as well. His biographer concedes that he was excommunicated by the synod but claims that it was an unjust action over a trifling matter. Will Durant, however, contends that his excommunication and departure for Britain were motivated by more than a trifling matter: "he was a fighter as well as a saint, 'a man of powerful frame and mighty voice;' his hot temper drew him into many quarrels, at last into

war with King Diarmuid; a battle was fought in which, we are told, 5000 men were killed; Columba, though victorious, fled from Ireland (563), resolved to convert as many souls as had fallen in that engagement at Cooldrevna."[42]

Whatever Columba's reasons were for embarking on the foreign field, the fact remains that he went, and through his years of service he made a tremendous impact on Britain. With twelve clerics to serve under him, he established his headquarters just off the coast of Scotland on Iona, a small bleak, barren, foggy island battered year-around by the pounding waves of the sea. Here he established a monastery that fostered the routine monastic life of prayer, fasting, meditation, Bible study, and manual labor, but in addition and more importantly it provided training for evangelists who were then sent out to preach the gospel, build churches, and establish more monasteries.

Columba himself was active in missionary work, and from Iona he traveled many times into Scotland proper and is credited with having evangelized the Picts who lived in the Scottish highlands. Through his witness, King Brude, who reigned over the northern Picts, was converted. Brude initially refused to allow Columba to enter the gates of his city, but Columba stayed outside and prayed until the king relented. As with Patrick more than a century earlier, Columba faced fierce opposition from the druids, but like his predecessor he challenged them to match their trickery against the power of God. Columba's theology, according to Latourette, "was as much a religion of miracles as of ethics and even more than of formal creeds...."[43]

As important as Columba's missionary efforts were, many scholars today would disagree with his admiring seventh-century biographer that he and his trainees at Iona were alone responsible for the evangelism of England and Scotland. There were many other missionaries, from Ireland and elsewhere, doing evangelism in this area who were in no way associated with him. The issue of Columba's importance relates in part to the importance of Roman Catholic missionaries, and many later historians have attempted to give the missionaries commissioned by the Pope a greater share of the credit than they rightly deserve. There was strong competition between Roman Catholic and Celtic missionaries, the Catholics eventually gaining the upper hand, but the initial work of evangelizing much of Britain and central Europe was accomplished by the energetic and faithful Celtic monks.

SELECTED BIBLIOGRAPHY

Allen, Roland. Missionary Methods: St. Paul's or Ours? *Chicago: Moody, 1956.*

Bruce, F. F. The Spreading Flame: The Rise and Progress of Christianity From Its First Beginnings to the Conversion of the English. *Grand Rapids: Eerdmans, 1979.*

Frend, W. H. C. Martyrdom and Persecution in the Early Church. *Oxford: Blackwell, 1965.*

Chapter 2

Roman Missions:
Baptizing the Masses

From the beginning, Roman Catholic missions were closely tied to political and military exploits, and mass conversions were the major factor in church growth. Political leaders were sought out and through promises of military aid became nominal Christians, their subjects generally following suit. In some instances the need for military aid was mixed with a superstitious belief that the Christian God was a better ally in battle than a pagan god or gods. Such was the case with Clovis, the fifth-century king of the Franks. He married a Christian princess but refused to turn from his pagan deities until he was on the verge of military defeat. At that moment he allegedly made a vow that he would serve the Christian God if his army was victorious. On Christmas Day of 496, he celebrated his victory by being baptized along with three thousand troops. The reason for his conversion, according to Norman Cantor, "was simple: he saw that if he would accept the Catholic religion, he would be the only orthodox Germanic king in Gaul,"

and "as the Catholic champion he would find it easier to gain the allegiance of the Gallo-Romans as his conquests proceeded."[1]

This mass conversion of Clovis's army was the first of many during the Middle Ages, and it was this method, writes Bruce Shelley, "that converted Europe." The concept of individual conversion was "the method used by Protestant missions under the evangelical movements of the nineteenth century, with individual change of heart," but it was "mass conversion" that expanded the Roman Catholic Church during the Middle Ages.[2]

During this time, however, there were individuals who were truly concerned about Christian missions. Among them was Gregory the Great (540–604), one of the most able and influential Bishops of Rome during the whole medieval period. He was a missionary statesman of the first rank, and it was through his persistent prodding that the first official mission team with papal backing was commissioned. As a monk, Gregory had been deeply concerned about bringing the Christian message to the pagans beyond the immediate borders of the empire, but it was not until he was made Bishop of Rome that he was able to transform his concern into action. The story is told of how he was touched when he saw blonde British boys in the slave market and said, "They are Angles, let them become angels."[3] Whether that particular story is true or not, Gregory made missions to Britain a top priority, and in 596 he dispatched Augustine and a company of monks to take the gospel to that part of the world, though not without problems and delays. Although he was sincere and pious, Augustine was not the best candidate for such a leadership role. On the way to Britain, while traveling through Gaul, he turned back with his monks, claiming "that they should not be compelled to undertake so dangerous, toilsome and uncertain journey" through such a "barbarous, fierce and unbelieving nation." His fears were unfounded, and Gregory wrote back insisting they go on. They did, and Augustine and his monks were largely responsible for planting the Roman Catholic Church in England. The service they rendered, however, was diminished by their refusing to accommodate themselves to the Celtic missionaries who were there first.

As Augustine and his contingent of monks evangelized England and baptized thousands of converts, they faced knotty problems relating to pagan traditions. Could pagan ceremonies coexist with Christianity, and what should be done with pagan temples? It was in response to these issues that Gregory set forth important Roman Catholic missionary policy standards and established a pattern for centuries to follow:

> The heathen temples of these people need not be destroyed, only the idols which are to be found in them.... If the temples are well built, it is a good idea to detach them from the service of the devil, and to adapt them for the worship of the true God.... And since the people are accustomed, when they assemble for sacrifice, to kill many oxen in sacrifice to the devils, it seems reasonable to appoint a festival for the people by way of exchange. The people must learn to slay their cattle not in honour of the devil, but in honour of God and for their own food.... If we allow them these outward joys, they are more likely to find their way to the true inner joy.... It is doubtless impossible to cut off all abuses at once from rough hearts, just as a man who sets out to climb a high mountain does not advance by leaps and bounds, but goes upward step by step and pace by pace.[4]

There were other monks who served the missionary cause during the early Middle Ages, most notably Boniface, the Apostle to Germany, but it was not until later in the Medieval period that large numbers of Roman Catholic clerics were making missions their lifetime calling. This transpired through the energetic participation of monastic orders, the four most active being the Franciscans, the Dominicans, the Augustinians, and the Jesuits. Through these orders, Roman Catholicism gained a foothold on every continent and eventually came to dominate the religious scene in many parts of the world.

Although Roman Catholics dominated Christian missions during the Middle Ages, they were not the only missionaries of the period. Entirely separate from Roman Catholicism was the Eastern or Nestorian church that spread out across Asia with the gospel as it fled persecution. According to historian John Stewart, the Nestorian church was "the most missionary church the world has ever seen." From their early strongholds in Asia Minor, they fled into Persia and the Arabian Peninsula to avoid persecution from Roman officials and Catholic church leaders. But there they met fierce opposition from Zoroastrians and later from Muslims, so they continued to push further east into central Asia, India, Afghanistan, and Tibet, areas that became "centers of Christian activity." "They were men of great faith, mighty in Scripture, large portions of which they knew by heart." Some, in fact, committed the entire New Testament to memory. Schools were established to train the young, and monasteries, resembling modern day Bible institutes, thrust young adults into full-time evangelistic activity.[5]

From Central Asia the Nestorians moved further East, and by the ninth century had moved into China and from there to Korea, Japan, and Southeast Asia. Their influence continued to grow, and by the thirteenth century it is estimated that there were no less than twenty-seven metropolitan patriarchs and two hundred bishops under them in China and surrounding areas. But then this powerful missionary church rapidly began to decline. The peace-conscious Nestorians were no match for the militant Islamic fanatics, and even worse were the armies of Genghis Khan and other barbarians who devastated large portions of Asia, including major centers of Nestorian Christianity.

An era of Christian missions was over and forgotten. Because of the early doctrinal differences between the Nestorians and Western church leaders over the issue of the two natures of Christ, Nestorians were viewed as heretics by Roman Catholics, and their great evangelistic endeavors were discounted. Only in recent years have scholars realized that the charges of heresy were far overstated, and only then did they begin to discover what a heritage the Christian missionary movement has in its Nestorian forebears.

The late medieval period was one of tremendous growth for Roman Catholic missions—one that continued on through the Renaissance and Reformation. But as religious orders spread out over the world, the missionary thrust of the Roman Catholic Church became more and more diversified and decentralized. In order to remedy this situation, Vatican officials consolidated their missionary outreach during the seventeenth century. The Sacred Congregation for the Propagation of the Faith, or simply the *Propaganda*, was established under direct Vatican control, in part to loosen the control that Spain and Portugal exerted over missions in the New World.

The *Propaganda* was essentially a board comprised of Catholic clerics who were charged with the responsibility of spreading the faith. Relying almost entirely on French missionaries, the *Propaganda* got off to a slow start, but by the early eighteenth century, missionary work in several areas of the world was thriving. It was not to last. Various factors, including liberal theological trends, rationalism, Protestant competition, the suspension of the Jesuits (forcing the return of some

3,500 missionaries), and the French Revolution combined to bring about a steep decline in Catholic missions, and by 1800 the number of missionaries directly accountable to *Propaganda* was only around three hundred.

During the course of the nineteenth century, Roman Catholic missions slowly began a rebuilding process, and by 1850 the church was clearly back in the business of foreign evangelism. There was an increase in women's work, most notably that of Anne-Marie Javouhey who began her work in Africa in 1822. When she died in 1851 she left behind some nine hundred blue-robed Sisters of Saint Joseph spread out all over the world. The twentieth century saw further expansion in Roman Catholic missions, and by the late 1960s there were nearly 100,000 professional and lay missionaries serving throughout the world. Approximately half of those were women—single Catholic sisters, many of the caliber of Nobel Peace Prize winner, Mother Teresa—giving their lives in the service of the church and mankind.

Boniface (Winfried)

The development of Roman Catholic missions in central Europe during the early Middle Ages was accomplished through the work of Boniface more than any other individual. He has been called "the greatest of all missionaries of the Dark Ages," "one of the most remarkable missionaries in the entire history of the expansion of Christianity," and "a man who had a deeper influence on the history of Europe than any Englishman who has ever lived."[6] Yet, despite his sincere efforts to carry on the task of missions as he and Roman Catholic Church officials understood that task, his career, according to V. Raymond Edman, "reflects the lowering spiritual tone of English and Continental Christianity, which had begun to emphasize Church more than Christ, Sacrament more than Scripture."[7]

Boniface was born in Devonshire, England, in the late seventh century. He entered monastic life as a youth, and at the age of thirty was ordained a priest. Though there were many opportunities to excel as a churchman in his homeland, his deep concern was for the unchristianized pagans on the Continent. His first tour of duty among the Frisians in Holland, however, was unsuccessful due to political opposition and turmoil. He returned home, tempted to stay there and accept a position as head of a monastery; but his burden for foreign missions would not go away, and in 718, three years after he left on his first venture, he went back to the Continent. This time he went to Rome first. He had learned a lesson from his first experience. Papal recognition and backing were essential, and that is what he sought and received in Rome—an endorsement that colored his entire career. He was no longer an independent missionary going out simply to evangelize the pagan world. He was an emmisary of Rome, commissioned to establish papal authority over the church in central Europe.

Boniface went first to Germany and then back to the Lowlands for three years before returning to Germany, where he served the remainder of his life. In 723 he made his second journey to Rome, at which time he was consecrated a missionary bishop to Ger-

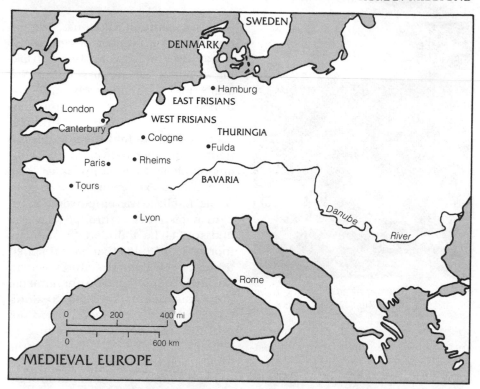

MEDIEVAL EUROPE

many by Pope Gregory II. Following his return to Germany, he began his missionary work in earnest and won a reputation for courage throughout the Rhineland. Many of the so-called Christians of the area had reverted to paganistic practices during his absence and were involved in spirit worship and magical arts. To counteract this sacrilege Boniface was convinced drastic measures were needed, so he boldly struck a blow to the very heart of the local pagan worship. He assembled a large crowd at Geismar, where the sacred oak of the Thundergod was located, and with the people looking on in horror he began chopping down the tree. It was a defiant act, but one that clearly drew attention to the fact that there was no supernatural power in either the tree or the god whom it honored. At the same time it

heightened the prestige of Boniface, and soon fanciful tales were associated with the incident, one alleging that when "the giant monster fell, its trunk burst asunder into four parts which, as they fell to the ground, miraculously shaped themselves into the arms of a cross, each arm of equal length."[8]

It was "a master stroke of missionary policy,"[9] according to Philip Schaff, and thousands of people recognized the superiority of the Christian God and submitted to baptism. Boniface was encouraged and relieved by the positive reaction and continued on in the same vein, destroying temples and shrines and smashing sacred stones into bits. Gradually he began to question the validity of this aggressive approach. He confided his doubts to another bishop, who advised him that

47

Boniface at Feismar after chopping down the sacred oak of the Thundergod.

such forceful methods were unwise and that a more meaningful and lasting approach was to "ask them questions about their gods, to enquire about their origins, their seemingly human attributes, their relationship with the beginning of the world, and in so doing elicit such contradictions and absurdities from their answers that they would become confused and ashamed."[10]

Whatever the impact the felling of sacred trees and smashing of shrines may have had on initial evangelistic work, it was obvious that much more was needed to build an enduring church. From his Celtic forebears, Boniface continued the concept of monastic missions that would prepare the way for a trained indigenous clergy. Several monks worked with him, and as each one was assigned to a new area, a cloister was established and training sessions were initiated for new converts. The only truly innovative aspect of his ministry was his enthusiastic recruitment of women to serve the cause of missions. "For the first time in a number of centuries," writes Latourette, "we find women taking an active part in missions.... Not again until the nineteenth century—unless it may be in the Moravian enterprise of the eighteenth century—do we find them so prominent as representatives of the faith among newly Christian peoples."[11]

In 737, following his third visit to Rome, Boniface was empowered to organize bishoprics through Bavaria, and in 744 he founded the famous monastery of Fulda that has remained a center for Roman Catholicism in Germany to this day. The phenomenal accomplishments credited to Boniface could not have been carried out without the powerful backing of Charles Martel, whose victory over the Muslims at the Battle of Tours in 732 marked a turning point in the struggle against Islam. "Without the protection of the prince of the Franks," wrote Boniface, "I can neither rule the people or the church nor defend the priests and clerks, monks and nuns; nor can I prevent the practice of pagan rites and sacrilegious worship of idols without his mandate and the awe inspired by his name."[12]

To the end Boniface's ministry was to bolster the Roman Catholic Church—to "turn the hearts of the heathen Saxons to the Catholic Faith," in his words, "and gather them among the children of Mother Church."[13] From that perspective, it is not surprising that the work of Boniface clashed with the missionary endeavors of Celtic and French monks. "He reaped the fruits of their labors," according to Schaff, "and destroyed their further usefulness, which he might have secured by a liberal Christian policy. He hated every feature of individuality. . . . To him true Christianity was identical with Romanism. . . ."[14] The fact that many Celtic missionaries had wives and defended clerical marriage was anathema to Boniface, but, imbued with the Roman passion for uniformity, even such trivial issues as the date for Easter, the right to eat certain meats, and the frequency of making the sign of the cross during mass caused him to denounce them as false prophets.

During the last years of his ministry, Boniface relinquished the administrative church work that had long consumed so much of his energy and went back to doing pioneer missionary work. "The spirit of the missionary prevailed," writes Neill, "and drove him out again into the lands where Christ had not been named."[15] In 753 he returned to Holland to minister to the Frisians, who still were largely unchristianized. It was there on the banks of the river Borne that he and some fifty assistants and followers set up their tents in preparation for a confirmation service of new converts. But the service never took place. Boniface and his companions were set upon and slain by a band of armed pagans, thus ending the ministry of Medieval Europe's most energetic and outwardly successful missionary.

Anskar

The earliest Roman Catholic missions to Scandanavia, like those to Germany, were very closely tied to political and military exploits. The first knowledge of Christianity came to that part of the world through traders, and then in 826 King Harold of Denmark, along with his wife and some four hundred court attendants and followers, submitted to baptism in hopes of obtaining Frankish military aid. Though such mass conversions were utterly devoid of spiritual commitment, they opened the way for missionaries, and Anskar was summoned to begin evangelistic work in Scandanavia following the king's turn to Christianity.

Anskar, often referred to as the "Apostle of the North," was born in France in 801 and schooled from the age of five at the monastery of Corbie, founded more than two centuries earlier by Columba. A mystic moved by visions and dreams, Anskar's highest ambition was to obtain a martyr's crown. Thus, he accepted his dangerous new assignment with eagerness. His hopes of converting the Danes, however, soon dimmed when the political and military impotence of King Harold became apparent, and in less than three years Anskar, along with the king, was expelled from Denmark.

No sooner had he been forced out of Denmark than an invitation came from the king of Sweden requesting missionaries. Anskar and another monk immediately accepted the challenge, only to have the ship they were sailing on attacked by pirates and all of their possessions stolen. On their arrival in Sweden, King Björn warmly welcomed them and gave them liberty to preach. There were many conversions, especially among the nobility—but as in the case of King Harold conversions were apparently politically motivated.

So significant was Anskar's work from a political perspective that Emperor Louis the Pious struck a deal with Pope Gregory IV to appoint Anskar Archbishop of Hamburg for the

EIGHTEEN CENTURIES OF ADVANCE

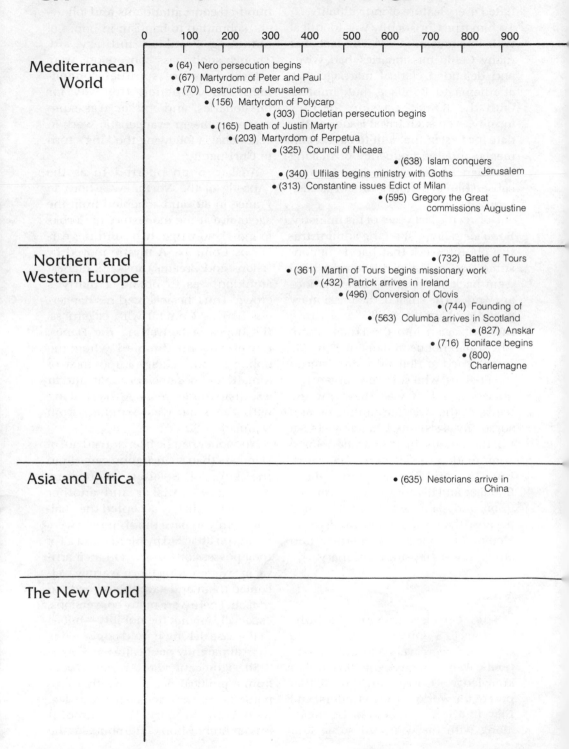

	0	100	200	300	400	500	600	700	800	900

Mediterranean World

- (64) Nero persecution begins
- (67) Martyrdom of Peter and Paul
- (70) Destruction of Jerusalem
- (156) Martyrdom of Polycarp
- (303) Diocletian persecution begins
- (165) Death of Justin Martyr
- (203) Martyrdom of Perpetua
- (325) Council of Nicaea
- (638) Islam conquers Jerusalem
- (340) Ulfilas begins ministry with Goths
- (313) Constantine issues Edict of Milan
- (595) Gregory the Great commissions Augustine

Northern and Western Europe

- (732) Battle of Tours
- (361) Martin of Tours begins missionary work
- (432) Patrick arrives in Ireland
- (496) Conversion of Clovis
- (744) Founding of
- (563) Columba arrives in Scotland
- (827) Anskar
- (716) Boniface begins
- (800) Charlemagne

Asia and Africa

- (635) Nestorians arrive in China

The New World

```
    1000    1100    1200    1300    1400    1500    1600    1700    1800
```

• (1095) Crusades begin
        • (1276) Lull opens monastery at Majorca
      • (1316) Death of Raymond Lull

Fulda

arrives in Denmark
missionary work

crowned emperor   • (1212) Francis of Assisi begins mission to Syria
        • (1219) Franciscans sent to North Africa
        •(1216) Founding of Dominicans
                    • (1534) Founding of Jesuits
                          • (1705) Founding of Danish-Halle Mission
                            • (1722) Zinzendorf establishes Herrnhut
                    • (1622) Founding of *Propaganda*
                        • (1773) Jesuits suppressed by pope

• (1219) Friar John arrives in Peking
        • (1542) Xavier arrives in India
      • (1583) Ricci arrives in China
     • (1606) de Nobili arrives in India
        • (1706) Ziegenbalg arrives in India
          • (1750) C. F. Schwartz arrives in India
        • (1737) George Schmidt arrives in South Africa

        • (1510) Dominicans arrive in Haiti
        • (1523) Las Casas joins Dominicans
          • (1646) John Eliot delivers first sermon to
                              Indians
          • (1675) King Philip's War
      • (1555) Calvin sends colonists to Brazil
        • (1722) Egede arrives in Greenland
        • (1733) Christian David arrives in Greenland
        • (1744) Zeisberger begins ministry to Indians
        • (1743) Brainerd begins missionary work
        • (1732) Moravians send missionaries to
                          Virgin Islands
      • (1625) Brébeuf commissioned to New France

Scandanavian and Slavic states of Northern Europe. To aid Anskar in his efforts, Louis gave him a rich monastery in West Flanders, a financial source that allowed him to bestow gifts on the provincial rulers. Anskar recruited monks from Corbie to assist him, and Catholicism made great strides in the next dozen years. The line between religion and politics, however, continued to be a fine one, and the gains were usually political in nature, motivated by what the Christian God and his temporal rulers could hopefully provide. Latourette relates one such incident recorded by Anskar's colleague and biographer: "An army of non-Christian Swedes in besieging a town faced a discouraging outlook. They cast lots to inquire whether any of their gods would help them. The answer was unfavourable and the Swedes were much disheartened. However, some merchants who recalled Anskar's teaching suggested that lots be cast to see whether Christ, the God of the Christians, would assist them. The outcome was propitious, the beleaguered purchased peace, and the victors, returning home, honoured Christ by observing fasts and giving alms to the poor."[16]

While political and military victories brought new areas under Roman Catholic influence, defeats often brought a return to paganism. Such was the case in 845 when Anskar saw fourteen years of labor destroyed by invading raiders from the north. A Danish fleet of plunderers led by King Horich I swept down on Hamburg and sacked and burned the city and drove Anskar into hiding, leaving him without a refuge. When he sought protection from the Bishop of Bremen, the bishop refused to help, still bitterly jealous that Scandanavia had not been included in his see.

With outside military aid, Hamburg was soon retaken, and Anskar was given the combined see of Hamburg and Bremen. King Horwich switched his allegiance to the side of the Christians, and the military threats lessened, allowing Anskar to devote more time to a spiritual ministry, the type of ministry he longed for. He was an ascetic at heart, and prayer and fasting were viewed as paramount—though never to be done at the expense of useful activity. He insisted his monks be ever occupied with work, and he himself was often seen knitting while he prayed. As with most medieval spiritual leaders he was credited with great miracles, but he personally sought to avoid all such praise, telling others that "the greatest miracle in his life would be if God ever made a thoroughly pious man out of him."[17]

Anskar died peacefully in 865 without the martyr's crown that he had longed for. But that certainly was not the greatest prize that eluded him. In spite of all his efforts he was unable to establish a permanent base for Christianity in Scandanavia. After he died, the people reverted to paganism, and it was not until after the tenth century that the Catholic Church gained a sure foothold in that area of the world.

Raymond Lull

The politically oriented missionary endeavors of the Roman Catholic Church during the medieval period amounted to very little compared to the Church's greatest expansionist effort—the Crusades, a two-hundred-year movement (1095–1291) to win back the Holy Land. It was hardly a missionary enterprise. The goal was to expand the territory controlled by Christians, not to convert the Muslims. It was a bloody ordeal, and tens of thousands of lives were lost. Though the early crusades were favored with a degree of military success, those gains were lost in the end. Far more significant was the loss of potential dialogue between the Saracens and the Christians. So bitter was the animosity of Muslims toward Christians, as a result of the savage cruelty manifested during the Crusades, that even today the memory has not been erased, and evangelism remains most difficult among the people of the Muslim faith.

Not all professing Christians of this period believed that military force was the appropriate way to deal with the Muslims. During the early thirteenth century, while the crusading spirit was still at high pitch, Francis of Assisi proposed that the Muslims should be won by love instead of by hate. His first two attempts to evangelize them were completely unsuccessful, but his third attempt in 1219 brought him into the presence of the sultan of Egypt. Restricted by language barriers, Francis, nevertheless, made a feeble attempt at presenting the gospel. Though there is no evidence that any actual conversions resulted from his efforts, his example paved the way for others to view Muslims as potential brothers in Christ, among them Raymond Lull, an outstanding missionary of this period.

Lull was born in 1232 into a wealthy Roman Catholic family of Majorca, an island off the coast of Spain in the Mediterranean which had been taken back from the Muslims not long before his birth. As a young man he went to Spain and served in the court of the king of Aragon, living a life of debauchery. Though he had a wife and children, he had mistresses on the side, and "by his own testimony lived a life of utter immorality."[18] His decadent lifestyle did not seem to diminish his intellectual and creative genius, and as a very young man he was recognized for his scholarship and literary talent.

During his early thirties, Lull returned to Majorca, and it was there that he underwent a profound religious experience. He was "born again," according to Samuel Zwemer. It was a mystical experience marked by visions. The first vision came one evening when he was composing an erotic song. Suddenly he was startled by an image. He saw "the Savior hanging on His cross, the blood trickling from His hands and feet and brow, look reproachfully at him." Though moved by the vision, Lull went back to his songwriting the following week, but again the vision appeared. This time he made his commitment to Christ, but immediately doubts arose: "How can I, defiled with impurity, rise and enter on a holier life?"[19] It was this feeling of guilt that prompted Lull to forsake his wealth and prestige and dedicate his life to serving God.

Lull's initial response to the call to Christian service was characteristic of the age in which he lived. He devoted his time to monastic living—to fasting, prayer, and meditation. The ultimate demonstration of love for God, he believed, was living a life as a reclusive monk, wholly separated from the temptations of the world. It was another vision that made him conscious of his responsibilities to those around him. In his book, *The Tree of Love*, he relates the vision that became his missionary call: while in the forest alone with God, far removed from worldly distractions, he meets a pilgrim, who, on learning of Lull's chosen vocation, scolds him for his self-centeredness and challenges him to go out into the world and bring others the message of Christ. It was this vision that prompted Lull to direct his energy to foreign missions and, in particular, missions to the Saracens—the most hated and feared enemies of Christendom. "I see many knights going to the Holy Land beyond the seas," he wrote, "and thinking that they can acquire it by force of arms, but in the end all are destroyed before they attain that which they think to have. Whence it seems to me that the conquest of the Holy Land ought ... to be attempted ... by love and prayers, and the pouring out of tears and blood."[20]

Following this vision, Lull devoted much of his time to Arabic language study—a nine-year ordeal that was marred by an unfortunate incident that almost ruined his future missionary career. To aid in his study of the language he purchased a Saracen slave, who apparently became annoyed with his master's oft-repeated and reasoned case for Christianity. At any rate, he lashed back one day by cursing Christ. Lull, losing control of his own emotions, hit the slave across the face, and the slave in turn grabbed up a weapon and severely wounded his master. For that crime the Muslim slave was arrested and imprisoned and soon afterwards committed suicide, fearing his fate would be worse. It was a traumatic ordeal for Lull, but it gave him an even greater passion to reach the Muslims for Christ.

Lull was past the age of forty when his actual missionary career began, and in later life he recalled what sacrifices that decision entailed: "I had a wife and children; I was tolerably rich; I led a secular life. All these things I cheerfully resigned for the sake of promoting the common good and diffusing abroad the holy faith."[21] He set aside a sufficient amount of money to provide for his wife and children, but the remainder—in the tradition of St. Francis of Assisi—he gave to the poor.

Lull's missionary outreach was three-pronged: apologetical, educational, and evangelistic. "He devised a philosophical ... system for persuading non-Christians of the truth of Christianity; he established missionary colleges; and he himself went and preached to the Moslems...."[22] Lull's contribution as a Christian apologist to the Muslims was immense. He wrote some sixty books on theology, many of them aimed at Muslim intellectuals. The theme that he developed most frequently related to the Godhead. His mission, as he saw it, was to "experiment whether he himself could not persuade some of them by conference with their wise men and by manifesting to them, according to the divinely given Method, the Incarnation of the Son of God and the three Persons of the Blessed Trinity in the Divine Unity of Essence." He sought to establish "a parliament of religions, and desired to meet the bald monotheism of Islam face to face with the revelation of the Father, the Son, and the Holy Spirit."[23]

In the area of missionary education, Lull, in the tradition of Columba viewed monasteries as the ideal training ground for evangelists. He traveled widely, appealing to church and political leaders to support him in the cause. King James II of Spain was one of those who caught his vision, and in 1276, with his enthusiastic support and financial contributions, Lull opened a monastery on Majorca with thirteen Franciscan monks and a curriculum including courses in the Arabic language and in the "geography of missions." Lull's dream was to establish training centers all over Europe, but to do that he had to convince the Roman Catholic hierarchy of their value—no easy task. When he visited Rome on various occasions, his ideas were either ridiculed or ignored by both popes and Cardinals, who seemed far more interested in worldly pleasures and personal aggrandizement than in missions. But despite the lack of support he found in many quarters, he was successful in establishing other missionary-oriented monasteries. His greatest victory in the area of education came at the council of Vienna when he won his battle to have Arabic offered in the European universities—a step that he believed would open up dialogue between Christians and Muslims.

Lull's own missionary career did not begin with the flair that one might expect from a seasoned missionary statesman who had promoted his pet project in the highest levels of society. It was one thing, he learned, to preach missions to others and quite another to go out himself. He was at the port in Genoa, ready to sail for Tunis. His belongings were on board ship, and crowds of well-wishers were preparing for a rousing send-off. Then at the last moment he was "overwhelmed with terror," as he later recalled; he was paralyzed "at the thought of what might befall him in the country whither he was going. The idea of en-

during torture or lifelong imprisonment presented itself with such force that he could not control his emotions."[24] His belongings were unloaded and the ship left port without him. Almost immediately he was overcome with remorse, and he determined to go on the next ship no matter what the consequences. Though racked by fever—probably caused by the emotional turmoil he was suffering—he was placed aboard another ship, and thus began his own foreign missionary career.

Lull's fears about conducting mission work in Tunis were certainly not unfounded. Tunis was a powerful center of Islam in North Africa that had held off repeated invasions. The Crusaders were viewed with hatred and bitterness. His arrival, however, was not greeted with as much hostility as he had expected. He made his presence known to the leading Muslim scholars and then called a conference to debate the relative merits of Christianity and Islam, promising that if Islam was demonstrated to be superior he would embrace it as his faith. The Muslim leaders agreed to meet and Lull had his first opportunity to demonstrate his missionary methods.

When Lull was given the opportunity to defend Christianity, he set forth a doctrinal position that, according to Zwemer, was "orthodox and evangelical to the core" with "little medieval theology and . . . very few Romish ideas." The basic tenets of his argument are fully valid today in a debate with Muslims:

Every wise man must acknowledge that to be the true religion, which ascribed the greatest perfection to the Supreme Being, and not only conveyed the worthiest conception of all His attributes, His goodness, power, wisdom, and glory, but demonstrated the harmony and equality existing between them. Now *their* religion was defective in acknowledging only two active principles in the Deity, His will and His wisdom, while it left His goodness and greatness inoperative as tho [sic] they were indolent qualities and not called forth into active exercise. But the Christian faith could not be charged with this defect. In its doctrine of the Trinity it conveys the highest conception of the Deity, as the Father, the Son, and the Holy Spirit in one simple essence and nature. In the Incarnation of the Son it evinces the harmony that exists between God's goodness and His greatness; and in the person of Christ displays the true union of the Creator and the creature; while in His Passion which He underwent out of His great love for man, it sets forth the divine harmony of infinite goodness and condescension, even the condescension of Him who for us men, and our salvation, and restitution to our primeval state of perfection, underwent those sufferings and lived and died for man.[25]

The reaction to Lull's defense of Christianity was mixed. A number accepted his arguments or at least showed an interest in hearing more, but the majority were stung by the verbal attack. Not surprisingly, Lull was thrown into prison, where he waited in terror, fully expecting the death penalty. Instead, he was stoned by a mob and ordered out of the country—an order he secretly defied. For three months he "concealed himself like a wharf-rat" in the coastal town of Goletta, "witnessing quietly for his Master."[26] Frustrated by his lack of freedom, he returned to Europe, where he spent several years in Naples and then went on to France, lecturing

and writing books on his "New Method," always seeking new recruits to join his mission.

While the Muslims were the primary object of Lull's missionary passion, Jews also caught his attention. The twelfth and thirteenth centuries were marred by horror stories of anti-Semitism. Jews were blamed for almost every ill in society, and as a result were expelled from France and England—punishment that seemed mild in comparison to that meted out by the Spanish Inquisition. Here and there, outspoken individuals defended the Jews, and among them was Lull. He reached out to them in love as he had the Saracens, presenting Christ to them as their Messiah.

Lull's travel and varied activities kept him busy in Europe, but in 1307 at the age of seventy-five, after a fifteen-year absence, he returned to North Africa—this time to Bugia, east of Algiers. As in Tunis years earlier, he immediately sought a forum for public debate, and he boldly challenged the Muslims to compare their religion with Christianity. Though Lull claimed to reach out to the Muslims in love, his message was often very offensive and may have embittered the Muslims toward Christianity almost as much as the Crusades themselves did. One of his arguments, as Zwemer relates, was to hold up the Ten Commandments "as the perfect law of God, and then showing from their own books that Mohammed violated every one of these precepts. Another favorite argument of Lull with Moslems was to portray the seven cardinal virtues and the seven deadly sins, only to show subsequently how bare Islam was of the former and how full of the latter!"[27]

Again, Lull's public debate did not

continue long. He was sent to prison and for six months his captors "plied him ... with all the sensual temptations of Islam."[28] Following his imprisonment he was banished from Bugia, and he returned to Europe. His career as a foreign missionary, though, was not over. In 1314, when he was past the age of eighty, he returned to Tunis, where his age alone apparently brought him some protection. Perhaps, too, he had mellowed over the years, for he was granted more liberty than had ever before been accorded him by Muslim authorities, and he won some converts. He was ever aware that ministering to Muslims was a downhill battle. "For one Saracen who becomes a Christian," he wrote, "ten Christians and more become Mohammedans."[29]

Although Lull's stay in Tunis was rewarding, it did not allow for the ultimate reward he wished to obtain— the crown of martyrdom. Lull was influenced by the spirit of the times in which he lived, and "Among the Franciscan order a mania for martyrdom prevailed."[30] To die in the service of his Master would be the highest privilege. So in 1314 he returned to Bugia to see his little band of converts and to put his defense of Christianity to the final test. "For over ten months the aged missionary dwelt in hiding, talking and praying with his converts and trying to influence those who were not yet persuaded.... At length, weary of seclusion, and longing for martyrdom, he came forth into the open market and presented himself to the people as the same man whom they had once expelled from their town.... He pleaded with love, but spoke plainly the whole truth.... Filled with fanatic fury at his boldness, and unable to

reply to his arguments, the populace seized him, and dragged him out of the town; there by the command, or at least the connivance, of the king, he was stoned on the 30th of June, 1315,"[31] and he died shortly thereafter.

Lull's life and work are a testimony to the power of true Christianity to endure even in the darkest periods of church history. The Roman Catholic Church, for the most part, either ignored him and his passion for missions or condemned him as a heretic. Yet he remained faithful to his calling, always conscious of his personal duty to spread the message of Christ.

Las Casas

The age of discovery that began in the late fifteenth century ushered in a new era of foreign missions for the Roman Catholic Church. The New World was seen as a potential field of expansion, and both Popes and political leaders were eager to do their part to bring it under Catholic domination. Queen Isabella, who relentlessly hunted down Protestant "heretics" in Spain, regarded the evangelism of the Indians as the most important justification for colonial expansion, and she insisted that priests and friars be among the first to settle in the New World. The Franciscans and Dominicans (and later the Jesuits) eagerly accepted the challenge, and within a matter of decades Catholicism had become a permanent and influential force. The speed with which Christianity took hold was phenomenal. In 1529 a Franciscan missionary in Mexico wrote about the mass conversions that were almost impossible to record: "I and the brother who was with me baptized in this province of

Mexico upwards of 200,000 persons —so many in fact that I cannot give an accurate estimate of the number. Often we baptized in a single day 14,000 people, sometimes 10,000, sometimes 8,000."[32]

The greatest obstacle to missions in the New World was the colonists themselves and their cruel treatment of the native Indians. Though Queen Isabella had decreed that the freedom of the Indians was to be honored, in practice the Indians were treated inhumanely in a system that fostered their virtual slavery. Such treatment did not go unnoticed by the missionaries, and a number of them risked the wrath of the colonists to make their stand on the side of right. Among them was Las Casas, who, though slow to recognize and admit the evil, became the greatest champion of the Indians during the Spanish colonial period. In Las Casas the spirit of missions and of humanitarianism were knitted together in a unity rarely equalled by missionaries before or since.

Las Casas was born in Spain in 1474, the son of a merchant who had sailed with Columbus on his second voyage. After receiving his law degree from the University of Salamanca, he sailed to the island of Hispaniola to serve as the governor's legal advisor. He quickly settled into the affluent lifestyle of the colonists, accepting the conventional view of the native population. He participated in raids against them and enslaved them as laborers on his plantation. Then in 1510, when he was in his mid-thirties, he underwent a spiritual change and sought ordination, becoming the first priest ordained in America. Yet outwardly he changed little, moving easily into the lavish lifestyle that characterized most of the clergy. Gradually, however, he was coming to realize that the treatment of the Indians was not consistent with Christian precepts, and at the age of forty he turned his back on the cruel system he had become a part of and began fighting against it. He later joined the Dominicans, where he found sympathetic support for his views.

As the New World's most vocal advocate for the Indians, Las Casas traveled to and from Spain, pleading their cause with government officials and anyone who would listen, sometimes presenting a naïve and oversimplified case: "God created these simple people without evil and without guile. They are most obedient and faithful to their natural lords, and to the Christians whom they serve. They are most submissive, patient, peaceful, and virtuous. Nor are they quarrelsome, rancorous, querulous, or vengeful. They neither possess nor desire to possess worldly wealth. Surely these people would be the most blessed in the world if only they worshipped the true God."[33]

Las Casas's ministry was more than mere humanitarianism. Evangelism was a priority, and for a number of years he traveled in Central America doing pioneer work. In one instance he convinced a native chief who had been terrorizing the colonists to lay down his weapons and to let all his tribe be baptized. Due to colonial opposition, most of his conversions did not come that easily.

At the age of seventy, Las Casas was appointed Bishop of Chiapa, an utterly impoverished see in southern Mexico that he chose above another far more prosperous diocese, even though, according to Latourette, "he must have known [it] would be one of the most trying tasks of his career."[34] Most of the Spanish planters there blamed him for the New Laws enacted by the Spanish crown that were designed to give the Indians protection and liberty. The enforcement of these laws would ruin the plantation economy—so said the Spanish landowners—and they simply ignored them. Las Casas, in turn, ordered his priests to deny absolution to any such lawbreakers, and the battle lines were drawn. Many of Las Casas's own priests defied him, and after three years he gave up his bishopric, discouraged and defeated. In 1547, at the age of seventy-three, he sailed from the New World, never to return again. His battle for human rights continued on in Spain until his death almost two decades later, and he is still remembered as one of Christendom's greatest humanitarian missionaries.

Francis Xavier

The sixteenth century that was dominated by the events of the Protestant Reformation was also marked by a Catholic Reformation—a reformation to counteract the gains of the Protestants, to shore up the crumbling walls of the Medieval church, and to expand the church to the distant shores where the name of Christ had never been spoken. This expansion was aimed not only at the New World, where colonial development was making rapid headway, but also toward India and the Far East, where lucrative trade routes were being established. The Roman Catholic Church was anxious to cash in on this new wave of overseas travel, and adventurous missionary

monks and friars eagerly volunteered for duty. It was the late medieval religious orders, the Dominicans and Franciscans, that supplied many of these courageous volunteers, but it was the Jesuits (the Society of Jesus), founded in 1535, that became the Counter Reformation's most active participant. The founding of that organization, writes Stephen Neill, "is perhaps the most important event in the missionary history of the Roman Catholic Church."[35]

Ignatius of Loyola, a Spanish nobleman, was the founder of the Jesuits, and under his control the little band of dedicated disciples grew into a highly centralized, military-like organization that viewed loyalty to the Pope and the Roman Catholic Church as its highest ideal. The order expanded rapidly and by the time of Loyola's death in 1556 there were over a thousand members, and in less than a century after its founding there were more than fifteen thousand members spread out all over the globe. The most famous of these early Jesuit missionaries (and perhaps of all times) was Xavier, one of Loyola's inner circle of six and a charter member of the order. In 1541 he sailed for India, representing both the Pope and the king of Portugal, to begin his short but extraordinary missionary career.

Xavier was born in 1506 into a Spanish noble family and grew up living in a castle in the Basque countryside. As a youth he attended the University of Paris, where his interests inclined toward philosophy and theology. It was there that he began spending time with a group of Protestants—dedicated young Christians who were risking their lives for the gospel in the Catholic stronghold of Paris. But then Xavier met Loyola, a man fiercely devoted to the Roman Catholic Church, whose dynamic personal magnetism had a powerful effect on the spiritually unsettled young student. It was not long before Xavier joined with Loyola, turning his back on the Protestants and on the tempting lucrative career he might have had in the Catholic church. Instead he took a vow of poverty and celibacy, and committed himself wholly to spreading the Catholic faith.

Xavier's call to foreign missions came suddenly and with no supernatural attachment. Two other Jesuits had been chosen to go to India as missionaries, and when one became ill Xavier was assigned to take his place. With less than twenty-four hours warning he was on his way to India. He arrived at the port city of Goa in 1542, where he found the society influenced far more by European culture than by religion. It was a morally corrupt environment, and Xavier was frustrated from the very beginning. How could such people steeped in immoral living be brought to Christ? It was here that Xavier developed his customary procedure for missionary work—one of concentrating on the children. They were much more easily swayed than their parents, and it was his hope that he and the priests who would follow him could train them from early childhood to become effective Christian leaders in their own communities.

Xavier did not remain in Goa long. The westernized society with its mixture of Jews and Muslims was not to his liking. When his exhortations failed to make an impact on the city, he pleaded with the king of Portugal to introduce the Inquisition and force the people to adhere to Catholic

Francis Xavier.

dogma and morality. But before that could be arranged he left, seeking a more fruitful vineyard. "I want to be where there are . . . out-and-out pagans," he wrote, believing that in such an environment conversions would come more easily.[36]

From Goa, Xavier moved further south in India to work among the impoverished pearl fishermen along the coast. Although Catholicism had been introduced to the area several years earlier, there were few signs of it when Xavier arrived. The people were Hindus and their response to Christianity depended largely on caste. The high-caste Brahmans were antagonistic, only one being converted, but the low-caste Paravas were much more open to change, realizing their status in society could not be worsened by such a move. Great crowds came out to learn and recite creeds, and baptisms were plentiful—so many that on some days Xavier was so tired from performing the sacrament that he could hardly move his arms. Yet baptism was to him the most important aspect of the ministry, and he would not deny anyone, no matter how tired he was. Appealing to Loyola for more workers he wrote, "In these heathen places the only education necessary is to be able to teach the prayers and to go about baptizing little ones who now die in great numbers without the Sacrament because we cannot be everywhere at once to succour them."[37]

Xavier's emphasis on baptism and his concentration on children went hand in hand. To a fellow worker he wrote, "I earnestly recommend to you the teaching of the children, and be very diligent about the baptism of newly born babies. Since the grown-ups have no hankering for Paradise, whether to escape the evils of life or to attain their happiness, at least let the little ones go there by baptizing them before they die."[38] But Xavier's emphasis on children was not just to ensure them a place in Paradise, but to use them in the evangelism of others—a task that he alone could not keep up with: "As it was impossible for me to meet personally the ever growing volume of calls ... I resorted to the following expedient. I told the children who memorized the Christian doctrine to betake themselves to the homes of the sick, there to collect as many of the family and neighbours as possible, and to say the Creed with them several times, assuring the sick persons that if they believed they would be cured.... In this way I managed to satisfy all my callers, and at the same time secured that the Creed, the Commandments, and the prayers were taught in the people's homes and abroad in the streets."[39]

Perhaps far more exciting for the youngsters than visiting the sick and reciting creeds were the other types of religious activities in which Xavier encouraged them to become involved. "They detest the idolatries of their people," he wrote with pride, "and get into fights with them on the subject. They tackle even their own parents if they find them going to the idols, and come to tell me about it. When I hear from them of some idolatrous ceremonies in the villages ... I collect all the boys I can, and off we go together to those places, where the devil gets from them more despiteful treatment than their worshipping parents had given him of honour. The little fellows seize the small clay idols, smash them, grind them to dust, spit on them and trample them underfoot."[40]

Xavier's evangelism in India was superficial at best. Whether the children and adults who were baptized even knew the most fundamental truths of Christianity is doubtful. After three years of working among the pearl fishermen along the coast, he still had not begun to master the very difficult Tamil language, and even the simple prayers and creeds he taught the people were later found to be very poorly translated. Church services were ritualistic and repetitious, as Xavier's own account would indicate:

On Sundays I assemble all the people, men and women, young and old, and get them to repeat the prayers in their language. They take much pleasure in doing so, and come to the meetings gladly.... I give out the First Commandment, which they repeat, and then we all say together, Jesus Christ, Son of God, grant us grace to love thee above all things. When we have asked for this grace, we recite the Pater Noster together, and then cry with one accord, Holy Mary, Mother of Jesus Christ, obtain for us grace from thy Son to enable us to keep the First Commandment. Next we say Ave Maria, and proceed in the same manner through each of the remaining nine Commandments. And just as we say twelve Paters and Aves in honour of the twelve articles of the Creed, so we say ten Paters and Aves in honour of the ten Commandments, asking God to give us grace to keep them well.[41]

Xavier had not come to India to settle down in one area and establish a long-term ministry. He considered himself a trailblazer and was anxious to move on and lay the groundwork for Jesuit missions elsewhere. When he left India in 1545 for the Far East, his place was quickly filled by others, and within a few decades there were more than a dozen Christian villages, each led by a Jesuit priest.

From India, Xavier went to Malacca on the Malay peninsula, where he ministered for a time; but his dream was to visit Japan and establish Christianity there. While back in Goa in 1548 he met Anjiro, a Japanese man who convinced him that with proper conduct and logical reasoning a missionary could expect great results in Japan: "The king, the nobility, and all other people of discretion would become Christians, for the Japanese, he said, are entirely guided by the law of reason."[42]

Xavier arrived in Japan in 1549 and quickly realized that his ministry there would be much more difficult than the glowing predictions had indicated. The language barrier stymied any attempt at evangelism: ". . . we are like so many statues amongst them, for they speak and talk to us about many things, whilst we, not understanding the language, hold our peace."

Nevertheless, Xavier could write only months after he arrived that the people were very fond of hearing about the things of God, "chiefly when they understand them."[43] Some apparently did understand, for when Xavier left the country after two years he left behind some one hundred converts.

The freedom to disseminate their beliefs that was granted to Xavier and his companions resulted from Japan's unstable political environment. There was no centralized government, and Buddhism was on the decline. That situation continued after Xavier departed, and the Jesuit missionaries who followed him witnessed impressive results. In the 1570s large numbers of Japanese began turning to Catholicism. Some fifty thousand in one region alone were baptized, and by the close of the sixteenth century it is estimated that there were some three hundred thousand professing Christians. This all occurred despite a dramatic change on the Japanese political scene. Foreign missionaries were no longer made welcome, and Japanese Christians faced severe persecution, sometimes resulting in death by crucifixion. In 1638 several thousand Christians took part in the Shimabara Rebellion, protesting persecution and exorbitant taxes. They finally took refuge in a castle where, after weeks of holding their own, they were defeated and slaughtered. But despite such setbacks, Catholicism continued to be a noticeable influence in Japan for more than two centuries.

Xavier returned to Goa following his departure from Japan, and from there he made plans to go to China, hoping to penetrate that land with the gospel. But it would be left to another Jesuit to pioneer the work there. For while Xavier was arranging entry he contracted a fever and died on an island just off the coast of China, only ten years after his missionary career had begun.

Matthew Ricci

"Barbarians Not Welcome." If there was one slogan that would have characterized China during its long history, it would have read that way. China was a proud and isolationist realm, and as such eluded for many centuries the permanent planting of Christianity on its soil. Attempts were made, but without success. Nestorians who traveled overland from Syria during the sixth century were the first known Christian missionaries to China. Their influence began to decrease by the thirteenth century when the first Roman Catholic missionary, Friar John, arrived. He found considerable freedom to preach under the protection of the Mongols who were then ruling China, and thousands were baptized. During the fourteenth century, however, when the Ming Dynasty came to power, missionaries were expelled, and again all signs of Christianity were quickly erased. It was not until the end of the sixteenth century that Christianity actually gained a permanent foothold in China, and it was Matthew Ricci, an Italian Jesuit, who was most responsible for that breakthrough, a man who "became and has ever remained the most respected foreign figure in Chinese literature."[44]

Ricci was born in 1552, the year of Xavier's death. His father was an Italian aristocrat who sent his son to Rome to study law. While there, however, young Ricci fell under the influence of the Jesuits, and after three years he turned away from his pursuit of a secular career and entered the Jesuit order. So distressed was his father when he heard the news that he left immediately for Rome to remove his son from the order. On the first night of his journey he became ill with a violent fever and was unable to go on. Accepting this sudden attack as a sign of God's anger with him, the elder Ricci returned home, fearing what might happen if he were to offer further resistance.

Ricci's acceptance into the Society of Jesus did not signal an end to his secular studies. In fact, it was at the Roman College, a Jesuit school, that he studied under one of the most widely recognized mathematicians of the day, and it was this secular education that later paved the way for his very effective ministry with the *literati* of China.

Ricci's first assignment was in Goa, where Xavier had begun his missionary career. Unlike Xavier, he did not go alone. With him were thirteen other Jesuit missionaries. Following the example and instructions that Xavier had left behind, they were involved mainly in educational work, training children who would become the next generation's Christian leaders. Educating children was not Ricci's idea of missionary work, but there was no immediate response to his request for reassignment. After four years in India Ricci, according to his biographer, "received the marching orders for which he had been praying so long."[45]

Exciting things had been happening in Jesuit missions in the Far East, and Ricci had desperately wanted to be in on the action. So when a call came from the Portuguese port city of Macao on the coast of China, he eagerly accepted. Ruggieri, his friend, had gone there earlier; and even though he was hopelessly bogged down in language study and depressed by the discouragement of the veteran missionaries in residence, Ricci sailed for his new post with anticipation.

Ricci's arrival in China signaled the breakthrough that had long been awaited. Though missionaries had for some time resided in Macao, entering China proper had not been permitted. But when word of Ricci's expertise in such fields as mathematics, astronomy, and geography reached Wang P'an, the governor of Shiuhing, he invited Ruggieri and Ricci to come and live in his province. Though they initially feared the invitation might be a ploy to dispose of them, they accepted the risk and went. It was not a trick, and Ricci quickly demonstrated the value of his secular learning in foreign missionary work. With him he brought a supply of mechanical gadgets, including clocks, musical instruments, and astronomical and navigational devices, as well as books, paintings, and maps—all of which drew widespread interest from scholars. The maps were particularly intriguing for these men who had previously refused to believe that the world consisted of more than China and her immediate neighbors.

Ricci's primary aim was not to bring Western learning, but to bring the gospel. To make that point, both he and Ruggieri shaved their heads and took on the garb of a Buddhist monk. After only two years there were converts, and the two missionaries dedicated a small church and private residence they had built with the help of Chinese labor. In 1588, five years after they entered China proper, Ruggieri returned to Europe, and Ricci was left in charge of the work with several Jesuit priests helping him.

In the meantime Ricci had switched from a Buddhist monk's attire to that of a Confucian scholar, realizing such dress would win him greater respect. Confucianism was the religion of the Chinese intelligencia, and more and more Ricci was trying to win that segment of the population. If the Chinese could view Confucianism as merely a philosophy, then they could accept Christianity as well and not be forsaking their traditional beliefs.

While Ricci was seeking to contextualize Christianity in China, another Jesuit missionary, Robert de Nobili, was doing the same thing in India—in essence, becoming a Brahmin to reach that caste for Christ. He observed the laws and wore the clothes of the Brahmin caste, and he disassociated himself from the existing Christian church. Not, however, without a barrage of criticism. Both he and Ricci were highly controversial figures within Roman Catholicism.

Ricci's effort to make Confucianism compatible with Christianity appealed to the Chinese and it no doubt increased the number of so-called converts, but in many ways it compromised basic tenets of Christianity. The name for God, for instance, was considered by many Western Christians to have been downgraded by the Chinese term Ricci used. The term Lord of Heaven (T'ien for heaven and Shang-Ti for sovereign lord) from the ancient classics was the name he used. Likewise, Ricci permitted Chinese converts to participate in ceremonies honoring ancestors through prayers and incense. He argued that such traditions only indicated a healthy respect for deceased family members.

Ricci's methods came under fire almost immediately, especially from competing orders, the Dominicans and Franciscans. As was the case in Japan, there was considerable resentment among the latter two directed at the Jesuits. In China, where the Jesuits had maintained a virtual monopoly on spreading Catholicism for a number of years, the other two orders were quick to find fault. By the early seventeenth century the issue had blown up into what became known as the Chinese Rites Controversy, the most heated debate ever to confront Roman Catholic missions. Papal pronouncements generally took the side of the Dominicans and Franciscans, forbidding Christians to sacrifice to Confucius or to their ancestors. The Chinese emperor, on the other hand, took the side of the Jesuits, threatening to expel those who opposed ancestor worship. The controversy raged for centuries without ever being fully resolved.

In defense of Ricci himself, it should be noted that the bitter disputes that his methods engendered were entirely unintentional, and his leniency toward Confucianists may have been influenced by the intellectuals with whom he associated. "It is conceivable," writes A. J. Broomhall, "that to them the ceremonial, civic and political aspects of these rites could have been distinct from the religious and superstitious, but not to the average Chinese with his animistic beliefs."[46]

For Ricci himself, the acceptance of Confucianist ideas came naturally. As he studied and translated the Chinese classics, he developed a tremendous respect for what this ancient culture had to offer. He dismissed the doctrine of the *tabula rasa* — the belief that non-Christian philosophies and religions must be entirely eradicated before Christianity can be effectively introduced. So also was the conclusion of Xavier after he came in contact with the Japanese and their highly developed culture. Earlier in India he had sought to debunk non-Christian systems and had met with little success. The policy of accommodation thus became a pattern for the Jesuits.

Ricci's great respect for the Chinese people and his eagerness to share his scientific knowledge with them brought him unusual opportunities that have been accorded few other foreigners before or since. In 1601, at the invitation of Wan Li, he was permitted to locate in Peking and continue his mission work right under the nose of the Emperor, while living on a stipend from the imperial government. With him he brought a large striking clock that he presented to the emperor, and he and his fellow priests became the official clock-winders of the imperial court. "When enemies tried to oust him," writes Broomhall, "the powerful palace eunuchs were afraid they could not keep it going and saw to it that Ricci was not expelled."[47] "It is a miracle of the omnipotent hand of the Most High," wrote Ricci, and "the miracle appears all the greater in that not only do we dwell in Peking, but we enjoy here an incontestable authority."[48]

Ricci ministered in Peking until he died in 1611, nearly ten years after he arrived in that city. During that time a significant number of scholars and government officials professed faith in

Christ, among them Paul Hsü, one of China's leading intellectuals and a member of the Imperial Academy. His faith was real and he passed it on to his children who kept it alive for generations. His daughter devoted her time to training professional storytellers to take the gospel out into the villages. Two other female descendants of Paul became famous through their marriages—one became Madame Sun Yat-sen, and the other, Madame Chiang Kai-shek. Though the number of Chinese converts at the time of Ricci's death (some two thousand) was miniscule in comparison to China's vast population, their influence was far greater because of their high status in society, and in the seventeenth and eighteenth centuries Christianity continued to grow, despite periodic outbreaks of violent persecution. During the half century following Ricci's death, the church increased a hundredfold.

How evangelical and personal this early Christianity in China was is debatable, but in dogma and practice it unfortunately differed little from Medieval Catholicism in Europe. In his journal, Ricci writes of Paul Hsü bowing "before the statue of the Blessed Virgin" before he entered the residence of one of the Jesuit priests, and how after he was baptized "he attended the sacrifice of the Mass every day" and "found a great consolation in going to confession."[49] Yet the gospel message was intertwined, and, according to Broomhall, "much pure doctrine was taught, whatever else was added."[50] One pamphlet on God, written by a Jesuit priest during this period, was widely circulated in the provinces and later used by Protestant missionaries, and it was just such literature that kept the message alive following a 1724 edict that expelled the missionaries and forced the Chinese Christians to worship in secret.

SELECTED BIBLIOGRAPHY

Brodrick, James. **Saint Francis Xavier.** New York: Wicklow, 1952.

Cronin, Vincent. **The Wise Man From the West.** New York: Dutton, 1955.

Cuming, G. J., ed. **The Mission of the Church and the Propagation of the Faith.** Cambridge: The University Press, 1970.

De Vaulx, Bernard. **History of the Missions.** New York: Hawthorn, 1961.

Edman, V. Raymond. **The Light in Dark Ages.** Wheaton: Van Kampen, 1949.

Greenaway, George William. **Saint Boniface.** London: Adam & Charles Black, 1955.

Zwemer, Samuel M. **Raymund Lull: First Missionary to the Moslems.** New York: Funk & Wagnalls, 1902.

Chapter 3

The Moravian Advance:
Dawn of Protestant Missions

The upsurge of Roman Catholic missions that occurred during the sixteenth-century Catholic Counter Reformation had no parallel among the Protestants. World-wide missions was not a major concern of most of the Reformers. Just holding their own in the face of Roman Catholic opposition and breaking new ground in Europe were significant achievements in themselves, and there was little time or personnel for overseas ventures. The Protestants, moreover, lacked the opportunities for overseas missions that were readily available to Roman Catholics who dominated the religious scene in most of the seafaring nations, and who consequently were able to travel with and live under the protection of explorers and commercial companies. The landlocked Swiss and German states, early strongholds of Protestantism, offered Protestants no such access to foreign lands. Furthermore, the Protestants did not have a ready-made missionary force like the Roman Catholic monastic orders.

Protestant theology was another factor that limited the vision of missionary enterprises. Martin Luther was so certain of the imminent return of Christ that he overlooked the necessity of foreign missions. He further justified his position by claiming the Great Commission was binding only on the New Testament apostles who had fulfilled their obligation by spreading the gospel throughout the known world, thus exempting succeeding generations from responsibility. Calvinists generally used the same line of reasoning, adding the doctrine of election that made missions appear extraneous if God had already chosen those he would save. Calvin himself, however, was at least outwardly the most missionary-minded of all the Reformers. He not only sent dozens of evangelists back into his homeland of France, but also commissioned four missionaries, along with a number of French Huguenots, to establish a colony and evangelize the Indians in Brazil. Unfortunately, the venture that began in 1555 ended shortly in tragic failure when the renegade leader, Villegagnon, defected to the Portuguese, who then plundered the fledgling colony and left the few remaining defenseless survivors to be slain at the hands of the Jesuits.

The seventeenth century saw more scattered Protestant missionary efforts, but aside from the work carried on in the American colonies (see chapter 4), none of the ventures had real staying power. The Quakers had more than a passing interest in foreign missions, and in 1661 George Fox commissioned three of his brethren as missionaries to China; but the party never reached its destination. Some years later Justinian von Weltz, the first Lutheran foreign missionary, sailed to Surinam, located along the Atlantic Coast of South America, where he gave his life in an unsuccessful effort to establish a mission there.

It was the eighteenth century that witnessed the first great thrust of Protestant missions, for it was only then that Protestants in any significant numbers began recognizing their responsibility in evangelizing those without the gospel. Among the first to recognize this responsibility were Lutherans—Lutheran Pietists such as Philip Jacob Spener and August Hermann Francke, who had turned away from the cold formalism of the state churches. Francke, a professor at the University at Halle, turned that school into the center of continental Pietism and of eighteenth-century evangelism and foreign missions. Foreign missions, however, was not an acceptable course of action for most eighteenth-century church leaders and theologians, and Pietists were scorned and ridiculed. They were dubbed "enthusiasts," "priests of Baal," "heretics," "false Lutherans," and "dangerous people," but their confidence in the rightness of their position propelled them forward.

The first breakthrough in Protestant missions came when King Ferdinand IV of Denmark, a Pietist himself, appealed to Halle for missionaries to evangelize the people in his overseas holdings—particularly in Tranquebar, along the southeast coast of India. Bartholomew Ziegenbalg and Henry Plütschau (see chapter 5) volunteered to go, and the Danish-Halle mission was born. The following decade, in 1714, a missionary college was opened in Copenhagen that trained missionary recruits, including the great Hans Egede, who established a missionary colony in Greenland in 1722.

The most notable eighteenth-century missionary to serve with the Danish-Halle mission was Christian Frederick Schwartz, a devout Lutheran, who went to India in 1750 and served faithfully until his death forty-eight years later. Much of his missionary career was spent traveling along the coast of India, preaching the gospel and planting churches, an accomplishment that would have been impossible without his mastery of several languages and dialects. Though he remained unmarried and without children of his own, he conducted an effective ministry with children, who matured in the faith and swelled the ranks of his church in Tanjore to a membership of some two thousand. During his lifetime the Danish-Halle mission had seen significant growth, with approximately sixty of its missionaries coming from Halle alone, but the enthusiastic spirit of earlier years was waning. At the time of his death there were few new volunteers to fill the vacant posts.

Fortunately, the decline of the Danish-Halle mission did not sound the death knell of early Protestant missions. Another group, also influenced by the Pietism at Halle, had come to the fore and soon developed into one of the greatest missionary churches in all history. The Moravian Brethren (Unitas Fratrum), stirred by the indominable Count Zinzendorf, took the Great Commission to heart, paving the way for the great era of modern missions. During the eighteenth century alone the Moravians planted mission stations in the Virgin Islands (1732), Greenland (1733), North America (1734), Lapland and South America (1735), South Africa (1736), and Labrador (1771). Their all-consuming objective was to spread the gospel to the ends of the earth, a passion that was clearly evident in their proportion of missionaries to lay people. The ratio was 1:60, a noteworthy attainment in comparison to the ratio of 1:5000 in Protestantism as a whole.

One of the unique features of Moravian missions that made it possible for such a large percentage to serve as foreign missionaries was the fact that all missionaries were expected to be self-supporting. Moravianism was a movement that had risen out of the artisan class, and it seemed natural that the missionaries should take their trade with them as they traveled abroad. Voluntary contributions, according to Moravian mission theory, were simply inadequate to finance the task of world evangelism. The only alternative, then, was for Christians to be missionaries while pursuing their vocations.

In Labrador, Moravian missionaries supported themselves through trade, with enough money left over to provide basic necessities for needy Eskimos. They owned ships and trading posts, and through their example they interested Eskimos in productive pursuits. The effect of their ministry was not only to bring the gospel to the people but also to significantly upgrade the economy. In Surinam, on the northeast coast of South America, the Moravians established a variety of businesses, including tailoring, watchmaking, and baking. As their economic influence grew, so did their spiritual influence, and a thriving Moravian church emerged in that country.

"The most important contribution of the Moravians," writes William Danker, "was their emphasis that every Christian is a missionary and should witness through his daily vocation. If the example of the Moravians had been studied more carefully by other Christians, it is possible that the businessman might have retained his honored place within the expanding Christian world mission, beside the preacher, teacher, and physician."[1]

Count Nicolaus Ludwig von Zinzendorf

One of the greatest missionary statesmen of all times and the individual who did the most to advance the cause of Protestant missions during the course of the eighteenth century was a German-born nobleman, Count Nicolaus Ludwig von Zinzendorf. Zinzendorf had a powerful influence on early Protestant Christianity that in many respects equaled or excelled that of his personal acquaintances, John Wesley and George Whitefield. He pioneered ecumenical evangelism, founded the Moravian church, and authored scores of hymns, but above all else he launched a world-wide missionary movement that set the stage for William Carey and the "Great Century" of missions that would follow.

Zinzendorf was born in 1700 into wealth and nobility. The death of his father and the subsequent remarriage of his mother left him to be reared by his grandmother and aunt. It was their warm evangelical Pietism that turned his heart toward spiritual matters. His early teaching was reinforced by his education. At the age of ten he was sent away to study at Halle, where he sat under the inspiring teaching of the great Lutheran Pietist, August Hermann Francke. Here Zinzendorf banded together with other dedicated youths, and out of their association came the "Order of the Grain of Mustard Seed," a Christian fraternity committed to loving "the whole human family" and to spreading the gospel. From Halle, Zinzendorf went on to Wittenberg to study law in preparation for a career in state service— the only acceptable vocation for a nobleman. But he was unhappy with his prospects for the future. He longed to enter the Christian ministry—yet to break with family tradition would be unthinkable. The decision weighed heavily on his mind until 1719, when an incident during a tour of Europe changed the course of his life. While visiting an art gallery he viewed a painting (Domenico Feti's *Ecce Homo*) that depicted Christ enduring the crown of thorns, with an inscription that read, "All this I did for you, what are you doing for me?"[2] From that

moment on, Zinzendorf knew he could never be happy living the life of a nobleman. No matter what the cost, he would seek a life of service for the Savior who had suffered so much to save him.

The opportunity for Zinzendorf to become involved in meaningful Christian service did not come until 1722, when a group of Protestant refugees sought shelter on his estate at Berthelsdorf, later named Herrnhut, meaning "the Lord's watch." Zinzendorf's invitation to these refugees to settle on the land, despite opposition from other family members, was a turning point in the development of the Moravian movement. Herrnhut grew rapidly as word of the count's generosity spread. Religious refugees continued to arrive, and soon the estate turned into a thriving community dotted with newly constructed houses and shops. But with the increasing numbers came problems. The diverse religious backgrounds of the residents created discord, and on more than one occasion the very existence of Herrnhut was in jeopardy.

Then in 1727, five years after the first refugees arrived, the whole atmosphere changed. A period of spiritual renewal was climaxed at a communion service on August 13 with a great revival, which, according to participants, marked the coming of the Holy Spirit to Herrnhut. Whatever may have occurred in the spiritual realm, there is no doubt that this great night of revival brought a new passion for missions, which became the chief characteristic of the Moravian movement. No longer were minor doctrinal differences a source of contention. Instead, there was a strong spirit of unity and a heightened dependence on

God. A prayer vigil was begun that continued around the clock, seven days a week, without interruption for more than one hundred years.

Direct involvement in foreign missions did not come until some years after the great spiritual awakening. Zinzendorf was attending the coronation of Danish King Christian VI, and during the festivities he was introduced to two native Greenlanders (converts of Hans Egede) and a Negro slave from the West Indies. So impressed was he with their pleas for missionaries that he invited the latter to visit Herrnhut, and he himself returned home with a powerful sense of urgency. Within a year the first two Moravian missionaries had been commissioned to the Virgin Islands, and in the two decades that followed, the Moravians sent out more missionaries than all Protestants (and Anglicans) had sent out in the previous two centuries.

Count Nicolaus Ludwig von Zinzendorf.

Although Zinzendorf is known primarily as a missionary statesman, he willingly helped in foreign mission ventures himself. In 1738, some years after the first missionaries had gone to the Caribbean, Zinzendorf accompanied three new recruits who had been commissioned to join their colleagues there. When they arrived they were distressed to find their colleagues in prison, but Zinzendorf wasted no time in using his prestige and authority as a nobleman to secure their release. During his visit he conducted daily services for the Negroes and revamped the organizational structure and territorial assignments for the missionaries. When he was satisfied that the mission work was on a solid footing, he returned to Europe, after two years to sail again, this time to the American colonies. Here he labored alongside the brethren who were working among the Indians, and he visited Moravian and Lutheran congregations, seeking to unify them into one body; but in neither area was he successful. The Lutherans resisted his ecumenical endeavors, and the Indians were apparently even less impressed with him.

Although Zinzendorf had renounced his life as a nobleman, he was never able to suppress his arrogance and conceit, and he found it difficult to lower himself to the life of a rank and file missionary. He openly despised living in the wilderness and enduring the drudgery of day-to-day missionary work. He viewed the Indians as uncivilized and crude, and he resented their invasion of his privacy. Surprisingly, his inability to relate to them or even get along with them did not dim his enthusiasm for evangelizing them. Zinzendorf was above all a missionary statesman, and before leaving America he appointed twenty more missionaries to American Indian mission work.

As a missionary statesman, Zinzendorf spent thirty-three years as the overseer of a world-wide network of missionaries who looked to him for leadership. His methods were simple and practical and ones that endured the test of time. All of his missionaries were lay people who were trained not as theologians but as evangelists. As self-supporting laymen, they were expected to work alongside their prospective converts, witnessing their faith by the spoken word and by their living example—always seeking to identify themselves as equals, not as superiors. Their task was solely evangelism, strictly avoiding any involvement in local political or economic affairs. Their message was the love of Christ—a very simple gospel message —with intentional disregard for doc-

trinal truths until after conversion; and even then, an emotional mysticism took precedence over theological teaching. Above all else, the Moravian missionaries were single-minded. Their ministry came before anything else. Wives and families were abandoned for the cause of Christ. Young men were encouraged to remain single, and when marriage was allowed, the spouse was often chosen by lot.

The chief example of single-mindedness was Zinzendorf himself. His wife and children were frequently left behind as he traveled through Europe and abroad, and his exile for more than a decade from his homeland further complicated his family life. While he was away, his business and legal affairs were handled by his very capable wife, Erdmuth, but she was less adept at keeping their marriage relationship intact. It was no secret that he and Erdmuth had grown cool

THE MORAVIAN CHURCH
AROUND THE WORLD

Erdmuth Zinzendorf, Count Zinzendorf's wife.

toward each other and that the last fifteen years of their marriage was a marriage in name only. Nevertheless, her death was a time of bitter grief for Zinzendorf. According to John Weinlick, his biographer, "... the count's sorrow was aggravated by remorse. He had not been fair to Erdmuth. Cynics to the contrary, he had not been unfaithful to her during their long periods of separation; but he had been extremely thoughtless. He had forgotten that she was a woman, a wife, and a mother."[3]

After the year of mourning for Erdmuth was over, Zinzendorf married Anna Nitchmann, a peasant woman who, along with others, had been his traveling companion for many years. The marriage was kept secret for more than a year, partly to avoid a family controversy over his stooping to marry a woman so far beneath his social rank. Despite her lowly status, Anna was a dedicated

Moravian sister who had had a strong ideological influence on Zinzendorf, particularly in the area of mysticism, and it was this very phenomenon that brought on grave problems for the mission.

Under the count's leadership, the Moravian church had placed great emphasis on the death of Christ. As a child he had meditated on the death and agony of the Lord, and his call to the ministry had become evident while viewing a painting depicting Christ's agony. As time passed, what once had been an emphasis turned into a gruesome obsession, and the whole church seemed to be carried away in a radical form of mysticism. Both the Moravian brothers and the sisters began denigrating their own worth as they morbidly depicted the death of Christ. In a circular letter to the churches, Anna (years before she and Zinzendorf were married) wrote, "Like a poor little worm, I desire to withdraw myself into his wounds," and Zinzendorf himself spoke of the brethren as "little blood worms in the sea of grace." An "Order of Little Fools" was formed, and Zinzendorf encouraged the members to behave like little children and to think of themselves as "little fish swimming in the bed of blood" or "little bees who suck the wounds of Christ."[4]

While some may view the Moravians' obsession with the physical death of Christ as merely a strange aberration of the evangelical Christian heritage, the significance lies far deeper than that in its relation to Christian missions. The more mystical and introspective the Moravians became in their personal identification with the Lord's physical suffering, the less they cared about the needs of others, particularly regarding world evangelism. They viewed their mystical, sensual experiences as evidence of ultimate spirituality and neglected the practical side of their faith. Active missionaries were actually looked down on because they had not yet reached the mystics' high plane of spirituality, and the cause of missions, therefore, suffered.

All this may have brought a quick demise to this great missionary movement, but, fortunately, the count came to his senses before that occurred. Admitting that the condition of the church had "greatly degenerated," and that he himself had "probably occasioned it," Zinzendorf was able to put that "brief but fearful"[5] period behind him and to steer his following back on course again. Certainly that factor alone adds to the stature of this great man.

Zinzendorf's contribution to missions is best seen in the lives of the men and women who accepted his challenge to forsake all for the sake of the gospel. Their sole motivation was Christ's sacrificial love for the world, and it was with that message that they went to the ends of the earth.

Christian David and Hans Egede

Apart from Count Zinzendorf, the individual most involved in the founding of the Moravian church was Christian David, who was responsible for bringing exiled brethren (Unitas Fratum) from all over Europe to Zinzendorf's estate. David was born in Moravia in 1690 into a Roman Catholic family. As a youngster he was a devout Catholic, zealous in his observance of rituals, holidays, and in his adoration of the Virgin Mary. Later he recalled that his heart burned like a stove with religious devotion. But despite his deep sincerity, he had no real understanding of true Christianity until he was sent away from home to be apprenticed to a master who, along with his family, secretly embraced a warm evangelical faith. But even then David's exposure to Christian teachings was limited. It was not until he was twenty that he acquired a Bible, a book that he had never before laid eyes on.

In 1717, at the age of twenty-seven, David was converted, and soon after that, through the encouragement of his devoted wife, Anna, he became a traveling lay preacher. During his travels he met hundreds of disheartened, persecuted Christians who longed for a refuge where they could worship freely; and it was with that background that David met Zinzendorf in 1722, which led to their joint efforts to establish Herrnhut. During the years that followed, David represented Herrnhut as he traveled around Europe recruiting settlers.

Although he was a carpenter by trade and had been effective in recruiting settlers, Christian David was eager to become involved more directly in evangelism, and in 1733 his opportunity came. He, along with two other Moravians, was commissioned as a missionary to Greenland to revitalize the mission work there. Two years before their departure for Greenland, Zinzendorf had heard rumor that Lutheran missionary Hans Egede was about to abandon his work there, and it was this erroneous information that prompted Zinzendorf to come to the rescue. He immediately called for volunteers among his Moravian following to fill the gap, and David was chosen to be the leader.

Christian David, Moravian missionary to Greenland.

The arrival of Moravian missionaries came as a surprise to Egede. He welcomed them, but almost immediately problems and misunderstandings arose. Both Egede and David were hard-headed and stubborn, and a language barrier further complicated matters. Egede, a native of Norway, had difficulty understanding the German spoken by the Moravian newcomers, and they could not comprehend his Norwegian tongue at all. David and his companions, however, quickly realized that Egede had no intention of forsaking his mission.

Hans Egede and his family had been in Greenland for more than a decade when the Moravians arrived; and despite setbacks, they remained wholly dedicated to the mission. Born in Norway in 1686 (four years before Christian David), Egede grew up in a devout Lutheran family and was deeply influenced by a warm spirit of Pietism that had penetrated the Scandanavian countries. He studied for the ministry and then spent a stormy ten years in the pastorate. Conflict with another minister in his diocese over money matters resulted in his being fined more than once by an ecclesiastical court. Apparently Egede was not receiving enough money to keep his family out of poverty, but the manner in which he sought to handle the situation was out of line.

Since his childhood Egede had heard tales of Greenland and of the Christians who centuries before had migrated there from Scandanavia— Christians whose descendants had not been heard from for more than two hundred years. He had learned from his Norwegian history that the gospel had been carried to Greenland hundreds of years before by Leif the Lucky (the son of Eric the Red, a violent man who had been ordered first to leave Norway and later to leave Iceland due to separate incidents of manslaughter). Leif, accompanied by a priest, propagated Christianity among the Greenlanders, and by the twelfth century the church there had grown to the point that it was permitted to have its own bishop; but as time passed, the church deteriorated and relapsed into paganism.

These stories, combined with Pietistic missionary fervor, impelled the young Norwegian pastor to pursue the possibility of beginning a mission to Greenland to those "poor people, who in former times had been Christians and enlightened in the Christian faith, but who now for lack of teachers and instruction had again fallen into heathen blindness and savagery."[6] With no mission board to sponsor him, Egede sent a proposal "for the conversion and enlightenment of the Greenlanders"[7] to the King (of the joint kingdom of Denmark-Norway) and to church authorities, but a war being waged with Sweden delayed action on his request for a number of years.

In the meantime Egede confronted strong personal opposition to his plans. His mother-in-law was incensed when she heard the news, and his wife, Giertrud (thirteen years his senior), was stunned and hinted that she regretted ever marrying him. Her attitude soon changed. After she and her husband prayed together about the matter she became his most faithful supporter, and they moved forward together in what now had become a joint calling. When others pressured him to forsake his plans, she held firm in her support: "My dear wife gave a proof of her great faith and constancy by representing to me that it was now too late to repent of what had been done. I cannot say how much she encouraged me by speaking in this way and by the fact that she, a frail woman, showed greater faith and manliness than I."[8]

In the summer of 1718, Egede, along with his wife and four children, left his parish in the North and sailed south to the seaport at Bergen, where he hoped to secure passage to Greenland. This first leg of the journey, along the treacherous Norwegian coast, turned out to be a perilous nightmare that might have crushed a weaker commitment. Egede fell overboard and would have perished but for a hairbreadth rescue by a fisherman. Rather than discouraging him, the mishap buoyed his faith and convinced him that his rescue was a clear sign from God that he had been spared for a divine purpose.

After more than two years of delays

and uncertainty in Bergen, the Egedes obtained passage through the Bergen Company and arrived in Greenland in the summer of 1721. After hastily building a dwelling to shelter his family during the cold months ahead, Egede settled down to the very unromantic life of being a foreign missionary. The pleasant summer weather was spoiled by swarms of ever-present gnats. But even more troublesome than the gnats was the language barrier. Egede had hoped to find a language similar to his own, brought to Greenland centuries before by his own people, but his hopes were soon dashed. Trying to communicate even the simplest phrases turned into a lengthy ordeal, and to make matters worse, Egede failed to detect even a trace of Christian beliefs that he had hoped might have been passed down through the centuries.

Communication was not the only cultural barrier that Egede had to overcome. The lifestyle of the Eskimos was so vastly different from his own. They lived in primitive dwellings, four to six feet high, often overcrowded with several families in one dwelling and torturously overheated in the winter. The sickening stench of spoiled meat and fish, combined with the repulsive odor of the urine tubs (for soaking hides), made the atmosphere almost unbearable for the Norwegian preacher; but home visitation was his only effective means of contact with the Eskimos during the long winter months.

Egede's ministry to the Eskimos got off to a slow start. While his young sons, Paul and Niels, quickly picked up the difficult language as they played with their friends, Egede struggled for years with the complexities of the grammar, and even then he found it very difficult to communicate spiritual values. He depended heavily on Paul and Niels, and they proved to be a tremendous asset in his ministry. Egede's most effective method of winning the friendship and the audience of the Eskimos during his early years in Greenland was through music. According to his biographer, Louis Bobé, "he won their hearts by singing to them."[9]

Nevertheless, the progress of evangelism was painfully slow. Egede insisted the Eskimos forsake their heathen ways, and he forcefully proclaimed that there could be no compromise between Christianity and paganism. He was adamant in his stance against heathen religious rituals, demanding that the Eskimos abolish their sacred protective charms, their superstitious drumdances and songs, and their "devilish jugglery." He had little understanding of their beliefs and thus was unable to establish any common ground between their pagan religion and Christianity. Furthermore, it was his objective to transform them into "human beings" before attempting to convert them to Christianity. It was this approach that prompted him to concentrate his efforts on children. Since they had not been steeped in pagan superstitions like their parents, they were more teachable. With their parents' permission, he baptized them and began teaching them the truths of Christianity as soon as they could grasp the meaning.

Egede never abandoned his dream of finding Greenlanders whose heritage could be traced back to his own native land. Through his searching he discovered remnants of European architecture, including the foundation of a church preserved from the Norse ruins; but he never was able to detect a trace of Christianity that may have been passed down from the earlier generations of Christians.

The slow progress of Egede's mission work and the lack of commercial success of the Bergen Company combined to dim the early enthusiasm there had been for the Greenland venture back home. Then in 1730, King Frederick IV, a strong supporter of the Greenland missionary venture, died, and his successor, King Christian VI, came to power. The following year Christian VI decided to abandon the Greenland commercial enterprise, and the company officials and workers were recalled. Egede himself was permitted to stay, but even his residence there was in question. It was this situation that led to the rumor that Egede was giving up his missionary work and that prompted Zinzendorf to commission Christian David and his Moravian colleagues to continue the work that Egede had begun.

Problems between the newly arrived Moravians and the veteran missionary Hans Egede were virtually inevitable. Egede, with his domineering and harsh personality, offended the Moravians, who believed in a softer approach to evangelism. "What followed," according to historian Stephen Neill, "is typical of what almost always happens when a second mission enters a territory where an older mission is already established. The newcomers pick on the weaknesses of the old, with little regard for what the pioneers have endured."[10]

The conflict between the two groups focused on the method of evangelism. To the Moravians, Egede was a rigid and doctrinaire Lutheran who was more concerned with teaching his cold orthodoxy than with saving souls. How, they asked, could the Eskimos ever be expected to understand complex doctrine until God had given them the light of salvation? Egede, on the other hand, viewed the Moravians as preaching a deplorably sentimental religion, with little concern for Christian doctrine and the eradication of heathen superstitions. Their one-sided gospel of the love of Christ, with little reference to a holy, righteous, almighty God, he maintained, failed to present Christianity as it really was.

Despite the differences, Egede and the Moravians worked side by side, at times maintaining a reasonably warm relationship. Egede shared all of his linguistic notes and material with the Moravians as they struggled to come to grips with the language (though the language barrier between them made the notes of little value); and when they were ill with scurvy, he visited them often, doing what he could to relieve their suffering. His wife, Giertrud, also showed kindness to them, and was loved and respected by them. Nevertheless, the conflict was ever present, causing a contemporary observer to comment that the Greenlanders "are apt to doubt the whole of the Christian faith and to say: 'How can it be truth, which you yourselves are quarrelling about?'"[11]

The first real breakthrough for Egede in his ministry to the Eskimos came in 1733, around the time of the arrival of Christian David and his co-workers. Good news arrived from Denmark that their new king had decided to continue the Greenland mission work. But with this good news came a converted Greenlander returning from a visit to Denmark, who had become a carrier of the smallpox germ. On his return he traveled from village to village, ministering with Egede and unknowingly spreading the deadly germ wherever he went. Soon the Eskimos were ravaged with disease and fighting for their lives, and it was only then that the tender warmth and sacrificial love of this otherwise stern churchman was clearly demonstrated to them. What could not be transmitted in words was shown through weeks and months of selfless service as the disease continued to rage. Egede was on continual call, and when he was not out in the villages nursing the sick he was besieged at his own home. Hearing of his generosity, Eskimos came from miles around for treatment, and the sickest among them, wretched as they were, were brought into his own home, where he and his wife gave them beds and lovingly cared for them.

After the danger had passed and a calm had returned to the region, Egede noticed a greater interest in spiritual things among the people. He had endeared himself to them, and the Eskimos were now seeking him out for spiritual counsel. A dying Greenlander who had ignored the teaching of Egede when he was in good health poignantly expressed the feelings of the people toward their Norwegian missionary: "You have been more kind to us than we have been to one another; you have fed us, when we were famished; you have buried our dead, who would else have been prey to dogs, foxes, and ravens; and in particular you have told us of God and how to become blessed, so that we may now die gladly, in expectation of a better life hereafter."[12] The terrible epidemic of 1733 lasted less than a year, but the scars were permanent. Egede never fully regained his health, and his wife remained ill until her death in 1736.

In the meantime, the Moravians had become established in their missionary work and soon began seeing tremendous success. In 1738 a revival broke out, and in the years that followed hundreds of Eskimos were converted to Christianity. Bitter with envy and resentment, Egede accused Christian David of having "reaped what I have ploughed."[13] Egede's charge certainly had an element of truth, but the fact remains that the Moravians' methodology was more suited to the Eskimos than was Egede's. Their simple gospel, filled with emotional sentimentality, appealed to people whose mystical superstitions were in some ways not so far removed from the mysticism of the Moravians. Soon the little chapel at New Herrnhut was overcrowded, and a new church was constructed by the missionary-carpenter, Christian David.

After the death of his wife, Hans Egede returned to Copenhagen and remarried. From there he supervised the mission work in Greenland and trained young men for missionary service, but he saw very little fruit from his labors. His greatest joy was seeing his sons continue in the work of evangelizing Greenland. His son Paul, in particular, carried out a very effective ministry in the area of Disko Bay, where religious revival broke out and people came from great distances to hear him preach. His ministry, though, was cut short due to failing eyesight, but his heart was still in missions. He returned to Copenhagen, where he continued his Bible translation work and collaborated with his father in developing a doctrinal guide for the Greenlanders. Hans Egede died in 1758 at the age of seventy-two, and Paul lived on another thirty years, supporting the cause of missions in Greenland to the very end.

George Schmidt

At the very time that Christianity was being planted in Greenland, it was also being introduced in other remote areas of the world by dedicated Moravian missionaries. In South Africa, George Schmidt, an unmarried Moravian brother, was struggling against almost overwhelming odds to bring the gospel to the native population there. Schmidt was born in Moravia in 1709, and was converted at the age of sixteen during a revival among the Moravian brethren. Soon after that he journeyed to Herrnhut and was there at the time of the great revival on August 13, 1727.

At Herrnhut, Schmidt became a messenger who, along with other brethren, was sent out to preach the gospel. His assignment was to return with two colleagues to his homeland of Moravia, where it was well-known that persecution by Roman Catholic authorities was rife. Soon after they arrived their meetings were detected, and Schmidt and his companions were imprisoned. After their releases, the three young Moravians returned to Herrnhut, but it was not long before Schmidt was again sent out to preach—this time to Austria, an even harsher environment. Once again Schmidt, along with his traveling companion, sought to elude the authorities and conduct secret religious meetings, and once again arrests were made, and Schmidt found himself in prison. For three years he languished in a dungeon cell. Conditions were deplorable, and after less than a year his comrade died, leaving Schmidt to suffer alone. Were his suffering only physical Schmidt's trials would not have been so unbearable, but he also suffered mental anguish. Daily he was pressured to recant by the imperious Jesuits who were holding him, but he steadfastly refused. After three years of misery and torment, Schmidt was sentenced to hard labor, which lasted for another three years until finally he broke down and signed a revocation of his beliefs to satisfy the Roman Catholic authorities.

Having endured so much suffering and humiliation, Schmidt returned to Herrnhut, expecting to be warmly embraced by his brethren. Instead, he was met with a cool reception and was treated as an apostate by some because of his "weakness." He was devastated, and to prove he was not a coward he left the security of Herrnhut once again and went back into Roman Catholic strongholds to preach. But he was not happy, and he gratefully welcomed a change in 1736 when he was sent to Holland to learn the Dutch language and then dispatched to South Africa in 1737 to work among the Hottentots. Zinzendorf had heard the reports of Ziegenbalg and Plütschau (see chapter 5) who, on their way to India, had become burdened for these oppressed Africans.

South Africa was undoubtedly as difficult a mission field as any during the early eighteenth century. The Dutch colonists did not look favorably on missionary endeavors that might raise the social status of the Africans, and, not surprisingly then, Schmidt's arrival among them was viewed with antagonism. Moreover, the Calvinistic Dutch Reformed ministers who were in the Cape Colony deplored the emotional and sentimental Pietism of the Moravians. Schmidt himself did little to endear himself to the Dutch colonists. According to one account, "He was definitely a hypocrite and a sham, sometimes climbing on the low roof of the house.... There he knelt so that all ... could see him, and pretended to pray."[14]

After residing at a military post for a time, Schmidt traveled inland to a region known as "Ape Valley" to work among the Hottentots. The Hottentots, characterized by their lack of Negroid features and their small size, were regarded as "black cattle" by the colonists and were hunted down like animals in the colonists' effort to enslave them. They cautiously welcomed Schmidt, and, with the help of a Hottentot interpreter, he began preaching to them; and in a very short time he had established a school with some fifty pupils.

As with other Moravian missionaries, Schmidt's ministry was not financed by supporters back home. All Moravians were expected to be evangelists, and there was little differentiation between those who ministered on the home field and those who went abroad. Schmidt worked among the people, and personal evangelism was simply conducted during his daily contacts with them. For a time he worked as a day-laborer, butchering, tanning hides, threshing wheat, pruning fruit trees, and doing other farm chores; and after a time he acquired some livestock of his own as well as his own garden.

Life was not easy for Schmidt in

South Africa. The winter of 1740 was particularly severe, and he and his neighbors survived a food shortage only by shooting a hippopotamus, an animal not normally used for sustenance. But to Schmidt, matters of day-to-day living were secondary. His sole purpose for being in Africa was evangelism of its people; but in this area, too, he faced hard times and setbacks. His little flock of believers was unstable and given to backsliding. Even Africo, his interpreter, fell back into his old ways. He went on drinking binges with his friends and almost shipwrecked the fledgling little church. Schmidt reacted harshly, and a few days later the men involved repented; but spiritual lethargy persisted. So discouraged was Schmidt that he wrote to Zinzendorf that he intended to return home.

Schmidt's problems in building a sound fellowship of Christians were not only with the Africans but also with the Dutch residents and colonial authorities. Local farmers maliciously besmirched his reputation, some charging that he was living with a Hottentot woman, others claiming that he was a spy. And the colonial authorities, both religious and secular, deeply resented his continuing presence—the presence of an unordained laborer who had the audacity of assuming a position of spiritual leadership.

In an effort to stabilize the situation, Zinzendorf intervened. In a letter to Schmidt, he gave advice, outlined mission policy, and at the same time ordained him (obviously hoping to quell the criticism): "Why don't you baptise the children of the Hottentots who die in infancy? [Presumably he meant before they died.] He who comes with water and blood, has died for them too. I ordain you for the case of a baptism or a communion ... a minister of our church in the name of the Father, the Son and the Holy Ghost, Amen. ... I am very pleased with you. But, my dear, you aim too much at the skin of the Hottentots and too little at the heart. ... You must tell the Hottentots, especially their children, the story of the Son of God. If they feel something, pray with them, if not, pray for them. If feeling persists, baptise them where you shot your hippo."[15]

Receiving ordination was a great encouragement to Schmidt, and he immediately exercised his rights to administer the sacraments by baptizing Wilhelm, who had been his first Hottentot convert. Soon others were baptized, and word spread to Dutch officials of what was happening. Rather than calming the situation, Schmidt's ordination only intensified the animosity of the Dutch officials toward him. Reformed ministers at Cape Town insisted that the baptisms were invalid. They summoned two of the converts to come before them to undergo the standard catechism instruction, and were surprised to find them as knowledgeable of doctrine as some of their own candidates for baptism. Nevertheless, Schmidt was ordered to leave South Africa and face officials back in Holland. Thus in the spring of 1744 he sailed for Europe to argue the validity of his ministry before the Dutch authorities there.

Despite the efforts of Schmidt and other Moravian leaders, permission to return was never granted, and the little church among the Hottentots remained without a shepherd for nearly half a century until 1792. It was in that year that Moravians returned to the valley; and to their amazement they found an old woman whom Schmidt had baptized more than fifty years before still cherishing the New Testament he had given her.

The second missionary endeavor in the Cape Colony by the Moravians was far more successful than the first.

Under the capable direction of Hans Hallbeck, the mission work thrived, and by the mid-twentieth century there were thirty-eight stations and nearly fifty thousand professing Christians under Moravian jurisdiction.

SELECTED BIBLIOGRAPHY

Bobé, Louis. **Hans Egede: Colonizer and Missionary of Greenland.** *Copenhagen: Rosenkilde and Bagger, 1952.*

Hamilton, J. Taylor and Kenneth G. **History of the Moravian Church: The Renewed Unitas Fratrum, 1722–1957.** *Winston-Salem: Moravian Church in America, 1967.*

Hutton, J. E. **A History of Moravian Missions.** *London: Moravian Publication Office, 1923.*

Kruger, Bernhard. **The Pear Tree Blossoms: A History of the Moravian Mission Stations in South Africa, 1737–1869.** *South Africa: Genadendal Printing Works, 1967.*

Langton, Edward. **History of the Moravian Church.** *London: Allen & Unwin, 1956.*

Weinlick, John R. **Count Zinzendorf.** *Nashville: Abingdon, 1956.*

Chapter 4

American Indian Missions:
Seeking the "Noble Savage"

"Redskins." "Aborigines." "The noble savage." "The lost tribes of Israel." No other native population of the world has been both more ardently solicited and more pushed around by government officials, politicians, and church leaders than the native American Indians. For centuries Indians were a prime target of Christian evangelism. The heyday of Catholic missions climaxed in the new world where the mighty force of the Roman Catholic establishment was mobilized to convert the natives to Catholicism. But an equally great zeal for reaching the Indians was advanced by the Protestants, led by English politicians, merchants, and churchmen, and carried out by a band of courageous missionaries. The story of American Indian missions is an intriguing one—a story of high-pitched emotion, of zeal, and of dedication, but ultimately a story of extensive failure. How could so much consecrated effort result in so little fruit? Two centuries of aggressive land grabbing, cultural clashes, and slow extermination tell the story.

The first missionaries to come to North America were Roman Catholics. In the sixteenth century Spanish priests, mainly from the Franciscan order, began working among the Pueblos in what is now the Southwest United States. A number of missions were established, and many of the Indians became nominal Christians, though they insisted on retaining many of their ancient religious traditions. A century later Catholic missions, represented by the French Jesuits, entered the St. Lawrence Valley (present-day Ontario) and began working among the Hurons. By the middle of the seventeenth century, half of the tribe was nominally Christian, but then disaster struck. The Iroquois League launched an all-out military campaign against the Hurons, and before it was over most of them were either killed or scattered. Jean de Brèbeuf, the leader of the mission, was tortured and murdered, and an era of Jesuit missions to the Hurons was over. Work continued in Quebec and elsewhere, but not with the enthusiasm it had once had.

Later on Roman Catholic missionaries began working among Indians on the Great Plains and in the Oregon Territory, but it was the Protestant missionary venture, more than the Roman Catholic, that made a lasting impact on the North American Indians. From the very beginning of English exploration of the new world there was a strong impulse to win the native population to Christianity. Writings of navigators, trading companies, and government magistrates indicate a calculated missionary zeal. Christianizing the natives became a powerful rationale for colonialism, and colonial charters emphasized Indian evangelism. The Virginia charter of 1606 opens with the king's blessing on the colonists "in propagating the Christian religion to such people as yet live in darkness and miserable ignorance." The Massachusetts Bay charter pledged to "wynn and incite the natives of the Country to the Knowledge and obedience of the only true God and Savior of Mankinde, and the Christian fayth." And the seal of the colony testified to this need; its emblem was a figure of an Indian crying out "Come over and help us." The charter of Connecticut asserted that "evangelization" was the "onlye and principal end" for the colony's establishment. Likewise Pennsylvania and other colonies were founded with the declared purpose of converting the Indians.

In many instances, however, the pronouncements of the government charters were little more than hollow rhetoric. As settlers staked out their land claims, the "poor savage" became a threat and hindrance rather than a potential brother in Christ. Greed overpowered the sentiments of humanitarianism and evangelism, and the work of the missionaries was openly despised. Thus, missionaries not only faced hostile natives, but also encountered the ridicule and opposition of their own people. There were exceptions. Massachusetts, more than any other colony, sought to fulfill its charter obligations. Ministers of the gospel were highly respected in that colony, and they were charged with a dual responsibility: to convert the Indians as well as to minister to the colonial settlers. Frequently, though, ministers were too busy to devote time to both facets of their ministry, and Indian evangelism was neglected; but in other instances colonial ministers took the dual charge seriously and established impressive missionary outreaches.

John Eliot

One of the first and probably the greatest of all missionaries to the American Indians was John Eliot, often referred to as the "Apostle to the Indians." But despite the greatness he achieved as a missionary, Eliot's primary vocation was his ministry at the Roxbury church. He was a Congregational minister—a colonial New England church father—not a missionary in the strictest sense of the word. Nevertheless, his devotion to the task of bringing Christianity to the Indians makes him one of the great missionary leaders of all history, and many of his methods carry a timeless quality.

John Eliot was born in England and educated at Cambridge where, after training for the ministry, he graduated in 1622. Although he was ordained in the Anglican Church, he was a Nonconformist, and thus any pulpit ministry he sought to have in England would have been insecure and limited in scope. So after serving as a school teacher for several years under the great Puritan father, Thomas Hooker, he sailed to America where his options in the ministry were wide open. The summer of 1631 brought him safely to Massachusetts, a colony that had not yet celebrated its second birthday.

Though the New England wilderness appeared remote and uncivilized, Eliot soon felt very much at home. His three brothers and three sisters as well as his fiancée all joined him in the New World within a year. After spending a year in Boston as a substitute pastor, Eliot accepted a call to the church in Roxbury, where many of his friends and neighbors from England had settled. Roxbury was a small frontier settlement just two miles outside Boston, and there in October of 1632 John Eliot and Hanna Mumford were married in a civil ceremony—the first wedding recorded in that town.

As with many colonial pastors, Eliot's early years in the ministry were filled with the needs of his flock. There were Indians close by, but their occasional visits to Roxbury attracted little attention. They were peaceable, and the settlers accepted their presence with little thought of evangelizing them. In fact, many New Englanders, including ministers, looked on the growing death rate of Indians due to imported European diseases as God's means of "clearing the land" for "His people." Indians were an annoying nuisance that slowed down the progress of civilization.

It was not until 1644 when Eliot was forty years old that he seriously began his missionary endeavor. There was

John Eliot, Puritan missionary to the Algonquin Indians.

no Macedonian call. There was no solemn commission. There was simply a need, and he was available. His first step was language study—two years of mental anguish learning the Massachusetts dialect of the Algonquin tongue, an unwritten language composed of gutteral sounds and voice inflections. This difficult task was aided by Cochenoe, a young Indian captured in the Pequot War. Cochenoe served as Eliot's teacher and also accompanied him as an interpreter and assistant for a number of years.

In the fall of 1646 Eliot delivered his first sermon to a group of Indians who lived nearby. It was the first crucial test of his ability to effectively communicate, and he longed for success. Despite his efforts, his message fell on deaf ears; the Indians "regarded it not" nor gave "heed unto it, but were weary and despised what I said." A month later Eliot preached again, this time to a larger group of Indians who congregated at Waban's wigwam. The response was greatly improved. The Indians listened intently for more than an hour, and when the sermon was over they asked questions—questions Eliot later described as "curious, wonderful, and interesting." Eliot answered some of the questions, but then with perceptive missionary psychology he closed the question time and "resolved to leave them with an appetite." Before leaving the encampment, Eliot passed out treats, including sweetmeats and apples for the children and tobacco for the men. He had his first taste of success, and he "departed with many welcomes."[1]

Two weeks after this encouraging meeting Eliot returned, accompanied by two pastors and a layman (as he had been on his first visits). More curiosity-seeking Indians turned out and the meeting was profitable. Following his opening prayer, Eliot drilled the children in recitation of catechism, and of course the parents learned while they listened. He then preached on the Ten Commandments and on Christ's love, to which some Indians responded with tears and weeping. Again there were questions that followed—the most difficult of which to answer was, "Why has no white man ever told us these things before?"

Eliot continued making bi-weekly trips to Waban's wigwam in the months that followed, always with catechism lessons and evangelistic sermons that were carefully prepared and rehearsed in the complex Algonquin language. Although he carried a heavy share of the ministry himself, he actively recruited the help of others, including neighboring pastors and his own parishioners. Their enthusiasm buoyed his spirits and kept the mis-

sion going during difficult times. Travel was always slow and cumbersome. Trudging through the rugged wilderness trails was fatiguing, but Eliot's optimism could not be dampened: "We never had a bad day to go preach to the Indians all the winter. Praised be the Lord."[2]

As the weeks and months passed, some Indians were converted and noticeable changes were seen in their lives. A report published less than a year after Eliot's first meeting documented the following progress:

> The Indians have utterly forsaken their powwows.
>
> They have set up morning and evening prayers in their wigwams.
>
> They not only keep the Sabbath themselves, but have made a law to punish those who do not. Whoever profanes it must pay twenty shillings.
>
> They begin to grow industrious and are making articles to sell all the year long. In winter, brooms, stoves, eelpots, baskets; in spring they sell cranberries, fish, strawberries.
>
> The women are learning to spin.[3]

One of the first concerns of the Indians as well as of Eliot was to have an area of land specifically designated for the Christian Indians. Eliot's rationale was that new converts needed to be separated from those who had no interest in the gospel. The Indians, on the other hand, wanted some place to call their own. White settlers had been homesteading and building fences, leaving the Indians restricted in their hunting and fishing. Eliot made an appeal in their behalf to the General Court, and the Indians were granted several thousand acres eighteen miles southwest of Boston in an out-of-the-way corner of the Natick territory. The Indians raised no objections to

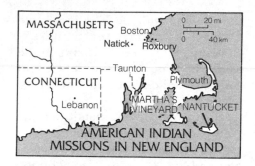

AMERICAN INDIAN
MISSIONS IN NEW ENGLAND

moving, and soon they established Natick, commonly referred to as a "praying town."

Natick was not a typical Indian settlement. Streets were laid out, and each family was given a lot. Some buildings, through the encouragement of Eliot, were constructed European style, but most of the Indians chose wigwams for their own homes. A Biblical form of government, based on Jethro's plan in Exodus 18:21, was set up by Eliot; the town was divided into tens, fifties, and hundreds, each division with a ruling adult male. The white man's civilization became the standard, and Christian Indians were expected to fall in line. To Eliot, true Christianity not only changed the heart and mind, but also the lifestyle and culture. He could not envision a truly Christian community apart from European culture, and this factor can, in hindsight, be seen as the one grave weakness of his ministry. Unfortunately, generations of missionaries that followed him, with few exceptions, perpetuated the same fallacy.

There were problems in establishing Natick, particularly from white settlers who resented the Indians' permanent residence among them, but Eliot periodically petitioned the Massachusetts General Court for more grants of land, and by 1671 he had gathered more than eleven hundred

Indians into fourteen "praying towns." His ministry was carefully scrutinized by the General Court, and he eagerly accepted all public funding they appropriated for his projects.

Although Eliot spent time and effort with temporal matters, his primary concern was the spiritual welfare of the Indians. He was slow and meticulous in his evangelism, and though he witnessed his first conversions after preaching to them only three times, he never tried to hurry the process. In fact, he purposefully delayed baptism and church membership until he was convinced the Indians were committed to their new faith. The first baptisms were delayed until 1651, five years after the first conversions. Likewise, the establishment of a church was put off until Eliot and his fellow ministers decided the Indians were ready to assume church offices and responsibilities.

Eliot was interested in more than professions of faith. He sought spiritual maturity in his Indian followers, and in his view that could be accomplished only if the Indians could read and study the Bible in their own language. Therefore, in 1649, three years after his first sermon at Waban's wigwam, amid a hectic schedule, he began his translation work. His first completed project was a catechism printed in 1654. The following year the Book of Genesis and the Gospel of Matthew were published; and in 1661 the New Testament was completed, with the Old Testament following two years later. Despite this noteworthy accomplishment, Eliot was harshly criticized for wasting his time in the Indian language when he could have been teaching the Indians English.

As the years passed and as the praying towns grew in numbers and the Christian Indians grew spiritually, Eliot concentrated more and more on training Indian leaders. By 1660 twenty-four Indians had been trained as evangelists to minister to their own people, and several churches had ordained Indian ministers. Schools were established in every town, and the Indians were seemingly adapting well to European culture. On the surface the future looked bright, but time was running out. Decades of European encroachment on Indian lands could not go unchecked indefinitely. The land encroachment, dishonest bargaining, and ill treatment of the Indians were bound to bring retaliation. There was unrest among the Indians of the Northeast, and even the praying Indians would not escape the horror looming on the horizon—the bloodiest war in American colonial history.

King Philip's War (named for the Wampanoag chief who initiated the fighting) broke out in the summer of 1675, after three of the chief's braves were hanged for the murder of a friendly Indian who had tipped off a colonial governor of the chief's plan to attack. This war was nearly lost by the settlers in what almost became a parallel on a much larger scale of the ill-fated settlement in Virginia. Even so, before the fighting was over, more than a year after it began, thirteen towns and many more settlements had been utterly devastated. Whole families—grandparents, aunts, uncles, and little children—were obliterated from the registers of colonial record books.

The saga of the praying Indians during this bloody war was a tragic one—a story repeated again and again in American history. Although even the praying Indians had legitimate complaints against the white encroachment on their land and, in the words of Eliot, "the business about land giveth them no small matter for stumbling,"[4] they nevertheless stood loyally by the white settlers when the Wampanoags and later other tribes attacked. Moreover, they aided the colonial militia as scouts and fighters. Their aid tipped the scales in favor of the settlers. But their loyalty and service were not enough. Tensions were high. All Indians were suspect, and thus hundreds of Christian Indians were exiled to a "bleake bare Island" in Boston Harbor—"harried away" before they could gather possessions and forced to endure a harsh winter without sufficient food or supplies.

Eliot visited the Indians several times during that dire winter and pleaded with officials on their behalf for more food and medicine, but his concern and sympathy produced little material help. Notwithstanding, these exiled Indians were more fortunate than the families they left behind. Many who remained were indiscriminately murdered by cowardly settlers seeking vengeance on anyone who fit the description of a redskin. When the violence ended, most of the surviving Christian Indians trickled back to their devastated towns. Efforts were made to rebuild, but life was never the same. The Indians had been weakened not only numerically, but also spiritually. Many of the Indians who became soldiers were enticed by the white man's liquor and no longer cared for spiritual things.

King Philip's War was a tragedy for the many Indians and whites directly involved, as well as for one aging seventy-two-year-old saint. John Eliot had poured decades of selfless service into his missionary work, and it was difficult to view the wreckage of the war. But he was not one to give up: "I can do little, yet I am resolved through the grace of Christ, I will never give over the worke, so long as I have legs to go."[5] As the years passed his output decreased, but he remained faithful to the work until his death in 1690 at the age of eighty-five.

Although much of Eliot's work was ravaged by the devastation of war, his place as a missionary statesman of the first rank was not blemished. His example as an evangelist and Bible translator paved the way for further missionary efforts among the Indians, and his influence in the founding of the SPG (Society for the Propagation of the Gospel), a missionary arm of the Anglican church that actively worked in the American colonies, cannot be overestimated.

What was the secret behind Eliot's exceptional life of service? What carried him through the years of opposition, hardship, and disappointment? Three characteristics are worth noting: his unbending optimism, his ability to enlist the help of others, and his absolute certainty that God, not he, was saving souls and was in control of the bad times as well as the good.

The Mayhews

Eliot was only one among several colonial New England pastors who was ministering effectively among the Indians. Another noteworthy mission to the native population was conducted on Martha's Vineyard by the Mayhew family. Thomas Mayhew, Sr., came to America in the 1630s at about the same time that Eliot arrived. Soon after he arrived he settled on Martha's Vineyard, where he purchased the proprietary rights and became governor. His son, Thomas, Jr., studied for the ministry and was ordained in his early twenties, and then he returned home to Martha's Vineyard to serve as a minister.

Although young Mayhew's primary ministry was to white settlers, he, like Eliot, soon became burdened for nearby Indians. He patiently worked on a one-to-one basis with them, and in 1643 he had his first convert, an Indian named Hiacoomes. From then on young Mayhew and Hiacoomes traveled together evangelizing other Indians—Hiacoomes serving as an interpreter until Mayhew learned the native language. In less than ten years there were nearly three hundred converts, and Mayhew was operating a school in their behalf. There was great promise for the ministry of this young pastor who was yet in his early thirties, and he had the rest of his life to build up the work. In the meantime, he wanted to publicize the work abroad, and he decided to sail to England with one of his converts. Despite pleas from associates to remain with the work, young Mayhew said good-by to his wife and children and set sail for England in 1655, never to be heard from again.

After it became apparent that his son had been lost at sea, Thomas Mayhew, Sr., the then seventy-year-old governor and landlord of Martha's Vineyard, took over the mission work. Though not a minister himself, he was respected by the Indians because he had honored their land titles and social structure, and they readily accepted him as their spiritual leader. With a grave sense of responsibility he assumed his son's duties and served as a missionary for twenty-two years until he died at the age of ninety-two. His grandson, John Mayhew, was also associated with the work, and after his death, Experience Mayhew, the fourth generation of Mayhews, took over the work for thirty-two more years.

David Brainerd

One of the most intriguing missionaries to the American Indians, and perhaps of all time, is David Brainerd, an heir of New England Puritanism and a product of the Great Awakening. Brainerd was a zealot. Bringing the gospel to scattered wandering tribes of Indians was his single mission. He spent his life for that cause. At the age of twenty-nine, after a mere five years of missionary work, he died as a result of his strenuous labors. Brainerd's place in history is based largely on the tremendous inspiration his personal life has had on others. His journal, diary, and biography, published by Jonathan Edwards, are classics of Christian literature, and missionaries through the centuries, including William Carey and Henry Martyn, have been deeply influenced by his life. But his methods of evangelism have been questioned. Brainerd's methods differed markedly from those of his great missionary predecessor to the American Indians, John Eliot, and in spite of the intensity of Brainerd's efforts the results of the work were meager.

David Brainerd was born in 1718 in Haddam, Connecticut. His father was a country squire who lived with his wife and nine children on a substantial estate overlooking the Connecticut River. David's father died when David was only eight years old, and his mother died when he was fourteen—a tragedy that ever lingered in his memory. Death was very real to him, and in many respects he missed the joys of a happy carefree childhood. He was sober and studious and very concerned about the condition of his soul.

At the age of twenty, after living with his sister and working on a farm for a time, Brainerd returned to Haddam to study in the home of an elderly minister. This pious old gentleman had a genuine concern for his young disciple, but his advice "to stay away from youth and cultivate grave, elderly people"[6] was hardly the counsel Brainerd needed. It only seemed to perpetuate his roller coaster religious pilgrimage that took him from peaks of lofty spirituality to valleys of mortifying despair. Brainerd's spiritual struggle climaxed with an experience of "unspeakable glory," which gave him assurance of his salvation, but his spiritual highs and lows persisted the rest of his life.

In September of 1739, at the age of twenty-one, Brainerd enrolled at Yale College. It was a time of transition at Yale. When he first entered the school he was distressed by the religious indifference he saw around him, but the impact of George Whitefield and the Great Awakening soon made its mark, and the whole atmosphere changed. Prayer and Bible study groups sprang up overnight—usually to the displeasure of school authorities who were fearful of religious "enthusiasm." It was in this atmosphere that young Brainerd made an intemperate remark about one of the tutors, commenting that he had "no more grace" than a chair, judging him to be a hypocrite. The remark was carried back to the school officials who were no doubt looking for an incident to discredit the spiritual revival, and David, a convenient scapegoat, was expelled after he refused to make a public apology for what he had said in private.

It was an unfortunate situation for Brainerd, causing him distress for years afterward and contributing to his melancholy disposition. Despite his own efforts and those of influential friends, he was not reinstated nor allowed to graduate from Yale. Nevertheless, his years of schooling were not a waste. It was during his student days that he heard Ebenezer Pemberton deliver a stirring message about the opportunities for missionary work among the Indians. Brainerd never forgot that message, and in November of 1742, following his expulsion from Yale, he eagerly responded to Pemberton's call for him to come to New York City to discuss a possible role for him in missionary work to the Indians. Pemberton was an American minister who also served as field secretary for The Society in Scotland for the Propagation of Christian Knowledge. Only recently had the society inaugurated its work among the Indians, and Brainerd was being considered as one of two missionary appointees whose ministry would be funded.

Although Brainerd viewed himself as unworthy of the task, the commissioners saw otherwise and enthusiastically offered him the appointment. Brainerd's first term of service was in Kaunaumeek, New York, where he was to spend time in language study with John Sergeant, a veteran missionary serving in nearby Stockbridge, Massachusetts. John, with his wife Abigail, had ministered effectively for eight years among the Indians, baptizing more than one hundred converts and translating portions of Scripture. What an opportunity it would have been for a raw recruit like Brainerd to work with and learn from this experienced missionary. But it was not to be. David Brainerd's spirit of independence and his eagerness for his own converts caused him to plunge into the task alone, though he was ignorant of the native tongue and utterly unprepared for life in the wilderness.

His first days as a missionary were lonely and depressing: "My heart was sunk.... It seemed to me I should never have any success among the Indians. My soul was weary of my life; I longed for death, beyond measure." Though he later was assisted by an Indian interpreter from Stockbridge, for several weeks Brainerd attempted to preach to the Indians without an interpreter. His efforts were fruitless and his life was miserable: "I live in the most lonely melancholy desert, about eighteen miles from Albany; ... I board with a poor Scotchman; his wife can talk scarce any English. My diet consists mostly of hasty-pudding, boiled corn, and bread baked in ashes.... My lodging is a little heap of straw laid upon some boards. My work is exceeding hard and difficult: I travel on foot a mile and a half, the worst of ways, almost daily, and back; for I live so far from my Indians."[7]

The following summer Brainerd built his own hut near the Indian settlement, but his attempt to evangelize the Indians remained unsuccessful. His first winter in the wilderness was one of hardship and sickness. On one occasion he was lost for a time in the woods, and on another he "was very much exposed and very wet by falling into a river." In March of 1744, after a year at Kaunaumeek, Brainerd preached his last sermon. He was discouraged with his missionary career, but despite offers from established churches to be their pastor, he "resolved to go on still with the Indian Affair."[8]

Brainerd's next assignment was in Pennsylvania, north of Philadelphia within the Forks of the Delaware River. Here he was well received by the Indians and was often allowed to speak to them in the chief's house. Progress, however, was slow. His new Indian interpreter, Tattamy, not only had a drinking problem, but also was devoid of spiritual knowledge, and thus he was wholly ineffective in delivering Brainerd's message. Brainerd viewed his prospects for winning converts "as dark as midnight."

After several months at the Forks of the Delaware, Brainerd traveled west to reach Indians along the Susquehanna River. It was an arduous journey: "We went our way into the wilderness; and found the most difficult and dangerous traveling by far, that any of us had seen; we had scarce anything else but lofty mountains, deep valleys, and hideous rocks to make our way through." To make matters worse, Brainerd's horse fell in a "hideous place" and broke her leg, which left Brainerd with no alternative but to kill her and continue on to the nearest house some thirty miles away. After preaching with little success, Brainerd returned to the Forks of the Delaware, where, except for frequent travels, he remained during his second year of missionary service.[9]

Illness and depression continued to plague Brainerd. His high hopes of revival among the Indians had long since dimmed. With the exception of Tattamy and his wife, who had been converted and were making remarkable spiritual progress, Brainerd regarded his year at the Forks of the Delaware a loss. He was guilt stricken in believing he had accomplished nothing for his pay and was tempted to quit. Then, in the summer of 1745 his spirits brightened. He heard about a group of Indians eighty-five miles to the south, in Crossweeksung, New Jersey, who were more open to Christianity. Once again, Brainerd pulled up stakes and moved on. But this time his fortune would improve. The Indians in New Jersey were more eager to hear the gospel. Soon Indians as well as whites were coming from miles away to hear him preach. Anxious for results, Brainerd baptized twenty-five converts within a matter of weeks, and the following winter he organized a school.

The real fruit of Brainerd's labors became evident in the summer of 1745 when revival broke out among the In-

David Brainerd preaching to the Indians.

dians. Although Brainerd still depended on an interpreter and the Indians understood only the most elementary tenets of Christianity, they responded to his preaching, and the emotionally charged scenes so characteristic of the Great Awakening suddenly appeared among the Indians of Crossweeksung. As his diary shows, it was an exhilarating time for Brainerd as he witnessed the visible results of changed lives.

August 6. In the morning I discoursed to the Indians at the house where we lodged. Many of them were then much affected and appeared surprisingly tender, so that a few words about their souls' concerns would cause the tears to flow freely, and produce many sobs and groans.

In the afternoon, they being returned to the place where I had usually preached among them, I again discoursed to them there. There were about fifty-five persons in all, about forty that were capable of attending divine service with understanding. I insisted upon I John 4:10, "Herein is love." They seemed eager of hearing; but there appeared nothing very remarkable, except their attention, till near the close of my discourse. Then divine truths were attended with a surprising influence, and produced a great concern among them. There were scarce three in forty that could refrain from tears and bitter cries.

They all, as one, seemed in an agony of soul to obtain an interest in Christ; and the more I discoursed of the love and compassion of God in sending His Son to suffer for the sins of men; and the more I invited them to come and partake of His love, the more their distress was aggravated, because they felt themselves unable to come. It was surprising to see how their hearts seemed to be pierced with the tender and melting invitations

of the gospel, when there was not a word of terror spoken to them.

It was very affecting to see the poor Indians, who the other day were hallooing and yelling in their idolatrous feasts and drunken frolics, now crying to God with such importunity for an interest in His dear Son! Found two or three persons, who, I had reason to hope, had taken comfort upon good grounds since the evening before. These, with others that had obtained comfort, were together and seemed to rejoice much that God was carrying on His work with such power upon others.[10]

In the spring of 1746 Brainerd convinced the scattered Indians in New Jersey to settle together at nearby Cranbury, and soon thereafter a church was established. More revivals followed, and after a year and a half the converts numbered nearly one hundred and fifty. But Brainerd's health was broken. His fourth and final journey back to the Susquehanna, though more successful than previous preaching tours, was too much for his frail constitution. He was dying of tuberculosis. His missionary work was over.

After spending the winter in the home of a pastor-friend in New Jersey, Brainerd traveled to Northampton, Massachusetts, where he spent his last months in the home of the great preacher and scholar, Jonathan Edwards, whose daughter, Jerusha, he hoped to marry. This dream, however, was never realized. For nineteen weeks Jerusha tenderly nursed him, but to no avail. He died on October 9, 1747. The following Valentine's Day Jerusha joined him, dying of consumption that she apparently contracted from him.

Eleazer Wheelock

If Brainerd was ill-prepared for his ministry, there were other early Indian missionaries more worthy of emulation. Among those are the innovative educational ideas developed by Eleazer Wheelock. Dr. Wheelock was a native New Englander who graduated from Yale in 1733. As with other New England ministers before him, he was burdened for the Indians. In 1743 he brought an Indian youth, Samson Occum, into his home and spent four years educating him. His success with Occum led him to develop a concept that historian R. Pierce Beaver has termed "the most original scheme of operations in the entire history of New England missions to the Indians."[11]

Wheelock's plan was to bring Indians and whites together for training in missionary service. In the process, the white students would learn the language and culture of the Indians, and the Indian youths would be schooled in the white man's ways. Both whites and Indians would be trained for Indian evangelism, though there would be an emphasis on recruiting Indians because they would be free of cross-cultural barriers and because they could live and work on far less financial support than their white counterparts.

Wheelock opened his school in Lebanon, Connecticut, in 1754 with two Indian students sent by John Brainerd, who had succeeded David at the New Jersey mission (and was a far more successful missionary than his famous brother). The school met in a house donated by Joshua Moor, and the institution became known as Moor's Training School. At its peak there were twenty-two students enrolled, and Wheelock's missionary work was the most extensive of any in New England. Altogether Wheelock trained nearly fifty Indian students, and approximately one third of those returned to their home communities to serve as evangelists or teachers.

A shining story of success? No, unfortunately not. What the project possessed in innovative ideas it lacked in effective leadership. Wheelock's personality and prejudices obstructed the path of progress. Instead of mutual sharing of culture, the school became dominated by white culture. Wheelock could never overcome his contempt for Indians and their civilization (or lack of it). Though he successfully trained Indian students and sent them out to minister, he was unable to work with them as equals—particularly Samson Occum, his first student, who became a highly respected missionary in his own right. As time went on, Wheelock's school declined in numbers and was eventually moved to Dresden where it turned to the education of whites and became known as Dartmouth College.

David Zeisberger

The greatest thrust for Indian missions during the colonial period came from New England, but there was effective work going on elsewhere in the colonies, in many cases carried out by European missionaries—particularly Moravians (see chapter 3). The most famous of the Moravian missionaries to the Indians was David Zeisberger, who labored amid tragedy and hardship for sixty-three years. His story is just one of many that graphically illustrates the cruel injustices dealt to the native Americans as

Europeans took over the land.

Zeisberger began his ministry in 1744 in the Hudson River Valley, but because of adverse public opinion to the evangelization of Indians he soon found himself, along with his associate, in jail, where they were confined seven weeks until a government official secured their release. As a Moravian missionary Zeisberger not only endured vociferous opposition to his calling, but also faced prejudice against his faith. Moravians were "sect people" who were looked down on by members of the traditional Protestant denominations. But despite persecution Zeisberger persisted in missionary work. In 1746 he helped establish Gnadenhuetten, a Christian Indian village in Pennsylvania that became a prosperous farming community of some five hundred Indian residents. So respected was he that the Indians made him a sachem and "keeper of the archives."

The good times, however, did not last. Both whites and unfriendly Indians viewed Gnadenhuetten with suspicion, and in 1755 at the outbreak of the French and Indian War a band of raiding Indians attacked the settlement and killed eleven people and burned the buildings, while most of the residents fled for their lives. Zeisberger remained with a segment of Indians who did not scatter and tried without success to establish a permanent settlement in Pennsylvania. Finally in the 1770s he secured a tract of land in Ohio.

For several years Zeisberger and the Indians lived peacefully and prospered in their new land, but again the calm was broken. The American Revolution brought unrest to the frontier, and in 1781 Zeisberger and his as-

sociates were accused by the English forces of being spies. The Indians were evacuated to the Sandusky River where they nearly starved during the harsh winter. The following spring more than one hundred of these Christian Indians returned to their settlement in Ohio to gather some unharvested corn. While there, ninety of their number (twenty-nine men, twenty-seven women, and thirty-four children) were captured and brutally murdered by a company of American militia.

For the next decade Zeisberger and his Christian following moved from place to place in northern Ohio and southern Michigan, and then finally settled in Ontario in 1792 when Zeisberger was past the age of seventy. There he established a mission station that survived for more than a century. In 1798 Zeisberger returned to work among the Indians of Ohio, where he remained until his death a decade later.

Isaac McCoy

Protestant missions to the American Indian changed considerably during the late eighteenth century. The Great Awakening that had fanned the flames of colonial missions had died down, and for many years following the American Revolution there was a lull in Protestant missions. Moreover, ministers no longer found unreached Indians within the bounds of their own parish. Many Indians had perished from wars and the white man's diseases, and most of those who survived found the eastern seaboard too populated for their native lifestyle. With the steady march of civilization westward, Indians were pushed further and further back into the uncharted wilderness. Those who sought to evangelize them could no longer stay home and carry on a dual ministry as colonial ministers had done; rather, they had to pull up stakes and follow the wagons westward, pushing beyond the white settlements to reach the Indians. Some missionaries like Zeisberger were pushed westward along with their Indian followers.

Interestingly though, as the Indians were pushed westward there was a renewed interest in Indian missions. While this was due in part to the Second Great Awakening that swept across much of the East during the early nineteenth century, it was also due to the fact that many people found Indians easier to love at a distance than in close proximity. Lay people and ministers alike found it simpler and less bothersome to send missionaries to some distant outpost than to become involved right in their own neighborhoods. During these years denominations developed missions to the Indians, and already existing missionary organizations increased their efforts.

Methodists were aroused to the need of Indian missions by John Steward, a black man from Ohio who felt called to preach to the Wyandot Indians at Upper Sandusky, Ohio, after he was converted at a camp meeting. He was well received by the Indians when he arrived in 1816, and to his surprise, he learned that another black man, Jonathan Painter, a runaway slave from Kentucky, was living among them. Steward immediately tried to conscript him to be his interpreter, but Painter refused, saying, "How can I interpret the Gospel to the Indians

when I have no religion myself?" That night, with Steward's encouragement and prayer, Painter made his peace with God, and together he and Steward preached to the Indians. Steward was licensed as a Methodist preacher, and in 1819 the Methodist Missionary Society was formed, and trained missionaries were appointed to the Upper Sandusky area.

Baptist missions to the Indians began with Isaac McCoy and his wife, who opened a mission at Fort Wayne in 1820. After only two years in that location they moved the mission to southern Michigan because of what they believed was an adverse effect of white neighbors. There they founded the Carey Mission, a thriving missionary compound. A United States military officer visiting the mission only seven months after its establishment found an impressive, efficiently run mission compound that included a large mission house, a school, a blacksmith shop and other buildings as well as well-cultivated, enclosed gardens and pastures. The school enrolled some forty children, and the mission showed every sign of success, but within two years McCoy was again anxious to move on, again fearing the encroachments of whites and the dire consequences he believed would result from Indians living in close proximity to whites. He believed that the only solution to the detrimental influence of neighboring whites was to establish an Indian colony "west of the State of Missouri." In 1824 McCoy traveled to Washington to offer his plan at the annual meeting of the Baptist Board of Missions. With the board's approval he set up a meeting with Secretary of War John C. Calhoun, who supported the proposal.

From that meeting onward, McCoy's efforts turned to political lobbying and away from evangelistic work among the Indians; his subordinates took over the missionary work.

Although Baptists historically fought for the separation of church and state, it is paradoxical that through McCoy's influence Baptist Indian missions became closely tied to the government. This was a period in the nation's history when government was becoming deeply involved in Indian missions, and the Baptists more readily than any other denomination accepted this role. The Carey Mission received considerable government funding, and McCoy actively allied himself with the government on the issue of Indian removal. The most notable case in which he became embroiled was the removal of the Cherokees from Georgia. McCoy's rationale for Indian removal was that Indians had to be segregated from whites to be Christianized, and politically he sided with the state of Georgia in its claims on Cherokee land. He had no qualms about initiating this controversial and drastic measure, and he readily accepted a government commission to explore and survey land in the West suitable for an Indian colony.

The removal of the Cherokees was one of the greatest injustices committed by the United States government in the nation's history. In 1837, several years after the discovery of gold on their lands, the peaceful and culturally advanced Indians of the Cherokee nation were forced by government decree and nine thousand troops to leave their homes in Georgia. They were herded into stockades while their property was auctioned off. Thousands of them were then trans-ported by riverboat while others were forced to march overland beyond the Mississippi River. It was a perilous journey, and the mortality rate was high. McCoy's strong support of this removal policy was not characteristic of all missionaries. In fact, many missionaries valiantly fought against the measure, and before the ordeal was over four Presbyterian and two Methodist missionaries were arrested, tried, convicted, and sentenced to hard labor because of their sharp protests. Accounts of missionaries being dragged from their homes in chains were not unusual.

In defense of McCoy, it should be pointed out that though he was one of the strongest advocates of removal, he did have the courage to condemn the wanton cruelty in carrying out the procedure. In the end, the forced removal of the Cherokees no doubt hurt the cause of the gospel among the Indians far more than any evil influence their white neighbors may have had.

Fortunately, the brutal mass removal of the Cherokees was the exception and not the norm. Most of the Eastern tribes that survived white intrusion were pushed West from their homes and beyond the borders of white civilization. But not without resistance. The Indians frequently fought vicious battles for their land, sometimes at the expense of the missionaries who came to serve them. The story of Waiilatpu in the Oregon country vividly illustrates this.

Marcus and Narcissa Whitman

The Louisiana Purchase and the opening of the West for settlement gave birth to a new breed of missionaries. They were courageous men and women with a spirit of determination and adventure. Inspired by the Second Great Awakening, they were committed to spreading the gospel. But they were also committed to carrying the white man's civilization. Indeed they could not see how it could be possible to evangelize without civilizing. The two seemed inseparably joined, a factor that with increasing white encroachment produced tremendous obstacles to the evangelization of Indians.

Typical of this new breed of missionaries were Marcus and Narcissa Whitman. Born in the early years of the nineteenth century, they both experienced spiritual awakenings as young people (Narcissa in New York and Marcus in Massachusetts). Narcissa, the daughter of Judge Stephen Prentiss, was well educated and bright. She was career-minded and conducted a kindergarten, but her heart was in missions, particularly in reaching the Indians of the far West. The missionary challenges of Rev. Samuel Parker, as well as the oft-repeated story of the Nez Perce Indians pleading for someone to bring them the "Book of Life," weighed heavily on her mind. Parker traveled extensively in the East, raising funds and recruiting missionaries for the American Board of Commissioners for Foreign Missions (a Congregational missionary society actively involved in Indian evangelism). The need for volunteers was great, but the American Board did not accept single women.

Marcus, too, had long been interested in missions. His Sunday school teacher was the father of one of the five who took part in the "haystack prayer meeting" and had another son who went to Hawaii as a missionary. Marcus dreamed of going to seminary and entering the ministry, but seminary was a costly pursuit. Entering the field of medicine was a more realistic option, and at the age of twenty-one he began "riding with a doctor." In the years that followed he taught school part-time and took formal medical training. As with Narcissa, it was Rev. Samuel Parker who influenced him in the direction of Indian missions. He applied to the American Board as a single unencumbered man, but he was not close-minded regarding marriage. He had heard through friends that Narcissa Prentiss was available and that she was still brooding over the fact that single females were considered unfit for missionary service. With the possibility of marriage in mind, Marcus visited Narcissa to discuss Indian missions. He was planning an exploratory trip west, and if he found the journey to be suitable for a woman, he would return to marry Narcissa. He left with no promises. It was not a love affair nor an engagement. It was more of a business arrangement.

Following their meeting, the thirty-two year old Whitman, accompanying Rev. Parker, traveled to Missouri to join up with the American Fur Company in its expedition west in the spring of 1835. Though Whitman's intended destination was Oregon, he never made it that far. In late August, having just crossed the Continental Divide, Whitman turned around and returned home with a caravan of fur traders, arriving only months after he had left. Although the American Board was not entirely pleased with his sudden return, Narcissa was. She and Whitman were married in February of 1836, and

Statue of Marcus Whitman.

sonality problems combined to make the overland journey a very difficult one, but there were delightful moments along the way. Unlike David Brainerd, who nearly one hundred years before despised the "hideous" wilderness, Narcissa was intoxicated by it. She was overwhelmed with the breathless beauty of God's creation, as her journal so descriptively records. She was happy and she was in love, and somewhere under the night sky between the Elkhorn and the Loup, she became pregnant with her first child.

After nearly two thousand miles of grueling hardships, the expedition was approaching its destination, the missionary party being much poorer than when it began. Precious posses-

the following day they left for Missouri in order to join the expedition to Oregon in the spring.

The Whitmans were not the only American Board missionaries heading for Oregon that spring. With them were Henry and Eliza Spaulding. Though Spaulding was a well-trained minister, his personality was not suited for the teamwork required for the Oregon project. Moreover, he had known Narcissa years before, and her refusal of his marriage proposal caused bitterness that continually surfaced for years to come. It was not an ideal situation, but the call to Oregon seemed too compelling to lay aside for personality differences.

Strenuous travel, illness, and per-

Narcissa Whitman, wife of Marcus Whitman.

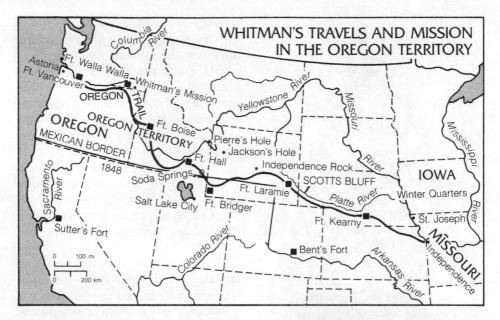

WHITMAN'S TRAVELS AND MISSION IN THE OREGON TERRITORY

sions had to be thrown out all along the way to lighten the load. "We scatter as we go," Narcissa lamented, concluding that it would be better to travel with nothing, "then you lose nothing."[12] This same conclusion could have been applied to missionary colleagues. By the time the Whitmans had reached Oregon they had already decided to part company with the Spauldings. After nearly five months of traveling together and sleeping together in the same tent, their relationship was so strained they could no longer work together. Contemporary reports generally placed most of the blame on Spaulding and his jealousy of Whitman, though Whitman himself, by many accounts, was not always easy to deal with. More than one tribe of Indians was asking for missionaries, however, so their decision to work separately was beneficial. Whitman settled in Waiilatpu, a lush green valley, while Spaulding settled at Lapwai, a bleak, dry mountainous area. Spaulding looked at Whitman's site at

Waiilatpu with envy, not realizing that ultimately his location would prove to be the superior one. His mission was to the Nez Perce Indians, who received him warmly and were anxious to learn of his God. Whitman, on the other hand, sought to reach the Cayuse, a more treacherous tribe of only a few hundred, who resented the coming of the white man.

During the first months in Oregon, neither Whitman nor Spaulding had much time for evangelizing Indians. To their great disappointment, Reverend Parker had returned east by way of ship, not even waiting to welcome them or bothering to leave behind a letter of advice and instructions. So the new missionaries were entirely on their own. Far removed from each other they spent their days building shelters for the winter months ahead. Whitman built a rough lean-to with a roof of mud and boughs and with only blankets at the windows and doors. On December 10 he and Narcissa moved in, and Narcissa immediately began giving the home some finishing touches. Waiilatpu was a desolate and lonely place that winter, but spring brought new hope. On March 14, 1837, the eve of Narcissa's twenty-ninth birthday, a baby daughter, Alice Clarissa, was born.

The first summer in Oregon was spent in constructing buildings and fences and in planting and harvesting crops. There was time for medical work, language study, and evangelism, but not enough. Unlike the Catholic missionaries who lived simply and sometimes followed the wandering Indians, the Protestant missionaries built compounds and in some instances maintained large farming ventures. The task was enormous, and they sometimes felt overwhelmed. They were desperate for additional supplies and workers, and they forcefully poured out their frustrations in a lengthy letter back home to the American Board. Before the letter ever reached its destination new recruits arrived. The fall of 1838 brought three new missionary couples, whose presence brought further conflict. In the words of one biographer, "It seemed that the 'reinforcements' had brought not help, but dissension only." Instead of unified prayer and sweet fellowship, the joint planning meetings of these missionaries were often stormy and bitter. One of the wives described a typical flare-up: "It came on so sharp that I was compelled to leave. . . . It is enough to make one sick to see what is the state of things in the mission."[13]

There were times of unity, but they were sometimes the result of tragedy. Such was the case in the summer of 1839. Sympathy and sorrow healed the wounds of bitterness, as the Whitmans suffered the pain of a heart rending ordeal. It was a late June Sunday afternoon at Waiilatpu. It was not just Sunday, but the Sabbath—a day of rest from the week's heavy labor. Marcus and Narcissa were engrossed in reading and little Alice was playing close by—or so they thought. When they suddenly realized she was missing, it was too late. The precious little two-year-old had wandered off and drowned in a nearby stream. The Spauldings came immediately to share the sorrow at the first funeral for the Oregon missionaries. A year later a package arrived from back east with the little shoes and dresses Narcissa had requested from her mother. A weaker woman could not have endured; but Narcissa's faith carried her through. It was God's divine purpose, and she resolutely accepted his will. Though she could see the little grave on the hill every time she stepped out of her door, she knew her dear Alice was in God's care: "My thoughts sel-

Henry Spaulding.

101

dom wander there to find her."[14]

Time marched on at Waiilatpu. There was work to be done, and sorrow was not permitted to stay the progress. The Whitmans' time was consumed with more than medical missions. They were farmers—and prosperous ones at that. After only six years at Waiilatpu, their "plantation" consisted of a large whitewashed adobe mission house, a guest house, a gristmill, and a blacksmith shop, all surrounded by well-cultivated fields. Dr. Whitman was not the only Protestant missionary in Oregon to be tempted by the richness of the land. Jason Lee, a Methodist missionary had fallen prey to materialism and spent his time in politics, immigration, and land ventures. This was clearly without the sanction of the Methodist Board, which reprimanded him for his consuming interest in worldly affairs.

In the case of Whitman, the materialism was not so blatant, but the consequences were far greater. Waiilatpu became a receiving station for new missionaries and other immigrants, as well as a school for Indian and white children. For that reason Whitman had to concern himself with more than subsistance forming, but soon Waiilatpu resembled an immigrant inn more than a missionary compound. Whitman began selling produce to immigrants as they passed through and was often accused of overcharging and exploiting their circumstances (though this charge was no doubt made about anyone who sold to the immigrants). The American Board, on hearing such rumors, scolded Whitman for the over secularization of the mission, but their letters were slow in coming and they knew little of the actual circumstances under which he worked. But the greater condemnation came from the Cayuse, the Indians whom Whitman came to serve. Though he sacrificially worked among them as a minister and doctor, the Indians resented his prosperity and all the white immigrants they believed he was attracting to their land. There was friction between Whitman and the Cayuse, but Whitman refused to be intimidated.

For Henry Spaulding, the situation was different. Spaulding had less time for worldly pursuits. He was too busy with his missionary activities. He established a church among the Nez

The Whitman mission in 1845.

Perce, and Eliza ran a school for the children and made hand-painted books and translated hymns into their language. With her artistic talent she made large brightly colored charts illustrating Bible truths. (She had heard how Father François Blanchet's famous "Catholic Ladder," depicting Bible history, had intrigued the Indians, and she was not to be outdone in visual aids.) The Spauldings faced opposition, but they also reaped a harvest of souls through their mission work.

By 1844, after less than eight years in Oregon, the Whitmans' missionary work for all practical purposes was over. Narcissa had long since lost the excitement and zeal she initially had for Indian missions. She was moody and depressed. She spent her days feeding and housing immigrants and her adopted family, including the seven Sager children whose parents both died on the overland trip from the East. Marcus, too, was consumed by the needs of the white immigrants. He continued treating the Indians' physical needs, but he was discouraged by their lack of response to spiritual values, and like so many other missionaries throughout history, Whitman could not separate salvation from civilization. If the Indians refused the white man's civilization, including his work ethic, how could they be saved?

Time was running out for Waiilatpu and the Whitmans. Despite repeated warnings, Whitman never fully appreciated the Cayuse's reputation for treachery. It was a difficult period of time for the Cayuse. Their villages were ravaged by a plague, and within the space of eight weeks nearly half of the four-hundred-member tribe had

suffered painful deaths. Though Whitman had tried to help, the situation only grew worse, and suspicion mounted among the Indians that he was purposely poisoning them with his "medicine."

The end for Waiilatpu came suddenly. It was a dreary late November afternoon in 1847. Two Indians, one with a personal vendetta against Whitman, appeared at the mission house door. Others were stationed outside. Without warning, the massacre began. It was not a mass uprising with a hoard of savage Indians suddenly descending on a helpless compound. There were seventy-two people living at the mission, including more than a dozen men, and the murderers were Indians whom the Whitmans knew well. Pulling tomahawks out from under the blankets they were carrying, the small party began the slaughter, starting with Dr. Whitman. When it was over, fourteen were dead. With the exception of Narcissa, the women and children had been spared, only to be held in terrifying captivity until their release some five weeks later.

News of the Whitman massacre spread rapidly. American troops were sent in, and the missionaries in the interior were ordered out. In the spring of 1850 the five Cayuse Indians responsible for the murders were brought to trial, convicted, and sentenced to die; and on June 3 all of Oregon, it seemed, came out to watch the hangings.

It was not until 1871, twenty-four years after he was ordered out, that Spaulding returned to Lapwai, without Eliza who had long since died. There he witnessed revival among the Nez Perce and Spokane Indians and

The massacre at Waiilatpu in 1847.

claimed to have baptized more than a thousand of them (although colleagues suspected that he baptized some of the Indians twice to pad the numbers). After three years of service, Spaulding died among the Indians he so loved, thus ending a difficult and controversial era of Protestant missions in Oregon. The work at Lapwai was taken over by two single sisters, Kate and Sue McBeth. A training school for Indian preachers was set up, and the Nez Perce, perhaps more than any other Indian tribe, became active in evangelizing other Indian tribes.

As the nineteenth century progressed, missionary work among the Indians decreased. The emphasis was on exotic foreign lands where the native population could not interfere with the advance of American society. Many scholars agree that Indian evangelism, as a whole, was not a story of success, the greatest reason being the intense conflict between the two cultures for supremacy over the land. But perhaps equally important was the deep-seated belief of white America that Indians were racially inferior and that their culture was not worth saving.

SELECTED BIBLIOGRAPHY

Beaver, R. Pearce. Church, State, and the American Indian. *St. Louis: Concordia, 1966.*

_____. Pioneers in Mission: The Early Missionary Ordination Sermons, Charges and Instructions. *Grand Rapids: Eerdmans, 1966.*

Berkhoffer, Robert F., Jr. Salvation and the Savage: An Analysis of Protestant Missions and American Indian Response, 1787–1862. *Louisville: University of Kentucky Press, 1965.*

Bowden, Henry Warner. American Indians and Christian Missions: Studies in Cultural Conflict. *Chicago: University of Chicago, 1981.*

Drury, Clifford M. Marcus and Narcissa Whitman and the Opening of Old Oregon. *2 vols. Glendale: Arthur H. Clark, 1973.*

Edwards, Jonathan. Life and Diary of David Brainerd. *Chicago: Moody, 1949.*

Hinman, George W. The American Indian and Christian Missions. *New York: Revell, 1933.*

Humphreys, Mary G., ed. Missionary Explorers Among the American Indians. *New York: Scribner, 1913.*

Jones, Nard. The Great Command: The Story of Marcus and Narcissa Whitman and the Oregon Country Pioneers. *Boston: Little, 1959.*

Winslow, Ola Elizabeth. John Eliot, "Apostle to the Indians." *Boston: Houghton Mifflin, 1968.*

Wynbeek, David. David Brainerd: Beloved Yankee. *Grand Rapids: Eerdmans, 1961.*

PART II

THE "GREAT CENTURY"

PART II

The
"Great Century"

The spread of Protestant Christianity in the three centuries following the Reformation, though notable, gave little indication of what was about to occur in the nineteenth century. In 1800, according to Stephen Neill, "It was still by no means certain that Christianity would be successful in turning itself into a universal religion."[1] Christianity might have appeared, in some circles, to be little more than a Caucasian religion that was being severely battered about by a wave of rationalism that was sweeping across the Western world. Would the profound power of the Evangelical Awakening in the eighteenth century make a difference? Would Christianity survive the modern era? The nineteenth century was crucial; and, instead of falling before the onslaught of rationalism, Christianity continued to be reinvigorated by an evangelical fervor that soon penetrated every continent on the globe. It truly was the "Great Century" for Christian expansion.

There were a number of factors that made the nineteenth century conducive to world-wide Protestant missions. The Age of Enlightenment and the eighteenth-century rationalism had been largely replaced by a new Age of Romanticism. It was a time to reject the excessive reliance on reason and to put more stock in the emotions and the imagination. And it was a time to put theory into practice. Reform movements sprang up in the newly industrialized nations, and churches and Christian organizations were reaching out as never before through the participation of volunteer workers.

Changes in the world's religious environment no doubt contributed to the rapid spread of Christianity in the nineteenth century. It was a period of decline for the non-Christian religions. "Hinduism, Buddhism, and Mohammedanism were relatively quiescent in the nineteenth century," according to Martin Marty, and "Christians sensed that they could fill a vacuum."[2] Catholicism, too, was on the decline in many parts of the world. The French Rationalism of the sev-

109

enteenth and eighteenth centuries had taken its toll on the church, and the French Revolution effectively cut the economic purse strings of Roman Catholic missions. In Latin America, especially, Roman Catholicism witnessed many reverses. National movements saw the church as "the last bulwark of an outmoded and oppressive regime."[3]

Protestantism, on the other hand, was thriving. The nineteenth century was a "Protestant era," and more specifically an era dominated by evangelical Protestantism. In the British Isles the evangelical Christians exercised powerful influence in the highest levels of government and commerce, and in America church membership increased from ten to forty percent during the course of the century. Denominations were developing rapidly, and the Sunday school movement in both Britain and America was growing at a fast pace.

Politically, the nineteenth century witnessed tremendous changes as well. Although there were revolutions and social upheavals in Europe and a bloody civil war in America, it was an era of relative world peace. Western nations, through scientific and technological advances, were quickly becoming world powers, and their wealth and prestige were viewed with envy and admiration by many nonindustrialized nations. Politically, it was also a period of secularization. "From the era of Constantine and the Christianization of the Roman Empire to the latter days of the eighteenth century," writes Martin Marty, "western men assumed . . . that religion was to be established by law and sanctioned by the legal arm of the state."[4] But by the nineteenth century that was no longer true. Individuals were taking command of their own personal spiritual condition and their responsibility to reach out to others.

The eighteenth-century evangelical revivals that began in England with Whitefield and Wesley played an important role in awakening Christian leaders and laymen to the responsibility for evangelism world-wide. "No longer," according to Harold Cook, "was the state held responsible in any sense for the propagation of the Christian faith."[5] Evangelism was the responsibility of the church and its leaders, and it was this once again rediscovered truth that launched the modern missionary movement with William Carey in England and Samuel Mills in the United States.

But belief was not enough. A vehicle was needed to turn the belief into action, and that vehicle emerged in the form of the mission society. The volunteer mission society, independent in some instances and denominationally oriented in others, transformed Christian missions, opening the way for ecumenical activity and lay involvement. "Never before," according to Latourette, "had Christianity or any other religion had so many individuals giving full time to the propagation of their faith. Never had so many hundreds of thousands contributed voluntarily of their means to assist the spread of Christianity or any other religion."[6] The first of these new societies was the Baptist Missionary Society (1792), soon to be followed by the London Missionary Society (1795) and the Church Missionary Society (1799). From Continental Europe came the Netherlands Missionary Society (1797) and the Basel Mission (1815); and from the United States, The

American Board of Commissioners for Foreign Missions (1810) and the American Baptist Missionary Board (1814). There would be dozens more as the century progressed, for it was, as Neill has pointed out, "the great age of societies."[7]

As important as the evangelical awakening and the new mission societies were to the spread of the gospel world-wide, without certain secular trends the foreign missionary cause would have been significantly curtailed. Both colonialism and industrialization had far-reaching effects on the expansion of Christianity. The Industrial Revolution had brought new power to Europe, and with that power came an urge to conquer. Colonialism and imperialism were on their way to becoming accepted government policies, and as such they had a significant impact on missions. "Commercial and colonizing schemes had brought the ends of the earth into new contact," according to R. H. Glover. "The great East India Companies, Dutch and English, had—without intention or desire, it is true—paved the way for the missionary by making travel to, and residence in, Eastern countries more practicable and safe."[8]

The close tie between colonialism and missions has caused many historians to charge that the missionaries were merely "following the flag" as tools of imperialism. This is an issue that has been hotly debated by historians. In many cases the missionaries did "follow the flag" and aided colonial and imperialistic schemes. Others preceded the flag but even then, in many cases, bolstered colonialism. Livingstone, among others, pleaded for European commerce and settlements in Africa, and missionaries

everywhere welcomed any privileges a favorable colonial power would grant them. Protestant missionaries strongly favored rule by Protestant countries and feared Catholic rule, and vice versa. However, by the year 1900 the majority of missionaries were not working in colonial territories ruled by their own home countries.

But despite this sometimes too cozy relationship between missionaries and the perpetrators of imperialism, the two groups were more often than not at considerable odds with each other. The commercial companies frequently stood in the way of the missionaries, and the missionaries, with few exceptions, decried the life-style of the traders and colonists. Rarely was the association harmonious. "The relation between missions and colonial expansion is complex," writes A. F. Walls. "But one thing is clear. If missions are associated with the rise of imperialism, they are equally associated with the factors which brought about its destruction."[9] Likewise, they are associated with social progress in underdeveloped nations. "Protestant missionary efforts in this period," writes Ralph Winter, "led the way in establishing all around the world the democratic apparatus of government, the schools, the hospitals, the universities and the political foundations for new nations."[10]

But valuable as such social progress was, it was not accomplished without the introduction of Western culture, accompanied in some cases by an almost wholesale destruction of native traditions and customs. As the missionaries spread out across every continent and into the island worlds, they brought a culture that bristled with strange new knowledge and power. It was generally hopeless to try to prevent the adoption of many aspects of their own Western cultures by the nationals in the foreign field, and in many cases the missionaries allowed and even encouraged such things as literacy and freedom from slavery and rank superstition. It is also true that within the environment of commercial and colonial circles "missionaries in the nineteenth century had to some extent yielded to the colonial complex. Only western man," continues Neill, "was man in the full sense of the word; he was wise and good, and members of other races, in so far as they became westernized, might share in this wisdom and goodness. But western man was the leader, and would remain so for a very long time, perhaps for ever."[11]

Imperfect as they were, it was the nineteenth-century missionaries—a tiny company in comparison to other forces impacting the nonwestern world—who, in a relatively short period of time, turned what some may have thought to be a declining Caucasian religion into the largest and most dynamic religious faith in the world. They were common people turned heroes, whose commitment and courage inspired succeeding generations to follow their example. This century was an age when little children dreamed of true greatness—of becoming a Carey, a Livingstone, a Judson, a Paton, a Slessor, or a Hudson Taylor.

Chapter 5

South Central Asia: Confronting Ancient Creeds

South Central Asia. What an ironic setting for the first major thrust of Protestant foreign missions. It was here in the subcontinent of India where the world's oldest and most complex religions were born and where religious beliefs pervaded every facet of society. It is no wonder, then, that the teeming millions who elbowed their way through the crowded marketplaces looked with scorn on those who would bring them a new religion. What could a "Western" religion offer them that Hinduism, Buddhism, Islam, Sikhism, or Jainism could not? And what appeal could there be in a dogmatic religion like Christianity? Hindus, with their thousands of gods, prided themselves in their tolerance and looked down on the exclusive claims of Christianity.

But Christianity, as William Carey and those who followed him demonstrated, had everything to offer the people of Central Asia. Even aside from the free gift of salvation and eternal life, only Christianity offered the people a release from the binding chains of the age-old caste system and from the endless process of reincarnation that enslaved them. Only Christianity reached out to the "untouchables" and offered them hope for the here and now. Only Christianity was willing to sacrifice its young men and women to the perils of tropical South Central Asia in a selfless love to uplift its people.

The sacrifices of William Carey, Adoniram Judson, and others who toiled in India and other parts of Central Asia were immeasurable. The cruelty of the climate was unrelenting and tropical fevers exacted a high toll. Carey and Judson each buried two wives as well as little children, but no price was too high for the privilege of bringing Christianity to this area of the world. Foreign missionary work was not for spiritual dwarfs, and the early pioneers never anticipated an ideal climate or a receptive population. But what they could not anticipate was the ultimate insult against them and their faith—the intense opposition of their own countrymen (the East India

Company in particular) who withstood every effort to propagate the gospel, though the company officials themselves claimed to be sheltered under the umbrella of Christianity.

In spite of the tremendous barriers, Christianity was planted in India and elsewhere in South Central Asia, and through the influence of William Carey, who ushered in the "Great Century" of foreign missions, the evangelism of the world began to be viewed as a primary obligation of the Christian Church. South Central Asia, however, would never be a fertile field for Christianity, where still today only a tiny minority (less than three percent) of the population profess the Christian faith.

Although Carey was the great pioneer missionary to India, he was not the first. Centuries before him came Francis Xavier (see chapter 2) and other Roman Catholic emissaries; and ninety years before him came Bartholomew Ziegenbalg and Henry Plütschau, Lutheran missionaries supported by the Danish-Halle Mission. Ziegenbalg and Plütschau, who worked near the southern tip of India in Tranquebar, were hampered by the commercial opposition of the Danish East India Company, but they nevertheless made progress and witnessed many converts during their years of service. After six years Plütschau returned home due to ill health, while Ziegenbalg remained to shepherd the church and translate all of the New Testament and a large portion of the Old Testament into one of India's many languages. He died in 1719 after fourteen years of service.

Ziegenbalg's translation was completed by another Danish-Halle missionary who in turn influenced Christian Frederic Schwartz to go to India. Schwartz arrived in 1750 and served faithfully for forty-eight years until he died in 1798, four years after Carey began his work more than a thousand miles to the north.

William Carey

William Carey, an impoverished English shoemaker, was an unlikely candidate for greatness. Yet, he has been appropriately designated as the "Father of Modern Missions." More than any other individual in modern history, he stirred the imagination of the Christian world and showed by his own humble example what could and should be done to bring a lost world to Christ. Although he faced many oppressive trials during his forty-year missionary career, he demonstrated a dogged determination to succeed, and he never gave up. His secret? "I can plod. I can persevere in any definite pursuit. To this I owe everything."[1] Carey's life profoundly illustrates the limitless potential of a very ordinary individual. He was a man who, apart from his unqualified commitment to God, no doubt would have lived a very mediocre existence.

Carey was born in 1761 near Northampton, England. His father was a weaver who worked on a loom in the family living quarters. Though poverty was the norm for families like Carey's, life was simple and uncomplicated. The Industrial Revolution had only begun to replace the cottage industries with grimy sweat shops and noisy textile mills. Carey's childhood was routine, except for persistent problems with allergies that prevented him from pursuing his dream of becoming a gardener. Instead, he was apprenticed, at the age of sixteen, to a shoemaker and continued in that vocation until he was twenty-eight. He was converted as a teen-ager and shortly afterwards became actively associated with a group of Baptist Dissenters and devoted his leisure time to Bible study and lay ministries.

In 1781, before he had reached his twentieth birthday, Carey married his master's sister-in-law. Dorothy was more than five years older than he, and, like many eighteenth-century English women of her background, she was illiterate. From the beginning it was a mismatched union, and as time passed and Carey's horizons broadened the chasm dividing them grew even wider. The earliest years of their marriage were filled with hardship and poverty. For a time, Carey not only had the responsibility of his own wife and fast-growing family, but also cared for the family of his late master's widow and her four children.

Despite the economic hard times, Carey did not turn aside from his study and lay preaching; and in 1785 he accepted a call to become the pastor of a tiny Baptist church where he served until he was called to a larger church at Leicester, though even here he was forced to seek other employment to support his family. During these years in the pastorate his philosophy of missions began to take shape, sparked first by his reading of *Captain Cook's Voyages*. Slowly he developed a biblical perspective on the subject, and he became convinced that foreign missions were the central responsibility of the church. His ideas were revolutionary. Many, if not most, eighteenth-century churchmen believed that the Great Commission was given only to the apostles, and therefore converting the "heathen" was no concern of theirs, especially if it were not tied to colonialism. When Carey presented his ideas to a group of ministers, one of them retorted: "Young man, sit down. When God pleases to convert the heathen, He will do it without your aid or mine."[2] But Carey refused to be silenced. In the spring of 1792 he published an eighty-seven page book that had far-reaching consequences and has been ranked alongside Luther's Ninety-five Theses in its influence on Christian history.

The book, *An Enquirey Into the Obligation of Christians to Use Means for the Conversion of the Heathens* (and that being a shortened title), very ably presented a case for foreign missions and sought to deflate the arguments dramatizing the impracticality of sending missionaries to faraway lands. After publishing the book, Carey spoke to a group of ministers at a Baptist Association meeting in Nottingham, where he challenged his audience from Isaiah 54:2–3 and uttered his now famous quote: "Expect great things from God; attempt great things for God." The following day, largely through his influence, the ministers decided to organize a new mission board, which became known as the Baptist Missionary Society. The decision was not made lightly. Most of the Association ministers were, like Carey, living on very meager incomes, and involvement in foreign missions meant tremendous financial sacrifices from both them and their congregations.

Andrew Fuller, the most prominent minister in support of the new society, became the first home secretary, and

William Carey, the "Father of Modern Missions."

the first missionary appointee was John Thomas, a Baptist layman who had gone to India as a doctor for the royal navy and stayed on after his term of service to minister as a free-lance missionary doctor and evangelist. Carey immediately offered himself to the new society as a "suitable companion" to Thomas and was eagerly accepted.

Although Carey had long been avidly interested in missions, the decision to offer himself for foreign service was nothing less than rash. The fact that his church was distressed at losing its pastor and that his father judged him "mad" could be easily overlooked, but his wife's response should have at least slowed him down. With three little ones and another on the way, it is no wonder Dorothy adamantly opposed leaving her home-land to embark on a hazardous five-month voyage (complicated by France's very recent declaration of war against England) to spend the rest of her life in the deadly tropical climate of India. Other women had willingly made such sacrifices and thousands more would in the future, but Dorothy was different. If there is a "Mother of Modern Missions," it is certainly not she. She defiantly refused to go.

If Dorothy thought her refusal to accompany her husband would change his mind, she was wrong. Carey, though distressed by her decision, was determined to go, even if it meant going without her. He went ahead with his plans, which included booking a passage for Felix, his eight-year-old son. In March of 1793, after months of deputation, Carey and Thomas were commissioned by the Society; and the following month they, along with Felix and Thomas's wife and daughter, boarded a ship on the Thames River that was to take them to India. But the trip to India ended abruptly at Portsmouth, England. Money problems (centering around Thomas and his disgruntled creditors) and failure to have a license prevented them from going further.

The delay was a disappointment for the missionaries, but it led to a dramatic change in plans. Dorothy, having delivered her baby three weeks before, grudgingly agreed to join the mission party with her little ones, providing Kitty, her younger sister, could accompany her. Obtaining funds for the additional passengers was a difficult hurdle, but on June 13, 1793, they boarded a Danish vessel and set sail for India. The long and dangerous voyage around the Cape of Good Hope was not without its terrifying moments, but on November 19 they arrived safely in India.

The time of their arrival was not favorable for establishing mission work. The East India Company was in virtual control of the country, and its hostility to mission work was soon made plain. The company feared anything that could possibly interfere with its profitable commercial ventures, and Carey quickly realized he was very unwelcome. Fearing deportation, he moved with his family to the interior. Here, surrounded by malarial swamps, the Careys lived in dire circumstances. Dorothy and the two oldest boys became deathly ill, and family cares required Carey's constant attention. His idealistic dreams of missionary work were rapidly fading. Likewise, it grieved him that his wife and Kitty were "continually exclaiming against"[3] him and were resentful of the Thomas family, who were living in affluence in Calcutta. After some months their plight was alleviated by the kindness and generosity of Mr. Short, an East India Company official who, though an unbeliever, took pity on them and welcomed them into his home for as long as they desired to stay. Soon, however, the Careys moved on to Malda, nearly three hundred miles north, where Carey was able to obtain a position as a foreman in an indigo factory.

The years in Malda were difficult ones. Although Carey was happy in his new position and found the indigo factory to be a choice language school and field for evangelism, family troubles persisted. Kitty, who stayed back to marry Mr. Short, was no longer with them, and Dorothy's health and mental stability steadily declined. Then, the tragic death of the little bright-eyed five-year-old Peter in 1794 pushed her over the brink. She never did fully regain her mental faculties. It was a pitiful situation, and she was later described by co-workers as being "wholly deranged."

Despite his traumatic family situation and his continued factory work, Carey did not forget his purpose for being in India. He spent hours every day in Bible translation work, and he preached and set up schools as well. By the end of 1795 a Baptist church had been established in Malda. It was a start, even though its entire membership equaled only four, and they were Englishmen. The services, however, drew large crowds of Bengali people, and Carey could confidently assert that "the name of Jesus Christ is no longer strange in this neighborhood." But there was no fruit. After nearly seven years of toil in Bengal, Carey could not claim even one Indian convert.[4]

In spite of his lack of outward success, Carey was satisfied with his missionary work in Malda and was keenly disappointed to leave in 1800. New missionaries had arrived from England, and in order to avoid continual harassment from the East India Company, they settled near Calcutta in the Danish territory of Serampore. Carey's help was urgently needed in setting up the new mission station to accommodate them, so he reluctantly departed with his family from Malda.

Serampore soon became the center of Baptist missionary activity in India, and it was there that Carey would spend the remaining thirty-four years of his life. Carey and his co-workers, Joshua Marshman and William Ward, known as the Serampore Trio, would become one of the most famous missionary teams in history. The mission compound, which housed ten missionaries and their nine children, enjoyed a family atmosphere. The missionaries lived together and kept all things in common, even as the early church had done in the Book of Acts. On Saturday nights they met to pray and to air their grievances, always "pledging themselves to love one another." Responsibilities were divided according to abilities, and the work progressed smoothly.

The great success of the Serampore Mission during the early years can be credited to a large extent to Carey and his saintly disposition. His own willingness to sacrifice material wealth and to go beyond the call of duty was a continual example to the rest. Moreover, he had an uncanny ability to overlook the faults in others. Even in regard to Thomas, who mismanaged the mission funds and was an embarrassment because of careless indebtedness, Carey could say, "I love him, and we live in the greatest harmony." Describing his co-workers, Carey wrote: "Brother Ward is the very man we wanted. . . . He enters into the work with his whole soul. I have much pleasure in him. . . . Brother Marshman is a prodigy of diligence and prudence, as is also his wife. . . ."[5]

Serampore was a harmonious example of missionary cooperation, and there were results to show for it. Schools were organized, a large printing establishment was set up, and, above all, translation work was continually being done. During his years at Serampore, Carey made three translations of the whole Bible (Bengali, Sanskrit, and Marathi), helped in other whole Bible translations, and translated the New Testament and portions of Scripture into many more languages and dialects. Unfortunately, his quality did not always match his quantity. Home Secretary Andrew Fuller scolded him for inconsistent spelling and other problems in the copy he sent back to England for printing: "I never knew a person of so much knowledge as you profess of other languages, write English so bad. . . . You huddle half a dozen periods into one. . . . If your Bengal N.T. shd be thus pointed I shd tremble for its fate. . . ."[6] Fuller's fears were well-founded, and Carey, to his bitter disappointment, found that some of his work was incomprehensible. But the indefatigable translator did not give up. He went back to the drawing board and completely reworked his translation until he was satisfied it could be understood.

Evangelism was also an important part of the work at Serampore, and within a year after the mission was established the missionaries were rejoicing over their first convert. The following year there were more converts, but on the whole evangelism progressed slowly. By 1818, after twenty-five years of Baptist missions to India, there were some six hundred baptized converts and a few thousand more who attended classes and services.

Despite his busy schedule of translation and evangelistic work, Carey always found time to do more. One of his greatest achievements was the founding of Serampore College in 1819 for the training of indigenous church planters and evangelists. The school opened with thirty-seven Indian students, more than half of whom were Christians. Another area of educational achievement involved his secular teaching. Soon after he arrived at

Serampore he was invited to become the Professor of Oriental Languages at Fort William College in Calcutta. It was a great honor to Carey, an uneducated cobbler, to be asked to fill such an esteemed position, and with the enthusiastic support of his colleagues he accepted. The position not only brought in much needed income to the missionaries, but also placed them in better standing with the East India Company and gave Carey an opportunity to improve his language skills while being challenged by his students.

As busy as he was, Carey was unable to give his children the fathering they so desperately needed. Even when he was with them his easy-going nature stood in the way of firm discipline, a lack that was plainly exhibited in the boys' behavior. In speaking of this situation, Hannah Marshman wrote, "The good man saw and lamented the evil but was too mild to apply an effectual remedy."[7] Fortunately, Mrs. Marshman stepped in. Had it not been for that dear woman's stern reprimands and William Ward's fatherly concern, the Carey boys would have gone entirely their own way.

In 1807, at the age of fifty-one, Dorothy Carey died. It was no doubt a relief to Carey. She had long since ceased to be a useful member of the mission family. In fact, she was a hindrance to the work. John Marshman wrote how Carey often worked on his translations "while an insane wife, frequently wrought up to a state of most distressing excitement, was in the next room. . . ."[8]

During his years at Serampore, Carey had developed a friendship with Lady Charlotte Rumohr, born into Danish royalty and living at Serampore

in hopes that the climate would improve her poor health. Though she came to Serampore as a skeptic, she attended services at the mission, was converted, and was baptized by Carey in 1803. After that she began devoting her time and money to the work of the mission. In 1808, only a few months after the death of Dorothy, Carey announced his engagement to Lady Charlotte, and in so doing caused an upheaval in the usually tranquil mission family. So great was the opposition that a petition was circulated in an effort to prevent the marriage; but when his colleagues realized his mind was made up, they backed down and accepted the inevitable. The marriage, conducted by Marshman, took place in May, just six months after Dorothy had been laid to rest.

Carey's thirteen-year marriage to Charlotte was a happy one. During that time he was truly in love—perhaps for the first time in his life. Charlotte had a brilliant mind and a gift for linguistics, and she was a valuable assistant to Carey in his translation work. She also maintained close relationships with the boys and became the mother they had never had. When she died in 1821, Carey wrote, "We had as great a share of conjugal happiness as ever was enjoyed by mortals." Two years later, Carey, at the age of sixty-two, married again, this time to Grace Hughes, a widow seventeen years younger than he. Though Grace was not as well-endowed intellectually as Charlotte had been, Carey praised her for her "constant and unremitting care and excellent nursing" during his frequent illnesses.[9]

One of the most devastating setbacks that Carey faced during his forty uninterrupted years in India was the loss of his priceless manuscripts in a warehouse fire in 1812. Carey was away at the time, but the ominous news that his massive polyglot dictionary, two grammar books, and whole versions of the Bible had been destroyed could not be concealed. Had his temperament been different, he may have never recovered; but as it was, Carey accepted the tragedy as a judgment from the Lord and began all over again with even greater zeal.

Carey's first fifteen years at Serampore were years of cooperation and teamwork. Except for occasional problems such as the one relating to his second marriage, the little Baptist community in India lived in harmony. Perhaps the situation had been too good to be true, but at any rate the peace did not last, and the fifteen years that followed were filled with turmoil. The spirit of unity was broken when new missionaries arrived who were unwilling to live in the communal fashion of the Serampore missionaries. One missionary demanded "a separate house, stable and servants." There were other differences, too. The new missionaries found their seniors—particularly Joshua Marshman—dictatorial, assigning them duties and locations not to their liking. The new missionaries no doubt were justified in feeling slighted. The senior workers were settled into their system, and they were not open to change. But had the junior missionaries manifested the love and longsuffering that had been so characteristic of the Serampore team, the differences could have been worked out. Unfortunately, that was not the case. Bitter accusations were made against the senior missionaries, and the result was a split between the two groups.

The junior missionaries formed the Calcutta Missionary Union and began working only miles away from their Baptist brethren. "Indelicate" was the word William Ward used to describe the situation.[10]

The ordeal became even more critical when the Home Committee received the news and became involved. The original committee headed by Andrew Fuller no longer existed. That little committee of three had increased its size several times, and most of the members knew Carey only through his letters. Fuller and one of the other original members had died, leaving the home committee clearly stacked in favor of the junior members whom it had personally commissioned as missionaries. While Fuller had been at the helm he had insisted for two reasons that Serampore be self-governing: "One is, we think them better able to govern themselves than we are to govern them. Anor is, they are at too great a distance to wait for our direction."[11] But the reconstructed home committee strongly disagreed. The members believed that all the important affairs of the Serampore Mission should be under their direct control. Finally in 1826, after years of wearying conflict, the Serampore Mission severed its relationship with the Baptist Missionary Society.

The final split between Serampore and the Baptist Missionary Society was a financial blow to the Serampore missionaries. Although the Serampore team had been financially self-sufficient during most of its history, receiving only a small percentage of its funds from England, times were changing. There were missionaries at more than a dozen outstations who needed support, and medical care was needed for others. No longer could the Serampore team support them all. Carey and Marshman (Ward having since died) had no choice but to swallow their pride and submit themselves and the mission to the authority of the Society. Soon after that a substantial sum of money and kind letters arrived from the home committee. The healing process had begun.

Carey died in 1834, but not before leaving his mark on India and on missions for all times. His influence in India went beyond his massive linguistic accomplishments, his educational institutions, and the Christian following he shepherded. He also made a notable impact on harmful Indian practices through his long struggle against widow burning and infanticide. But otherwise, he sought to leave the culture intact. Carey was ahead of his time in missionary methodology. He had an awesome respect for the Indian culture, and he never tried to import Western substitutes, as so many missionaries who came after him would seek to do. His goal was to build an indigenous church "by means of native preachers" and by providing the Scriptures in the native tongue, and it was to that end that he dedicated his life. But it was not just in India where Carey's influence was felt. His work was being closely followed not only in England, but also on the Continent and in America where the inspiration derived from his daring example outweighed in importance all his accomplishments in India.

The Adoniram Judsons

Associated for a time with Carey, and particularly with his son Felix,

were Adoniram and Nancy Judson, who arrived in India in 1812. The Judsons, along with six other young missionaries, had come from the United States, and they held the distinction of being America's first foreign missionaries. Like so many missionaries before them, these Americans discovered the East India Company to be an unyielding barrier to missionary work, and they were forced to leave India. After months of complications and delays, the Judsons, separated from their colleagues, arrived in Burma, where they would spend the rest of their lives under extreme hardship and privation in an effort to bring the gospel to the people of that closed and uninviting land.

Adoniram Judson was born in Massachusetts in 1788, the son of a Congregational minister. He was barely sixteen when he entered Brown University, and he graduated three years later (from a four-year course) as valedictorian of his class. During his student days he had grown close to a fellow student, Jacob Eames, who espoused Deism, a doctrine anathema to the conservative Congregationalism in which he had been raised. But Eames's views made a strong impact on young Judson, who was no longer intellectually satisfied with the faith of his father. After graduation, Judson returned to his hometown, where he opened an academy and published two textbooks; but he was unhappy. Disregarding his parents' pleas, he set out to see the world, heading for New York City where he hoped to become a playwright.

Judson's stay in New York was short and unfulfilling. After a matter of weeks he was on his way back to New England, dejected and frustrated about his future. He was heading for nowhere in particular when he stopped one evening at an inn. His sleep that night was interrupted by the painful groans of a sick man in the room next to his. In the morning he inquired about the unfortunate traveler, only to be informed that the man—Jacob Eames—had died during the night. It was a brutal shock to the twenty-year-old Judson, and it was a time for soul-searching as he slowly made his way home.

There was an air of excitement at the parsonage at Plymouth when Adoniram arrived home in September of 1808. His father was one of several ministers involved in establishing a new seminary at Andover that, unlike Harvard and the other New England divinity schools, would stand on the orthodox tenets of the faith. With the encouragement of his father and the other ministers, Adoniram agreed to continue his search for truth at this new seminary. He was admitted as a special student, making no profession of faith, but after only a few months he made a "solemn dedication" of himself to God.

Soon after his dedication, Judson read a printed copy of a stirring missionary message given by a British minister. So moved was he that Judson vowed that he would be the first American foreign missionary. Andover Seminary was not a beehive of missionary zeal, but there were other students who were sympathetic, including Samuel Mills from Williams College who had been the ringleader of the "Haystack Prayer Meeting" some years before. This outdoor prayer meeting, an unplanned event, was a landmark in American foreign missions. A group of missionary-minded Williams College students, known as the Society of the Brethren, were in the habit of meeting outside for prayer. Caught in a thunderstorm one afternoon, they took shelter under a nearby haystack. It was there under that haystack that they pledged themselves to missionary service. Mills, having since transferred to Andover, was a strong supporter of Judson and the other Andover students who were interested in missions. He went on to become a great missionary statesman, though he never served overseas as a missionary.

The heightened concern for missions among this small group of Andover students led to the formation of the American Board of Commissioners for Foreign Missions, commonly referred to as the American Board—the same society that commissioned the Whitmans to Oregon more than two decades later (see chapter 4). Though there was a great deal of enthusiasm, the American Board got off to a bumpy start. Paralyzed by lack of finances, the

Adoniram Judson, pioneer missionary to Burma.

Ann (Nancy) Hasseltine Judson, the first wife of Adoniram Judson.

commissioners sent Judson to England in hopes of obtaining funds through the London Missionary Society. While the directors of the LMS were willing to sponsor American missionaries, they were clearly not willing to finance them under the American Board. Judson was prepared to offer himself and his colleagues to the LMS, but then word came of a sizable inheritance received by the American Board, and he returned home.

Before he had gone to England, Judson had "commenced an acquaintanceship" with Ann Hasseltine, better known as Nancy. Nancy, like Adoniram, had undergone a life-changing religious conversion that turned the flighty wayward teen-ager into a serious but vivacious adult. Unlike Dorothy Carey, Nancy was burdened for the heathen and insisted that her going to India was not because of "an attachment to an earthly object," meaning Adoniram, but because of

"obligation to God . . . with a full conviction of its being a call. . . ."[12] In February of 1812, she and Adoniram were married, and thirteen days later they set sail for India, arriving in Calcutta in mid-June.

For Adoniram and Nancy, the long sea voyage was more than an extended honeymoon. They spent many hours in Bible study—particularly searching out the true meaning of baptism, a subject which had been weighing heavily on Adoniram's mind. The more he studied the more convinced he became that the Congregational view of infant baptism by sprinkling was wrong. Nancy at first was upset with his new ideas, arguing that the issue was not crucial and stating that even if he became a Baptist she would not. After a thorough investigation, however, she became convinced of believers' baptism by immersion, and after arriving in India Adoniram and Nancy were both baptized by William Ward of Serampore.

When word reached the United States that the Judsons as well as Luther Rice (one of the other six missionaries commissioned to India by the American Board) had moved into the Baptist camp, there was an uproar among the Congregationalists. How could their star missionary desert them after all they had invested in him? The Baptists, however, were elated, and they quickly moved to form their own missionary society and underwrite his support.

The Judsons' stay in India was short-lived. They were no match for the powerful East India Company. Unable to remain in India, they sailed to the Isle of France off the coast of East Africa; but when their prospects for missionary work there seemed dim, they returned to India, en route to Penang on the Malay Peninsula where they hoped they could conduct missionary work. But with no vessel sailing for Penang, and once again under threat of deportation, the Judsons boarded a ship sailing for Burma. Interestingly, Burma had originally been Adoniram's first choice for a mission field, until he heard frightening reports of brutal treatment meted out to foreigners.

The Judsons' arrival in Rangoon was a depressing time for them. Nancy had undergone a stillbirth on the voyage and had to be carried off the ship to their new land. Unlike India, Burma had no European community, and there was no caste system. The people appeared rather independent and free, in spite of the cruel tyrannical regime that ruled them. Poverty was everywhere. The narrow, filthy streets of Rangoon were lined with run-down huts, and there was a sense of oppression behind the happy smiles that greeted them. The Judsons were not the first Protestant missionaries in Burma. Others had come and gone, but only Felix Carey (William Carey's oldest son) and his wife remained; and they left soon after the Judsons arrived, when Felix was offered a position by the Burmese government (to which his father had bitterly commented, "Felix is shrivelled from a missionary into an ambassador"). Later on Felix returned to India to work with his father and ably assist in the mission work there.

At last, two years after they had sailed from America, Adoniram and Nancy were finally alone to establish their own missionary work. They had

America's first foreign missionaries commissioned February 5, 1812.

The Judsons aboard the *Caravan* leaving from Crowninshield's Wharf in Salem, February 18, 1812.

the large Baptist mission house in Rangoon to themselves, and there they spent up to twelve hours a day studying the difficult Burmese language. Nancy, through her daily contacts with Burmese women, caught on to the spoken tongue quickly; but Adoniram struggled laboriously with the written language, a continual sequence of letters with no punctuation or capitals, and no divisions between words, sentences, or paragraphs.

The language was not the only barrier standing between the Judsons and the Burmese people. They discovered that the Burmese had no concept of an eternal God who personally cared about mankind, and their first attempts to share the gospel were discouraging: "You cannot imagine how very difficult it is to give them any idea of the true God and the way of salvation by Christ, since their present ideas of deity are so very low." Buddhism was the religion of Burma, a religion of ritual and idol worship: "It is now two thousand years since Gaudama [Gautama], their last deity, entered on his state of perfection; and though he now ceases to exist, they still worship a hair of his head, which is enshrined in an enormous pagoda, to which the Burmans go every eighth day."[13]

The Judsons' status as the only Protestant missionaries in Burma was brief. Not long after they moved into the spacious mission house their privacy ended as they made room for George and Phebe Hough and their children. Hough, a printer, came with his press and type and soon was printing portions of Scripture that Adoniram had slowly been translating.

125

Within two years, two more families arrived, but death, disease, and early departures kept the mission force small.

Burma was a discouraging field for the cultivation of Christianity. Every seedling of progress, it seemed, was beaten down before it could take root. At times there were encouraging signs of interest, but then the inquiries would suddenly drop off as rumors of official crackdowns surfaced. Toleration of the missionaries fluctuated from one extreme to another with the continual turnover of viceroys in Rangoon. When the Judsons were in favor at the court, they were free to propagate the gospel, and the Burmese responded to the relaxed controls; but when they were out of favor, they laid low, spending their time at the mission house in translation work.

From their early days in Rangoon, the Judsons were unhappy with the out-of-the-way location of the mission house. They were in Burma to minister to the people, and they wanted the people to have easy access to them. For a short while they moved out of the mission house and lived among the teeming population of the city, but a fire ravaged through their section and drove them back to the secluded mission house. But they were not satisfied. They wanted to mingle with the people and reach them on their own level. How could this be accomplished in a culture so vastly different from their own? A zayat provided the ideal solution.

A zayat was a shelter open to anyone who wanted to rest or to discuss the day's events, or to listen to Buddhist lay teachers who often stopped by. It was a place to relax and forget the pressures of the day, and there were many such shelters in Rangoon. Judson was convinced that such a building would put him in touch with the people, but he was hampered in his plans by lack of finances. Finally, in 1819, five years after arriving in Burma, he was able to secure a reasonably priced piece of property not far from the mission house on the Pagoda Road, a well-traveled thoroughfare, and he and Nancy began building their zayat (a twenty-by-twenty-foot hut with a wide veranda, all elevated on poles several feet off the ground). But merely constructing a zayat was not enough. Adoniram and Nancy wanted the Burmese people to feel at ease, so they attended a religious service at a nearby zayat to familiarize themselves with seating patterns and other cultural peculiarities. They understood clearly that they were not opening a New England meeting-house, but rather a Burmese zayat.

The concept worked. Almost immediately visitors, who would never have come to the mission house, began stopping by. Though Adoniram found little time for his translation work, he was excited about this new phase of his ministry, and in May of 1819, only a month after the zayat opened, Maung Nau made a profession of faith in Christ at a Sunday service in the zayat packed with Burmese people. Slowly the little Burmese church in Rangoon grew, and by the summer of 1820 there were ten faithful baptized members. From the beginning, the Burmese converts took an active role in evangelism: one woman opened a school in her house, a young man became an assistant pastor, and others distributed tracts. The work went forward, even when the Judsons were gone.

Next to official harassment, tropical fever was the greatest setback to the work in Burma. Both Adoniram and Nancy suffered frequently from bouts of fever that endangered their very lives. Death, they discovered, was always a very real threat. Baby Roger, born to them the year after they settled in Rangoon, filled their hearts with joy for six months before he suddenly succumbed to fever. In 1820 they left Rangoon for several months to seek medical care for Nancy in Calcutta. Then in 1822 Nancy parted with Adoniram for an extended sick leave that took her to England and back to the United States.

While Nancy was away, Adoniram buried himself in his translation work, completing the New Testament in less than a year. In the meantime, his situation had drastically changed. Dr. Jonathan Price, a medical missionary working with Adoniram, was ordered to appear before the emperor at Ava, several weeks' journey up river. Adoniram's fluency in the Burmese language obligated him to accompany Price on this important meeting, so he reluctantly packed his belongings for the journey. For a time the two missionaries enjoyed the favor of the royal court, but by early 1824 the political situation in Burma began to look ominous. Nancy had returned from the United States, and she joined Adoniram in Ava; but their reunion was brief. War broke out between Burma and England, and all foreigners were suspected of being spies. Both

INDIA AND BURMA

Adoniram and Price were arrested and confined in a death prison, where they awaited execution.

Life in death prison was appalling. The missionaries were confined with common criminals in a filthy, vermin-infested, dark, dank prison house, with fetters binding their ankles. At night the Spotted Faces (prison guards whose face and chest were branded for being one-time criminals themselves) hoisted the ankle fetters to a pole suspended from the ceiling, until only their heads and shoulders rested on the ground. By morning the weary prisoners were numb and stiff, but the daytime offered them little relief. Each day executions were carried out and the prisoners never knew who would be next.

Adoniram's suffering affected Nancy as much as, or more than, it did him. Daily she sought out officials, explaining to them that, as an American citizen, Adoniram had nothing to do with the British government. Sometimes her pleas and bribes were heeded and Adoniram was given temporary relief; but more often than not she felt helpless to do anything about her husband languishing in prison. To make matters worse, she discovered she was pregnant. The only bright spots during the months that followed were the visits she was allowed to have with Adoniram through bribing officials and guards. Her visits stopped for a time, but then on February 15, 1825, eight months after Adoniram had been arrested, she came carrying a small bundle—baby Maria, less than three weeks old.

The following May, with British troops marching toward Ava, the prisoners were suddenly removed from the prison house and forced on a death march to a location further north. Having been bound in prison for most of a year without exercise, the prisoners were unprepared for the arduous pace under the scorching sun, and some did not make it alive. Adoniram's blistered feet were soon raw and bleeding. Each step was excruciating torture. As they marched, they crossed over a bridge that spanned a dry rocky river bed, and for a moment Adoniram was tempted to go over the edge and end it all. It would have been the easy way out, but he suppressed the temptation and kept on going, only to be confined once again in prison.

Within days, Nancy, who had not heard about the transfer until after the fact, arrived at the new location, once again pleading her husband's case. But whatever she hoped to accomplish was soon obscured by baby Maria's and her own ill health. She became so sick that she could no longer nurse Maria, and only the mercy of the guards kept the baby alive. They allowed Adoniram to go out of the prison twice daily to carry the baby around the village to suckle from nursing mothers. Slowly mother and baby began to recover, but never would their health be fully restored.

Finally, in November of 1825, after nearly one and a half years of prison confinement, Adoniram was released to help interpret peace negotiations with the British. While working on the negotiations, the Judsons spent a short time with the British officials, and for the first time in nearly two years they were able to enjoy themselves. To her brother-in-law Nancy wrote, "No persons on earth were ever happier, than we were during the fortnight we passed at the English

Camp."[14] It was the last time of relaxation they would have together. They returned to Rangoon for a short time and then went to Amherst, where Nancy stayed alone with Maria while Adoniram returned to help wind up the negotiations. The weeks dragged into months, and before he was able to return he received a letter with a black seal. Nancy, his beloved companion, had died of fever. A few months later baby Maria also died.

Judson's immediate reaction to Nancy's death was to drown his sorrows in work. For more than a year he kept up a hectic pace of translation work and evangelism, but his heart was not in his labors. Beneath the surface was a pressure of guilt and grief that had to be released. He could not forgive himself for not being with Nancy when she needed him most, and he could not rid himself of the overwhelming sorrow that only seemed to grow more intense. As the depression increased, his output decreased. He began meditating for long periods and avoided any social contact with others. He even stopped eating with the other missionaries at the mission house. Finally, about two years after Nancy's death, he stopped social intercourse altogether and went into the jungle, where he built himself a hut and lived as a recluse. He went so far as to dig a grave where he kept vigil for days on end, filling his mind with morbid thoughts of death. Spiritual desolation engulfed him: "God is to me the Great Unknown. I believe in him, but I find him not."[15]

Fortunately, Judson's mental breakdown did not last indefinitely (as Dorothy Carey's had). There were no psychiatrists, there was no psychoanalysis, and there was no group therapy. There was, however, a tremendous outpouring of love and prayer both by his colleagues and by the native converts. But more important, there was a solid foundation to his faith that was able to endure even the most trying times of doubt. Slowly, he recovered from the paralyzing depression, and as he did he acquired a new depth of spirituality that intensified his ministry. He began traveling around in Burma, helping other missionaries at their outposts. Everywhere he went, the response was the same—throngs of inquirers, converts, and signs of spiritual growth. He sensed a new spirit of interest "through the whole length and breadth of the land." It was an awesome feeling: "I sometimes feel alarmed like a person who sees a mighty engine beginning to move, over which he knows he has no control."[16]

As exhilarating as Judson's itinerant ministry was, he knew that there was an even greater job to be done—completing the Burmese Bible. It would take more than a snatch of time here and there between travels; it would take total concentration, and that meant setting aside two years and keeping up a pace of translating between twenty-five and thirty Old Testament verses each day from the original Hebrew into Burmese—two enormously complex languages. Judson met his goal of completing the initial translation, but there were years of less concentrated revision work ahead of him. It was not until 1840, fourteen years after Nancy's death, that he sent the last page of his Burmese Bible to the printer.

In the meantime, Judson had been concentrating on more than his revisions. In 1834, at the age of forty-six, he married Sarah Boardman, a thirty-year-old widow, who had gallantly stayed on in missionary work after her husband had died three years earlier (see pp. 131ff.). They were well-suited for each other, but Sarah's missionary work decreased as her family increased. During the first ten years of their marriage she gave birth to eight children. But the strain was too much. In 1845, the year after her last child was born, while en route to the United States on medical leave, she died.

Judson and three of their children had accompanied Sarah, and the tragedy that had befallen them deeply saddened what would have been a joyous reunion with family and friends. It had been thirty-three years since Judson had last seen his native land, and what tremendous changes he found. He could not help being impressed by the country towns and fishing wharves that had turned into great cities and seaports, but the land of his childhood was forever gone. He hardly recognized the once familiar New England countryside. But the thirty-three years of progress were not all that prevented him from quietly returning to his boyhood haunts to assuage his grief. He suddenly found himself a celebrity. Everybody, it seemed, wanted to see and hear this man whose name had become a household word and whose missionary work had become a legend. Though he disdained publicity, Judson, nevertheless, accommodated his enthusiastic supporters and began a tiring circuit of speaking engagements. The people, however, were disappointed with their hero. They wanted to hear exciting stories about exotic people and customs, but all he preached was the gospel, and they had heard that before.

During his travels, Judson was introduced to Emily Chubbock, a young author of popular fiction written under the pseudonym Fanny Forrester. Judson was delighted with her lively writing style, but he was astounded that such brilliant talent of a professing Christian (and a Baptist at that) would be wasted on secular endeavors. His suggestion that Emily write a biography of Sarah was enthusiastically received, and their friendship quickly blossomed. He proposed marriage in January of 1846, less than a month after their first meeting.

The decision to marry Emily was a controversial one. She had contemplated missionary work when she was younger, and there was no reason to believe that she could not be a faithful wife to Judson and a valuable asset to the missionary effort in Burma. But Judson was a venerated saint of Protestant America, and as such the expectations of him were inordinately high. Marrying a secular author still in her twenties, and only half his age, was not the proper thing to do, so said the American public. But the barrage of criticism only seemed to make their commitment deeper, and in June of 1846 they were married.

The following month they sailed for Burma, leaving the three children in care of two different families—never to see their father again. There were three more children who had been left behind in Burma, who would never know the mother who had suckled them in infancy. The Judson saga, as much as any missionary story, illustrates the trauma that missionary work has brought to families—the trauma of crying, frightened little ones clinging to their parents, never comprehending why they were being torn from the only love and security they had ever known. Nevertheless, the children somehow weathered these ordeals. Of Judson's five children by Sarah who grew to adulthood, two became ministers, one a physician, another a headmistress of an academy, and another served honorably in the Union Army until he was disabled in battle.

In November of 1846 Judson and his new bride arrived in Burma. Emily had faired the voyage well and was ready to fill Sarah's shoes to the best of her ability. She became a mother to Judson's little ones (only two of whom had survived to greet them), and she enthusiastically plunged into language study and missionary work, never forgetting her talent for writing. Through her pen came some graphic pictures of the stark reality of missionary life. She was bothered by the "thousands and thousands of bats," but most of the other little creatures she took in stride: "We are blessed with our full share of cockroaches, beetles, lizards, rats, ants, mosquitoes, and bed-bugs. With the last the woodwork is all alive, and the ants troop over the house in great droves.... Perhaps twenty have crossed my paper since I have been writing. Only one cockroach has paid me a visit, but the neglect of these gentlemen has been fully made up by a company of black bugs about the size of the end of your finger—nameless adventurers."[17]

Adoniram and Emily served three years together in Burma. The birth of a baby girl brought happiness to them, but much of the time was marred by illness. In the spring of 1850, with Emily soon expecting another child, Adoniram, who was seriously ill, left on a sea voyage, hoping to recover. Less than a week later, he died and was buried at sea. Ten days later Emily underwent a stillbirth, and not until August did she hear of her husband's death. The following January she, along with little Emily and Judson's two young sons, sailed for Boston to make a home for the children in the United States; but her own health was broken, and three years later she died at the age of thirty-six.

George and Sarah Boardman

Sarah and George Boardman arrived in Burma from the United States at the close of the Anglo-Burmese War, soon after the death of Nancy Judson. They knew well the perils of coming to such a land. In fact, their concern for Burmese missions and their subsequent marriage was stimulated by the untimely death of James Coleman, one of Judson's missionary colleagues. So deeply moved by this sacrifice was George Boardman, a graduate of Colby College, that he enrolled at Andover Seminary to prepare for missionary service. In much the same way Sarah Hall, a sober-minded teen-ager and the oldest of thirteen children, was touched by the tragedy. Her response was to write a poem about Coleman —lines that would change the course of her life. The poem, published in a religious journal, stirred the curiosity of Boardman, who was impressed by the sincerity of its author. He was not satisfied until he located her, and within months after their initial meeting they became engaged.

The Boardmans were known for their ministry among the Karens, a mountain tribe looked down on by the more sophisticated Burmese. Shortly after they arrived in Burma they left the comfortable mission confines of Moulmein to move to Tavoy for pioneer work among the Karens. With them they brought Ko Tha Byu, a criminal who by his own admission had committed some thirty murders before his conversion. Ko Tha Byu, a native Karen, had a vibrant testimony, and for three years he accompanied the Boardmans in their evangelistic ministry from one mountain village to another. It was a fruitful ministry, but slowly George Boardman's health was giving out. He died in 1831 after less than five years in Burma. Unlike Judson, who served several years before he saw even one convert, Boardman had the privilege of seeing many come to Christ. During the last two months of his life, fifty-seven Karens were baptized, and the Tavoy church alone had seventy members.

After her husband's death, Sarah was tempted to return to the United States with little George, her two-year-old son; but through Judson's urging, she decided to stay on in the work. She had established a girls' school and feared that it would falter were she to leave. For three years she remained with the Karens, spending her time teaching and continuing her husband's itinerant ministry into the mountain villages with her little boy, whom the Karens affectionately called "Little Chief."

In 1834, Adoniram Judson came to Tavoy to visit Sarah, and during his extended visit they were married. The following year the six-year-old "Little Chief" was sent to the United States to be properly educated. It was a traumatic experience for the little boy

whom Sarah described as having "a clinging tenderness and sensitivity which peculiarly unfitted him for contact with strangers."[18] He never saw his mother again. The emptiness in Sarah's life was soon filled with more little ones, and she became encumbered with the duties of motherhood; but she never entirely set aside her ministry to the Burmese people. In addition to teaching a girls' school, she made effective use of her language skills. She wrote hymns and curriculum material in Burmese and translated other material, including part of *Pilgrim's Progress*, which she was working on at the time of her death.

Sarah's marriage to Judson did not end the evangelistic endeavors to the Karens. Ko Tha Byu had become a fiery evangelist, who stimulated a mass movement of the tribe toward Christianity. Other missionaries came to minister to the Karens and to translate Scripture, and by the 1850s there were more than ten thousand church members. Recent estimates have shown some one hundred thousand baptized believers among the Karens.

Henry Martyn

Adoniram and Nancy Judson's rebuff by the East India Company that catapulted them to Burma was seen as providential; and through them, the Boardmans, and others, that once hostile country slowly opened up to the gospel. In the meantime, however, missionaries continued to arrive in India. Though the East India Company remained obstinate, the Baptist Missionary Society, the Church Missionary Society, and the London Missionary Society all managed to get by the annoying regulations and send additional recruits to bolster their work in India. One way to enter India as a messenger of the gospel with a minimum of hassle was to come as a chaplain for the East India Company. The most famous of these chaplains was Henry Martyn, who arrived in India in 1806 and during his short term there became one of the greatest Bible translators of Central Asia.

Martyn was born in Cornwall, England, in 1781. His father was a merchant who provided well for his gifted child. Martyn found his schooling a pleasure, and after completing his formal training he went on to Cambridge, where he graduated with top honors in mathematics. Though he had turned his back on God during his youth, he was impelled by a combination of factors to reassess spiritual values. The death of his father, the prayers of his sister, the counsel of a saintly minister, and the written words of David Brainerd united to bring him into submission to God, and only then did he begin contemplating foreign missions. David Brainerd's sacrificial example and William Carey's pioneering efforts in India were a powerful source of inspiration, and soon foreign missions became his single objective.

Like his hero David Brainerd, Martyn spent many hours each day in prayer and devotion to God: "I thought of David Brainerd and ardently desired his devotedness to God. I feel my heart knit to this dear man. I long to be like him. Let me forget the world and be swallowed up in a desire to glorify God." In his effort to glorify God, Martyn began practicing self-denial, which included eating his breakfast and reading, "standing at a distance

from the fire . . . though the thermometer was at freezing point."[19]

Celibacy was another aspect of his self-denial. He was thankful he was "delivered from all desires for the comforts of married life," preferring a "single life in which are much greater opportunities for heavenly mindedness." But that was before he fell helplessly in love with Lydia, his cousin's sister-in-law, who was six years older than he. It was this "idolatrous affection" which more than anything else distracted him from his single-minded goal of evangelizing the heathen: "I felt too plainly that I loved her passionately. The direct opposition of this to my devotedness to God in the missionary way excited no small tumult in my mind." Lydia had captured his heart. He could not stop thinking about her, waking "in the night with" his "mind full of her."[20]

Martyn would not have been the first (nor the last) to have been deterred from foreign missions by romance; but though Lydia consumed his thoughts, he refused to be turned aside from his spiritual commitment. He was convinced he could more effectively serve God unencumbered by marriage, and it was highly doubtful whether Lydia would have accompanied him to a foreign land anyway. He spent most of a year making plans to sail to India, all the while pining over Lydia, but claiming to be "cheerfully resigned to do the will of God and to forego the earthly joy" of marriage.[21]

In the spring of 1805, Martyn was ordained an Anglican priest. The following month he was appointed a chaplain to the East India Company, and in the summer of 1805 he said good-by to Lydia and sailed for India.

On his arrival he met William Carey and the other Serampore missionaries, who immediately recognized his brilliance and encouraged him to do Bible translation work. As a chaplain, his main responsibilities were to the employees and families of the East India Company; but his heart was in missions, and he was thrilled with the opportunity of making the New Testament available to millions of Asians. For four years he served at military posts, preaching to both Europeans and Indians, establishing schools and at the same time translating the New Testament into Hindustani, Persian, and Arabic. But the torrid temperatures of Central India aggravated his already frail health, so in 1810, with his Hindustani New Testament ready for the printer, he left on a sea voyage to Persia, hoping to restore his health and at the same time revise his Persian and Arabic translations.

Martyn's health did improve for a time, and he was able to perfect his

Henry Martyn, Bible translator in India and Persia.

translation with the help of some of the most qualified scholars in Persia, but by 1812 his physical condition had again deteriorated. An overland trip to England seemed like the only solution for his health problems, and it would also be an opportunity for him to renew his relationship with Lydia. Although she had rejected his invitations for her to come to India and marry him, he longed to see her again and to tell her in person what he had been saying in letters for the past six years. But the opportunity never came. He died in Asia Minor in the fall of 1812, at thirty-one years of age. When he had first arrived in India, he had written in his diary, "Now, let me burn out for God." That he did.

Alexander Duff

One of the most innovative missionaries to serve in India was Alexander Duff, who arrived in Calcutta with his wife in 1830. Duff had not been impressed with the reports of missionary work in India, some of which claimed evangelism among the Indians was a complete failure. The critics charged that the few converts that had been made were largely among the outcastes, who then remained dependent on the mission, with no influence on their fellow countrymen. While the reports were unduly pessimistic, it was true that no concerted effort had been made to win the upper classes to Christianity, and it was Duff's mission to remedy that situation.

Duff was born and raised in Scotland and educated at the University of St. Andrews. The evangelical awakening that brought Scotland to its knees in the 1820s also fired up this young university student, and at the age of twenty-three he became the first foreign missionary of the Church of Scotland. Duff's missionary career began on an inauspicious note. On his voyage to India he endured two shipwrecks, during one of which he lost his entire personal library—a crushing blow to one as consumed with scholarship and education as he was.

On arriving in India, Duff immediately put into action his plans for reaching India's upper classes by means of higher education. His concept was to teach Western arts and sciences in English to India's educated elite, who were very interested in Western ideas and education. The Bible would also be taught and studied, and through this method Duff was convinced that Christianity would be firmly planted in India. Duff's critics were numerous—both missionaries and Indian educators—but he had two notable supporters: the aged and highly respected William Carey and Ram Mohum Roy, an educated and liberal Brahman. Roy was a popular reformer with a wide following, and it was largely his influence that paved the way for Duff. Roy prided himself in being open-minded and did not object to Duff's emphasis on the Bible. He had read the Bible without becoming a Christian, and he urged Duff's students to do the same and judge for themselves.

Within a few short months after he arrived in India, Duff opened his school. He started out with five students under a banyan tree, but word spread like wildfire, and by the end of the week there were more than three hundred students clamoring to enroll. The school was a tremendous success in its efforts to disseminate Western education, and perhaps only slightly less so in its efforts to disseminate the gospel. Within three years Duff had baptized four converts, a small number for the size of his school. But even the news of those few conversions created such a disturbance that students left, and Duff's work for a time was jeopardized. Slowly students returned, however, and by the end of his first decade in India his school enrollment averaged eight hundred. Later he opened a school for high-caste girls, which also attracted wide interest.

The major criticism of Duff's work was that the vast majority of his students came to his school only for the secular education, and of these thousands there were only thirty-three recorded converts during Duff's lifetime. It must be remembered, though, that most of those thirty-three

Alexander Duff, missionary educator in India.

135

were young men from influential families, who themselves became influential Christians. Some of them served as missionaries and ministers, and others became prominent Christian lay leaders.

Duff was a staunch, sober, humorless Presbyterian whose monumental achievements were not fulfilled without sacrifice to his family life. His work was his life, and his family dared not interfere. In 1839 he and his wife returned to India after their first furlough, leaving their four little children (including their infant boy) behind with a "widow-lady," and they did not return until 1850, when that little boy was eleven years old. Unfortunately the little boy's recollection of his parents' homecoming was not all joyous. Wasting no time to drill his son on his catechism, Duff, who was obviously not schooled in the principles of positive reinforcement, rebuked him, saying: "The heathen boys in my Institution in Calcutta know more of the Bible than you do."[22]

Young Duff later described his father as having "no wit, no humour, and still less of rollicking fun." He resented his father's aloofness, and his own recollections of his parents' departure for India in 1855, when he was a teen-ager, certainly bear this out: "I ... well remember how my mother's and my own heart were wellnigh breaking, and how at the London Bridge my father possessed himself of the morning *Times*, and left us to cry our eyes out in mutual sorrow. ... And so we parted ... a sadder parting as between mother and son there never was. The father buried in his *Times* ...

parted from the son without any regret on the latter's part."[23]

If Duff failed as a father, he certainly succeeded as a missionary statesman. During his second furlough he toured England, Ireland, Scotland, Wales, and the United States, and everywhere he went he was highly acclaimed. In the United States he preached to Congress and had a private meeting with the President. Duff has been described as "the most eloquent missionary orator"[24] of his century, and his impact on foreign missions was colossal. Through his influence hundreds volunteered for foreign missionary service, and tens of thousands contributed financially to the cause. His concept of combining education and evangelism was copied the world over, despite the controversy the method frequently aroused.

While Duff was being hailed as an innovator in evangelizing the elite, others continued to work with the dregs of society—the untouchables and the members of the degraded low castes. In 1865, Dr. and Mrs. John Clough of the American Baptist Mission began their work at the Lone Star Mission at Ongole, India, and they soon witnessed a tremendous revival among the outcastes. The mass movement to Christianity continued, and on a single day during the summer of 1878 Clough baptized 2,222 believers. During the century since that time more than a million Mala outcastes professed faith in Christ. So whether through intellectual reasoning or through egalitarian love, the gospel was planted in India, and in certain areas and in certain hearts it took root.

SELECTED BIBLIOGRAPHY

Anderson, Courtney. To the Golden Shore: The Life of Adoniram Judson. *Grand Rapids: Zondervan, 1972.*

Bentley-Taylor, David. My Love Must Wait: The Story of Henry Martyn. *Downers Grove, Ill.: InterVarsity, 1975.*

Brumberg, Joan Jacobs. Mission for Life: The Story of the Family of Adoniram Judson. *New York: Free, 1980.*

Drewery, Mary. William Carey: A Biography. *Grand Rapids: Zondervan, 1979.*

Padwick, Constance E. Henry Martyn: Confessor of the Faith. *New York: Doran, 1922.*

Paton, William. Alexander Duff: Pioneer of Missionary Education. *New York: Doran, 1922.*

Richter, Julius. A History of Missions in India. *New York: Revell, 1908.*

Chapter 6

Black Africa: "The White Man's Graveyard"

Black Africa, known for centuries as the "white man's graveyard," has claimed the lives of more Protestant missionaries than any other area of the world. Evangelism has been a costly undertaking, but the investment has paid rich dividends. Although Protestant missions got a late start in Black Africa (in comparison to Asia), it has been one of the most fruitful "mission fields" in the world. It is estimated that by the end of the twentieth century fifty percent of the population of that region (Africa south of the Sahara) will be professing Christian. Most of this growth, however, has come in the twentieth century. Church growth in the nineteenth century was often painfully slow, but it was the nineteenth-century missionary pioneers who risked all to open the way for Christianity in Africa.

Modern Protestant missions to Africa began during the eighteenth century in the Cape Colony with the Moravians (see chapter 3). By the end of that century the London Missionary Society had entered South Africa and, with Robert Moffat, began penetrating into the interior, though the majority of the missionaries remained in the healthier environment south of the Orange River and in the coastal regions. The thrust of Protestant missionary activity moved from south to north, and by the mid-nineteenth century the Baptists, Anglicans, and Presbyterians each had a solid foothold on the west coast. These were soon followed by permanent mission stations on the east coast, with almost all of Black Africa opened up to missionaries by the end of the century.

In spite of the tremendous sacrifice, African missions have been harshly criticized, particularly in regard to the missionaries' ties to colonialism and their exporting of European civilization Moffat's philosophy of the "Bible and plough" was expanded by Livingstone's philosophy of "Commerce and Christianity," and even Mary Slessor insisted on the necessity of trade to raise the African standard of living and make the people more suited to Christian ethical standards.

The future of Christianity in Africa, in the eyes of the missionaries, depended on European influence and trade, and few missionaries opposed the underlying concepts of imperialism that have come under fire in recent years. Nevertheless, the harsh criticism is unwarranted. Granted, missionaries were an integral part of colonialism, unashamedly identifying European civilization with the Christian message. But they, more than any other outside influence, fought against the evils colonialism and imperialism brought. They waged long and bitter battles (sometimes physically) against the heinous traffic in human cargo. And after the demise of slave trade, they raised their voices against other crimes, including the bloody tactics King Leopold used to extract rubber from the Congo. The vast majority of missionaries were pro-African, and their stand for racial justice often made them despised by their European brothers. Indeed, it is no exaggeration to say that without the conscience of Christian missions, many of the crimes of colonialism would have gone entirely unchecked.

That missionaries were imperialists and colonialists is only one area of criticism that has been leveled against them. In recent years it has become fashionable to look back at the nineteenth-century missionaries (particularly those who served in Africa) as racists of the first order. There is little doubt that they were racist (by twentieth-century standards), but what is more significant is that they never attained the degree of racism that was so prevalent in their day. It was the nineteenth-century intellectuals of high society who viewed black Africans as inherently inferior—many rungs below Caucasians on the ethnologists' evolutionary ladder. Missionaries, on the other hand, were ridiculed in scholarly journals for their shallow thinking in regard to race, and most educated Englishmen would have agreed with Mary Kingsley (whose Africa travelogue was widely circulated) when she criticized missionaries for their "difficulty in regarding the Africans as anything but a Man and a Brother" and their belief in "the spiritual equality of all colors of Christians."[1]

If missionaries frequently sounded like true nineteenth-century racists it was because they viewed Africans (or any unchristianized peoples) to be degraded because of their lack of Christian moral teaching. Henry Drummond's views were characteristic. He described Africans as "half animal and half children, wholly savage and wholly heathen," but qualified his blatant racism by concluding that "they are what we were once."[2]

Perhaps the greatest criticism of African missions has come from social scientists and anthropologists who have charged that Christian missions have wreaked havoc on African culture. It is true that missionaries of the nineteenth (and even the twentieth) century often failed to appreciate the distinctive qualities of unfamiliar cultures and failed to make Christianity compatible with the customs of primitive societies. But it must also be remembered that much of African culture was unhealthy and in desperate need of major surgery. The Africans were destroying themselves at an alarming rate through intertribal warfare, and in some instances through time-honored traditions of headhunting, twin-murder, human sacrifice, cannibalism, and witchcraft. The missionaries' efforts to eradicate these practices helped preserve Africa's most valuable cultural asset—the people themselves—and only through the preservation of its people could Africa become the great Christian stronghold it is today.

Protestant missions to Africa began in the Cape Colony with the Moravians in the eighteenth century. By the early nineteenth century missionaries were penetrating three major beachheads. They tackled the west coast beginning with Sierra Leone, the east coast starting with Ethiopia and Kenya, and from the south they established their mission base at Capetown.

Robert and Mary Moffat

Robert Moffat was the patriarch of South African missions, a man who had a significant influence in that section of the world for more than half a century. Yet, even during his own lifetime he was overshadowed by his famous son-in-law, often being referred to as "the father-in-law of David Livingstone." Moffat, nevertheless, was the far greater missionary of the two. He was an evangelist, a translator, an educator, a diplomat, and an explorer, and he effectively combined those roles to become one of Africa's greatest missionaries of all time.

Born in Scotland in 1795, Moffat was raised in humble circumstances that afforded him a very limited education and no formal biblical training. His parents were Presbyterians with a strong missionary zeal, and on cold winter evenings his mother gathered the children around her while she read aloud stories of missionary heroes. But Moffat was not inclined toward spiritual things. He "ran off to sea" for a time, and at the age of fourteen he became apprenticed to a gardener, learning a skill that he carried with him the rest of his life.

At the age of seventeen, Moffat moved to Cheshire, England, to begin his career in gardening. It was here in 1814 that he joined a small Methodist society that met in a nearby farm house. This association warmed his heart even as Wesley's heart had been "strangely warmed" nearly a century before at Aldersgate Street, and it gave him a harmonious blend of Scottish Calvinism and Methodist "enthusiasm." The following year, after hearing a missionary message delivered by Rev. William Roby, a director of the London Missionary Society, Moffat applied to that board for missionary service. Though he was recommended by Roby, the society responded by saying that they could not "receive all who offered their services for missionary work" and were thus "obligated to select those who possess the most promising acquirements," which in their view apparently did not include Moffat. He was turned down.[3]

Undaunted by his rejection, Moffat secured a new gardening position near Roby's home and began studying theology with him on a private basis. After a year Moffat again applied to the LMS, and this time he was accepted. The LMS, founded in 1795, the year of Moffat's birth, was an interdenominational evangelical mission board. In its twenty years it had seen steady growth and had missionaries stationed all over the globe. Moffat was sent to South Africa with four other novice missionaries, and after eighty-five days at sea they arrived in Capetown to launch their missionary careers.

Moffat had hoped to begin his life as a missionary as a married man. During his last year as a gardener in England he had become interested in his employer's daughter, Mary Smith, whom he perceived as having a "warm missionary heart." Though Smith was enthusiastic about Moffat's missionary plans, he was less excited about sending his only daughter to a distant foreign field. So, Moffat went to South Africa single, waiting more than three years before Mary's parents relented and agreed to let their twenty-four-year-old daughter join him.

In the meantime, Moffat was introduced to the realities of missionary work and African culture. He was disturbed by the strong prejudice against missionaries by both the English and the Dutch colonists, and he was impatient when, for that very reason, government officials stood in the way of evangelism of the interior. But if he was disturbed by government policy, he was shocked by the open immorality and dissension among the missionaries themselves. Writing to the LMS secretary in London, Moffat lamented that "... never was there a period when a body of missionaries were in such a confused and deplorable (& awful to add) degraded condition."[4]

While the LMS had seen its share of problems (including moral lapses) with some of its Cape Colony missionaries, there were many who served honorably. The first missionary to South Africa was John T. Vanderkemp, a physician from Holland. Though the son of a Dutch Reformed pastor, the well-educated young Vanderkemp had become a religious skeptic and remained so until the tragic deaths of his wife and daughter in a

boating accident, which he himself witnessed, turned his life around and brought him to Christ. Vanderkemp arrived in the Cape Colony in 1799 when he was past the age of fifty. He worked mainly among the Hottentots, where, despite discouraging setbacks, he won hundreds of converts. He was greatly distressed by the slave trade he daily witnessed and spent thousands of dollars in freeing slaves, including a seventeen-year-old Malagasy slave girl whom he married at the age of sixty—an act which created an uproar among the colonists and missionaries as well. Vanderkemp died in 1811 after only twelve years of missionary service, but he was recognized then and in the years that followed as one of the great pioneers of the LMS. Had Moffat looked closely he would have seen many faithful, hard-working missionaries, but unfortunately, the unfaithful ones (as generally is the case) were the most conspicuous.

After several months of delays, Moffat and a married couple were granted permission to journey into the bleak arid regions of Namaqualand, hundreds of miles north of Capetown. It was here that Moffat first met Afrikaner, a fearsome Hottentot chief who had only recently been tamed by a Dutch missionary who left the area after Moffat arrived. Moffat spent nearly two years at Afrikaner's camp and then invited him to travel to Capetown so that the white colonists could see for themselves the dramatic change Christianity had wrought in this outlaw, whose reputation for raiding colonists' farms was known far and wide. It worked. Everywhere Moffat went people were impressed with his trophy, and Moffat's star as a missionary statesman began to rise.

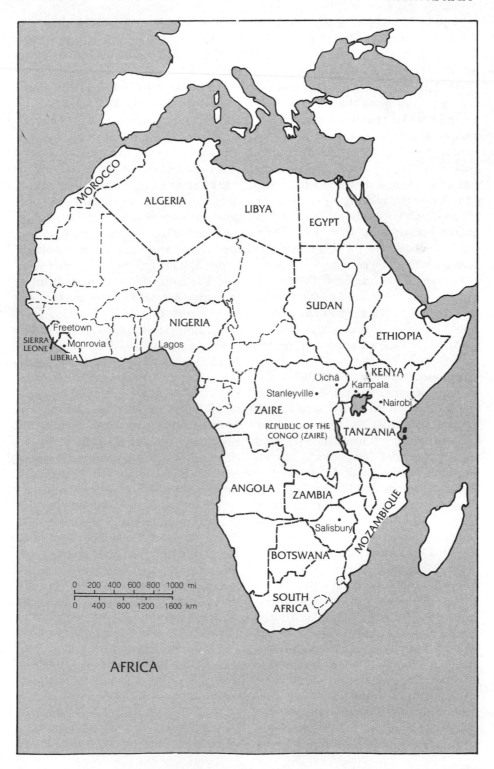

AFRICA

Showing off Afrikaner was not Moffat's only reason for traveling back to Capetown. In December of 1819 Mary Smith arrived from England, and three weeks later they were married. It was a happy union from the start and remained so for fifty-three years. Their honeymoon, a six-hundred-mile wagon trek northeast to Kuruman, was not all romance. There were parched deserts, dense forests, quagmire swamps, and raging rivers to be crossed, which no doubt made them grateful they were not alone. With them throughout their honeymoon was a single male missionary.

Kuruman was, in Moffat's eyes, a choice spot for a mission station. He had hoped Afrikaner and his people could move to the location, but, regretably, Afrikaner died before the move could transpire. The mission compound was situated at the mouth of the Kuruman River, fed by an underground spring that gushed forth crystal clear water. As a gardener, Moffat envisioned bountiful fruit and vegetable gardens watered by irrigating canals and tilled and harvested by industrious natives. Christianity and civilization could develop hand in hand. His ideals were high, and eventually, after many years of struggle, Kuruman became a model station.

The Moffats' early years in Kuruman were filled with hardships. They lived in primitive conditions, their first home being a mud hut, with the kitchen separate from the house. Although Mary was not used to doing heavy domestic work, she adapted to African life remarkably well. She washed clothes by hand in the river and cooked on an open fireplace. She soon overcame her aversion to cleaning the floors with cow dung and even

recommended it: "It lays the dust better than anything, and kills the fleas which would otherwise breed abundantly."[5]

The greater hardship at Kuruman related to their ministry. The Bechuanas, with whom the Moffats worked, were not at all receptive to Moffat's message. Tribal superstitions prevailed, and when the official rainmaker could not prevent long periods of drought, Moffat was blamed. Theft also was common among the people, and the Moffats' house was ransacked on many occasions. "Our labours," wrote Moffat, "might be compared to the attempts of . . . a husbandman labouring to transform the surface of a granite rock into arable land . . ."[6]

As time passed, however, Moffat's prestige among the Bechuanas grew. In 1823, after only a few years at Kuruman, the tribal situation in the area began to change. Waves of nomadic tribes began sweeping across the arid plains, and the very existence of the Bechuanas was in danger. It was at this time that Moffat exercised his diplomatic prowess, and through compromise efforts and military arrangements with another tribe he was able to avert the impending destruction of the Bechuanas. Moffat became a civilian general of sorts and rode out to meet the enemy. Though his peace efforts failed, and a fierce battle ensued, the invading Mantatee tribe was severely weakened and driven back.

From this point on, Moffat's leadership role at Kuruman was secure. As a diplomat and military leader he commanded the highest respect. Unfortunately, there was little corresponding success in his evangelistic efforts. His converts were few. Polygamy was a nagging problem for him as it has been for African missionaries since. What is the solution for a convert who comes into this new-found faith with many wives? There was and is no easy answer, and consequently church membership remained small. It was a discouraging situation, and Mary, particularly, was inclined to periods of despondency: "Could we but see the smallest fruit, we could rejoice midst the privations and toils which we bear; but as it is, our hands do often hang down."[7]

Perhaps the greatest reason for the slow progress of Christianity among the Bechuanas was simply a lack of understanding. Neither Moffat nor the Bechuanas fully comprehended the other's beliefs in spiritual matters. Moffat had little interest in the Bechuana religious traditions, and he sought to evangelize them with the mistaken impression that the tribe had no concept of God or word for "God" in their language. But an even greater handicap to his ministry was his failure to learn their language. For several years his sole means of communication was Cape Dutch, a trade language that some of the Bechuanas understood for rudimentary business transactions, but hardly suitable for presenting a clear picture of the gospel. Moffat wasted years of precious time trying to squeeze by on this short cut, but he finally realized that learning the language, as difficult as it was, was the only solution to communicating the gospel. So convinced was he of this necessity that in 1827 he left Mary with their little ones, turned his back on his gardens, and went out into the bush with several tribesmen, and for eleven weeks he immersed himself in language study.

On his return, Moffat was ready to

begin the translation of the Bible, a task that began very slowly and took him twenty-nine years to complete. Beginning with the Gospel of Luke, he agonized over each sentence, and even then he was painfully aware that his translation was filled with errors. (In one instance, the natives were shocked to learn that the apostle Paul insisted on being armed with guns.) Only the patience of continual revising made the translation comprehensible. But translating was not the only problem Moffat faced in bringing the written Word to the Bechuanas. Printing the text also became a complicated ordeal. After traveling all the way to Capetown in 1830, he found printers unwilling to print Scripture in a tribal tongue, fearing the equalizing tendencies it might have on the "inferior" race. Thus, Moffat, with the use of the government press, was forced to print the Gospel of Luke himself, which in the long run proved to be a valuable experience. On his return trip to Kuruman he brought an iron press donated by the mission for use in printing the rest of the Bible.

Translation and printing the Bible often seemed like a fruitless, thankless task, but it also had its rewards. In 1836, while conducting a service in an outlying area, Moffat was astonished when a young man stood up and began quoting passages from the Gospel of Luke. To Mary he wrote: "You would weep tears of joy to see what I had seen."[8]

But even before he was able to make his translation available to the people, Moffat was seeing positive results from his language study. His ability to speak the language of the people brought a new understanding of his teaching. He started a school with forty pupils, and soon his message began to take hold and a religious awakening followed. The first baptisms took place in 1829, nearly a decade after the Moffats' arrival in Kuruman. In 1838 a great stone church was built that still stands today.

Although Moffat's career is generally associated with Kuruman, his work extended far beyond that area. In fact, the nucleus of believers at Kuruman never exceeded two hundred, but his influence was felt hundreds of miles around. Chiefs or their representatives from distant tribes came to Kuruman to hear Moffat's message. The most notable instance of this occurred in 1829 when the great and fearsome Moselekatse, one of Africa's most infamous tribal chiefs, sent five representatives to visit Moffat and to bring him back with them on their return journey. The meeting of Moffat and Moselekatse was an unforgettable encounter. The naked Moselekatse was overwhelmed that the great white "chief" would come so far to visit him, and so began a thirty-year friendship built on a deep respect of one man for the other. Though Moselekatse himself was never converted to Christianity, in later years he did allow missionaries, including Moffat's son and daughter-in-law, John and Emily, to establish a mission station among his tribe.

As far away as Moffat often traveled, his thoughts were never far from Kuruman. Kuruman, over the years, had become a showpiece of African civilization, where Moffat's philosophy of "Bible and plough" was practiced. The man-made canal was lined with some five hundred acres of garden plots cultivated by Africans. The Moffats' own home consisted of a

Robert Moffat, missionary patriarch of South Africa.

stone house and a large enclosed back yard where their five servants did domestic chores around a huge open brick oven. It was a homey atmosphere with children always at play. (The Moffats had ten children, though only seven survived to adulthood, and of those, five became actively involved in African missions.) Though Kuruman was an out-of-the-way settlement, not on the main route to the interior, it attracted so many visitors that Moffat sometimes regretted the circus atmosphere that interfered with his Bible translation and revisions.

After fifty-three years in Africa with only one furlough (1839–1843), the Moffats were ready to retire. They had suffered some severe tragedies, particularly the deaths of their two oldest children within the space of a few months in 1862, but the work was moving forward. There were several native pastors active in the work, and their son John, who had joined them at Kuruman, was prepared to take over the mission. It was a sad departure from Kuruman and perhaps an unfortunate mistake. Kuruman was the only home they had known for half a century, and readjustments back in England proved difficult, particularly for Mary, who died only months after their return. Moffat lived on another thirteen years, during which time he became a noted missionary statesman, traveling throughout the British Isles challenging adults and youth alike with the tremendous needs of Africa.

David Livingstone

Never in the annals of missionary legend has a man been more lionized than David Livingstone. He was the hero that Victorian England so desperately needed, and the recognition he was accorded fueled African missions for most of a century. He became a hero for all generations to follow, and "after his death and his burial in Westminster Abbey, David Livingstone's reputation was secure from assault by anyone but the most reckless heretic. Even in the middle of the twentieth century, historians would still acknowledge him as the greatest missionary of them all. For almost a hundred years he would take his place in the pantheon of English-speaking Christians as a figure of inspiring sanctity and devotion, to be considered in the same breath as St. Francis of Assisi and St. Joan of Arc."[9]

There is little debate over the unparalleled influence Livingstone has had in the realm of African missions,

but as to his own missionary work there remain doubts. Livingstone was not the "super-saint" so many of his early biographers created. Rather, he was a frail, temperamental human being with serious personality flaws that hindered his ministry throughout his entire life. But despite his weaknesses, he was the man God used more than any other to focus the world's attention on the appalling needs of Africa.

Livingstone was born in Scotland, the birthplace of so many missionary "greats" (including Robert Moffat, whom he followed to Africa; Mary Slessor; and Charles Mackay, who followed him). As with his father-in-law, Robert Moffat, Livingstone was raised in humble surroundings, but unlike his father-in-law his brilliant mind and insatiable desire for learning impelled him to seek a higher station in life. His long days of toil (from 6 A.M. to 8 P.M.) at a textile mill beginning at the age of ten did not halt his education. He bought a Latin grammar book with his first week's pay, and he continued his schooling by enrolling in evening classes. He survived his difficult years of schooling by snatching glances at a book propped up on his spinning jenny and pouring over homework assignments until midnight.

Livingstone was raised in a pious church-going family. During his youth his parents left the established Anglican church to attend an Independent chapel. After his conversion as a teenager, he planned to become a missionary doctor to China; but family priorities delayed further education until 1836, when he was twenty-three years old. Even then his education was restricted. He studied during the winter term at Anderson's College in

Glasgow and spent his summers back at the textile mills. He studied both medicine and theology, and in 1840, at the age of twenty-seven, he was ready to begin his missionary career.

Livingstone's application to the LMS was accepted in 1839, but his plans to sail for China were foiled by international politics. Missionary work to China was being curtailed by the LMS due to the friction between Britain and China, which eventually led to the Opium War. The LMS directors thought Livingstone should go to the West Indies instead, but in the meantime Livingstone had been introduced to the striking, six-foot-tall veteran missionary to Africa, Robert Moffat. Moffat had a profound influence over the eager missionary candidate and tantalized him with the thrilling opportunities for evangelism beyond Kuruman in "the vast plain to the north" where he had "sometimes seen, in the morning sun, the smoke of a thousand villages, where no missionary had ever been."[10]

It was with great anticipation that Livingstone sailed for Africa in December of 1840. After spending thirteen weeks in language study aboard ship, he arrived at the Cape in March of 1841 and remained there a month before beginning his journey to Kuruman, where he was to help with the work until the Moffats returned. Livingstone immediately fell in love with Africa and thoroughly enjoyed his overland travel to Kuruman, describing it as a "prolonged system of picnicking." He was not so impressed, though, with African missionary work. He sharply criticized, and rightly so, the work at Capetown, where too many missionaries concentrated in a small area discouraged indigenous

leadership. Further disappointment awaited him at Kuruman. With the mental image of "a thousand villages," he was surprised to find the region so sparsely populated, and he was shocked to discover the discord among the missionaries: "The missionaries in the interior are, I am grieved to say, a sorry set. . . . I shall be glad when I get away into the region beyond—away from their envy and back-biting." Livingstone's presence only complicated the situation, and most of the missionaries were only too anxious for him to "get away into the region beyond." He complained that there was "no more Christian affection between most if not all the 'brethren'" and himself than between his "riding ox and his grandmother."[11]

While waiting for the Moffats to return from their furlough, Livingstone made several treks northward to explore the area. Of his two-and-a-half-year apprenticeship at Kuruman, more than a year was spent away from his base, and this practice of "riding off" continued during the rest of his career. In 1843 Livingstone rode off to stay. He set out for the wooded and well-watered area of Mabosta, two hundred miles north, to establish a second Kuruman. With him was Roger Edwards, a middle-aged artisan-missionary, and his wife, both of whom had served for ten years at Kuruman. There were problems from the start. Edwards resented the imposed leadership of Livingstone, who was not only new on the African scene, but also eighteen years his junior.

Mabosta became Livingstone's first African home. Here he built a "substantial hut 50 feet by 18 feet," with glass windows brought up from Kuruman. It was here also that he first encountered the ever-present dangers of the African jungle. While taking part in a lion hunt he was attacked by one of the beasts and was badly mauled. Though he was grateful to have survived, thanks to his brave African companions and a thick jacket, his left arm was severely injured and maimed for life.

By May of 1844, three months after the incident, Livingstone was feeling well enough to travel—especially since it involved important business. He headed for Kuruman "to pay his addresses" to the Moffats' oldest daughter, Mary, who at twenty-three had just returned with her parents from England. Livingstone's period of convalescence no doubt convinced him that there were drawbacks to being single, and so during that summer he "screwed up . . . courage to put the question beneath one of the fruit trees." What Mary's immediate response was is unclear, but later that year Livingstone wrote to a friend, "I am, it seems, after all to be hooked to Miss Moffat," whom he had described to another friend as being a "sturdy" and "matter-of-fact lady."[12]

The wedding took place at Kuruman in January of 1845 and in March the Livingstones left for Mabosta; but their stay there was short lived. Further problems developed with the Edwards, making it next to impossible for the two families to work together; so later that year, after delivering his first child, Livingstone pulled up roots and moved his family to Chonwane, forty miles north. The time at Chonwane was a happy one for the Livingstones, but it only lasted eighteen months. Severe drought in that area necessitated a move with the tribe northwest to the Kolobeng River. In

David Livingstone, the world-famous missionary-explorer.

the summer of 1847, after their second child was born, the Livingstones moved into their third home.

For seven years, the Livingstones lived a semi-nomadic life in Africa. Sometimes Mary and the children stayed home alone, while at other times she brought the children and accompanied her wandering husband. Neither situation was satisfactory. On one occasion when Livingstone was away from Chonwane for an extended period of time he wrote: "Mary feels her situation among the ruins a little dreary and no wonder, for she writes me that the lions are resuming possession and walk around our house at night."[13] But accompanying her husband was hardly the answer either. In 1850, after an exploratory trip with her husband, she gave birth to her fourth child, who died soon after while Mary was suffering from temporary paralysis. All this became too much for the more sedentary Moffats of Kuruman to tolerate. In 1851 when they heard from their daughter (who was again pregnant) that Livingstone was planning to take her and the "dear children" on another long jungle trek, Mrs. Moffat wrote her son-in-law a stinging letter in characteristic mother-in-law style:

> ... Mary had told me all along that should she be pregnant you would not take her, but let her come out here after you were fairly off. . . . But to my dismay I now get a letter—in which she writes 'I must again wend my weary way to the far Interior, perhaps to be confined in the field.' O Livingstone what do you mean—was it not enough that you lost one lovely babe, and scarcely saved the others, while the mother came home threatened with Paralysis? And still you again expose her & them on an exploring expedition? All the world still condemn the cruelty of the thing, to say nothing of the indecorousness of it. A pregnant woman with three little children trailing about with a company of the other sex—through the wilds of Africa among savage men and beasts! Had you *found a place* to which you wished to go and commence missionary operations the case would be altered. Not one word would I say were it to the mountains of the moon—but to go with an exploring party, the thing is preposterous. I remain yours in great perturbation, M. Moffat.[14]

Whether the letter would have changed Livingstone's mind is impossible to say, but the fact is, he did not receive it until he and the family were well into their journey. On September 15, 1851, a month after departure, Mary delivered her fifth child on

LIVINGSTONE'S TRAVELS
IN SOUTHERN AFRICA

the Zouga River, an event to which Livingstone devoted only one line in his journal, leaving more space for his exciting discovery of crocodile eggs. Apparently ignoring his own culpability, Livingstone bemoaned his wife's "frequent pregnancies," comparing the results to the output of "the great Irish manufactory."[15] Yet, Livingstone genuinely loved his children, and in later years regretted he had not spent more time with them.

By 1852 Livingstone had come to realize that African exploratory trips were no place for a mother and her little children. Earlier he had justified the risk:"It is a venture to take wife and children into a country where fever —African fever—prevails. But who that believes in Jesus would refuse to make a venture for such a Captain?" But no longer could he endure the criticism of his in-laws and others, so in March of 1852 he saw Mary and the children off from Capetown en route to England. How could he sacrifice his family for African exploration? "Nothing but a strong conviction that the step will tend to the Glory of Christ would make me orphanize my children."[16]

The next five years were depressing for Mary. A biographer wrote that she and the children were not only "homeless and friendless" but also "often living on the edge of poverty in cheap lodgings." And, it was rumored among the resident LMS missionaries that Mary had lapsed into spiritual darkness and was drowning her misery in alcohol.[17] But for Livingstone, the period was one of exhilaration and success, far more exciting than his previous time in Africa. He had little to show for his first eleven years. He had no mature converts. He had no thriving mission station nor church. He was a frustrated explorer, hemmed in by his surroundings and tied down by his family. Now he was free to move. The interior of Africa was beckoning.

Livingstone's first and greatest expedition took him across the continent of Africa along the Zambezi River. After seeing his family off at Capetown, he leisurely headed back north, stopping at Kuruman and then going on to his favorite tribe, the Makololos, where he recruited a number of them to accompany him on the expedition. Beginning in central Africa, they followed the river northwest to the coast at Luanda. It was a hazardous journey with continual threats from hostile tribes and the dread of the deadly African fever, but Livingstone was never tempted to turn back. Although he was primarily an explorer, he never entirely abandoned evangelism. With him he carried a "magic lantern" (an early version of a slide projector) with pictures depicting biblical scenes. He was sowing the seed for future missionary work. After six months of arduous travel, Livingstone and his men made history when they came out on the coast alive.

Despite offers from ship captains to return him to England, Livingstone, under a personal obligation to return the Makololo tribesmen to their homeland, turned back and started his trek down the Zambezi to the east coast. His journey east moved at a slower pace, hampered by dozens of bouts with African fever. In twelve months he reached Linyanti, his original starting point, and from there he continued on to the great falls that he named Victoria, in honor of his queen. From this point, Livingstone's single aim was to explore the Zambezi as a possible trade route from the East. The more he encountered the inhumane slave traffic of the Portuguese and the Arabs, the more convinced he became that only the combination of "Commerce and Christianity" could save Africa. He was well aware that foreign slavers could not stay in business without the Africans' cooperation (one tribe capturing slaves from an enemy tribe), and his solution was to bring legitimate commerce to Africa; and this, he believed, could only be done if a navigable trade route could be found.

Although the Livingstone expedition did not follow the Zambezi the entire route, Livingstone nevertheless arrived on the coast in May of 1856, confidently (though incorrectly) proclaiming the Zambezi to be navigable. It was a happy occasion, though Livingstone was disappointed again, as he had been on the west coast, not to find a letter from Mary among all his mail.

Back in England in December of 1856, after fifteen years in Africa, Livingstone was heralded as a national hero. After only three days with his family, he went to London where he launched a year-long whirlwind speaking tour before adulating crowds, accepting some of the nation's highest awards. During his year in England, Livingstone also wrote his first book, *Missionary Travels and Researches in South Africa*, and he inspired the founding of new mission societies. It was a high point in his life and also a time of decision making. Before returning to Africa in 1858, Livingstone severed his connection with the LMS and accepted a commission from the British government that allowed him more funds and equipment.

The remaining fifteen years of Livingstone's life could never recapture the glory of 1857. He returned to Africa with an official entourage for his second expedition, only to discover that the Zambezi River was not navigable. The section of the river he had passed by on his previous journey contained rocky gorges and white rapids. Disappointed, he turned northward (nearer the east coast) to explore the Shire River and Lake Nyasa. Unfortunately, slavers followed in the wake of his discoveries, and thus, for a time, his exploration was doing more to open the area to slave traffic than to missions.

Missionaries also followed his paths to the Shire River region, but not without painful sacrifice. The Universities Mission to Central Africa (UMCA), founded as a result of Livingstone's rousing speech at Cambridge, entered the area with enthusiasm and false assurance of favorable living conditions. Livingstone was not an organizer, and soon the mission was in chaos. Bishop Charles Mackenzie, the leading cleric in the party, was a controversial figure. He was said to have "arrived in East Africa with a crozier [bishop's staff] in one hand and a rifle in the other," and he did not hesitate to use his rifle and distribute others to friendly Africans for military action against the vile slave-trading Ajawa tribe.[18] His behavior created a scandal and seriously hurt the UMCA. In less than a year, however, Mackenzie was dead, and others in the mission party soon perished, including Livingstone's wife, Mary, who had left the children in England to join her husband in 1861.

Livingstone returned to England in 1864, this time to much less acclaim. His second expedition had not been the success he had hoped it would be, and his reputation had been tarnished. Most of the members of his party, once enamored by their fearless leader, were complaining bitterly about his autocratic rule and difficult personality.

In 1865 Livingstone returned to Africa for the last time to begin his third and final expedition, this time for the purpose of discovering the source of the Nile. He took no Europeans with him, and, in fact, did not see another European for nearly seven years. It was a difficult time for him. His body was racked by malnutrition, fever, and bleeding hemorrhoids, and often his supplies were stolen by Arab slave traders. Yet, it was not an unhappy period of his life. While he failed to discover the source of the Nile, he made several other significant discoveries, and he was at peace with himself and his surroundings (except for the ever-present slave trade that tortured his conscience). As time passed, the Africans became used to the bearded, toothless, haggard old man who often spoke to them of his Savior.

During Livingstone's last years in Africa, rumors periodically surfaced that he had died. Though his reputation had been marred, people the world over still held him in awe and were strangely curious about this eccentric old man in the wilds of Africa. It was this curiosity that spurred the editor of the New York *Herald* to send his versatile and ambitious reporter, Henry Stanley, to find Livingstone dead or alive. After several months of searching, Stanley caught up with Livingstone at Ujiji, near Lake Tanganyika, late in 1871. The initial meeting was awkward. After dismounting his horse, Stanley bowed and uttered the ridiculous phrase (that soon became the butt of jokes): "Dr. Livingstone, I presume."

Stanley was a welcome sight to Livingstone. He brought medicine, food, and other supplies that Livingstone desperately needed. And, perhaps more importantly, he brought companionship and news from the outside world. The two men developed a close and tender relationship; and, in a moving tribute, Stanley described the months they shared together:

> For four months and four days I lived with him in the same hut, or the same boat, or the same tent, and I never found a fault in him. I went to Africa as prejudiced against religion as the worst infidel in London. To a reporter like myself, who had only to deal with wars, mass meetings, and political gatherings, sentimental matters were quite out of my province. But there came to me a long time for reflection. I was out there away from a worldly world. I saw this solitary old man there, and I asked myself, "Why does he stop here? What is it that inspires him?" For months after we met I found myself listening to him, wondering at the old man carrying out

the words, "leave all and follow me." But little by little, seeing his piety, his gentleness, his zeal, his earnestness, and how he went quietly about his business, I was converted by him, although he had not tried to do it.[19]

Livingstone lived a little more than a year after Stanley departed. His African servants found him dead, kneeling beside his cot on the morning of May 1, 1873. They loved the old man and knew of no other way to pay their respects than to deliver his body and personal papers to his former associates at the coast. After burying his heart under a Mpundu tree, the body was dried in the hot African sun until it was mummified, and then carried overland fifteen hundred miles to the coast.

In England, Livingstone was given a state funeral at Westminster Abbey, attended by dignitaries from all over the country. It was a day of mourning for his children, who came to say good-by to the father they had never really known; but it was a particularly sad hour for the seventy-eight year old Robert Moffat, who slowly walked down the aisle in front of the casket bearing the man who decades before in that same city had caught a vision of "a thousand villages, where no missionary had ever been."

Henry M. Stanley

The death of David Livingstone had a tremendous psychological impact on the English-speaking world. Missionary fervor reached a high pitch as zealous young men and women volunteered for overseas duty, no matter what the cost. Part of this fervor was inspired by the exploratory work of Henry Stanley, who picked up the

Livingstone mantle and carried it with grim determination. His 999-day journey across Africa intrigued the world and sent missionary societies scrambling to stake their claims in the Dark Continent.

Although Henry Stanley professed conversion through the influence of Livingstone and was determined to carry on the work of his dear friend, he was an unlikely candidate for missionary work. He was born John Rowlands in 1841 (the year Livingstone arrived in Africa), an illegitimate son of Britain's industrial masses. At the age of six he was placed in the custody of a cruel workhouse master, where he remained until he ran away to New Orleans as a teen-ager. There he was adopted by Henry Stanley, a wealthy childless merchant, who soon sent his troublesome youngster away to work on a plantation. During the Civil War, young Stanley (who had taken his adopted father's name) joined the Confederate forces, only to be wounded and taken prisoner at Shiloh. After serving a portion of his prison term he switched to the Union side; but he was soon discharged for medical reasons. Following this, Stanley worked as a deckhand and as a clerk; he then joined the Federal Navy but deserted after a short time and became a free-lance journalist. In this capacity he traveled to Asia Minor, but before he completed his assignment he was captured and beaten by a band of pirates. In 1867 Stanley was back in the United States covering General Hancock's military campaign against the Indians, and later that year he began working for the New York Herald. He was on assignment in Africa for this newspaper in 1871 when he first laid eyes on David Livingstone,

the man who would become a hero and a father to him.

After his four months in Africa and after completing his hastily written best seller, How I Found Livingstone, Stanley made plans for his own exploratory expedition to Africa, which he began a year after Livingstone's death. Stanley regarded himself as an explorer as well as a free-lance missionary, and when he arrived in Uganda he tried his hand at Bible translation work for a short time. But his greatest contribution to missionary work was his writing. He did more for the cause of missions in one emotional letter (published in the Daily Telegraph) than many missionaries have done in a lifetime. He passionately pleaded for missionary volunteers: "Oh, that some pious, practical missionary would come here! ... What a field and harvest ripe for the sickle of civilization.... It is the practical Christian tutor who can teach people how to become Christians, cure their diseases, construct dwellings.... You need not fear to spend money on such a mission...."[20]

Stanley's 999-day expedition across Africa from Mombasa to the mouth of the Congo River was a costly one, not only in British pounds but also in lives. He started out with 3 other Europeans and 356 Africans, and he emerged on the west coast having lost all but 82 of the Africans through death and desertion. Unlike Livingstone, Stanley hated Africa and feared its people: "The greatest danger, an ever-recurring one, is that which we have to encounter each time the wild howling cannibal aborigines observe us.... The sense of danger is ever present and pervades our mind whether in our sleeping or our waking hours."[21] Stanley was not adverse to taking up arms and firing on menacing natives, apparently ignoring the issue (as Mackenzie had) of whether missionary exploration should even be undertaken if it necessitates military force. For Stanley it was a matter of life and death and it was not the time for philosophical reasoning.

Despite the danger and the tragic loss of life, Stanley's expedition was a monumental achievement, and missionary societies were eager to follow in the wake. The first to follow was the Livingstone Inland Mission, an undenominational society patterned after the China Inland Mission. It established seven stations along the southern tributaries of the Congo River, but the deadly perils of the African jungle took their toll, and the mission was short-lived. Other missions followed the path of Stanley and struggled for decades to link the east coast with the west through a chain of mission stations.

George Grenfell

George Grenfell was one of the many British citizens inspired by the work of Livingstone and drawn to Africa in the wake of his death. Grenfell was born in Cornwall, England, in 1849. Though his family belonged to the established Anglican church and sent the children to Sunday school there, George and his younger brother switched to a Baptist Sunday school to avoid the taunts and harassment of another youngster. It was here that George's spiritual interests were awakened. He was converted at the age of ten, and soon after that, through reading Livingstone's first book, he committed himself to African missions. After working in a

warehouse for a number of years while serving as a lay minister, Grenfell enrolled for a year at the Baptist College in Bristol to prepare for his missionary service.

In November of 1874, at the age of twenty-five, Grenfell was accepted by the Baptist Missionary Society (the same mission that commissioned William Carey some eighty years before), and the following month he left for the Cameroons. In 1876, he was back home in England for his marriage to a Miss Hawkes, who returned to Africa with him but died less than a year later, leaving Grenfell bereaved and regretful: "I have done a great wrong in taking my dear wife into this deadly climate of west Africa." Grenfell remarried two years later, this time to a "colored" woman from the West Indies who was also widowed.[22]

After a three-year apprenticeship in the Cameroons, Grenfell was assigned to do pioneer work on the Congo River, following on the discoveries of Stanley's 999-day journey. It was Grenfell's hope to pave the way for a network of mission stations across Africa, and he eagerly accepted the challenge. His mode of travel was a river steamer, the *Peace*, which he assembled himself after three engineers who were sent one at a time to carry out the task all died. For years the *Peace* was a home for Grenfell and his family, who accompanied him on his exploratory trips.

The Congo, as much as any area of Africa, lived up to the reputation of a "white man's graveyard." Only one out of four missionaries survived the first term of service. Yet, Grenfell pleaded for more missionaries: "If more men don't soon come, the Congo mission will collapse, and the work that has cost so much will be thrown away." His own family did not escape the clutches of death. Four of his children were buried in the Congo, including his oldest daughter, Pattie, who had come from England as a teen-ager to help in the work.[23]

But the disease-ridden jungle was not the only obstacle standing in the way of bringing Christianity to the Congo. Unfriendly tribesmen, known for their cannibalism, were a constant threat. Grenfell recalled as many as twenty harrowing experiences of "running away from cannibals." "The people are wild and treacherous, for several times after a period of apparently amicable intercourse, without any other cause than their own sheer 'cussedness,' as the Yankees would say, they let fly their poisoned arrows at us."[24]

The biggest obstacle Grenfell faced, however, was not disease or cannibalism, but rather the Belgian government. King Leopold viewed the Congo as his own private domain, and the missionaries were restricted at every turn. Government officials demanded Grenfell's private maps and his written observations for their own imperialistic endeavors, and later they confiscated his steamboat. The formation of the Congo Free State was a welcome development for the missionaries, and Grenfell, the most experienced explorer in the area, accepted a government commission to settle the southern boundary; but this working relationship did not last long. Belgian atrocities committed against the Congolese (in an effort to extract rubber) began to surface, and Grenfell could not contain his wrath. In an effort to silence him, officials appointed him to the Commission for the Protection of the Natives; but when he realized the commission was a sham, he defiantly resigned. Following this, the government refused to grant him new sites for mission stations, and he was notified that certain children in his mission school would be turned over to priests because "being a Roman Catholic State it had no power to place orphans under any other than Roman Catholic tutelage."[25]

Despite the overwhelming obstacles, Grenfell saw surprising success during his years in the Congo. His exploratory pioneer work was only a portion of his great accomplishments. He supervised Baptist missions in the Congo for twenty years and he witnessed a great spiritual awakening at his own mission station at Bolobo. In 1902 he wrote: "You will be glad to know that here at Bolobo, short-handed as we are, we are not without evidence of progress and blessing. People are more willing to hear, and give heed to the message they have so long slighted. In fact, many are professing to have given their hearts to the Lord Jesus, and there are signs of good times coming." Growth did continue, and soon there was a need for a larger chapel. As he traveled Grenfell also saw marked changes. He told of where twenty years before he had been driven off by spears he now was greeted with the singing of "All Hail the Power of Jesus' Name."[26]

Though Grenfell was prevented by the Belgian government from completing a network of mission stations linking up with stations of the Church Missionary Society from the east, he continued to do pioneer work until his death from African fever in 1906.

Alexander Mackay

While Grenfell and the Baptists were penetrating Africa from the west, the Church Missionary Society (an arm of the Anglican church) was moving from the east in an effort to fulfill Stanley's dream of spanning the continent with Christian mission stations. Johann Ludwig Krapf, a German Lutheran, was the first great CMS missionary to have this dream. He was one of many godly Lutherans from Germany who filled the ranks of the CMS when few Englishmen were willing to make the necessary sacrifices. Long before Stanley's expedition he pioneered Protestant missions on the east coast. In 1844, after being driven out of Ethiopia, Krapf founded a station at Mombasa on the Kenya coast, a victory that was overshadowed by the death of his wife and baby. Krapf continued in pioneer missionary work for more than twenty years, making some notable discoveries but never realizing his dream of spanning Africa with the gospel.

The most noted missionary commissioned to the east coast by the CMS was Alexander Mackay, who arrived in Africa in 1876, a year and a half after the arrival of Grenfell on the west coast. Mackay was a well-educated Scot, an engineer by profession but a jack-of-all-trades with a keen mind for linguistics and theology. He was one of eight missionaries sent out by the CMS in 1876 in response to Stanley's rousing challenge to the Christian world that King Mtesa of Uganda had requested missionaries.

As the leader of this team of missionaries, Mackay felt an awesome responsibility, but his farewell message reflected the courageous determination such a venture required: "I want to remind the committee that within six months they will probably hear that some one of us is dead. Yes, is it at all likely that eight Englishmen should start for Central Africa and all be alive six months after? One of us at least—it may be I—will surely fall before that. When the news comes, do not be cast down, but send someone else immediately to take the vacant place.'[27] Mackay's words were still ringing in the directors' ears when the news came that one of the eight had died. A ghastly total of five of them succumbed to the African graveyard in the first year, and by the end of the second, Mackay was the only one left.

Though at times Mackay was at the point of death, he refused to give up. By 1878, two years after his arrival, he had constructed (with the help of African labor) a 230-mile road from the coast to Lake Victoria. But there was no joyous welcome. He arrived shortly after the murder of two fellow missionaries, and the rest of his colleagues had all left due to ill-health.

On reaching Lake Victoria, Mackay constructed a boat and then crossed the lake to Entebbe where he met with King Mtesa. While Mtesa and his people welcomed him, there was extreme opposition to his presence from other sectors—particularly Roman Catholics and Muslims. Mtesa himself was an unsavory character who almost daily executed his subjects for trivial offenses and allegedly had the largest store of wives of any man in history. Mackay utilized all the freedom Mtesa allowed him and immediately began preaching the gospel to the Baganda people, whom he found lovable and eager to learn. He was always surrounded by children, and people of all ages begged him to teach them to read, so Mackay began translating the Scriptures. Long hours were spent at the printing press, but his labors were richly rewarded. Late in 1879, only a year after his arrival, he wrote: "Hosts of people come every day for instruction, chiefly in reading."[28] In 1882 the first baptisms took place, and two years later the local church had eighty-six African members.

Church growth was not without hazards. There were numerous attempts on Mackay's life by both Arabs and Roman Catholics, and the situation became critical after Mtesa died in 1884 and was succeeded by his son, Mwanga. Cold-blooded persecution of Christians followed. In 1885 more than thirty Christian boys were burned alive for refusing to succumb to Mwanga's homosexual passions. Later that year, James Hannington, an Anglican bishop, attempting to enter Uganda from the east, was murdered by orders of Mwanga. Tensions reached a climax when full-scale civil war broke out between Protestant and Catholic natives, ending with the bloody battle of Mengo. It was a shameful episode that was remedied only through British military intervention and the division of the country into Protestant and Catholic spheres of influence.

During these years Mackay was threatened repeatedly with expulsion, but his value as a skilled engineer prevented the threats from being carried out until 1887 when the Arabs finally convinced Mwanga to expel him. Mackay continued his ministry in Tanganyika on the southern end of Lake Victoria, where he persisted in his translation and printing of the Bible and ministered to Christian refugees from Uganda. In 1890, at the age of forty, this single and often solitary missionary died of malaria. After his death one of his grief-stricken colleagues lamented the irreplaceable loss in a simple but telling eulogy: "A score of us would never make a Mackay."

Mackay's death did not end the struggle to bring the gospel to Uganda. The CMS refused to be intimidated. In 1890, the year of Mackay's death, Alfred R. Tucker, a saintly Anglican bishop, arrived in Uganda, and through the invaluable assistance of African evangelists built a church membership of sixty-five thousand. His unswerving commitment to racial equality stirred opposition among fellow missionaries, but his ideals triumphed and the church in Uganda thrived.

Mary Slessor

The exploration and missionary work of Livingstone and Stanley inspired scores of others to embark on Africa—women as well as men. Most of the women, not surprisingly, envisioned their ministry sheltered within the confines of an established mission station, such as Kuruman where Mary Moffat spent most of her life. Exploration and pioneer work was not even an option for a single female missionary—at least not until Mary Slessor arrived on the scene.

The story of Mary Slessor, as much as the life of any missionary in modern history, has been romanticized almost beyond recognition. The image of her as a Victorian lady dressed in high-necked, ankle-length flowing dresses, pompously escorted through the African rain forests in a canoe by painted tribal warriors, is far removed from the reality of the barefooted, scantily clad, red-haired, working-class woman, who lived African-style in a mud hovel, her face at times covered with boils, and often without her false teeth. Yet, her success as a missionary pioneer was amazing, and the oneness she felt for the Africans has been equaled by few. She held the distinction of being the first woman vice-consul in the British Empire, but the greatest tribute she ever received was paid to her before her death by fellow missionaries who knew her well and, in spite of her faults and eccentricities, honored her for the great woman of God she was.

Mary Mitchell Slessor, the second of seven children, was born in Scotland in 1848. Her childhood was marred by poverty and family strife, due largely to the sporadic work habits of her alcoholic father, who had been known to throw Mary out into the streets alone at night after he had come home drunk. At age eleven, Mary began working alongside her mother at the textile mills as a half-timer while she continued on in her schooling. By the time she reached fourteen she was working ten-hour days to support the family due to her mother's confinement in the birth of her seventh child. For the next thirteen years Mary continued in the mills and was the primary wage earner in the family.

Though she later referred to herself as a "wild lassie," Mary's early years were spent mainly at work, both at the mills and at home. There was little time or opportunity for leisure in the crowded, polluted working-class district where her family lived. Fortunately, church activities provided a fulfilling outlet from her miserable home life. Converted as a youngster through the concern of an elderly widow in the neighborhood, Mary soon became very active in her local Presbyterian church. She taught Sunday school, and after the death of her father she volunteered for home missionary work. When she was in her early twenties she began working with the Queen Street Mission, which provided practical experience for her future missionary endeavors. How many times she had to stand up to foul-mouthed thugs and bawdy street gangs who sought to break up her open-air meetings. The courage she would need in later years was developing in the blighted neighborhoods of Dundee.

Foreign missions, since early childhood, deeply interested Mary. Missionary meetings were a common occurrence in her church, and furloughed missionaries pleaded for workers. The progress of the Calabar Mission, established two years before her birth, was followed with lively interest, and Mary's missionary-minded mother hoped her only living son, John, would become part of the foreign missionary force. His death, when Mary was twenty-five, shattered her mother's dreams. But for Mary, it was an inducement to escape the mills and to take her brother's place. The Calabar Mission had always made room for women, and Mary knew she would be a welcome addition to the staff. The death of David Livingstone clinched her decision, and all that was left was to sever the close physical ties she had with her family.

In 1875 Mary applied to and was accepted by the Calabar Mission, and in the summer of 1876, at the age of

Ikpe

NIGERIA

Niger River

ENYONG

Okpo

Mbiabo

IBIBIO

OKOYONG

EFIK

Uyo

Abak

Creek Town

Oron

Cross River

Eket

Jamestown

0 5 10 mi

CALABAR-WEST AFRICA

twenty-seven, she sailed for Calabar (located in present-day Nigeria), long known for its slave trade and deadly environment. Mary's earliest years in Africa were spent at Duke Town, where she taught in a mission school and visited with the Africans, picking up the language as she went. She learned the language quickly, but she was dissatisfied with her assignment. As a mill girl, she never felt quite at ease with the social niceties and ample lifestyle of the several missionary families comfortably stationed at Duke Town. (And, no doubt they had reservations about her—a twenty-nine-year-old woman who admittedly had climbed every tree worth climbing between Duke Town and Old Town.) Life was too routine. She wanted more out of her missionary career than what she was offered at Duke Town. Only a month after her arrival she had written, "One does need a special grace to enable one to sit still. It is so difficult to wait." Her heart was set on doing pioneer work in the interior, but for that "privilege"[29] she would have to wait.

After less than three years in Africa and weakened by several attacks of malaria (and many more of homesickness), Mary was allowed a furlough to regain her strength and reunite with her family. She returned to Africa refreshed and excited about her new assignment at Old Town, three miles further inland along the Calabar River. Here she was free to work by herself and to maintain her own lifestyle—living in a mud hut and eating local produce that allowed her to send most of her mission salary to her family back home. No longer was her work routine. She supervised schools, dispensed medication, mediated disputes, and mothered unwanted children. On Sundays she became a circuit preacher, trudging miles through the jungle from village to village, sharing the gospel with those who would listen.

Evangelism in Calabar was a slow and tedious process. Witchcraft and spiritism abounded. Cruel tribal customs were embedded in tradition and almost impossible to subdue. One of the most heartrending of these customs was twin-murder. Superstition decreed that a twin birth was a curse caused by an evil spirit who fathered one of the children. In most cases both babies were brutally murdered, and the mother was shunned by the tribe and exiled to an area reserved for outcasts. Mary not only rescued twins and ministered to their mothers, but also tirelessly fought against the perpetrators of this heathen ritual, sometimes risking her own life. She courageously intervened in tribal matters and eventually gained a respect unheard of for a woman. But after three years Mary was once again too ill to remain on the field.

On her second furlough Mary was

Mary Slessor, pioneer missionary to Calabar, West Africa.

accompanied by Janie, a six-month-old twin girl she had rescued from death. Though she desperately needed rest, Mary was inundated with speaking requests. She and Janie were a sensation, and so great was the demand for their appearance that the mission committee extended Mary's furlough. Mary was further detained by obligations to her sickly mother and sister; but finally in 1885, after nearly three years' leave, she returned to Africa, determined to penetrate further into the interior.

Soon after she returned, Mary received word of her mother's death, and three months after that of her sister's. Another sister had died during her furlough, and now Mary was left alone with no close ties to her homeland. She was despondent and almost overcome with loneliness: "There is no one to write and tell all my stories and troubles and nonsense to." But along with the loneliness and sorrow came a sense of freedom: "Heaven is now nearer to me than Britain, and no one will be anxious about me if I go up-country."[30]

"Up-country" to Mary meant Okoyong, an untamed area that had claimed the lives of other missionaries who had dared to penetrate its borders. Sending a single woman to the Okoyongs was considered by many to be an exercise in insanity, but Mary was determined to go and would not be dissuaded. After visiting the area a number of times with other missionaries, Mary was convinced that pioneer work was best accomplished by women, who, she believed, were less threatening to unreached tribes than men. So in August of 1888, with the assistance of her friend, King Eyo, of Old Town, she was on her way north.

For the next quarter of a century and more, Mary would continue to pioneer missions in areas in which no white man had been able to survive. For fifteen years (minus two furloughs) she stayed with the Okoyongs, teaching them and nursing them and arbitrating their disputes. Her reputation as a peacemaker spread to outlying districts, and soon she was acting as a judge for the whole region. In 1892 she became the first vice-consul to Okoyong, a government position she held for many years. In that capacity she acted as a judge and presided over court cases involving disputes over land, debts, family matters, and the like. Her methods were unconventional by British standards (often refusing to act solely on the evidence before her if she personally was aware of other factors), but they were well suited to African society.

Although Mary was highly respected as a judge and had influenced the gradual decline in witchcraft and superstition, she saw little progress in bringing Christianity to the Okoyongs. She considered herself a pioneer and she viewed her work as preparatory and was not unduly anxious about the fact that she could not send glowing reports back home of hosts of converts and thriving churches. She organized schools, taught practical skills, and established trade routes, all in preparation for missionaries (ordained men being her preference) to follow. She saw some fruit from her evangelistic endeavors, but it was mainly in her own family of adopted children. In 1903, near the end of her term at Okoyong, the first baptism service was held (with seven of the eleven children baptized being her own), and a church was organized with seven charter members.

Mary's life as a pioneer missionary was a lonely one, but she was not entirely without social contacts. Furloughs back to England and periodic trips to Duke Town reacquainted her with the outside world. During one of her sick leaves to the coast she met Charles Morrison, a young missionary teacher, eighteen years her junior, serving in Duke Town. As their friendship grew they fell in love, and Mary accepted his marriage proposal, providing he would work with her in Okoyong. The marriage, however, never took place. His health did not even permit him to remain in Duke Town, and, for Mary, missionary service came before personal relationships.

Mary was not really suited for marriage anyway. Her living habits and daily routine were so haphazard that she was better off by herself. Single women had tried to live with her, but

usually without success. She was careless about hygiene, and her mud huts were infested with roaches, rats, and ants. Meals, school hours, and church services were irregular—all much more suited to Africans than to time-oriented Europeans. Clothing, too, was a matter of little concern for her. She soon discovered that the modest tightly fitted long dresses of Victorian England were not suited to life in an African rain forest. Instead, she wore simple cotton garments, often clinging to her skin in the dampness (causing one male missionary to insist on walking ahead of her on jungle treks so he would not have to look at her, even though she was the one who was familiar with the trails).

Though Mary often failed to take the most basic health precautions and "lived native" (as other missionaries were prone to say), the fact is that she outlived most of her fellow missionaries who were so careful about health and hygiene. Nevertheless, she did suffer recurring attacks of malaria, and she often endured painful boils that appeared on her face and head, sometimes resulting in baldness. At times, however, she was surprisingly healthy and robust for a middle-aged woman. Her many children kept her young and happy, and she could heartily say that she was "a witness to the perfect joy and satisfaction of a single life."[31]

In 1904, at the age of fifty-five, Mary moved on from Okoyong with her seven children to do pioneer work in Itu and other remote areas. Here she encountered great success with the Ibo people. Janie, her oldest adopted daughter, was now a valuable assistant in the work, and another woman missionary was able to take over the work at Okoyong. For the remaining decade of her life, Mary continued doing pioneer work while others followed behind her—their ministry made much easier by her pioneering efforts. In 1915, nearly forty years after coming to Africa, she died at the age of sixty-six in her mud hut, a great testimony to Christian missions in Africa.

During the span of her ministry in Africa there had been a dramatic increase in missionary work. It was a period of time when independent faith missions were rapidly developing. The denominational missions supported by the Anglicans (who grew from a little over a hundred to more than a thousand during this period), Presbyterians, Methodists, and Baptists made dramatic increases in their overseas outreach, but by 1915 such missions as the Christian and Missionary Alliance, The Evangelical Alliance Mission, the Sudan Interior Mission, and the Africa Inland Mission had all gained a solid foothold in the interior and were on their way to becoming a major missionary force in Africa.

SELECTED BIBLIOGRAPHY

Christian, Carol and Plummer, Gladys. God and One Red Head: Mary Slessor of Calabar. Grand Rapids: Zondervan, 1970.

Falk, Peter. The Growth of the Church in Africa. *Grand Rapids: Zondervan, 1979.*

Livingstone, W. P. Mary Slessor of Calabar: Pioneer Missionary. *London: Hodder and Stoughton, 1915.*

Morrison, J. H. The Missionary Heroes of Africa. *New York: Doran, 1922.*

Mueller, J. Theodore. Great Missionaries to Africa. *Grand Rapids: Zondervan, 1941.*

Northcott, Cecil. David Livingstone: His Triumph, Decline, and Fall. *Philadelphia: Westminster, 1973.*

_____. Robert Moffat: Pioneer in Africa, 1817–1870. *London: Lutterworth, 1961.*

Ransford, Oliver. David Livingstone: The Dark Interior. *New York: St. Martin's, 1978.*

Chapter 7

The Far East:
"Barbarians Not Welcome"

The impressive missionary enterprises established in India and Africa during the late eighteenth and early nineteenth centuries found no parallels in the Orient. Japan, Korea, and China were all strongly isolationist, and Christianity was clearly unwelcome. It was not until the late 1850s that Protestant mission boards entered Japan, and even then the progress was painfully slow. Korea remained closed even longer, with the first Protestant missionary not arriving until 1865. But in China, despite extreme opposition, the genesis of Protestant missions began during the first decade of the nineteenth century. During that period of time only the small area of land known as Canton and the Portuguese colony of Macao were open to foreign residence, and thus missionary work was obviously limited; but at least it was a start— enough to arouse Christian concern for the heathen in that vast land.

The underlying motivation for Oriental isolationism was national pride. Orientals were proud of their civilizations and generally regarded outsiders as barbarians or, worse yet, "foreign devils." China could boast a four-thousand-year uninterrupted national history, the longest this world has known, and for that reason rightfully resented the implied superiority of the West. Both the culture and religion possessed a distinctly Oriental flavor that proved difficult for Western minds to grasp. Early Oriental religion developed around spirit and ancestor worship and was consequently diverse and disorganized; but with the introduction of the philosophies of Confucianism and Taoism in the sixth century B.C. and the later advance of Buddhism into China in the first century A.D. (and from there to Korea and Japan) the religious scene dramatically changed. Organized religious teachings and nationalistic pride blended together, and all efforts to introduce Christianity were rebuffed.

Christianity came to the Orient, particularly China, in four stages. Nestorian Christians of the seventh century, who lived in Persia, were the first to try to evangelize China. Persecution was at times fierce, but the church maintained a foothold until the fourteenth century. The Roman Catholics entered China at the end of the thirteenth century. In 1293, Friar John, a Franciscan monk, was commissioned by the Pope to establish the faith in China. In less than a decade he had founded a church in Peking of some six thousand adherents, but after a short time persecution brought a sudden end to the work. In the sixteenth century the Roman Catholics, inspired by Francis Xavier (see chapter 2), reentered China under the banner of the Jesuits. This time the Roman Catholic foothold remained, though the terrors of persecution were certainly not over. The fourth and final stage of missionary enterprise to China was the Protestant thrust that began with Robert Morrison in the early nineteenth century. But China, for all practical purposes, was still closed. Chinese authorities were fiercely resisting opium imports, and the only solution for a time seemed to be to ban all trade and close the coastal ports to foreign merchants—a defiance that Britain would not tolerate.

Why Britain insisted on smuggling opium to China's millions of opium addicts was simply a matter of economics, and the issue of morality was given very little consideration. Marketing opium from India was a highly profitable venture for the East India Company, and those profits helped pay for Britain's colonial administrative expenses. For that reason British officials ignored the emperor's ban on opium in the early 1830s, and by 1836 opium production had tripled. The fact that debilitated opium addicts were dying in the streets, and that the emperor's own three sons had died of addiction, was conveniently ignored as many Britishers argued that opium was no worse than tobacco.

By 1839 the tense situation erupted into open warfare. At the same time heated debates erupted in Parliament. The hawks won and Britain used its military might to force China to open her ports. The Opium War ended with the treaty of Nanking that ceded Hong Kong to Britain and opened five coastal ports to foreign trade. It was an economic victory, but hardly a moral one. "We have triumphed," wrote Lord Shaftesbury, "in one of the most lawless, unnecessary and unfair struggles in the records of history, this cruel and debasing war."[1]

There were other voices of protest —some from the missionary ranks— but many church and mission leaders believed that China should be opened to the gospel at all costs, even if it could only be accomplished by military force. Regrettably, some missionaries were associated with opium smuggling itself. But smuggling ended in the 1850s when opium was officially legalized following a second Anglo-Chinese military outbreak. With this final humiliation of China, mission societies quickly moved in. Christianity along with opium could now be legally marketed in China, but not without paying a high price.

Robert Morrison

Robert Morrison was the first Protestant missionary to go to China, a noteworthy distinction considering the formidable obstacles confronting foreigners in that hostile land during the first half of the nineteenth century. His prayer had been that "God would station him in that part of the field where the difficulties are the greatest, and to all human appearance the most insurmountable."[2] His prayer was answered. He persevered for twenty-five years in China, seeing fewer than a dozen converts, and at the time of his death there were only three known native Christians in the entire Chinese empire.

Morrison was born in England in 1782, the youngest of eight children. While yet a young child he was apprenticed to his father, who manufactured wooden forms used in shoemaking and repair. It was a hard life for young Robert, who was ever under the watchful eye of his stern, but devout, Scotch-Presbyterian father, and there was little time for play. His "free" time was spent studying the Scriptures under the tutelage of a local minister. At the age of fifteen he was converted, and in the next few years his interests turned to foreign missions—particularly as he read articles in missionary magazines. To be a missionary was his dream, but for one obstacle—his mother. There was a powerful bond of affection between them, and he bowed to maternal pressure, promising not to go abroad so long as she lived. The delay was brief. She died in 1802 when he was twenty years old. He never regretted his decision to wait, ever treasuring the opportunity he had to minister to her during her dying hours.

Soon after his mother's death, Morrison went to London for ministerial training. He studied for two years and then applied to the London Missionary Society for foreign service and was accepted. The joy of being accepted was dampened by the attitudes of his family and associates.

Why would a promising young minister want to waste his life in a heathen land when there were so many opportunities for an effective home ministry? Despite their arguments and pleadings, Morrison stood firm. China weighed heavily on his mind, and once the decision was made for him to go there, the door opened for him to study with a Chinese scholar living in London, his sailing being delayed in order to find a suitable colleague to accompany him.

A partner was not to be found, and so Morrison made plans to go alone; but obtaining passage to China was no simple task. The East India Company refused to take him. Finally, in January of 1807, nearly five years after the death of his mother, he set sail on an American vessel to Canton via the United States. While in the United States, Morrison met with Secretary of State James Madison, who gave him a letter of introduction to the American consul in Canton. It was in America, also, where Morrison had his oft-quoted conversation with the ship's owner who sarcastically probed the young missionary: "And so, Mr. Morrison, you really expect to make an impression on the idolatry of the great Chinese Empire?" To which Morrison responded, "No, sir, but I expect God will."[3]

Morrison reached Canton in September of 1807, seven months after he had left England. It was only then that his real problems began. Further study of the Chinese language could be done only in the strictest secrecy; and his presence in Canton was under the constant scrutiny of the East India Company, whose officials prohibited any activity that in the least way bordered on evangelism of the Chinese. As was the case in India, they feared

FAR EAST ASIA

for their commercial ventures. To make matters worse, Morrison had little choice but to live in the high style of the company official, a waste that tried him sorely. Loneliness, too, was a grievous trial. Working without a partner was difficult enough, but his lack of communication from home (despite regular mails) was inexcusable and caused him unnecessary depression. A year after his arrival he wrote to a friend: "I yesterday received your very welcome letter. It is but the second that I have received, after having written at least two hundred." The reason for the dearth of mail from family and friends? They were too busy.

In spite of the restrictions placed on him, Morrison's residence in Canton was not a wasted period of time. Soon after he arrived he located two Roman Catholic converts who were willing to tutor him in Chinese, though they so feared the authorities that they carried lethal poison with them in order to end their lives quickly and avoid the torture they would surely suffer should they be found out. Morrison studied with them and began compiling a dictionary and secretly translating the Bible. So impressed were the East India Company officials with his dictionary that less than eighteen months after he arrived they offered him a position as a translator. Although Morrison was distressed at having to succumb to secular employment, he knew that such a move was the only way he could come to terms with the company, and the generous salary was a further inducement.

At the very time that Morrison was negotiating with the East India Company, he was also negotiating a significant change in his personal life. After a brief courtship, he married Mary Morton, the daughter of an English doctor who was living in China at the time. Women were not allowed in Canton, so Morrison arranged to live with her in Macao, a Portuguese colony, six months a year and spend the rest of the year in Canton working for the East India Company. In Macao he found the Roman Catholics more restrictive than the company officials had been in Canton.

Morrison's early years of marriage were not happy ones. His separation from Mary, as well as her ill health and spiritual condition, contributed little to Morrison's well-being. To a friend he confided: "Yesterday I arrived in Canton. . . . I left my dear Mary unwell. Her feeble mind much harassed. . . .

My poor afflicted Mary, the Lord bless her . . . she 'walks in darkness and has no light.'"[4] Mary's condition did improve for a time, but in 1815, six years after their marriage, her ill health obliged her to return to England with their two small children. After a six-year separation, she and the children returned for a brief and joyful reunion before she died unexpectedly in the summer of 1821. The following year Morrison painfully parted with his nine-year-old Rebecca and seven-year-old John. He sent them back to England "to be brought up in a plain way; but above all things, to be taught the fear of the Lord. . . ."[5]

Morrison's long separations from his wife and children, as depressing as they were, had allowed him precious time for Bible translation, a task that he carried out with tireless energy. He re-

Robert Morrison translating the Bible into Chinese with the help of his assistants.

sented the time he had to devote to the East India Company (though that very work greatly expanded his knowledge of the language), always considering himself first and foremost a missionary of the gospel, though never openly so. His first convert (coming seven years after beginning his missionary career) was baptized "away from human observation" so as to avoid the wrath of both the British and Chinese officials. How well he knew that his very residence in China was at the mercy of the East India Company. This was seen in 1815 when his translation of the New Testament was made public. He was promptly ordered dismissed by company officials. Although the ordeal caused Morrison anxiety, the dismissal was never carried out. His work proved to be indispensable to the company.

That the East India Company would be irritated by Morrison's translation work was to be expected, but that other Christians would resent his labors caused him additional anxiety. How unfortunate it was that there was to be bitter competition in the effort to translate the Bible into Chinese, but such was the case. In 1806, before Morrison even arrived in China, Joshua Marshman, Carey's colleague at Serampore, had begun to study Chinese with a view to translating the Bible. When Morrison heard of Marshman's plans in 1808, he immediately wrote to Serampore but never received an answer. Marshman apparently wanted to be remembered as the first to have translated the Bible into Chinese. There was a sharp rivalry (though never expressed to each other personally), including an unfair accusation of plagiarism against Marshman by some of Morrison's colleagues. In the end, Marshman won the race, but it was a Pyrrhic victory. His translation, according to his own son, "was necessarily imperfect," to be valued "chiefly as a memorial to his missionary zeal and literary perseverance"[6] and, it might be added, stubborn pride. Morrison's translation, which was thoroughly revised before printing (and thus delayed), was considerably better; and Morrison rather than Marshman is generally remembered for pioneering the translation of the Chinese Bible.

After completing his translation of the Bible, Morrison returned to England in 1824 for his first furlough in more than seventeen years. Though often ignored while he was in Canton, he found himself a celebrity in England, continually besieged with invitations to speak. Morrison was concerned that his ministry have more depth than the usual one-night stands accorded to missionaries, so he offered lecture series and language lessons for those who were truly interested in serving in China. So burdened was he for missions and for women's work in particular that he organized a special class for women in his own home. Interestingly, one of the first to join this class was nineteen-year-old Mary Aldersey, who would later be remembered for being the killjoy in one of the greatest missionary love stories in history (see Taylor section).

In 1826, after two years in England, Morrison returned to Canton, accompanied by his two children and his new wife, Elizabeth. He continued his translation of Christian literature and his clandestine evangelism; but his time was not his own and there were increasing demands for him to serve

Old Canton, mission base for Robert Morrison.

as a negotiator between the conflicting commercial interests of England and China, which eventually culminated in war. In the midst of his busy schedule, he fathered four more children and was increasingly burdened by family responsibilities until 1832 when he tearfully saw his wife and children off to England. The company work continued to be demanding, and Morrison labored until his strength was gone and his frail constitution could take no more. It was a depressing time but it did not last long. He died in China in 1834 before word came that his family had arrived safely in England. His death coincided with the forced departure of the East India Company from China and with the death of another great missionary pioneer, William Carey, who had died less than two months earlier in India.

Karl F. A. Gutzlaff

The story of Christian missions in the Orient would not be complete without a discussion of Karl Gutzlaff, who according to historian Stephen Neill "may be variously judged as a saint, a crank, a visionary, a true pioneer, and a deluded fanatic."[7] Gutzlaff was born in Germany in 1803, attended school at Basel and Berlin, and was in his early twenties when he was commissioned by the Netherlands Missionary Society as a missionary to Indonesia. There he began working with Chinese refugees, though without the approval of the society, which led to his withdrawal from the society after two years to become independent.

As a free-lance missionary, Gutzlaff savored his independence. From Indonesia he went to Bankok, Thailand, where he donned native dress and lived the native lifestyle. During his three-year residence there he and his wife realized the incredible task of translating the entire Bible into Siamese and portions of the Bible into the Cambodian and Laotian languages. His stay in Thailand was cut short, due to the untimely death of his wife and infant daughter and due also to his own ill health.

After leaving Thailand in 1831, Gutzlaff began making journeys along the China coast in whatever sailing vessel he could obtain passage, be it a Chinese junk or an illicit opium clipper. On these journeys, which took him as far as Tientsin and Manchuria, with brief stops at Korea and Formosa, he preached the gospel and distributed tracts and portions of Scripture, some of which were supplied to him by Robert Morrison in Canton. In 1833, after two years of traveling along the coast, Gutzlaff began penetrating inland, again distributing literature and preaching. His Chinese dress and his fluency in the language allowed him to move about virtually unnoticed until the outbreak of the Opium War in 1839.

During the Opium War, Gutzlaff, following the footsteps of Morrison, served as an interpreter for the British and helped to negotiate the Treaty of Nanking in 1842. After that he made his home in Hong Kong and from that base began to formulate his dream of reaching all of China with the gospel. His plan was to train Chinese nationals as evangelists and to send them inland to preach and distribute literature. His goal was to evangelize China in one generation. Within a half a dozen years Gutzlaff had more than three hundred Chinese workers and

the reports of success were phenomenal. Thousands of New Testaments and countless more books and tracts were being distributed. People everywhere were flocking to hear the gospel messages, and the greatest news of all was that no fewer than 2,871 converts had been baptized "upon examination and satisfactory confession of their faith." It was a testimony for which every missionary dreams and a success story for which Christians back home were longing. Gutzlaff's detailed letters were met with an outpouring of enthusiasm, and missionary organizations and individual Christians from all over Europe sent financial support.

In 1849, after recruiting two European associates, Gutzlaff arrived in Europe in person to share the wonderful news of what God was doing in China. He triumphantly traveled and preached throughout the British Isles and on the Continent. His story was thrilling, and it almost seemed too good to be true. It was. In 1850, while he was in Germany, his bubble burst. The whole endeavor turned out to be a grand hoax perpetrated by his Chinese workers, most of whom were thoroughly dishonest. The literature, instead of being distributed, was sold back to the printers, who then resold it to the gullible Gutzlaff. The tales of converts and baptisms were fabricated, and the money that had been so sacrificially donated had quickly found its way to the black-market opium trade.

As shocking as the news was to his supporters, Gutzlaff himself, as evidence indicates, was aware of the shady state of affairs before he left China for his European tour. Pride apparently compelled him to protect his own reputation and to turn his back on the mounting evidence. Following the exposure, Gutzlaff returned to China, vowing to reorganize the work, but he died in 1851, his reputation still tarnished. To some he remained a hero, and out of his missionary efforts was born the Chinese Evangelization Society, the organization that commissioned Hudson Taylor to China in 1853. Gutzlaff, more than anyone else, influenced the missionary methods and goals of the enthusiastic young Taylor, and in later years Taylor referred to him as "the grandfather of the China Inland Mission."

The J. Hudson Taylors

No other missionary in the nineteen centuries since the apostle Paul has had a wider vision and has carried out a more systematized plan of evangelizing a broad geographical area than Hudson Taylor. His sights were set on reaching the whole of China, all four hundred million people, and it was to that end that he labored, though not single-handedly. He had a knack for organization, and he possessed a magnetic personality that drew men and women to him and to his point of view. The China Inland Mission was his creation and the pacesetter of future faith missions. In his own lifetime the missionary force under him totalled more than eight hundred, and in the decades following his death it continued to grow. But Hudson Taylor did not develop this vision alone. His first wife, Maria, was indispensable in setting the plan in motion, and his second wife, Jennie, was in the front lines carrying out the plan. Taylor's story is more than a story of a great missionary leader. It is a story of love, adventure, and unswerving faith in

God, though not the story of the flawless saint that his early biographers created.

Hudson Taylor was born in Yorkshire, England, in 1832. His father was a pharmacist as well as a Methodist lay preacher, and he instilled in the mind and heart of his son a passion for missions. Before he had reached his fifth birthday little Hudson Taylor was telling visitors that he wanted to some day be a missionary, and China was the land that intrigued him the most.

Although family Bible reading and prayer were an integral part of his upbringing, Taylor was not converted until he was seventeen years old. It was in the summer of 1849 when his mother was away for an extended visit with a friend. Young Taylor was at home idly paging through papers in his father's library when he came on some religious tracts. More interested in the stories than the spiritual applications, he picked one out and took it outside to read. As he read he fell under a "joyful conviction . . . light was flashed into my soul by the Holy Spirit. . . . There was nothing in the world to be done but to fall down on one's knees and, accepting this Savior and His Salvation, to praise Him forevermore."[8] When his mother returned home two weeks later and he told her the news, she was not surprised. She related to him how that two weeks earlier while at her friend's home she suddenly felt the urge to pray for his salvation, so she went to her room and prayed until she was certain God had answered her.

From that point on, Taylor began focusing his goals on missionary work in China. Although evangelism was his sole motivation, he realized the importance of gaining an entrance with the

J. Hudson Taylor, founder of the China Inland Mission.

people, and so at the age of eighteen he began training in medicine, first as an assistant to a small-town doctor, and then as a trainee at the London Hospital. During this time the zealous young Taylor began a rigorous program of self-denial as additional preparation for missionary work. It was an effort to live entirely by faith. His diet was meager, a pound of apples and a loaf of bread each day, and his attic room was barren of the comforts he had been used to. He even refused to remind his employer of his long overdue wages. His rationale was simple: "... when I get out to China I shall have no claim on anyone for anything; my only claim will be on God. How important, therefore, to learn before leaving England to move man, through God, by prayer alone."[9] Prayer alone did not

sustain Taylor's physical strength. His already frail health declined with his meager diet, and his contact with an infected corpse during his anatomy training certainly did not help the situation. He contracted a "malignant fever" that nearly ended his young life, forcing an interruption in his medical studies for several months.

Foregoing the physical necessities and comforts of life came much easier for young Taylor than foregoing his romantic interests. "Miss V.," as he referred to her in his letters, had become the object of his affections. She was a young music teacher introduced to him by his sister, and for Taylor it was love at first sight. Soon after their first meeting he wrote to his sister: "I know I love her. To go without her would make the world a blank."[10] But Miss Vaughn had no vision for China. She viewed Taylor's passion for missions as a passing fancy, apparently confident that he would not give her up merely to fulfill some wild dream in a faraway land. Taylor was equally convinced that she would change her mind and come with him. Twice they were engaged, but each time the engagement was broken. Taylor's commitment to God proved more powerful than his love for a woman.

The opening for Taylor to go to China came unexpectedly. His plans to complete his medical training were suddenly interrupted when word reached England that Hung, a professing Christian, had become the emperor of China. The prospect of China being freely opened to the gospel was an answer to prayer for the directors of the Chinese Evangelization Society, who had sponsored Taylor's medical training, and they were anxious that he leave immediately. So, in September of 1853, the twenty-one-year-old Taylor sailed for China.

He arrived in Shanghai in the early spring of 1854. It was a strange and exciting place to be for a young Englishman who had never before ventured far from his Yorkshire home. Shanghai was a city of dragon-roofed Buddhist temples, narrow shanty-lined streets, cheap coolie labor, submissive dwarfed-feet women, pig-tailed men, and a snobbish international settlement. It was the international settlement where Taylor found his first home and where loneliness soon engulfed him. The CES was a small disorganized mission board, and there was no one in China to welcome or work with the young missionary recruit. Missionaries were plentiful in the international settlement, but they looked down on the uneducated, unordained boy that had the audacity to call himself a missionary.

Soon after his arrival, Taylor found himself in financial straits. The support money that had been promised him did not arrive, and the money he did have was a paltry sum when faced with Shanghai's inflationary prices. The visionary dream of evangelizing China quickly faded, and the memories of his boyhood days in Yorkshire filled his thoughts. Feelings of homesickness pervaded his letters to his family: "Oh I wish I could tell you how much I love you all. The love I have in my composition is nearly all pent up, and so it lets me feel its force. I never knew how much I loved you all before."[11]

Taylor's efforts to master the Chinese tongue only added to his frequent bouts of depression. His early months in Shanghai were filled with long hours of language study, and there were times when he feared he would never learn the language. Fortunately, he did have an outlet—his hobby of plant and insect collecting. A far greater source of consolation for him was his deep personal faith in God. Writing to the CES directors in England he pleaded: "Pray for me, for I am almost pressed beyond measure, and were it not that I find the Word of God increasingly precious and feel His presence with me, I do not know what I should do."[12]

After a few months of living at the London Missionary Society compound, Taylor temporarily moved out of the international settlement and bought his own shanty, which he described as having "twelve rooms, doors without end, passages innumerable, outhouses everywhere, and all covered with dust, filth, rubbish, and refuse."[13] It was hardly an ideal living situation. To make matters worse, civil war was raging close by, and the frigid temperatures of winter mercilessly invaded his walls. After some months of independence, he was grateful to be back in the international settlement.

Taylor was never happy living among the other missionaries. In his eyes they lived in luxury. There was no "place in the world where missionaries" were "more favored than in Shanghai." He viewed most of them as lazy and self-indulgent, and beyond that, he characterized the American missionaries as "very dirty and vulgar." He was only too anxious to get away from their "criticising, backbiting and sarcastic remarks,"[14] and so less than a year after he arrived in China he began making journeys into the interior. On one of these trips he traveled up the Yangtze River and stopped at nearly sixty settlements that had never before been visited by a Protestant missionary. It was an exciting time for him, sometimes traveling alone and sometimes with a companion, but more importantly it was an enlightening education that intensified his burden for inland China.

Foreign missionaries had become commonplace in Shanghai, and the Chinese people took little notice of them. In the interior the situation was entirely different. Early in his travels, Taylor discovered he was a novelty and the people were far more interested in his dress and manners than in his message. To him there was only one logical solution: to become Chinese, to adopt Chinese dress and culture. Jesuit missionaries had long taken up Chinese ways and had ministered with great success, but most Protestant missionaries considered such behavior a radical departure from acceptable missionary methods. For them, Christianity was not "kosher" unless it was clothed in Western culture.

Becoming Chinese was a complicated ordeal for the blue-eyed, sandy-haired, Yorkshire-bred Taylor. The baggy pantaloons "two feet too wide around the waist," the "heavy silk gown," and the "flat-soled shoes" with turned up toes would have been trial enough, but to blend in with the Chinese people, black hair and a pigtail were essential.[15] Taylor's first attempt at dying his hair was a fiasco. The top blew off the ammonia bottle and burned his skin and nearly blinded him. Fortunately, a missionary doctor was close by, and within a week Taylor had recovered

sufficiently to be out and about again. Despite the bad experience, Taylor went ahead with his plans and "resigned" his "locks to the barber" and dyed his hair. But it was no fun. He found it to be "a very sore thing to get one's head shaved for the first time, when the skin is so irritable as the prickly heat makes it," and "the subsequent application of hair dye for five or six hours after does not do much to soothe the irritation." But the end result was worth the pain. With some "false hair plaited" in with his own to form a pigtail and with some Chinese spectacles, Taylor blended in with the crowds: "You would not know me were you to meet me in the street with other Chinese.... I am not suspected of being a foreigner."[16]

As pleased as Taylor was with his new appearance, most of his fellow missionaries were unimpressed. He was an embarrassment to them and soon became the object of ridicule. Even his own family was shaken when they heard the news. But if Taylor had second thoughts about his decision, he never made them known, and his adoption of Chinese dress and culture became his trademark. Not only could he move about more freely in the interior, but also he found Chinese dress to be better suited to the climate than Western dress. So impressed by Taylor's ease and comfort was veteran missionary William Burns, Taylor's traveling companion, that he adopted Chinese dress himself.

Chinese dress by no means solved all of Taylor's problems related to working in the interior. As he traveled and dispensed medical treatment he found himself in direct competition with the local doctors, and he was consequently driven out of town on different occasions. Traveling itself was risky. On one occasion Taylor's servant, who was hired to carry his belongings, absconded with his money and everything Taylor owned, forcing him to return to Shanghai, where he found refuge with fellow missionaries until he received a private donation in the mail from England—forty pounds, the exact amount of money that had been stolen.

Taylor could not have survived his early years in China without private donations. Though his adopting Chinese culture and his residence in the interior had drastically reduced his living expenses, his support from the CES was erratic and far less than he was able to live on, causing him to charge that the society had "acted disgracefully" in regard to its support of him and another missionary. In 1857, after three years of strained relations, Taylor resigned from the CES. From that point on he was entirely on his own, still unsettled and wandering through the interior of China, "not idle, but aimless," as one missionary characterized him.

The loneliness that Taylor had experienced during his early months in China still plagued him. He desperately longed for a wife. Although Miss Vaughn had refused to come to China with him, he could not forget her: "I am glad to hear of any news of Miss Vaughn you may have. She may get a richer and a handsomer husband but I question whether she will get one more devoted than I should have been."[17] Finally, with all hope for her fading, Taylor turned his attention to Elizabeth Sissons, another young woman whom he had known in England. He wrote to her, requesting a lock of her hair, and after he received it he wasted no time in proposing marriage. Elizabeth accepted, but it was a short-lived engagement. Perhaps it was the news of his Chinese dress and pigtail that made her wary, but whatever the reason, she could not go through with her promise. She did not answer his letters, and for a time he contemplated "giving up the missionary work" and returning to England to woo her.

It was during this time of depression and uncertainty that Taylor arrived at Ningpo, an important coastal city south of Shanghai, and met Maria Dyer. There was no apparent romantic interest at first. Taylor was still pining over Elizabeth, and Maria was a bit leary of the robed and pigtailed Englishman. She had mixed emotions: "I cannot say I loved him at once, but I felt interested in him and could not forget him. I saw him from time to time

Maria Dyer Taylor, Hudson's Taylor's first wife.

and still this interest continued. I had no good reason to think it was reciprocated; he was very unobtrusive and never made any advances." If Taylor seemed reticent to show any feelings for Maria, it was because he was still waiting for Elizabeth to write, and he no doubt feared a third rebuff were he to show interest in Miss Dyer. But in his diary he described her "a dear sweet creature, has all the good points of Miss S. and many more too. She is a precious treasure, one of sterling worth and possessed with an untiring zeal for the good of this poor people. She is a *lady* too...." As for the "very noticeable" and "decided cast in one of her eyes," the insecure Taylor was grateful: "I felt it gave me some chance of winning her."[18]

Maria Dyer had been born in China of missionary parents. Her father died when she was a small child, and her mother some years later. After that, Maria and her brother and sister were sent home to London for their education; but for Maria and her older sister, China was home. They returned when they were in their late teens to serve as teachers in Miss Mary Ann Aldersey's school for girls. Miss Aldersey was the first woman missionary to China, and she opened the first school for girls in that male-dominated country. She was a truly remarkable woman, whose dedication to the Lord and to missions was never in question; but in the ensuing romance between Hudson Taylor and Maria Dyer she played the role of the spoilsport, and it is unfortunately that role for which she is remembered.

In March of 1857, several months after Taylor and Maria became acquainted, Taylor made his first advance, and, typical of his style, it was a bold one—a letter containing a marriage proposal. A mutual friend brought the letter to Maria while she was teaching school. Maria secretly hoped the letter was from Taylor, but she waited until her classes were over to open it and find out: "I then opened my own letter and read of his attachment to me, and how he believed God had given him that love for me which he felt. I could hardly understand that it was a reality. It seemed that my prayers were indeed answered . . . he asked me to consent to an engagement to him." Taylor went on to plead with Maria not to "send him a hasty refusal," intimating it would cause him "intense anguish." But, of course, considering Maria's feelings toward him, his fears were unfounded. No. She sent him a "hasty refusal": ". . . I must answer your letter as appears to me to be according to God's direction. And it certainly appears to be my duty to decline your proposals. . . ."[19] Why? How could this young missionary teacher brazenly turn her back on the man of her dreams—the very husband she had prayed for? Here is where the very domineering and protective Miss Aldersey (whom Maria loved and respected) enters the drama. She stood over her timid teen-age charge and dictated the response, and with that accomplished, she wrote to Maria's uncle and legal guardian in England, pungently outlining her objections to Hudson Taylor. Her objections? He was uneducated, unordained, unconnected (with a mission society), and uncouth. And if that was not enough, he was short (Maria was tall), and he wore Chinese clothes.

Although Taylor was dejected when he received the response, he "strongly suspected that the hindrance lay with Miss Aldersey," and he refused to give up hope. In July of 1857, some months after his letter of proposal, Taylor secretly arranged an "interview" with Maria in the presence of another missionary. They shook hands, exchanged a few words, prayed, and then parted—a seemingly harmless meeting, but one that hurled the normally tranquil missionary community at Ningpo into the throes of dissension. Miss Aldersey threatened Taylor with a lawsuit; and Reverend W. A. Russell, her strongest ally, suggested Taylor "ought to be horsewhipped." Some were calmer in their reactions, suggesting that were Taylor to return to England and finish his education he would be worthy of her. Maria's response was eloquent: "I would wait if he went home in order to increase his usefulness. But is he to leave his work in order to gain a *name* for the sake of marrying me? If he loves me more than Jesus he is not worthy of me—if he were to leave the *Lord's* work for world's honour, I would have nothing further to do with him."[20]

Unfortunately, reason did not prevail. Maria was virtually placed under house arrest, and Reverend Russell would not allow her to take communion until she "should give evidence of repentance." In a letter home, Taylor wrote: "Dear Maria is charged with being a maniac, being fanatical, being indecent, weak-minded, too easily swayed; too obstinate and everything else bad."[21]

The months passed with only one brief meeting in October. Then in mid-November, with the help of a sympathetic friend, the two lovers met secretly, and what a meeting it was! For six hours it was sheer ecstasy. They became secretly engaged, and they hugged and kissed and prayed and talked and kissed some more—with no apologies to make. Wrote Taylor, "I was not long engaged without trying to make up for the number of kisses I ought to have had these last few months."[22]

Back in England, William Tarn, Maria's uncle and guardian, was in a quandary. He had received not only Miss Aldersey's letter, but also a letter from Maria and one from Taylor himself. Thousands of miles away, Tarn was outside the fray, and common sense directed him to calmly check out who this Hudson Taylor really was. So impressed was he with the reports that he gave his unqualified approval of the match, and at the same time "condemned" Miss Aldersey's "want of judgement." His letters arrived in December, and the following month, on January 20, 1858, Hudson Taylor and Maria were married.[23]

Maria was the very woman Taylor needed to polish the rough edges of his personality and to help focus his enthusiasm and ambitions, and from the start their marriage was a true partnership. They remained in Ningpo for three years, during which time Taylor was unexpectedly thrust into the supervision of the local hospital, a position that was clearly beyond his capability. Through that experience he became convinced that he needed more medical training, though the decision to leave their post in China was not an easy one.

In 1860 the Taylors arrived in England for an extended furlough, one that would serve a number of purposes. Both Hudson and Maria had suffered severe health problems, and so it was a time of relaxation and recuperation. It was also a time for further education. Taylor enrolled at the

London Hospital, where he completed the Practical Chemistry course, the Midwifery course, and the Diploma for Membership of the Royal College of Surgeons. Another priority during their furlough was translation work. Accompanying them to England was a Chinese assistant, and, together with him and another missionary, Taylor made a revision of the Ningpo New Testament—an arduous task, sometimes consuming his energies for more than thirteen hours a day. But the most significant accomplishment during their extended furlough was their organizational work. It was during this time that the China Inland Mission came into being.

The China Inland Mission was not the brainchild of a man who desired recognition or wanted to head up his own organization. Rather, it evolved slowly in the mind and heart of a man who was deeply burdened for the millions in China who had never heard the gospel. As Taylor traveled through England people were moved, not by his eloquence of speech or by his impressive knowledge, but by his passion for lost souls: "A million a month dying without God," rang in the ears of his listeners, and many responded. The foundation of a great mission society was being laid.

The CIM was a unique missionary society, molded around the experiences and personality of Hudson Taylor. It was undenominational and appealed largely to the working classes. Taylor knew that China would never be evangelized if he had to wait for highly educated, ordained ministers to go, and so he looked for dedicated men and women among England's massive laboring classes. By appealing to this segment he avoided competition with other mission boards, thus maximizing the missionary effort in China. His experience with the CES led him to establish the headquarters for the mission in China, where it could be more responsive to the needs of the missionaries. Though he at first was reluctant to take control, he realized the need for strong leadership, and as time went on he became a virtual dictator, though always sensitive to the personal needs of those under him. As to finances and personal support, the CIM missionaries were offered no set salary but rather were to depend entirely on God for their needs. To avoid even the appearance of relying on human resources, offerings and other forms of direct appeals for money were strictly taboo.

In 1865 the CIM was officially established, and the following year Taylor was once again prepared to embark on China. With him were Maria, his four children, and fifteen raw recruits, including seven single women, who were ready to unite with the eight recruits that had been sent out earlier. During his furlough, Taylor had left his mark on England. In the words of the great Charles Haddon Spurgeon, "China, China, China is now ringing in our ears in that special, peculiar, musical, forcible, unique way in which Mr. Taylor utters it."[24]

The voyage to China was a remarkable one. Never before had such a large mission party set sail with the mission's founder and director on board, and the impact on the ship's crew was dramatic. By the time they had rounded the Cape, card playing and cursing had given way to Bible reading and hymn singing. But there were problems as well. The "germs of ill feeling and division" had crept in

The Lammermuir Party that sailed from London on May 26, 1866 (from left to right) seated, 3rd and 4th, Mr. and Mrs. Lewis Nichol; 5th, Jennie Faulding; 6th and 7th, Hudson and Maria Taylor; standing, 4th, Emily Blatchley.

among them, and the once harmonious band was sounding dissonant chords before it reached its destination. Lewis Nicol, a blacksmith by trade, was the ringleader of the dissenters. He and two other missionaries began comparing notes and came to the conclusion that they of the CIM had received less substantial outfits than were usually received by Presbyterians and other missionaries. With that complaint came others, and soon Taylor found himself in the center of a barrage of poisoned arrows: "The feeling among us appears to have been worse than I could have formed any conception of. One was jealous because another had too many new dresses, another because someone else had more attention. Some were wounded because of unkind controversial discussions, and so on."[25] By talking to each missionary "privately and affectionately" Taylor was able to calm the wrangling, but underlying feelings of hostility remained that would soon culminate in a near fatal disruption of the infant CIM.

On arriving in Shanghai, Taylor ordered tailor-made Chinese clothes for each of his missionaries. The missionaries were well aware of his stand on the issue of Chinese dress and had agreed to it in principle; nevertheless, the change, complicated by the ordinary pressures of culture shock, was a brutal psychological jolt. The initial discomfort of the clothing and the hair dyeing and head shaving were torture enough, but the ridicule heaped on them by the resident missionary community in Shanghai was more than some could cope with, and the situation only seemed to worsen after the missionaries moved to the CIM compound at Hangchow. Taylor's leadership was challenged, and again the mission was caught up in strife. Even Taylor's most loyal supporters, Jennie Faulding and Emily Blatchley, had a falling out. Nicol and others flatly refused to wear native dress and began meeting separately for meals and devotions. The situation was tense, and the prospects for renewed fellowship seemed dim. Could anything save this visionary dream that had fallen in such shambles?

The price was high, but the mission was saved. It was during the heat of the summer of 1867, a year and a half after the missionaries had arrived in China. Little eight-year-old Gracie Taylor, whom her father idolized, became ill. For days her father sat beside her, giving her the best medical attention he was capable of giving, but her situation did not improve. The climate had also taken its toll on others; and during his vigil with Gracie he left on a one-day business trip, during which time he was called to another station to treat the critically ill Jane McLean, one of his own missionaries who had vehemently opposed him. Her illness was not as serious as supposed, and she soon recovered; but Taylor's delay in returning home to Gracie proved critical. He diagnosed water on the brain, but he was too late to be of any help. Within days Gracie died. It was a heartrending tragedy, but it saved the CIM. The grievances were forgotten, and the outpouring of sympathy brought the missionaries back together, except for Nicol and his wife and the two single sisters, one of whom was Jane McLean. In the fall of 1867 Nicol was "put away" from the mission, and the McLean sisters resigned, allowing the mission family to move ahead in harmony.

The death of Gracie by no means ended the problems of the CIM. The greater crises were yet to come, and they revolved around the age-old hostility of Chinese for foreigners—a hostility that was magnified many times over in the interior. The first violent attack against the CIM missionaries occurred at Yangchow in 1868. The mission house was attacked and set on fire, and the missionaries, including Maria Taylor, barely escaped with their lives. As peaceable as the missionaries had been, it seems incredible that the incident could have brought on them the charge of their being warmongers, but such was the case. Although Taylor never sought for revenge or even requested British protection, certain hawkish politicians viewed the Yangchow incident as the perfect excuse to dispatch the gunboats of the Royal Navy to humiliate China, and the CIM suffered the consequences. Though shots were never fired, the *Times* of London despaired that England's "political prestige had been injured" and blamed it on "a company of missionaries assuming the title of the China Inland Mission."[26] The adverse publicity was devastating. Financial support plummeted, and prospective recruits suddenly lost interest.

While international controversy raged over the Yangchow incident, the CIM missionaries quietly returned to that city and continued their ministry. Their courage was a testimony to the Chinese people who had observed their brutal treatment by a minority of hoodlums, and the door was now open for an effective witness. A church was begun, and, according to Emily Blatchley, "The converts here are different from any others we have known in China. There is such life, warmth, *earnestness* about them."[27]

Criticism of Taylor and the CIM did not end with the Yangchow controversy. Newspaper editors and private citizens continued to rail against him until he was beaten down. So great was his despair that he lost his will to go on, succumbing to "the awful temptation ... even to end his own life." While outside forces contributed to his dark depression, it was inner strife that afflicted him the most: "I hated myself; I hated my sin; and yet I gained no strength against it." The more he sought to attain spirituality, the less satisfaction he found: "Every day, almost every hour, the consciousness of failure and sin oppressed me." Where was it all to end? But for the concern of a friend, Taylor may have suffered a complete mental collapse. Aware of Taylor's problem the friend, in a letter, shared his own secret to spiritual living: "To *let* my loving Savior work in me *His will....* Abiding, not striving or struggling.... Not a striving to have faith, or to increase our faith but a looking at the faithful one seems all we need. A resting in the loved one entirely...." With that letter Taylor's life was changed: "God has made me a new man."[28]

Taylor's spiritual renewal came in time to sustain him through a period of severe personal testing. Soon after the Christmas season was over in January of 1870, the Taylors began making preparations to send their four older children back to England for their education. Emily Blatchley, who knew them well, offered to return with them and to care for them in England, but it was nevertheless a time of trauma for the close-knit family. So much so, that frail little five-year-old Sammy could not endure. He died in early February. Despite the tragedy, the decision to send the children away was firm. In March, the Taylors sorrowfully parted with the other three children, who could not know that their kisses and hugs were the last their mother would ever receive from them in this world. During the hot summer that followed, Maria, who was late in another pregnancy, became seriously ill. In early July she delivered a baby boy, who lived less than two weeks. A few days after his death, Maria, at the age of thirty-three, died also.

Without Maria, Taylor was a lonely man. He had relied heavily on her support and good judgment, and he deeply missed her warm affection. He longed for the female companionship of which he had been deprived, and that no doubt influenced his decision to visit Hangchow in the months after Maria's death, where he spent time with Jennie Faulding, a twenty-seven-year-old single missionary who had been a close family friend since coming to China with the Taylors. The following year they sailed to England together and were married.

Back in England, Taylor was overjoyed to be reunited with his children, but he found himself burdened with administrative work. His home secretary of many years, W. T. Berger, could no longer carry his responsibilities, and thus most of the office duties fell on the shoulders of Taylor. During his year of furlough he organized a council to take over Berger's duties; and after that matter was settled, in the fall of 1872, he and Jennie returned to China.

As the CIM grew, Taylor spent most of his time traveling about China, supervising the work at various stations. He served as a troubleshooter and was continually called on to settle problems throughout China's many provinces, as well as back in England. In 1874, after a two-year absence, he returned to England to regroup his children, who had been scattered due to Emily Blatchley's ill health, which prevented her from continuing her

Jennie Faulding, Hudson Taylor's second wife.

care; and again in 1876 he returned to keep the fires burning on the home front. Each time he returned to China he brought with him more missionaries, and with them more controversy. Despite the success of the CIM, criticism continued, especially with reference to the poor quality of missionary candidates. Education was a prized attainment for a nineteenth-century Englishman, and those who lacked it were considered inferior.

CIM missionaries, though sometimes lacking in worldly wisdom, excelled in dedication and zeal. They willingly served in the interior in spite of the danger and the deprivations, often because they had endured the greatest of personal sacrifices just to get to China. Elizabeth Wilson was one such missionary. For years she longed to serve the Lord in China, but due to the ill health of her parents she was prevented from going. For thirty years she patiently cared for them; and then at the age of fifty, three weeks after her last surviving parent died, she applied to the CIM and was accepted. Her age, accentuated by her silvery hair, made her an honored resident of China, and she served faithfully.

Single women were commonplace in the CIM. Taylor had long recognized not only their eagerness to volunteer, but also their potential for ministry. There was an openness among Chinese women not found among the men, and only women missionaries could effectively reach them. The true test of Taylor's confidence in women came in 1877 while he was back in England with Jennie and the children. Word came of the devastating famines that were wreaking havoc on North China and the desperate need for relief work. It would be a tremendous opportunity for evangelism, and there were volunteers—women—but there was no one to lead them. Taylor himself had been unwell, and who else knew China and its people and language well enough to lead a missionary party? The answer was obvious— Jennie did. But the decision was not easy. Leaving a husband in poor health and seven children (two of her own, four of Taylor's by Maria, and an adopted daughter) was not her idea of good mothering, but she realized her ministry extended beyond the bounds of her own family, and Taylor strongly encouraged her to go. Missionary wives, in his opinion, were not just wives, they were missionaries as well. Writing to potential candidates, he had charged: "Unless you intend your wife to be a true missionary, not merely a wife, home-maker, and friend, do not join us."[29] Jennie was a "true missionary." Accompanied by single women, she set out for the interior of North China, where she and her companions served until Hudson joined her the following year, bringing still more recruits with him.

The more Hudson Taylor worked and traveled in China the greater his burden for evangelizing that immense population became, though the responsibility was overwhelming: "Souls on every hand are perishing for lack of knowledge; more than 1,000 every hour are passing away into death and darkness."[30] It seemed like an impossible task, but Taylor had a plan. If he could muster up one thousand evangelists, and if each of those evangelists could reach two hundred and fifty people a day with the gospel, the whole of China could be evangelized in a little more than three years. It was an unrealistic vision, and, of course, his goal was never reached, but the CIM did leave an indelible mark on China. By 1882 the CIM had entered every province, and in 1895, thirty years after its founding, the CIM had more than six hundred and forty missionaries investing their lives in China.

That Taylor sought to reach all of China with the gospel was certainly a lofty ambition, but that very goal may have been the decisive weakness of the CIM. In its effort to reach all of China the policy of diffusion (as opposed to concentration) was implemented. According to the great missions historian, Kenneth Scott Latourette, "The main purpose of the China Inland Mission was not to win converts or to build a Chinese church, but to spread a knowledge of the Christian Gospel throughout the empire as quickly as might be.... Nor, although Chinese assistants were employed, did it stress the recruiting and training of a Chinese ministry."[31] Such a policy was unwise. The hostility toward foreigners unleashed in the Boxer Rebellion, and the Communist takeover some decades later glaringly illustrate the inherent weakness of a policy that did not make the building of a strong local ministry and church its number one priority.

The dark days were not long in coming for the CIM. The closing years of the nineteenth century were years of tension and unrest. The forces of modernization (and westernization) were clashing with the forces of tradition and antagonism toward foreigners. With imperial power moving to the side of the conservatives, the position of Westerners became more precarious. Then in June of 1900 an imperial decree from Peking ordered the death of all foreigners and the extermination of Christianity. The greatest holocaust in the history of Protestant missions followed. One hundred and thirty-five missionaries and fifty-three missionary children were brutally murdered, and it was the courageous CIM missionaries of the interior, many of them single women, who suffered the most. Ninety-one CIM missionaries in the Shansi Province alone were mercilessly slain.

For Taylor, who was isolated in Switzerland, recuperating from severe mental and physical exhaustion, the news from China, though muted by those caring for him, was almost too much to endure, and he never fully recovered from the trauma. In 1902 he resigned his position as General Director of the mission, and he and Jennie

THE "GREAT CENTURY"

	1800	1810	1820	1830	1840	1850

India and Central Asia

(1793) William Carey arrives in India
● (1836) John Scudder begins
● (1834) Death of Carey
● (1812) First American missionaries set sail
● (1819) Founding of Serampore College
● (1830) Alexander Duff arrives in India
● (1824) Judson imprisoned
● (1845) Judson's
● (1806) Henry Martyn arrives in India
● (1850)

Black Africa

● (1799) Vanderkemp arrives at Cape
● (1816) Moffat begins missionary service
● (1825) Moffat settles at Kuruman
● (1841) Livingstone
● (1852)
● (1844) Krapf

The Far East

● (1807) Morrison arrives in Canton
● (1814) Morrison baptizes first convert
● (1842) Treaty of
● (1840) Gutzlaff begins
●

The Pacific Islands

● (1817) Williams arrives in South Seas
● (1819) Baptism of Pomare
● (1820) Hawaiian mission begins
● (1848)
(1796) *Duff* sails for South Pacific
● (1837) Coan begins revival
● (1838) Bible published
● (1839) Martyrdom of

Europe and North America

● (1810) Founding of the American Board of Commissioners for Foreign Missions
(1795) Founding of London Missionary Society
● (1799) Founding of Church Missionary Society
● (1837) Cherokee removal
● (1835) Whitman leaves for
● (1847)

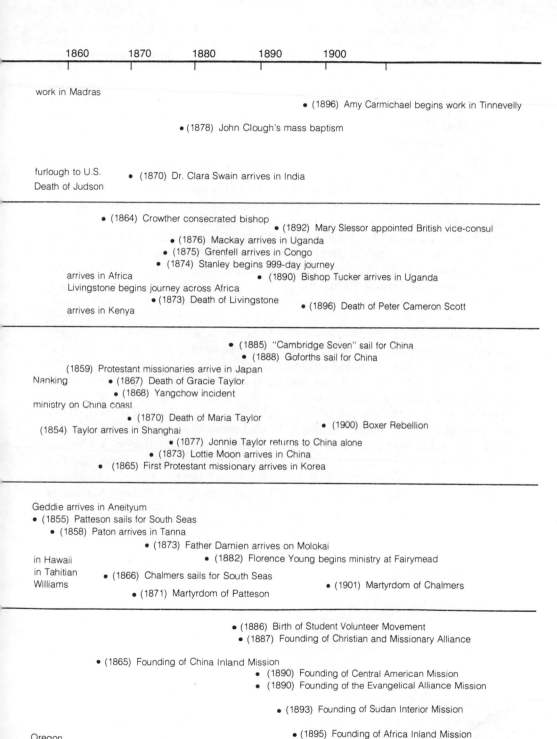

1860	1870	1880	1890	1900

work in Madras

● (1896) Amy Carmichael begins work in Tinnevelly

● (1878) John Clough's mass baptism

furlough to U.S.   ● (1870) Dr. Clara Swain arrives in India
Death of Judson

● (1864) Crowther consecrated bishop
       ● (1892) Mary Slessor appointed British vice-consul
● (1876) Mackay arrives in Uganda
● (1875) Grenfell arrives in Congo
● (1874) Stanley begins 999-day journey
arrives in Africa   ● (1890) Bishop Tucker arrives in Uganda
Livingstone begins journey across Africa
● (1873) Death of Livingstone
arrives in Kenya   ● (1896) Death of Peter Cameron Scott

● (1885) "Cambridge Seven" sail for China
● (1888) Goforths sail for China
(1859) Protestant missionaries arrive in Japan
Nanking   ● (1867) Death of Gracie Taylor
● (1868) Yangchow incident
ministry on China coast
● (1870) Death of Maria Taylor
    ● (1900) Boxer Rebellion
(1854) Taylor arrives in Shanghai
● (1877) Jennie Taylor returns to China alone
● (1873) Lottie Moon arrives in China
● (1865) First Protestant missionary arrives in Korea

Geddie arrives in Aneityum
● (1855) Patteson sails for South Seas
● (1858) Paton arrives in Tanna
● (1873) Father Damien arrives on Molokai
in Hawaii   ● (1882) Florence Young begins ministry at Fairymead
in Tahitian
Williams   ● (1866) Chalmers sails for South Seas
    ● (1901) Martyrdom of Chalmers
● (1871) Martyrdom of Patteson

● (1886) Birth of Student Volunteer Movement
● (1887) Founding of Christian and Missionary Alliance

● (1865) Founding of China Inland Mission
● (1890) Founding of Central American Mission
● (1890) Founding of the Evangelical Alliance Mission

● (1893) Founding of Sudan Interior Mission

● (1895) Founding of Africa Inland Mission
Oregon   ● (1892) Grenfell arrives in Labrador

Waiilatpu massacre

stayed on in Switzerland until 1904 when Jennie died. The following year Taylor returned to China, where he peacefully died the month following his arrival. In the years that followed, the CIM continued to grow. By 1914 it had become the largest foreign mission organization in the world, reaching its peak in 1934 with 1,368 missionaries. After the Communist takeover in 1950, the CIM, along with the other mission societies, was expelled from China, and after one hundred years of ministry, the CIM changed its name, in 1964, to the Overseas Missionary Fellowship, a name that was more indicative of its expanding missionary endeavors in the Orient.

The contribution Hudson Taylor made to Christian missions is incalculable. It is difficult to imagine where missions would be today without his vision and foresight. He was a "young upstart," in the words of Ralph Winter, whose impact on Christian missions rivaled or surpassed that of William Carey's—an impact that Winter goes on to perceptively summarize in light of later developments:

> With only trade school medicine, without any university experience much less missiological training, and a checkered past in regard to his own individualistic behavior while he was on the field, he was merely one more of the weak things that God uses to confound the wise. Even his early anti-church-planting missionary strategy was breathtakingly erroneous by today's church-planting standards. Yet God strangely honored him because his gaze was fixed upon the world's least-reached peoples. Hudson Taylor had a divine wind behind him. The Holy Spirit spared him from many pitfalls, and it was his organization, the China Inland Mission—the most cooperative servant organization yet to appear—that eventually served in one way or another over 6,000 missionaries, predominantly in the interior of China. It took 20 years for other missions to begin to join Taylor in his special emphasis—the unreached, inland frontiers.[32]

Jonathan and Rosalind Goforth

Of all the missionaries who served in the Orient during the nineteenth and early twentieth centuries, none saw a greater immediate response to his personal ministry than did Jonathan Goforth, who, according to J. Herbert Kane, was "China's most outstanding evangelist." China was Goforth's base, but he also ministered in Korea and Manchuria; and wherever he went, revival followed.

Goforth, the seventh of eleven children, was born in western Ontario in 1859. He was converted at the age of eighteen and dedicated himself to the Lord's service after reading the *Memoirs of Robert Murray M'Cheyne*. His call to missions, however, did not come until later, when he was moved by the appeal of Dr. George Mackay, a veteran missionary from Formosa. Mackay had traveled "for two years . . . up and down Canada trying to persuade some young man to come over to Formosa," but, as he told his audience, all his travels had been in vain, and he had no choice but to return to Formosa without anyone to carry out the work he had begun. Mackay's message stung the conscience of young Goforth: "As I listened to these words, I was overwhelmed with shame. . . . From that hour I became a foreign missionary."[33]

In preparation for his ministry, Goforth attended Knox College, where

Jonathan Goforth, missionary evangelist to China, Manchuria, and Korea.

he had expected to find warm Christian fellowship and eager Bible scholars. Instead, the naive country boy, clad in homemade garments, found himself alone in his dedication to the Lord and in his zeal for missions. He soon became a popular subject of campus humor, especially after he began devoting his time to rescue mission work; but as time went on attitudes changed, and by the time of his graduation, Goforth had become one of the most respected students on campus.

While active in city mission work in the spring of 1885, Goforth met Rosalind Smith, a talented and sophisticated art student—and an unlikely prospect for a missionary wife. But somehow Rosalind looked beyond "the shabbiness of his clothes" and

perceived the great potential he had as a servant of God. For her, it was love at first sight: "It all happened within a few moments, but as I sat there, I said to myself, 'That is the man I would like to marry!' "[34] Later that year they became engaged, and at that time Rosalind got her first taste of the sacrifice she would encounter the rest of her life as the wife of Jonathan Goforth. Her dreams of an engagement ring were dashed when he told her that the money he would have spent for a ring must instead go for Christian literature.

After graduation from Knox College, Goforth applied to the China Inland Mission, since his own church, the Presbyterian Church of Canada, had no missionary work in China. Before he received a response from the CIM Presbyterian students from Knox rallied to his cause and vowed to raise the money themselves to send him to China. Prior to his sailing, Goforth traveled through Canada, speaking out for missions. His messages were powerful, and everywhere he went he witnessed changed lives. The testimony of a Knox College graduate regarding Goforth poignantly illustrates this:

I was going up to the Alumni meeting in Knox College, Toronto, determined to do everything in my power to frustrate the crazy scheme which the students of the college were talking about, i.e., starting a mission field of their own in Central China. I also felt that I needed a new overcoat; my old one was looking rather shabby. So I thought I would go to Toronto to kill two birds with one stone. I would help side-track the scheme and buy an overcoat. But this fellow here upset my plans completely. He swept me off my feet with an enthusiasm for missions which I had never experienced before, and my precious overcoat money went into the fund![35]

In 1888 the Goforths sailed for China to serve in the province of Honan, where they began a life of hardships and lonely separations. They both suffered frequent illnesses, and they saw five of their eleven children die in childhood. Fire, flood, and theft took its toll on their possessions, and on several occasions they encountered life-threatening situations. The most terrifying trial they faced was their one-thousand-mile harrowing flight to safety during the Boxer madness of 1900. Through it all, their vision for lost souls in China never dimmed.

From his early years in China, Goforth was known as a powerful evangelist, sometimes speaking to

Rosalind Goforth, wife of Jonathan Goforth.

crowds numbering as many as twenty-five thousand. His message was simple: "Jesus Christ and Him crucified." Early in his ministry a seasoned missionary advised him not "to speak of Jesus the first time when preaching to a heathen audience" because of the "prejudice against the name of Jesus," advice that Goforth consistently ignored. A straightforward approach was the only one he knew.

The Goforths' efforts to reach the Chinese were unconventional by most missionary standards, particularly their "open-house" evangelism. Their home, with its European interior design, and their furnishings (including a kitchen stove, a sewing machine, and an organ) were subjects of intense curiosity to the Chinese people, and the Goforths willingly relinquished their privacy and effectively used their house as a means to make friends and contacts among the people of the province. Visitors came from miles around, once more than two thousand in one day, to tour the house in small groups. Before each tour began, Goforth gave a gospel message, and sometimes visitors stayed on after the tour to hear more. He preached an average of eight hours a day, and during a five month period some twenty-five thousand people came to visit. Rosalind ministered to the women, sometimes speaking to as many as fifty at a time who were gathered in their yard.

It was this type of evangelism that paved the way for Goforth's future ministry of traveling from town to town conducting revivals, but not all of his colleagues approved: "Some may think that receiving visitors is not real mission work, but I think it is. I put

Boxer poster showing Chinese attitude toward foreigners.

myself out to make friends with the people and I reap the results when I go to their villages to preach. Often the people of a village will gather around me and say, 'We were at your place and you showed us through your house, treating us like friends.' Then they almost always bring me a chair to sit on, a table to lay my Bible on, and some tea."[36]

The Boxer Rebellion in 1900 interrupted the Goforth's mission work, and after they returned to China their family life radically changed to accommodate Goforth's new plan for a broad itinerant ministry. He had developed his idea before Rosalind returned from Canada to join him in China, and soon after her arrival he confronted her with the scheme: "My plan is to have one of my helpers rent a suitable place in a large centre for us to live in, and that we, as a family, stay a month in the centre, during which time we will carry on intensive evangelism. I will go with my men to villages or on the street in the daytime, while you receive and preach to the women in the courtyard. The evenings will be given to a joint meeting with you at the organ and with plenty of gospel hymns. Then at the end of a month, we will leave an evangelist behind to teach the new believers while we go on to another place to open it in the same way. When a number of places are opened, we will return once or twice a year." As Rosalind listened, her "heart went like lead." The idea itself was impressive, but it simply was not suited to a family man. Exposing their little ones to the infectious diseases that were so prevalent out in the villages was too risky, and she could not forget the "four little graves" they had already left behind on Chinese soil.[37] Although Rosalind initially objected, Goforth went ahead with his plan, convinced it was God's will.

While Rosalind fully supported her husband's dedication to the Lord, she was naturally concerned at times about his dedication to her and the children. Of course God's will was paramount, but must it be at odds with what was in the best interest of the family? As a wife, she never doubted his love, but she did on occasion feel less than fully secure in her position. Before she and the children returned to Canada alone in 1908, she probed him concerning his commitment to her: "Suppose I were stricken with an incurable disease in the homeland and had but a few months to live. If we cabled you to come, would you come?" Goforth obviously did not want to answer the question. An outright 'no' would have been too harsh, but Rosalind persisted until he gave his answer—in the form of a question to her: "Suppose our country were at war with another nation and I, a British officer in command of an important unit. Much depended upon me as commander as to whether it was to be victory or defeat. Would I, in that event, be permitted to forsake my post in response to a call from my family in the homeland, even if it were what you suggest?" What could she say? She had no choice but to sadly reply, "No."[38]

The itinerant ministry that Goforth began in the early years of the twentieth century was a stepping stone that led to the great revivals he conducted in the years that followed. His revival ministry began in 1907 when he and another missionary toured Korea and inspired the revival movement that had swept through the churches there, resulting in an "amazing increase of converts" and a strengthening of the local churches and schools. From Korea they went to Manchuria "with hearts stirred to the depths at what they had been witnessing," and mighty revivals followed. In his wife's words, "Jonathan Goforth went to Manchuria an unknown missionary. . . . He returned a few weeks later with the limelight of the Christian world upon him."[39]

As he traveled through China and Manchuria in the years that followed, Goforth's revival ministry mushroomed. Some of his colleagues and supporters back home were wary of his evangelistic zeal. They were uncomfortable hearing reports of weeping and confession of sin and of the outpouring of the Holy Spirit, and some charged that it was a movement of "fanaticism" and "Pentecostalism." Goforth ignored the criticism and kept on preaching. One of the high points of his revival ministry was in 1918 when he held a two-week campaign with Chinese soldiers under the command of General Feng Yu-Hsiang, himself a Christian. The response was overwhelming, and at the end of the campaign nearly five thousand soldiers and officers took part in a communion service.

Along with his success, Goforth faced setbacks and problems. Early in his ministry he confronted a "danger which threatens to absorb our infant church in North Honan . . . a Romanist invasion." The Roman Catholics, it seems, were following on his heels, and in one town they "captured almost the whole number of enquirers . . . sweeping away in a week the work of years." What would motivate these "enquirers" to turn to the Catholics? According to Goforth, the Catholics offered the Chinese employment and free education, including room and board. (Protestants were guilty of this, too, sometimes going so far as to actually pay the Chinese to attend their schools.) But Goforth was adamant in his convictions: "We could offer no such inducements, and we have a horror of making 'rice Christians.' We cannot fight Rome by competing with them in buying up the people...."[40] Though Goforth refused to match the offers made by the Catholics, most of those who had been swayed by the Catholics later returned to the fold.

Another problem Goforth faced involved his own mission board. He regarded the "Holy Spirit's leading" above the "hard and fast rules" of the Presbytery under which he served, and thus, according to his wife, "with his convictions concerning Divine guidance *of himself,* he naturally came often into conflict with other members of the Honan Presbytery," making him "not easy to get along with." Goforth did not demand special privileges for himself, but rather insisted that each missionary should have "freedom to carry on his or her work as each one felt led." It was a knotty problem, and Goforth often

"found himself hampered and held back from following fully what he deemed was for him the Holy Spirit's leading."[41]

As Goforth served over the years in China, his problems did not diminish. Confrontations continued and friction increased particularly in the 1920s when the Fundamentalist-Modernist controversy, that was tearing churches apart in his homeland, found its way to China (see chapter 11). New missionaries, steeped in higher criticism, were arriving on the field, and Goforth "felt powerless to stem the tide." His only recourse was to "preach, as never before, salvation through the cross of Calvary and demonstrate its power...."[42]

Long after most missionaries had succumbed to disease or gone into retirement, Goforth, at seventy-three, kept up his hectic pace of revival meetings. Even after being stricken with blindness he continued his ministry, aided by a Chinese assistant. At the age of seventy-four he returned to Canada, where he spent the last eighteen months of his life traveling and speaking at nearly five hundred meetings. He carried on to the very end, speaking four times on the Sunday before he peacefully died in his sleep. He left behind a striking testimony of what one man could do for God among the teeming millions of the Orient.

SELECTED BIBLIOGRAPHY

Barr, Pat. To China With Love: The Lives and Times of Protestant Missionaries in China 1860–1900. *Garden City, N.Y.: Doubleday, 1973.*

Broomhall, A. J. Hudson Taylor & China's Open Century. *Book One:* Barbarians at the Gates. *London: Hodder & Stoughton, 1981.*

Broomhall, Marshall. Robert Morrison: A Master-builder. *New York: Doran, 1924.*

Goforth, Rosalind. Goforth of China. *Grand Rapids: Zondervan, 1937.*

Latourette, Kenneth Scott. A History of Christian Missions in China. *New York: Macmillan, 1929.*

Pollock, J. C. Hudson Taylor and Maria: Pioneers in China. *Grand Rapids: Zondervan, 1976.*

Taylor, Dr. and Mrs. Howard. J. Hudson Taylor: God's Man in China. *Chicago: Moody, 1978.*

Chapter 8

The Pacific Islands:
Preaching in "Paradise"

The islands of the Pacific: a paradise on earth. No other geographical location in the history of man—save for the Garden of Eden—has received more glowing press reviews. Explorers and traders came away with dazzling accounts of breathtaking beauty, and writers, including William Melville, Robert Louis Stevenson, and James Michener, masterfully adorned their novels with the enchantment of the island world. "Writers have vied with each other in their glowing descriptions of the wondrous picturesqueness of the scenery, the rugged mountains, deep valleys, and tranquil lagoons; the glistening fringe of sandy beach, the stately trees, feathery palms, and luxuriant creepers; the profusion of bright blossoms, delicious fruits, and gorgeous birds."[1] It was into this setting that missionaries came, first Roman Catholic monks who accompanied explorers and later Protestants who were commissioned by missionary societies.

Oceania, the term generally used to designate the Pacific islands, consists of some 1500 islands divided into three major groupings: Polynesia, the largest group, extends from Hawaii in the north to New Zealand in the south; Micronesia, the group of small islands, is located between Hawaii and the Philippines, including the Marianas and the Caroline, Marshall, and Gilbert Islands; and Melanesia, the islands south of Micronesia and north of Australia, includes Fiji, Santa Cruz, New Guinea, the New Hebrides, New Caledonia, and the Solomon Islands. The size of the islands ranges from New Guinea, the second largest island in the world, to tiny dots in the ocean such as the Marshall Islands, whose total land area is less than one hundred square miles. In fact, all of Micronesia is smaller in land area than the state of Rhode Island, and the population of Micronesia, and all of Oceania, was correspondingly small—excluding New Zealand, probably fewer than two million.

Nevertheless, there were souls dying without Christ, so despite the geographical drawbacks, many mission societies were willing to expend whatever money and human resources were needed to evangelize this sprawling mission field. The first European missionary endeavor to the South Pacific was carried out by Magellan and his party of explorers and Franciscan friars in 1521, less than one decade after Balboa's great discovery of the Pacific Ocean. After landing in the Marianas the little fleet of four ships (one had been abandoned earlier) sailed on to the Philippines, where some three thousand islanders were received into the Catholic Church. While there is no indication they understood even the most basic tenets of Christianity, the occasion was, nevertheless, considered a high point in Roman Catholic South Seas missions. For Magellan, this historic expedition would be his last. He, along with a number of his crewmen, was killed after trying to force natives on another island to pay homage to the king of Spain. Later, during the sixteenth century, Roman Catholic missionaries returned to the islands, but again their mission was short-lived.

It was Captain Cook who more than any other individual awakened Protestantism to the potential opportunity for evangelism of the Pacific islands. His discoveries stirred the imaginations of church leaders and lay people alike, and as a result the London Missionary Society was formed in 1795 by an interdenominational group of ministers and laymen for the purpose of sending missionaries to Tahiti "or some other of the islands of the South Sea." Soon other mission societies (particularly those representing the Wesleyan Methodists, Congregationalists, Presbyterians, and Anglicans)

followed, and by the end of the nineteenth century Oceania was the shining success story of Protestant missions.

In the Pacific islands, as with so many other areas of the world, the first Protestant missionaries were British; other Protestants from Australia, America, and Germany came later on. Roman Catholics were comparatively late in entering the Pacific islands, not gaining a strong foothold until around the middle of the nineteenth century. As was the case elsewhere, there was a bitter rivalry between Protestants and Catholics, and anti-Catholic sentiment was a prominent theme among the missionaries. The common criticism was that the Catholics were perpetrating a superficial religion based on sacraments while ignoring the moral decadence of the natives. "Popery rises its hideous head," wrote Joseph Waterhouse (a Wesleyan missionary), "sanctioning the eating of human flesh, polygamy, adultery, and fornication!!"[2] Perhaps the greatest source of tension between Protestants and Catholics, however, was nationality. The Catholics were French, and there was a genuine fear among Protestants that French political and military power might prevail on the islands.

During the earliest years of Protestant missionary work in the South Pacific, most missionaries had been negative toward the idea of British or American political involvement in the islands. With the arrival of the French Catholics, however, missionaries began clamoring for protection, suggesting either a British or American protectorate. Neither was instituted, and by the mid-nineteenth century British missions in the South Seas were on the decline.

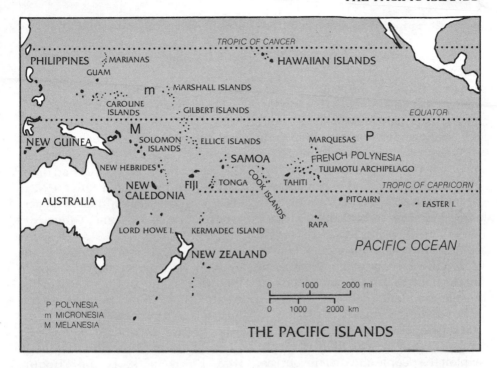

THE PACIFIC ISLANDS

The geographical uniqueness of the Pacific islands had from the very beginning obvious implications on mission strategy. Transportation became an all-encompassing issue. It was simply not enough to send missionaries out to the South Seas and drop them on isolated islands and expect them to be satisfied for a year or more until the next passing ship arrived. The small size and population of most of the islands fostered an overwhelming sense of claustrophobia, and the brave missionaries who had ventured so far from their native land were suddenly isolated and hemmed in by the vast Pacific Ocean. Mission-owned ships soon became the logical solution to the problem. The *Morning Star* in Micronesia, the *John Williams* in Polynesia, and the *Southern Cross* in Melanesia—each name taken by a succession of mission ships that almost took on personalities of their own—played a key role in the evangelization of the island world.

With the use of mission ships, many of the European missionaries became traveling field directors who coordinated the work of native evangelists and teachers. It was sound strategy, and, according to one missions historian, "... the native missionaries were to prove the main strength of Christian missions in the South Seas. They did remarkable work. Lacking the prestige of the Europeans they were ignored, bullied, and sometimes killed by islanders with whom they cast their lot, but almost to a man persevered, and between 1839 and 1860 most faiths owed more than they cared to admit to these island missionaries who went where few Europeans dared to venture."[3]

As with early missionary ventures elsewhere in the world, there were tremendous sacrifices made to introduce Christianity to the Pacific islands. Most of the islanders had a dread fear of their European visitors, and with good cause. The accounts of the horrendous activities of the traders had spread to many of the islands, and at first sight missionaries could not easily be differentiated from their surly brothers. Moreover, the religion of most of the islanders was a primitive form of animism; and acceptance of strangers, it was believed, even if they came in peace, would surely invite a curse by the evil spirits. As a result, many of the great missionaries, foreign and native, were added to the roles of martyrdom as they reached out to hostile islanders.

But often the greatest resistance to the missionaries came from the traders and sailors who had come to exploit the people and their resources. To them, the missionaries were an unbending obstacle standing in the way of pleasure and financial gain; and thus the missionaries were sometimes betrayed by their own countrymen, who incited the wrath of the natives against them. According to Robert H. Glover, the Europeans for the most part were "dissolute and unprincipled, and left a shameful trail wherever they went. They reveled in the heathen immorality, imported rum wherewith to frenzy the natives, and firearms to add to the horrors of tribal warfare; they deceived and exploited the islanders and were guilty of the greatest excesses and cruelties."[4]

It was against such obstacles that the Christian missionaries struggled, but sometimes even more devastating were the inner conflicts they encountered. The ever present prospect of material gain took its toll on the mission force, and worse yet was the free lifestyle and sexual openness that proved to be a moral quagmire into which some missionaries could not resist falling. The practice of "going native" was, according to Stephen Neill, "a much commoner happening than is generally reflected in the edifying accounts of these early missions. . . ."[5] Here in this island paradise they faced temptations that had never before confronted them in the confines of their often sheltered background. Some overcame. Others did not.

Despite the personal failures of the missionaries, the saga of missions in this area of the world is one of the great success stories in Christian history. It is a story of individuals turning from destructive tribal customs to a vibrant faith in Christ. But more than that, it is a story of "people movements"—movements that have occurred throughout Christian history in every area of the world, but ones that were particularly striking in the island world. Such movements that brought large families and sometimes whole tribes to Christianity have been meticulously documented by Professor Alan R. Tippett in his books *People Movements in Southern Polynesia* and *Solomon Island Christianity.* He points out that in many instances there was no appreciable church growth until the missionaries realized the vital significance of the family and tribal unit. It was this realization then that helped bring about the unparalled success missionaries to the South Seas achieved. Today this area of the world has a larger percentage of Christians than does any other comparable area.

Henry Nott and the *Duff* Missionaries

Unlike early Protestant missionary ventures elsewhere in the world where missionaries trickled in one by one or in small groups, the entry into the Pacific islands began with a big splash. It was a foggy London morning in August of 1796 when thirty missionaries, along with six wives and three children, all sponsored by the London Missionary Society, boarded the mission ship *Duff* and began their seven-month ocean voyage to Tahiti. Such an extensive Protestant missionary assault had never before been launched, and it was a day to remember. There was an enthusiastic send-off as crowds of earnest supporters came down to the river bank "singing the praises of God," with high expectations of what their Christian ambassadors would accomplish in this most "uncivilized" area of the world.

After a less than tranquil voyage, the missionaries landed safely on Tahiti on Saturday, March 4, 1797, and on the following day they conducted a European-style church service, viewed with more than passing interest by the islanders. With the Sabbath behind them, the missionaries wasted no time getting settled, and within a matter of weeks Captain Wilson, himself a Christian, felt they were secure enough to be left on their own. He then proceeded to Tonga to establish ten missionaries on that island. The atmosphere at Tonga was less inviting than that of Tahiti; the friendly curiosity at Tahiti was not to be found on Tonga, and Wilson left the missionaries with mixed emotions. But his job as a missionary chauffeur was still not finished; he had two remaining missionaries, William Crook and John Harris, to drop off on the Marquesas.

It was on the islands of the Marquesas that the LMS encountered its first of many setbacks in the Pacific islands. Here the problem was an unexpected one. The missionaries confronted not the terrifying reception of spears and clubs, the dreaded and all too real vision of their nightmares, but a too friendly welcome—one their missionary orientation had not prepared them for. Hardly had the ship anchored when two beautiful unclad native women swam out into the surf and around the ship shouting "Waheine! Waheine!" (We are women.) Although Wilson refused to let them board the ship and tried to discount their behavior, he, a seasoned sailor, could not have been oblivious to what was ahead for his two rookie missionaries. Nevertheless, Crook and Harris had a job to do, and they dutifully loaded their belongings into a small boat and paddled to shore.

The following morning before lifting anchor, Wilson sent crewmen ashore to check on the missionaries. There on the beach they found Harris with his belongings, discouraged and very anxious to leave. It seems he had endured a most humiliating night. After being separated from Crook, he was left alone in the company of the chief's wife, who proceeded to make indecent advances toward him. Having encountered white men before, she no doubt believed such behavior would be well received, but she could not have been more mistaken. Harris's contemptuous rebuffs so shocked her that she began to question if he were truly of the male gender. Leaving him alone, she went back to the village and, according to Graeme Kent, returned "accompanied by other women" and "swooped on the sleeping man and conducted a practical examination in order to clear up the matter."[6] So distraught was Harris by the ordeal that he absolutely refused to remain on the island, so the crewmen brought him back to the ship, leaving Crook to establish the work on the Marquesas. But before the year had ended, he, too, had given up, and the LMS was left with only two outposts in the South Pacific, Tahiti and Tonga.

On Tonga, the missionaries faced entirely different problems. It did not take them long to discover they were not the only Europeans on the island. Sailors who had deserted their ships sometimes made the islands their home, and Tonga had three such beachcombers in residence. From the very beginning they were a "thorn in the flesh" to the missionaries, seemingly going to any length to make life miserable for them. They viewed the missionaries as a threat to their easygoing lifestyle, and thus they sought to incite the natives against them. But physical danger was not their only ploy. They also tried to break down the missionaries psychologically and spiritually, taunting them with their free and easy access to sexual pleasures and mocking the missionaries' strait-laced celibate existence. Despite the pressure, the missionaries held firm in their convictions—all except one, George Veeson, a bricklayer, who only a year before had dedicated himself, along with his twenty-nine colleagues, to the Lord's service. But he weakened in the face of temptation and left his brethren to join the beachcombers in their loose living among the natives. The chief gave him land and servants, and he took for himself a harem of "wives."

The disgrace caused by Veeson was a deep humiliation for the LMS, but there were even greater problems facing the missionaries on Tonga. Civil war had erupted on the island, and the fighting was playing havoc with all attempts to coordinate missionary work. Three missionaries, caught in the middle of the warring factions, lost their lives, and the surviving six hid in caves until they were rescued by a passing ship. Only the renegade missionary, Veeson, remained, and even his days on the island were numbered. His conscience, though temporarily seared, prevented him from enjoying his promiscuous lifestyle, and he returned to England a repentant man and publicly confessed his sin, assuring his supporters that his experience was an isolated incident: "Considering all the obstacles, it must be a great satisfaction to the promoters of the South Sea Mission . . . that no other of the missionaries . . . acted unbecoming their sacred character"[7] (an assumption that, unfortunately, was untrue). Though abandoned for a time, Tonga was again visited by missionaries in the 1820s—this time by Wesleyan Methodists. The most notable of their number was John Thomas, a blacksmith, who witnessed encouraging progress during his twenty-five-year tenure on that island.

Meanwhile, the LMS work on Tahiti had been slowly moving ahead despite numerous setbacks there. Three of the missionaries, like Veeson, had "gone native," and others had left, discouraged and ill. But for the perseverance of a stubborn, uneducated bricklayer, Henry Nott (who worked for sixteen years without any visible signs of success), the work there would no doubt have been abandoned. Nott was born in Broomsgrove, England, in 1774, and at the age of twenty-two sailed aboard the *Duff* as a single missionary, determined to invest his life in the evangelization of the Pacific islanders. At first he was only one of many missionaries struggling to make even the slightest impact on the hearts and minds of the people. But as dangers and problems multiplied, other missionaries gave up (eleven departing at one time), and Nott found himself left with only three others, and even they spoke of going home. Times were hard for the missionaries. In 1808 their house and printing press were destroyed and most of their belongings were stolen. And to make matters worse there was virtually no contact from the outside world. The *Duff* was captured by the French during the Napoleonic wars, and thus more than four years elapsed during which the missionaries received no news or supplies from home. Their clothing became torn and ragged, and their shoes wore through to the soles of their feet. And with their food supply depleted, they were forced to forage in the mountains for wild berries and fruits. Nevertheless, Nott shunned any talk of retreat.

From the very beginning, the Tahitian missionaries had to contend with the hedonistic and authoritarian king, Pomare. He had a reputation for brutality which was fostered in part by his record of offering some two thousand human sacrifices. Though he represented heathendom at its worst, the missionaries needed him as an ally and they sought to win his friendship. At times he responded favorably, but on other occasions he treated them as enemies. When he died in 1804, his son, Pomare II, came to power, and for

a time the missionaries feared he would be worse than his father. Soon Pomare II, however, began to view the missionaries as potential sources for European goods, particularly muskets and ammunition; and apparently to gain their confidence he made a profession of Christianity, which was dubious at best. He pleaded for weapons to put down rebel forces, a request which first made the missionaries wary. But with increased rebel threats on their own lives they gave in and decided to supply Pomare and his professing Christian followers with guns and ammunition. How could such involvement be justified by missionaries? To them it was a pragmatic move, a move that their very survival depended on. According to a native observer, the rebels would have won, "had not the native missionaries been taught to shoot as they have been taught to pray, and been given guns along with Bibles."[8]

During the rebellion the missionaries all fled Tahiti, except for Nott. He bravely held his post, refusing to leave the island, weakening only once when he journeyed briefly to Australia to claim a special delivery from the LMS. She was one of four "godly young women" who had been sent out as wives for the lay missionaries. (No doubt the LMS had come to realize that the Pacific islands were not a conducive atmosphere for single men.) Nott, as with a number of other single missionaries, had taken a native wife, but bowing to the objections of his fellow missionaries, the union was apparently "annulled by common consent, and no doubt conveniently forgotten when the four 'godly young women' arrived by special shipment."[9]

Nott may have been far happier and more compatible with his native wife than the "godly woman" that was sent to him. Though described physically as having a "perfect curvature," she received less favorable reviews in regard to her temperament. A fellow missionary wrote: "Her Tong is daily employed in abusing her Husband in the most cruel manner and to slander others with the lest [sic] just cause. . . . Her Feet of late are never directed to the place where prayer is wont to be made but daily she joines with those who are studious in their design to perplex and thwart us."[10] She was generally regarded as a disgrace to the mission. Dr. Ross, an LMS missionary, lamented her drinking problem and claimed that "when intoxicated she is absolutely mad and cares not what she does or says." It was his opinion when she died some months later that she "drank herself to death."[11]

After the rebellion was over, Nott continued his forthright evangelism, ever pleading with Pomare to forsake his sinful ways. Pomare was not only a drunkard and polygamist but also a homosexual, and he seemingly had little intention of letting his professed Christianity interfere with such activities. Nevertheless, his final victory over the rebels in 1815 did signal a breakthrough for Christianity on the island. Pomare publicly denounced the heathen idols and altars, and to demonstrate his sincerity he gathered up his twelve personal idols and presented them to the missionaries (no doubt in response to their own prompting) to be shipped to London and delivered to the LMS directors as evidence of what was taking place on Tahiti. The discarded idols made a great sensation in England where spe-cial prayer meetings had been held to pray for Pomare's conversion. They were just the curios the LMS needed to reestablish its reputation in the South Seas, and contributions began pouring in.

For Pomare, though, the renunciation of his idols was not enough. He wanted full status as a professing Christian, and that included water baptism, a request that posed a real dilemma to the missionaries. His baptism, they believed, would influence hundreds, perhaps thousands, to turn to Christianity, but would the act be a mockery, considering his continued lapses into immorality? It was a difficult decision, but finally after prolonged discussion and prayer they decided there was more to gain than to lose from his baptism, though they managed to delay the act for seven years. When it finally did occur in 1819, it was a momentous occasion with some five thousand people looking on, and it paved the way for many of Pomare's subjects to make their faith public. Although Pomare himself had soon backslidden into his old sinful pleasures, great changes took place among the Tahitian natives. A visiting Russian nobleman was amazed by the absence of infanticide, cannibalism, and war—a tremendous credit to the European missionaries.

Elsewhere in the South Pacific, the progress of missions during the early decades of the nineteenth century was laboriously slow. Other islands besides Tahiti were being evangelized, but for every apparent victory there seemed to be a comparable setback. Only in Hawaii, far to the north, was there marked evidence of God's working in the hearts of men.

Hiram Bingham and
Hawaiian Missions

The story of Christian missions in Hawaii (or the Sandwich Islands, as they were then called) is a unique account of how a handful of American missionaries moved into an unfamiliar culture and within a few short decades dominated every facet of society. It is an intriguing tale of struggle and interpersonal conflict, so fascinating that in recent years it became the subject matter for one of James Michener's best-selling novels, *Hawaii*, a novel that has unfortunately misrepresented Christian missions in Hawaii. Michener's ranting, bigoted missionary, bent on destroying the native culture, is not typical of missionaries sent to Hawaii. True, they were tainted by the pervasive nineteenth century sentiments of racial superiority, but their genuine concern for the well-being of the Hawaiians was their overriding sentiment.

The Hawaiian Islands are believed to have become inhabited around A.D. 900. As with most of the islands of the South Seas, cannibalism and infanticide were commonplace, and spirit worship was the universal religion. It was not until 1778 that Hawaii became known to the western world, and then only by accident. Captain James Cook was sailing from Tahiti to the west coast of North America when he discovered this island paradise. During his first visit he was thought to be a god by the Hawaiians, but on his second visit in 1779 their reverence for him began to wane; and during a quarrel with one of the chiefs, Cook was killed. Despite this incident, contact with Hawaii continued, and the breach was soon mended. In the decades that followed trade was established with the western world, and the islands became a favorite stopover for ships trading in the Far East. During these layovers, native boys were sometimes invited to sail with the crew, and some of the Hawaiian youths found their way to the United States.

It was this contact with the native Hawaiians that sparked American interest in Hawaiian missions. The best known of these youths was Obookiah, who was found crying one morning on the steps of Yale College because of his unfulfilled desire for learning. Edwin Dwight, a student, had compassion on him and began tutoring him and also explaining the gospel to him, hoping that one day Obookiah could return to Hawaii and evangelize his people. Dwight's hopes soared when Obookiah made a profession of faith, but the dream of seeing him return to his own people was dashed when Obookiah became ill and died during the winter of 1818. Interestingly, he stirred more hearts in death than he had in life, and scores of New Englanders turned their attention to bringing the gospel to Hawaii.

It was the American Board that took the initiative in starting a work in Hawaii. Within a year after Obookiah's death, the Board had a contingent of missionaries and Christian workers ready to sail to Hawaii. Perhaps fearing the enthusiasm might die down, the directors moved with a sense of urgency. Potential candidates were contacted and interviewed in record time, and on acceptance by the Board they were urged to secure wives and prepare to leave as soon as possible. They were no doubt aware of the problems single missionaries faced in the South Seas. Of the seven couples who

Hiram Bingham, missionary to Hawaii.

left for Hawaii in October of 1819, six of them were married within a matter of weeks before departure.

During the five-month voyage, Hiram Bingham, a graduate of Andover Seminary, assumed the leadership of the little band. He and Sybil had been married less than two weeks before sailing, and exactly two weeks after they first met. Fortunately, they were well suited for each other, and their leadership held the sometimes faltering missionaries together. On arriving in Hawaii the New Englanders, wholly unprepared for what lay ahead, were shocked by what they found, as is evident from Bingham's telling description of their first encounter with Hawaiian civilization: "The appearance of destitution, degradation, and barbarism among the chattering and almost naked savages ... was appalling. Some of our number, with gushing tears, turned away from the spectacle. Others with firmer nerve continued

their gaze, but were ready to exclaim, 'Can these be human beings? ... Can such things be civilized? Can they be Christianized? Can we throw ourselves upon these rude shores, and take up our abode for life among such people, for the purpose of training them for Heaven?'"[12]

Whether the Hawaiians made any adverse observations about their priggish New England visitors is unknown, but at least they had the courtesy to warmly welcome them, "far more courtesy," according to one historian, "than they deserved."[13] Fortunately for the missionaries, the timing of their visit was perfect—an unexplainable "coincidence" apart from the providence of God. A tremendous change had recently occurred in their society, since the new king had come to power. Idolatry and human sacrifice had been outlawed, and the long history of tribal warfare seemed to be over. The missionaries were given permission to go ashore and to begin their work as Christian missionaries.

The task that lay ahead for the missionaries was a mighty challenge, especially if they hoped to fulfill the assignment they had received from the Board: "You are to open your hearts wide and set your marks high. You are to aim at nothing short of covering these islands with fruitful fields, and pleasant dwellings and schools and churches, and of raising up the whole people to an elevated state of Christian civilization...."[14] A "state of Christian civilization" naturally meant civilization New England style, far removed from the easygoing lifestyle of the Hawaiians. Not surprisingly there was resistance, or if not resistance, at least a complete lack of understanding of the Puritan moral code that the missionaries brought with them. The work ethic, particularly, was a stumbling block for many of the new Christians.

The real resistance the missionaries confronted (as was the case in the South Pacific) came from their own people—sailors who were infuriated by the missionaries' interference in the native lifestyle, which encouraged young women to go on board the trading vessels and sell themselves for a few cheap trinkets. As the missionaries' influence increased, the practice declined, and more than once Bingham and his fellow workers faced the wrath of those to whom sexual favors had been denied. In one incident, sailors from the *Dolphin* came ashore and attacked Bingham with knives and clubs and would have no doubt killed him but for a harried rescue by faithful Hawaiians.

Despite the opposition, the progress of missions in Hawaii moved with amazing speed. Churches and schools were established, and soon they were overflowing with eager students anxious to hear more of Christianity and to learn to read. One of these schools, organized by Sybil Bingham, enrolled several of the female chiefs, and soon there were professions of faith, one of the first being the king's mother, who was baptized in 1823. Perhaps the most dramatic conversion was that of Kapiolani, a chieftainess who like many Hawaiians had lived in dread fear of the goddess Pele who, according to tradition, resided in the fuming volcanic crater of Kilauea. After turning to Christ, Kapiolani, in front of hundreds of horrified onlookers, flaunted Pele by climbing up the volcanic mountain and descending into the crater to demonstrate the impotence of this false god. In bold defiance Kapiolani cast rocks and "sacred" berries into the lake of lava as she ridiculed the superstition of the people. Then, returning to the bystanders, she testified to the power of Jehovah. It was a dramatic incident that did more to pave the way for Christianity in Hawaii than all the missionary diatribes against Pele put together.

By 1830, after only a decade in Hawaii (and after a second contingent of missionaries had arrived), the missionaries had spread out to all the islands. Bingham was held in high esteem, and many chiefs looked to him as far more than just their spiritual leader. According to one cynic, they even let "King Bingham" tell them what law to make. "The blue laws of Connecticut are the laws of Hawaii," wrote another critic.[15]

But all the laws of New England put together could not overcome the centuries of moral laxity that characterized the islands. It was a most frustrating situation, according to Bradford Smith, particularly in dealing with sexual sins: "Patiently the brethren tried to explain the seventh commandment. But in rendering it into Hawaiian they learned to their horror that there were about twenty ways of committing adultery Hawaiian-style. If they used any one of the twenty names, that left all the other avenues to pleasure wide open. They ended up with the vague phrase, 'thou shalt not sleep mischievously,' thus making the whole thing a state of mind."[16]

Even the most faithful Hawaiian Christians had problems with sexual immorality. In summing up the situation, missionary teacher Lorrin Andrews wrote that "adultery has been the crying sin of native teachers. . . ." And another missionary wrote, "Most teachers have lain with many or all of their scholars." The missionaries had believed they were aiding the cause of morality when they insisted converts wear clothes, "only to discover," according to Smith, "that the clothes the girls put on became a source of allurement to men who all their lives had taken nudity for granted!"[17]

The missionaries themselves, unlike some of their brethren in the South Pacific, managed to stay above the lax moral environment in which they lived, but they did face other temptations, particularly in the area of materialism. Some of the missionaries were accused of marketing goods in competition with the foreign merchants and traders. Artemas Bishop, for example, was employing natives to manufacture cigars in exchange for educational materials, while he was using the proceeds to build himself a home. Another missionary, Joseph Goodrich, acquired a sugar cane plantation and built his own sugar mill, and still another was raising coffee beans.

Such commercial activity was clearly not sanctioned by the American Board, and a hot debate over this issue and others raged between some of the missionaries and the directors. Writing home to his father, Lorrin Andrews castigated his superiors: "Are we to be made slaves of? . . . You are now paying your money to the A.B.C.F.M. to keep your son in bondage to the Prudential Committee."[18] Andrews and others wanted freedom from what they described as dictatorial control. Ironically, the economic situation in America gave them just that. Hard times caused by the Panic of 1837 forced the Board to cut back its support, and the missionaries had little choice but to diversify and to earn their own support.

Amid all of the problems of morality and materialism and the controversy between the missionaries and the directors, evangelistic work continued with surprising success. By 1837 the missionary force numbered sixty, the majority of whom were hard-working, dedicated, spiritually-minded servants of God. For nearly twenty years they had been meticulously laying the groundwork for a solid Christian church in Hawaii, and with that work accomplished, a spiritual awakening took place. Revival swept through the islands, particularly in the wake of Titus Coan's itinerant evangelistic ministry. Unlike some of his staunch New England brethren, he was not afraid of emotionalism and welcomed "the gushing tear, the quivering lip, the deep sigh, and the heavy groan."[19] Coan preached as many as thirty sermons a week as he traveled, and thousands professed salvation in Christ. Churches grew rapidly, some reaching a membership of two or three thousand and more. More than twenty thousand Hawaiians were accepted into church membership during the revival, boosting the church roles almost twenty-fold.

By 1840, after twenty years of missionary work, the New England missionaries could look back with a real sense of accomplishment, but problems lay ahead. Their strict puritanical churches were being undermined by the influx of Roman Catholic priests whose methods, according to Bradford Smith, had more appeal. "Instead of asking for contributions, Catholic priests were giving presents, especially to children who were brought to be baptized. They held short services with no sermons, had no objections to smoking or drinking, promised indulgence to the sinners and willingly received any to membership. Instead of building good Yankee houses they adopted the Hawaiian style of living."[20] Many of the Hawaiians who had flocked to hear Coan now turned to the less demanding Roman Catholics, and in less than a decade evangelical Christianity was on the decline.

The ministry of Roman Catholics in certain instances was characterized more by sacrificial love than was the ministry of the Protestants. One striking example is that of Father Damien, a Belgian priest who, in 1873, volunteered to work on Molokai, a desolate, rocky, barren island inhabited only by the leprous refuse of the other islands. On his arrival he immediately set up social programs and began an intensive evangelistic outreach. So successful was he that news of his work was carried all over the world, and financial assistance and supplies began pouring in. After more than a decade of tireless work, however, he realized that he himself had contracted leprosy. For four more years he continued his labor of love, now able to totally identify with those around him in the world of the "living dead." When he died in 1889 at the age of forty-nine his work was world famous.

Besides the influx of Roman Catholics, the departure of the Binghams (who returned permanently to the United States due to Sybil's ill health) contributed to the decline of Protestant missions. The most serious impediment to a vigorous missionary enterprise, however, was an ever increasing drift toward materialism among the missionaries. Several missionaries had left their calling for dreams of land and wealth, and many of those who remained were charged with land grabbing and were too involved in "moonlighting" to give themselves wholly to the work. Many of the missionary children remained in Hawaii, but not to serve with the mission. Instead they held high political positions or became wealthy landowners. All this brought Hawaii into a close political relationship with the United States, but at the same time adversely affected the church. By the turn of the century the once vibrant Christian church that had numbered well over twenty thousand had dropped to less than five thousand. The missionaries had succeeded in their commission to bring "civilization" to Hawaii, but the more difficult assignment of making that civilization "Christian" had slipped through their fingers.

John Williams

One of the most innovative and far-sighted missionaries to the Pacific islands was John Williams, sometimes referred to as the "Apostle of the South Seas" or the "Apostle of Polynesia" because of his widespread influence in missions in that part of the world. He was born in England in 1796, the year the *Duff* was dispatched to the South Pacific by the London Missionary Society. Williams grew up in a working class district of Tottenham, England, and at the age of fourteen was apprenticed to an ironmonger with the agreement that he would live in his master's home for seven years while he learned the trade. During this time Williams fell in with a rowdy gang of youths and turned away from the spiritual training of his childhood, but not without rousing the concern of his master's wife. One January night in 1814 while he was waiting on a street corner for his companions, she deliberately went out of her way and exhorted him to come with her to church instead of partying with his friends. He reluctantly agreed, and that night in the Old Whitefield Tabernacle his life was irrevocably changed. From that time on his leisure hours were spent for the Lord—teaching Sunday school, distributing tracts, and visiting the sick.

The pastor of the Tabernacle Church, Matthew Wilkes, took a keen interest in Williams and invited him to join a special class for young men interested in entering the ministry. Soon Wilkes's passion for foreign missions began to rub off on his young disciple, and through his encouragement Williams applied to the LMS. Although he was only twenty years old and had no formal Bible or missionary training, he was accepted as a candidate. There was an urgent need for reinforcements in the South Pacific, and thus the society was not inclined to turn down eager recruits. During the weeks before his departure Williams continued his informal study with his pastor, and also found time to squeeze in a hastily planned marriage to Mary Chawner.

On arriving in the South Pacific, Williams, his wife, and several other missionaries took residence on Moorea, a small island near Tahiti, but their stay there lasted less than a year. In 1718 they moved further west to another small island where they spent three months before finally settling on the island of Raiatea, Williams's base for the next thirteen years. Although

Raiatea was a small island with a population of less than two thousand, it held great significance for the Polynesians because it was the home of the Polynesian god, Oro, whose shrine was a center of human sacrifice. Williams and his family were warmly welcomed by the natives, but behind the cordial façade was a cultural heritage that placed little value on human life. Besides human sacrifice and the all-too-common practice of infanticide (usually burying the little one alive), the natives seemed almost oblivious to any type of moral code. According to Williams, "men and women, boys and girls, completely naked, bathe together in one place, without shame and with much lasciviousness.... Promiscuous intercourse is as common, also, as it is abhorrent. When a husband is ill, the wife seeks his brother and when the wife is ill, the husband does the same.... When we tell them of the necessity of working they laugh at us...."[21]

How to approach these people was Williams's first challenge. How could Christianity ever reach the hearts of people within such a culture? He was not trained in cross-cultural evangelism, so his first priority was to change the culture. He had come not just to bring Christianity but to bring civilization, Western civilization, which he viewed as a prerequisite to church planting and a significant aspect of the missionary's divine commission: "For the missionary does not go to barbarise himself, but to elevate the heathen; not to sink himself to their standard, but to raise them to his." To demonstrate the superiority of Western civilization, Williams erected a large seven-room house with a verandah overlooking the water and land-scaped gardens on all sides. His skill and industry apparently impressed the natives, for soon, on his urging, they were following his example: "Many have built themselves very neat little houses and are now living in them with their wives and families. The king, through seeing ours and by our advice, has a house erected near to us. . . . Perhaps the advocates of *civilisation* would not be less pleased than the friends of *evangelisation*, could they look upon these remote shores and upon a portion of natives diligently employed in various useful arts."[22]

Fortunately, Williams's emphasis on civilization did not diminish his zeal for evangelism. Despite all his secular activities, he conducted five services on Sunday and others during the week, and personal evangelism was a regular part of his daily routine. The bulk of missionary work, however, he assigned to native converts, who he believed could reach their own far more effectively than he could.

From his first months in the South Seas, Williams had felt confined by the small populations of the individual islands and the inability to travel freely from island to island. Commercial vessels visited the islands on occasion, but their irregularity made any hope of planned travel impossible. The obvious solution to the problem, at least from Williams's perspective, was for the mission to have a ship of its own. He was not the first to come to this conclusion. A few years earlier missionaries on Tahiti, with the help of Pomare, had constructed a trading vessel for the purpose of transporting products from their sugar and cotton mills, but the entire undertaking

ended in failure. Other missionaries had tried to construct vessels, only to discover the task was more complex than they had anticipated. One such abandoned project was just the enticement that Williams (an ironmonger by trade) needed to fulfill his dream of moving freely from island to island. He recruited the help of other missionaries, and soon the ship was ready for launching, a day that called for celebration among the missionaries.

Perhaps not unexpectedly, the joyous celebration of the missionaries was not shared by the mission directors back home. Viewing the situation from a distance, they failed to recognize the necessity of better transportation and communication for the island missionaries. They vetoed the course of action the missionaries had taken and resolved that "the Society cannot allow itself to enter into any engagement with regard to ownership or employment of the vessel. . . ." With this, the battle lines were drawn. While some missionaries were willing to accept the verdict of the directors, Williams was not; and the years that followed were tainted by conflict— sometimes heated and bitter—as Williams, in flagrant violation of the directors' mandate continued his nautical activity. The first vessel that Williams had helped salvage was disposed of, but in 1821 on a visit to Sydney, Williams solicited funds from businessmen and contributed money of his own to purchase the *Endeavour* in order to expand the evangelistic work of the mission as well as transport native goods to market. Needless to say, the directors were furious when they received the news, even though Williams had already turned a profit of some 1800 British pounds through his commercial ventures. They viewed the purchase as a "great evil" and accused Williams of "engaging in . . . commercial transactions" which were "calculated to divert . . . attention from the great object of their mission."[23]

How such a difference of opinion could persist and Williams remain in the mission can be explained only by the slow communications between England and the South Pacific. By the time the directors' mandates reached him, the situation had usually changed, and their stinging rebukes no longer applied to the current situation. His commercial ventures had dwindled after heavy custom duties were imposed by New South Wales, and so, in response to the directors' indignation, he promised to "avoid any and every future entanglement of every kind." But that was not to imply that he was backing down on his basic premise that a ship was indispensable to the evangelization of the islands. He was determined that he would have his way or he would leave the islands: "A missionary was never designed by Jesus to get a congregation of a hundred or two natives and sit down at ease as contented as if every sinner was converted, while thousands around him are eating each other's flesh and drinking each other's blood with a savage delight. . . . For my own part I cannot content myself within the narrow limits of a single reef and if means is not afforded, a continent to me would be infinitely preferable, for there if you cannot ride, you can walk."[24]

Partly due to financial problems, Williams reluctantly agreed to give up the *Endeavour*, but not without the suggestion that the directors themselves may have been the devil's tools in staying the progress of evangelism in the islands: "Satan knows full well that this ship was the most fatal weapon ever formed against his interests in the great South Sea; and therefore, as soon as he felt the effects of the first blow, he has wrested it out of our hands."[25]

Without ready access to a vessel, Williams's travel to other islands was curtailed, and he spent the next years building up the believers on the island of Raiatea and translating Scripture. Still he was frustrated by his confinement and the lack of additional reinforcements coming out from England. Evangelism of the South Seas was progressing too slowly. The LMS strategy simply was not getting the job done. Someone had to come to the rescue with forceful leadership, and Williams saw himself as that one. His firsthand experience convinced him that he knew better than the directors how to carry out the evangelism of the South Seas, which he maintained must involve extensive use of native missionaries. His plan was to commission and transport native missionaries to the various islands and then periodically visit them and guide them in their ministry.

Williams's plan would obviously require a ship and would once again put him in an adversary relationship with the mission directors; but despite the consequences he began constructing a ship, and after only a matter of months, the fifty-ton *Messenger of Peace*, a curious-looking craft, was ready for sailing and Williams was ready to begin his Polynesian itinerant ministry. By the time the directors received the news, the plan was already in operation, and there was little they could do so many thousands of miles away.

Once again Williams had flouted the will of the directors—in one sense, indefensible behavior, but in another sense, visionary action. Was he wrong? Should his actions be condemned or praised? To see only his defiance of the directors in this situation without seeing Williams's tremendous burden for evangelism would be a disservice to a great missionary. He had sacrificed too much for the cause of missions to be held back from his goal. His health and that of his wife had been severely weakened, and seven of his ten children had died in infancy. There was too much at stake to relinquish his dream.

As Williams sought to renovate the LMS missionary work in the South Seas, he met with opposition from many of his fellow missionaries. Many were critical of him because he refused to settle down; he moved on before the work was established or before problems were settled. But as one historian has commented, "He had never made a secret of the fact that he regarded himself as a planter, not a cultivator." While many missionaries were grateful for the increased communication and freedom the *Messenger of Peace* brought, others resented the implied power and prominence Williams was gaining over the mission work. The directors, too, feared the consequences of his growing influence and prestige: "Take care that you give the glory to God—take care that you appropriate none of it to yourself—instead of yielding to the temptation ... to become high-minded...." Williams was stung by the implied rebuke, as his response indicates: "The calculating suspicious spirit evident in your letter I am not aware of having merited at your hands. Letters written in such a strain produce in our minds feelings and sentiments toward the Directors of the Society that I never wish to cherish."[26]

Despite continued hard feelings toward the directors and frequent setbacks in the ministry, Williams's basic plan moved forward with great success. Under his supervision, evangelism was carried out almost entirely by native teachers, most of whom had very limited training and very little Christian maturity to face the obstacles before them. Nevertheless, they courageously left their homes and tribal security and entered into strange surroundings and learned unfamiliar languages, risking their lives to bring the gospel to their fellow islanders. In the words of Stephen Neill, "But few marvels in Christian history can equal the faithfulness of these men and women, left behind among peoples of unknown speech and often in danger of their lives, to plant and build Churches out of their own limited stock of faith and knowledge, supported only by the invigorating power of the Holy Spirit and the prayers of their friends. Many watered the seed with their own blood; but the Churches grew, and far more widely than if reliance had been placed first and foremost on the European missionary."[27]

By 1834, after nearly eighteen years in the South Pacific, Williams's work and the work of others had expanded to the point that he was able to announce that "no group of islanders, nor single island of importance, within 2000 miles of Tahiti had been left unvisited." It was a tremendous accomplishment but it was only a beginning.

More funding and reinforcements were needed from home, and Williams knew that the only way to obtain the help he needed was to return home and make an appeal in person.

Arriving with his family in England in the summer of 1834, the thirty-eight-year-old Williams found that his reputation had preceded him. The Archbishop of Canterbury had proclaimed that his ministry was adding a new chapter to the Book of Acts, and others, too, had been lavish in their praise. In person, he was an overnight sensation. People flocked to hear the exotic tales of the Pacific islanders and the danger-filled life of a missionary. Williams played to their fancy, sometimes parading about in native costume, but sometimes with less than his hoped-for response. After one service he lamented, "I tried to work on their sympathies by giving them affecting accounts of heathen cruelties and wrung tears from their eyes, but only four pounds from their pockets. They are a cold-blooded lot."[28]

While Williams's meetings aroused lively interest and were generally very well attended, it was his book, *A Narrative of Missionary Enterprises in the South Seas*, that stimulated the solid financial support his work needed. Copies were sent to wealthy and influential individuals, several of whom responded with substantial gifts—gifts that would be used to purchase another mission ship for the South Seas. This time the directors did not object. They were grateful for the unexpected influence their star missionary was having with prominent individuals, and they clearly did not want to discourage the enthusiasm he had created in the LMS missionary work in the islands. The

Camden (twice the size of the *Messenger of Peace*) was purchased in the spring of 1838, and, after nearly four years of furlough, Williams was ready to sail with his family and new recruits (including his son and new daughter-in-law) back to his home in the Pacific. It was a rousing send-off, and, as usual, the speeches were laced with hyperbole. He was being hailed by some as the greatest missionary statesman of the day. With the finances he needed, what could prevent him from conquering all of Oceania for Christ? He was the man of the hour. But could he ever live up to their expectations?

Back in the South Pacific, Williams quickly jumped into the work, visiting island stations and reinforcing the work of native missionaries, but disappointment met him on every hand. According to one historian, Williams "found that in spite of the glowing reports still being returned to Britain by LMS missionaries, matters had gone from bad to worse.... The islanders were turning away from Christianity, disillusioned and tired of the constant demands of the missionaries." There were problems, too, between the missionaries themselves, especially between the LMS missionaries and the Wesleyan Methodists. And even worse in Williams's eyes, the Roman Catholics were making "a most desperate effort to establish Popery in the islands."[29]

It was a time when Williams's recognized authority and years of experience were desperately needed to help stabilize the situation and restore continuity to the scattered islands he had opened to Christianity. But Williams was basically more of a salesman than a repairman, and the unreached islands to the west were beckoning him. For years he had dreamed of expanding westward as far as the New Hebrides, and now, with the acquisition of the *Camden*, there was nothing, besides the reported savagery of the natives, standing in his way. He had risked his life before as a missionary pioneer, and he was ready and willing to do so again, despite his wife's objections.

In early November of 1839, after saying good-by to his wife and family, Williams, along with several native missionary volunteers, boarded the *Camden* and set sail for the island of Erromango in the New Hebrides. Little was known of the people of these islands except that they had viciously attacked European traders who had mercilessly exploited their precious sandalwood trees.

After a two-week voyage the *Camden* reached Erromango. Natives soon appeared on the shoreline and waded into the bay to receive gifts from their visitors who had come near shore in a small boat. After the initial encounter, Williams and two other European missionaries went ashore and began walking with the natives to their village. Suddenly, without any provocation, the attack came. Williams had time to turn and make a dash for the beach, but he was clubbed to death in the water as he tried to outswim his assailants. One of the missionaries made it safely to the boat, and he and Captain Morgan rowed back to the *Camden*. Unable to go ashore to recover the bodies, Morgan sailed for Sydney to secure help. Two months later they returned and, after negotiating with the natives, were given the bones of Williams and his comrade, the flesh of which had been eaten by the natives.

The tragic death of Williams was in many ways a baffling enigma to his colleagues and friends. Knowing the treachery of the natives, especially in the wake of the sandalwood traders, why did he not send native missionaries ashore first as was generally the practice? (Their presence was far less threatening than that of Europeans, who would naturally be associated with the traders.) Likewise, why did Williams not sense danger when he saw no women present? As a seasoned South Seas missionary he certainly was aware that such a situation signaled impending peril. Why did he seem to blatantly ignore obvious precautions? Having just come down from a mountain peak of praise and adulation back home in England, Williams may have been dispirited by the dull routine of missionary work. He was a courageous hero in the minds of his supporters. He had an illustrious reputation to uphold, and perhaps for a fleeting moment he lost himself in fanciful visions of his own invincibility.

John G. Paton

The international publicity surrounding the tragic news of the death of John Williams sent a shock wave through the Christian church, particularly in the British Isles, where dozens of young men vowed to take his place. The Presbyterians, represented by John Geddie, were the first Protestants with staying power to enter the New Hebrides in the years following the Williams's tragedy. Geddie, described as a "tough, humorless, single-minded and incredibly brave" missionary, had been intrigued by the accounts of missionary heroism in the South Seas since his early childhood in Nova Scotia. In 1848 he and his wife sailed for Aneityum, the most southerly of the islands of the New Hebrides, and there they spent their lives translating Scripture, conducting evangelism, and training native workers. So effective were they in their evangelistic work that virtually the entire population of the island turned to Christianity. An inscription commemorating Geddie in one of the churches he established underscored his powerful influence: "When he landed in 1848 there were no Christians here; when he left in 1872 there were no heathen."

Geddie's success stimulated more interest, and soon other Presbyterian missionaries began to arrive. One of these was John G. Paton, perhaps the best known of the South Seas missionaries, who became immortalized largely because of his own play-by-play coverage of natives clubbing missionaries, published in his widely-read, tension-filled autobiography. Paton, by his own account, tasted so many close calls at the hands of the natives that it was impossible to enumerate them all. Mere survival was a constant mental and physical strain, and staying alive was in itself an achievement worth noting.

John Paton was born in 1824 in Dunfries, Scotland, and grew up in a little three-room thatched-roof cottage where his father earned a living by knitting stockings. The family was poor, and before John reached the age of twelve he was forced to quit school and spend his days working alongside his father to help support the family. The Patons were staunch Presbyterians who centered their lives in their church activities, but it was not until he was seventeen that John was converted—a life-changing experience that set his sights on full-time Christian service.

Paton's first real taste of Christian service came during his early twenties when he became a missionary for the Glasgow City Mission, a position that paid two hundred dollars a year. Here he worked in the ghettos of Glasgow, where the impoverished industrial masses were spilling into the streets and where "sin and vice walked about openly and unashamed." It was a difficult assignment, but one that prepared him well for the trials he would one day face in the New Hebrides. There was violent opposition to his evangelistic street work, but Paton's philosophy did not allow for retreat: "Let them see that bullying makes you afraid, and they will brutally and cruelly misuse you, but defy them fearlessly, or take them by the nose, and they will crouch like whelps beneath your feet."[30]

After ten years of city mission work, Paton heard of the great need for missionaries in the South Pacific through his own church, the Reformed Presbyterian Church of Scotland. At first he was inclined to think he should stay at his post, knowing how much he was needed there; but he could not get the Pacific islanders out of his mind. Yet, he was needed at the city mission, and how would he ever break the news to the mission directors that he was leaving? On the other hand, how could he stay home in Scotland when thousands of islanders were going into eternity without ever hearing the name of Christ? It was a difficult decision, but once it was made, not even offers of a higher salary and a manse to live in could tempt him to stay with the city mission work. Nor could the voices of fear dissuade him. "You'll be eaten by cannibals," they warned. But Paton needed no reminder of the cannibals. The fate of the great John Williams was never far from his thoughts.

In the spring of 1858, after a three-month speaking tour in Presbyterian congregations, he was ready to go. Before leaving he attended to two final matters, his ordination and his marriage to Mary Ann Robson, and on April 16 set sail for the South Seas. On arriving in the New Hebrides, the Patons were immediately assigned to the island of Tanna, where they were almost overcome by a severe case of culture shock: "My first impressions drove me to the verge of utter dismay. On beholding these natives in their paint and nakedness and misery, my heart was as full of horror as of pity. . . . The women wore only a tiny apron of grass . . . the men an indescribable affair, like a pouch or bag, and the children absolutely nothing whatever!"[31]

As Paton became settled on Tanna it did not take him long to discover the harsh realities of the native lifestyle, and the problem of nakedness quickly paled by comparison. The natives were deeply involved in deadly and often subtle games of warfare among themselves. Killings occurred almost daily and were accepted as a routine part of life, with occasional violent eruptions that threatened the whole population. It was a tension-filled time with hardly a moment for relaxation. Complicating their situation were the ever-threatening bouts with tropical fever. Mary was plagued by illness more than her husband, and childbirth only made her condition worse. On March 3, 1859, she died of fever, and less than three weeks later their infant boy died also. It was a time of despair for Paton. Only one short year had passed since they had solemnly repeated their wedding vows, and now it was over. It was almost too much to bear: "But for Jesus . . . I must have gone mad and died beside that lonely grave."[32]

The first years of Paton's missionary service saw very little progress in establishing Christianity among the people of Tanna, and what was accomplished was largely a result of the efforts of the native teachers who had come from Aneityum where John Geddie was serving. They not only effectively preached the gospel, but also lived the Christian life before their fellow islanders in a way that no European could do. This was particularly true in the area of family relationships, especially as it related to women. Women in the Tanna social structure were virtual slaves, often beaten by their husbands and sometimes even killed. The example set by the native teachers and the protection they offered to the Tanna women were not surprisingly a threat to the men. Violent attacks were made on Paton and the native teachers, and Namuri, one of Paton's most faithful assistants, was killed. Disease also took its toll on native teachers. When measles were brought to Tanna by European sailors, thirteen of the Aneityum teachers died, and the rest, except for one faithful couple, all left. So severe was the outbreak, according to Paton, that one third of the population of Tanna was wiped out.

By the summer of 1861, three years after Paton had arrived, the natives of Tanna were on the verge of civil war, and Paton himself was in the center of much of the conflict. At one point,

Paton and his one remaining Aneityum teacher locked themselves in a room for four days as natives waited outside to kill them. It was the coastal natives who despised Paton the most, and they were threatening all-out war against the inland tribes unless Paton left. Finally in mid-January of 1862 the daily outbreaks of violence turned into a full-scale civil war. Using his gun for protection, Paton made his escape from Tanna to a trading vessel, leaving all of his belongings behind.

On leaving Tanna, Paton went to Aneityum and then to Australia, where he immediately began a tour of Presbyterian churches, telling the people of the horrors he had endured in the New Hebrides. He was an effective speaker, and by the time his tour ended the offerings had netted him more than twenty-five thousand dollars to be used for the purchase of a mission ship, the *Dayspring*. In the spring of 1863 Paton sailed for the British Isles, where he continued his tour of Presbyterian churches, raising thousands more dollars for missions in the South Seas. While on tour, Paton remarried, and in late 1864 he and his bride, Margaret, sailed for Australia, where they boarded the *Dayspring* and went on to the New Hebrides.

Soon after he arrived in the islands Paton became embroiled in a controversy that nearly ruined his ministry and that of other missionaries in the South Seas. His own past experience with the islanders and the experience of other Europeans had convinced a bellicose British commodore to sail his man-of-war through the islands and punish the natives of Tanna by destroying some of their villages —particularly the coastal natives who

had so strongly opposed Paton. Paton later denied having "directed" the punishment, but he did accompany the expedition as an interpreter, thus making a direct link between missions and military action. Although the natives had been forewarned and there were few casualties, the incident, nevertheless, created a tremendous uproar. According to Paton, "The common witticism about 'Gospel and Gunpowder' headed hundreds of bitter and scoffing articles in the journals; and losing nothing in force, was cabled to Britain and America, where it was dished up day after day with every imaginable enhancement of horror for the readers of the secular and infidel press." Some of Paton's harshest critics, however, were not infidels, but his own colleagues. John Geddie, a fellow Presbyterian missionary, who was on furlough at the time, was incensed when he heard the news, and he blamed Paton for this incident. As a result of the incident, there was negative fallout for missions, how much is impossible to determine, but Paton himself complained that it made the "task of raising funds for our mission ship all the more difficult."[33]

Paton's second term in the New Hebrides was spent on the small island of Aniwa since Tanna was still considered unsafe for Europeans. Once again Paton was accompanied by teachers from Aneityum, and he and his wife soon settled down to their new mission post. Although Aniwa was considered more peaceful than Tanna, the Patons and their native teachers still faced hostile threats, but now Paton had a psychological (if not physical) weapon to use against them. He warned them "not to murder or steal, for the man-of-war that punished Tanna would blow up their little island."[34]

As the Patons continued their ministry on Aniwa in the decades that followed, they witnessed impressive results as Christianity found its way into the hearts of the people. With the help of native Christians they built two orphanages, established a thriving church, and set up schools—one a girls' school taught by Margaret. Paton, supported by converted chiefs, became a powerful political influence, and strait-laced puritanical laws became the standard by which all residents were to live. Crimes such as Sabbath breaking were not looked on lightly. In one instance, after a number of "heathen" were discovered fishing on the Sabbath, they were visited the following morning by Paton and eighty of his Christian followers and were quickly persuaded to mend their ways [35]

Although Paton's attitude toward the Pacific islanders often seemed harsh, he was wholly dedicated to the task of winning them to Christ, and he had a genuine love for them. Describing the first communion service he conducted on Aniwa, he wrote: "At the moment I put the bread and wine into those dark hands, once stained with the blood of cannibalism, now stretched out to receive and partake the emblems and seals of the Redeemer's love, I had a foretaste of the joy of Glory that well nigh broke my heart to pieces. I shall never taste a deeper bliss, till I gaze on the glorified face of Jesus himself."[36]

With the church on Aniwa well established, Paton spent the later years of his life as a missionary statesman, traveling in Australia, Great Britain, and North America, raising funds and

John G. Paton, pioneer missionary to the New Hebrides.

speaking out for the mission needs in the New Hebrides. Great progress was being made in those islands, due in part to his broad influence. By the end of the century all but a few of the thirty inhabited islands had been reached with the gospel. A school had been established to train native evangelists, who numbered more than three hundred, and some two dozen missionaries and their wives were serving with them.

Paton labored diligently to the very end, translating the Bible into the Aniwan language and speaking out for missions. At the age of seventy-three, while on a preaching tour, he wrote of his busy schedule: "I had three services yesterday, with driving twenty miles between; as I go along I am correcting proof sheets."[37] The Patons returned to the islands for a brief visit in 1904. The following year Margaret

217

died, and two years later she was joined by her eighty-three-year-old husband, leaving their work in the New Hebrides to be carried on by their son Frank.

James Chalmers

While Paton, Geddie, and others were evangelizing the small islands of the South Pacific, other missionaries were looking even further west, eyeing the unpenetrated mountainous rain forests of New Guinea. One of the greatest nineteenth-century missionaries to New Guinea was James Chalmers, another Scottish-born Presbyterian missionary, who, like so many other missionary pioneers in the South Seas, was martyred in his quest to bring Christianity to that region.

The son of a stonemason, Chalmers was awakened to the needs of South Seas missions as a teen-ager one Sunday afternoon in Sabbath school when his pastor read a moving letter from a missionary serving in Fiji. With tears in his eyes, the minister pleaded with the young people: "I wonder if there is a boy here who will by and by bring the Gospel to the cannibals." Chalmers vowed to be that one, but the vow was quickly forgotten until some three years later at the time of his conversion.[38]

In 1866, a decade after he made his initial vow to be a missionary, Chalmers and his young bride, Jane, sailed for the South Pacific under the auspices of the LMS. For ten years they worked on the island of Rarotonga, where John Williams had served for a time, but Chalmers was dissatisfied. He was a pioneer at heart, and he wanted to evangelize where the gospel had never been preached—where he would have "direct contact with the heathen." Others could carry out the work at Rarotonga. His heart was set on reaching the vast unexplored regions of New Guinea, where Rarotonga teachers had begun working in 1872.

In 1877 the Chalmers left the relative security of Rarotonga and took up residence in New Guinea in an area where Stone-Age cannibalism continued as it had for centuries, undisturbed by Western civilization. There were many obstacles facing Chalmers, not the least of which was the trail of blood left by missionaries to New Guinea who had preceded him. Only two years before his arrival, a Methodist missionary, Rev. George Brown, accompanied by a force of some sixty armed men, marched into the jungles in retaliation against Talili, a native chief who had ordered the killing of several of Brown's native Fiji teachers. For Brown it was a choice between giving up the mission work in New Guinea or teaching Talili a lesson he and other chiefs would never forget, and he opted for the latter. In the words of historian Graeme Kent, "It must have been a bizarre expedition, the men of God marching through the steaming undergrowth, burning villages in their path and destroying banana plantations thought to be the property of Talili and his followers." Talili managed to escape attack, but his followers surrendered, agreeing to compensate the missionaries by giving them certain valuable items as well as the bones of the murdered Fijian missionaries. Although Brown won an apparent victory in the jungles of New Guinea, his action generated a storm of controversy throughout the world, causing some to call for his arrest on manslaughter charges.[39]

From the very beginning, Chalmers's attitude toward the people of New Guinea was entirely different. He, too, was involved in a punitive expedition, one led by Commodore Wilson after eight native teachers were murdered; but his role was that of a peacemaker, reluctantly agreeing to go, hoping that his presence could help prevent bloodshed. Though not successful in his mission, his presence did prevent wholesale slaughter of the natives, which may have otherwise occurred.

Back at his own post, Chalmers conducted effective evangelistic work. He had a way with people that few other missionaries could match. Chalmers, known affectionately by the natives as "Tamate," was "the least conventional of missionaries, able to make friends with men of every type and to command their respect." He brought gifts to the people and freely accepted gifts from them. He gladly joined in their feasts, declining only when human flesh was being served. In an age when most missionaries were still wearing long black coats and top hats, he dressed casually and felt at ease with the native people. Although he was deficient in language skills, he made up for his weakness by a nonverbal communication of love. It was this attitude, according to Neill, that "won the heart of Robert Louis Stevenson, and turned him from a hater of missionaries into a steadfast supporter of their work—with reservations."[40]

Nevertheless, the Chalmers's work was not easy—especially for Jane. In 1879, only two years after coming to New Guinea, she sailed for Australia for medical treatment, where she died that year. The grief only seemed to motivate Chalmers to greater dedication. He vowed to bury his "sorrow in work for Christ," recognizing similar sacrifices native teachers had made.

But Chalmers's sacrifice paid off. Within five years after he came he could find "no cannibal ovens, no feasts, no human flesh, no desire for skulls" in the region in which he worked. Instead, the heathen temples were packed out for gospel services —sometimes continuing all through the night. The natives that Chalmers worked with genuinely loved him and were not hesitant to express their feelings openly. After a furlough in England he returned to an enthusiastic welcome: "One dear old lady threw her arms round my neck and kissed (rubbed noses) in a most affectionate manner. I was then on my guard. It was very affectionate, but it is not nice to come into too close contact with faces."[41]

Chalmers's furlough had come after nearly twenty years in the South Seas. On his return he was accompanied by his second wife, but the marriage was short-lived. Once again he endured the sorrow of losing a wife to jungle fever. And once again his zeal for reaching the lost was only magnified by his sorrow. Bringing the gospel to unreached areas was ever his passion, and it was that passion that ended his life in the spring of 1901. He and a young colleague, Oliver Tomkins, were on an exploratory trip along the coast of New Guinea in the Fly River region, an area known for ferocious cannibals. The men went ashore; and when they did not return, a search party went in and came out shortly with the grisly news. Chalmers and Tomkins had been clubbed to death, chopped into pieces, cooked and eaten before the search party even arrived. It was a shocking incident that stunned the Christian world, but one that Chalmers himself had always been prepared to endure.

John Coleridge Patteson

One of the most effective missionaries to the South Pacific was John Coleridge Patteson, the first Anglican bishop of Melanesia, and a great nephew of the famous English poet, Samuel Taylor Coleridge. Patteson was born in 1827 into a well-to-do English family. His father, a distinguished judge, saw to it that his little "Coley" received the best education available, first at Eton and then Oxford. While he was attending Oxford, Bishop George Selwyn, a family friend, encouraged him to consider entering the Christian ministry, and so, on graduation, Patteson sought ordination as an Anglican priest and then served twelve months in a local parish before sailing to the South Seas in 1855. Again it was Bishop Selwyn's influence that had changed the course of his life.

George Augustus Selwyn, the first Anglican bishop to New Zealand, was, like Patteson, affluent and well-educated. He had served in the South Pacific for more than a decade, and he needed the assistance of Patteson in overseeing his enormous diocese, the size of which was a controversial issue. A clerical error in his letters patent mistakenly granted him authority over a vast area of the Pacific, including Melanesia, and he possessively guarded the whole territory almost as though it were his personal domain. From the beginning of Patteson's missionary career he and Selwyn worked as a team, though it was Patteson's ministry as the bishop of Melanesia (an appointment he received through the recommendation of Selwyn) that had the most far-reaching influence. In 1856, soon after he arrived in New Zealand with Selwyn, Patteson was given his first tour of Melanesia. It was far more than a sightseeing tour, and it was what opened the door for Patteson's education and evangelistic ministry among the Melanesians. As they sailed from island to island on their mission ship, the *Southern Cross*, they recruited native boys to join them on the ship and be taken back to New Zealand (and later to Norfolk Island) to be trained in a mission school. It was a somewhat unorthodox scheme, but Selwyn and Patteson were convinced that bringing the boys apart for a proper education and sending them back to their own people as evangelists and teachers was the only viable method of evangelizing the South Seas. Other missionaries had made good use of native teachers, but generally without giving them adequate education and training to effectively lead their native churches without depending on the European missionaries. Back in New Zealand, the responsibility of directing the training school fell on Patteson's shoulders—and a tremendous responsibility it was. The youngsters had brought with them their own languages and social customs, and the task of bringing a sense of continuity to the school was a mighty challenge. Patteson, however, seemed to be uniquely qualified for the job. Among other things, he had a brilliant mind for linguistics, and during the course of his missionary career he became

Home of John Coleridge Patteson at St. John's College, New Zealand.

fluent in some twenty different Melanesian languages and dialects.

Unlike most of his predecessors, Patteson had no desire to Anglicize the natives. He strictly avoided saddling them with any sort of European dress or lifestyle. He often praised their culture and intelligence and insisted they not be discriminated against. Describing them as "friendly and delightful," he sarcastically queried, "I wonder what people ought to call sandalwood traders and slave masters if they call my Melanesians savages."[42]

After reaching the Melanesian boys with the gospel and training them as evangelists, Patteson returned them to their homes and then helped establish them in their ministry. As he did this he developed warm friendships with the island people and their chiefs and became a trusted figure in their eyes. He not only placed the young men that he had trained, but he also did

evangelistic work himself; and as he did so he recruited more young men and women for his school, which for a time had an enrollment of over fifty from twenty-four different islands.

But as he continued to minister in Melanesia, Patteson could not but help notice the change that was occurring in the attitudes of the people toward him and his ministry. The trust and confidence that they had once had in him seemed to be slipping, and not through his own doing. The outside commercial interests in the islands were rapidly expanding, and by the middle of the nineteenth century sugar and cotton plantations (particularly on the islands of Fiji and Queensland) were emerging as a highly profitable venture—one that required an enormous labor force able to endure the tropical heat. This need created a new business in the South Pacific known as blackbirding, a pursuit that made sandalwood traders appear mild by comparison. According to one historian, "The scum of the earth came to the Pacific in search of easy money in the blackbirding trade." Sometimes young men and boys were bribed or tricked into coming along willingly, but more often they were kidnapped. "Gangs of white seamen would go ashore and carry off men and youths at gunpoint." All in all, it has been estimated that some 70,000 young men were thus captured into slavery, rarely having the opportunity of seeing their native island again.[43]

It was this terrible European blight on the islands of the South Seas that more than anything else signaled the end to Patteson's ministry. Despite his condemnation of the blackbirders and his efforts to disassociate himself from them, his very methods created suspicion in the minds of some of the islanders. It became much more difficult for him to persuade young boys to come with him for schooling. But though the prospects seemed discouraging, Patteson kept up his hectic pace, and in April of 1871 he again set out on another tour of Melanesia in the *Southern Cross.*

It was a disappointing journey from the very start. Everywhere Patteson went it seemed he was following in the wake of blackbirders. There were some happy times, including a large baptismal service for more than two hundred people on the island of Moto, but everywhere he went he saw fear in the eyes of the people. No longer did he receive a warm welcome as he had in the past when the natives came down to the shore and joyfully greeted their "bishopi." They lived in terror, and if he wanted to see them he had to seek them out.

It was during this tour on September 21, 1871, that the brilliant young Anglican bishop made his final island stop. On board ship were the crew, another missionary, and several young Melanesians who were on their way to Norfolk Island for training. After the morning Bible lesson, on the martyrdom of Stephen, Patteson went ashore. It was a routine stop, but he sensed trouble almost as soon as he touched shore, and others who sought to follow him inland were driven back to the ship by a barrage of arrows. Back on ship, they anxiously waited for some sign of their missionary leader, but he did not return. Finally, Joseph Atkin (though fatally wounded) and some native boys decided to go in after him. As they headed toward shore, they saw natives pushing what appeared to be an unmanned canoe out into the water toward them. When they reached the canoe they found Patteson's body, marked by five separate wounds and covered by a palm with five knotted fronds, signifying that Patteson's life had been taken in revenge for five of their own men who had been seized by blackbirders. Despite the universal hatred for blackbirders, many of the islanders were appalled by the murder of this kind and gentle man, and for that reason his body had been washed and returned to the ship. Patteson's body was buried at sea, and shortly afterward Joseph Atkin and a native Christian died of the wounds they had sustained.

Patteson's death drew world attention to the despicable business of blackbirding and helped eventually to bring about its demise. It also inspired many young men to dedicate their lives to South Seas missionary work.

But all the gains did not diminish the tragic loss to the island peoples—the loss of one of the truest friends and supporters they had ever had, a man who had forsaken the joys of marriage and family and had sacrificed his wealth to bring them saving faith in Christ.

Florence Young

The blackbirding business that had wrought such havoc in the islands of the South Pacific was ironically the very gateway that opened portions of the Solomon Islands to Christianity. While some missionaries such as John Coleridge Patteson bitterly fought this insidious traffic in human cargo, others such as Florence Young seemed to accept it and work within the system. A native of Sydney, Australia, Miss Young was the first to publicly express concern for the spiritual welfare of the South Seas plantation laborers. Her brothers were the owners of Fairymead, a large sugar cane plantation on Queensland, and her visit to that estate changed the course of her life. Whether her brothers were actually involved with the blackbirders is unclear (some of the plantation owners apparently contracted laborers through legitimate means), but it is clear that Florence was willing to work within the system to reach the wretched laborers with the gospel.

A member of the Plymouth Brethren, Miss Young had studied the Bible since early childhood and was well-suited for her teaching ministry that began in 1882. Her first little class of ten men was an inauspicious beginning, but the numbers grew and soon she had eighty in her Sunday class and half that many coming out each eve-

Florence Young, Plymouth Brethren missionary to Queensland and later to the Solomon Islands. She also served a ten-year term in China under the China Inland Mission.

ning. The response was far greater than Florence ever could have imagined. Cutting cane in the scorching sun twelve or more hours a day was killing work—literally killing. Many workers died under the strain, including Jimmie, her first convert. Nevertheless they sacrificed their precious hours of rest to come out and hear the gospel.

The success of Miss Young's ministry at Fairymead encouraged her to branch out to other plantations on Queensland, where some ten thousand laborers lived in similar or even worse conditions. A monetary gift from George Mueller (also Plymouth

Brethren) was the stimulant she needed for the Queensland Kanaka Mission ("Kanaka" being the term used for imported laborers). She secured the help of a male missionary teacher and wrote a circular letter to the planters in her district, and by the end of the century, through the work of nineteen missionaries, thousands had enrolled in classes, some carrying the message back to their own people.

In 1890, Florence had felt the call of missions to China, and had left to serve under the China Inland Mission, but she returned to the South Seas in 1900 to direct the work of the mission as it moved into a different phase of the ministry. Laws forbidding black-birding and the use of forced labor had

been enacted, and by 1906 most of the islanders had been sent home. But this did not mean an end to the work. Follow-up was needed, and Florence and other missionaries sailed to the Solomon Islands, where they worked with recently returned converts to establish churches.

In 1907 the mission changed its name to the South Sea Evangelical Mission, and Miss Young's two nephews and niece, Northcote, Norman, and Katherine Deck, became very active in the work. As the years passed, ten more of her relatives found their way to the Solomon Islands as missionaries, and a vibrant evangelical Christianity took root that still thrives today.

SELECTED BIBLIOGRAPHY

Bell, Ralph. John G. Paton: Apostle to the New Hebrides. Butler, Ind.: Higley, 1957.

Griffiths, Allison. Fire in the Islands: The Acts of the Holy Spirit in the Solomons. Wheaton: Shaw, 1977.

Gunson, Neil. Messengers of Grace: Evangelical Missionaries in the South Seas, 1797–1860. New York: Oxford University Press, 1978.

Gutch, John. Beyond the Reefs: The Life of John Williams, Missionary. London: McDonald, 1974.

Kent, Graeme. Company of Heaven: Early Missionaries in the South Seas. New York: Nelson, 1972.

Lennox, Cuthbert. James Chalmers of New Guinea. London: Melrose, 1902.

Paton, John G. The Story of Dr. John G. Paton's Thirty Years With South Sea Cannibals. New York: Doran, 1923.

Pierson, Delavan L. The Pacific Islanders: From Savages to Saints. New York: Funk & Wagnalls, 1906.

Smith, Bradford. Yankees in Paradise: The New England Impact on Hawaii. New York: Lippincott, 1956.

Tippett, Alan R. People Movements in Southern Polynesia: A Study in Church Growth. Chicago: Moody, 1971.

PART III

THE
EXPANDING INVOLVEMENT

The Expanding Involvement

Profound changes were occurring in the world as the nineteenth century came to a close. The "European century throughout world history"[1] was over. The colonialism and imperialism unleashed by Western powers were being resisted and challenged, and the era of relative world peace was coming to an abrupt end. As the twentieth century opened, there were rumblings of war in Asia, and by 1904 Russia and Japan were battling each other in armed conflict. The outcome was a victory for Japan, and on a larger scale for Asia. No longer could the Western nations assume they were the only military powers in a rapidly expanding world.

The real break in international stability did not come until a decade later when, in the words of Stephen Neill, "The European nations, with their loud-voiced claims to a monopoly on Christianity and civilization . . . rushed blindly and confusedly into a civil war which was to leave them economically impoverished and without a shred of virtue." And "the second world war,"

he continues, "only finished off what the first had already accomplished. The moral pretensions of the West were shown to be a sham."[2]

If Christianity was not the answer to the world's problems, then what was? To many people in Europe it was Marxism. The revolutionary ferment that had erupted periodically during the nineteenth century had not been purged, and the disillusionment resulting from World War I only added to the dissatisfaction with capitalism and its class-oriented structure of society. The Bolshevik Revolution of 1917 was just one manifestation of this discontent, but it was a significant one. With a solid foothold in Russia, Marxism was on its way to becoming a grave threat to Western capitalism. This turn of events brought an added incentive to twentieth-century missionaries, many of whom viewed their mission as one of disseminating a combined philosophy of Christianity and capitalism to combat atheistic Marxism.

Along with the threat of Marxism came an anti-Western sentiment that was seen in much of the third world. Nationalism was on the rise and there was a growing movement toward independence. Westerners, though armed with advanced technology and social programs, were associated with economic exploitation. The white man was seen as both a "deliverer and destroyer," according to Neill, and "the missionary, too, would come to be regarded as both friend and foe."[3]

Western society itself was undergoing major social changes. In the United States, the late nineteenth century had seen growing discontent among farmers and laborers. The Populist movement championed a wide variety of rural causes, and William Jennings Bryan became a symbol of rural radicalism. In the cities, labor unions were on the upswing and strikes were numerous and violent. The Progressive Movement was the middle class expression of social concern, out of which came a variety of legislative reforms, including antitrust laws, child labor prohibition, and laws to protect industrial workers. In the churches, the social gospel was gaining momentum as clergymen turned away from the emphasis on an individual's inner relationship with God and began to emphasize the broad human social needs in the here and now.

One of the most far-reaching social concerns of the late nineteenth and early twentieth centuries related to women's rights. The suffrage movement that had begun decades earlier climaxed in 1920 with the passage of the nineteenth amendment. But the women's movement involved much more than suffrage. World War I had created a vacuum in the labor force, and women more than ever before were entering the work place in large numbers. With the close of the war, young women began entertaining dreams of professional careers, and more and more were enrolling in the nation's colleges and universities.

This new liberation for females had a direct impact on foreign missions. As in other professions, women began entering the field in vast numbers. When the nineteenth century opened, missionaries were men. Many of these men had wives, and the wives served faithfully alongside their husbands, but they were not generally viewed as missionaries in their own right. By the close of the century, however, the situation was vastly different. Single women had begun pouring into foreign missionary service, and married women were beginning to assume a more active role. No longer was foreign missions a male profession.

The social changes taking place in society were accompanied by intellectual changes, most noticeably in the fields of philosophy and religion. By the twentieth century the theological liberalism so prominent in Germany had begun to draw a wide following in America. Higher criticism—based on rationalism and the scientific method —was in vogue, and much of traditional Christianity was being stripped of its essential beliefs. "In essence, it stripped Christianity of its supernatural elements," writes Robert Linder, "especially its miracles and the deity of Christ. It taught instead what it considered to be the essential Christian virtues of the fatherhood of God, the brotherhood of man and the necessity of living in love. The Bible, historically the authority for faith and practice in the Protestant churches, was no longer considered trustworthy, but embracing errors and contradictions. Critical studies seemed to have undermined its authority."[4]

All this had a profound effect on foreign missions. Virtually one hundred percent of Protestant missionaries during most of the century were evangelicals who held a literal interpretation of Scripture and staunchly defended the cardinal doctrines of the faith. But by the end of the century, carrying the title of missionary was no guarantee that an individual was orthodox in his Christian beliefs. The fallout from higher criticism, the Darwinian theory of evolution, and the social gospel was beginning to be felt on the mission field. Relatively fewer liberals, however, were willing to be missionaries and the dominant majority of all missionaries continued to be evangelicals.

This trend toward theological liberalism at home and abroad, however, did not go unchallenged. In Europe, Neoorthodoxy was the answer for many. The teachings and writings of Germany's Karl Barth and his American counterpart, Reinhold Neibuhr, were widely respected by Protestant intellectuals as a compromise between the old orthodoxy and the new liberalism. In America, the reaction was much more conservative. Neoorthodoxy gained a wide following, but the more prominent opposing force was Fundamentalism. "For nearly a generation," writes Linder, "Christians fought an exhausting war for the minds and souls of American church members. When the smoke of battle cleared, every major denomination had been affected and a number of them split by the quarrel."[5]

In part as a reaction to this trend, another new breed of missionaries emerged, not necessarily so different from their forebears, but intensely determined to keep the faith pure and to trust God only for their needs. They were largely Bible institute and Christian college graduates, and they founded and filled the ranks of the new faith mission societies that arose in the late nineteenth and early twentieth centuries. Unlike a certain few of their predecessors, they had no qualms about evangelizing "nominal" Christians; and areas of the world traditionally regarded as already evangelized were not off limits, Latin America and Europe being prime examples.

One of the most significant changes in Protestant missions during the first half of the twentieth century related to the nationality of the missionaries themselves. After the turn of the century, the home base of missions shifted from England to North America. Although thousands of missionaries continued to pour out of England, Europe, Australia and New Zealand, and Scandinavian countries (Norway and Finland sent out an amazing number in proportion to their Christian population), America took the lead. This was due in part to the active role the United States began playing in international affairs. "American imperial expansion," writes Winthrop Hudson, "was accompanied by a mounting enthusiasm among the churches for overseas missions."[6] Foreign policy was in some cases justified in the name of world evangelism. In regard to the acquisition of the Philippines, President McKinley explained, "There was nothing left for us to do but to take them all and to educate the Filipinos and uplift and civilize and Christianize them, and by God's grace do the very best we could by them, as our fellow men for whom Christ also died."[7]

So by the middle of the twentieth century the United States had become the missionary "sender" of the world. Who were these Americans, and why were they so willing to leave the luxuries of the freest and most prosperous nation on earth? Their profile had changed in some significant respects. They were different in many ways from their missionary forebears. They were women in increasing numbers, and they were better educated with stronger theological views— university-educated liberals, avowed Fundamentalists, and everything in between. Like their predecessors, they were hardy individualists, tempered by waves of revivals and spurred on by a pioneering spirit. They, too, sought to conquer new frontiers, and as the western frontier vanished the mission field became for many the last frontier. In the eyes of some nationals, they were just another form of the "ugly American," and even some of their "proper" English colleagues considered them undiscriminating. But by and large it was the Americans who brought missions into the modern age, who anticipated the tremendous need for specialized skills, modern communication techniques, and an effective cross-cultural dialogue.

Chapter 9

Single Women Missionaries: "Second-Class Citizens"

From the earliest times women have contributed to the cause of world evangelism. Beginning in the New Testament, through the early church and Middle Ages, and into the period of modern missions, women have served nobly. Moravian wives particularly stand out for their dedicated missionary service, and so also the wives of later missionaries (such as Adoniram Judson and Hudson Taylor). But there were other wives thrust into missions who did not want to be there. Dorothy Carey is a notable example. How many missionary wives served faithfully despite the fact that they were not doing what they truly wanted to do will never be known. Edith Buxton, in her book *Reluctant Missionary*, tells of her struggles and unhappiness as a foreign missionary before she received peace that foreign missions was God's will for her; and Pearl Buck writes of the many years of discontentment her mother spent as a missionary wife in China before she felt satisfied with her lot. But how many other wives never received that peace or satisfaction and lived their lives longing to be serving the Lord in some other capacity?

Yet if some married missionary women secretly resented their station in life, there were countless more single women who believed the mission field was precisely where God wanted them. They were challenged by the tremendous needs on the foreign field. Married women missionaries, with household duties and little children to care for, simply could not carry the load. "They glimpsed the promise of what might be achieved in women's work for women and children," according to R. Pierce Beaver, "but they longed for colleagues who would have more freedom and who could devote themselves solely to such activity."[1] Some men also saw the need for single women on the mission field, but public opinion throughout much of the nineteenth century was opposed to the idea. Nevertheless, beginning in the 1820s single women began to trickle overseas.

The first single American woman

231

(not widowed) to serve as a foreign missionary was Betsy Stockton, a black woman and former slave, who went to Hawaii in 1823. Believing that God had called her to serve as a foreign missionary, she applied to the American Board, and the directors agreed to send her abroad—but only as a domestic servant for another missionary couple. Despite her lowly position, she was considered "qualified to teach" and was allowed to conduct a school. Later on in the 1820s, in response to a need for a single woman teacher, Cynthia Farrar, a native of New Hampshire, sailed for Bombay, where she served faithfully for thirty-four years under the Marathi Mission.

Although a few single women did receive sponsorship from established mission boards in the early decades of the nineteenth century, the discrimination they faced created a new concept of foreign missionary support—the "female agency." The idea for a separate organization for women first surfaced in England; but it quickly spread to the United States. By 1900 there were more than forty women's mission societies in the United States alone. Largely because of the "female agencies," the number of single women in missions rapidly increased, and during the first decade of the twentieth century women, for the first time in history, outnumbered men in Protestant missions—in some areas by large proportions. In the Chinese province of Shantang, for example, the 1910 statistics relating to Baptists and Presbyterians show seventy-nine women as compared to forty-six men. In the decades that followed, the ratio of single women missionaries overall continued to climb until women in

some areas outnumbered men by 2:1 (with single women, married women, and married men each comprising approximately one-third).

In her classic book on missions, *Western Women in Eastern Lands*, published in 1910, Helen Barrett Montgomery wrote of the amazing strides taken by women in world evangelism:

> It is indeed a wonderful story.... We began in weakness, we stand in power. In 1861 there was a single missionary in the field, Miss Marston, in Burma; in 1909, there were 4710 unmarried women in the field, 1948 of them from the United States. In 1861 there was one organized woman's society in our country; in 1910 there were forty-four. Then the supporters numbered a few hundreds; to-day there are at least two millions. Then the amount contributed was $2000; last year four million dollars was raised. The development on the field has been as remarkable as that at home. Beginning with a single teacher, there are at the opening of the Jubilee year 800 teachers, 140 physicians, 380 evangelists, 79 trained nurses, 5783 Bible women and native helpers. Among the 2100 schools there are 260 boarding and high schools. There are 75 hospitals and 78 dispensaries.... It is an achievement of which women may well be proud. But it is only a feeble beginning of what they can do and will do, when the movement is on its feet.[2]

But why so many single women? What would motivate them to leave the security of their families and homelands for a life of loneliness, hardship, and sacrifice? Foreign missions attracted women for a variety of reasons, but one of the most obvious was that there were few opportunities for women to be involved in a full-time ministry in the homeland. Christian service was considered a male profession. Some nineteenth-century women, such as Catherine Booth, broke into this male-dominated realm, but not without opposition. Wrote Catherine, herself a Bible scholar, "Oh, that the ministers of religion would search the original records of God's Word in order to discover whether . . . God really intended woman to bury her gifts and talents, as she now does, with reference to the interests of his Church." Other women simply entered secular work. Florence Nightingale above all else wanted to serve God in a Christian ministry, but there were no opportunities. "I would have given her (the church) my head, my hand, my heart. She would not have them."[3] So the mission field, far away from the inner sanctums of the church hierarchy, became an outlet for women who sought to serve God.

Besides the opportunities for Christian service, the mission field was an outlet for adventure and excitement. While men could fulfill their heroic fantasies as soldiers, seamen, and explorers, women had no such available options. For them foreign missionary service was one of the opportunities to venture into the unknown. Likewise, women (such as Mary Slessor) from poor working-class backgrounds were able to raise their station in life through foreign missionary careers. But perhaps an even greater influence on women entering foreign missions was feminism. R. Pierce Beaver refers to the surge of American women into missions as "the first feminist movement in North America." Although most women missionaries were not overtly feminist, their very willingness to swim against the current in a man's world was evidence of

an underlying feeling of equality, fostered in part by the upsurge of "female agencies."

Once on the field, single women had unique opportunities for ministry not afforded to men. In some areas of the world, it was only through women's work that the gospel penetrated the age-old cultural and religious barriers (though, it must be pointed out, in other areas women's work had very little impact until after the men had been reached). Single women also were free from the family responsibilities that distracted so from the ministry of their married male and female colleagues. Referring to that freedom, H. A. Tupper, secretary for the Southern Baptist Foreign Mission Board, wrote to Lottie Moon in 1879: "I estimate a single woman in China is worth two married men."[4] But with that freedom often came loneliness and depression, maladies few single women missionaries entirely escaped.

Women excelled in almost every aspect of missionary work, but the fields of medicine, education, and translation work were particularly affected by their expertise. Hospitals and medical schools were among their achievements, including one of the best mission-run medical schools in the world, located in Vellore, India. Schools were established by them all over the world, including an eight-thousand-student university in Seoul, Korea. And Scripture was made available for the first time to hundreds of different language groups as a result of their persistence. But if there is any one generalization that can be made about single women missionaries and their ministries, it is perhaps their bent for difficult pioneer work. "The more difficult and dangerous the work," writes Herbert Kane, "the higher the ratio of women to men."[5]

Another unique feature of women in missions relates not so much to their particular ministry as to their appraisal of that ministry. Women, by and large, found it easier to admit their weaknesses and vulnerabilities and to present a truer picture of living the life of a "super-saint" missionary. Their honest soul-searching and admission of faults and failures has shed light on a profession that has often been clouded in myth. And thus it is the Lottie Moons, the Maude Carys, and the Helen Roseveares that provide the student with some of the clearest understanding of the realities of modern missions.

Charlotte (Lottie) Diggs Moon

If a divine calling, an adventuresome spirit, and a feminist impulse were some of the main factors influencing the surge of single women into missions, they were the very ingredients that combined to thrust Lottie Moon into a fruitful life of missionary service. But Lottie was far more than just a successful lady missionary to north China. Though certainly not the first single woman to enter the ranks of foreign missions, she was one of the first and most prominent female missionary activists. Her impact on missions—particularly Southern Baptist missions—was enormous, and still today she is referred to as the "patron saint" of Baptist missions.

Lottie Moon was born in 1840 into an old Virginia family of Albemarle County and grew up on Viewmont, a tobacco plantation close by three famous presidential homes—Monticello, Montpelier, and Ashlawn. She

was one of seven children, all of whom were deeply influenced by the staunch faith, ambitious drive, and independence of their mother, who was widowed in 1852. The oldest child, Thomas, became a respected physician, but it was the Moon daughters who distinguished themselves the most. Orianna, also a physician (and reputedly the first female doctor south of the Mason-Dixon line), served as a medical missionary among the Arabs in Palestine until the outbreak of the Civil War and then returned home to serve as a medical doctor in the Confederate Army. Edmonia, the youngest of the seven, was one of the first two single women missionaries to be sponsored by the Southern Baptist Convention. But it was Lottie who truly made the family name famous.

Lottie, like her brothers and sisters, was well educated and cultured. During her college years she rebelled against her strict Baptist upbringing, but during a campus revival her life was changed: "I went to the service to scoff, and returned to my room to pray all night." After college she returned home to help run Viewmont, while other family members, both male and female, "marched out to fight for the Stars and Bars," performing "splendid service" as spies and elite guerrilla soldiers. Lottie was left out of the excitement, and it was this vacuum, according to Irwin Hyatt, "that would eventually send her to China."[6]

Following the war Lottie pursued a teaching career, but she longed for a Christian ministry and for adventure beyond what her little school in Cartersville, Georgia, offered her. And, unlike so many women, she did not feel deterred by her sex. The strong

Lottie Moon, "Patron Saint of Southern Baptist Missions."

women in her family who had performed as "doctors, executives, and spies," according to Hyatt, "further demonstrated what determined females could do." In 1872 Edmonia sailed for China, and in 1873, Lottie followed.[7]

If Lottie is perceived by some as beginning her missionary career as a follower, she soon demonstrated her independence and commitment to missions, apart from her sister's calling. Edmonia, who was only in her late teens when she sailed for China, was unable to cope with the pressures of missionary life in Tengchow. Besides physical ailments, she suffered from seizures and, according to co-workers, did "queer and unreasonable things" and was "very burdensome" to the missionary community. Even Lottie was exasperated by her "good for nothing" behavior, and finally in 1877, after four years in China, Edmonia returned home to Virginia. Although her

departure freed Lottie from the drudgery of being her sister's nursemaid and allowed her to actively participate in missionary work, it also plunged her into a period of depression. To her home committee she wrote: "I especially am bored to death living alone. I don't find my own society either agreeable or edifying.... I really think a few more winters like the one just past would put an end to me. This is no joke, but dead earnest."[8]

Loneliness, however, was not the only factor frustrating Lottie's ministry in China. Her old boyfriend, Crawford Toy, a Confederate Army chaplain, who had first "come a-wooing" while she was living at Viewmont following the war, had entered her life again. Now a professor at a Southern Baptist seminary in South Carolina, he proposed marriage and suggested they work as a missionary team in Japan. It was an offer many lonely single women would have quickly accepted, but one that Lottie reluctantly felt forced to refuse. While the prospect of going to Japan appealed to her, considering her dissatisfaction with the situation in China, there were more important factors, in her mind, to consider. Toy, "influenced by the new ideas of the German scholars," held to the Darwinian theory of evolution, a view that had already created controversy for him within the Southern Baptist Convention. Lottie was aware of his position, and after reading all that was available on the subject she concluded that evolution was an "untenable position" and an issue significant enough to preclude plans for marriage. Years later, when asked if she had ever had a love affair she responded, "Yes, but God had first claim on my life, and since the two conflicted, there could be no question about the result." Toy went on to become a professor of Hebrew and Semitic languages at Harvard University, and Lottie, in her own words, was left to "plod along in the same old way."[9]

Lottie's work in China in the years that followed Toy's marriage proposal continued to be drudgery, and the romantic ideal of missionary work had long since faded. As a well-educated and cultured Southern belle, she found it extremely difficult identifying with the Chinese people, and as a teacher she found it almost impossible to penetrate their "dull" minds. Had she really given up her thriving school in Cartersville, Georgia, for this? She had come to China to "go out among the millions" as an evangelist, only to find herself chained to a school of forty "unstudious" children. Relegating women to such roles, she charged, was "the greatest folly of modern missions." "Can we wonder," she wrote, "at the mortal weariness and disgust, the sense of wasted powers and the conviction that her life is a failure, that comes over a woman when, instead of the ever broadening activities she had planned, she finds herself tied down to the petty work of teaching a few girls." "What women want who come to China," she went on to write, "is free opportunity to do the largest possible work. . . . What women have a right to demand is perfect equality."[10]

Such a view was a radical position for a female missionary, but the startling aspect about Lottie's comments was that they were not penned in private letters but in articles that were published in missionary magazines. There was immediate reaction, particularly by those who found such

signs of female liberation "replusive." One such response came from one of her colleagues, a Mrs. Arthur Smith, wife of a Congregational missionary to China, who suggested Lottie was mentally unbalanced for craving such "lawless prancing all over the mission lot." Mrs. Smith argued that the proper role of a female missionary was to attend "with a quivering lip" her own children.[11]

With no children of her own, there was obviously no way that Lottie could adhere to Mrs. Smith's standard for a female missionary, but there were many obstacles preventing her from expanding her ministry to fit her own concept of fulfillment. She knew that such a ministry would be highly controversial and that there would be many dangers for a single woman living in China outside the missionary community—especially considering the ever-present xenophobia. Nevertheless, she began traveling out into the country villages, and by 1885 she concluded that her ministry would be more effective if she were to move to P'ing-tu and begin a new work there on her own. Besides her desire to be involved fulltime in evangelistic work, she wanted to get out from under the high-handed authority of her field director, T. P. Crawford. His philosophy of missions did not allow for mission schools, so Lottie's teaching ministry was in jeopardy anyway, and his dictatorial methods of dealing with other missionaries had even alienated his own wife. Moreover, Lottie feared that under his authority single women missionaries might be relegated to the place of Presbyterian women missionaries who had no vote in their mission, and she threatened to resign over this very issue. "Simple justice," she wrote, "demands that women should have equal rights with men in mission meetings and in the conduct of their work." Before moving to P'ing-tu, Lottie wrote to the home board, severely criticizing Crawford and his new plan of operation (including the closing of schools and the "regulation of mission salaries") and concluded with the terse comment, "If that be freedom, give me slavery!"[12]

Lottie's derisive remarks, it must be remembered, were not those of a heady adolescent struggling with life's incongruity of freedom and authority. She was forty-four years old and a twelve-year veteran of China missions, and she justifiably resented the lack of free choice women were accorded. But her move to P'ing-tu did not solve all her problems. Pioneer evangelism was extremely difficult work. The cries of "devil" followed her as she walked down the narrow village streets, and only slowly and after weary persistence did she win friends among the women, and even then it was difficult to win the women to Christianity without first reaching the men.

Lottie's first opportunity to reach Chinese men came in 1887, when three strangers from a nearby village appeared at her door in P'ing-tu. They had heard the "new doctrine" being whispered about by the women, and they were anxious that Lottie tell them more. Lottie visited their village, and there she found "something I had never seen before in China. Such eagerness to learn! Such spiritual desires!" So excited was she that she canceled plans for a long-overdue furlough and summoned Martha Crawford, the wife of her field director, to come and help her. Their efforts were duly rewarded, and Lottie wrote home, "Surely there can be no deeper joy than that of saving souls." Despite local opposition, she established a church, and in 1889 the first baptisms were conducted by an ordained Baptist missionary. The church witnessed steady growth, and within two decades, under Lottie's policy of keeping "the movement as free from foreign interference as possible," Li Shou Ting, the Chinese pastor, had baptized more than a thousand converts, and P'ing-tu had become the "greatest" Southern Baptist "evangelistic center . . . in all China."[13]

Between 1890 and her death in 1912, Lottie lived two separate lives in China. Part of the year was spent in villages doing evangelistic work, and the other part was spent in Tengchow, where she trained new missionaries, counseled Chinese women, and enjoyed her Western books and magazines. During this period she also continued her writing, and it was this writing that paved the way for her extraordinary influence in the Southern Baptist Church. Although she returned home on furloughs and occasionally spoke before large audiences, it was her pen that more than anything else stirred the hearts of Baptist women in the South.

Most of Lottie's writing was directed to Baptist women in an appeal for greater support of foreign missions, but sometimes she stepped hard on the toes of men. "It is odd," she wrote, "that a million Baptists of the South can furnish only three men for all China. Odd that with five hundred preachers in the state of Virginia, we must rely on a Presbyterian to fill a Baptist pulpit [here]. I wonder how these things look in heaven. They certainly look very queer in China. . . ."

But if the men would not come to the rescue of foreign missionary work, how could the work be saved? Lottie saw the answer to that question in the example that had been set by the Southern Methodist Church. The China missionary work in that denomination had almost collapsed before it was rescued by "enlisting of the women." And if Methodist women could save their foreign missionary program, why could not Baptist women do the same?[14]

To follow up her appeal with specifics, Lottie called for a week of prayer and a special Christmas offering to be handled solely by women and to be directed exclusively toward missions. She also called on "vigorous healthy women" to fill the ranks that had been left vacant by men. The response was immediate. It seemed that women were only too anxious to become involved. The first Christmas offering in 1888, according to Hyatt, "exceeded its goal by a thousand dollars, enough to pay for three new ladies instead of two." Lottie responded with enthusiasm: "What I hope to see is a band of ardent, enthusiastic, and experienced Christian women occupying a line of stations extending from P'ing-tu on the north and from Chinkiang on the south, making a succession of stations uniting the two ... a mighty wave of enthusiasm for Women's Work for Women must be stirred."[15]

In the years that followed, the Christmas offering increased and there were more single women to serve in China, but the early years of the twentieth century following the Boxer uprising (for which Lottie was evacuated to Japan) were devastating times in China. Outbreaks of the plague and smallpox, followed by famine, and then topped by a local rebellion in 1911 brought mass starvation to the area of Tengchow. Lottie organized a relief service and pleaded for funds from the United States, but the board, unable to meet other financial obligations, declined assistance. Lottie contributed from her personal funds and gave all the help one person could possibly give, but her efforts seemed so trifling in the face of such tragedy. With the last of her savings drawn out of her small bank account, Lottie lapsed into a period of deep depression. She quit eating, and her mental and physical health declined. A doctor was sent for, and only then was it discovered that she was starving to death. In hopes of saving her life, her colleagues made arrangements for her to return home in the company of a nurse, but it was too late. She died aboard ship while at port in Kobe, Japan, on Christmas Eve, 1912, one week after her seventy-second birthday.

What Lottie could not do in life she accomplished in death. In the years that followed, the "Lottie Moon Christmas Offering" increased, and the Lottie Moon story was repeated over and over again. By 1925 the offerings had surpassed three hundred thousand dollars, and in recent years more than twenty million dollars annually has been collected for Southern Baptist missions in the name of Lottie Moon. For Southern Baptist women, Lottie had become a symbol of what they themselves could accomplish for God. She was a shining example of Christian womanhood and sexual equality—an example that was no doubt lost on some. The highest compliment the *Foreign Missions Journal* could pay her at the time of her death was to say she was "the best man among our missionaries."[16]

Amy Carmichael

What Lottie Moon was to Southern Baptist women in America, Amy Carmichael was to Christian women of all denominations in the United Kingdom. Her thirty-five books detailing her fifty-five years in India made her one of the most beloved missionaries of all time, and her own self-effacement and truly sweet and genuine personality has placed her in that rare category of "too good to be true" individuals. Sherwood Eddy, a missionary statesman and author, who knew her well, was deeply impressed by the "beauty of her character"; and character, according to Eddy, was the key to successful world evangelism. "Here is the point where many a missionary breaks down. Every normal missionary sails with high purpose but as a very imperfect Christian.... His character is his weakest point.... It was just here that Miss Carmichael was a blessing to all who came into intimate and understanding contact with her radiant life.... Amy Wilson Carmichael was the most Christlike character I ever met, and ... her life was the most fragrant, the most joyfully sacrificial, that I ever knew."[17]

Amy Carmichael was born in 1867 into a well-to-do North Ireland family whose little village of Millisle was dominated by the prosperous Carmichael flour mills. She lived a carefree live until she was sent to boarding school as a teen-ager. Her father died when she was eighteen, and as the oldest of seven children, heavy responsibility fell on her shoulders. Her father had made a large personal loan that could not be repaid, leaving the family in severe financial straits. Soon afterward the family moved to Belfast, and it was here that Amy was introduced to the rewards of city mission work. Through this opportunity of lay evangelistic work, spiritual concerns became paramount in her life, but it was the Keswick Movement (an interdenominational Bible Conference that stressed "deeper life theology"—a viewpoint that holds that victorious living in the Spirit can overcome a Christian's tendency to sin) more than anything else that turned her life around and stimulated her spiritual growth.

Amy's call to missions was as direct and personal, in her mind, as any missionary call has ever been. The words "Go ye" were from God to her, and she had no choice but to obey. But her decision was not made without opposition—particularly from Robert Wilson, the chairman of the Keswick Convention. That a young woman would give her life to foreign missions was indeed a commendable act in the eyes of Wilson, as long as the young woman was not Amy. Following the death of his wife and daughter, Amy had become as an adopted daughter to him. She had lived with him and cared for him, and he was deeply shaken on hearing her intention to go abroad. Although he reluctantly gave his blessing, his pleading for her to return to him caused her heartache in the intervening years until his death in 1905.

Amy received her "Macedonian call" in 1892 at the age of twenty-four, and the following year she was in Japan. She eagerly jumped into the work, but like so many missionaries

Amy Carmichael, founder of Dohnavur Fellowship in India.

before her there were disappointments. The Japanese language seemed impossible to her, and the missionary community was not the picture of harmony she had envisioned. To her mother she wrote, "...we are here just what we are at home—not one bit better—and the devil is awfully busy.... There are missionary shipwrecks of once fair vessels." Amy's health was also a problem. To Sherwood Eddy she later confided that she had "broken down from nervous prostration during the very first year of ... service, suffering, as some foreigners do, from what was called Japanese head." "The climate," she had written her mother, "is dreadful upon the brain."[18]

After fifteen months as a missionary, Amy became convinced that Japan was not where God wanted her, so

without even notifying the Keswick Convention, the mainstay of her support, she sailed for Ceylon. But how could she defend such an impulsive decision? "I simply say that I left Japan for rest and change, that when at Shanghai I believed the Lord told me to follow Him down to Ceylon, and so I came."[19] Amy's stay in Ceylon was cut short by an urgent plea for her to return home to care for Mr. Wilson who was seriously ill. But after less than a year in the British Isles, she was back in Asia—this time in India, where she would remain for more than fifty-five years without a furlough.

From the beginning, Amy was regarded as a bit eccentric by her fellow missionaries as well as by some of her supporters back home. Her claim to a direct line of communication to God bothered some, especially when it interfered with their programs or ministries. And her determination to not paint a rosy picture of missionary work was a sore point with certain other individuals. One of her manuscripts that had been sent home for publication was returned because the mission committee "wanted it altered a little to make it more encouraging." Amy refused, and later it was published under the title, *Things as They Are.*

Within a few years after Amy arrived in southern India she moved to Dohnavur and became involved in the work that her life is remembered for—saving temple children (particularly girls) from a life of painful degradation. The sale of children as temple prostitutes to be "married to the gods" and then made available to Hindu men who frequented the temple was one of the "secret sins" of Hinduism, and even some of the foreign missionaries refused to believe it was as prevalent as Amy claimed. Some believed she was wasting her time searching for children who did not even exist. But Amy would not be deterred. Through the help of converted Indian women, who in some cases scoured the country as spies, she slowly began to uncover this terrible blight. Though she was not alone in her campaign (Indian reformers were also outraged by the practice), she confronted tremendous opposition. More than once she faced criminal charges of kidnapping, and the threat of physical danger was always present. Nevertheless, Amy persisted in her rescue operation, and by 1913, twelve years after she began her controversial ministry, she had one hundred and thirty children under her care. In the decades that followed, hundreds of children were rescued and housed at Dohnavur.

Dohnavur Fellowship (as her organization became known) was a unique Christian ministry. The workers (including the Europeans) all wore Indian dress, and the children were given Indian names. Foreign and Indian staff members all lived communally. The children were educated and physically cared for, and special attention was paid to the development of their "Christian character." To critics who charged her emphasis on physical needs, education, and character-building was not evangelistic enough, Amy responded, ". . . one cannot save and then pitchfork souls into heaven. . . . Souls are more or less securely fastened to bodies . . . and as you cannot get the souls out and deal with them separately, you have to take them both together."[20]

Amy sacrificed all for Dohnavur Fellowship and expected her co-workers to do the same. Years before, while in Japan, she had come to grips with the prospect of remaining single the rest of her life. It was a difficult struggle and one that she was unable to write about for more than forty years—and even then she only shared it privately with one of her "children," whom she was admonishing to follow the same course: "On this day many years ago I went away alone to a cave in the mountain called Arima. I had feelings of fear about the future. That was why I went there—to be alone with God. The devil kept on whispering, 'It's all right now, but what about afterwards? You are going to be very lonely.' And he painted pictures of loneliness—I can see them still. And I turned to my God in a kind of desperation and said, 'Lord, what can I do? How can I go on to the end?' And He said, 'None of them that trust in Me shall be desolate.' That word has been with me ever since. It has been fulfilled to me. It will be fulfilled to you."[21]

That others should follow her in forsaking marriage and a family was to Amy a practical as well as a spiritual commitment. Dohnavur Fellowship needed staff members who could give themselves wholly as mothers and spiritual counselors to the children. And it was for that reason that she formed the Sisters of the Common Life—a Protestant religious order for single women. It was a voluntary association, originally made up of Amy and seven young Indian women who were not bound by vows, but who could not remain in the order should they at a later date decide to marry.

For Amy, the Sisterhood was in part a spiritual and mystical alternative to married life. Single women now had a "family" to cling to and a feeling of belonging, instead of being plagued by loneliness and the unending hope of marriage in the future. The concept was patterned after a fourteenth-century religious community, the Brothers of the Common Life, founded by a Roman Catholic mystic, Gerhard Groot, and mysticism was an integral part of the sisterhood. A mystical union with Christ compensated for the absence of physical love, and Amy and her "sisters" testified of a deep and satisfying peace. By the 1950s there were three groups of Sisters of the Common Life, but efforts to form a corresponding Brotherhood failed.

In spite of the Sisterhood and the sense of unity it fostered, Dohnavur Fellowship, like other Christian organizations, faced internal as well as external problems. Though Amy often wrote in vague terms and avoided specific details, she did allude to times of friction within the Fellowship, and she herself suffered from recurring bouts of anxiety and tension. So Dohnavur was not the idyllic utopia some visitors claimed it to be, but it was a remarkable organization developed and carried on by a remarkable woman. Though her final twenty years (following a serious fall) were spent as an invalid, Amy continued to write books and to plead for the cause of her dear children. She died at Dohnavur in 1951 at the age of eighty-three.

Maude Cary

By the early twentieth century, women were equaling or outnumbering men in most mission societies, and in some countries the mission work would have virtually collapsed had it not been for the single women. Such was the case for a time in Morocco with the Gospel Missionary Union. The GMU, one of five Protestant missions in that country, had struggled since 1894 to reach the Muslims with the gospel. Despite the efforts, there was little visible progress against the seemingly impenetrable wall of Islam, and discouragement as well as disease took its toll on the missionary force. For some, the logical solution would have been to close the mission stations and concentrate on other fields; but the single women, among them Maude Cary, remained and served with unusual distinction during a difficult time in that very unresponsive country.

Maude was born on a Kansas farm in 1878, and it was there that she was introduced to missions by the traveling evangelists and missionaries who frequently conducted meetings in the Cary home. Maude's mother, a very independent woman, was a talented musician who had trained at the Boston Conservatory of Music and was an outstanding Bible teacher as well. Maude inherited this independent spirit, and at age eighteen she enrolled at the GMU Bible Institute in Kansas City, Missouri, to be trained for a ministry in foreign missions.

In 1901 Maude sailed to Morocco with four other GMU missionaries to begin her fifty years of service there. The first months were devoted to language school, and from the beginning there was evidence of personality friction between Maude and the other students. A bright and competitive student, Maude was not about to be outscored by the others, including F.C. Enyart, the only male in the small class. Although Enyart was as competitive as Maude, he felt that since he was a male it was "his prerogative to maintain the highest grades in class," (and, in fact, he outscored her by a fraction of a percentage point). But it was Maude who was accused of pride and aggressiveness. Women had to be independent and courageous enough to forsake all for a foreign missionary career, but when it came to outshining their male counterparts, they had gone too far. Maude, however, realizing the error of her ways, "prayed daily," according to her biographer, "for cleansing from the sin of pride."[22]

Maude's first summer in Morocco was filled with new experiences. It was the mission policy to spend the summer months doing itinerant evangelistic work in the villages, and it was an exciting time as the missionary caravan started out into the rural areas. The excitement soon faded as the harsh realities of the primitive camp life became apparent. And the difficulty in presenting the gospel proved to be even more frustrating. Every family kept a "pack of fierce dogs whose bite was worse than their bark," but "even when they were held back from attacking the foreign visitors, they would bark noisily in the background," drowning out what the missionaries had to say. There were encouraging times, especially for the women missionaries, who, once outside the village, were able to talk with the women at a river or spring where they carried water or washed their clothes. Many listened with interest, "but if a man appeared in the distance the women melted away, apparently fearful of being caught listening to the heretics."[23]

More threatening than the dogs and men, who occasionally caught their wives giving audience to the missionaries, was the general political situation in Morocco that soon turned against the missionaries, forcing them to relocate near the coast a little more than a year after Maude arrived. Work continued, but not without heartache for Maude. At the field mission conference, following her second year in Morocco, one of the meetings was opened to group discussion on the topic of gripes and irritants the missionaries had toward each other; and, according to her biographer, Maude soon found herself to be the brunt of much of the criticism: "From all that was said, her first two years on the field had been a total failure. The mission would have been better off without her. She was selfish and forgetful. She had written at least one unspiritual letter. She didn't always pray with the Muslims to whom she witnessed. Gaiety, friendliness, laughter—these had all been misconstrued. Added to her tendency to idle talk and her pride of dress, they became a mountain over which her co-workers had stumbled."[24]

Within weeks after that devastating meeting, the president of the GMU, who was visiting Morocco at the time, advised Maude to prepare to return home. Her health problems along with her personality quirks combined to make her a greater liability than asset to the mission. Maude was crushed. How could she ever face her family and friends back home?

Ironically, the ordeal Maude endured relating to her pride (both during her language school days and again at the annual field meeting) was not an unusual or isolated occurrence for women in missions. Many other single women faced the same kind of devastating circumstances. The very qualities that made them supremely capable for missionary service were viewed with suspicion by their weaker sisters and were threatening to their male colleagues. Isobel Kuhn in her book, *By Searching*, tells of a similar experience when she was applying for mission candidacy to the China Inland Mission. On the basis of a personal reference she was charged with being "proud, disobedient, and likely to be a trouble-maker." Though "conditionally" accepted, her departure for China was delayed, allowing the council time to keep an eye on her. She was promised that if she "conquered" her problems she would be "fully accepted." Dr. Helen Roseveare, similarly, was nearly denied candidacy because of the council's judgment that she was "proud, always knowing better than others, unable to be told things or warned or criticized, difficult to live with, and so on."[25]

In Maude's case, she was already on the field, and sending her home would have been devastating; in the end she was allowed to stay. There would, however, be more humbling experiences ahead of her. In addition to her language study in Arabic she was studying Berber, the language of the Berbers, an ancient tribe that inhabited the area long before the Arabs

moved across North Africa—the tribe with whom she had initially worked before her relocation near the coast. But as she struggled with the language, she searched her motives, wondering to herself if she would be so interested in going back to those people if it were not for a single male missionary, George Reed, who was working among them. She and George had corresponded with each other, and Maude secretly hoped her study of the Berber language would stimulate further interest in her. It apparently did, and soon after the 1907 field conference they became engaged. But whether it was her ill health or a combination of reasons, George soon had doubts about his decision. He encouraged her to go back to the United States, and when she refused he returned to work with the Berbers without her, though not officially breaking off their engagement.

Still single on her thirtieth birthday, Maude, according to her biographer, "chose a new motto for her life. It was 'Seek Meekness,' chosen, in part at least, because George Reed said he wanted a humble wife."[26] But humility or not, the marriage never took place, though Maude was to be strung along for six more years before she would know for sure. In 1914 George decided to leave Morocco and open a new work in the Sudan (a decision that may have been precipitated by his seeming inability to call off the engagement), and his departure signaled the end of their relationship. Only then did Maude reluctantly accept her fate—spending the rest of her life, as she put it, as an "old maid missionary."[27]

After twenty-three years Maude returned home for her first furlough, still wearing the same style dress and hat she had worn when she left the United States in 1901. America was reveling in the lively era of the 1920s, and Maude seemed entirely out of place. Yet it was a time to care for her aged parents, both of whom died during her furlough; and it was also a time for reflection. What had she accomplished in those twenty-three years? Had churches been founded? Were mission schools overflowing with eager students? Were converts winning their own people to Christianity? No. In terms of outward success, very little had been accomplished against the power of Islam; and of the handful of "converts" the most promising one had turned away from Christianity in the face of persecution. Was it truly worth the sacrifice? Maude was convinced it was; and besides, at forty-seven, she was now alone and the only home she really knew was in Morocco.

Back in Morocco the very slow progress of the previous decades seemed to be starting to reverse itself, and Maude began to see signs of success. More women were openly defying their cultural mores and coming out for Bible teaching. Likewise, there were two young male converts whose courageous stand inspired the whole Moroccan missionary community. But despite Maude's optimism, the GMU missionary force continued to dwindle, and new recruits were few in number. By 1938 she found herself alone with one other single missionary to "man" the GMU stations in that most discouraging field. Two more single women arrived just before the outbreak of World War II, but then the doors were closed. It was a troubling time, and the four single women could have isolated themselves in an out-of-the-way station and waited out the war. Instead, they split up in order to keep the three stations in operation —Maude and the other more experienced missionary each to a station by themselves, and the two new missionaries working together. Finally in 1945 the war was over, and surprisingly, according to Maude's biographer, "The work had suffered very little, thanks to the faithful, sacrificial labors of four single women who chose to remain on the job."[28]

Following the war, new GMU missionary recruits began entering Morocco, eleven by 1948, and most impressive of all was the fact that "3 of them were men!" Maude, now the mission's elder statesman, conducted language school and helped new recruits get situated, but her pioneering days were not over. Still plagued by a shortage of workers, the GMU assigned her, at the age of seventy-one, to "open the city of El Hajeb to resident missionary work," to be accompanied only by a young woman still in language study. Elsewhere the work also went forward, and in 1951 a Bible institute was organized to train young Moroccan men. The enrollment was three, two of whom were from Maude's new station at El Hajeb.

Although the Bible institute had long been a dream of Maude's, she was not present at its dedication in January of 1952. Some months before, she had been flown back to the United States for medical treatment. No one expected her to return, but late that year at the age of seventy-four she was back and once again involved in the work. For three years she continued her ministry, but due to recurring health problems the mission began arranging for her retirement. Her departure in 1955 coincided with the end of the French occupation of Morocco and an exciting new era of relaxed restrictions against the missionaries. For twelve years the missionaries worked openly and freely among the Muslims, and the Muslims responded. Some thirty thousand of them enrolled in correspondence courses, and Bible studies flourished.

But the good times were not to last. In 1967 the Moroccan government closed the door to all foreign missions. Seventy-five years of service ended for the GMU. Radio broadcasts continued to beam the gospel to those who would listen, but for all practical purposes the tiny Moroccan church was on its own. In that same year, back in the United States, an obituary appeared in the local newspaper, and "a small handful of people, seven of whom were ministers, attended the funeral. There were only two sprays of flowers and hardly any tears."[29] Maude Cary had gone to be with her Lord.

Johanna Veenstra

Perhaps the most striking aspect of single females in foreign missions was the status the profession conferred to otherwise very ordinary women. This was also true in certain cases with men, but not to such a great extent. A man had to excel. He had to attain some kind of distinction in his missionary service to be rated a "missionary hero," but a woman, particularly a single woman, became a "heroine" just by having the courage to strike out as a foreign missionary pioneer. Such was the case with Johanna Veenstra, who in many ways is representative of the vast army of single women who went abroad after the turn of the century. Johanna, who was repeatedly referred to as a "heroine" by her admiring biographer (the late Henry Beets, Director of Missions of the Christian Reformed Church), turned from an obscure stenographer into a local celebrity (both in Grand Rapids, Michigan, and Paterson, New Jersey), and yet her missionary service was in many ways very ordinary. Her life, however, sheds light on the sacrifice as well as the expectations placed on all her fellow "heroines" of the faith.

Johanna was born in Paterson, New Jersey, in 1894, two years before her father decided to give up his trade as a carpenter and train for the ministry. With that decision, the family moved to Grand Rapids, Michigan, where William Veenstra attended the Theological School (now Calvin College and Seminary) to be trained as a Christian Reformed Church pastor. On graduation he was ordained, and he accepted a call to a rural church in western Michigan, only to be struck down eight months later with typhoid fever. His death brought hardship and poverty to the widow and her six small children, she soon returned to Paterson where she opened a general store. Johanna attended Christian parochial schools until she was twelve and then entered a two-year business college. At the age of fourteen, to help support the family, she became a stenographer in New York City, commuting every day from Patterson.

Although the temptations of riches and worldly pleasures did not entirely pass Johanna by, she was a serious youngster, and church activities in her Christian Reformed Church consumed much of her leisure time. It was while attending a Baptist church that

Johanna was converted—a decision her mother and pastor no doubt wistfully wished might have taken place in her home church.

After her conversion she became involved in lay missionary work, and at the age of nineteen she enrolled at the Union Missionary Training Institute in New York City to prepare to become a city missionary. Before she graduated, however, she was challenged by the needs of overseas missions and consequently applied to the Sudan United Mission, an undenominational organization committed to stopping the spread of Islam into Black Africa. Because of a mission policy, Johanna had to wait three years until she was twenty-five to begin her overseas service, so in the interim she moved back to Grand Rapids. Here she worked with a city mission and took further schooling at Calvin College, where she became the first woman member of the Student Volunteer Board. Before sailing to Africa (via England) she went back to New York City for medical training and graduated from the midwifery course.

Johanna's assignment under the SUM involved pioneer work at Lupwe, not far from Calabar (where Mary Slessor had served so faithfully not many years before). The station at Lupwe was new and consisted only of a few unfinished and unfurnished huts with dirt floors. But Johanna adjusted to the very primitive conditions quickly. The white ants were an annoyance, but she took them in stride: "When having my evening meal, here were those creatures, in swarms, sticking fast in hand, dropping in the food— and I concluded a plague was upon us. There was no 'shutting' them out because in these native huts we have

Johanna Veenstra, Christian Reformed missionary to Africa.

no ceiling." The rats, too, were bothersome, but she refused to complain. The expectations placed on her were high, and if missionary work was not as romantic or fulfilling as she had dreamed it would be, she never hinted that she had second thoughts: "There has never been a single regret that I left the 'bright lights and gay life' of New York City, and came to this dark corner of his vineyard. There has been no sacrifice, because the Lord Jesus Himself is my constant companion."[30]

Johanna's work, like that of most single women of her day, was varied. One of her first projects was to set up a boarding school to train young men as evangelists, a school that enrolled as many as twenty-five at a time. Though it was a time-consuming project, she still found time for medical and evangelistic work. Sometimes her treks into neighboring villages lasted for several weeks at a time, with alternating periods of success and failure. Success rarely included outward professions of faith. Johanna was a pioneer laying the groundwork, and thus merely obtaining an attentive audience was a major sign of success.

But if on "rare occasions" she saw "people weep as they were hearing the story of the death of our Lord" and "gasp with wonder and clap their hands in gratitude to God for His gifts," there were "very discouraging" times too:

> I took one trek through the hills, walking from place to place for nine days. . . . We planned to stay over Sunday at a certain village but it proved that we were not welcome. They did not want to provide food for the carriers and the others who were with me. So they suffered a good deal of hunger. Rain hindered the people coming to meetings. I sat at a hut door, with an umbrella to keep me dry, while the people were huddled together inside the hut about a fire. On Sunday afternoon a heavy thunderstorm arose. The rain came down in torrents. The hut where I camped was a grass-walled one, and the rain came rushing in until the whole place was flooded. . . . Early the next morning we started off for a long walk to another hill. . . . The chief was at home, but he was sick. We stopped here one night, and decided to go home. How glad we were to see our Lupwe compound.[31]

Johanna's usual means of transportation from village to village was a bicycle, but it was slow and very tiring peddling uphill in rough terrain, especially considering her tendency to be overweight. She secretly envied some of the male missionaries who were moving about in relative ease on their motorcycles, and so after her second furlough in 1927 she returned to Africa with a new motorcycle. Her matronly appearance no doubt made for a curious sight as she began her motorized journey inland over the bumpy trails, but no one could question her pluck. Despite her initial enthusiasm and determination, she soon discovered that "dirt-biking" was not her niche. Less than forty miles out, she unexpectedly hit sand and was thrown from the bike. Badly bruised in body and spirit, she sent for help and resigned herself to go back to peddling.

Although Johanna willingly lived in a native hut and accepted the Africans for what they were, she always maintained a sense of superiority over those she worked with. "It is necessary," she wrote, "that the missionary continually hold an attitude of superiority. Not in the sense of 'we are better than you.' God forbid! But rather in the sense of claiming and using authority. The missionary must prove himself or herself to be 'boss' (not bossy), commanding and demanding obedience."[32] This kind of paternalism (or maternalism in this case) was the norm, and Johanna, as much as any missionary, was a product of her generation. But such attitudes, nevertheless, contributed to the bitter animosities that led to violent revolution in that part of the world only a few decades later.

But during the 1920s and '30s, while Johanna was pouring her life into Africa, there seemed to be no outward feeling of resentment. Her medical work was particularly appreciated, and it was considered a privilege to attend her boarding school. It was thus a great sorrow to the people of Lupwe and neighboring villages when they received word of their missionary's untimely death in 1933. She had entered a mission hospital for what was thought to be routine surgery, but she never recovered.

Back home in Paterson and Grand Rapids the news was received by her family and friends with disbelief and sorrow. But they were God-fearing Christian Reformed people who never questioned God's sovereignty in such matters. Their "heroine" had merely been promoted to a higher position and was now enjoying far greater riches than she so willingly relinquished on earth. Ironically, a letter that arrived from her after her death, though written about an African Christian who had died, was titled appropriately for Johanna herself, "From a Mudhut to a Mansion on High."[33]

Gladys Aylward

If sex discrimination had been a factor in the past for women who had been denied missionary appointments, it was certainly not the case with Gladys Aylward. She applied to the China Inland Mission in 1930 (a mission with a long-standing reputation for its eager acceptance of women) only to be turned down after a probationary term at the mission's training center. She simply was not missionary material. At twenty-eight, her age was not in her favor (though Elizabeth Wilson had been accepted at the age of fifty), but the main reason for rejecting her was her poor academic showing—which may have been caused by a profound learning disability. Although Gladys was bright conversationally, book learning seemed impossible for her. She studied as hard as the other students, but, according to one biographer, "when it came to imbibing knowledge by normally accepted methods, Gladys's powers of

mental digestion seemed automatically to go into neutral, and occasionally reverse."[34] But despite this handicap, Gladys became the most noted single woman missionary in modern history.

Gladys was born in London in 1902 into a working-class family, and it was among that segment of society that she seemed doomed to carry out her existence. She entered the work force at the age of fourteen and settled into a life of domestic service. She was a parlor maid, a genteel term for a house servant—a position that included heavy chores, long hours, and low pay—and a job that trapped some single women for the whole of their lives. The days were routine and dull, and the occasional nights off were cut short by an early curfew. Only in her fantasies did she break out of her drab existence. Here she moved in fast circles—drinking, smoking, dancing, gambling, and attending theaters.

It was with a combination of fantasy and reality that Gladys moved through her twenties, and perhaps would have continued on into her thirties and beyond but for a significant change in her life—a spiritual change. Although she had attended church off and on and was familiar with the gospel message, she did not identify with Christ personally until one night at the close of a church service, when she was confronted by a stranger concerning her spiritual need. This led her to seek out the pastor, and finding him gone she agreed to talk with the pastor's wife, who led her to a saving knowledge of Christ.

With her conversion, Gladys's life changed. She began attending Young Life campaigns and dreaming about serving the Lord as a foreign mission-

249

ary. It was this dream that brought her to the CIM headquarters in 1929, and it was that same dream that would not die when she was not invited to continue her training after her probationary term was over. She was convinced that God was calling her, and if she could not obtain a mission's sponsorship she would go on her own. So, alone in her little bedroom, once again employed as a parlor maid, she committed herself and her scant earnings to God, convinced that he would get her to China. But of course she could not stand idly by. She began saving every penny she earned and depositing it with the ticket agent at the railway station. (Rail passage through Europe, Russia, and Siberia was the cheapest transportation available.)

She also began reading and inquiring about China every opportunity she had, which brought her in contact with Jeannie Lawson, an elderly widowed China missionary who was anxious that someone come out to assist her. If Gladys needed a direct sign from God, that was it, and on October 15, 1932, tickets in hand, she departed from the Liverpool Street Station en route to China.

Bundled up in an orange frock worn over a coat, Gladys was a curious looking traveler, resembling a gypsy more than a missionary. Besides her bedroll she carried two suitcases (one stocked with food) and a bag clanking with a small stove and pots and pans. Despite the language barriers, Gladys had a relatively uneventful trip through

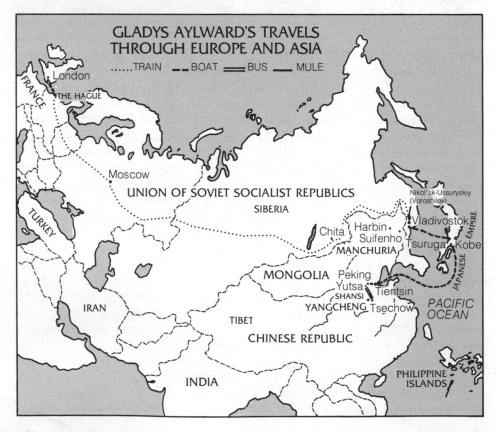

GLADYS AYLWARD'S TRAVELS THROUGH EUROPE AND ASIA

Europe, but in Russia the situation began to change. Russia was in the midst of an undeclared border war with China, and after passing through Moscow the train was packed with Russian troops. At every stop the validity of her tickets and passport was questioned, and it was only by the grace of God that the non-English-speaking authorities allowed her to continue.

Alone with hundreds of soldiers, crossing the stark Siberian landscape, Gladys had second thoughts about her decision, but it was too late to turn back. She had to go on despite the war and uncertainty. The whole venture seemed so unreal as the train clanged along the frozen tracks, but then, almost without warning, she was told that she had gone as far as she would be allowed to travel. Only soldiers were allowed to stay on the train. But Gladys refused to get off. She insisted that she be allowed to go on until the train stopped, thinking that every mile was bringing her closer to China. The train continued on several miles down the track, and then it stopped. The sound of gunfire could be heard in the distance as the soldiers and supplies were unloaded, and Gladys found herself all alone in a deserted train only hundreds of yards away from the war zone. She had no choice but to trudge back on the snow-covered tracks to Chita. Her biographer, Alan Burgess, vividly recounts the ordeal:

> The Siberian wind blew the powdered snow around her heels, and she carried a suitcase in each hand, one still decorated ludicrously with kettle and saucepan. Around her shoulders she wore the fur rug. And so she trudged off into the night, a slight, lonely figure, dwarfed by the tall, somber trees, the towering mountains, and the black sky, diamond bright with stars. There were wolves near by, but this she did not know. Occasionally in the forest a handful of snow would slither to the ground with a sudden noise, or a branch would crack under the weight of snow, and she would pause and peer uncertainly in that direction. But nothing moved. There was no light, no warmth, nothing but endless loneliness.[35]

By dawn, after having taken a two-hour rest next to her little alcohol stove, she could see the lights of Chita in the distance. The worst ordeal of her journey was over. From Chita she was able to get rail passage into Manchuria, but even then she was able to get into China only after making an unscheduled trip to Japan, where she received help from the British consul.

Once in China, Gladys began the arduous trek across the mountains to Yangcheng, where Jeannie Lawson was faithfully continuing the work she and her husband had begun so many years earlier. Jeannie welcomed Gladys, but in her own way. She was a brusque woman who had survived the harsh xenophobic environment she lived in by being tough-skinned, and she was hardly the one to be impressed by any sacrifice that Gladys had endured. Gladys was shown around and then, without any celebration, got settled into the work of being a missionary. The work was not what Gladys had expected. Her first assignment consisted of operating an inn for muleteers who passed through Yangcheng on their route west. For Jeannie it was an opportunity to share the gospel with the muleteers each evening, but for Gladys it was hard work—making her housework back in London seem like a genteel profession.

Gladys Aylward shortly after her arrival in China.

Despite the hard work and few rewards, Gladys was making progress. What she never could have learned in formal language training, she was readily picking up as she dealt with the muleteers. The Chinese tongue was not just a language of complex written characters, but a language of emotion and feeling, and it was through this facet of the language that she learned to communicate. But if Gladys was making progress in communicating with the Chinese, she was regressing in her ability to communicate with Mrs. Lawson—if, in fact, they ever had truly communicated. Jeannie's set ways and Gladys's independ-

ent spirit clashed, and finally after one heated eruption (less than a year after her arrival), Gladys was ordered to leave. With nowhere else to go, she moved in with some CIM missionaries in another town; but when word came some time later that Mrs. Lawson was ill, Gladys rushed back to be at her side and cared for her until she died several weeks later.

With the death of Mrs. Lawson, Gladys no longer had the financial support she needed to operate the inn, but a new opportunity opened up—one that gave her a far wider influence than the inn had. She was asked by the Chinese magistrate of Yangcheng to become the local foot inspector. It became her job to go from house to house, making sure the new laws against female footbinding were being complied with. It was an exciting opportunity for her to improve her language skills, to get to know the people, and to share the gospel.

As Gladys traveled around, her ministry blossomed. Wherever she went people came out to see her and to listen to her Bible stories, sometimes embellished almost beyond recognition. As she visited and revisited villages, her prestige grew and the people began to view her as an authority figure—so much so that on one occasion she was called on to use her prowess to put down a prison riot.

During the years that Gladys spent traveling from village to village, she made friends and converts, and the future for her ministry seemed bright. But outside her little world around Yangcheng in the Shansi Province, massive plots and military maneuvers were taking place. It was a period of time when the yet-obscure guerrilla leader, Mao Tse Tung, was building his revolutionary force, and when Japan was amassing thousands of troops on the Manchurian border. But life went on in Yangcheng as usual until the summer of 1937. The once peaceful mountain villages of Shansi suddenly became targets of Japanese bombing raids. Gladys, who had recently become a Chinese citizen, stayed on; and in the spring of 1938, when Yangcheng itself was bombed, she refused to leave until the last casualties were accounted for.

The war had two very different effects on Gladys. On the one hand it brought courage and physical endurance that even amazed herself. She moved behind enemy lines, bringing supplies and assistance to villagers, and served so effectively as a spy for the Chinese military that she had a high price on her head. But on the other hand, the ravages of war made Gladys realize how very alone and vulnerable she really was. To those around her she was strong, but deep down inside she longed for strong arms to hold her when she could do no more.

Marriage was something that Gladys had never ruled out. Even before the war she had prayed for a husband and dreamed that one day her Prince Charming would come walking into Yangcheng. He never came, at least the one of her fantasies, but the war did bring another man into her life. His name was Linnen, and he was a Chinese military officer—the man who convinced her to become a spy against the Japanese. At first it was only mutual patriotism that brought them together, but as time went on it turned into love. How could she justify such a relationship? "She was a missionary dedicated to God. But,"

continues Burgess, "God had also made her a woman full of the natural tides and forces which stir womankind. If she was falling in love, she reasoned, then it was God who allowed it to happen."[36] As the suffering and hardships of war increased, Gladys's desire for marriage and security grew more intense. She became convinced that Linnen was the one for her, and she wrote home to her family in England that she was planning to marry him. But the marriage never took place. In the devastated war-torn countryside nothing short of death seemed certain, and plans were made to be broken.

There were others who needed Gladys's love and attention far more than Linnen. Her children. Ninepence was her first child—a tiny abandoned girl she had purchased for that amount. And as the years passed she "adopted" more, and besides her own there were dozens of war orphans that depended on her for sustenance. It was this overwhelming responsibility that loomed above all else, impelling Gladys to leave Shansi with her brood of nearly one hundred children in the spring of 1940 and to cross the mountains and the Yellow River into safety beyond the Siam border.

The journey was a harrowing one. Enemy troops were never far away, and moving unnoticed with nearly one hundred noisy children was a constant emotional strain. When at last they reached their destination, Gladys collapsed from mental and physical exhaustion, and the children were scattered around in refugee housing. They had made it out safely, but not without paying a price.

After months of care by a missionary couple in Siam, Gladys slowly regained her strength, but mentally she remained impaired—suffering hallucinations and wandering around the village unable to find her way home. It was a difficult time for her; but as the months passed, the period of mental confusion decreased, and she was able once again to reestablish contact with her scattered children and minister to others.

By 1943, with the Japanese retreating, Gladys was back again in China, but not back to Yangcheng. She lived for a time with CIM missionaries in Lanchow, but she was restless and soon moved on to Tsingsui and finally settled in Chengtu, where she eventually became employed by a local church as a Bible woman—a role heretofore that had always been reserved for native Chinese women, but Gladys had become so assimilated into Chinese society that she seemed perfectly suited to that lowly position of serving the church in evangelism and charity work.

In 1949, after nearly twenty years in China, Gladys was persuaded to make a visit home, and it was on that furlough that the "small woman" of China won her way to the hearts of the British people. Gladys, ill at ease in Western culture, would have preferred to remain in the background, but her mother had different ideas for her. According to one biographer, she was "an official unconscious publicity agent of the first order." For many years she had eagerly accepted speaking invitations to deliver her one and only address, "Our Gladys in China," and now that Gladys had returned she could hardly wait to bring her to her listeners in person.

In the years that followed, through a popular biography (The Small Woman by Alan Burgess), a film ("The Inn of Six Happinesses," starring Ingrid Bergman), and a "This Is Your Life" feature on BBC, Gladys became an internationally known celebrity. Though she returned to minister and make her home in Taiwan in 1957, she continued her world travel and was never out of the limelight, speaking in such places as the Hollywood First Presbyterian Church and dining with such dignitaries as Queen Elizabeth. Yet through all the service she had rendered and the fame she had acquired, she was never fully secure in her calling—particularly that God really wanted to entrust a woman with the responsibilities he had given her. In an interview during her later years she confided her doubts to a friend: "I wasn't God's first choice for what I've done for China. There was somebody else.... I don't know who it was—God's first choice. It must have been a man—a wonderful man. A well-educated man. I don't know what happened. Perhaps he died. Perhaps he wasn't willing.... And God looked down ... and saw Gladys Aylward."[37]

Helen Roseveare

By the mid-twentieth century the vital necessity of women in missions was an accepted fact, and virtually no area of the world had been left unpenetrated by these hearty female pioneers. But if few questioned the strategy of sending women in as rugged soldiers to fight in the front lines of combat, the same was not true when it came to commissioning them as officers. The "brass" had always been exclusively male, despite the abilities or leadership qualities of the other sex, and most women passively accepted the circumstances, convinced that the standard of church authority outlined by the apostle Paul excluded them from any sort of leadership role in the church. But even outside the local church, women missionaries faced the same type of discrimination and thus were often limited in their ministry for the Lord. "The single missionary ... remained for decades a second-class citizen of the mission station."[38] Such was the case with the highly intelligent and efficient Helen Roseveare, a missionary medical doctor to the Congo, whose role as a woman created not only inner struggles but also struggles with fellow missionaries and with nationals.

Helen was born in England in 1925 into a proud and well-respected Cornwall family of many generations. Her father, who had been knighted for his patriotic service during the war, was a renowned mathematician, keenly interested in the education of his children. At twelve Helen was sent away to an exclusive girls' school, and after that to Cambridge, where she received her medical degree.

It was during her freshman year at Cambridge that Helen underwent a conversion experience that caused her to turn away from her Anglo-Catholic background and join the ranks of evangelicalism. Her commitment for missionary service was natural. Her father's brothers and her mother's sister had served as missionaries, and from childhood she had looked forward to being a missionary herself. That day came in 1953, when she sailed for the Congo to serve with the Worldwide Evangelization Crusade there. The emphasis of the WEC was evangelism, and medicine was only a secondary sideline, which well suited Helen who envisioned her own ministry as primarily evangelism. Once in the Congo, Helen found the medical needs to be overwhelming, and it was impossible for her to view the situation without trying to improve it. She immediately realized that the traditional concepts of missionary medicine would never even begin to solve the serious health problems all around her. Instead of establishing a regional medical center where a doctor worked around the clock and still fell short of meeting the needs of the sick, she envisioned a training center where nurses would be taught the Bible and basic medicine and then sent back to their villages to handle routine cases, teach preventive medicine, and serve as lay evangelists. It was a far-reaching plan, but from the start Helen was blocked at every turn by her colleagues, who believed that a mission had no business involving itself in training the nationals in such fields as medicine.

Two years after arriving in the Congo and after spending months in building a combination hospital and training center in Ibambi, and just after she had bathed in the glorious victory of seeing her first four students pass their government medical exams, Helen was forced to relocate at Nebobongo, where there was an old leprosy camp that had become overgrown by the jungle. Helen bitterly argued against the move, but to no avail. Nevertheless, she accepted the decision, moved to Nebobongo, built another hospital, and continued training African nurses.

Despite her setbacks, Helen loved her work. She particularly loved teaching, and she loved the Africans with whom she worked—perhaps too much—at least in the eyes of her colleagues. When differences prevented warm fellowship between her and other foreign missionaries, she spent time with her African friends; and it was an old African pastor to whom she went for spiritual counsel. That a missionary would humble herself before an African in such a way was unacceptable even for the 1950s, and thus her associations created even greater strain between her and her colleagues.

Although Helen had rebelled against her relocation to Nebobongo, she did not allow the decision to slow her down, and within two years she could look with pride on her accomplishments there. And she did look with pride—a sin that by her own admission she constantly struggled with. She had worked so hard against insurmountable odds, and she had succeeded. It was hers, and at least subconsciously she felt that she had a right to be proud, and perhaps dictatorial at times.

Without defending Helen's attitude, it is safe to say that such traits might have been overlooked in a male medical doctor, but as it was, the strong-willed Dr. Roseveare seemed to be a threat to many of her male colleagues. So in an effort to keep her in her place, it seems, a decision was made at the annual field conference in 1957 to relocate John Harris, a young British doctor, and his wife to Nebobongo and to make him Helen's superior. Helen was devastated, and as her biographer has so vividly portrayed, Harris's takeover was a bitter pill to swallow: "In her terms, he'd just taken over Nebobongo—*her* place, which she'd built up out of nothing, out of her dreams, out of her heart, out of the

money she'd raised. This was the place where she'd dug the water holes, cleared the ditches, fired the bricks. She had acknowledged the facts that you could not have two people in charge, that he was a man, and that in Africa a man was the superior being, so she handed over the keys. Then she found she couldn't take it. Perhaps she had been her own boss too long. But now she had lost everything. She had always taken Bible class; Dr. Harris took it now. Dr. Harris organized the nurses, and Helen had always done that. Everything that had been hers was now his."[39]

From the beginning there was almost continual tension between Helen and John Harris that more than once culminated in bitter controversy. On one occasion Harris arbitrarily fired Daniel, Helen's chauffeur, on the grounds that he had misused the van by making an unauthorized trip to see his parents. Helen was furious that Harris had fired Daniel without even consulting her, but it was indicative of the problems she had to contend with as a woman doctor.

WEC missionaries were scheduled for furloughs every seven years, but Helen, who was suffering ill health, was all too ready to go home for a break when she was offered leave in 1958 after only five years on the field. She left for England, disillusioned with missionary work and, according to her biographer, "feeling that it was unlikely she would ever return to Congo."[40] But Helen was too dedicated to the cause of missions to quit that easily, and she began to convince herself (as she had suspected while she was serving in Congo) that her real problem was her singleness. If she had a doctor-husband who would work

Helen Roseveare, missionary doctor to the Congo.

with her and stand by her during the difficult times, everything, she reasoned, would be all right. Was it too much to ask? Surely God understood her need.

Helen had asked God for a husband (in fact, she had "told" him she would not go back without one), but God, like most humans, did not work fast enough to satisfy her. (In the words of a missionary colleague, "... she couldn't drag everybody after her at her speed. You can't keep pace. You're walking stride for stride and suddenly she's a hundred yards ahead. And just when you're catching up, she's off two hundred yards in another direction.")[41] So, in her desire for a husband, Helen went full speed ahead, planning and scheming, too impatient to allow God to simply work out his will in her life.

It was while she was taking additional medical training (to better prepare her for her work in Congo) that Helen met a young doctor—a Christian doctor whom she decided would be a perfect mate for her. She bought new clothes, got her hair permed, and even resigned from the mission in an effort to win him, but to no avail. He truly cared for her, but not enough to marry her. It was a very trying time for Helen, and she struggled against what she knew was best: "The Lord spoke very clearly during my furlough that he was able to satisfy me. . . . I wasn't interested in a spiritualized husband. I wanted a husband with a couple of arms. Well, in the end I jolly near mucked up the whole furlough. . . . I couldn't find a husband in the mission, so I got out of the mission. God let me go a long way, and I made an awful mess. Then God graciously pulled me back and the mission graciously accepted me back."[42]

Helen's return to Congo in 1960 coincided with that country's long sought after independence. It was an uneasy time for whites, and many missionaries believed the risks were too high. Some wanted to leave with their families immediately. Helen, however, had no intention of turning around and going home. If God had truly called her back to Congo she was convinced he would protect her. Her stand, along with that of other single women, made it difficult for the men. How would it look if they slunk away while the women bravely stayed on, and who would protect the women if they were gone? But in Helen's mind, such reasoning had no merit and was, in her biographer's words, "pure male chauvinism." The very fact that most of the men were married made their circumstances different from hers. Obviously they had heavy family responsibilities to consider; and as to protection, there was little a male missionary could do (besides relinquish his own life) if truly perilous conditions did develop.

Helen's decision to stay offered her tremendous opportunities for service. John Harris and his wife left for a well-deserved furlough, and she was once again in charge of the medical facilities at Nebobongo. Much was accomplished in the three years that followed, despite the political uneasiness as the Simba Rebels gained strength in their opposition to the new government. Reports came periodically of attacks against missionaries elsewhere, including reports of missionary women who had "suffered" at the hands of the rebels—an act so degrading and humiliating it could not even be named. Helen herself endured a burglary and an attempted poisoning, but always in her mind the situation was improving— and even if it was not, too many people depended on her. She had to stay.

By the summer of 1964, the Congo was in the throes of a bloody civil war as the Simba Rebels violently took control of village after village. On August 15 the mission compound at Nebobongo was occupied by soldiers, and for the next five months Helen was in captivity, though she remained at the compound, living in her own house until November. Brutal atrocities were committed in the name of black nationalism, and few whites escaped the violence and bloodshed. Helen was no exception. On the night of October 29, while the compound was under rebel occupation, she was overpowered by a black rebel soldier in her little bungalow at Nebobongo. It was a night of terror. She tried to escape, but it was useless: "They found me, dragged me to my feet, struck me over head and shoulders, flung me on the ground, kicked me, dragged me to my feet only to strike me again—the sickening, searing pain of a broken tooth, a mouth full of sticky blood, my glasses gone. Beyond sense, numb with horror and unknown fear, driven, dragged, pushed back to my own house—yelled at, insulted, cursed." Once in the house, it was all over in a few minutes. According to her biographer, the soldier "forced her backwards on the bed, falling on top of her.... The will to resist and fight had been knocked out of her. But she screamed over and over again.... The brutal act of rape was accomplished with animal vigor and without mercy."[43]

"My God, my God, why have you forsaken me?" rang over and over again through Helen's numbed consciousness. Though she never could have understood it at the time, the terrible violation of her body that night allowed her to have a ministry to others that she could not have otherwise had. Her depth of spiritual maturity gave her complete assurance that she had not failed God or in any way lost any supposed purity because of the rape. Whatever she had suffered physically, her relationship with God had not been damaged.

But not all the rape victims had such assurance. Helen discovered this to be true some weeks later while imprisoned in a convent with Catholic nuns. One young Italian nun on the verge of a mental collapse due to the repeated brutal rapings was convinced she had lost her purity and thus her salvation. The Mother Superior had tried in vain to reason with her and only reluctantly sought out Helen to counsel with her. Helen's frankness about her own experience and her spiritual depth was what the young nun needed, and it was a cathartic time for both of them—a time that prepared Helen for more sexual brutality she would endure before her release.

Helen's rescue on the last day of 1964 was more than she had dared hope for. For months she had faced the almost daily threat of death, and she hardly knew how to deal with her new found freedom and the rude shock of suddenly being back home. There was a sense of joy and relief, but also a sense of great sorrow as she listened to horror stories of the martyrdom of some of her dearest friends and colleagues. At first the thought of returning seemed remote, but as the Congo political situation improved and as heartrending letters from African co-workers and friends arrived, the pull to Africa became intense. She was needed now more than ever. How could she say no?

Helen returned to Africa in March of 1966 to resume her duties as a medical missionary and particularly her work of training nationals. Her initial arrival at the devastated mission compound was greeted with jubilation, but she soon discovered that life in the Congo had irrevocably changed since her first term in the 1950s. Things would never be the same. The new spirit of independence and nationalism had penetrated every area of society, including the church, and no longer was there an automatic feeling of respect and admiration—especially from the younger generation—for the lady doc-

tor who had sacrificed so much for the Congo.

Had she simply been caring for the sick her work would have been more appreciated, but as it was, her seven-year term was filled with turmoil and disappointment. Blacks were now in control, and as a white she was denied the authority she needed as a teacher. Students rudely challenged her on almost every issue. Moreover, their sometimes careless work habits and expectations of a good life clashed with her own drive and dedication.

Despite her remarkable sacrifice and great accomplishments during those seven years, Helen left Africa in 1973 broken in spirit. Students had rebelled against her authority, and even her colleagues questioned her leadership ability. It was a tragedy, at least in human terms, that her twenty years of service in Africa ended in such a way. Her own words tell the story best: "When I knew I was coming home from the field and a young medical couple were taking my place at the college and an African colleague was taking over the directorship of the hospital, I organized a big day. It was to be a welcome to the two new doctors, a handover to my colleague, graduation day for the students in the college, and my farewell. A big choir had been practicing for five months. I got lots of cassettes to record everything and films to snap everything. Then at the last moment the whole thing fell to bits. The student body went on strike. I ended up having to resign the college where I'd been the director twenty years."[44]

Helen returned home to face a "very, very lonely period" in her life, but again as with so many other disappointing experiences, she turned to

God. Instead of bitterness there was a new spirit of humility and a new appreciation for what Jesus had done for her on the cross. God was molding her for an even greater ministry—one of which she herself could never have dreamed. In the years that followed she became a much sought after internationally acclaimed spokeswoman for Christian missions. She continues today to write and speak from the heart, and her honest forthrightness has been a refreshing breeze in a profession that too long has been stifled by its image of supersainthood.

SELECTED BIBLIOGRAPHY

Allen, Catherine. The New Lottie Moon Story. *Nashville: Broadman, 1980.*

Beaver, R. Pierce. American Protestant Women in World Mission. *Grand Rapids: Eerdmans, 1969.*

Beets, Henry. Johanna of Nigeria: Life and Labors of Johanna Veenstra. *Grand Rapids: Grand Rapids Printing Company, 1937.*

Burgess, Alan. Daylight Must Come: The Story of a Courageous Woman Doctor in the Congo. *New York: Dell, 1975.*

_____. The Small Woman. *New York: Dutton, 1957.*

Houghton, Frank. Amy Carmichael of Dohnavur. *London: Society for the Propagation of Christian Knowledge, 1954.*

Hyatt, Irwin. "Charlotte Diggs Moon" in Our Ordered Lives Confess: Three Nineteenth-Century American Missionaries in East Shantung. *Cambridge, Mass.: Harvard University Press, 1976.*

Roseveare, Helen. Give Me This Mountain. *London: Inter-Varsity, 1966.*

_____. He Gave Us a Valley. *Downers Grove, Ill.: InterVarsity, 1976.*

Stenbock, Evelyn. "Miss Terri": The Story of Maude Cary, Pioneer GMU Missionary in Morocco. *Lincoln, Neb.: Good News Broadcasting, 1970.*

Thompson, Phyllis. A Transparent Woman: The Compelling Story of Gladys Aylward. *Grand Rapids: Zondervan, 1971.*

Veenstra, Johanna. Pioneering for Christ in the Sudan. *Grand Rapids: Smitter Book, 1926.*

Chapter 10

Student Volunteers:
Forsaking Wealth and Prestige

Unlike the single women who for the most part raised their status in life by entering foreign missions, the student volunteers were mainly young men who in the eyes of the world lowered their status; and, unlike the women, they generally went to the field married or else married soon after they arrived. In the minds of many people it was commendable that the Gladys Aylwards, the Maude Carys, and the Johanna Veenstras went to the distant shores to evangelize the "heathen," for all they would have amounted to was parlor maids or stenographers anyway; but to send brilliant young university graduates to "waste" their lives among the "heathen" was a crying shame.

The Student Volunteer Movement was born in Mount Hermon, Massachusetts, in 1886, though the impetus for its development occurred even earlier when seven Cambridge University students turned their backs on their career ambitions and committed their lives to foreign missions. The movement prospered for some fifty years, during which time, according to J. Herbert Kane, "It had been instrumental in sending 20,500 students to the foreign mission field, most of them from North America." During the early twentieth century it is estimated that student volunteers constituted half of the total Protestant foreign missionary force. Most of them worked among the people of old, well-developed civilizations. There was a strong bias toward China among the volunteers. Approximately one third of them served there. The next largest concentration was in India, where some twenty percent of the student volunteer force ministered. Mission leaders passionately pleaded for "men and women of literary tastes" to go to China, and the call was answered. By 1920 at the Des Moines Convention, the movement had passed its peak, and from then on it declined. "It was inevitable," writes Harold R. Cook, "that the same liberal trend affecting the major denominations should touch the Student Volunteer Movement. By the late 1920s it was already losing ground. Then came the

Great Depression and the critical 'Laymen's Report' on foreign missions with disastrous effects on the whole missionary enterprise."[1]

Despite their failures, the student volunteers were among the most dedicated missionaries ever to enter foreign missionary service. In an era when some (or "most," in the evaluation of Hudson Taylor) missionaries had become "self-indulgent and idle," the student volunteers were a striking contrast. They were driven by an intensity of purpose that has rarely been equaled, and they were committed to evangelizing the world by whatever means was necessary.

Such intensity combined with their liberal university training often lead the student volunteers to adapt their faith to their new culture in order to bring greater numbers under the umbrella of Christianity. They were different from their missionary forebears, whose chief education had been centered in the Bible. Many of the student volunteers, while trained in theology, had also spent their formal education grappling with Kant's *Critique of Pure Reason* and Darwin's *Origin of Species*. Many had entered their work as laymen, quite unprepared for the type of ministry they had been sent to fulfill. Moreover, their avid interest in world religions led to a heretofore unheard of respect for those religions by professing Christians, which also opened the way for a re-examination and adaptation of their beliefs in the name of Christian evangelism.

Because of the regularly scheduled Quadrennial Conventions sponsored by the Student Volunteer Movement, there was an interdenominational bond among the student volunteers that had never before occurred in a broad-based missionary movement. The outcome of this association was a beneficial cooperative effort among missionaries that had rarely been seen before; but it also paved the way for the ecumenical movement. This concern for unity along with the modernist approach to Scripture had long-term effects on world evangelism. "Protestant liberalism, deemphasizing and demythologizing miracles and biblical authority, introduced the powerful but crippling secularism into Chinese Christianity." According to Kenneth S. Latourette, this "secularizing movement" was the most important factor influencing Christianity's losses in China in the face of communism.[2]

For many student volunteers, the whole world rather than one country was their mission field. While many did settle on one field and dedicated their lives to one small area, a great many others changed fields and traveled throughout the world in an effort to reach the elite—the educated classes who could wield the most influence on their peers. With them the student volunteers brought the YMCA and other organizations that provided a network for Christian students throughout the world.

During the first half of the twentieth century, the student volunteers made an indelible impact on foreign missions. Their names—C. T. Studd, J. E. K. Studd, Robert Wilder, John R. Mott, Joseph H. Oldham, Robert E. Speer, W. Temple Gairdner, William Paton, Fletcher Brockman, E. Stanley Jones, and others—will forever be remembered in the annals of missionary literature as ones who willingly forsook professional careers, wealth, and comfort to serve in a cause to which they were wholeheartedly committed.

Sherwood Eddy spoke for many student volunteers when he movingly wrote of his own experience and of the movement as a whole:

In restrospect, I find I have spent half a century along the far-flung battle line of missions. I was one of the first of six-teen thousand student volunteers who were swept into what seemed to us nothing less than a missionary crusade. We were considered fanatical by some, and we made numerous mistakes which we ourselves came to realize later in bitter experience. Many sacrificed early plans and ambitions for wealth, power, prestige or pleasure, to go to some distant country about which they knew little save its abysmal need. Not wholly unlike the unity of Christendom achieved during the Middle Ages was the feeling of these student volunteer missionaries that they were one team, working for one world, under one Cap-tain. We felt much as Wordsworth did about the French Revolution—which he doubtless idealized as we did our crusade:

Bliss was it in that dawn to be alive, But to be young was very Heaven![3]

C. T. Studd

Perhaps the most famous of the stu-dent volunteers was C. T. Studd, an illustrious college athlete and son of a wealthy Englishman. Charlie Studd strikingly exemplifies the willingness of the student volunteers to sacrifice wealth and prestige and to boldly con-front the task of world evangelism with intense dedication. He possessed al-most frantic zeal—particularly in later life—zeal that caused him to disre-gard his own well-being and the well-being of his family in his effort to fur-ther the Kingdom of God. It was this unrelenting discipline, combined with

personality flaws, that made him one of the most controversial missionary leaders the evangelical church has known in modern history. His role as founder and director of The World-wide Evangelization Crusade illus-trates the paramount importance of a missionary candidate's familiarity with the particulars of the mission board and the personality of its leader.

Wealth and luxury surrounded the young C. T. Studd as he grew up in the 1870s on Tedworth, the family estate in Wiltshire. Edward Studd, C.T.'s father, had made a fortune as a planter in India and then had returned to Eng-land to live a life of leisure. Horse rac-ing was his passion, and it was a great day of celebration when his own horse won the Grand National. With such a reputation, it naturally came as a shock to many people when word spread that Edward Studd had been converted at one of D. L. Moody's evangelistic campaigns. The effect was immediate. He sold his horses, gave up racing, began holding gospel meetings at Tedworth, and invested his energy in saving the souls of his friends and relatives. His three sons were special targets of his persistent witness, and, according to C. T., "Everyone in the house had a dog's life of it until they were converted."[4]

All three sons were converted before their father's untimely death two years later, but it was not until some six years after that, following a near fatal illness of his younger brother, that C. T. went to a Moody campaign on his own and there dedicated his life to God and to foreign missionary service. His decision created a sensation. At both Eton and Cambridge he had managed to outshine even his talented brothers as a cricket player, and, as

The "Cambridge Seven" after they arrived in China (C. T. Studd, standing on the left).

captain and best all-around player of the famed Cambridge Eleven, he was considered by many to be "England's greatest cricketer." Added to the sensation of Studd's decision was the fact that six other brilliant and talented Cambridge students made the same commitment, and the "Cambridge Seven," as they were dubbed, vowed to sail to China together to serve under the CIM. "Never before in the history of missions," wrote a newspaper reporter, "has so unique a band set out to labor in the foreign field."[5] To many people, including members of Studd's own family, the decision of the seven university students was a rash move and a tremendous waste of intellect and ability.

Studd's tenure in China lasted less than a decade, but it was filled with activity. Soon after he arrived he met and married Priscilla Steward, who was serving in China with the Salvation Army; and four daughters were born to them on Chinese soil. The years of labor in the interior of North China were filled with difficulties. "For five years," wrote Studd, "we never went outside our doors without a volley of curses from our neighbors."[6] But as they established themselves their ministry expanded—Priscilla in her evangelistic work with women and C. T. in his work with opium addicts. Although C. T. had received a substantial inheritance (equivalent to more than a half million dollars by today's standards) from his father's estate, he gave it all away and chose to live entirely by faith as other CIM missionaries did, facing many times of severe financial hardship.

Ill health forced Studd to return to England with his family in 1894, and the next six years were spent speaking out for missions in the United States and England in behalf of the Student Volunteer Movement. According to J. Herbert Kane, "... students by the thousands flocked to his meetings, sometimes six a day ... and hundreds, caught up in the revival movement, volunteered for missionary service."[7] In 1900, Studd moved with his family to India for six years to minister to planters and English-speaking people there, but these years away from direct missionary evangelism were unfulfilling for him. Back in England, again plagued by ill health, Studd continued his itinerant speaking ministry, but missing was the confidence that he was in the center of God's will.

It was a sign on a door, inscribed with the words "Cannibals Want Missionaries," that changed the course of Studd's life. On further inquiry he heard of hundreds of thousands of tribal people in Central Africa who had never once heard the gospel because "no Christian had ever gone to tell of Jesus." "The shame," according to Studd, "sank deep into" his soul. "I said, 'Why have no Christians gone?' God replied, 'Why don't you go?' 'The doctors won't permit it,' I said. The answer came, 'Am I not the good physician? Can I not take you through? Can I not keep you there?' There were no excuses, it had to be done.'"[8]

Studd's decision to go to Africa was devastating to Priscilla, who was suffering from a debilitating heart condition. How could he just leave her and

C. T. Studd, missionary to China, India, and Africa.

pursue such a wild scheme? He was fifty years old, sickly, and without financial backing. She strongly objected, but Studd, convinced of his calling, left for an exploratory trip in 1910, returning the following year to make plans for his new mission to Africa, HAM—the Heart of Africa Mission. In 1913, with one assistant, Alfred Buxton, who would later become his son-in-law, Studd began his eighteen-year venture to the Belgian Congo in "the heart of Africa." Though he received word on his journey that Priscilla had suffered further heart complications, he refused to turn back. The work of the Lord, he firmly believed, came before family concerns. When he returned home in 1916 (his only furlough) to bring back recruits to Africa, he found Priscilla no longer an invalid and more active than she had been in years, effectively carrying out the work of the home office.

In the years that followed, more re-

265

Priscilla Stewart Studd, wife of C. T. Studd.

cruits arrived in Africa, including his daughter Edith, who married Alfred Buxton, and his daughter Pauline, who arrived with her husband Norman Grubb. But as more missionaries came, doctrinal and personal differences surfaced that continually plagued the infant mission. Even Studd's daughters and sons-in-law found him to be a most difficult individual to work with. He had sacrificed everything for Africa, and he expected his missionaries to do the same. He worked eighteen-hour days, and, according to Norman Grubb, "There was no let-up . . . no diversions, no days off, no recreation." The missionaries were expected to live African style, avoiding any appearance whatever of affluent European lifestyles.

Doctrinal controversies also arose between Studd and many of the missionaries—particularly between him and new recruits arriving on the field. Studd had written home about the great headway he was making. In fact, in 1918, after only five years on the field, he wrote: "The progress is simply wonderful; people are coming to us from every quarter and from very long distances. We are having pretty nearly weekly baptisms. The converts are evangelizing far and near." But when the missionaries arrived, they found quite a different picture. "But what shocked us most," wrote Norman Grubb, "was his attitude toward professing African Christians, five hundred of whom would gather on a Sunday morning. Where we had been told to expect a concourse of shining saints, C. T. was saying that sin was rampant, and nobody who continued in sin entered heaven, no matter how much he was supposed to have been born again; and that he doubted, holding up the fingers of his two hands, whether ten of these five hundred would really get there. We thought this awful. Our theology was . . . that once a person was born again . . . he could not be unborn. C. T. took no count of that. His stand was 'without holiness no man shall see the Lord.'"[9]

Living in sin, to C. T., did not just mean gross immorality. It included a wide range of "sins," including ones related to a man's work ethic. "One of the worst sins of these people," wrote Studd, "is a terrible laziness. To sit about on a chair and talk is the desire of everybody. To work is folly." For Studd, the regular work day began at 6 A.M., and he expected Africans and missionaries alike to follow suit. Personal devotions were to be over with by then, so that the day's activities could begin. When Grubb suggested on one occasion that the Africans and missionaries hold special prayer meetings for revival, C. T. responded, "I don't believe in praying in work hours. Let's have a meeting at 4 A.M." When Grubb rose at 4 A.M. for his own devotional time, he could hear from across the compound "the old man's banjo going. He had gathered a 4 A.M. prayer meeting of some of the Africans."[10]

Living such a rigorous Christian life was too much for many of the Africans and missionaries as well, but Studd had no time for anyone who, in his mind, was less than totally committed, even if it meant dismissing his own daughter and son-in-law, Edith and Alfred Buxton. It was a demoralizing time for them, especially for Alfred who had sacrificed so much to begin the work in Africa with Studd. "To Alfred's nursing and care," he had written some years before, "I certainly ... owe my life; and truly no mother ever nursed her child more tenderly and efficiently than he nursed me."

Other close relationships of past years were also deteriorating, and by the late 1920s, despite his hard work and dedication, Studd was rapidly losing the support of the home committee—particularly after Priscilla's death in 1929. His rigorous demands on missionaries and his negative view of African Christians were well known to the home committee, but now other issues were creating controversy—one surrounding a booklet C. T. had written, entitled "D.C.D." In response to the lethargy he had found among Christians, C. T. had said, "I want to be one of those who doesn't care a damn except to give my life for Jesus and souls." "D.C.D." was an expansion of that expression of commitment, and the initials stood for

"Don't Care a Damn," a phrase that shocked and offended many Christians, including some of his staunchest supporters.[11]

If the pamphlet was not enough to spur the committee into action against him, reports that he had become a morphine addict were. Studd's ill-health and eighteen-hour days were taking a toll on him physically and emotionally, and after discovering the relief that a shot of morphine gave him, he began taking morphia tablets dispensed by a medical doctor from Uganda and brought in by missionaries "without declaration because of difficulties which might have been raised." "With this news reaching home ... the Committee," according to Grubb, "decided that the only thing to do was to remove him from the mission." What followed, in the words of Grubb, "was the darkest chapter in the mission's history."[12] With the home committee prepared to reorganize and start a new mission without Studd, Grubb (who, with Studd, had also been dismissed from the mission) and David Munro, also Studd's son-in-law, took the "drastic action" of going into the mission headquarters early one morning and removing the records to their own safekeeping.

But even with the records in hand, the mission was in shambles, and there seemed to be little hope of recouping the losses. Was there anything that could give the fledgling WEC (The Heart of Africa Mission was now the Worldwide Evangelization Crusade) a fresh start? There was. Within weeks came the news of Studd's death. A tumultuous era was over, and with the courageous leadership of Norman Grubb the mission got a fresh start— but it never forgot the tireless dedication of the mission's founder, C. T. Studd.

What went wrong? How could one of Britain's most prestigious young missionaries come to such an end? There are, no doubt, many underlying factors that influenced the course of Studd's life, but certainly the intensity of his dedication contributed to his downfall—an intensity that was characteristic of the student volunteers and one that sidetracked many of them into extraneous issues while it catapulted others into outstanding service. "We do need to be intense," wrote Studd, "and our intensity must ever increase."[13] But it was that intensity, viewed by many as "fanaticism" or "extremism," that brought him down. C. T. often referred to himself as a "Gambler for God." But it could be said that he gambled and lost.

In the years since Studd's death, the WEC witnessed steady growth, and by the 1970s it was reaching all over the globe with more than five hundred missionaries—among them the courageous Dr. Helen Roseveare, who began her service in Ibambi where Studd himself tirelessly served. In analyzing the phenomenal comeback of the WEC, it would be difficult to overestimate the outstanding leadership of Norman Grubb, a man possessed of a rare honesty in admitting his own shortcomings and, though a relentless defender of his father-in-law, wise enough to recognize his flaws and to learn from them.

John R. Mott

While it was C. T. Studd and his fellow classmates of the "Cambridge Seven" that captured world attention as student missionary volunteers, it was John R. Mott who more than any other individual influenced the surge of students onto the mission field in the decades that followed. Though a layman and never an actual missionary in the strictest sense of the word, his influence in missions rivaled—and perhaps surpassed—that of his idol, David Livingstone, "whose heroic, Christ-like achievements," in the words of Mott, "furnished the governing missionary motive of my life."[14] Like so many of the student volunteers, Mott passed over opportunities of wealth and prestige in his commitment to world evangelism. But though he declined diplomatic posts and opportunities for financial gain, he could not elude fame. He was a friend and counselor of presidents, a winner of the Nobel Peace Prize, and the most influential world religious leader of the twentieth century.

John R. Mott was born and raised in Iowa, the son of a prosperous lumber merchant. He was converted as a youth and became active in the local Methodist Episcopal church. In 1881, at the age of sixteen, he left home to attend Upper Iowa University, and there he became a charter member of the YMCA, an international organization then committed to Christian evangelism. After four years at Upper Iowa University, Mott transferred to Cornell University, where he studied political science and history. It was here, under the preaching of J. E. K. Studd, that he underwent a life-changing experience that made spiritual growth and evangelism his priorities. J. E. K. Studd, C. T. Studd's brother, had come to the United States to tour university campuses at the invitation of D. L. Moody and YMCA leaders. It was hoped that Studd, according to Mott's biographer, "would attract students to hear his missionary message and description of the 'Cambridge Seven' who had rejected status and wealth to volunteer for foreign missions."[15]

Although Studd emphasized missions, Mott did not personally commit himself to the cause until the following summer, when he attended the first Christian Student Conference at Mount Hermon, Massachusetts (sponsored by D. L. Moody and later held at the nearby Northfield conference grounds). As a delegate from Cornell, along with some two hundred and fifty other students from nearly one hundred colleges and universities, he spent a month under the tutelage of D. L. Moody and other renowned Bible teachers. On the last day of the conference, Robert Wilder, a missions enthusiast from Princeton, presented a missionary challenge that turned into an aggressive appeal for personal commitment. As a result, one hundred students, later dubbed the "Mount Hermon Hundred," signed the "Princeton Pledge" ("I purpose, God willing, to become a foreign missionary") that would soon become the initiation oath into the Student Volunteer Movement. Mott was among the one hundred who signed, and that meeting was the beginning of the Student Volunteer Movement for Foreign Missions (officially organized in 1888), an organization that he would lead for more than thirty years.

Following this famous meeting, Wilder, at the encouragement of D. L. Moody and others, began a tour of college campuses to make his challenge nationwide. With his moving appeal, his urgent slogan ("The Evangelization of the World in This Generation"), and

his "Princeton Pledge," he provided the real impetus for the movement at home, in England, and on the Continent. Wilder's own missionary fervor had come from his experience of growing up in India with his missionary parents; and his concern to motivate students was inspired in part by his father, who had been a member of the "Society of the Brethren" at Andover, a missions-oriented club that had originated in 1806 with Samuel Mills and the Haystack Group. Following his effective college tour, Wilder returned to India and worked with students there, while Mott and others took over the leadership on the home front.

As a leader and organizer of the SVM, Mott confronted an enormous task, especially if the movement's slogan, "The Evangelization of the World in This Generation," was to be taken at face value; and the best way this could be accomplished, in his view, was to mobilize thousands of students to carry the gospel to the ends of the earth. But why the SVM? How could it accomplish a feat that organized religion had failed to do? Mott was convinced of the need of collaboration, and the SVM which encompassed young people from a wide spectrum of religious backgrounds seemed to be the ideal solution.

Closely associated with Mott's activities with the SVM were his activities with the YMCA, an organization he ably served for more than forty years, sixteen as general secretary. In these capacities, travel became a way of life, and as soon as one world tour was over he was already planning for another. As he traveled, he worked with resident missionaries as well as national students and sought to develop a world-wide network of

THE TWENTIETH CENTURY

	1900	1910	1920	1930

Black Africa

- (1915) Death of Mary Slessor
- (1910) C. T. Studd arrives in Africa
- (1931) Death of
- (1913) Schweitzer arrives in Africa
- (1928) Carl Becker sails

The Far East and Pacific Islands

- (1932) Martyrdom
- (1930) Gladys Aylward
- (1907) Goforth begins revival ministry in Korea and Manchuria
- (1905) Martyrdom of Eleanor Chestnut
- (1934) Martyrdom

Latin America

- (1936)
- (1917) W. C. Townsend arrives in Guatemala
- (1929) Townsend
- (1931) HCJB begins

The Near East, North Africa, and Central Asia

- (1901) Maude Cary sails to Morocco
- (1933) Death of
- (1928) Jerusalem World
- (1907) E. Stanley Jones arrives in India
- (1938)
- (1912) Zwemer begins work in Cairo
- (1900) Ida Scudder begins medical work in India
- (1918) Ida Scudder founds Vellore Medical College

Europe and North America

- (1910) Edinburgh Missionary Conference
- (1939)
- (1920) SVM Des Moines Convention
- (1932) *Rethinking*
- (1908) Grenfell rescued from drifting ice
- (1934) Founding

1940	1950	1960	1970	1980

• (1977) Festo Kivengere escapes Uganda

• (1953) Helen Roseveare arrives in the Congo

C. T. Studd

• (1960) Congo independence

for the Congo

• (1964) Simba rebellion

• (1964) Death of Paul Carlson

• (1964) Attack on Kilometer Eight

• (1945) Death of R. A. Jaffray in Japanese prison camp

of eleven TEAM missionaries   • (1962) Capture of Mitchell, Gerber, and Vietti

goes to China   • (1958) Cho begins tent ministry in Korea

(1940) Gladys Aylward leads children to safety

• (1968) Death of Betty Olsen

• (1945) Death of Eric Liddell

• (1962) Don Richardson arrives in Irian Jaya

of the Stams   • (1954) Myron Bromley enters Balim Valley

• (1948) FEBC begins broadcasting in Manilla

Ken Pike begins work in Mexico

• (1981) Martyrdom of Chet Bitterman

• (1943) Martyrdom of five New Tribes missionaries in Bolivia

• (1941) Walter Herron begins aviation ministry

• (1964) TWR broadcasts from Bonaire

• (1956) Auca massacre

• (1948) Nate Saint arrives in Ecuador

completed Cakchiquel NT   • (1956) Marianna Slocum completes Tzeltal NT

broadcast from Quito   • (1957) Rachel Saint and Dayuma tour U.S.

• (1951) Death of Amy Carmichael

Johanna Veenstra

Missionary Conference

• (1967) Morocco closed to missionaries

Madras World Missionary Conference

• (1973) Death of E. Stanley Jones

• (1962) Viggo Olsen arrives in East Pakistan

• (1972) JAARS crash in New Guinea

Joy Ridderhof founds Gospel Recordings

• (1955) Death of Mott

• (1954) Founding of Trans World Radio

Missions published

• (1950) Founding of World Vision

• (1976) Founding of the U.S. Center
for World Mission

• (1942) Founding of New Tribes Mission

• (1945) Founding of MAF

• (1946) First triennial "Urbana" Missionary Convention held by IVCF in Toronto

of Summer Institute of Linguistics

• (1974) Lausanne Conference on
World Evangelization

271

unified missionary activity. In realizing this goal, he helped to organize the World Student Christian Federation, a loose international organization of Christian students that under his leadership grew to include societies in some three thousand schools.

One of the most receptive fields for Mott's appeal to students was, surprisingly, China, among the literati, "the scholars of that great land of scholars." During his first tour of that country in 1896 the prospects for reaching that class seemed dim, but, according to Mott, the atmosphere soon changed: "Five years later the walls of Jericho were beginning to crumble.... The ancient literati were beginning to give way to the modern literati.... When I reached Canton, I found to my surprise that they had hired the largest theater in China, a building that holds thirty-five hundred people. On the night of the first meeting as we neared the theater, I saw crowds in the streets and asked, 'Why do they not open the doors?' Someone came to tell us that the doors had been opened for an hour and that every seat was taken.... On the platform were about fifty of the leading educated Chinese of Canton, many of them young men who had studied in Tokyo and in American universities." By the time the series of meetings was over, more than eight hundred had become "inquirers," and within a month nearly one hundred and fifty of those "had been baptized or were preparing for baptism." In two other Chinese cities where Mott conducted meetings, he received a similar response.[16]

The highlight of Mott's career as a missionary statesman was the Edinburgh Missionary Conference of 1910, which he organized and chaired. This ten-day conference, composed of 1,355 delegates, was the first interdenominational missionary conference of its kind and became the impetus for the ecumenical movement that took shape in the decades that followed. The conference was a high point of missionary enthusiasm; and the call to evangelize the world "in this generation" was still in the air. With some forty-five thousand missionaries on the field and the prediction that the number might be trebled in the next thirty years, some delegates truly believed the complete evangelization of the world was imminent.

But in the years following Edinburgh the interest in foreign missions waned in most mainline denominations, and the SVM, in its tension-filled meeting in Des Moines in 1920, moved, according to C. Howard Hopkins, "to take a big step toward correcting that fateful fascination with the wonder and mystery of the Orient that had hypnotized their forebears and sent them off to China ... out of sight, sound, and smell of the slums of Chicago or the injustices of sweated labor. They wanted to concentrate on the visible pressing social maladjustments at hand rather than 'traditional questions of missionary work.'"[17]

Mott had all along stressed the social dimensions of world evangelism, but never to the extent of making it a primary focus. Yet, he was forced to come to terms with "social gospel shift" that was beginning to be seen in missions. Social service, he insisted, is "one of the most distinctive calls of our generation," and one intrinsically tied to personal evangelism: "There are not two gospels, one social and one individual. There is but one Christ who lived, died, and rose again, and relates himself to the lives of men. He is the Savior of the individual and the one sufficient Power to transform his environment and relationships."[18]

It was Mott's conservative stance and strict adherence to the primacy of evangelism in missions that led to his declining influence during the last years of the SVM. A younger generation of "volunteers" no longer found his "narrow" emphasis relevant to their expanding concept of missions. There were others who criticized Mott as well. His name was associated with the Laymen's Foreign Missions Inquiry and its report, *Rethinking Missions*, and for that reason he was viewed by some as having become more liberal in his foreign missionary outlook. That report sought to redefine the aim of missions: "to see the best in other religions, to help the adherents of those religious to discover, or to rediscover, all the best in their own traditions, to cooperate with the most active and vigorous elements in the other traditions in social reform and in the purification of religious expression. The aim should not be conversion."[19] Although Mott acknowledged the value of the inquiry and subsequent report, it clearly did not reflect his own position. Throughout his life he viewed conversion of non-Christians to be the most important aim of missions.

The last years of Mott's life were filled with activities on the mission fields and at home. He had a part in the formation of the World Council of Churches, an organization he believed could strengthen the influence of Christianity in the world. Though he sought to remain above the bitter Fundamentalist-Modernist debate that was raging at home and abroad,

John R. Mott at Whitby World Conference meeting in 1947.

he, along with Robert Speer became a target for criticism among fundamentalists. Yet, throughout this period, his own personal faith and vibrant love for his Savior never dimmed, and he maintained his warm friendships with many of his more conservative colleagues.

Throughout his life, despite all his travels, Mott remained a strong family man. Leila, his wife of sixty-two years, traveled and worked with him, often speaking to groups of college women and ministering to women missionaries all over the world. Her death in 1952, at the age of eighty-six, came as a heavy blow to Mott, but he continued his travel in behalf of world evangelism without her. In 1953, at the age of eighty-eight, he remarried, and in 1954 he made his final public appearance at the World Council of Churches assembly in Evanston, Illinois. But his traveling days were not over. "Death,"

273

he told a reporter, "is a place where I change trains," and he made that transfer on January 31, 1955.

Robert E. Speer

A close associate and lifelong friend of Mott, and a man decribed as "the incarnation of the spirit of the Student Volunteer Movement," was Robert E. Speer, who, like Mott, served the foreign missionary cause as a layman. Unlike Mott, his ministry was dedicated largely to a single denomination—the Presbyterian Church—serving for forty-six years as the Secretary of the Board of Foreign Missions. The Presbyterian Church was one of the most fervent of the mainline denominations in its missionary zeal, and Speer's own enthusiasm for foreign missions only enhanced the church's stand. Though Speer was a highly respected and popular figure within his own denomination and in ecumenical circles, his ministry spanned a stormy period of his denomination's history; and despite his efforts to play the role of peacemaker, bringing opposing factions together, he was often the brunt of criticism. Nevertheless, during his tenure the Presbyterian Church greatly expanded its role in overseas evangelism.

Speer was born in Pennsylvania in 1867, the son of a lawyer and two-term Democratic congressman, who brought up his children in a strict Puritan-Presbyterian atmosphere. He was educated at Andover and Princeton, where he twice held office of class president and gained a reputation as a hard-hittung defensive tackle on the varsity football team. It was during his sophomore year at Princeton that Speer, under the powerful and persuasive preaching of Robert Wilder, became a "pledge-signing" student volunteer, along with several of his classmates. He left behind his ambition to follow his father into the legal profession and began setting his sights on the mission field. "There are many," he wrote, "who regard us as possessed of a strange delusion, many who count us carried away by some fanatical madness...."[20]

After graduation from Princeton, Speer became the traveling secretary for the Student Volunteer Movement; and though he served for only one year in that capacity, he signed up more than a thousand volunteers for the foreign field. With the intention of going to the mission field himself, Speer returned to Princeton for seminary training, but after less than two years his studies were interrupted when he unexpectedly received a call from the Presbyterian Board of Foreign Missions to fill its highest administrative post. The call, according to Sherwood Eddy, "upset Speer's equilibrium, and he fought hard against it. He certainly did not want to stay at home when he had asked a thousand volunteers who had signed the declaration to undergo the hardships of the foreign field."[21] But Speer reluctantly accepted the offer, challenged by the potential influence he could exert for missions through such a key position.

Although Speer was an activist, he is best remembered for the philosophical influence he had on foreign missions of his day. During a time when many voices from the younger generation were calling for social activism in missions, he insisted that the "Supreme and Determining Aim" of missions be religious: "We cannot state too strongly in an age when the thought of men is full of things, and the body has crept up on the throne of the soul, that our work is not immediately and in itself a philanthropic work, a political work, a secular work of any sort whatsoever; it is a spiritual and a religious work. Of course, religion must express itself in life, but religion is spiritual life. I had rather plant one seed of the life of Christ under the crust of heathen life than cover that whole crust over with the veneer of our social habits on the vestiture of Western civilization."[22]

Speer took a strong stand against the Laymen's Foreign Missions Inquiry Report of 1932, again separating himself from many of his more liberal colleagues, but the real clashes that he confronted as a missionary statesman were not with the liberals but with the Fundamentalists, though he himself had helped write the last volume of *The Fundamentals.* The Modernist-Fundamentalist controversy that was being waged in the Presbyterian Church at home had also found its way to the mission field, and Speer seemed to be caught in the middle, distressed by the unfortunate effect the infighting was having on the work of evangelism. "I wish we could get up such a glow and fervor and onrush of evangelical and evangelistic conviction and action," he wrote to a missionary in China, "that we would be swept clear past issues like the present ones so that men who want to dispute over these things could stay behind and do so, while the rest of us could march ahead, more than making up by new conquests for all the defections and losses of those who stay behind."[23]

During this time Speer himself was attacked for alleged unorthodoxy and was accused by J. Gresham Machen and others of "malfeasance in appointing allegedly unorthodox missionaries." It was a trying time for one who had served so long and so faithfully for his church (even filling its highest position as moderator in 1927), but he weathered the storm and was vindicated by the General Assembly, which gave him an overwhelming vote of confidence.

Unlike so many other mission board leaders of his day, Speer had an unusually open view toward women in Christian service. He argued that "it would be strange and anomalous to deny to women equality in the church, which is the very fountain of the principle of equality. It is Christ who has made women free and equal. Is she to be allowed this freedom and equality elsewhere and denied it in the Church, where freedom and equality had their origin?" Likewise, he praised "the Christian Churches on the foreign mission field" that were "apprehending the measure of the Gospel in this better than we. . . . God shuts no doors to His daughters which He opens to His sons."[24]

At the age of seventy, after forty-six years of service, Speer retired from his leadership position in Presbyterian missions. For the next decade he traveled, lecturing at campuses and conferences, never letting up in his all-consuming commitment to foreign missions; and the intensity that had so characterized him in his earlier years continued to the very end. ("When he boarded a train," according to his biographer, "his bag of papers and books were with him. Out of the battered brown bag came papers and reports from the office, or a book.

He plunged at once into their perusal. . . .")[25] Although terminally ill, suffering from leukemia, he insisted on keeping a previously arranged speaking commitment only three weeks before he died in 1947, even though he was so weak he was unable to stand. In spite of the fact that Speer was one of the great missionary statesmen of this century, he always depreciated his own service as compared to those serving in the front lines; and when a friend requested to write his biography, he replied: "Nix on the biography . . . merely say the cuss lived; he worked; he died; there are others coming along."[26]

Samuel Zwemer

The intensity that so characterized the educated young student volunteers who spread out over the world beginning in the late nineteenth century was a quality that spurred on the missionary effort in the Islamic world, where resistance to Christianity was fierce. The first significant Christian mission to the Muslims was conducted by Raymond Lull in the thirteenth century (see chapter 2), who was almost alone among Christians in his concern to evangelize the Muslims rather than fight them. And in the centuries following, according to Stephen Neill, the "Muslim lands" were "neglected by Christian missions in comparison with more productive fields." That changed in the late nineteenth century, a period "marked by the beginning of a real encounter between the faith of Jesus Christ and the faith of Mohammed."[27] Anglicans entered the area in the 1860s, and other denominations hesitantly followed, but it was Samuel Zwemer, a student volunteer, initially without denominational support, who coordinated Muslim missionary efforts and focused the attention of the world on the Muslim population and its need for Christ. Many other student volunteers, including W. H. Temple Gairdner, Dr. Paul Harrison, and William Borden, also gave their lives in this most difficult and unrewarding missionary endeavor.

Samuel Zwemer, the "Apostle to Islam," was born near Holland, Michigan, in 1867, the thirteenth of fifteen children. His father was a Reformed Church pastor, and it seemed natural for Samuel as he was growing up that he should enter Christian service. Four of his five surviving brothers entered the ministry, and his sister, Nellie Zwemer, spent forty years as a missionary to China. It was while attending Hope College that Zwemer sensed the urgency of foreign missions. During his senior year, under the persuasive preaching of Robert Wilder (the same missionary enthusiast who had stirred John R. Mott and the Mount Hermon Hundred), he and five of his seven classmates volunteered for foreign missionary service.

After seminary studies and medical training, Zwemer and a fellow seminarian, James Cantine, offered themselves to the Reformed Board to serve in the Arab world; but they were turned down because of the prevalent belief that such a mission would be "impractical." Undaunted, the enthusiastic pair formed their own mission, the American Arabian Mission, and began raising support, Zwemer traveling some four thousand miles and visiting "nearly every church in our denomination west of Ohio" while Cantine traveled in the East. Their method of deputation was unique. Instead of appealing for funds for themselves, "Zwemer . . . pled for Cantine's support and Cantine pled for Zwemer's. . . ." "Lethargy of the pastors," wrote Zwemer, "is the great drawback," but there were petty annoyances, too: "Last Sabbath I preached in the afternoon on missions —although I was not allowed to hang up my chart because it was Sunday! That same congregation had a singing school for its youth after the service(!)—'O consistency, thou art a jewel'—but by God's help I can speak without a chart—and I did."[28]

By 1889 Cantine's tour was over and he sailed for Arabia, with Zwemer following in 1890. Their determination and dedication did not go unnoticed by their church leaders, for in 1894 the mission was invited to become incorporated into the Reformed Church of America. The slow progress and opposition Zwemer faced during the early years of his ministry in the Persian Gulf region did not discourage him but only verified what he had anticipated. Initially he and Cantine lived with Anglican missionaries, but when the Anglican couple was relocated, they were on their own, except for a young Syrian convert who had come to work with them. His untimely death, less than six months after he arrived, was a painful setback to the work.

In 1895, after five lonely years as a single missionary, Zwemer fell in love with Amy Wilkes, a missionary nurse from England, sponsored by the Church Missionary Society of the Anglican Church. But even as with his evangelistic work, Zwemer's courtship and marriage were not without obstacles. Sidestepping the Church Missionary Society's "very strict rules about their young lady missionaries having gentlemen friends" was an ordeal in itself, but marriage faced even greater roadblocks, especially for a young missionary with limited finances. "True it is," writes Zwemer's biographer, "that the Church Missionary Society did not surrender their prize without something of a struggle. As is the custom with most Societies, a portion of transportation cost must be refunded if a new person does not remain a certain time on the field. It was necessary to meet this rule, so . . . Samuel Zwemer purchased his wife in true oriental fashion."[29]

After sailing to the United States for furlough in 1897, the Zwemers returned to the Persian Gulf to work among the Muslims on the island of Bahrein. They passed out literature and conducted evangelism in public thoroughfares and in private homes, but rarely did they witness any positive response. Living conditions further complicated efforts for a successful ministry. In an age before air conditioning, the heat was almost unbearable—"107 in the coolest part of the veranda." Personal tragedy also interfered with the work. In July of 1904, the Zwemers' two little daughters, ages four and seven, both died within eight days of each other. Despite the pain and hardship, Zwemer was content in his ministry, and he could look back on this period some fifty years later and say, "The sheer joy of it all comes back. Gladly would I do it all over again. . . ."[30]

By 1905, Zwemer's Arab mission had established four stations, and, though they were few in number, the converts showed unusual courage in professing their new-found faith. In that year, the Zwemers returned to the United

States, and, though unknown to them at the time, it would mark the end of their pioneer missionary work to the Muslims. Back in the United States, Zwemer traveled and spoke out in behalf of missions to the Muslims. He aggressively raised funds, shunning any sort of Hudson Taylor philosophy of not letting the financial needs be known. Then in 1906 he served as chairman of the first general missionary conference on Islam that convened in Cairo.

While in the United States, Zwemer accepted an urgent call to become the traveling secretary for the Student Volunteer Movement, a position that suited him well. At the same time he served as field secretary for the Reformed Board of Foreign Missions, so that his time was taken up in traveling and speaking. Unlike his work with the Muslims, this work elicited an enthusiastic response, and many students answered the call to foreign missions. Nevertheless, Zwemer was anxious to go back to his post in Arabia; and in 1910, following the great Edinburgh Missionary Conference and a return trip to America, he sailed for Bahrein to continue his work.

Zwemer's wife and two youngest children accompanied him back to the Gulf region, but not to remain long. Living arrangements for the two older children back home had not been satisfactory, nor had the education of the two younger children on the field. Thus, Amy returned to the United States to oversee the family matters, a situation that placed the family, as Zwemer described, on "three horns of a dilemma"—a problem with no real solution. "If the wife went home with the children some would remark that the missionary did not love his wife to let her go like that. If the children were left in the homeland they were thought to be neglected by their parents. If husband and wife both spent more than usual furlough time at home they would be accused of neglecting the work on the field."[31]

Back on the field, Zwemer found it difficult to reestablish himself in the work. His leadership abilities were in great demand, and conference planning and speaking engagements frequently called him away from his post. Then in 1912 he received a call from the United Presbyterian Mission in Egypt that was seconded by the Church Missionary Society, also located there, requesting that he relocate in Cairo and coordinate the missionary work to the entire Islamic world. The Nile Mission Press, known for its literature distribution to Muslims, also joined in the call, and so did the YMCA and the American University of Cairo, leaving Zwemer with little choice but to respond in the affirmative.

In Cairo, Zwemer found a far more open society, where educated young adults were eager to listen to the impressive missionary intellectual from the West. He spent hours each week on university campuses and, according to Sherwood Eddy, even "gained access to the leaders of the proud and influential Muslim University El Azhar." Sometimes he conducted meetings with as many as two thousand Muslims present, but actual conversions were rare, and opposition remained intense. On one occasion he was forced to leave Cairo on the grounds that he had illegally distributed tracts among university students, but the incident contributed to the conversion of one of those students.

An infuriated professor tore to bits one of Zwemer's tracts in front of his class; and a student, curious as to why a small leaflet should create such an outrage, later picked up the fragments and pieced them together, and subsequently was converted to Christianity.

During his first year in Cairo, Zwemer was joined by William Borden, a young student volunteer from Yale who had signed the "Princeton Pledge" as a result of Zwemer's own preaching. Borden's humility and eagerness to pass out tracts as he rode through the steaming Cairo streets on his bicycle belied the fact that he had been born into wealth and was an heir to the vast Borden fortune. Before venturing to the mission field he had given hundreds of thousands of dollars to various Christian organizations, while at the same time refusing to succumb to the temptation of buying himself a car—"an unjustifiable luxury." His single-minded goal was to serve out his life as a missionary. That he did, though his term was short. After four months in Cairo he died following an attack of spinal meningitis.

For seventeen years Zwemer made Cairo his headquarters, and from there he traveled all over the world, participating in conferences, raising funds, and establishing work among Muslims in India, China, Indochina, and South Africa. Zwemer's evangelistic methods were a combination of traditional evangelism and the more contemporary concept of "sharing" that was characteristic of the student volunteers. He dealt with Muslims on a plane of equality—sharing his own faith (a very conservative theology) as he sought to learn more about theirs, always showing them the utmost respect. Although his converts were few—probably fewer than a dozen during his nearly forty years of service—he made great strides in awakening Christians to the need for evangelism among the Islamic peoples.

In 1918 Zwemer received a tempting offer to join the faculty at Princeton Theological Seminary, but the urgency for him to continue the work in Cairo was too great, and he rejected the call. In 1929 his work was well established, and when a call again came from Princeton he was able to leave with good conscience and to begin a new career as chairman of History of Religion and Christian Missions.

Besides his teaching, the remainder of Zwemer's life was filled with speaking and writing. For forty years he edited the *Moslem World* ("the most prestigious journal of its kind in the English-speaking world," according to J. Herbert Kane), and he wrote hundreds of tracts and nearly fifty books. To the very end he was filled with "nervous energy" and incessant mental activity. A traveling companion once grudgingly recounted his overnight stay with Zwemer: "... he could not stay in bed for more than half an hour at a time ... for then, on would go the light, Zwemer would get out of bed, get some paper and a pencil, write a few sentences and then again to bed. When my eye-lids would get heavy again, up would come Zwemer, on again the light, and another few notes.... Then off to bed again."[32]

Throughout his life, Zwemer faced tragedy and hardship. He mourned the deaths of his little daughters, of close associates, and of two wives (his first in 1937 and his second in 1950). Yet, he remained remarkably happy

279

and optimistic, and he always had time for fun and joking. On one occasion his fun became so "hilarious and riotous" in a restaurant in Grand Rapids, Michigan, that the headwaiter had to step in and restore order. He had a lively appreciation for the lighter side of life, and in many ways his personality was uniquely suited to his years of toil in the barren ground of the Islamic world.

Fletcher Brockman

The thrill of seeing the brilliant young men of the Student Volunteer Movement dedicate their lives to foreign missions was tempered when the methods and ideology of some of their numbers became known. Conservative evangelical missionaries were many times appalled by the new concepts brought to the field by the young intellectuals, and many believed that the course of Christianity was being irrevocably damaged. This conflict of philosophy was particularly evident in China, and one of the young missionaries who vocally expressed his progressive views was Fletcher Brockman.

Brockman was reared on a cotton plantation in Georgia and educated at Vanderbilt University, graduating in 1891. On graduation he served as the national secretary for the YMCA, working with college students in the South and promoting foreign missions. As a Methodist, Brockman first offered his services to his own denominational mission board, but his bishop suggested that interdenominational sponsorship of the YMCA might be more appropriate for the broad based ministry he hoped to have with students in China. The YMCA eagerly accepted his services, anxious to respond to the invitation of many China missionaries who had called on the organization to enter that field.

In 1898, along with his wife and small son, Brockman sailed for China, arriving at a critical time just prior to the Boxer uprising. Although he survived the terrors of that violent period, other student volunteers did not. Horace Pitkin, the leader of the Yale volunteer band, had been in China only four years when he was brutally executed in Paoting by a Boxer mob in the summer of 1900. But his death was not in vain. Fourteen years later, Sherwood Eddy, another Yale volunteer, visited that same city in China at the invitation of Brockman, and he reminded his audience (that included some three thousand students) of Pitkin's sacrifice: "When I came to the story of the cross and of Pitkin's death the interpreter broke down under deep emotion and stood silent, unable to speak. It is considered a shameful disgrace for a Chinese to weep in public. The audience bowed their heads in sympathy and shame. Many were in tears. When, after a pause, we quietly gave the invitation, some decided for Christ and many became honest inquirers. More than ten thousand Christian books were sold in a single day in the city where Pitkin had been martyred."[33]

With the Boxer uprising over, Brockman settled into missionary work, but he soon discovered that his concept of missions was rapidly changing. "In America," according to Sherwood Eddy, "Brockman had been preparing to go out and work for the conversion of what he then called the 'heathen' in the Orient. It was only after he had reached China and had humbly sat at the feet of Confucius, in his language study, that he learned that 'all within the four seas are brothers.'" In his book, *I Discover the Orient*, he wrote of his search for the meaning of Chinese philosophy and religion: "The next ten years were largely taken up with discovering and untangling the true from the false without destroying my sense of mission."[34]

Brockman, like some of the other student volunteers in China, was well received by the Chinese "literati" because he was so tolerant and sympathetic toward Confucianism, Buddhism and other Oriental religions —an attitude that was a bold departure from traditional evangelical missionary strategy. Though he always remained a Christian missionary and evangelist, he shocked many of his fellow missionaries and supporters back home by his open view toward other world religions and their leaders. "I am rich," he wrote in *I Discover the Orient;* "I have come into a great inheritance. My wealth has been gathered for thousands of years. Confucius, Mencius, Mo Ti, Buddha, Abraham, Moses, Isaiah, Paul, Jesus—I have entered into their inheritance. I am heir of the ages. I am sent not to dig up roots but to gather in the harvest."[35]

As Brockman studied the Chinese writings and learned from Chinese scholars, he won their hearts. But learning was not enough. He believed that he should reciprocate and teach them of his way of life, which naturally included sharing his Christian faith; but more importantly from the Chinese standpoint it also included teaching them of modern science and technology—a subject students

craved to learn more about. Realizing his own deficiency in this area, Brockman wrote to John R. Mott and, in the words of Eddy, "implored him to secure the best man in America with scientific training to meet China's need." C. H. Robertson, professor of mechanical engineering at Purdue University, who had been in the Christian Association during his student days, was sent, and "within a few years Brockman's dream was realized in a remarkable way. The popular young educational genius Brockman had secured from America was addressing the largest audiences of officials, gentry, ancient scholars, and modern students that had ever listened to any man, Chinese or foreign, in all the history of China."[36]

One of Brockman's main tasks in China was to establish the YMCA in cities across the land. Such work required financial backing, and Brockman relied heavily on the Chinese— particularly the more tolerant Confucianists for this help. Although the control of the YMCA was to be in the hands of the Christians, some of the organizations later fell into the control of other segments of the population, and today the YMBA (Young Men's Buddhist Association) has become a part of Oriental society.

So respected was Brockman in China that after less than fifteen years there he was offered the post of presidency of Peking University. At the advice of John R. Mott, he declined the offer. Mott believed that Brockman's organizational ministry with Chinese students was too great a calling to forsake for a secular pursuit. But then only three years later, Mott himself called upon Brockman to leave China in order to help shore up the YMCA in

Fletcher Brockman and John R. Mott with a Chinese Christian leader.

America. Brockman left China with deep regrets. "Mott," according to Latourette, "almost forced him to do so," and the years that followed were not happy ones. Brockman's tenure under Mott's direct authority was "self-denying," "difficult," and "exhausting." Before he retired in 1927, Brockman was able to make return trips to the Far East and to again work among the people whom he loved and respected so much.

E. Stanley Jones

The enthusiasm that Brockman had for introducing Western science and technology to China found no parallel in E. Stanley Jones's effort to reach the intelligentsia of India. In fact, Jones shunned any effort to align Christianity with Western civilization, believing rather that Christ should be interpreted by the Indian people according to their own customs and civilization. Even using science lectures as an opening for the gospel, he believed, was making an association that should not be made. One of the greatest detriments to the growth of Christianity in India, in his view, was the inseparable relationship between Christianity and Western civilization, and missionaries were the culprits in perpetuating this ill-advised marriage.

Jones was born in Maryland in 1884, making him only two years old when Wilder inspired the hearts of the "Mount Hermon Hundred." His commitment as a student volunteer came many years later while attending Asbury College, and his first inclination was to serve as a missionary in Africa (a calling that Jones humorously related was only fulfilled in the mind of a student who wrote on an exam that it was "Stanley Jones" who was sent in to find Livingstone after his long disappearance); but before he left Asbury, the Methodist Missionary Society wrote to him, requesting him to serve in India.

Before going to India, Jones endured a humiliating experience that changed the course of his ministry —an experience that focused his message on Christ rather than on doctrinal intricacies. The occasion was his "very first sermon."

The little church was filled with my relatives and friends, all anxious that the young man should do well. I had prepared for three weeks, for I was to be God's lawyer and argue His case well. I started on rather a high key and after a half dozen sentences used a word I had never used before and I have never used since: indifferentism. Whereupon a college girl smiled and put down her head.... Her smiling so upset me that when I came back to the thread of my discourse it was gone. My mind was an absolute blank. I stood there clutching for something to say. Finally I blurted out: "I am very sorry, but I have forgotten my sermon," and I started for my seat in shame and confusion.... As I was about to sit down, the Inner Voice said: "Haven't I done anything for you? If so, couldn't you tell that?" I responded to this suggestion and stepped down in front of the pulpit—I felt I didn't belong behind it—and said, "Friends, I see I can't preach, but you know what Christ has done for my life, how He has changed me, and though I cannot preach I shall be his witness the rest of my days." At the close a youth came up to me and said he wanted what I had found. It was a mystery to me then, and it is a mystery to me now that, amid my failure that night, he still saw something he wanted. As he and I knelt together he found it. It marked a profound change in his life, and today he is a pastor, and a daughter is a missionary in Africa. As God's lawyer I was a dead failure; as God's witness I was a success. That night marked a change in my conception of the work of the Christian minister—he is to be, not God's lawyer to argue well for God; but he is to be God's witness, to tell what Grace has done for an unworthy life.[37]

Jones began his missionary career in 1907 as an ordained Methodist minister of an English-speaking church in Lucknow. He preached on Sundays and spent most of the rest of the time in language study. After three years he transferred to Sitapur, where he ministered mainly to outcastes— the segment of society among whom most missionaries concentrated because outcastes offered them the least resistance. But as Jones lived among the people, he realized that India was far more than a land of impoverished outcastes, and he became burdened for others, particularly the high caste intellectuals, and soon he began a ministry to them.

Working among the educated classes was challenging but also debilitating. Jones often found himself on the defensive, being challenged by some of the keenest intellects he had ever encountered. The strain was too much. After eight and a half years and several nervous breakdowns, he returned to the United States to recuperate and rest. But back in India, after his furlough, his mental problems continued. "I saw that unless I got help from somewhere I would have to give up my missionary career.... It was one of my darkest hours." It was then that Jones underwent a deep spiritual experience: "A great peace settled into my heart and pervaded me. I knew it was done! Life—abundant life—had taken possession of me." Never again was Jones plagued with the agony of mental illness.[38]

With his life changed, Jones became one of the world's most distinguished evangelists to work among the educated elite, and as his reputation spread he traveled beyond the borders of India with his message of Christ. It was Christ who was the focal point of Jones's evangelism, not Christianity, and he was quick to emphasize the difference. Christianity as the world knew it was a Western institutional church; and it was Christianity, brought to India by the Western missionaries, not Christ, that had been rejected by the Indian intellectuals. Jones was convinced that if the educated Indians had the opportunity to see Christ, without all his Western garb, they would glady receive him.

But Jones went further than merely disassociating Christ from Western civilization; he also disassociated him from the Old Testament: "Christianity must be defined as Christ, not the Old Testament, not Western Civilization, not even the system built around him in the West, but Christ himself...." Jones viewed his own mission as to "refuse to know anything save Jesus Christ and Him crucified." Eliminating the Old Testament from his preaching was naturally controversial, but Jones defended his action on practical grounds:

> I still believed in the Old Testament as being the highest revelation of God given to the world before Jesus' coming; I would inwardly feed upon it as Jesus did. But the issue was further on. A Jain lawyer, a brilliant writer against Christianity, arose in one of my meetings and asked me a long list of questions regarding things in the Old Testament. I replied, "My brother, I think I can answer your questions, but I do not feel called on to do so. I defined Christianity as Christ. If you have any objections to make against Him, I am ready to hear them and answer them if I can." He replied, "Who gave you this authority to make this distinction? What church council gave you this authority?" I replied that my own Master gave it to me.... Revelation was progressive, culminating in him. Why should I, then, pitch my battle at an imperfect stage when the perfect was here in him? My lawyer friend saw with dismay that a great many of his books written against Christianity had gone into ashes by my definition.[39]

It was not the Bible or Christian doctrine, according to Jones, that made Christianity unique among the world's religions, but rather it was Christ, and thus he believed that Christ alone should be exalted. On one occasion when he was complimented by a Hindu for being a "broad-minded Christian," he responded: "My brother, I am the narrowest man you have come across. I am broad on almost anything else, but on the one supreme necessity for human nature I am absolutely narrowed by the facts to one—Jesus." Jones went on to explain, "It is precisely because we believe in the absoluteness of Jesus that we can afford to take the more generous view of the non-Christian systems and situations."[40]

Jones's "generous view of the non-Christian systems" made him a target for criticism, especially among Fundamentalists who believed he was compromising Christianity in order to make it more appealing to other religious groups. "Jones accommodates himself to sinful pride, heathen thought and the growing nationalism," wrote Chester Tulga, a Conservative Baptist. "His Christ looks much like an Indian nationalist. His Biblical universality shrinks to Indian nationality.... The Christ of the modernist missionary ... becomes a false Christ, with no saving power and no historical authenticity."[41]

In presenting Christ to the non-Christians of India, Jones sought to use methods that were a natural part of Indian society. His Round Table Conferences and his Christian Ashrams were examples of this. The Round Table Conferences began after he had been invited to a Hindu home to join other intellectuals in philosophical discussions as they all sat in a circle on the floor. With that example, Jones began doing the same thing, inviting Christians as well as adherents of Hinduism, Jainism, and

Islam. These discussions, though intellectually oriented, became an avenue for evangelism: "There was not a single situation that I can remember where before the close of the Round Table Conference Christ was not in moral and spiritual command of the situation."[42]

The Christian Ashram movement that Jones founded was also an accommodation to Indian social life —an alternative to the Western church. "The Church is for the most part a worshiping institution used once or twice a week. This makes the fellowship a momentary thing of an hour or two in seven days. After those few hours, each goes back into his compartmentalized life. The Indian mind—in fact, the human mind— wants something that will gather the whole of life into a central control and make it into a fellowship which will not be for an hour or two, but something continuous and all-embracing."[43]

The setup of the Christian Ashram was very similar to its Hindu counterpart. The "family" was required to rise at 5:30 A.M. and spend its day in a combination of activities, including private devotions, manual labor, and group discussions, the latter being eliminated on the one day a week that was specified as a day of "complete silence." While the main purpose of the ashram was for personal spiritual growth, its greatest effect in India was to break down the caste and political barriers that otherwise separated Christians in their daily workaday life. By 1940 there were some two dozen Christian Ashrams located throughout India.

Jones's reputation as an evangelist and Christian statesman made him a highly respected individual in India and all over the world. He counted Mahatma Gandhi and Jawaharlal Nehru among his friends, and both men paid him great respect, though neither converted to Christianity. But Jones was more than just a missionary to India. In the words of Sherwood Eddy, "No one can more appropriately be called a world evangelist, no one has more consistently maintained his evangelistic work—for over forty years—in the spirit of a crusader, than E. Stanley Jones." Japan was just one of the countries he visited on his evangelistic tours, and, according to J. Herbert Kane, the meetings there "attracted vast audiences in all parts of the country and tens of thousands registered their decision for Christ."[44]

As a renowned world evangelist and Christian leader, Jones was an influential voice in the twentieth-century ecumenical conferences, but he was frequently at odds with his colleagues—particularly on the issue that Jesus, rather than institutional Christianity, must be paramount. At the Madras Conference in 1938, for example, he took issue with Hendrick Kraemer and others who supported the proposition, "The Church is, under God, the hope of the world." Only God, as seen through Jesus Christ, Jones argued, was absolute. "The church is a relativism.... The Conference was thus betrayed...."[45] Because of his weak view of the institutional church, Jones did not entirely fit in with other ecumenically-minded missionary statesmen, and he was often criticized by both liberals and conservatives.

Although Jones had long since turned away from denominational exclusiveness in his ministry, and had embraced a broad concept of Christian unity, he was, nevertheless, regarded highly among peers in the Methodist Church and was elected Bishop at the General Conference. Before the consecration ceremony, though, he resigned. "I am an evangelist," he wrote, "not a bishop."

Jones always was first and foremost an evangelist. Though he "revered all that was good and true in Oriental religions and did his best to meet them halfway," according to Kane, "he spoke on the finality of Jesus Christ and the uniqueness of the Christian Gospel" and "always ended up with 'Jesus and the Resurrection.'" His task as an evangelist was not to expand the institutional church but to introduce people to Jesus and then let them come to know Him in their own way. "There is a beautiful Indian marriage custom," he wrote, "that dimly illustrates our task in India, and where it ends. At the wedding ceremony the women friends of the bride accompany her with music to the home of the bridegroom. They usher her into the presence of the bridegroom—that is as far as they can go—then they retire and leave her with her husband. That is our joyous task in India: to know Him, to introduce Him, to retire—not necessarily geographically, but to trust India with the Christ and trust Christ with India. We can only go so far—He and India must go the rest of the way."[46]

That philosophy of world evangelism was the theme of Jones's widely circulated book, *The Christ of the Indian Road*, a book that has had a significant impact on twentieth-century missions. Until his death in 1973, he was first and foremost a sincere Christian evangelist, but his view of the institutional church and his concern for peace and social justice may have contributed to the abandonment by many missionary societies of true evangelism in exchange for a social gospel.

SELECTED BIBLIOGRAPHY

Brockman, Fletcher S. I Discover the Orient. New York: Harper & Row, 1935.

Eddy, Sherwood. Pathfinders of the World Missionary Crusade. Nashville: Abingdon-Cokesbury, 1945.

Fairbank, John K., ed. The Missionary Enterprise in China and America. Cambridge, Mass.: Harvard University Press, 1974.

Grubb, Norman P. C. T. Studd: Cricketer & Pioneer. Fort Washington, Pa.: Christian Literature Crusade, 1972.

_____. Once Caught, No Escape: My Life Story. Fort Washington, Pa.: Christian Literature Crusade, 1969.

_____. With C. T. Studd in Congo Forests. Grand Rapids: Zondervan, 1946.

Hogg, William Richey. Ecumenical Foundations: A History of the International Missionary Council and Its Nineteenth-Century Background. New York: Harper & Row, 1952.

Hopkins, C. Howard. John R. Mott, 1865–1955: A Biography. Grand Rapids: Eerdmans, 1979.

Johnston, Arthur P. The Battle for World Evangelism. Wheaton: Tyndale, 1978.

Jones, E. Stanley. Along the Indian Road. New York: Abingdon, 1939.

_____. The Christ of the Indian Road. *New York: Abingdon, 1925.*

Mackie, Robert. Layman Extraordinary: John R. Mott, 1865–1955. *New York: Association, 1965.*

Mott, John R. The Larger Evangelism. *Nashville: Abingdon-Cokesbury, 1944.*

Tulga, Chester E. The Case Against Modernism in Foreign Missions. *Chicago: Conservative Baptist, 1950.*

Wheeler, W. Reginald. A Man Sent From God: A Biography of Robert E. Speer. *London: Revell, 1956.*

Wilson, J. Christy. The Apostle to Islam: A Biography of Samuel M. Zwemer. *Grand Rapids: Baker, 1952.*

_____. Flaming Prophet: The Story of Samuel Zwemer. *New York: Friendship, 1970.*

Chapter 11

"Faith" Missionaries: Depending on God Alone

During the same period of time that the Student Volunteer Movement was recruiting young intellectuals from the universities and colleges, another missionary movement was building momentum as a vibrant missionary force focused on the unreached "inland" territories of the world. The "faith" missionary movement, as it has been loosely termed, had its origins in 1865 with the founding of the China Inland Mission by Hudson Taylor, who directly or indirectly influenced the founding of over forty new mission boards. With the founding of such missions as the Christian and Missionary Alliance (1887), The Evangelical Alliance Mission (1890), the Central American Mission (1890), the Sudan Interior Mission (1893), and the Africa Inland Mission (1895), independent "faith" missions became a significant feature of world evangelism, whose "glorious achievements," according to Herbert Kane, are "stranger than fiction and more marvelous than miracles." While most of the infant faith missions struggled for survival, others such as TEAM, founded by Fredrik Franson as the Scandinavian Alliance Mission, grew with amazing speed. Within eighteen months it had commissioned some one hundred missionaries to China, Japan, India, and Africa.

From the very beginning, faith missions have been associated with conservative evangelicalism, and the majority of the recruits have been either without higher education or graduates of Bible institutes or Christian colleges such as Nyack, Moody, and Wheaton. Moody Bible Institute particularly stands out as a training ground for faith missionaries, having "chalked up a fantastic record," according to Kane. "Since 1890 over 5,400 Moody alumni have served under 245 mission boards in 108 countries of the world. Of this number over 2,022 were still in active service in 1976. This means that one out of every eighteen North American missionaries in the world today is an alumnus of Moody Bible Institute," and the vast majority of those serve under faith missions.[1]

The term "faith" mission is often associated with those missions whose financial policy guarantees no set income for its missionaries, and some such missions carry the policy to the point of refusing to solicit funds or even make known the needs of the missionaries, thus professing to rely entirely on God for financial needs. But the concept of living entirely by faith went far beyond the matter of finances. The missions were born out of faith, often at great risks and resulting in a high mortality rate among the early faith missionary pioneers.

Risking life and limb to bring the gospel to those who had never heard was not taken lightly. The "faith" missionaries were motivated by a vivid picture of hell. For them, the purpose of missions was to save lost souls from the eternal torment of hellfire and brimstone. "May we who know Christ," implored Jim Elliot, "hear the cry of the damned as they hurtle headlong into the Christless night without ever a chance. . . . May we shed tears of repentance for those we have failed to bring out of darkness."[2]

While faith missionaries have not been oblivious to the physical and social needs of the people to whom they minister, and have thus been active in medical and educational ministries, evangelism has always been paramount; and to facilitate the spreading of the gospel, new concepts of evangelism emerged. "Most of the innovations in twentieth-century missions have been introduced by the faith missions," according to Kane, "including radio, aviation, Bible correspondence courses, gospel recordings, tapes, cassettes, saturation evangelism, and theological education by extension."[3] One prime example of this was Harry Strachan's founding of the Latin America Mission in 1921 for the unique purpose of mass campaign evangelism. Using the latest techniques in advertising and communications, he, his wife Susan, and other missionary personnel conducted wholesome, entertaining programs in theaters and public halls throughout South and Central America, attracting huge crowds. The gospel was clearly presented, and converts were left in the care of local mission societies and churches. "There is hardly a mission of any size in Latin America," according to Kane, "which does not count among its members converts won in the campaigns conducted through the years by the LAM."[4]

This emphasis on evangelism by faith missions sharply increased the spread of Christianity, and the faith missions grew to meet the challenge. Today, spurred on by the dedication and perseverance of their founders and early pioneers, faith missions are among the largest mission societies in the world. Though diverse in their geographical emphasis and their evangelistic methods, they have effectively worked together in a spirit of cooperation on an individual basis and through the Interdenominational Foreign Mission Association (founded in 1917 to promote the growth of faith missions) and other loose organizational ties. Through this joint effort the independent evangelical faith missions combine to make the most powerful missionary force the world has known.

A. B. Simpson and the Christian and Missionary Alliance

Like the great missionary statesmen Samuel Mills and John R. Mott, A. B.

Simpson never served as a foreign missionary himself; but like Mills and Mott, his influence for missions was enormous, particularly in the growth of the late nineteenth- and early twentieth-century mission societies in America. The founders of both the Sudan Interior Mission and the Africa Inland Mission were deeply influenced by him and studied at his missionary training school; and evangelical denominations, particularly ones within the holiness movement, were stimulated into missionary activity largely through his missionary zeal. Beginning in 1883, he inaugurated interdenominational conventions held in cities throughout the United States and Canada, featuring foreign missionaries from various denominations and mission societies. These conventions brought foreign missions to the people and led to the formation of Simpson's own highly effective international mission society, the Christian and Missionary Alliance. Largely through his influence, foreign missions in the twentieth century became the most vital outreach of the North American evangelical churches.

Simpson's introduction to foreign missions began early in life. He was born on Prince Edward Island in Canada in 1843 and was baptized when he was a few weeks old by John Geddie, the first Canadian missionary to the South Seas. The "missionary atmosphere" in his home had a lasting impact on him, and as a youth he was deeply affected by a biography of John Williams, martyred on the island of Erromango. At Knox College in Toronto, foreign missions continued to interest Simpson, but on graduation, a call to the large and fashionable Knox Church in Hamilton, Ontario, pulled him into the pastorate instead. It was Simpson's exceptional preaching ability that won him a place in one of Canada's most prestigious churches when he was only twenty-one years old; and it was that same preaching ability that paved the way for his great influence as a missionary statesman. But qualities other than great preaching ability were needed for the role Simpson would play in world missions, and these qualities would require years of development.

Simpson's reputation as a flaming preacher brought him calls from other churches, and after eight years at the Knox Church he accepted one such call to the large Chestnut Street Church in Louisville, Kentucky, that offered him an impressive yearly salary of $5,000. His ministry there was effective in his efforts to reconcile this city church which was still divided by latent Civil War hostilities, but he remained unsatisfied with the genteel Christianity so prevalent in that city. He did not feel comfortable with the dignified respectability that pervaded his congregation, nor with his own tendency toward self-gratification that catered to the wealthy and ignored the urban masses. It took a great spiritual crisis before he realized how "barren and withered" his ministry had become and that his "true ministry had scarcely begun." After a "lonely and sorrowful night . . . and not knowing but it would be death in the most literal sense before the morning light," his "heart's first full consecration was made." After that his Chestnut Street Church became a soul-winning center for evangelism in Louisville.[5]

During his Louisville pastorate, Simpson traveled to Chicago to visit friends, and there again he passed through a deep spiritual experience. In a vision:

> The burden of a Christless world was rolled upon him by the spirit of God.... "I was awakened one night from sleep, trembling with a strange and solemn sense of God's overshadowing power, and on my soul was burning the remembrance of a strange dream through which I had that moment come. It seemed to me that I was sitting in a vast auditorium, and millions of people were there sitting around me. All the Christians in the world seemed to be there, and on the platform was a great multitude of faces and forms. They seemed to be mostly Chinese. They were not speaking, but in mute anguish were wringing their hands, and their faces wore an expression that I can never forget. I had not been thinking or speaking of the Chinese or the heathen world, but as I awoke with that vision on my mind, I did tremble with the Holy Spirit, and I threw myself on my knees, and every fibre of my being answered, 'Yes, Lord, I will go.'" [6]

Following that vision, Simpson "tried for months to find an open door, but the way was closed." The greatest obstacle confronting him was his family—his wife Margaret and his six children. "The missionary vision," according to A. E. Thompson, "had not yet come to Mrs. Simpson. She had been willing to leave her beloved Canada at the call of the people of the sunny South. But China! Her practical nature, her mother instinct, and perhaps her womanly ambition for her brilliant husband all answered *No*." She was content in the comfortable lifestyle the Chestnut Street Church afforded them, and she was not eager to give those comforts up: "I was not then ready for such a sacrifice. I wrote him that it was all right—he might go

to China himself—I would remain home and support and care for the children. I knew that would settle him for a while."[7]

Simpson was not a Livingstone, and he simply could not abandon his wife and six children, but as time passed "God showed" him that he "was to labor for the world and the perishing heathen just the same as if" he "were permitted to go among them."[8] But Louisville was not the place to launch his enterprise for world evangelism, so in 1879 he accepted a call from a church in New York City, and it was there that his world-wide ministry began.

Simpson soon discovered that the Thirteenth Street Church where he had been called to minister did not have the same vision for lost souls that he had. Nor did they share his views on divine healing that had recently developed through his own healing experience. So after only two years at the church he announced his resignation, a decision that in the eyes of many was pure folly. Without any steady income, he launched his new ministry. New York City would be his own personal mission field, and from that base he would reach out to the ends of the earth—and at the same time keep his family intact.

It was a bold move and one that stunned not only the church and his associates, but his wife Margaret. A. W. Tozer poignantly described her feelings:

> The wife of a prophet has no easy road to travel. She cannot always see her husband's vision, yet as his wife she must go along with him wherever his vision takes him. She is compelled therefore to walk by faith a good deal of the time—and her husband's faith at that. Mrs. Simpson

tried hard to understand, but if she sometimes lost patience with her devoted but impractical husband she is not for that cause to be too much censured. From affluence and high social position she is called suddenly to poverty and near-ostracism. She must feed her large family somehow—and not one cent coming in. The salary has stopped, and the parsonage must be vacated.... Mr. Simpson had heard the Voice ordering him out, and he went without fear. His wife had heard nothing, but she was compelled to go anyway. That she was a bit unsympathetic at times has been held against her by many. That she managed to keep within far sight of her absent-minded high soaring husband should be set down to her everlasting honor. It is no easy job being wife to such a man as A. B. Simpson was.[9]

With an advertisement in the newspaper, Simpson launched his new movement. His first meeting was held on a Sunday afternoon and was open to the public, except for his former parishioners whom he had specifically instructed not to attend. He did

A. B. Simpson, founder of the Christian and Missionary Alliance.

not want to be accused of splitting the church. That meeting was well attended, but only seven remained after the service to dedicate themselves wholly to his new ministry. These seven, however, along with Simpson, formed a nucleus, and through their zealous evangelism the crowds soon overflowed the rented hall in which the services were being held. For the next eight years the group moved from place to place until a permanent building, the Gospel Tabernacle, was erected.

Simpson's ultimate aim was to organize a body of believers fully committed to world evangelism, but he was not satisfied confining the movement to his New York City followers. To broaden the appeal he launched an illustrated missions journal, *The Gospel in All Lands*, and he began a convention ministry to North American cities. In 1887 the Christian Alliance was formed to bring missionary-minded believers together in a cohesive organization, and an outgrowth of that organization was a new mission society, the Evangelical Missionary Alliance. For ten years the organizations functioned separately, merging in 1897 to form the Christian and Missionary Alliance. In the meantime, Simpson established a missionary training school in New York City, and he was well on his way to becoming America's foremost missionary statesman.

There was a sense of urgency as Simpson pleaded in behalf of foreign missions—not just to save souls from hell, but to hasten the return of Christ. Simpson's key missionary text was Matthew 24:14: "And this gospel of the kingdom will be preached in all the world as a testimony to all nations, and then the end will come." It was this global thrust that made the Christian and Missionary Alliance unique among independent mission societies. Most missions focused on one particular area, or selected two or three fields, but the Christian and Missionary Alliance quickly spread out all over the world. Within five years it had nearly one hundred and fifty missionaries on fifteen fields.

But if the numbers sound impressive, they belie the fact the C&MA went through a period of severe testing during its earliest years. The first to go abroad were five young men who sailed to the Congo in 1884, three years before the mission was officially organized, and within only a few months after their arrival, John Condit, the leader of the party, had died. In both the Congo and the Sudan, the early attempts at evangelism were costly in lives. "Those deadly climates," according to Thompson, "exacted such an awful toll of lives that for years the missionary graves in both fields outnumbered the living missionaries."[10] The early work in China was also stained with the blood of martyrs. The Boxer Uprising of 1900 claimed the lives of thirty-five Alliance missionaries and children.

But the work went forward, and by the time of Simpson's death in 1919 the mission was securely grounded on every continent. By 1919 his missionary training school was also well established at its permanent location in Nyack, New York. His legacy in the area of Christian education extended far beyond the corridors of one institution. His missionary training school concept launched the Bible institute movement that spread out across North America and became the major recruiting source for independent faith mission societies in the decades that followed.

A. B. Simpson had an overwhelming burden for lost souls that was succinctly summed up in one of his plaintive hymns:

> A hundred thousand souls a day
>   Are passing one by one away,
> In Christless guilt and gloom.
>   Without one ray of hope or light,
> With future dark as endless night,
>   They're passing to their doom.

Such a burden for the lost was a heavy load for one man to carry, and at different times in his life, Simpson buckled under the weight. Soon after he moved to New York, he plunged "into a Slough of Despond so deep that . . . work was impossible." "I wandered about," he later recalled, "deeply depressed. All things in life looked dark and withered." He recovered, but was always susceptible to periods of despair. For a time prior to his death, "he went under a spiritual cloud," according to A. W. Tozer, and "felt that the face of the Lord was hidden from him. . . ."[11]

To many friends and associates his bouts of despair were puzzling. How could a spiritual giant like Simpson experience such profound depression? Tozer's analysis is poignant: "It is characteristic of the God-intoxicated, the dreamers and mystics of the Kingdom, that their flight-range is greater than that of other men. Their ability to sweep upward to unbelievable heights of spiritual transport is equaled only by their sad power to descend, to sit in dazed dejection by the River Chebar or to startle the night watches with their lonely grief."[12] Such highs and lows were a part of

Simpson's earthly pilgrimage, and if he seemingly lost his sense of direction on his descents into the valleys, it was while he was flying high that he caught and carried out his global vision of evangelism.

Rowland Bingham and the Sudan Interior Mission

Failure, death, and despair marked the beginnings of the Sudan Interior Mission. The idealistic dreams of a few inexperienced men to penetrate what was then known as the Sudan appeared to be nothing short of a hopeless cause. It was a vast, forbidding region south of the Sahara that has since been divided into a number of separate nations. Yet, through the undying persistence of one man, Rowland Bingham, SIM became one of the most dynamic mission ventures in Africa in the history of the Christian church, and today it is one of the largest mission societies in the world, with a missionary force that has at times exceeded thirteen hundred.

The story of SIM does not begin with Rowland Bingham. It was Walter Gowans, a young Canadian of Scottish descent, who first dreamed the dreams that led to the founding of SIM. After studying the needs of the world's mission fields he became convinced that the Sudan, with its more than sixty million people without one Christian missionary, was where God wanted him. But from the beginning, Gowans confronted obstacles, especially in obtaining sponsorship and support. No mission society in North America was prepared to risk sending personnel into the disease-infested Sudan. But Gowans would not be deterred. He left his home in Toronto and sailed to England, hoping to rouse some interest there.

In the meantime, Gowans's staunchest supporter—his mother—sought additional recruits to join in the venture with her son. The fact that she had already sent a daughter to China did not dampen her eagerness to send off her son. She was an ardent missionary enthusiast, as Bingham readily observed while talking with her in the parlor of her home. She had invited him to her home after hearing him speak at a meeting. Convinced that he would make an ideal partner for her son, she passionately presented to him the needs of the Sudan. She was a persuasive woman, and "the next morning," wrote Bingham, "when I went to call on Mrs. Gowans, it was to announce that I expected to sail in two weeks to join her son in a common enterprise. Was she glad? She was the whole board and I was accepted on the spot."[13]

Bingham was born in 1872 in Sussex, England, where he had a carefree childhood until financial devastation hit the family after the death of his father. At the age of thirteen he went to work full-time, and three years later he emigrated to Canada to sample the opportunities of the New World. He had been converted in England through the ministry of the Salvation Army, and soon after arriving in Canada, "God made it clear," he wrote, "that He wanted me to preach the Gospel, and following His leading I joined the Salvation Army as an officer." It was through this ministry that he first met Mrs. Gowans.

After committing himself to the new missionary endeavor, Bingham traveled to New York, where he contacted Thomas Kent, a "college chum" of Walter Gowans, and persuaded him to join the venture. They sailed together in the spring of 1893 to join Gowans and to begin their trek into Africa from the west coast. On arriving in Lagos, the young trio quickly learned why other missions had been so wary about sending missionaries into the Sudan. Their chances of survival, they were told, were nil. From the head of the Methodist Mission in West Africa they were given an ominous warning: "Young men, you will never see the Soudan; your children will never see the Soudan; your grandchildren may."[14] Missionaries from other societies also offered gloomy predictions, but the fact that no other missionaries were preaching the gospel in the Sudan was the very reason for which they had come, and they were not about to turn back. But their hope of setting off together as a team was dashed when Bingham became ill with malaria, and it was decided that he should remain on the coast and set up a supply base.

In less than a year after they left on their eight-hundred-mile overland journey both Gowans and Kent, true to the pessimistic predictions, were dead. While Kent had turned back for more supplies, Gowans, weakened by dysentery, had been captured by a slave-raiding tribal king, only to die several weeks after his release while he was being carried back to the coast by Africans. Meanwhile, Kent had been stricken by malaria on his return trip. He was nursed back to health by Bingham but died from another malaria attack on his way back to meet Gowans.

When word of their deaths, only three weeks apart, reached Bingham, he was devastated. He returned to England, uncertain about his future and his faith: "My faith was being shaken to the very foundation. . . . Why should those most anxious to carry out the Lord's commands and to give His gospel to millions in darkness be cut off right at the beginning of their career? Many questions faced me. . . . Was the Bible merely an evolution of human thought, even biased thought, or was it a divine revelation? For months the struggle over this great issue went on before I was finally brought back to the solid rock."[15]

Bingham returned to Canada, his faith renewed, determined to go forward with a mission to the Sudan. Realizing his own inadequacies for mission work, he took a basic medical course at a Cleveland hospital, and then in the fall of 1895 he enrolled in A. B. Simpson's Bible school in New York City, the school both Gowans and Kent had attended. During his student days there he was called to serve the pastorate of a small church, but his burden for the Sudan would not go away. He knew he would never have peace unless he returned to Africa to fulfill Gowan's dream. But to do that he was convinced he needed an organization, and in May of 1898 the Sudan Interior Mission was officially established. In that same month Bingham married Helen Blair, the daughter of a man to whom Bingham owed a debt of gratitude: "Just five years before, when her father had emptied his bank account to help send me to Africa, he little thought that I might some day return and ask his daughter to share in that work. In view of the fact that our first effort had nothing to show but two lonely graves, he found the first gift easier than the second."[16]

By 1900, seven years after his first

attempt, Bingham and two young volunteers were ready to try again to reach the Sudan. This time Bingham found "the missionaries in Lagos more than ever out of sympathy" with his plans, and "they did not hesitate to express themselves to the two young men" he had brought with him. More discouragement followed, and within weeks Bingham was seriously ill with malaria and ordered to return home. Though his young recruits had promised to go on without him, they lost heart after hearing more dismal predictions, and they decided to leave on the next ship.[17]

Once again Bingham was in the depths of depression: "It would have been easier for me, perhaps, had I died in Africa, for on the homeward journey I died another death. Everything seemed to have failed, and when while I was gradually regaining strength in Britain, a fateful cable reached me with word that my two companions were arriving shortly, I went through the darkest period of my whole life."[18] Still, Bingham refused to give up. He returned to Canada and met with the council and found four more recruits to join him for the third attempt to reach the Sudan.

This third attempt, made in 1901, was successful, resulting in the first SIM station in Africa, located at Patigi, some five hundred miles up the Niger River. But with each step forward there were two steps backward, and within two years only one of the original party of four remained. One had died and two were sent home physically debilitated, never to return. Though hanging on "only by a toehold at first," with only a few converts made during the first ten years at Patigi, the SIM gradually spread out to new stations and became firmly grounded in the desolate region.

One of the factors influencing the staying power of SIM in Africa after the turn of the century was the perfected use of quinine as a cure for malaria. With the proper use of that drug, missionaries no longer had to fear the dreaded disease. But another factor that affected the staying power of the SIM was prayer. Mrs. Gowans, according to Bingham, was "one of the greatest prayer helpers that ever blessed and strengthened" the SIM. "With her prayer and faith she carried us from the first seven barren years into the years of harvest."

With the dread of malaria behind them, the missionaries faced other obstructions that were in some ways equally frightening. "There is the constant invisible warfare," wrote Bingham,

that has to be waged against the powers of darkness.... It is fashionable in the Western world to relegate belief in demons and devils to the realm of mythology, and when mentioned at all it is a matter of jest. But it is no jest in West Africa or any other mission field for that matter. One has not to go far in the jungles of Nigeria, the Sudan or Ethiopia and visit a few of the African villages to believe in devils and demons. They are all around you, and soon, very soon, one begins to share the beliefs of the pagans as to the reality of these malign agencies without, of course, as a Christian sharing their fears or their vain oblations to propitiate them. Fetish men, devil men, ju-ju, lycanthropy, witches, wizards, ordeal by poison all flourished unchecked in the early days of the Mission....[19]

Missionaries frequently told "strange and macabre stories" of their "encounters with these sinister forces of evil. . . ." One missionary told of entering a village where satanic rites were being conducted: "The witch-doctors were . . . with hideous masks on . . . gesticulating, posturing, and gyrating, the mob shrieking and roaring, creating a noise . . . beyond description." "When I pushed my way to the centre of the ring," the missionary later recalled, "I saw to my utter astonishment a young woman rigid in the air. Her feet were some two feet off the earth and . . . the perspiration was coming out of that young woman's body like a fountain as she approached me in mid-air with no visible support beneath her."[20]

As the missionaries battled the unseen powers of darkness and preached the gospel, they realized they could not ignore the physical needs of the people around them. Leprosy, particularly, was a dreaded African disease, and SIM soon became actively involved in eradicating its awful scourge on the people. The work began among the lepers in the 1920s and by the 1960s the mission was treating more than thirty thousand leprosy patients in Nigeria alone. Many of the Africans who sought treatment were Muslims, and "many made their choice for Christ in spite of their early Muslim teaching and their parents' threats."[21]

As SIM grew and spread out across Africa, the needs of Ethiopia became apparent, and the church that was established there by SIM missionaries was a fitting climax to Bingham's sacrificial life of service for Africa. In 1928 Dr. Thomas Lambie had opened up the southern provinces of Ethiopia. He soon settled in the province of Wallamo, where he practiced medicine and conducted evangelistic work.

Other SIM missionaries joined the effort, and for several years they poured themselves into the work with few results. Then, in 1935, when the Italian military forces moved against Ethiopia, the situation became grim. The American and British embassies advised all their citizens to leave immediately, but the SIM missionaries stayed on—with the blessing of their general director, Rowland Bingham. "You are under higher orders than those of the King of England or the President of the United States. Get your instructions from Him and we are one with you."[22]

At this time there were only seventeen baptized believers in Wallamo, and the missionaries realized that their days were numbered. "Because we knew our time was short," wrote one missionary, "we did everything we could to teach the Christians and get the gospel message out. . . . It was unsafe to leave the mission compound, but the urgency and importance of using the little time which remained to further train the young Christians warranted the danger."[23]

Despite the fighting and daily threats to their lives, the last nineteen missionaries and seven children were not forceably evacuated until the spring of 1937—giving them nearly two years of "borrowed time" to build the little Wallamo church. But even with the added time the number of believers remained small—only forty-eight—and the missionaries left with a deep sense of sadness and doubt: "As we turned the last corner around the mountain and saw in the distance the wave of their hands in farewell, we wondered what would happen to the little flickering flame of gospel light that had been lit in the midst of so much darkness. Would these young Christians, with no more of the Word of God in their own language than the Gospel of Mark and a few small booklets of selected Scripture portions to guide and teach them, be able to stand under the persecution that would inevitably come?"[24]

And persecution did come—severe persecution that purified the church and magnified the Christians' testimony, even as it had in the early church. "At one point," according to Raymond Davis, "50 leaders had been arrested and put in prison when the Italians realized that their efforts to stamp out the church were only increasing its strength and size. Each of the leaders received 100 lashes, and one was given 400. None of them were able to lie on their backs for months, and three died." But despite this harsh persecution the church rapidly grew. Why? "The warm love displayed by the Christians toward one another in the times of severest persecution made a great impression on the unbelievers.... This kind of natural, living, unspoken witness brought many to know the Lord. Word of such love, hitherto unknown and unheard of, spread far and wide."[25]

By 1941 the war in Ethiopia was over, and the following year the first missionaries were allowed to return —though only by working under the British government. What they found was no less than a miracle to them. The forty-eight Christians they had left five years before had grown to some ten thousand, and instead of one fledgling church there were nearly one hundred congregations spread out across the province. It was the greatest story of Christian evangelism in African history—one that overwhelmed the sixty-nine-year-old Rowland Bingham. The painful losses of his early years in Africa had turned around, and he had just completed the story of this in a book recounting the fifty years of SIM in Africa, *Seven Sevens*. Amid the excitement, Bingham made plans to go to Ethiopia himself, but before he left Canada in December of 1942 he died suddenly of an apparent heart attack.

In the years since Bingham's death, SIM has witnessed some great victories in Africa, but also faced some discouraging setbacks. When Sudanese[26] independence was declared in 1955, the missionaries found themselves in the midst of political turmoil, and when civil war broke out between the southern tribal people and the northern Muslim Arabs, they were accused of aiding the southern rebels. The new government nationalized mission schools, and in 1964 the Muslim controlled government expelled all missionaries in the South. With the missionaries gone, life for the Sudanese Christians only seemed to get worse. The northern government armed some southern tribes to fight other southern tribes, exploiting tribal animosities to weaken southern resistance. Some of the tribes in the South were ruthlessly crushed, and over a half million died. Christians were tortured, churches were burned, and at least one Christian village was totally destroyed.

By the early 1970s, however, the political climate in Sudan turned around. The Soviet advisors were dismissed and the missionaries were allowed to return. A small Bible school was established, and a substantial primary health care program was conducted between 1977 and 1982.

With the completion of the health project the missionary force was decreased, but the churches continue to grow at an encouraging rate.

Meanwhile, in Ethiopia there was again political turmoil. This time the Soviet Union became involved, and eventually a Marxist government was firmly established. As pressure was brought on both the churches and missions, many missionaries transferred to other countries. By 1978 the SIM missionary force there had been reduced to approximately twelve percent of its peak level, but the number of churches in the SIM related fellowship stood at 2,500.

The late 1970s and early 1980s were times of severe testing for Christians in Ethiopia. Some were imprisoned, and hundreds of church buildings were closed by government order. Yet, the number of functioning churches remained nearly constant, and in 1982 the church was still operating more than sixty Bible training schools with more than three thousand students. The Ethiopian church continues to send out and support its own missionaries and thousands are being converted to Christ each month.

Peter Cameron Scott and the Africa Inland Mission

The Africa Inland Mission, like the Sudan Interior Mission, barely survived its turbulent infancy. The torture of the African environment took its toll on the Western missionaries, and for a time the dream of fulfilling Johann Krapf's vision of establishing a line of mission stations across Africa from the east coast seemed to have turned into a grueling nightmare. The venture that had begun with such hopeful promise

in 1895 was within a few years barely alive. Yet, by 1901 the situation had begun to reverse itself, and AIM was on its way to becoming the largest mission in East Africa.

The Africa Inland Mission was founded by Peter Cameron Scott, a young missionary who had served for a short time in Africa under the International Missionary Alliance (later the C&MA) but was forced to return home due to repeated attacks of malaria. Scott was born in Glasgow, Scotland, in 1867. When he was thirteen his family emigrated to America and settled in Philadelphia, where Peter, a gifted vocalist, trained with an Italian maestro. Although his parents objected to his pursuing a career in the opera and insisted he learn the trade of printing, the lure of the stage was strong, and it was on the steps of an opera house, as he was on his way to answer an advertisement for chorus singers, that Scott faced the crucial decision of his life. Would he seek a life of self-glory and applause under the spotlight of the entertainment world, or would he dedicate his life to God's service, no matter how humble and obscure the circumstances? It was a moment of crisis in the young man's life, but the decision was final. He chose to serve God.

With that decision behind him, Scott enrolled at the New York Missionary Training College, founded by A. B. Simpson, to prepare for missionary service in Africa. In November of 1890, at the age of twenty-three, he was ordained by Simpson, and the following day he sailed for the west coast of Africa to join the International Missionary Alliance in its work there. Within months after he arrived he was joined by his brother John, but the joyful reunion soon turned to sorrow. John could not withstand the African assault on his health, and thus one more missionary was laid to rest in the "white man's graveyard." Peter constructed a crude coffin and dug the grave himself. There were no church bells or flowers or eulogies, but, alone at the grave, Peter "reached another crisis" and recommitted himself to preaching the gospel in Africa.

That solemn moment must have seemed like a farce to Scott some months later as he arrived in England, broken in health. How could he ever carry out his pledge to God? He needed a fresh source of inspiration and he found it at a tomb in Westminster Abbey that held the remains of a man who had inspired so many others in their missionary service to Africa. The spirit of David Livingstone seemed to be prodding Scott onward as he knelt reverently and read the inscription, "Other sheep I have which are not of this fold; them also I must bring." He would return to Africa and lay down his life, if need be, for the cause for which this great man had lived and died.

From England, Scott returned to America and there he met with other men and women to plan the strategy of penetrating Africa from the east, moving beyond the coastal regions where the Anglicans were serving and on into the "unreached tribes of the interior." Among those involved in the first planning sessions were A. T. Pierson and C. E. Hurlburt, men who would play significant roles in AIM in the years to come. The Bible Institute of Pennsylvania became the headquarters for the new mission and the scene of the farewell service in August of 1895

Peter Cameron Scott, founder of the Africa Inland Mission.

when Scott and seven others, including his sister, Margaret, were officially commissioned to service in Africa.

In October the missionary party arrived in Zanzibar, and from there they traveled inland to establish the first of several mission stations that would be located in Kenya. Within months after founding the first station, Scott was off seeking new mission sites so the missionaries could spread out and maximize their resources. More recruits, including Scott's parents and younger sister, Ina, were on the way, and Scott was optimistic about the future.

In 1896 Scott submitted his first annual report of AIM, enthusiastically recounting the significant accomplishments that had occurred in only one year. Four stations had been opened, houses had been built, educational and medical programs had been set up, and there was steady progress in language work. Scott clearly enjoyed his work, and, unlike so many of his missionary contemporaries, he had a real appreciation for the people and their culture; and their attire or lack of it did not seem to bother him: "The men (a great many of them) are naked, with the exception of the brass wire, which is freely worn about their necks, arms, waists and legs. They also make very fine chains out of fine brass wire, and great bunches of these are worn in the ears. They are generally well-built fellows, tall, thin, but muscular. As a rule, they have straight-cut features, are high in the forehead, and rather intelligent in appearance.... The women do not wear so much brass wire, but the quantity of beads some of them carry around their waists and necks is really wonderful."[27]

Hardly had Scott's first annual report been issued when word came that he had become ill. The brutal African environment had once again brought him down, and his hectic travel schedule on foot—covering some 2,600 miles in a year—only aggravated the situation. His mother patiently nursed him, but to no avail. He died in December of 1896, just fourteen months after he and his mission party had set foot on Africa.

Scott had been the lifeblood of AIM, and with his death, according to Kenneth Richardson, "The young mission passed through deep waters.... One after another, several of its valuable workers passed away. Others had to give up for health reasons. Still others—including the remaining members of the Scott family—left to serve Africa in other ways." By the summer of 1899 the only missionary remaining on the field was William Gangert, a solitary symbol that AIM was in Africa to stay. He was soon joined by two new recruits, and the AIM rebuilding process had begun. Then in 1901, C. E. Hurlburt, who had been appointed General Director of the mission, uprooted his wife and five children (all of whom later became AIM missionaries themselves) and relocated in Africa, where he could have a closer scrutiny of the work and actually become involved himself.

By 1909, AIM had expanded its work into Tanzania, and in the years following the northeastern part of the Congo was opened to the gospel—but not without powerful political influence. In 1908, while on furlough in the United States, Hurlburt had been summoned to the White House to meet President Theodore Roosevelt and to advise him concerning a safari he was planning to take in East Africa. When he visited Africa the following year, Roosevelt renewed his acquaintance with Hurlburt and laid the cornerstone for Rift Valley Academy, offering at that time to lend his influence should the mission ever need it. Hurlburt remembered that pledge in 1910 when he confronted Belgian authorities blocking AIM's entrance into the Congo, and he called upon the ex-President for help. True to his word, Roosevelt contacted the Belgian government and permission for AIM to enter was granted. A communications mix-up caused the local chiefs to believe Roosevelt himself was on his way in, so the first contingent of missionaries received an unexpected royal welcome.

Hurlburt's concept of effective missionary strategy did not simply involve an increase of mission stations and an expansion of evangelism, but it encompassed the total life of the missionary—particularly family life. He had surprised many by bringing his own five children to the mission field, but he was convinced of the importance of a stable family life and did not agree with the concept of sending children back to the homeland for their education. Hurlburt thus became one of the pioneers of the missionary children's school—a boarding school located on the field. Rift Valley Academy was established soon after he arrived in Africa; and in the years since, has expanded to meet the family needs of the several hundred AIM missionaries in East Africa, with a curriculum schedule of three months in school and one month home, allowing the children to return to their families three times each year.

Hurlburt was a strong, effective leader of AIM who was not afraid to face controversial issues head-on. He was a leading spirit in the 1913 Kikuyu Conference in Kenya that sought to establish a federation for missionary cooperation in East Africa based on strict adherence to the Scriptures and to the Apostles' and Nicene creeds. "It seemed tragic," writes Richardson, "that the denominational differences which divided Christians in the homelands should be imported into Kenya."[28] Although there was adverse reaction to the proposals of unity (especially from some Anglican leaders who denied the validity of communion from anyone who was not episcopally ordained), a loose alliance was formed that fostered cooperation among mission societies.

There were other controversial problems of church unity that Hurl-burt had to deal with—particularly ones relating to the Africans and their tribal customs. During the 1920s the practice of female circumcision created a crisis that nearly destroyed the young Kenyan church. It was a senseless practice accompanied by tribal rites that involved circumcising girls at the age of puberty. The young girls were taken to a secluded forest camp where they were operated on without anesthesia by older women using unsterilized, crude instruments that frequently resulted in serious infections as well as complications at the time of childbirth.

Within the African churches the feelings ran high on both sides of the issue, and when it appeared as though the problem would not only split the churches but create civil strife, some missionaries sought a compromise solution, proposing that the girls come to the mission hospital to have the surgery performed. The already overworked hospital staff, however, vehemently objected to any such compromise, and they were supported by the majority of missionaries who decided to take a hard line on the issue, demanding that the African church leaders who were supported by the mission condemn the practice or be fired. Only twelve refused to comply, but the crisis was not over. For taking a stand against this time-honored tribal practice, the African Christians were persecuted, and self-appointed circumcisers scoured the villages in search of uncircumcised girls.

Then came the ultimate humiliation. "It was bound to happen," write James and Marti Hefley. "An elderly, deaf AIM missionary, Hilda Stumpf, was found choked to death. First reports said she had been killed by a thief. Then the real facts came out. She had been brutally mutilated in a fashion that pointed to the work of circumcision fanatics." This "shocking murder caused some of the tribal zealots to back off. But the deeper conflict between Africans and Europeans dragged on and culminated in the bloody Mau Mau rebellion of the 1950s."[29]

Following the Mau Mau rebellion, AIM leaders realized the urgent necessity of releasing more control of the mission activities to the Africans themselves. The church had been in control of its own affairs for more than a decade, but in 1971 AIM turned over its properties to the Africa Inland Church and submitted to its leadership and authority. AIM continues in its evangelization of Africa as set forth by Peter Cameron Scott in 1895, but today its missionaries serve at the invitation and under the authority of a strong African leadership that the early pioneers worked hard to establish.

C. I. Scofield and the Central American Mission

During the same decade that A. B. Simpson was commissioning missionaries all over the globe and Bingham and Scott were penetrating central Africa, another American, who would later become famous for his popular edited Bible, was laying the groundwork for a gospel witness in Central America. C. I. Scofield was not the first evangelical Christian to catch a vision for Central America, but when that area of the world came to his attention in the late 1880s, "there was only one Spanish-speaking Gospel witness," according to a CAM histo-

rian, "in all of the Central American Republics." American missionaries, while venturing halfway around the world, had all but forgotten their next-door neighbors. Basing his strategy on what he viewed as a missionary principle in Acts 1:8, Scofield was determined to right that wrong: "Jerusalem and in all Judea, and in Samaria—that Central America is the nearest unoccupied field to any Christian in the United States or Canada! We have passed over our Samaria!"[30]

C. I. Scofield was born in Michigan in 1843 and raised in Tennessee. When he was in his late teens, the Civil War broke out and by conviction he joined the Confederate forces and served valiantly in Lee's army, winning the Confederate Cross of Honor for his courageous service at Antietam. Following the war he studied law; and after he was admitted to the Kansas bar in 1869 he served in the Kansas State Legislature and then became a United States Attorney under President Grant. Later, in 1879, while practicing law in St. Louis, Scofield was converted to Christianity by a client who boldly witnessed to him. For Scofield, "a slave . . . to drink," the conversion was dramatic. He began an intense study of the Bible, and in 1883 he was ordained a Congregationalist minister. For the next thirteen years he served as a pastor in Dallas and later became a conference speaker, a renowned Bible scholar, and the founder and first president of Philadelphia College of the Bible; but it was during his first pastorate in Dallas that he became burdened for the spiritual needs of Central America.

Hudson Taylor, the founder of the China Inland Mission, was the one who made the greatest impression on Scofield in the area of missions. For several summers Scofield attended the Niagara Bible Conference in Niagara, New York, and there he formed a lasting friendship with Taylor, who heightened his sensitivity toward foreign missions. Then in the summer of 1888 he learned specifically of the needs of the people in Costa Rica, who were devoid of religion, except for the "dissolate priests making a mockery of ministering to the people spiritually."

When Scofield returned to Dallas he called together some of the leaders of his church and shared with them the spiritual poverty of Costa Rica and formed a prayer fellowship for the 280,000 people of that tiny nation. Soon after that meeting, one of the men who had attended began an investigation of other Central American countries and discovered that they also, except for Guatemala, were entirely without Spanish-speaking Christian missionaries.

With this information, Scofield could not remain passive. In the fall of 1890 he called his church leaders together in his home to organize the Central American Mission, and within four months the new mission had its first candidate, William McConnell, on the field in Costa Rica, soon to be joined by his wife Minnie and their three sons.

But there was more behind the founding of CAM than an enthusiastic pastor, a supportive congregation, and a willing missionary couple. When McConnell arrived in Costa Rica he met two godly women, Mrs. Ross and Mrs. Lang, who were both married to coffee plantation owners living in the English-speaking community of San José and active in a church founded by

C. I. Scofield, Bible editor and founder of the Central American Mission.

the Scotch Presbyterians. These two women, like Scofield, had been burdened for the spiritual needs of Costa Rica, and they had been meeting together to pray for missionaries. As the months passed they became discouraged and were tempted to forego their prayer meetings, but they persisted and were duly rewarded when McConnell arrived early in 1891. Years later McConnell described the women as "the first to heartily welcome us to the country and encourage us in the work," adding that they had been "loyal friends and helpers ever since."

By 1894 there were seven CAM missionaries in Costa Rica, and the mission was seeking other fields of service. The first efforts of expansion were stymied when two missionaries en route to El Salvador both died of yellow fever. In 1895, H. C. Dillon was sent to survey the prospects for further work in Central America, and on his return he wrote, "It seems strange to me that such a great field lying just at our door with its many nations should

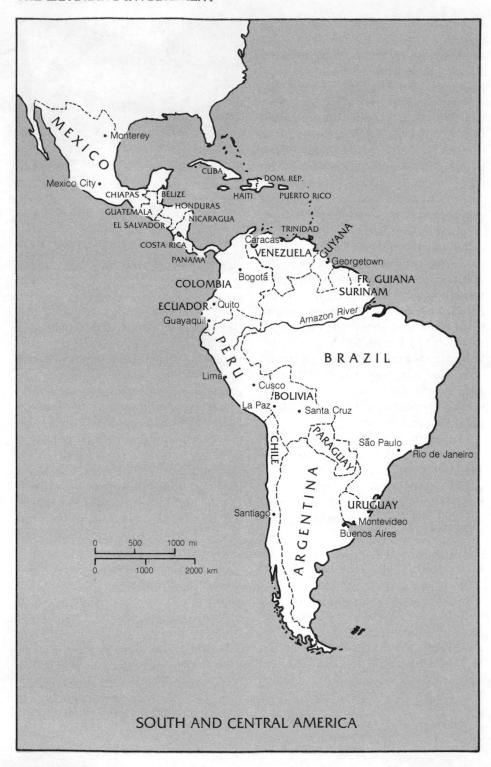

SOUTH AND CENTRAL AMERICA

have been absolutely neglected during the whole century of missions.... There are large tribes that can be reached in ten days from New Orleans, and at a cost of $50.00. Who will go?"[31] The following year CAM opened two new fields, Honduras and El Salvador, and in 1899 Guatemala was opened and the following year Nicaragua. After one decade the mission had twenty-five missionaries working in five Central American fields, and despite setbacks the mission continued to grow and is actively serving today with nearly three hundred missionaries in six Central American republics plus Mexico.

Joe Moreno and New Tribes Mission

Although Scofield's concern was specifically for Central America, all of Latin America had been for centuries neglected by Protestant missions. By the end of the nineteenth century, however, there was a growing awareness of this oversight. *The Neglected Continent*, a book by Lucy Guinness, underscored the "spiritual neglect of South America" and helped awaken many Christians to their responsibility. It is estimated that in 1900 there were only fifty thousand evangelical Christians in all of Latin America, a figure that increased nearly one hundredfold in the fifty years that followed and that exceeds twenty million today. "Nowhere," according to Herbert Kane, "has Christianity grown so rapidly in this twentieth century."[32]

Why Protestant mission boards neglected Latin America is a puzzling aspect of the "Great Century" of foreign missions. R. H. Glover has written that there is "no satisfactory explanation ... for the aloofness and inaction."

Harold Cook, another missions historian, however, has given some reasons, if not a "satisfactory explanation," for this neglect. One factor was that "violent Roman Catholic opposition made Protestant missions to Latin America unattractive if not impossible." Another factor Cook mentions was that Latin America "lacked the glamour that was somehow attached to areas like the Orient, Africa or the South Seas." Likewise, some of the leaders of Protestant mission societies "argued that Latin America was nominally Christian, so Protestant activity in that area could not properly be classified as missions in the same sense as the work in India, China and Africa." This was particularly true of some of the delegates at the Edinburgh Missionary Conference of 1910.[33] It was also true of some of the "faith" mission leaders whose prime concern was to reach inland frontiers where Christ had not even been named.

But if certain individual mission societies hesitated to enter Latin America, most mainline denominational societies and newer "faith missions"—especially those being forged around the turn of the century—had no such compunctions. They moved into the region, according to Stephen Neill, "with the express purpose of 'converting' Roman Catholics." Most of the Latin Americans, particularly the native Indians, were Roman Catholic in name only, and had never had even minimal instruction in the Roman Catholic religion.

It was on these aboriginal peoples —some ten million of them in western South America—that many of the new missions focused their attention. The South American Indian Mission, the

Andes Evangelical Mission, Wycliffe Bible Translators, and New Tribes Mission were all founded for the purpose of reaching these primitive people, of whom Charles Darwin wrote, "One can hardly make one's self believe that they are fellow creatures."[34] To the missionaries, however, there was no difficulty in believing that they were fellow creatures and far more—priceless souls for whom Christ died. And they were willing to risk their lives to bring these people hope of eternal life. Among them were five young men with New Tribes Mission who disappeared in the jungle of Bolivia, never to be seen or heard from again.

New Tribes Mission was founded in 1942 by Paul Fleming, a sickly missionary returnee from Malaysia, who was encouraged and assisted by Cecil

Dye, a young pastor from Michigan. They both had a concern for remote tribes that had never been reached by the gospel, and after lengthy discussions they formulated the guidelines for an undenominational mission society specifically for the purpose of reaching "new tribes." By the fall of 1942, Cecil Dye was ready to lead a party of sixteen (including his wife and three children) into the unexplored Bolivian jungle while Fleming remained in the United States to man the home office. Inquiries about Indian tribes were made with the Bolivian Embassy in Washington, D.C., but precisely where they would be going and what tribe they would be attempting to reach was still an uncertainty when the mission party arrived in Santa Cruz, Bolivia, on Christmas Eve of 1942. There was no uncertainty as to

1 The mission begins
2 Jungle camp, June, 1943
3 The five last seen, November 10, 1943
4 The confrontation with the Ayorés, November 19, 1943
5 First friendly contact, August 12, 1947
6 Joe Moreno makes an airstrip, June, 1948
7 Contact with the killers, May, 1953

God's leading them, however, and not even the most hair-raising stories of savage ferocity against white men could dim their faith.

After discussing their aims with a Bolivian doctor who was familiar with the lush hot jungle lowlands, the missionaries decided that a tribe known as the *bárbaro* was the tribe for them—a tribe they were told "uses short arrows with such deadly effect that even the neighboring tribes . . . are terrified of them." Others who heard of the missionaries' plans also warned of danger: "They . . . attack any civilized person who comes near them"; "impossible to tame"; "you won't come back alive"; "they'll club their victims in their hammocks at night." But the determined party refused to be dissuaded. "God had called them to reach this so-called 'hardest tribe' first." "Of course it is risky going to them," wrote George Hosback, the youngest member of the team, "but didn't God stop the mouths of lions by His angels, and 'quench the violence of fire' by His presence? And is He not 'the same yesterday, today and forever'?"[35]

The speed with which the missionaries began their search for the *bárbaro* or Ayorés (a tribe whose actual name they did not even know when they began the search) has been a sharp point of controversy in the years since. That they "just jumped off the truck and ran into the jungle" (as some critics suggested) is obviously not true; but by any standard they appear to have acted in undue haste. Except for Cecil Dye, who flew in ahead with the women and children, the mission party did not reach Roberé, the base station, until February of 1943. The next few months were con-

sumed with situating the families, recovering from malaria, and learning the basics of jungle survival. Then, "all activities were brought to a halt for two weeks of special prayer." By June, "at long last" wrote one of the wives, the men (though admittedly still "greenhorns") were "ready to move on into the jungle."[36]

The march into the jungle was acknowledged to be undertaken by faith. Though accompanied for the first several weeks by a Bolivian familiar with the area, the missionaries were unarmed and unfamiliar with the customs and language of the people they were seeking. Since the Ayorés were nomadic the missionaries did not even know precisely where the Ayorés lived, but nevertheless they began cutting a swath wide enough for pack animals through the jungle in the territory believed to be inhabited by the tribe.

During the summer and early fall the men took turns returning to the base station for supplies, and two of the wives were relocated in a small town in the heart of the jungle near where the men expected to emerge. From there Cecil Dye, his brother Bob, and their three companions planned to launch their final leg of the journey that they expected would result in a face to face meeting with the *bárbaro*. November 10 was set for the day of departure. "Our hopes were high," wrote Jean Dye, "that the five were about to have that long awaited contact." She was unaware of the message her brother-in-law Cecil had left with the two remaining men: "If you don't hear anything inside a month, you can come and make a search for us."[37]

With no specified date for the return of their husbands, the missionary

The five New Tribes martyrs, killed in 1943: (from left to right) Dave Bacon, Cecil Dye, George Hosback, Bob Dye, and Eldon Hunter.

wives anxiously waited as the days and weeks went by. Finally a month passed, and a small search party made up of the two remaining male missionaries and four Bolivians went into the jungle. Christmas passed, but still there was no word from the missionaries. Then in early January word from the search team reached the women, and it was not encouraging. After following the river, the search team discovered where the Ayorés had been camped, and there they found a machete, a sock, pieces of a camera, and other fragments of items belonging to the five missing missionaries. Though important finds, the items formed no conclusive evidence, but plans to continue the search were suddenly called off when Wally, one of the missionaries, was wounded by an arrow from an enemy lurking in the undergrowth.

After the first search party returned, another larger team made up of Bolivians was sent in. They quickly picked up the trail of the Ayorés and again found items belonging to the five missing men, but still no evidence regarding their whereabouts. On the second expedition the search party was well armed, and when a lone Ayoré allegedly threatened them, one of the men in the party shot and killed him. The wives were devastated when they

heard of the tragedy and were discouraged that their husbands had not been found, but they refused to give up. Even though one of the missionaries who had gone in on the first search had written that there was "no hope," they clung to the possibility that their husbands had been taken captive and would one day walk out of the jungle.

During the years that followed, rumors surfaced periodically about the men—one in 1946 reporting that the men had emerged from the jungle in a remote area of Brazil. "We wondered," wrote Jean Dye, "how much more we could bear of these waves of hope—raised only to be dashed." In the meantime the wives of the missing men remained in Bolivia. "Depleted as our ranks were," wrote Jean, "our outlook had not changed. We were more determined than ever to win these souls to Christ.... But how? Where? When? What should we do?" Important questions, but how unfortunate they had not been pondered at greater length before the five missionaries went in.[38]

The answers came only slowly as the women and remaining men became familiar with the area in which they lived. It was learned that there were captive Ayoré servants living in San José, and so Jean relocated there to study their language and learn their customs. While she was away, Joe Moreno took up the search for the Ayorés. He was a middle-aged farm laborer—a sixth-grade dropout—who, with his three children, had joined the first party of New Tribes missionaries after his wife had abandoned the family. Though Joe did not think of himself as a missionary, only a "flunky for Cecil Dye," it was his patient efforts that eventually resulted in peaceful encounters with the Ayorés.

Joe quickly realized that pioneer missionary work to primitive Indian tribes was a slow and tedious process. He began by following (at a distance) the movements of the Ayorés, studying the patterns in the trails and directions they took. From Jean he learned Ayoré greetings and other phrases, and he constantly inquired about their customs, noting that such things as knives, wire, and pieces of metal would be considered priceless gifts. As time passed, Joe became familiar with the jungle and was often close on the trail of the Ayorés, though never confronting them directly. He began leaving gifts in their abandoned camps. Finally, more than three years after his comrades had disappeared, there were signs that Joe's patient efforts were paying off—"to his joy he found two Ayoré items left in that camp, exactly where his gifts had been."

It was in August of 1947 that the first real breakthrough with the Ayorés occurred. The painstaking work of Joe had apparently convinced members of the tribe that the cojñone (the civilized ones) did not want to kill them, as previous experience had taught them to believe; and on the morning of August 12, a number of them appeared at a railway camp, "wanting to be friends."

Joe was immediately summoned, and he arrived in time to take part in the first friendly face to face meeting that had ever taken place between the cojñone and the Ayorés. "For once in his life," wrote Jean, "Joe was speechless. From the depths of his heart he thanked God for bringing all this about. He knew . . . that a miracle was passing before his eyes. . . ." "The greatest miracle of all," she continued, "was that bárbaro themselves had taken the first step in seeking a 'friendly contact' with the cojñone."[39]

That the Ayorés be allowed to determine the time and place of their first friendly meeting with the cojñone was a key element in Joe's strategy of success. If they were ever to be reached they had to come on their own terms, and he had allowed them that privilege. After the first meeting there were more, and in less than a year the Ayorés had developed such confidence in the cojñone that a group of them literally moved in on Jean Dye and her partner, sleeping on the floor of their house. To deal with the problem of overcrowding, the missionaries moved to an abandoned ranch with one whole tribe and later moved back into the jungle with them. There were serious logistical and health problems, but the gospel was being preached and the Ayorés were responding.

As the missionaries built a friendship with the Ayorés, they began questioning them about the five missing men. Some of the Ayorés had heard stories about five cojñone being killed by another Ayoré tribe, but none of their information was conclusive. Then in 1949, some six years after the tragedy had occurred, an Ayoré tribesman from the region where the men were found missing gave for the first time an eyewitness account of the slaying of the five missionaries. Six years of clinging to the hope that they were still alive had come to an end.

"Was it worth the price?"—five missionaries and one Ayoré. That question has often been asked and answered. The wives and other surviving missionaries all answered in the affirmative. But is such a question relevant? Perhaps no price is too high to pay for the miracles of conversion that took place among the Ayorés. The issue is not the amount of the price but whether the price was necessary at all. Was it necessary to sacrifice lives to reach the Ayorés? Joe Moreno, with his meager sixth grade education, answered that question by his own tireless efforts. He performed no glorious heroic feats, but he patiently persevered.

Was there nothing then to be gained by the sacrifice? There was. In January of 1944, when word had reached the United States that five missionaries were missing and presumed dead, a factory worker from Lansing, Michigan, read the account in the evening newspaper, and that night he dedicated himself as a missionary to help make up for the loss. His name was Bruce Porterfield, and in the years since he has effectively ministered as a missionary to Bolivia, as a representative of New Tribes Mission, and as the author of *Commandos for Christ* and other exciting missionary books. Others, too, inspired by the willingness of the five missionaries to risk all for the sake of the gospel, dedicated themselves to missionary service.

But the new mission seemed to be plagued with adversity. In the years following the martyrdom of the five missionaries, there were several more painful tragedies. In 1949 the mission established its own aviation program with the purchase of a DC-3. The following year that plane went down in Venezuela, and all on board died. A second plane was purchased, and on its first flight it went down during a storm over the Grand Tetons in Wyoming, killing all on board, including Paul Fleming, the mission's founder. The following year, news of another mishap reached the home office. David Yarwood, Bruce Porterfield's partner, was killed while seeking to make contact with a hostile tribe of Indians. Then only a year and a half later, in the summer of 1953, a tragic disaster occurred at the mission's boot camp when fourteen promising young students died fighting a forest fire. But through it all, New Tribes Mission continued to grow, and by 1980 the mission was sponsoring more than 1,600 missionaries who were carrying the gospel to more than one hundred and forty tribes around the world.

Pete Fleming and Operation Auca

The tragedy that accompanied the early years of New Tribes Mission in Bolivia was strangely repeated the following decade in Ecuador. How such an incident could recur in such similar circumstances illustrates how truly independent many twentieth-century "faith" missionaries had become, and it also shows the degree of cooperation that existed among missionaries from different evangelical mission societies. Operation Auca, which claimed the lives of five brilliant young men, was not a project designed by a mission society, and it is doubtful whether any established mission society would have approved it. Rather, it was a hastily drawn-up plan devised by members of three different missions with virtually no consultation with their leaders or with senior missionaries on the field. They were proceeding "by faith," depending on direct guidance from God.

That is not to suggest, however, that they ignored pertinent data relating to the Indians and the experience of other missionaries. Indeed, as they planned the contact with the Aucas they poured over the details of the New Tribes tragedy in Bolivia the previous decade, noting with grave interest their mistakes and vowing not to fall into any of the same traps themselves.

The five missionaries involved in Operation Auca were all what might be termed junior missionaries. Nate Saint, a pilot working under Missionary Aviation Fellowship, was the most experienced, having served in Ecuador for seven years. The others had only two or three years of experience each. Roger Youderian was serving with the Gospel Missionary Union, and Jim Elliot, Pete Fleming, and Ed McCully were with Christian Missions in Many Lands, a Brethren organization that channels money to some thirteen hundred missionaries, though it claims it is "not a mission board, nor ... in any way a mission society." As such, CMML encourages its missionaries to "depend directly on the Lord for guidance in their work," reminding them that they are not "answerable to any mission board—only to God." It was this philosophy, then, that opened the way for such a project as Operation Auca.

Operation Auca was born in the Ecuadorian jungle in the fall of 1955 in an effort to reach one of the most hostile Indian tribes in all of South America with the gospel. For centuries the Aucas had been the subject of hair-raising stories. "Spanish conquistadors, Catholic priests, rubber hunters, oil drillers—all had been targets of Auca spears. Dozens, perhaps hundreds, had been killed. No outsider had ever been able to live in Auca territory"—so said Dave Cooper, a veteran missionary to Ecuador. The most recent publicized killings by the Aucas had occurred in 1943, when eight Shell Oil employees lost their lives at the hands of this most unfriendly tribe. But it was these very accounts that held a certain fascination for the five young missionaries. What a glorious victory it would be if such a tribe could be converted to Christianity.

Pete Fleming was born in 1928 in Seattle, Washington. Following his conversion as a teen-ager he went on to excel athletically and academically in high school, earning letters in basketball and golf and becoming valedictorian of his graduating class. After high school he enrolled at the University of Washington, where he earned both his bachelors and masters degrees. It was his intention to go on to Fuller Theological Seminary to prepare for a Bible teaching ministry, but then he met Jim Elliot whose well publicized story has since become almost synonymous with Operation Auca. Jim had graduated from Wheaton College in 1949 and was preparing for missionary service in Ecuador, and his single-minded enthusiasm to reach South American Indians deeply influenced Pete. In 1952 they left together for the mission field, both still single, though that would soon change.

Also arriving in Ecuador that year

was Ed McCully, with his wife Marilou. Ed, like Jim, was a graduate of Wheaton College, where he had been a star football player. Also a Wheaton alumnus was Nate Saint, who, with his wife Marj, had served in Ecuador since 1948. Roger Youderian, a World War II paratrooper and graduate of Northwestern College in Minneapolis, was the most recent arrival, coming in 1953 with his wife Barbara and infant daughter.

Although Roger was an enthusiastic participant in Operation Auca, his brief tenure as a missionary working among the headhunting Jivaros had not been a satisfying time, and he had been on the verge of giving up and going home. "There is no ministry for me among the Jivaros or the Spanish," he had written in his diary, "and I'm not going to try to fool myself. I wouldn't support a missionary such as I know myself to be, and I'm not going to ask anyone else to. Three years is long enough to learn a lesson and learn it well . . . the failure is mine. . . . This is my personal 'Waterloo' as a missionary."[40]

But Operation Auca changed all that. The excitement of being involved in what was hoped to be one of the great missionary breakthroughs in modern history brought new life into his missionary work. For the others, too, Operation Auca provided, in the words of Nate Saint, "high adventure, as unreal as any successful novel,"[41] a welcome change in the midst of routine missionary work. Though Jim, Pete, and Ed had been invited by Chief Atanasio to come and teach his tribe of Quichuas, it was the fearsome Aucas that captured their imaginations.

The dream of reaching the Aucas had been in the minds of the missionaries for years. Ever since Nate had arrived in Ecuador and heard stories of them he had dreamed of one day sharing the gospel with them. Pete and Jim had also been deeply burdened for them. In December of 1953 Pete wrote of this burden in his diary:

Last night with Nate and Cliff [a visitor from the States] we talked a long time about the Auca problem. It is a grave and solemn one; an unreachable people who murder and kill with a hatred which causes them to mutilate the bodies of their victims. It came to me strongly then that God is leading me to do something about it . . . for I have some qualifications for it that no one else has. I am still single. I know both Quichua and Spanish which would probably be essential for gathering of linguistic data, I know something of jungle life and I strongly believe that God is *able* for anything. I know that this may be the most important decision of my life but I have a quiet peace about it. Strangely enough I do not feel my coming marriage as prohibiting myself from being eligible for this service. I feel that if pushed to it that Olive would rather have me die after we had lived together than to indefinitely postpone our wedding in the possibility that something fatal might happen. Our life has become one and I do not feel that God will separate us in our discernment of the will of God.[42]

Not long after he made that commitment, Pete suffered several serious bouts of malaria and was unable to carry through with his plans. Back in the States at the University of Washington, his fiancée Olive was praying for a successful contact with the Aucas and doing research on Indians of South America in her anthropology course.

It was not until September 19, 1955, that the first breakthrough came. As

Nate flew over Auca territory in his single-engine Piper Cruiser he spotted for the first time an Auca village. In the weeks that followed, regular visits to the "neighbors" began. As Nate manned the controls, one of the other missionaries would drop gifts (including machetes, knives, clothing, and life-sized pictures of themselves) and shout friendly Auca greetings learned from Dayuma, an Auca woman living outside the tribe. On one occasion while circling above, Nate used a rope to lower a bucket containing gifts, and he was delighted to pull it back up filled with gifts from the Aucas—a live parrot, peanuts, and a smoked monkey tail. This response was taken as a genuine sign of friendship, and there was a strong feeling among at least some of the five missionaries to move in expeditiously.

The speed with which the missionaries moved forward in this dangerous undertaking, and the secrecy that surrounded it, have in the years since been the most controversial aspects of the effort. "The whole project," wrote Ed McCully to Jim Elliot, "is moving faster than we had originally dared to hope...." But why such haste? "The reason for the urgency," wrote Nate, "is the Brethren boys feel that it is time now to move." Presumably he was referring only to Jim and Ed, as Pete had warned against moving ahead quickly —especially before they had a better command of the language. Jim, who was "always quick to make decisions," was described as "chewing the bit" while Nate was cautioning that nothing be done suddenly, allowing each advance to "soak in" before another step was taken. Nevertheless, in less

315

than three months after the first gift drop the men had landed in the midst of Auca country.[43]

But if speed was a top priority, secrecy was even more so. A code system was developed so that the missionaries could communicate over shortwave radio without others finding out what they were up to. The missionaries themselves were sworn to secrecy. No one other than their wives and Johnny Keenan, an MAF pilot who would provide backup support should they need it, was to know. Nate wrote to his family back home requesting special prayer, hinting at what was underway, but couching even the vaguest clues in such phrases as "do not mention," "CONFIDENTIAL," "guard your talk," and "tell no one."[44]

The reason for the strict secrecy, according to James Hefley, was that "they feared that if word got out, a horde of journalists, adventurers, and curiosity seekers would make contact impossible." But the veil of secrecy extended to others who could be trusted and who could have given invaluable assistance. Frank Drown, with twelve years experience among the Ecuadorian Indians was not told of the venture until the plans had been finalized.

Another key individual left out of the planning was Rachel Saint, Nate's sister, who had spent months studying the Auca language with Dayuma, who had fled from her people. Rachel hoped to reach them with the gospel herself, but she knew the necessity of extreme caution. From Dayuma she had been warned: "Never trust them. . . . They may appear friendly and then they will turn around and kill."[45] Were such warnings ones the missionaries did not want to be reminded of? Were they afraid Rachel might influence their wives or foil the project in some other way? Would she report the operation to her supervisors at Wycliffe, forcing delays and inviting interference from government officials?

Certainly the five missionaries were aware of the danger, but they were convinced that no risk was too great to take for God. "He is no fool who gives what he cannot keep to gain what he cannot lose," was Jim's motto; and Jim solemnly vowed that he was "ready to die for the salvation of the Aucas."[46] They were all looking to God for guidance, and they saw signs of what they viewed to be God's direct intervention. The Curaray River, for example, seemed to shrink from its banks, providing a beach airstrip at a time when the beach normally would have been flooded. Nevertheless, there was great trepidation as the time approached for the landing in Auca territory. Aside from the ferocious nature of the Aucas, there were other serious safety factors to consider, particularly concerning the landing and takeoff from the short sandy beach along the Curaray River. Could Nate, skilled as he was, accomplish such a feat? It was an awesome responsibility that kept him awake most of the night on January 2, 1956.

The alarm clocks rang before 6 A.M. on Tuesday, January 3, and the adrenaline was flowing as the men began dressing. For Olive Fleming, who had been married to Pete for only a year and a half, it had been a "rough night." Though her burden to reach the Aucas was as intense as it had ever been, her apprehension could not be disguised. Jim had initially advised against Pete's going since it would mean risking the lives of three of the four men missionaries who knew the Quichua language, but by late December the consensus of opinion seemed to have changed. On December 27, Pete wrote in his diary: "It was decided that perhaps I ought to prepare to go on the expedition in order to gain by numbers more relative security for all."[47] Added precautions were taken, however. It was decided that Pete should fly out with Nate each night. All reports of previous Auca attacks indicated they invariably took place during the pre-dawn hours.

The plan called for Nate to make several trips to Palm Beach (the name they had given a sandy shoreline along the Curaray River), ferrying the missionaries and equipment in. The first landing and takeoff were crucial: "As we came in . . . we slipped down between the trees in a steep side slip. . . . As the weight settled on the wheels I felt it was soft sand—too late to back out now. I hugged the stick back and waited. One softer spot and we'd have been on our nose—maybe our back. It never came." On takeoff, after leaving Ed alone on the beach, "the sand really grabbed the wheels," but within seconds Nate was airborne and on his way back to the base to begin his second trip.[48]

January 3 was a busy day on Palm Beach as Nate ferried in the missionaries and equipment. By nightfall the men had constructed a tree house, and three of them slept there while Nate and Pete flew back to the base at Arajuno to spend the night. They returned the following morning and spent a relaxing uneventful day with the other three on the beach before flying out again in the late afternoon. Thursday was much the same. Then on Friday, things began to happen. At

11:15 A.M., three naked Aucas (two women and a man) suddenly appeared out of the jungle from across the river. Jim waded out to meet them, and a friendly exchange took place. The Aucas gleefully accepted gifts and appeared to be entirely at ease with their hosts. The man, whom the missionaries dubbed "George," was invited to take a plane ride—an offer he eagerly accepted. That night the Auca visitors departed, and Saturday was another uneventful day.

By Sunday the missionaries were restless and anxious for something to happen. Surely their visitors had not forgotten them. Nate decided to fly over the Auca village to check things out. He found it almost entirely deserted, and on the way back he spotted a band of Aucas "en route" to Palm Beach. "That's it, guys! They're on the way," he shouted as he touched down on the beach. Now all the missionaries had to do was wait. At 12:30 P.M. Nate made his scheduled radio contact with Marj at Shell Mera, promising to contact her again at 4:30.

The 4:30 contact never came. Nate's watch (later found smashed against a stone) had stopped ticking at 3:12 P.M. But Marj refused to believe the worst. Perhaps the radio transmitters had broken down. It was a sleepless night as she prayed and thought of the unthinkable. Early the next morning Johnny Keenan was in the air flying over Palm Beach. His report back to Marj was grim—a report that Marj relayed on to Elisabeth Elliot: "Johnny had found the plane on the beach. All the fabric is stripped off. There is no sign of the fellows."[49]

"Suddenly, the secrecy barrier was down," according to Russell Hitt. Word spread rapidly. Missionaries and government officials organized a search party. A *Time* magazine correspondent and a *Life* magazine photographer were dispatched to the scene, and the whole world waited for news. On Wednesday afternoon two bodies were sighted from the air, and on Friday the ground search team reached the site. "The missionaries in the ground party," according to Hefley, "pulled four badly deteriorated bodies from the river. Some still had palm wood spears sticking through their clothing. From personal belongings, they identified Jim, Pete, Rog, and Nate. Ed McCully's body apparently had been washed away." It was a somber scene. "The darkening sky indicated a jungle storm would soon be upon them. Hurriedly, the missionaries dug a shallow grave. As the rain came down in sheets, Frank Drown offered a quick committal prayer. . . ."[50]

At Shell Mera the five widows congregated to hear the grim details. Ahead of them was the task of putting their lives back together. For the stoical Elisabeth Elliot, there were "no regrets." "This was not a tragedy. . . . God has a plan and purpose in all things."[51] For Olive, who was left alone with no children, the trauma might have been unbearable. During her brief marriage she had endured the strain of two miscarriages and now the tragic death of her husband. But the very Bible passages she and Pete had been reading together before his death became her strength during this time of desperation, especially 2 Corinthians 5:5: "For he who has prepared you for this very thing is God."

As with the slaying of the five missionaries in Bolivia the previous decade, the public response was mixed. From everywhere came an outpouring of sympathy for the families; and many Christians, on seeing the commitment of these five, dedicated themselves to God and to missionary service. But to others the incident was "a tragic waste" of young lives.

Despite the trauma that ended Operation Auca, the Aucas themselves were not forgotten. MAF pilots resumed the gift drops, and Rachel Saint continued her study of the Auca language. But no more dramatic entries into Auca territory were planned. The effort proceeded with caution, and after nearly two years, some of the Aucas slowly began to make overtures to others outside their tribe. Then in September of 1958, Dayuma returned to her tribe with two Auca women and three weeks later they reappeared and invited Rachel Saint and Elisabeth Elliot to visit them, and so began the evangelization of the Aucas. There were no newsmen or photographers to record the breakthrough, for there was nothing to record except that two women were once again venturing into the jungle to preach the gospel— routine missionary work.

Eliza Davis George and the Elizabeth Native Interior Mission

While many faith missions such as the Sudan Interior Mission, the Africa Inland Mission, the Christian and Missionary Alliance, New Tribes Mission, and Christian Missions in Many Lands grew rapidly during the course of the twentieth century, each sponsoring hundreds of missionaries, others remained small and obscure. Yet some of these tiny mission societies performed extraordinary service, and collectively they sent out a mighty force of dedicated men and women. One such mission is the Elizabeth Native Interior Mission, founded by Eliza Davis George for the purpose of training young Liberian nationals to evangelize their own people.

Eliza, a native Texan, was born in 1879. During her student days at Central Texas College she dedicated her life to African missions; but it was not until more than a decade later in 1913, when she was past thirty, that she was able to fulfill her dream. With the support of the National Baptist Convention, she sailed for Liberia as "the first black woman from Texas to go to Africa as a missionary."

During her missionary career, Eliza met and married C. Thompson George, who also had a burden for missions, but he did not have the stamina to face the trials of being a pioneer missionary. The continual setbacks in their work broke his spirit. As depression overcame him he began to drown his sorrows in alcohol, and in 1939 he died. Eliza continued on in the work until 1945, when her board called her home. She was sixty-five, and the committee believed it was time for her to retire. But retirement was not suited to Eliza, and at the age of sixty-seven, after raising her own support, she returned to Africa to serve for another quarter of a century. During her fifty-five years in Africa, "Mother" George established eight schools and more than one hundred churches. On January 20, 1979, she celebrated her one hundredth birthday in Texas, and the following March she died, but the legacy she left through one small "faith" mission—the Elizabeth Native Interior Mission—lives on.[52]

SELECTED BIBLIOGRAPHY

Davis, Raymond. Fire on the Mountains: The Story of a Miracle—The Church in Ethiopia. Grand Rapids: Zondervan, 1975.

Elliot, Elisabeth. Through Gates of Splendor. New York: Harper & Row, 1958.

Hitt, Russell T. Jungle Pilot: The Life and Witness of Nate Saint. Grand Rapids: Zondervan, 1973.

Hunter, J. H. A Flame of Fire: The Life and Work of R. V. Bingham. Scarborough, Ontario: Sudan Interior Mission, 1961.

Johnson, Jean Dye. God Planted Five Seeds. Woodworth, Wisconsin: New Tribes Mission, 1966.

Kane, J. Herbert. Faith Mighty Faith: A Handbook of the Interdenominational Foreign Mission Association. New York: Interdenominational Foreign Mission Association, 1956.

Richard, Kenneth. Garden of Miracles: The Story of the Africa Inland Mission. London: Africa Inland Mission, 1976.

Spain, Mildred W. "And in Samaria": A Story of More Than Sixty Years' Missionary Witness in Central America, 1890–1954. Dallas: The Central American Mission, 1954.

Thompson, A. E. The Life of A. B. Simpson. New York: Christian Alliance Publishing, 1920.

Tozer, A. W. Wingspread: A. B. Simpson: A Study in Spiritual Altitude. Harrisburg: Christian Publications, 1943.

PART IV

THE CALL
FOR SPECIALIZATION

The Call
For Specialization

The typical nineteenth century missionary, if there was one, was an evangelist. His time was largely consumed with saving souls and planting churches. Even if he practiced medicine or translated Scripture, he was first and foremost a preacher of the gospel. By the twentieth century that concept of a missionary was beginning to erode. Missionary work was becoming far more diversified. By mid-century many mission societies had been founded for the express purpose of promoting certain mission specialties, and today it is almost assumed that a missionary carries to the field some particular specialty. Only a minority of missionaries consider themselves general evangelists.

The base for this new trend in mission specialization was the United States, where advances in science and technology had fostered a movement toward specialization in almost every field. But the impetus for missionary specialization did not arise from a secular trend, but rather from a spirit of recommitment to spiritual values. It was a strong fundamentalist-evangelical current that propelled specialty missions into the mainstream of world evangelism while many traditional mission societies supported by liberal denominations declined.

During the years following World War I, as the nation careened through the roaring 20s, there was a noticeable decline in religious fervor, and this was reflected in an ambivalence toward foreign missions. "The mood of the Protestant churches in the 1920's" according to Winthrop Hudson, "was remarkably complacent." There was "a growing missionary apathy," and "missionary giving steadily declined during this period of booming prosperity."[1] The number of students volunteering for foreign missions, according to the Foreign Missionary Conference report, also fell drastically—from 2,700 in 1920 to only around 250 in 1928. Even the very philosophical basis for missions came under fire as William E. Hocking and his colleagues, who compiled the *Laymen's Inquirey*, warned against "conscious and direct evangelism."

But what seemed apparent in statistics and publicized reports failed to tell the whole story. In fundamentalist-evangelical circles the missionary spirit had never died, and during the 1930s, despite the woes of the Depression, there was a conscious and growing movement to speed the pace of world evangelism with whatever means were available. It was during that decade that Clarence Jones and some of his visionary colleagues initiated the earliest attempts to establish missionary radio, that William Cameron Townsend began training missionary linguists, that Joy Ridderhof implemented her ideas for gospel records, and that others were testing the practicality of aviation on the mission field. World War II, however, frustrated the plans of many of these missionary activists, and it was not until the end of the war that the real thrust of missionary specialization got underway.

The close of World War II brought a "surge of piety in America," as Roy Eckardt has suggested in the title of his book. By the 1950s, writes Winthrop Hudson, "the United States was in the midst of a religious revival," distinct from previous revivals—one that was "formless and unstructured, manifesting itself in many different ways and reinforcing all religious faiths quite indiscriminately."[2] But, while almost all religious groups played a role in this new religious spirit, it was the "evangelicals," according to Hudson, "that gave the revival its most vigorous leadership."[3] And such newly formed organizations as Youth for Christ and the National Association of Evangelicals gave the evangelical movement a broader base. In the area of foreign missions involvement, the close of the war saw the emergence of a new missions association, the Evangelical Foreign Missions Association, that was openly opposed to the religious liberalism of the twentieth century—a trend that had infected most mainline denominational missions.

Spurred on by this wave of evangelical fervor, the embryonic specialty missions conceived in the 1930s began to blossom forth. The future looked bright and personnel was available. No longer were America's young men being sent off to war, and with servicemen coming home from abroad, there seemed to be a new awareness and sense of urgency for world evangelism. Such organizations as Mission Aviation Fellowship, Far East Broadcasting Company, Far East Gospel Crusade, and Greater Europe Mission were all formed through the efforts of World War II veterans.

Another effect that the close of World War II had on foreign missions was the cold war that quickly ensued. An "iron curtain" had been formed around Eastern Europe, and by the 1950s vast portions of Asia were effectively closed to the gospel. In America it was a heyday for Wisconsin Senator Joseph McCarthy, who spewed forth virulent anti-communist rhetoric and made defamatory accusations of treason against his own countrymen. Prodded on by this mixture of hysteria and patriotism, Evangelicals infused the gospel with political freedom in a heightened concern for the millions whose freedom was denied by atheistic totalitarian regimes. (Ironically, no such intense concern had been evident in the late nineteenth and early twentieth centuries when the powerful Russian Orthodox Church harshly persecuted Baptists and other Evangelicals, who initially welcomed the

Russian Revolution, but when the spiritually dead Russian Orthodox Church became the object of persecution, then the Christian world took notice.) Radio and literature were seen as the only viable means of reaching such people, and as a result such missions as the Slavic Gospel Association, the Far East Broadcasting Company, and those promoting Bible smuggling found a solid base of support.

But not only were the Communist Block countries viewed as a new mission field, but the whole of Europe—the one-time bastion of Protestant Christianity. Even as Roman Catholic Latin America emerged as a mission field in the late nineteenth and early twentieth centuries, so the predominantly Protestant nations of Western Europe emerged as a mission field by the mid-twentieth century, when religion had become a nonpersonal matter of state, and church attendance was at an all-time low. Organizations such as Trans World Radio, Greater Europe Mission, Operation Mobilization, and Word of Life entered the scene to take up the slack.

The emphasis on specialization in missions, coming largely as a response to technological, political, social, and religious changes during the twentieth century, has been broad and varied. Medicine, translation work, radio, and aviation have attracted thousands of missionary specialists in recent decades, and other areas such as education, literature, and agriculture work have also grown at a steady pace. One of the factors influencing the growth of such specialized and sometimes secular-oriented ministries has been the increase in the number of Christian liberal arts colleges, many growing out of one-time Bible institutes and Bible colleges. Graduates from these schools, often through the aid of INTERCRISTO (a computerized Christian placement service) have discovered countless opportunities to utilize their education and skills on the foreign field. Likewise, Bible institutes and Bible colleges have broadened their curriculum to accommodate such specialized ministries as radio, aviation, and linguistics.

Involvement in the education of nationals has certainly not been exclusively a twentieth-century phenomenon. During the nineteenth century, Alexander Duff worked predominately in the field of education in India, and since then, spurred on by the Student Volunteer Movement, education has been considered an effective opening for evangelism. In Africa as well as in Asian nations such as Korea, primary, secondary, and college Christian education has had a significant impact on church growth. But while mission-supported schools still play an important role in mission work, in recent decades government education programs have opened their doors to missionaries. Some governments, as Herbert Kane has pointed out, "pay the missionaries to teach Christianity as a required course. The teacher is free to select his own textbook; so of course the Bible is used as source material. In this way the missionaries have a made-to-order situation—a captive audience in a structured program and the government paying the bill! . . . One missionary in Nigeria wrote: 'I am doing more direct missionary work now than I have done in my sixteen years in Nigeria.' Another missionary reports thirty-seven Bible classes a week in the government schools in Kano and more opportunities for personal witness than he can handle. In ... Indonesia and South Africa, missionaries were hired to write the curricula for the entire course on Christianity, from elementary school through high school. One could hardly imagine a more strategic ministry."[4]

The ministry of Christian literature, likewise, has had a significant impact on twentieth-century missions. In 1921, Arthur Brown's survey of contemporary missionary trends concluded that "one hundred and sixty presses are conducted by the Protestant missions boards in various parts of the world, and they issue annually about four hundred million pages of Christian literature."[5] Since World War II, Christian literature as a missionary tool has expanded rapidly. Several organizations have been founded that are geared almost exclusively to an overseas ministry, including the Christian Literature Crusade, the World Literature Crusade, Operation Mobilization, the Evangelical Literature League, the Pocket Testament League, and Evangelical Literature Overseas. One of the largest literature organizations is the Moody Literature Mission, which distributes literature in nearly two hundred languages. In addition to literature, films and other audiovisual materials are produced, the most widely distributed being Moody Science Films, available in more than twenty languages and distributed in more than one hundred countries.

Agriculture is another specialty field that has developed during the twentieth century. American expertise in this area has long been coveted by agriculturalists in developing nations, and thus agricultural missionaries have found an open door for a ministry that combines their agricultural know-how with their testimony for Christ. Some mission societies such as the Andean Indian Mission, founded in 1945 by Presbyterian, United Brethren, and Reformed churches, have well-developed agricultural programs. Others such as the Africa Inland Mission have used agriculture only in isolated instances, but no less effectively. Ben Webster is a notable example. He joined AIM as an experienced agriculturalist, having worked with UNESCO in Bangladesh. Assigned to Lokori in the Kenya Desert where the Kerio River was dried up, he drilled pipes into the dry riverbed and began an irrigation system that allowed Turkana tribesmen to leave their nomadic impoverished lifestyle and productively grow legumes in this otherwise arid region. His success was a satisfying accomplishment, but even more rewarding were the opportunities his work gave him to minister with other missionaries in evangelizing the tribe.

The mission specialties with the most numbers and the most profound impact on recent trends in world evangelism have been those centered around medicine, translation and linguistics work, radio and recordings, and aviation. These specialties have not been ends in themselves, but rather ministries that have bolstered and supported the work of missionary evangelists and national church leaders. But as important as these missionary specializations have been in recent decades, the trend in some areas, as missionaries serve at the invitation of national church leaders, is to assign more missionaries to work as evangelists and church planters.

Chapter 12

Medical Missions: "Angels of Mercy"

Since the time of Christ, the influence of medical work on evangelism has been immense. Christ's own evangelistic ministry as well as that of his disciples was enhanced by the ministry of healing; and in the centuries that followed, Christians continued to be known for their genuine concern for the sick and needy. During a series of plagues at Alexandria, it was the early Christians who remained to care for the sick and bury the dead after everyone else had fled, thereby increasing the reputation of Christianity as a religion of love and devotion.

From the onset of the modern missionary period, medical work has been a significant aspect of world evangelism, but it was not until the late nineteenth and early twentieth centuries that medical missions became a distinct specialty in its own right. By 1925, more than two thousand doctors and nurses from America and Europe were serving throughout the world, and mission-run hospitals and clinics were increasing rapidly.

The ministry of missionary medicine during the twentieth century has been without a doubt the greatest humanitarian effort the world has ever known, and, more than any other force, it has served to disarm the critics of Christian missions. How many times medical specialists forsook lucrative practices and modern facilities in their homelands to work long hours at a feverish pace in utterly primitive conditions. They devoted their lives to raising health standards around the world, often leading the research in diseases in which most Western doctors had little interest, and building hospitals and medical schools from funds they had personally donated or solicited. Among their credits are some of the finest medical schools and hospitals in the world, the Christian Medical College and Hospital in Vellore, India, being a prime example.

But despite their good will, medical missionaries had to counter the same obstacles confronting their nonmedical colleagues. Their work brought them into direct competition with witch doctors and medicine men, and the medical concepts they introduced often clashed with cherished cultural traditions. At times opposition was fierce. But aside from outright hostility, the medical missionaries had to contend with superstition, fear, and ignorance, all of which seriously hampered their efforts to improve health conditions. A missionary doctor in Africa had to wait eight long years before he treated his first native patient. In China, medical missionaries faced almost constant xenophobia; yet, in 1935 well over half of the hospitals in that country were mission-operated facilities.

While it has been medical doctors that have generally received the most acclaim for their service in medical missions, dentists and less trained medical personnel have also made noteworthy contributions to the cause. Likewise, some missionaries, with virtually no training in medicine, learned by trial and error how to treat diseases, thereby alleviating suffering and death, and always paving the way for an evangelistic ministry.

The first noted medical missionary in the modern period was Dr. John Thomas, who preceded William Carey to India and later worked alongside him. Though Thomas was emotionally unstable, Carey praised his work, claiming that the "cures wrought by him would have gained any physician or surgeon in Europe the most extensive reputation." Dr. John Scudder was the first American foreign missionary to specialize in medicine and was the patriarch of a whole line of medical missionaries to serve in India and elsewhere in the world. Other missionaries who were trained in medicine, including David Livingstone and Hudson Taylor, merely used medicine as a sideline.

One of the most noted medical missionaries of all times was the famed Albert Schweitzer, a medical doctor, musician, and biblical scholar, whose liberal and highly controversial theological views were widely disseminated in his book, *The Quest of the Historical Jesus.* His career as a medical missionary began in West Africa in 1913, where he established a hospital at Lambarene; and there, except for a period of imprisonment by the French during World War I, he devoted his life to medical work in Africa. Although he was a sought-after author, lecturer, and concert organist and could have enjoyed a life of mingling with the celebrity world, he chose instead to expend his energy on prolonging the life of "the brother for whom Christ died." Why? The reason he gave to those he served was the same reason that prompted thousands of other medical specialists to help their underprivileged brothers: "It is the Lord Jesus who has told the doctor and his wife to come...."[1]

Though the field of missionary medicine was dominated in the early years by men, women began entering the field in the late nineteenth century, and soon their achievements were being heralded all over the world. Clara Swain, serving under the Board of Missions of the Methodist Church, was the first woman missionary doctor from the United States. She arrived in India in 1870, and within four years she had opened her first hospital. The first missionary nurse was Miss E. M. McKechnie, who arrived in Shanghai in 1884 and later founded a hospital there.

By the middle of the twentieth century, significant developments in the Third World were making inroads on the traditional role of the medical missionary. As independence was granted, underdeveloped countries began forging their own medical programs, and the pioneer medical missionary no longer played the indispensable role that he once had. With this political and social change, medical missions has shifted away from pioneer work and has begun concentrating more on preventive medicine, field clinics, hospital work, and medical schools. Another recent trend in medical missions is the growth in support organizations such as MAP (Medical Assistance Programs), founded in the 1950s and today giving more than ten million dollars worth of medical supplies annually to Christian mission hospitals and clinics. A similar organization begun in Washington State by Ethel Miller sends drug samples and unwanted medical tools to missionary doctors in Africa and Asia and is operated almost entirely by retired volunteer workers.

Wilfred Grenfell

While most medical missionaries in modern history have spent their lives in tropical climates fighting against the ravages of fevers, leprosy, and other tropical scourges, Wilfred Grenfell, one of the most highly acclaimed missionary doctors of all times, carried out his ministry on the North American continent along the frozen coastline of Labrador. Though he was a medical doctor and commissioned primarily as a medical missionary, Grenfell branched out into many areas besides medicine. Medicine alone was not enough in a land where the people were enchained by poverty. Thus he sought to alleviate their suffering by improving the whole of society, causing some people to charge that he had become sidetracked from his calling as a missionary. Because of his wideranging activities, his efforts conflicted with the policies of his mission board and other interest groups, and he was frequently the center of heated controversy. But though his critics were numerous, his popularity only seemed to increase as he wrote and spoke out for the needs of Labrador.

Born near Chester, England, in 1865, Grenfell, like his forebears, grew up with a fascination for the sea. His dreams of seafaring adventure were cut short when his father sent him to prep school and then on to London to study medicine. Grenfell had been brought up in the Church of England, but to him, religion was a formality that had no personal meaning. Then in 1885, while completing his medical training in London, he stumbled on a Moody-Sankey revival one evening as he was returning home from a house call. As he edged his way through the crowd, he realized he was intruding on what seemed to be an endless prayer led by a man on the platform. As he was turning to leave he heard a commotion on the platform. It was Moody himself inviting the audience to sing a song "while our brother finishes his prayer." So amused was Grenfell by the unconventional style of the evangelist that he stayed to the end. That night he not only heard Moody preach and Sankey sing, but also listened as C. T. and J. E. K. Studd, two of England's greatest cricket players, gave their testimonies. Grenfell, a cricket player himself, was deeply moved, and that night he was converted to Christianity.

Following his conversion, Grenfell learned of a mission organization that immediately stirred his interest. It was the Royal National Mission to Deep Sea Fishermen. The mission needed a doctor who was willing to practice aboard a mercy ship commissioned to the North Sea to minister to the rough fishermen both physically and spiritually. Grenfell jumped at the chance, and so began his lifelong career as a medical missionary.

Grenfell's early years with the mission were as adventurous as his childhood dreams and were rewarding spiritually as well as professionally. He had found his niche in life and had no thought of ministering elsewhere. Then in 1892 his travels took him to North America along the rugged coast of Labrador, and suddenly his vision changed. Here was a people struggling for bare survival, living along the bleak rocky coastline with no hope for a better life in the present world or the hereafter, and no one seemed to care. Grenfell was overwhelmed by their physical and spiritual needs, and despite objections from his mission board, he was convinced that the rest of his life should be devoted to ministering to these long-neglected people.

Grenfell began his work in Labrador serving aboard a mercy ship as he had in the North Sea, but he soon realized that the greatest needs were in the scattered villages where families were entirely without medical services. To reach these villages, the adventurous doctor navigated his own steam powered launch along the dangerous coastline, "taking risks," according to a biographer, "that would have made a professional sailor die of fright." He simply trusted God as he "threaded the launch between islands and a fearful collection of submerged rocks ... through fog and ... against the strong winds and heavy seas...."[2] Everywhere he went, villagers gladly received his medical expertise, but despite his good will he quickly ran into strong opposition.

One source of opposition was the established Anglican church. "The Church is dead," wrote Grenfell. "The Bishop dare not say anything against us, but he is not with us, and told a great friend of mine here that our preaching the Gospel and people being converted was pulling down the work of the Church."[3] This attitude persisted despite the fact that the Anglican Church itself seemingly cared little about the destitute families out in the remote villages.

Another source of opposition was the merchants. Though they recognized the impressive medical work Grenfell was conducting in Labrador by building medical centers and serving as a village physician, they deeply resented his interference in the local economy. Grenfell, in turn, viewed the merchants as the great enemy of the people and was incensed by their exploitation of the vulnerable Labradorian fishermen who had no choice but to accept even their most niggardly prices. Though altogether lacking in business acumen, Grenfell soon became deeply involved in economic endeavors, setting up cooperatives, transporting pelts to market, importing reindeer, establishing lumber mills, and introducing cottage industries. Such activities drew a barrage of criticism, and Grenfell was accused by many of having come to Labrador, not for religious purposes, but for economic gain.

Such charges were entirely false. In fact, Grenfell lost vast sums of money in his various efforts to help the people of Labrador, all of which created another source of controversy and criticism—his own mission board. He had been commissioned as a medical and evangelistic missionary, and the fact that he had become sidetracked in economic ventures was, to the board, very disturbing. Grenfell was called on to account for his activities, but when he was questioned about such things, he retorted sharply "that these were no concern of the Council."[4] Rules, too, seemed not to apply to him. He did what he thought should be done, then informed, or did not inform, the Council.

The fact that Grenfell had become superintendent of the mission in 1890 may have contributed to his free-wheeling attitude, but even more important was his ever-increasing popularity, especially in America, where his fame spread quickly. "Grenfell Societies" sprang up across the United States and Canada, and money poured in, not for the Royal National Mission to Deep Sea Fishermen, the mission to which he belonged, but for his own special projects over which the mission had no control. The relationship between Grenfell and the Council was a stormy one, and as time passed, Grenfell became more and more independent, finally separating his work entirely from the Mission to Deep Sea Fishermen.

As Grenfell traveled across America presenting the needs of Labrador, he enthralled his audiences, not with polished sermons, but with stories of high adventure. "Following Christ," he told his listeners, "has given me more fun and adventure than any other kind

Winfred Grenfell, missionary doctor to Labrador.

of life." His life was full of daring exploits, and he urged his supporters to seek the same course: "When two courses are open, follow the most venturesome."[5]

The most hair-raising adventure Grenfell himself ever experienced occurred on Easter Sunday in 1908, when he received an urgent call to come and treat a gravely ill youth in a village some sixty miles away. Grenfell harnessed his dog team and set out for the village in a desperate attempt to reach the young man before he died. Although he was aware of the dangers accompanying the spring thaw, to save time, Grenfell decided to risk crossing the ice on a bay instead of winding around the rugged shoreline. It was an unwise decision. The ice was breaking and shifting, and Grenfell and the dogs suddenly plunged into the icy water. Though he managed to pull himself onto a large chunk of ice with three of his dogs, it was of little comfort with the wind driving the ice out to sea. But the struggle for life was intense, and to avoid freezing to death in his wet garments, he killed his three dogs and wrapped himself in their bloody skins.

The following morning, as he lay near death, Grenfell was rescued by men who risked their lives maneuvering between the surging ice chunks to save their beloved doctor. In the years that followed it was this story of courage and endurance more than any other that was associated with the famous doctor, and many young men and women, inspired by his heroism, came to serve with him in Labrador.

What had begun as a uniquely Christian ministry to Labrador developed over the years into what some viewed as a purely humanitarian endeavor. Like many medical missionaries before and after him, Grenfell faced the temptation to devote all his energy to the physical needs of the people to the neglect of their spiritual needs, and through the years his own philosophy of missions, as expressed in his many books, seemed to change. In his book *What Life Means to Me*, Grenfell wrote, "To me now any service to the humblest of mankind is Christ-service. . . . I believe absolutely in the socialism of Jesus." To him, true Christianity was activity: "The theory of Christianity would not convince the heathen of the Congo that religion is desirable," only "fraternity in action" would.[6] Grenfell, according to his biographer, "believed that if a person served others, he or she was living Christianity." His "perfect Christian was the Good Samaritan,"[7] and he welcomed the service of doctors and others in his mission work, without particular concern for their religious beliefs or their commitment to evangelism.

Many awards and honors were bestowed upon Grenfell for his forty years of service in Labrador. He was knighted in 1927, and soon after he was awarded an honorary doctorate from St. Andrews University. But to the impoverished villagers of Labrador, he was no less than a saint—and perhaps more. Said one devoted admirer, "If Wilfred Grenfell came through that door now I would feel that Jesus Christ had entered the room."[8] Though he died in 1940, the memory of Wilfred Grenfell lives on today along the rugged coasts of Labrador.

Ida Scudder

The most distinguished medical missionary family in all history was the Scudder family, beginning with John Scudder, a young medical doctor in New York City who, after reading a booklet appealing for missionaries left his growing practice and in 1819 sailed for Ceylon with his wife and child. The Scudders served for thirty-six years in Ceylon and India, and during that time thirteen more children were born to them, nine of whom survived to adulthood. Of those nine, seven became missionaries, most of them specializing in medicine like their father. In four generations, forty-two members of the Scudder family became missionaries, contributing well over one thousand combined years of missionary service. Among those forty-two was Ida, the daughter of

John Scudder's youngest son, also named John and also a medical missionary to India.

Ida was born in India in 1870 and grew up well acquainted with the trials of missionary life, particularly the pain of separation from loved ones. When she was a youth, her family returned to the United States for furlough, and then her father went back to India alone. Two years later her mother sailed to join him, leaving Ida with relatives in Chicago. It was a traumatic time according to her biographer: "The memory of that night could still bring a stabbing pain. The rain outside had been as wild as her own fourteen-year-old helpless grief. She had not even been allowed to go to the station to see her mother off for India. When her clinging arms had been finally, regretfully, unloosed, she had rushed upstairs and sobbed all night into her mother's empty pillow . . . With the passing weeks and months the aching loneliness had never ceased, merely subsided."[9]

After high school, Ida had remained in the United States to attend a "young ladies' seminary" in Northfield, Massachusetts, conducted by D. L. Moody. She had no intention of joining the family tradition and becoming a missionary, but shortly after her graduation in 1890 she received an urgent cablegram informing her that her mother was seriously ill. Within weeks Ida was on her way to India, that "horrible country, with its heat, dust, noise, and smells." She was going only to care for her mother, and when that obligation was met she would return to America to pursue her own dreams —or so she thought.

Ida's stay in India was longer than she had planned. Besides caring for her mother there was other work to be done. A girls' school was in need of a teacher, and Ida soon found herself in sole charge of sixty-eight pupils. And there were babies to baptize—a sacrament officiated by her father but one that, according to Ida's biographer, required assistance: "Since the babies were always oiled with coconut oil, their slippery bodies were hard to hold. Fearful lest her husband would drop one in the process, Mrs. Scudder made a white garment that could be slipped on each baptismal candidate before the service. It was Ida's duty to see that the transfer of the garment was properly effected."[10]

Although she was happy to be reunited with her family, Ida was not entirely comfortable with them. She felt pressure from all sides—uncles, cousins, and even parents—to not shirk the Scudder duty of becoming a missionary. But Ida wanted more for herself than the burdensome toil of missionary life, and family tradition was not enough to convince her otherwise. It took an extraordinary experience in her life that almost resembled a parable more than reality, but it became her own personal "call" to medical missions. Three different men—a Brahmin, another high-caste Hindu, and a Muslim—came to the door during the course of one night, pleading for her to come and assist in difficult childbirths, refusing the assistance of her doctor-father because religious customs prohibited such close contact by strangers of the opposite sex.

It was the most traumatic night Ida had ever endured: "I could not sleep that night—it was too terrible. Within the very touch of my hand were three young girls dying because there was no woman to help them. I spent much of the night in anguish and prayer. I did not want to spend my life in India. My friends were begging me to return to the joyous opportunities of a young girl in America. I went to bed in the early morning after praying much for guidance. I think that was the first time I ever met God face to face, and all that time it seemed that He was calling me into this work. Early in the morning I heard the 'tom-tom' beating in the village and it struck terror in my heart, for it was a death message. I sent our servant, and he came back saying that all of them had died during the night. Again I shut myself in my room and thought very seriously about the condition of the Indian women and after much thought and prayer, I went to my father and mother and told them that I must go home and study medicine, and come back to India to help such women."[11]

The following year Ida sailed for the United States, and in the fall of 1895 she enrolled at Women's Medical College in Philadelphia, where Clara Swain, the first American woman missionary doctor, had graduated. Then in 1898, when Cornell Medical College opened its doors to women, Ida transferred there to take advantage of its higher ranking accreditation, and it was from there that she received her M.D. degree. With her studies completed, Ida returned to India, and besides her degree she brought with her a ten thousand dollar check for a new hospital (given by a wealthy woman supporter) and Annie Hancock, her best friend from Northfield. Annie had come to conduct evangelism in conjunction with Ida's medical work.

Ida's initiation into medical missions was disappointing. Her dreams of serving her internship under the brilliant tutelage of her father were shattered when he unexpectedly died of cancer. To make matters worse, the Indian people, so desperate for medical attention, did not trust Ida, and for a time she had no patients at all. As the months passed, her practice slowly grew, but as it did she faced the same frustrations that all doctors in India faced. Superstitious practices of the people continually counteracted their best efforts. Medicine was prohibited on certain feast days, and sometimes critically ill patients were dragged from place to place to escape evil spirits. On one occasion after Ida had finished cleaning a serious wound, she stepped aside to prepare the dressing and when she turned back she was horrified to see that the girl had filled the wound with "holy ashes," a ritual that almost cost her her life. Even when her patients were willing to cooperate, ignorance often hindered recovery. Explaining how and when they should take their medication was a complicated ordeal, and in one instance when Ida gave a man a piece of cotton for his ear, he asked if he should eat it.

Soon after Ida arrived in India, construction began on the hospital at Vellore that she had so impassionately pleaded for before she had left America. But as she worked among the people she realized that a hospital would never be enough. The Indian people, especially the women, needed to be freed from their ignorance of medical treatment and taught basic health standards, and that could only be done if Indian women could be properly trained to go out among their own people in the villages. Thus, a medical school for Indian women became her all-consuming goal.

In order to reach that goal, Ida needed funds, and fund-raising became an important part of her ministry. While home on furlough she captivated her largely female audiences by her stories of the hopeless plight of the Indian women, and every meeting brought more money for her proposed medical school in India. Her first project was a nursing college, despite strong discouragement from government officials. The British Surgeon General told her to go ahead with her plans if she could get six applicants, but he doubted she could get more than three. She got one hundred and fifty-one. From that number she chose eighteen, and fourteen of those completed the four-year course. But the real test came when the girls confronted the government medical exams. An average of only one in five men passed the exams the first time they took them, and Ida was warned not to expect any of her girls to pass. What a thrill it was, then, when she learned that all fourteen had passed and four ranked in the top category.

As important as her medical work was, Ida was always conscious of her spiritual ministry to the people she served and particularly to the young women she trained. Her four-year Bible course on the apostle Paul and the Pauline epistles was a favorite among her students, and she repeated it several times. Medical work, however, consumed the vast majority of her sixteen-hour work days, but even then she took time to pass out Scripture cards. More important, her medical work paved the way for Annie Hancock, who spent her days doing evangelistic work in Vellore and in the outlying villages. When she had first come to India with Ida, rarely was she allowed into a home, but as Ida's reputation blossomed, so did Annie's, and eventually she was welcome in almost every home she visited.

In addition to running a hospital, a medical college, and village dispensaries, Ida, with her mother's help, operated a virtual orphanage. More than twenty homeless children were taken into the Scudder home, and frequently Ida brought one or more of them along on her rounds. For this ministry and others, Ida felt a deep loss when her mother died in 1925 at the age of eighty-six. Sixty-three years earlier this tenacious woman had been denied mission board support because it was believed she could not withstand the rigors of India. Her husband had accepted responsibility for her himself, and for a quarter of a century after he died she continued on in the work.

As Ida's medical work grew, vast sums of money were needed to defray expenses and update equipment. Women's groups from four denominations were supporting the work, but still the funds were inadequate. Then in the early 1920s she received word that her work along with other Christian schools in India would be eligible for a one million dollar Rockefeller grant if two million dollars could be raised elsewhere. Ida returned to America for the grueling fund-raising campaign that netted three million dollars; a large portion of which went to build a new medical complex at Vellore.

In spite of the new facilities, Vellore Medical College could not keep pace with the new government requirements during the years following independence. In 1937, the new minister of public health issued a new regulation requiring all medical schools to be affiliated with the University of Madras. For Ida, "it sounded the death knell for her beloved medical school."[12] How could she ever raise the needed funds when her homeland was still struggling through the greatest depression in its history? It seemed like an impossible situation. For the men's Christian medical schools, the future was less dismal. The administrators were making plans to consolidate; but Ida had no such option, as there were no other women's medical schools. But why not a coeducational college? That was the logical solution, at least in the mind of the great missionary statesman, John R. Mott, who visited India in 1938. The proposal was quickly espoused by others, some even suggesting that Vellore would be the ideal location.

Ida enthusiastically shared the proposal with her supporters back home, only to be thrown into the most bitter controversy she had ever endured. Thousands of women had been mobilized to raise money to support medical missions for women in India, and the thought of sharing all they had worked so hard for with the men was unthinkable to some. Hilda Olson, one of the members of the governing board of the Vellore Medical compound, responded tersely to the proposal: "Vellore is as you say, God's work, but I would like to add God's work *for women*. Every dollar would have to be given back to the givers."[13]

The governing board was bitterly divided on the issue, and Lucy Peabody, who had been one of Ida's staunchest supporters through the years, became her most caustic critic, accusing her of disloyalty to everything the board stood for. It was a depressing time for Ida, but in the end, after years of sharp debate, the board voted to join the men, believing such a merger the only alternative to closing down. Vellore would be the site of the new co-educational Christian medical school. Although Ida was pleased with the outcome, her happiness was tempered by the news that both Hilda Olson and Lucy Peabody had angrily resigned from the board.

Despite the barrage of criticism that had come over the issue of making Vellore coeducational, Ida was recognized the world over for her accomplishments. She was interviewed by reporters, and her story was written about time and again. The *Reader's Digest*, among other magazines, gave her flattering coverage: "This extraordinary white-haired woman has, at 72, a spring in her step, a sparkle in her eye and the skilled, strong hands of a surgeon of 45. For 18 years she had been head of the medical association in a district with a population of 2,000,000. Doctors all over India send her their most difficult gynecological cases. Women and children come just to touch her, so exalted is her reputation for healing."[14]

Ida retired in 1946 at the age of seventy-five and was succeeded by one of her most distinguished pupils, Dr. Hilda Lazarus. It was a graceful retirement, according to her biographer. "She who had been all her life a leader—some had called it dictator —now found it possible to be a follower."[15] But she remained active for more than another decade. She taught her weekly Bible class (to both men and women), advised doctors on difficult cases, entertained friends and dignitaries at Hill Top, her beautiful Indian residence, and played a fast game of tennis. Although she was not what she had been at the age of sixty-five (when during a tournament she had unmercifully trounced her teen-age opponent by winning every game in two sets, after hearing the girl scornfully object to having to play a "grannie"), she continued to play regularly, and even at the age of eighty-three, according to her biographer, "she was still serving a wicked tennis ball."[16]

In 1950, ten years before her death, a golden jubilee celebration was arranged in Vellore, marking Ida's fifty years of service to India. It was a day to commemorate the woman who had only reluctantly followed the Scudder family tradition, but whose success had far exceeded that of any other family member. Beginning with a ten-by-twelve room with a trickle of patients, she had lived to see the establishment of a modern medical complex with nearly one hundred doctors, a 484-bed general hospital, a 60-bed eye hospital, and numerous mobile clinics, all serving some two hundred thousand patients and training some two hundred medical students each year. So famous had she become that when a letter addressed simply "Dr. Ida, India" arrived on the subcontinent populated by some three hundred million people, it was directed immediately to her at Vellore.

Jessie and Leo Halliwell

Unlike Wilfred Grenfell and Ida Scudder, who were widely acclaimed for their service to humanity as medical missionaries, the Halliwells, though they ministered to thousands each year for decades, practiced their medicine in virtual obscurity. The

Ida Scudder at the hospital she founded in Vellore, celebrating her eighty-seventh birthday.

Amazon River valley was their mission field, and they devoted their lives to bringing the gospel and medical treatment to the river people, traveling some twelve thousand miles a year up and down a thousand-mile, jungle-lined stretch between Belém and Manaus. Though they possessed no medical degrees, they were the only "doctors" in the region, and their reputation for successfully treating tropical diseases was widely known and respected among the Indians.

The Halliwells' decision to embark on the mission field came almost on impulse soon after they were married. After hearing an emotionally charged plea for missionaries, Leo applied to the Seventh-Day Adventist mission board, and within a short time he and Jessie were on their way to Brazil, without any specialized missionary training. Jessie was a nurse, and Leo held a degree in electrical engineering.

Their first mission assignment was to conduct pioneer evangelistic work in Northern Brazil at Belém, a ministry they effectively carried out throughout the 1920s. Leo, however, was not satisfied with the limited scope of their ministry in Belém, especially when he thought of the thousands of unreached river people whose lives were made miserable by their poverty and disease. Smallpox, syphilis, hookworm, leprosy, malaria, and other tropical diseases took their deadly toll, and the Halliwells wanted to help. Evangelizing these neglected people and ministering to their physical needs became their goal, and during their furlough to the United States in 1930 they began making preparation for an expanded ministry. Leo took a course in tropical diseases, and Jessie took further training in nutrition, sanitation, and midwifery. They also raised money for a thirty-foot boat that would serve as their home as well as a floating clinic. The Seventh-Day Adventist Church was one of the pioneer missionary agencies in medical work and gave its enthusiastic support to the Halliwells' new venture.

At the very beginning of their ministry, the Halliwells faced almost daily threats to their lives from hostile tribes of Indians, but as their reputation became known, people began waiting on the shore for them to pass by. Others, at the Halliwells' prompting, hung out white scraps of cloth signifying they wanted them to stop. On some days they treated as many as three hundred malaria patients. A large part of such treatment involved dispensing the proper medication, and here the Halliwells confronted serious communi-cation barriers in attempting to explain the proper use of the medication. On one occasion they left medicine with a mother for her sick child and instructed her to give a dose each morning when the rooster crowed. When they returned some days later and inquired about the child, the mother replied, "My boy is fine now—but the rooster died!"[17]

Although the Halliwells avoided treating complex maladies, preferring rather to transport such cases to the nearest city where a doctor could be consulted, they frequently confronted emergency situations in their travels that could not wait. One such case involved a little girl who had been badly mangled by an alligator. The timing of the Halliwells' visit and their combined medical expertise saved her life.

Evangelism was an important part of the Halliwells' ministry, and they used innovative techniques to attract crowds. With the use of a generator on their boat they were able to show films and slides—an attraction that brought Indians in their canoes from miles away, and many were converted to Christianity. As the number of converts grew, the Halliwells helped establish churches and schools, and in many cases other missionaries moved in to carry on the work.

In 1956, after twenty-five years of serving the Indians along the Amazon, the Halliwells "retired" to begin a new work in Rio de Janeiro, supervising the ministry of all the Adventist medical launches in South America. Through their inspiring example the Amazon was becoming "crowded" with floating clinics, and their pioneer work was over.

Carl Becker

Perhaps more than any other continent, Africa has been favored by a long line of outstanding Christian medical missionaries, whose contributions to the evangelization of the Africans has been enormous. Names such as David Livingstone, Albert Schweitzer, Helen Roseveare, Paul Carlson, and Malcolm Forsberg all bring to mind the great service medical missions has rendered to Africa. And, of course, there were some less prominent individuals, such as Andrew P. Stirratt of the Sudan Interior Mission, who was only reluctantly accepted as a candidate (after he donated his estate to the mission and booked his own passage) because his age of thirty-eight was considered unacceptable. Yet he served faithfully for more than four decades, overseeing all the dispensary work and personally treating tens of thousands of patients during his lifetime. But if one medical missionary to Africa were to be singled out for his length of service combined with his extraordinary dedication to saving the lives and improving the health standards of the African people, it would surely be Carl Becker, the great *munganga* of the Congo.

It was in 1916 during President Wilson's campaign for his second term in office that the twenty-two year old Carl Becker began his medical studies at Hahnemann Medical College in Philadelphia. He had been out of school for several years, working at a foundary to help support his widowed mother and his sister, but with these obligations lessening and with his savings of a little more than one hundred dollars, he was ready to begin the six-year grind that would lead to financial security

that he had never before enjoyed. The outbreak of World War I soon after he entered medical school was a "godsend" for him, for it allowed him to enlist in the United States Medical Corps that provided him with free room, board, and tuition, in addition to a small salary.

Becker began practicing medicine in Boyertown, Pennsylvania, in 1922, and three months later he married Marie, a young woman whom he had met some years earlier at a church social. Before the marriage he had warned Marie that he had promised to give God his life if God would give him an education. "I don't know if it means I'll go to China or Africa as a missionary or what," he told her, "but he has first claim on my life."[18] As Becker became settled in Boyertown his practice and prestige grew and his promise to God seemed to be forgotten until one day he received a letter from Charles Hurlburt of the Africa Inland Mission, a man whom he had met some years earlier. Hurlburt's daughter-in-law, Elizabeth Morse Hurlburt, a medical doctor who was serving in the Congo, had died suddenly, and Hurlburt was urgently seeking another doctor to take her place. Torn by feelings of guilt, Becker rejected Hurlburt's request, explaining that he had a responsibility for the support of his mother. Hurlburt, however, would not give up, and the following winter he received a letter from Becker in which he agreed to go. In the summer of 1928, the Beckers sailed for Africa, leaving "a $10,000-plus income to earn $60 a month . . . to go to a primitive outpost he knew nothing about."[19]

The Beckers' first home in the Congo was located at Katwa, where they lived in a mud hut that Marie creatively turned into a "mud mansion." After serving at Katwa for a time, Becker transferred to Aba, where he replaced a furloughed doctor at an established hospital, and then in 1934 he moved with his wife and two children to the tiny mission station of Oicha in the dense Ituri forest to work among the Pygmies and other forest tribes.

It was at Oicha, an unlikely spot for a mission hospital, that Becker's ministry bloomed. Here, walled in by the giant mahogany trees, he built a highly effective medical compound out of nothing—primitive in comparison to the facilities he had been used to back home, but one that somehow met the needs of the African jungle. Becker was not an organizer or a long-range planner, nor was he public-relations minded. Otherwise, writes his biographer, "he might have raised a large sum of money by promoting it as a memorial hospital in honor of some dear-departed saint. . . ." As it was, Becker added room additions and buildings as they were needed, with "no overall general plan."[20] There was no budget for hospital construction, so much of the expense came out of the Becker's $60-a-month salary.

The medical services at Oicha expanded rapidly, and within two years some two hundred patients were being treated every day. But there were certain villages and tribes that remained outside the doctor's reach. Witch doctors held powerful sway over the people until gradually one-by-one they were converted to Christianity through the tireless evangelistic work of Becker and other missionaries.

Evangelism was the primary purpose for Becker's work in Africa, and weekends were devoted to itinerant work in the villages. Though without formal Bible training and not a Bible teacher per se, Becker communicated the gospel effectively to the Africans. Bible stories were related in an African context, and soon the American Sunday school pictures were discarded in favor of Becker's own crude drawings that became so popular that he began mimeographing them for distribution among his listeners, who in turn used them to evangelize others. On one occasion when Becker entered an outlying village, he noticed a crowd gathered in the middle of the road, and to his surprise he discovered an illiterate Congolese soldier sharing the gospel, using a set of picture stories that he had obtained from Becker a month earlier.

Despite his effective evangelistic work, Becker, as with countless other medical missionaries before and after him, was distressed by the fact that the vast majority of his time was consumed with the physical rather than spiritual needs of the people. "What is the spiritual value of all this?" he frequently asked himself. It was a question that could only be answered through seeing the results of his work. He gradually came to realize, according to his biographer, "that there was spiritual value in medical work. In fact, far from imagining that medical work was only the soil-breaker for the seed—only the John the Baptist for the Messiah—he came to see it was a complete missionary ministry. It was an opportunity for mass evangelism, for where else could he find several hundred needy Africans each day, coming from distant places to one site where the gospel could be preached? It was also an opportunity for Christian nurture. With the in-patients he had a chance to help young Christians grow in their Christian life, to provide a sort of hot-house climate for young plants. And Dr. Becker felt, too, that it was an unparalleled opportunity to build a responsible African church."[21]

In many instances, medical missions paved the way for evangelizing tribes that were otherwise very difficult to reach. Such was the case with the Pygmies of the Ituri forest. Long the brunt of discrimination by other Africans, the Pygmies withdrew into the jungle and shied away from all outsiders, white or black, but their need for medical services eventually overcame their extreme isolationism. They slowly developed a trust in the missionaries, and many were converted to Christianity.

Likewise, medical missions played a crucial role in reaching lepers with the gospel. They, too, had been the brunt of discrimination, but the love and care they received from Dr. Becker and his staff gave them a renewed sense of worth, and they turned by the thousands to Christ.

Although Becker treated every disease and injury imaginable, it was the problem of leprosy that concerned him the most, and he desperately sought to find a cure that would relieve the terrible suffering. Word of his compassion spread, and lepers by the thousands came to him for treatment. By the early 1950s he was treating some four thousand resident patients at his 1100-acre leprosy village, and the results were impressive—so much so that medical missionaries and leprologists from all over the world were visiting Oicha and borrowing the notes on his research. But though great strides had been made in relieving the suffering of lepers, Becker was not

Carl Becker, medical missionary to Zaire under the Africa Inland Mission, writing a prescription for an African patient. Dr. Ruth Dix is in the center of the photograph.

satisfied, and despite his hectic schedule he continued his search for a more effective treatment. Even Dr. Robert Cochrane from Cambridge, the world's leading authority on leprosy, was impressed with his findings.

During the time that he was conducting his medical research, Becker, the only medical doctor at Oicha, was performing upwards of four thousand operations and delivering some five hundred babies each year. But even with such a heavy load, he found time to branch out into areas most general practitioners would have avoided, including psychiatry, and he eagerly experimented with the most up-to-date treatment. Among his patients were some severely disturbed individuals, viewed by their families as demon possessed, but treated by Becker for mental illness. He established a mental ward and a psychiatric clinic, and was the first doctor in equatorial Africa to successfully use electric shock treatment on Africans. Although he successfully treated many patients with such methods, he "remained convinced that simple Christianity was the soundest general therapy for the mentally upset, that 'the Gospel of love and hope alone can banish superstition and fear.'"[22]

In spite of his tremendous service in behalf of the people of the Congo, Becker did not remain immune to the vicious outbreak of nationalism that arose in the 1960s. While most missionaries fled to East Africa for safety, he stayed on at Oicha until the summer of 1964, when it became certain that he could not remain at the compound and survive. When it was learned that he had been targeted by the Simbas to face a firing squad, he reluctantly agreed to leave. At the age of seventy, he bade farewell to his beloved African associates and, with his wife, three nurses, and young associate, evacuated, barely escaping the rampaging Simba guerrillas.

Considering Becker's age, the evacuation in 1964 would have been an opportune time to begin retirement. But for the Beckers, Africa was home. In the words of his biographer, Becker was "allergic to furloughs," and he had no desire to return to the United States. Since 1945 he had spent less than a year in the United States, and though he recognized that he was slowing down, he wanted to remain in Africa as long as he could be of useful service. So, after a year in the relative security of East Africa, and after the political situation had quieted down in the Congo, the Beckers were back in Oicha to rebuild what the guerrillas had destroyed and to reestablish medical services that were needed now more than ever. Though Becker suffered three heart seizures in 1966, he kept going, ignoring pleas that he rest: "If this is to be my last day on earth, I

certainly don't want to spend it in bed."[23]

It was not until he was eighty-three that Dr. Becker agreed to return to the United States and retire. His last years had been spent developing an interdenominational evangelical medical center that included a hospital and training school for Africans—a project that had long been a dream of his; but once that program was well under way in 1976, he realized it was time for him to step aside. He had served nearly fifty years as a medical missionary and had made an indelible imprint on Africa. Of him, Art Buchwald, the well-known American newspaper columnist, wrote: "In all of Congo, the man who made the greatest impression on us was an American missionary doctor named Carl K. Becker.... We couldn't help thinking as we left Oicha that America had its own Dr. Schweitzer in Congo."[24] But the greatest tribute ever paid Becker may have been made by an African medical trainee: "Many missionaries had preached Jesus Christ to me, and many missionaries had taught Jesus Christ to me, but in the *munganga* I have seen Jesus Christ."[25]

Viggo Olsen

Known best through his widely read autobiography, *Daktar: Diplomat in Bangladesh*, Viggo Olsen, as the title suggests, was more than a doctor. He was an unofficial diplomatic emissary who fought his way through what seemed to be miles of red tape, established a large medical compound, and courageously served the Bengali people in the hour of their deepest trouble.

It was not long after his 1944 high-school graduation in Omaha, Nebraska, that Olsen made the decision to study medicine. His higher education began at Tulane University, under a program sponsored by the United States Navy, and from there he enrolled at the University of Nebraska, where he graduated and was awarded his M.D. degree after seven grueling years of study. During his student days, Olsen met and married his wife, Joan, and together they looked forward to the affluent life the medical profession would offer them.

The lifestyle the Olsens planned had no room for Christianity. To them Bible reading and church attendance had no relevance to everyday life, but as much as they sought to avoid it, Christianity was a subject they could not escape. Joan's parents had both been converted after Joan had gone away to college, and they wanted desperately for Joan and Viggo to experience the same peace they had found through their faith in Christ. They shared their new found faith in letters and often enclosed tracts, and when Joan and Viggo visited them in Toledo, Ohio, on their way to begin Viggo's internship at Long Island College, they boldly brought up the subject in person. Viggo's initial reaction was negative: "I viewed Christianity and the Bible through agnostic eyes, feeling that modern science had outmoded much of this religious sentiment. When my father-in-law spoke of flaws in evolutionary laws and other scientific dicta, I boiled inwardly."[26]

Before their stay in Toledo was over things had begun to change. Viggo and Joan had a long discussion about spiritual matters with a Christian minister, and after that they agreed to study the "Christian religion and the Bible," making their "own, independent decision,"[27] and to attend a Christian church once they were settled in Brooklyn. It was that agreement that led to their eventual conversion, through the ministry of a Baptist pastor, his wife, and members of their congregation.

Following his internship in New York and a brief term of medical service for the Navy in the South Pacific Viggo set his sights on Mayo Clinic, applying there for the highly coveted fellowship in internal medicine. With such prestigious training he would be able to fulfill his dream of practicing and teaching medicine in the Northwest, at the same time providing all the material possessions his family could want.

But the dream that had once seemed so idealistic and satisfying to the Olsens was beginning to haunt them. They began to question what God's will for their lives was. Could it be service for him? Before leaving Brooklyn, Viggo had overheard an elderly woman in the church say, "Now that young Dr. Olsen has become a Christian believer, he'll no doubt be a missionary." At the time, Viggo had "inwardly curdled," but the remark stuck with him; and as the months passed, his and Joan's dreams for the future were slowly being transformed: "The more we thought, meditated, and prayed about the possibilities . . . the more medical missions seemed a live option."[28]

The following weeks of indecision were ended with a whole week of intense struggle. "On the seventh day, walking alone on the beach, pressed on every side by experience, human feelings, heredity, environment, biblical teaching, God's direction, and

343

many other forces, the crisis came." Viggo knelt on the beach and accepted "God's call" to overseas medical missions. "Three days later came the acid test." In the mail was a letter: "We are happy to inform you that you have been accepted for a fellowship in the department of Internal Medicine of Mayo Clinic." But Viggo did not waver: "Somehow I did not find it difficult to write back and decline the fellowship. God's work in my heart had been done thoroughly. I was at peace."[29]

The next five years, from 1954 to 1959, were busy ones. The Olsen family grew from three to six while Viggo continued his education in preparation for primitive medical work. At the same time, Viggo and Joan threw themselves into the work of their local church and researched various mission boards as they anticipated their future ministry. But Viggo did not wait for mission board acceptance or foreign residence to begin his missionary work. He considered evangelism part of his ministry as a doctor whether he was at home or abroad.

One afternoon while he was making his rounds at Milwaukee County Hospital, where he was completing his residence for surgical training, he "sensed considerable anxiety in a patient being prepared for surgery the next morning." Viggo explained to the man that his cancer was serious and that the operation would be extensive and then "talked to him about God and faith and God's son who loved him and gave his life for him." There on his hospital bed the man committed his life to Christ, and following his surgery he thanked Dr. Olsen, in the presence of others on the hospital staff, for explaining to him "the way of eternal life."[30]

The Olsens' choice of a mission board did not come easily. Since they were Baptists, the Association of Baptists for World Evangelism was recommended to them. One area being opened by ABWE that was in dire need of medical services was East Pakistan, and C. Victor Barnard, the missionary assigned to start that work, met with Viggo and encouraged him to consider that field. During their meeting, however, philosophical differences arose:

> Mr. Barnard's view of medical missions . . . clashed hopelessly with mine. He pictured a doctor moving about from village to village with a black bag in hand, treating minor illnesses as best he could. I visualized a small but capable hospital as the essential beginning. I felt we needed a team of doctors and nurses and other workers to provide excellent medical-surgical care worthy to represent the Lord Jesus Christ, and in that environment of love and concern, daily share His good news with others. As we discussed medical missions, I found that Mr. Barnard's views were fixed and nothing I presented changed them. As much as I appreciated this fine dedicated man of God, I was sure East Pakistan was no longer an option because I could not accomplish God's revealed plan for me within that framework.[31]

But Viggo could not erase East Pakistan from his mind: "With one missionary for every three-quarters of a million people, East Pakistan was more neglected by the Christian church than any other open land. No Christians or Christian work graced the extreme southern end of the country. There was a great Christian vacuum between the works of the earliest missionary pioneers, William Carey of India and Adoniram Judson of Burma. Visas were readily available to East Pakistan and religious freedom prevailed. Our eyes, furthermore, had been fixed on this very area of the world.... And ABWE seemed to be the mission agency to which all our guidance pointed."[32]

In the spring of 1959, the president of ABWE wrote to Viggo, inviting him to come before the board and present his philosophy of medical missions. Viggo presented his "thirteen basic principles," with the view that if the board members rejected them "we would know we must look further for another board and field." After a lengthy session, the board voted unanimously to support the implementation of the thirteen principles in East Pakistan. Although the cost would be high, the board members were convinced that Viggo was on target with all of his thirteen guidelines—guidelines that should be considered by any prospective medical missionary and supporting mission:

1. Only high caliber, compassionate medical work is worthy to represent the Lord.

2. Because "black bag" and clinic treatments fail to heal many patients, a hospital is a desirable beginning.

3. The site for a new hospital must be chosen with great care.

4. Two or more doctors are necessary to provide continuity of medical care.

5. The doctors should study tropical diseases before beginning a practice in the tropics.

6. The doctors and nurses must have adequate time for protected and uninterrupted language study.

7. At least one of the Home Board members should be a Christian physician.

8. Nonmedical missionaries should be appointed to the hospital to share in the administrative and spiritual work.

9. Nationals should receive training in medical-spiritual work.

10. A hospital in a poor area cannot be expected to be completely self-supporting, or charges will be excessive and the poor neglected in favor of the wealthy.

11. The medical work must be geared to spiritual sharing and spiritual healing.

12. Christian believers must be helped, baptized, loved, strengthened, and incorporated into an indigenous church.

13. The medical staff must have spiritual strength and stamina, plus an intimate walk with God so that the highest spiritual standards are maintained.[33]

It was not until January of 1962 that the Olsen family was on board an air flight to East Pakistan. The nearly three years that had intervened since the board had accepted his thirteen principles had been filled with further study in tropical medicine and eighteen months of deputation work. The fact that the promising young candidate was a highly qualified medical doctor did not exempt him from the sometimes condescending task of going from church to church presenting his future ministry and financial needs. In fact, that was the type of arrangement the Olsens had sought when they were contemplating a mission board: "We wished to affiliate with a mission that did not have money in the bank to send out a new appointee immediately. Rather, we would have to travel about the churches in deputation, presenting our program, and praying that God would stimulate the churches to undertake the necessary support. In this way we would learn how to trust our heavenly Father more fully and would become acquainted with dozens of churches and hundreds or thousands of individuals. These churches would likewise know us personally, understand our work, and would pray earnestly for us and our activities. Such prayer support would be priceless."[34]

On arriving in East Pakistan, Viggo immediately began making plans for the hospital he hoped to establish, but he quickly ran into roadblocks. Although East Pakistan had been relatively easy to enter as a missionary, the government inefficiency and the red tape involved in implementing medical work was exasperating. East Pakistan, though separated from West Pakistan by more than a thousand

miles and though inhabited by some seventy-five million people, was considered only a province of Pakistan (the other four provinces being in West Pakistan)—a situation that lent itself to government mismanagement and inefficiency. And the fact that the culture and religion of East and West Pakistan were so vastly different did not help matters; the Bengalis that made up the majority of East Pakistan's population were Muslim, while West Pakistan was overwhelmingly Hindu.

Although Viggo's patience was tried time and again, he finally secured the land and permits necessary for his proposed medical compound, and with the help of a builder from the United States who volunteered his time, construction began in 1964. During this time, the Olsens concentrated on language study, and Viggo performed routine medical work. But all was not well for the ABWE work in East Pakistan, and 1965 turned into a year of crisis: "We were hit from all sides by continuing visa obstructions, crippling of our tribal work, employee problems, storms of wind, storms of war, bombing, illness, and death! I had to call twenty-five special field council sessions to deal with the recurring problems and crises."[35]

As the months passed, the situation in East Pakistan progressively worsened. India began amassing troops on the West Pakistan border, and what followed was a seventeen-day war between India and Pakistan, during which time most of the women missionaries and children were evacuated until the situation began to return to normal. In 1966, Memorial Christian Hospital was opened, and the medical work began on a full-scale level, ready to face such emergencies as occurred in 1968 when a cholera epidemic broke out. Hundreds of patients were treated at the hospital for this killer disease, and only two died. But Viggo's ministry involved far more than just medicine. He was actively involved in evangelism, and he taught a pre-baptismal class for new Bengali Christians that was climaxed by seventeen baptisms, the largest Christian baptismal service ever conducted in that area.

As the decade of the 1970s opened there was a continuation of the political turmoil in East Pakistan. The Muslim majority there had long been dissatisfied with West Pakistan's domination of its affairs, and there was a growing movement toward independence. By the early months of 1971, West Pakistani military forces began to move into East Pakistan, and again most of the women missionaries and children were evacuated. Viggo and others remained to keep their much needed medical facilities functioning, sobered by the uncertainty of whether they would ever see their loved ones again. It was a terrifying time for the missionaries as well as the Bengali people: "... the Pakistan army smashed into cities and towns across the land. They followed the same scenario of kill, rape, loot, and burn!"[36]

For Viggo and his colleagues, these terror-filled days were climaxed by the harrowing night of April 23, 1971. Alarming news had come that afternoon from a Bengali friend that "armed bandits" were coming that night to attack the compound. To attempt an escape would mean losing the hospital and all they had worked so hard to build. There was no choice, in Viggo's mind, but to arm themselves and to risk their lives for the ministry they had been called to perform.

Complicating the situation was a broken elbow Viggo had sustained that afternoon in a motorcycle accident, but with the others he stationed himself on the compound, steeling his eyes into the shadows as the seconds on his watch ticked away toward midnight, when the government-run generator would be shut off and the lights on the compound would go out. "We were surrounded on three sides by dense forest and on the fourth by a river. In the thick darkness, the armed robbers could silently enter our property at a hundred different points. We would be like sitting ducks!"[37] But for some unexplained reason, the lights never went off, and the attack never came. "It was a miracle from Allah," explained one of the Bengali guards, but Viggo and his colleagues knew differently.

The following month Viggo left East Pakistan for furlough and for recuperation in the United States, and while he was gone the independent nation of Bangladesh was born, but not without terrible agony and devastation. Viggo knew he was needed back at his post more than ever before, and so as soon as he could arrange entry with the new government, he returned— his visa number being "001." And there amidst the pain and suffering he fruitfully served as a shining testimony to Christian medical missions and to his Lord.

Selected Bibliography

Dodd, Edward M. The Gift of the Healer: The Story of Men and Medicine in the Overseas Mission of the Church. *New York: Friendship, 1964.*

Hall, Clarence W. Adventurers for God. *New York: Harper & Brothers, 1959.*

Haskin, Dorothy. Medical Missionaries You Would Like to Know. *Grand Rapids: Zondervan, 1957.*

Hefley, James C. The Cross and the Scalpel. *Waco: Word, 1971.*

Kerr, J. Lennox. Wildred Grenfell: His Life and Work. *New York: Dodd, 1959.*

Miller, Basil. Wilfred Grenfell, Labrador's Dogsled Doctor. *Grand Rapids: Zondervan, 1948.*

Olsen, Viggo (with Jeanette Lockerbie). Daktar: Diplomat in Bangladesh. *Chicago: Moody, 1973.*

Peterson, William J. Another Hand on Mine: The Story of Dr. Carl K. Becker of Africa Inland Mission. *New York: McGraw-Hill, 1967.*

Wilson, Dorothy Clarke. Dr. Ida: The Story of Dr. Ida Scudder of Vellore. *New York: McGraw-Hill, 1959.*

Chapter 13

Translation and Linguistics:
"The Bible in Every Man's Tongue"

Although Bible translation, like missionary medicine, can be viewed properly as a twentieth-century foreign missions specialization, it has its roots early in the history of the Christian church. As the gospel spread through the Mediterranean world and beyond, Scripture translations appeared in Syriac, Georgian, Coptic, Gothic, Slavic, and Latin, and by the mid-fifteenth century there were more than thirty translations of the Bible. During the next three centuries, Bible translation accelerated and took on new meaning with the impetus it received from the Renaissance and Reformation. Translations appeared in most of the major European languages, and by the beginning of the nineteenth century, thirty-four more translations had been completed.

Not surprisingly, it was the modern missionary movement that changed the entire complexion of Bible translation work. No longer was the work delegated to meticulous scholars in monasteries or musty libraries. Instead, it was being undertaken by untrained missionaries stationed all over the world who carried out their translation work in thatched-roof huts with illiterate informants; it had become a sideline that had to compete with all the other missionary tasks. William Carey is of course regarded as the first and most prolific of these missionary translators, but more than a century earlier the dedicated and energetic John Eliot translated the Scriptures for the Algonquin Indians of Massachusetts. It was Carey who made Bible translation an accepted, integral part of missionary work; and following his example, almost all the pioneer missionaries of the "Great Century," including Robert Morrison, Adoniram Judson, Robert Moffat, Hudson Taylor, and Henry Martyn, were Bible translators. During the course of the nineteenth century alone, Bible translations appeared in nearly five hundred more languages.

But as significant as Bible translation was during the "Great Century," it was not until the twentieth century that the work took on a new image with the introduction of the science of linguistics. With the wide proliferation of Bible translations, missionaries were no longer forced to struggle with translation work before they could begin their evangelistic ministry. At the same time, however, more missionaries were beginning to view translation work as a specialized ministry in itself and felt compelled to provide the Word of God in *every* language. Since 1900, major portions of the Bible have been translated into some one thousand additional languages, half of those since 1950—an indication of what linguistic science has done for the ministry of Bible translation.

Linguistic science, however, would have influenced Bible translation work very little had it not been for the tireless efforts of W. Cameron Townsend and his twin organizations, Summer Institute of Linguistics and Wycliffe Bible Translators. SIL was founded in an Ozark farmhouse in 1934 as Camp Wycliffe by Townsend and L. L. Legters, both of whom were concerned about linguistics training for prospective Bible translators. Though not a mission society itself, it has made an invaluable contribution to the progress of world evangelism. Through its training sessions over the past half century (conducted at the University of Oklahoma and other universities in America and abroad), students have learned to phonetically write down unfamiliar languages, formulate alphabets, analyze grammar, detect idioms, produce primers, teach literacy, and translate Scripture; and at the same time they have benefited from the experience of those who have gone before them by appropriating their shortcuts and avoiding their pitfalls.

As important as SIL was to the work of Bible translation, it soon became evident that with its secular nature (for the purpose of better relations with foreign governments) it was not suitable as a mission support organization. Thus in 1942, Wycliffe Bible Translators (named for John Wycliffe, the fourteenth-century Bible translator known as "the Morning Star of the Reformation") was officially organized and headed up by a retired businessman, Bill Nyman. Its purpose was to receive funds for the support of missionary translators and to publicize the ongoing field work, even as its predecessor, the Pioneer Mission Agency, had done. The twin organizations, WBT/SIL, though separate, had interlocking directorates and the same goals and philosophy, but different duties to perform.

Other mission organizations besides WBT have been actively involved in Bible translation work, but most of these organizations soon discovered the tremendous value of topnotch linguistics training and began sending their trainees to SIL. New Tribes Mission and Unevangelized Fields Mission, among others, are actively pursuing translation work today. Bible translation work is also being done more and more by non-Western Christians. Students at SIL come from countries all over the world, including Mexico, China, Japan, and African nations. On occasion, tribal language informants have even accomplished outstanding translation work. Angel, a Mixtec Indian from Mexico with only six years of Spanish primary school, became a trustworthy translator in his own San Miguel Mixtec language and later came to the United States with SIL Director Ken Pike, and worked alongside him, translating New Testament books as well as typing and proofreading the copy.

Due to broad cultural gaps, the task of translation work is aided considerably by competent nationals such as Angel. Bible translation is not an exact science, and the linguist must be sensitive to cultural differences and know when to follow the biblical text precisely and when to allow for cultural deviations. Flexibility is the key, according to Eugene Nida of United Bible Societies. Many times, as Harold Moulton has pointed out, hard philosophical questions arise, and the answers do not come easily. "An Eskimo translator finds all references to agriculture difficult. Bread is a commodity that is not known in many tropical countries. Customs of greeting differ. Terms such as 'justification' do not have the background that they had for Paul. The danger of substituting some other food for bread is that it deviates from the original. The danger of retaining the Greek or English word is that it is incomprehensible. Translators must throughout use the *closest*, *natural* equivalent; but to work that out in practice is always difficult."[1]

While such problems continue to beset translators, many of the problems of Bible translation have been greatly alleviated by modern technology. Today, Bible translators are using battery-operated suitcase-size computers right out in the villages where they are working. Such technology is invaluable in the development of dictionaries, in cross referencing, in text editing, and in language research in general.

Despite technology, linguistic science, and the impetus WBT/SIL has given to Bible translation in recent decades, the task is far from finished. According to recent estimates there are more than five thousand languages spoken in the world today, but the Bible or the New Testament has been translated into only a third of them. Today, Wycliffe Bible Translators alone are working in more than seven hundred languages, and each year completed translations are published in some thirty new languages; but at that rate it will take almost another century to complete the task.

William Cameron Townsend

The one individual most responsible for the twentieth century surge in Bible translation work has been William Cameron Townsend, the founder of WBT/SIL. He was a man of strong conviction, and his leadership role in those organizations as well as in JAARS (Jungle Aviation and Radio Service) was a powerful one—one that was often accompanied by storms of controversy. Cam never quite fit into the classic conservative mold from which the majority of his supporters and associates were formed, and though his own personal faith was never called into question, his methods were viewed with skepticism by many evangelical leaders. Yet, Billy Graham called him "the greatest missionary of our time," and at the time of his death in 1982, Ralph Winter, of the United States Center for World Mission, ranked him with William Carey and Hudson Taylor as one of the three most outstanding missionaries of the last two centuries.[2]

Cam Townsend was born in California in 1896 during the difficult economic period following the Panic of 1893, and much of his early life was plagued by poverty. He was raised in the Presbyterian Church, and after high school he enrolled in Occidental College, a Presbyterian school in Los Angeles. During his second year there he joined the Student Volunteer Movement and was further challenged by missions when John R. Mott came to the campus to speak. Then, during his junior year, the Bible House of Los Angeles appealed for Bible salesmen for Latin America, and Cam felt called to go. He applied and was accepted and within a short time was assigned to Guatemala, but he soon realized that there were other pressing obligations to be dealt with. It was 1917, and, as a corporal in the National Guard, he knew he would be expected to join in the war effort—an obligation he accepted with a spirit of patriotism, believing it was his duty to forego missionary service to serve his country. That, however, was not the opinion of Stella Zimmerman, a single missionary on furlough from Guatemala, who rebuked him for being a "coward" by "going to war where a million other men will go and leaving us women to do the Lord's work alone."[3] Her chiding was enough to prompt Cam to apply for a discharge, and to his surprise his captain agreed to let him go, telling him that he would "do a lot more good selling Bibles in Central America than ... shooting Germans in France."[4]

Cam, accompanied by a college chum, left for Guatemala in August of 1917 and thus began his missionary career that spanned more than a half century. Selling Bibles in Central America, where so few Bibles were available, seemed at first like a worthwhile ministry, but he soon discovered that much of his effort was being wasted. His work was largely in remote rural areas where some two hundred thousand Cakchiquel Indians lived who had no use for the Spanish Bibles he was selling and whose own language was yet unwritten. As he traveled around and began to familiarize himself with their language, he became burdened for these people, but they were slow to respond and seemed offended by his preoccupation with selling Spanish Bibles. "Why, if your God is so smart," queried an Indian one day, "hasn't he learned our language?"[5]

Cam was taken aback by the blunt question, and it led to his dedicating the next thirteen years of his life to the primitive Cakchiquel Indians. His overriding goal was to learn their language proficiently, reduce it to written form, and finally and most importantly to make a Scripture translation. Without prior linguistic training, Cam immediately faced tremendous obstacles as he began to dig into the Cakchiquel language. There were four different "k" sounds that to him were barely distinguishable from each other, and the verb forms were mind-boggling. One verb could be conjugated into thousands of forms, indicating time, location, and many other ideas besides simple action. It all seemed like an impossible task until Cam met an American archaeologist who advised him to quit trying to force the Cakchiquel language "into a Latin mold," and instead seek to find the logical pattern on which the language is based. That advice changed the course of Cam's language study, and it led eventually to his forming a linguistics training program.

From the very beginning of his ministry, Cam's independent spirit often clashed with the more conservative views of those around him. When his work as a Bible salesman ended, he had joined the Central American Mission, only to realize that evangelism, not translation work, was what the mission expected him to concentrate on. The mission leaders did not understand his deeply felt concern for a translation ministry, a factor that frequently created strained relations and eventually led to his resignation.

Just prior to joining the Central American Mission, Cam was married to Elvira Malmstrom, a first-term missionary also serving in Guatemala. Though Elvira was a competent missionary and greatly augmented the translation and evangelistic ministry among the Cakchiquels, she found it difficult to cope with the frustrations of missionary life and was at times emotionally unbalanced. She was able to take advantage of professional counseling while on furlough in California, though, according to the Hefley's, it availed little.[6] Yet she continued to contribute significantly to the work until her premature death in 1944.

It was in 1929, after only ten years of arduous toil, that Cam completed the Cakchiquel New Testament. This milestone only solidified in Cam's mind the need for translation work. He was anxious to move on and translate Scripture for other tribes whose language was unwritten, but the Central American Mission leaders felt it was his duty to remain with the Cakchiquels and continue to build them in the faith. Because of these philosophical differences, Cam resigned, and in 1934 he and L. L. Legters

founded Camp Wycliffe in Arkansas —a disorganized and unimposing venture that grew into the world's largest independent Protestant mission organization.

Although Cam himself was an easygoing person, always eager to promote harmony among his fellow workers, his twin organizations, WBT/SIL faced numerous controversies over the years. The most common criticism was that Cam was attempting to gain an entrance with foreign governments under a false pretense, while at the same time deceiving home supporters. To government officials, critics charged, the linguists claimed to be secular language specialists and social workers teaching literacy, but to their supporters back home they called themselves missionary Bible translators. What really was their mission? So heated was the controversy that one veteran missionary returned home from Central America to warn churches about the "dishonesty" and "fakery" of Cam Townsend.[7]

Good relations with foreign governments were a top priority for Cam, but again it was an issue that raised criticism, especially among other missionaries. Cam's close working relationship with President Cardenas of Mexico and his defense of his socialistic programs was anathema to many missionaries. Likewise his eagerness to involve his translators in government-sponsored social programs was seen as a drift toward the secularism characteristic of the social gospel. His desire to cooperate with government officials led to his decision to authorize JAARS pilots to fly government missions, a policy that alienated some of his own pilots and outsiders alike.

Cam's eagerness to establish good public relations in his translation ministry extended not only to foreign governments, but also to other religious groups, and once again his policy met with criticism that resulted in WBT/SIL pulling out of the IFMA (Interdenominational Foreign Missions Association), where criticism had been the most rife. How should Bible translators react to Roman Catholics? Should they share the fruits of their labors with priests whose goal it was to expand the Roman Catholic Church? The vast majority of evangelical missionaries believed that there should be no cooperation whatever with Roman Catholic officials, but Cam was far more tolerant. "It's possible to know Christ as Lord and Savior," he wrote, "and to continue in the Roman Church," and as for him, he was "happy indeed if the translations are used by anyone and everyone."[8]

As volatile as this issue was, the real test came when Paul Witte, a young Catholic scholar, applied to become a translator under Wycliffe. He was a Christian believer engaged to a member of the Salvation Army. Though Witte viewed Bible truths above Roman Catholic dogma, he wanted to remain a member of the church. Cam's wholehearted support of him was sent in a letter to the entire Wycliffe membership: "We must not depart from our nonsectarian policy one iota if we are to keep entering countries closed to traditional missionary organizations."[9] But despite Cam's plea, Witte was denied membership by a two-thirds majority of the WBT voting delegates. Though upset by the outcome, Cam did not succumb to defeat. He promised to personally support Witte and his new bride

under some other sponsorship.

Roman Catholics were not the only unacceptable religious candidates for Wycliffe membership. In 1949, with the application of Jim and Anita Price, the issue of accepting Pentecostals flared into a heated floor debate. Most of the members, while not denying the sincere Christian faith of Pentecostal believers, felt that they would be incompatible with the noncharismatic evangelicals that filled the ranks of the organization. Cam, not surprisingly, however, upheld the nonsectarian policy of Wycliffe, asserting that the theological issues involved were "nonessentials," and that to deny the Prices membership would be to deny a tribe in Peru the privilege of having its own Scriptures. But argument alone was not enough to persuade the delegates, and Cam threatened to resign his position as General Director if the Prices were rejected. In the end the issue was resolved by a compromise proposal defining incompatibility in this area as holding the view that "speaking in tongues is essential for the indwelling of the Holy Spirit." Since the Prices did not subscribe to that view, they were accepted into membership.

It was simply part of Cam's nature to be tolerant, and this spirit of tolerance was reflected in all aspects of his work. During a time when many evangelicals were still defending segregationist policies, he was appealing to blacks and other ethnic minorities to become involved in Bible translation work. He deplored race prejudice, and in a letter to the board in 1952 he wrote, "Our constitution has nothing that savors of discrimination. You won't find it in the New Testament either. Please send along all the non-Caucasian workers you can, if they make out good in courses."[10]

Education was another area that demonstrated Cam's open-minded attitude. Although many of his translators had advanced degrees, including Ph.D.'s, he himself resisted any attempt to make a college or seminary education a prerequisite for Wycliffe members. He was a college dropout himself, and he insisted that a degree was not necessary for Bible translation work. Though he was offered a number of honorary doctorates, he declined them all, except one from a Peruvian university, in order to maintain an affinity with those translators without degrees.

Cam's open-mindedness toward women was another issue that aroused controversy among organization members and supporters. Allowing single women to work with married couples was an accepted fact in mission circles, but permitting them to go in pairs into remote tribal areas was quite another issue. Even Cam himself expressed doubts when single women first requested tribal work, but when they challenged him as to why God would not protect and care for them as he would men, Cam backed down and agreed that there would be no restrictions on their service. Despite loud objections from chivalrous protectors of the "weaker sex," by the 1950s there were several pairs of single women translators in Peru alone, and among those were Loretta Anderson and Doris Cox, who served as Cam's prime example in defense of women translators.

In 1950 they began their work among the Shapras, one of the most feared headhunting tribes of the Peruvian jungle, led by the infamous Chief Tariri, who had won his position by murdering his predecessor. Though "scared most of the time during the first five months," Loretta and Doris stayed on and "buckled down to the agonizingly slow job of learning the language."[11] Soon they had won the hearts of the people, including the chief. Tariri began helping them as a language informant, and after only a few years turned away from witchcraft and murder and became a Christian, setting an example that many in his tribe followed. Years later, Tariri confided to Cam, "If you had sent men, we would have killed them on sight. Or if a couple, I'd have killed the man and taken the woman for myself. But what could a great chief do with two harmless girls who insisted on calling him brother?"[12] What better argument could Cam have used to disarm his critics?

More than most mission founders and leaders, Cam attempted to avoid the powerful one-man rule that was often so easy to slip into. When SIL was first organized, the obvious choice for director was Cam, but to everyone's surprise he proposed that he be under the executive committee, and ultimately under the vote of the membership. This, according to Hefleys, "was something new in the history of missions—a founder-director telling a crew of young green members, some unhappy with past decisions, to take charge. But Cam believed it was dangerous for one man to have control. It meant he would have to use persuasion and charisma in attempting to put across his policies."[13] Because of this self-imposed policy, Cam was frequently stymied in carrying out his innovative plans. After one heated debate between Cam and his execu-

William Cameron Townsend ("Uncle Cam"), founder of Wycliffe Bible Translators and the Summer Institute of Linguistics.

tive committee, one of the committee members commented, "Uncle Cam is probably right. He may be ten years ahead of the rest of us as usual."[14]

Despite (or perhaps, in part, due to) the lively sparring that characterized WBT/SIL, the membership grew rapidly over the course of the decades and today has reached 4,500. Although Cam has been perceived as the human dynamo behind the organizations, there were many others who contributed significantly to the work, not the least of whom was Elaine, his second wife. Elaine was a school teacher from Chicago who at the age of twenty-seven had been promoted to a well-paying position that entailed supervising classes for the mentally retarded in some three hundred schools. The

work was rewarding and held great promise for the future, but she gave it up to become the first teacher for WBT/SIL children in Mexico and later to conduct reading campaigns among more than a dozen Indian tribes. In 1946 she and Cam were married in the home of their friend General Lazaro Cardenas, the ex-president of Mexico.

Following their marriage, Cam and Elaine served for seventeen years in Peru, during which time their four children were born. They then moved on to pioneer the work in Colombia. Though Cam became recognized the world over as a great missionary statesman, he always thought of himself first and foremost as a Bible translator. After fifty years of service, when most men would have been contemplating retirement, he was preparing to go to the Soviet Union with Elaine. Having learned that there were some one hundred languages spoken in the Caucasus, many of which had no Bible translation, he decided to become involved at the grassroots level once again. So, at the age of seventy-two, with Elaine at his side, he found himself in a hotel overlooking Red Square in Moscow, studying Russian several hours a day. After their initial period of study was completed, they traveled into the Caucasus to confer with linguists and educators. They also spent many hours with the common people, listening to local folklore of how an angel had long ago flown over Russia distributing languages, but ripped his bag on a cliff while flying over the Caucasus, and dozens of languages fell out at once.

Before leaving the Soviet Union, Cam made arrangements for a cultural exchange of linguists so that translators could study in the Caucasus. But despite his success, inevitable criticism followed. One longtime supporter accused Elaine of having been "taken in by the Communists," to which she replied, "We didn't go to the U.S.S.R. to find fault. We went to see how we could serve and pave the way for the Bible to be translated into more languages."[15]

Throughout his life there was one single philosophy that motivated Cam more than any other, and that centered around his high view of the Bible. "The greatest missionary is the Bible in the Mother tongue," he was fond of repeating. "It never needs a furlough, is never considered a foreigner."[16] It was that philosophy, articulated so forcefully by this single-minded man, that made WBT/SIL and JAARS what they are today, though no longer guided by that indomitable leader. In an April 1982 special WBT newsletter, Bernie May emotionally expressed the feelings of the entire organization: "When the word came that Uncle Cam was gone, I had the feeling I've had on several occasions when flying a twin-engine airplane and one engine suddenly goes dead. All at once your goal becomes very important. You instantly turn to your guidance system. You keep on flying, but with a new intensity of reaching your destination as quickly as possible.... There are still 3,000 languages without the Bible.... This is our challenge. This is our call."[17]

Kenneth Pike

One of the most brilliant and highly honored linguists of the twentieth century, recognized the world over in secular as well as Christian circles, is Ken Pike, for many years director and president of the Summer Institute of Linguistics. As a professor at the University of Michigan, the author of numerous scholarly books and articles, and a sought-after seminar and conference speaker, Pike could have so easily settled into a comfortable life in America, but his heart was in Mexico and other underdeveloped areas of the world where the Bible was unavailable in the native tongue. He felt as comfortable talking with an illiterate Mixtec Indian as he did with a distinguished French university professor; and with all his contributions to linguistic science, he remained first and foremost a missionary, eager to share the gospel with those who had never heard.

Pike was born in Connecticut in 1912, the son of a country doctor whose income barely stretched far enough to support his wife and eight children. As a youth, he was unpretentious and would have appeared to be an unlikely candidate for greatness. He was gangly and awkward, was plagued by motion sickness, had an almost paralyzing fear of heights, and possessed a nervous disposition that even in later years resulted in canker sores in his mouth and blisters on his feet. There was little impressive about him. He did excel at Gordon College and, in fact, graduated with distinction, but when he sought to enter his chosen vocation, he encountered roadblocks. He applied to the China Inland Mission and was accepted for candidate school, but when the term was over he was rejected for missionary service. Only two reasons were given for the decision: his nervous disposition and (incredible as it may seem) his language difficulty—particularly his inability to grasp pronunciation.

For more than a year Pike had been enthusiastically telling friends and relatives of his plans to go to China, so the rejection by the CIM was a humiliating blow. Yet he was determined to be a missionary. After a year of work with the CWA (Citizens Workers' Administration) he began writing to mission boards, inquiring about training they offered for linguists and Bible translators, refusing to be deterred by the language problems he had encountered at the CIM candidate school.

Of all the mission board leaders Pike contacted, only Legters of the Pioneer Mission Agency (later WBT) replied, inviting him to attend Camp Wycliffe. So the summer of 1935 was spent in Sulphur Springs, Arkansas, but even there the impression he made was not entirely positive. Observing the delicate-looking Pike in the rugged outdoor setting, Legters is reported to have uttered disappointedly, "Lord, couldn't you have sent us something better than this?"[18] But Cam Townsend saw beneath the unpolished exterior and recognized in Pike great potential for scholarship and ministry.

After the summer training program, Pike traveled to Mexico, where he began studying the language of the Mixtec tribe. Despite the frustration of breaking down such a complex tonal language, he found the task challenging, and his diligence quickly paid off as he made significant headway during his first year as a linguist. So impressed was Cam with his grasp of linguistics that he invited him to return to Camp Wycliffe the next summer as a teacher, and so began his lifelong ministry as a linguistics instructor.

Returning to Arkansas each summer to teach in the Summer Institute of Linguistics became a routine part of Pike's schedule, and it was there in the summer of 1938 that he renewed his acquaintance with Evelyn Griset, Cam's niece who was preparing to minister as a translator in Mexico. Evelyn was a bright young woman who had graduated from UCLA and had gone on to BIOLA for Bible training, an education that prepared her for more than being merely a wife and mother. Her marriage to Ken the following November forged a linguistic partnership that demonstrated teamwork at its best. She went on to earn her master's degree in linguistics at the University of Michigan, wrote a number of articles and books, and later served as a part-time instructor at the University of Michigan alongside her husband. Three children kept her busy as a mother and housewife, but Ken frequently stepped in and took over child care and household duties when outside pressures were mounting.

Ken's scholarly pursuit of linguistics began early in his missionary career. During his second year in Mexico he sustained a broken leg that left him hospitalized, and during that time he fulfilled a request from Cam to write a phonetics book to help Wycliffe trainees. He had dreaded the task, but once he was into the material he found the work very satisfying. From his hospital room he wrote to a friend, "Studying is the thing that makes me happy . . . when things begin to roll."[19] Before completing the manuscript he sent chapters to University of Michigan professor Edward Sapir, who was one of the world's leading experts on Indian languages. Sapir was impressed with the young scholar and encouraged him to come to the University of Michigan for further study. Prodded also by Cam Townsend, Pike began his graduate study in 1937, and in the summer of 1941 he completed the requirements for his Ph.D. degree.

Pike's writing, graduate study, SIL work, and troubleshooting for other translators with difficult problems kept him away for long periods of time from his number one priority— translating the Bible into the San Miguel Mixtec language. In 1941 with his doctoral work completed, he returned with Evelyn and his little daughter to reside in Mexico and to concentrate his efforts on one tribe and one language; and in 1951, after ten years and many interruptions, the New Testament was ready to be printed.

During the decade that Pike translated the New Testament, he was also occupied with many other duties. Each summer he continued to serve as the director and as an instructor for SIL. He also continued his writing and educational pursuits; and in 1945, on receiving a postdoctoral fellowship, he returned to the University of Michigan for a year of research while Evelyn remained in Mexico. Then in 1948, with four books in print, he became an associate professor at the University of Michigan, a position that allowed him to continue his other duties.

With the completion of the Mixtec New Testament, Pike's time was dedicated to helping other linguists in their struggles with language problems. Though his efforts were tied more and more to academic circles, his scholarship directly benefited the translators who were so dependent on his linguistic expertise. He was a demanding teacher, and students often dreaded his classes, but they knew that mastering his theory and techniques could save them years of time in the difficult task that lay ahead of them on the mission field.

Making courses practical was always a top priority for Professor Pike, and sometimes his lectures were as entertaining as they were scholarly. Even during his early days as a teacher, when SIL first moved to the University of Oklahoma, his classes were "good entertainment as well as good teaching." "Who said phonetics was a dull study?" wrote a reporter in the *Oklahoma Daily* of Pike's class. "His big roomful of students sit on the edge of their seats, gurgle with delight at every fresh comparison and seize every opportunity to make their contribution. It's a safe bet that there isn't a livelier class on the campus...."[20]

Even more entertaining than his lectures were his language demonstrations that were often given to large public audiences—demonstrations showing how quickly an unknown language could be learned without an interpreter. On stage with Pike along with several blackboards and a few props (sticks, leaves, and simple objects of various sizes), would be a stranger whom Pike had never met and whose language he did not know. Before the session was over, however, the two would be communicating amazingly well with each other. "After seeing one demonstration," writes Pike's sister, Eunice,

> you are sure that Ken will soon learn the difference between "one stick" versus "two sticks," "a big leaf" versus "a little leaf," etc. He'll probably get a verb or two, for example, "I sit down" versus "he sits down," and even "I am hitting you" versus "you are hitting me." Possessed

nouns, verb conjugations, etc., appear to be easy, but Ken doesn't stop there. He goes on to clauses with subjects, objects, and maybe even an indirect object. The last few years he has sometimes been able to build up to sentences with both dependent and independent clauses.... The speed with which he does it is always amazing, and it is fun to watch the reaction of the stranger helping him. It is apparent that he is enjoying the encounter. When Ken, reading from his scrawls on the blackboard, manages to make up and say his first sentence, the stranger is surprised and delighted. The audience is delighted too and they clap in appreciation.[21]

As Pike continued his research and teaching at the University of Michigan and SIL, he branched out into other areas of linguistics besides phonetics, and the more he studied and learned the more he was able to help linguists and Bible translators all over the world. He had helped establish translation work in South and Central America, where he had found many similarities in the various Indian languages, but as Wycliffe branched out from Latin America into other areas of the world, so did he. The new language groupings his SIL students encountered challenged him to dig deeper into his studies and glean information from other world-renowned linguists. World travel became an important aspect of his ministry, and by the 1960s he was conducting workshops in such remote areas as Papua, New Guinea, where he trained and counseled workers from twenty-two different languages.

Although Pike's travel had taken him to the far corners of the earth, it was not until 1980 that he was able to go to the one place he had his heart set on.

Nearly fifty years before, apparent language problems had prevented him from going to China; at that time he never could have dreamed that one day both he and his wife would be lecturing on linguistics at the Institute of Foreign Languages at Beijing in the People's Republic of China. Though the lectures were at a secular institution, he knew that in the providence of God the information he disseminated could one day be used to further Bible translation work in China, even as such secular lectures had aided Bible translators in other parts of the world.

Few linguists in history have received more personal honors and awards than Dr. Kenneth Pike. With his first book, *Phonetics*, he "revolutionized the thinking of the field," according to Professor Eric Hamp of the University of Chicago, and that was only the beginning. "It is fair to say," continues Hamp, "that something like one-half of all the raw data from exotic languages that has been placed at the disposal of theoretical linguists in the past quarter century can be attributed to the teaching, influence, and efforts of Kenneth Pike.... The boyish enthusiasm of Pike in all his studies and his modesty in attacking every fresh problem would scarcely suggest to the unprepared onlooker that he was in the presence of one of the few really great linguists of the 20th century."[22] And also, he might have added, one of the great missionaries of the twentieth century.

Marianna Slocum

One of the most frequent criticisms of Cam Townsend and his policies relating to Bible translation was that Wycliffe missionaries were expected

Ken and Evelyn Pike, Bible translators and linguistic scholars.

to concentrate their efforts on linguistics and translation work and then move on to another tribe when that work was complete. But what about evangelism and church planting, the critics howled. For Cam, the answer was simple. He and his followers had not been called to specialize in evangelism and church planting, but rather to bring the Word of God to those who did not have it in their native language. But all the criticism aside, Wycliffe Bible translators were vitally involved in evangelism, and through their encouragement and direction thousands of churches have been planted throughout the world. One shining example of such evangelism and church planting was the very effective ministry of Marianna Slocum in Mexico and later in Columbia.

Marianna was raised in Philadel-phia, where she graduated from college and then took courses at Philadelphia School of the Bible. Her father was a university professor and a prolific writer, and her own love for language and writing seemed to come naturally. It was during her junior year at college that she felt God's leading into tribal translation work, and when her schooling was completed she attended Camp Wycliffe and joined the ranks of WBT in the summer of 1940. Her first assignment was to the Chol tribe in the southernmost Mexican state of Chiapas, only one day's hike from the Tzeltal tribe where Bill Bentley, a young man whom Marianna had met at Camp Wycliffe, was also doing translation work.

In February of 1941, Bill and Marianna became engaged, and the following summer they returned to the United States to arrange for a small private wedding. It was a storybook romance, but it ended tragically on August 23, six days before their wedding date. Bill died in his sleep, apparently of a degenerative heart condition that he had unknowingly lived with for years. After his funeral in Topeka, Kansas, Marianna traveled on to Camp Wycliffe and vowed to take up the unfinished task among the Tzeltals that Bill had left behind.

Marianna departed for Mexico alone, but was soon joined by another single woman translator, and together they lived in the same room at the German-owned coffee ranch where Bill had lived as he worked with a lowland group of the Tzeltal tribe. The early months and years were difficult for Marianna. The Indians were given to heavy drinking and brawling and made no effort to disguise their hostility toward the young American women. After a time, Marianna's first partner left. Other temporary partners came and went until 1947, when Florence Gerdel, a nurse, came to help temporarily, and stayed on more than twenty years.

For both women, the task seemed insurmountable. Marianna worked long hours each day, struggling with the complexities of the language, and Florence struggled against the alcohol, filth, superstitions, and the demonic powers of the local witch doctors. And for all their struggles there were so few signs of success. Nearly seven years went by before a Tzeltal Indian—the son of a witch doctor—made a public profession of faith. His testimony, tested by harsh persecution, led to the salvation of others until there were nearly one hundred converts in the village of Corralito alone. Sunday services were begun, and soon hundreds of Indians were trudging in from the countryside even in the worst days of the rainy season when the muddy mountain trails and swollen streams made travel almost impossible.

August 6, 1956, was an exciting day for Marianna and the more than one thousand Tzeltal Christians. A small yellow MAF (Missionary Aviation Fellowship) plane arrived with precious cargo—the first New Testament editions in the Oxchuc Tzeltal language. A dedication service was held at the local church, and then Indians lined up by the hundreds to buy a copy of God's Word in their own language. It was the climax of fifteen lonely and difficult years and one of the happiest days of Marianna's life.

Having completed the translation of the New Testament as well as Old Testament stories, hymns, and primers, Marianna knew that her work with the Oxchuc Tzeltals was over. The church was well established under indigenous leadership, and Florence was prepared to turn the medical work over to the Indians she had trained. There were other Tzeltal Indians, the Bachajón people living in the dense rain forest, whose language was yet unwritten, and in April of 1957, after a short MAF flight and a six-hour hike, Marianna and Florence found themselves in a strange culture, starting all over again.

The experience Marianna had gained during her first translation assignment speeded up the task of her second, and in 1965, only eight years after she and Florence had arrived, they were once again marking a milestone in their ministry—distributing Bachajón New Testaments. And again, the translation work was not accomplished in a vacuum. Florence cared for the medical needs of the Indians and trained medical assistants, and great strides were made in evangelism. On the day the New Testaments arrived, Christians from more than forty congregations—some from many miles away—came to meet the MAF pilot, and once again there were tears of rejoicing as hundreds lined up to purchase Bachajón New Testaments.

"How much does it cost?" was the oft-repeated question as the Indians stood in line. Seventeen and a half pesos was, of course, the answer to the question they had in mind, but the actual answer could never be given in pesos. Loneliness, illness, unfriendliness, primitive living conditions, and the sacrifice of marriage and family all made up the cost of the Bachajón New Testament. It was a heavy price, but one Marianna gladly paid. And when her work with the Bachajón people was over, she and Florence started all over again in the Southern Andes Mountains of Columbia.[23]

Rachel Saint

The most publicized Bible translator of the twentieth century, with the possible exception of Cam Townsend himself, has been Rachel Saint, the sister of MAF pilot Nate Saint, who was martyred by the Aucas in 1956. Rachel's appearance on the popular television program "This Is Your Life" and at Billy Graham crusades brought welcome publicity to the ministry of Bible translation work, and it demonstrated what women with language skills could accomplish in remote jungle tribes where others had failed. It was Rachel's privilege to go in and live among her brother's killers and communicate to them in their own language the love and forgiveness she had for them through Christ.

Rachel's interest in missions developed in childhood, and it was contagious as she read missionary stories and shared her enthusiasm with her younger brother Nate. But though she was nine years older than he and had sparked his interest in missions, it was he who arrived on the mission field in South America first, though only months ahead of her. Rachel's decision to become a foreign missionary —a decision that signaled a drastic change in her life—did not come to fruition until she was approaching her mid-thirties. In the words of Ethel Wallis, it "meant leaving a comfortable, happy place of Christian service and heading toward a primitive home somewhere in the tangles of Amazonian jungle."[24]

It was translation work more than any other aspect of missions that intrigued Rachel, and so she applied to SIL and in 1948 traveled to the University of Oklahoma for an intensive session in linguistics taught by Ken Pike and his staff of linguistic specialists. Following her completion of the SIL program she applied to and was accepted by Wycliffe Bible Translators. On hearing of her acceptance, Nate wrote a letter of encouragement and support and emphasized the importance of her mission:"My own feelings toward the translation work is such that if the Lord had not definitely called me to aviation, I'm sure I would be in language work. What a priceless privilege, that of leaving something behind you ... which will enable the Lord to work with new tribes through His own Book...."[25]

Rachel's first assignment in Peru

was to the Piro Indians, an assignment that afforded her valuable experience but one that was less than fully satisfying. She had her heart set on working among an unreached tribe, and the Piros had already been evangelized. Also, she felt out of step with her partner, who was well into the language when Rachel arrived. A reassignment, therefore, came as welcome news. She was asked to take the place of Doris Cox and Loretta Anderson as each in turn took a furlough, thus assisting the remaining one in the work among the headhunting Shapras.

Following her two-year temporary assignment among the Shapras, Rachel took a vacation to Ecuador to visit Nate and his wife, and it was during that time that she felt a calling to learn the language of the Aucas, the most feared tribe in Ecuador, with the anticipation of one day bringing the gospel to them. But there was one major obstacle standing in her way. "I hardly knew what to do with this new assurance," she wrote, "for Wycliffe was not working in Ecuador and I had no leading to leave Wycliffe. I loved this group which was as dear to me as my own family, and I couldn't think of leaving. I didn't mention the matter to anyone except a Peruvian pastor, a godly man who promised to pray for me and the tribe to which I had been called."[26] Rachel's answer to prayer came sooner than she dared hope. Hardly had she returned to Peru for a field meeting when a startling announcement was made by Cam Townsend: "I would like to read a letter which has just come from the Ecuadorian ambassador to the United States, inviting us to work among the Indian tribes of Ecuador...."[27]

In February of 1955, Rachel, along with her partner, Dr. Catherine Peeke, arrived at Hacienda Ila, a ranch close to Auca territory where they had been invited to stay and study the Auca language with a field hand, Dayuma, a young Auca woman who had fled for her life during an intertribal war several years earlier. There were three other Auca women working on the ranch, but only Dayuma remembered enough of the language to be of any help, and even her speech was found to be mixed with Quichua, a tribe with whom she had lived after her escape. Despite the difficulties, by the end of the first month, Rachel had made significant progress. Previous vocabulary lists had been compiled by others, but in only a few short weeks Rachel's list of words and phrases was far more extensive than any other list that was available to her. Yet great obstacles remained. Dayuma spent long days working in the fields, allowing her little time to study with Rachel. Even when she was available, communication was slow and difficult, but it was often punctuated with humor: "Sometimes the bright Indian girl, capturing the idea, would act out the words for Rachel by crawling like a baby, or throwing herself down in a feigned fit of anger. Such antics were always accompanied by hilarious laughter, which made informant hours great entertainment."[28]

During the summer of 1955, Rachel, physically exhausted, left Hacienda Ila, and months of serious illness prevented her from returning until the following year. In the meantime the tribe she so longed to reach had stunned the world by another attack on outsiders—an attack that brought their murderous reputation painfully close to home for Rachel. Her kid brother Nate, so dear to her heart, had, along with his four companions, been slain by the very people God had called her to reach. For some, the ordeal of returning to Ecuador to continue Auca language study after such a personal tragedy would have been inconceivable, but for Rachel the opportunity of vindicating her brother's unsuccessful efforts only served to intensify her resolve.

Although Rachel was anxious to reach the Aucas, she was set against another premature contact that would risk lives and further alienate the Aucas. Others, however, did not possess her patience, perhaps thinking of the publicity that would be theirs in the event of a successful contact. Pressure mounted to use Dayuma to initiate the contact, but Rachel resisted. She argued strongly that since Dayuma was not yet converted to Christianity herself she would not be able to evangelize her people, even if the contact were successful, and that no one else besides Dayuma was fluent enough in the language to communicate spiritual truths. Reason prevailed, and the pressure to use Dayuma abated.

As concerned as Rachel seemed to be that Dayuma not be endangered or exploited unnecessarily, Rachel herself used questionable judgment when she involved Dayuma in a lengthy publicity tour that was clearly not arranged with Dayuma's personal interests in mind. In the early months of 1957, an unexpected invitation came from California, requesting Dayuma to appear on television. At first Rachel was opposed to the idea, convinced that it would be wrong to "snatch the jungle girl out of her environment and drop her suddenly into Hollywood," but, continues her biographer, "peace of mind finally came ... when the Lord assured her that the program would provide a means of sharing her own burden for Bibleless tribes with the American public."[29]

This was certainly not the first time the question of the value of such publicity versus the potential exploitation of the exotic "native" had arisen. More than a century earlier, Robert Moffat had traveled to Capetown with Afrikaner, his "tamed" Hottentot chief, and since that time other missionaries had felt inclined to carry out similar publicity tours. But with Dayuma, so utterly unprepared for the outside world, the potential for permanent damage seemed unacceptably great. Certainly no one could deny the value of Dayuma as a publicity gimmick, but was the delay in language study (Rachel's primary ministry) and the physical and psychological risk to Dayuma worth satisfying the curiosity of the American public and drawing attention to Wycliffe?

On arriving in the United States, Rachel, with Dayuma as the real celebrity, was featured on Ralph Edwards's "This Is Your Life," and Billy Graham, well aware of the publicity attention Dayuma would be, featured her as one of the guests for his 1957 New York Crusade in Madison Square Garden. Even Dayuma's baptism became a production geared to attract publicity. She was flown to Wheaton in R. G. LeTourneau's private jet, and there at the Wheaton Evangelical Free Church, pastored by Wilbur Nelson, she was baptized in front of a large audience by Dr. V. Raymond Edman before listening to an incomprehensible message in English by Dr. Carl Armerding.

If the well-being of Wycliffe was enhanced through the publicity tour, the same cannot be said for Dayuma. The Asian flu epidemic that swept across the United States in 1957 caught her without the resistance most Americans had. Her temperature soared, and for days she tottered between life and death. The crisis finally passed, but recuperation was slow, and Rachel found it necessary to keep her in the United States through the winter. The trip that had originally been scheduled for a month turned into a year—a very crucial year to be absent from Ecuador.

Back in the jungle an exciting event had transpired. Two Auca women had emerged from the forest and were staying with Elisabeth Elliot, who was stationed close by. If ever Rachel and Dayuma were needed it was then, but Dayuma was too ill to return. Tapes of the two Auca women were sent to Rachel and Dayuma, but it was not until the summer of 1958 that they were able to return and Dayuma was able to meet her kinfolk face to face. From that point, events moved rapidly. When several weeks of intensive language study with Rachel were finished, Dayuma and the two other Auca women began their journey back into the jungle, promising to return again. They kept their promise, and one month later they emerged from the jungle at Arajuno, where Marj Saint, Nate's widow, had the thrill of greeting them.

The next step in the long-awaited meeting with the Aucas came quickly. Rachel and Elisabeth Elliot (with her four-year-old daughter Valerie) began packing for the return trip to the Aucas, and within a week they had carried out a most historic undertaking—a peaceful and friendly en-counter with the fearsome Auca tribe. For nearly two months they lived among the Aucas, experiencing firsthand Auca lifestyle and perfecting their language skills.

It was an exciting time, but only a beginning. Gospel Recordings soon entered the picture, dispatching Marguerite Carter to work with Dayuma and Rachel to produce recorded gospel messages in the Auca tongue. Years of language study followed with Wycliffe's gifted Dr. Catherine Peeke, and nine years after the slaying of the five missionaries, the Gospel of Mark was published in the Auca language. Another significant event had occurred as well. Under the direction of Dayuma, the Aucas built an airstrip, and when that was completed, MAF pilot Johnny Keenan, the backup man for Operation Auca, landed with another pilot. For the first time in history, white men and Auca men, through the painstaking efforts of women from both sides, were meeting peacefully.

As significant as the translation work, the airstrip, and the face-to-face encounters with the Aucas were, the lasting rewards came when Auca tribesmen began turning to Christ. Among them were the six killers at Palm Beach, who told of their anxiety on that awful day in 1956 when they feared the white men had come to kill and eat them. One of the killers, Kimo, became the pastor to the tribe, and it was he who had the unique privilege of baptizing Steve and Kathy Saint, Nate's children, at Palm Beach in the Curaray River. There would be more high points in the continuing Auca story, but stretching between those mountain peaks would be days and months filled with the tiring and sometimes tedious task of linguistic and translation work so that one day Aucas would have their own Scripture and would no longer have to depend on the white man for guidance and growth in spiritual matters.

Myron Bromley

Though the specialty of missionary translation work has been associated with WBT more than any other organization and has been geographically linked with Latin America more than any other area of the world, the work in this field done by other organizations and in other areas of the world is well worth noting. The efforts of the Christian and Missionary Alliance, Unevangelized Fields Mission and other mission societies in the remote interior valleys of Dutch New Guinea (Irian Jaya) are prime examples. "The advance of the Christian and Missionary Alliance into West Irian, and particularly into the territory of the Baliem Valley, must rank as one of the greatest missionary achievements of this century,"[30] writes J. H. Hunter, and it was the linguistic work of Myron Bromley that made this advance possible.

The C&MA had been interested in reaching the isolated Dani tribes of the Baliem Valley since the 1930s, when the great missionary statesman, R. A. Jaffray, himself too ill to make the expedition, inspired two young and courageous missionaries to make the overland journey. World War II and the invasion of the Japanese, however, brought a halt to the effort. Death took its toll on the mission party, including Jaffray, who had recovered enough to join the pioneer effort but died in the Japanese prison camp in 1945 only two weeks before the cease-fire and release of prisoners.

It was not until 1954 that Myron Bromley entered the Baliem Valley with a small party of C&MA missionaries to establish the first mission station there. Bromley had been raised in Meadville, Pennsylvania, and educated at Nyack Missionary College, Asbury Theological Seminary, and the graduate school of the University of Minnesota. He was a brilliant linguist and was eager to use his skills in an area of the world entirely untested by the science of linguistics. He was a bachelor, and, according to Russell Hitt, "was more interested in getting to know the Dani people and to 'break down' the language than he was in his personal appearance. He went about in an old khaki army jacket to which his toothbrush was attached with a long metal chain.... Most of the time he was unshaven, and wore an old battered campaign hat. His tent was furnished with an unmade canvas cot surrounded by books, papers, medicines, canned goods, a tape recorder, and miscellany."[31]

Before coming to New Guinea, Bromley had learned Dutch in order to study the only scientific works available on Dani culture. But even with this background he was shocked by what he discovered firsthand about Dani society. "Death, death, death! When will it cease?" he wrote soon after he arrived. "Or when at least will it be illuminated by the Light of life that transcends its tragedy? The year ends with a week of death from war and disease and feuding. We pray that God will soon let new life be born in men's hearts here. I try to help our friends with pliers (to remove arrow tips). I try to help them with pills. But I am kicked in the face with the suddenness of death. We sometimes dream that the work could progress were there not the fightings and feuds—only to sit with mud-smeared mourners around the pyres of new victims. We dream of great achievement—only to be shaken by inexplicable personal failure."[32] The only answer was Christianity, and bringing Christ to the Danis depended on a breakdown of the language barrier, a goal that prodded Bromley along even faster in his linguistic mission.

But as much as Bromley wanted to concentrate solely on language, he found many hours each day consumed in "doctoring." The Danis had grave medical needs, and they quickly learned that the white man's medication performed wonders. Acquiring a suitable language informant was another difficult problem that Bromley had to overcome. After working with one tribesman for a time, he discovered the man had a speech impediment and that some of his pronunciations did not even resemble true Dani speech. Bromley took the matter in stride, commenting, "Well, that's still not as bad as Eugene Nida's story of the new missionary who ran into a stutterer as the only willing informant."[33]

Though Bromley ran into difficulty coming to grips with the Dani language, he nevertheless sought to share the gospel as soon as he was able to piece together some constructions that seemed meaningful to him. But he realized that sharing the gospel was more than merely a linguistic effort: "It was one of the most discouraging experiences I've ever had," he later recalled. "I used pictures from a scripture calendar and tried my best to say all I could as simply and intelligently as possible. But the natives looked as if I were talking in Latin about the price of corn in Asia. . . . Yet at some places in the Pugima Valley where I have talked to folk in a village for the first time, I have been greeted with a series of intelligent questions. Indeed, this is the work of His Spirit, and if He does not open men's minds and hearts, our task is helpless. Perhaps the Lord wanted to remind me that this message is not something to be casually huckstered but a redemptive cry of good news to be passionately shared in His Spirit's power."[34]

As a trained linguist, Bromley attempted to attack the Dani language systematically, and in the early months of 1955 he concentrated on tone, stress, and length of vowels. From that study he wrote a scholarly paper entitled, "The Phonetic Structure of the Language of the Lower Grand Beliem Valley." In it he told of the major breakthrough that had occurred in his language study when he discovered that there were four more vowels than he originally believed. What had escaped his notice were two "high-front double-E-like vowels" and "two high-back-W- or double-O-like vowels,"[35] a discovery that helped unlock the door to the difficult Dani language.

Although Bromley had made progress during his first year in phonetics, "the grammar," he wrote a friend in 1955, "is still in the diaper stage."[36] He found that the long-held belief that the most culturally backward peoples of the world spoke the simplest language was false, at least in the case of the Danis. They had a complex pattern of syntax and verb forms in some ways similar to the Cakchiquels of Mexico, where one verb could have as many as two thousand forms.

Coming to terms with such a complicated language was terribly frustrating as can be seen in Bromley's effort to teach the Danis one simple Bible verse. He wrote his mother in the summer of 1955:

I've tried to talk about John 3:16, but I'm sure I made a lot of blunders. . . . You can imagine how faulty my interpretation must have been, since we have no adequate terms for "God," "believe," or "everlasting life." I talk about "Jesus' father" because we know as yet of no belief of these people that would furnish a good term for "God." They know of the ghosts of their dead, of noise-making, heart-stealing spirits of the lowland peoples that cause people to lose their minds. They speak of the sun and moon as husband and wife and they think of the rain as a person. Also they talk about a tiny man up in the sky called *Hulisogom*, but they are vague about the origin of earth. So far I have not discovered that they have a creation story.

For the word "believe" I get along with the term that means "hear" or "understand." I can say "I think he's telling the truth," but that's something different from Biblical faith.

As for everlasting life, I can say that we will remain alive, but that is not Jesus' or John's idea. Or I can say our skin and bones and our meat and blood will die but our souls will live, but this is not the Biblical idea either. How to say that God creates in us a new kind of life that will be ours right now and forever is something I don't know yet.

When I try to explain the whole concept of Jesus' dying for us, I say that he died in our interest that we may remain alive . . . but the whole central concept of the atonement is beyond the grasp of our language. Probably this is because we don't really know how to talk about sin. I usually use the expression "bad acting," but that's quite different from the true concept of sin. One could talk about breaking taboos, but that's exactly the idea we don't want to use, since we are so uncertain about the meaning of *wesa*, or taboo, in the thought and culture of these people. Acts that are so obviously sinful to us are items of cultural praise—killing, cruelty to enemies, hatred, pride, jealousy, disdain of the weak and the inferior.[37]

Bromley's language ministry among the Danis involved more than breaking down the language and translating Scripture. It also involved the training of other missionaries. In 1956 six new Alliance couples arrived in the Baliem Valley, and Bromley spent long hours in language study with them. He also worked with missionaries from other mission societies, including Wal Turner, a UMF (Unevangelized Fields Mission) missionary who was convinced after completing the Summer Institute of Linguistics course that the only thing he had really learned was that he would "never be a linguist."[38] But once he arrived in the Baliem Valley he realized he could not function without the language, and with the help of Bromley he eventually became a highly competent linguist and an effective evangelist to the Dani people.

As Bromley and his fellow missionaries continued working in the Baliem Valley they began spreading out among the previously uncontacted tribes, and as they did so they often met with resistance, sometimes manifested in life-threatening attacks. More than once Bromley and his colleagues ran for their lives to escape Dani arrows. But with persistence, more tribes were reached, and with each new tribal contact came more work for Bromley. He discovered that in the

Baliem Valley alone (some forty miles in length), there were three major dialects and a number of offshoots from each of the three. But with each new dialect the speed and proficiency of his linguistic ability increased.

The tremendous accomplishments Bromley made in linguistic work during his early years in the Baliem Valley may have been due in part to his singlemindedness and the fact that he was unencumbered by family responsibilities. As appreciative as his associates were for his tireless efforts, at least some felt his life would be enhanced by marriage. One of the Alliance leaders commented as much to his mother, who in turn passed it on to Bromley himself, who was more than a little irritated by the suggestion. "I know that bachelorhood can get to be a habit," he tersely wrote back to the leader, "and I've asked God to deliver me from obstinacy in this matter. However, one factor has rather strongly turned me from this possibility—so many other folks have felt God's direction. Somehow I feel God is gentleman enough to talk to me about my life before He speaks, or at least while He speaks, to others about me, if I am willing to hear."[39]

Apparently God did speak to Bromley and deliver him from obstinacy, for in 1957 when he traveled to Melbourne, Australia, to attend a linguistics institute he met Marjorie Teague, a medical doctor who had a heart for missionary service. The following year they married and then furloughed in the United States before returning to the Baliem Valley, where they worked as a team among the Danis.

As time passed and as the language barrier was broken down, the Danis began turning to Christianity. By 1961, C&MA reported more than twenty churches and some eight thousand believers in the valley alone. The cost of such an accomplishment was high, especially when tallying up the deaths of the several Alliance missionaries beginning with the Japanese occupation in 1940, but it was a price worth paying. No longer were the Danis killing and eating each other. Lifelong enemies were now sharing the same communion cup.

SELECTED BIBLIOGRAPHY

Cowan, George M. The Word that Kindles: People and Principles that Fueled a Worldwide Bible Translation Movement. Chappaqua, New York: Christian Herald, 1979.

Hefley, James and Marti. Uncle Cam: The Story of William Cameron Townsend, Founder of the Wycliffe Bible Translators and the Summer Institute of Linguistics. Waco: Word, 1974.

Hitt, Russell T. Cannibal Valley: The Heroic Struggle for Christ in Savage New Guinea. New York: Harper & Row, 1962.

Nida, Eugene A. God's Word in Man's Language. New York: Harper & Row, 1952.

Pike, Eunice V. Ken Pike: Scholar and Christian. Dallas: Summer Institute of Linguistics, 1981.

Wallis, Ethel E. The Dayuma Story: Life Under Auca Spears. New York: Harper & Row, 1960.

Wallis, Ethel E. and Bennett, Mary A. Two Thousand Tongues to Go: The Story of the Wycliffe Bible Translators. New York: Harper & Brothers, 1959.

Chapter 14

Radio and Recordings:
Harnessing the Air Waves

It was not long after commercial broadcasting began on a wide scale in the 1920s that farsighted Christians jumped at the opportunity to use this new media for spreading the gospel. John Zoller in Jackson, Michigan, Paul Rader in Chicago, R. R. Brown in Omaha, and Charles E. Fuller in Santa Ana, California, were all pioneers in the field of Christian broadcasting. And as these Christian broadcasters broke new ground in America, still other farsighted Christians began to dream of what the impact of radio could be on the foreign mission field. Dr. Walter A. Maier, who inaugurated "The Lutheran Hour" in 1930, was one of the foremost pioneers in missionary radio, and by the 1960s he was broadcasting over hundreds of stations world-wide. It was Clarence Jones, however, who more than any other individual brought missionary radio into vogue; and on seeing his success with HCJB, other independent missionary broadcasting organizations came into being, the two largest being the Far East Broadcasting Company and Trans World Radio.

From the beginning, missionary radio was not seen as a tool to be used independently of traditional missionary outreach. Though some missionaries were skeptical at first, they soon realized the value of having radio pave the way for them. "It has given traditional missionary effort a tremendous weapon and means to spread the gospel," according to Abe Van Der Puy of World Radio Missionary Fellowship. "Until recently, in many parts of Latin America, missionaries had a very difficult time getting people to talk with them about the gospel. These same people, however, have been willing to listen in the privacy of their own home.... Many times when personal workers are dealing with individuals about the gospel, the person being dealt with will say, 'Oh, that means you are like those of HCJB.'"[1]

The value of missionary radio, however, goes far beyond paving the way for personal evangelism. "Radio has expanded the scope and potential of traditional missionary endeavor," according to Peter Deyneka, Jr., Director of Slavic Gospel Association, because "it goes where missionaries cannot and reaches people who otherwise might not respond to more conventional approaches."[2] Radio also has been used effectively to strengthen the local church on the mission field. One of the primary reasons for establishing HLKX in Korea by TEAM (The Evangelical Alliance Mission) was to produce programs that would relate to the local church. ELWA, owned and operated by the Sudan Interior Mission, also broadcasts programs geared primarily to Christians, not only in Liberia where the station is located, but also to surrounding African countries.

In most countries missionary broadcasters have had to deal with government regulations that place limitations on religious programming, and in some cases Christian broadcasting has been barred altogether. In rare instances missionary radio has received favored treatment by government, Kenya being a prime example. There the government owned and operated station, the 100,000-watt Voice of Kenya, reserves free of charge twenty-two hours a week for religious programs—much of that time being allotted to the Africa Inland Mission. In 1978 when President Jomo Kenyatta died, the government declared thirty days of official mourning and preempted all broadcasting except for news and Christian music, a significant decision in light of the fact that a large percentage of the population is Muslim.

The value of radio has led many missions besides AIM to become actively involved in broadcasting by producing their own programs and buying time from established stations, thus avoiding the expense and responsibility of operating their own station. The Slavic Gospel Association and the Bible Christian Union, for example, both spend large portions of their mission budget to produce programs that are beamed into the Soviet Union. Some missions such as LARE (Latin America Radio Evangelism) concentrate entirely on radio programming and develop their ministry around key personalities. "Hermano Pablo" Finkenbender, their most well-known radio host, was on the air during the 1960s more than two hundred times a day on scores of different stations throughout Latin America.

Today with the increasing size of transmitters and the greater affordability of transistor radios, Christian broadcasts are reaching more people than ever. According to Barry Siedell, "There is virtually no square foot on earth that isn't reached sometime during the day by a gospel radio broadcast."[3] But as all-encompassing as it is, radio fails to reach large numbers of the world's population whose language or dialect represents too small a number of people to make radio practical. To fill that void, records have become an important part of audio evangelism, taking the gospel to remote tribes whose language in many cases is yet unwritten. Gospel Recordings, more than any other mission, has spanned the world over with this type of mechanized ministry.

Clarence W. Jones and HCJB

Like other specialized areas of missions, missionary radio had to fight its way into acceptance with the Christian public; and without the foresight of a visionary like Clarence W. Jones, missionary radio would not be where it is today. Jones was not afraid to use this "tool of the devil" for evangelism and was thickskinned enough to endure the ridicule that was heaped on him. "Jones's folly" is what the people from his home church termed it. Only a fool would go off to a foreign land to set up a radio station when there were only six receiving sets in the whole country. But Jones was convinced that missions had to be in the forefront of the field of communications if the world was to be evangelized; and if the more traditionally minded Christians were offended, that was not his concern.

Born in 1900 in Illinois, Jones's life from his earliest recollections centered around Christian service, both his parents being Salvation Army officers. At the age of twelve, after years of pleading with his father, he was allowed to join the Salvation Army band, where he quickly learned to play several instruments and later specialized in the trombone—an instrument that became his trademark. It was under the ministry of Paul Rader at Moody Memorial Tabernacle that Jones was converted; and following his conversion he enrolled at Moody Bible Institute, where he graduated in 1921 as class president and valedictorian, even though he had only completed two years of high school.

During the years following his graduation, Jones worked with Paul Rader. He first helped in the tent meeting evangelism and later served on the staff of Rader's new ministry at the Chicago Gospel Tabernacle that soon became a base for world-wide missionary outreach—a ministry that attracted such talent as Lance Latham, Merrill Dunlop, and Carlton Booth. Jones played his trombone in the brass quartet and became program director for the Tabernacle's radio broadcasting that began with the onset of Chicago's first commercial radio station.

Although Jones had been a missions major at Moody Bible Institute, foreign missions work had been pushed aside in his thinking during the busy years he spent working with Rader. But in 1927, while assisting Rader as music director during a Bible conference, the urgency of world evangelism was again impressed upon him as he listened to an emotional missionary appeal from Rader, and in the weeks and months that followed he became convinced that God wanted him to go to South America to pioneer the field of missionary radio.

In 1928, despite the skepticism of many of his friends and associates, Jones made an exploratory trip to South America, hoping to gain entrance into Venezuela with his radio ministry. As he traveled through the villages and towns, he was overwhelmed with the need for evangelism, as his diary indicates: "How endless the task of missions seems here in Venezuela at our present slow rate of response! This country is only a small portion of a whole great continent, with many places having no witness for missions. Missionary work could be supplemented and speeded up by the perfectly possible procedure of regular Spanish radio broadcasts. I am more and more impressed with the opportunity for evangelism in all Venezuela, and am spending much time in prayer these days, asking the Lord to do *the great and mighty things*."[4] But instead of "great and mighty things," God shut the door to Venezuela. Government officials flatly refused his request. Before returning home, Jones visited Columbia, Panama, and Cuba with similar requests, but the answer was the same.

Back home, Jones was frustrated and embarrassed. All the time and money that had been invested in his exploratory trip had come to naught. At times he was tempted to think that maybe his idea was as crazy as so many people believed. Katherine, his wife, was secretly "elated," according to his biographer. "Her initial reckless zeal had worn off, and with two little ones to care for, she just did not want to go to 'the foreign field.' Not at all."[5] For Jones it was a depressing period in his life. "Then there was the day of such discouragement that Clarence, desperately needing some money for his family, unable to shake off the feelings of total inadequacy and failure, and chagrined that this obsession with South America had made him look like a fool, decided to chuck it all—his work at the Tabernacle, his call to the mission field, his family— and went down to enlist in the Navy. He was rejected for lack of 20/20 vision."[6]

It may have been that Jones's dream of missionary radio would have faded away had it not been for a devoted couple that entered his life in the months that followed. Reuben and Grace Larson had been serving in Ecuador under the Christian and Missionary Alliance since 1924, and during their furlough in 1930 they visited the Chicago Gospel Tabernacle to present their work. To the Larsons, Jones's trip to South America was not a fiasco; he had simply gone to the wrong countries. He had passed by the beautiful land of Ecuador, providentially not even seeking entrance until after he had met Reuben and Grace, two individuals that would provide the key to missionary radio in South America.

Cooperative teamwork was an essential part in establishing the world's first missionary radio station, and Jones often quoted Jonathan Goforth, saying, "God never asked me to do a job but that he sent along men to help me do it." There were several men and women who contributed invaluable service to Jones as he carried out his vision, but Reuben Larson's work in making initial contacts with Ecuadorian officials was indispensable. While Jones remained in the United States raising funds, the Larsons returned to Ecuador and made necessary arrangements with government officials.

Though Ecuadorian officials were at first skeptical about a Protestant radio station, Larson was persistent; and on August 15, 1930, he sent a cable to Jones, urging him to come as soon as possible and announcing that a twenty-five-year contract had been granted. "Clearly we saw the hand of God moving on the whole Congress of Ecuador," he wrote, "causing them to allow, in this closed Catholic country, a ministry of gospel radio."[7] Jones, however, had not waited for Larson's cable. So anxious was he to begin his work that he was already on his way to South America when the cable arrived.

The weeks following Jones's arrival in Ecuador were discouraging ones. Hardly had the ink on their permit dried when the missionaries were told by engineers as well as American State Department officials that Ecuador— particularly Quito—would never be suitable for radio transmission. The mountains and the close proximity to the equator would be insurmountable obstacles. But "unreasonable, illogical though it seemed," in the words of his biographer, "Clarence was absolutely certain that Quito was God's place for his voice to South America."[8] So he went ahead with plans, and in the year that followed, despite more disappointments, Radio Station HCJB (Heralding Christ Jesus' Blessings) became a reality. It was a historic day. The world's first missionary radio program was broadcast live on Christmas Day in 1931, coming from a 250-watt transmitter located in a sheepshed in Quito, Ecuador. With organ music in the background, Clarence played his trombone, and Reuben preached in Spanish. All thirteen receiving sets in the country were tuned in, and the Voice of the Andes was on the air.

In the months that followed, the World Radio Missionary Fellowship was officially incorporated, and the daily broadcasts continued, but not without periods of crisis. As the depression deepened back in the United States, contributions fell off. During the entire year of 1932, less than one thousand dollars was donated to the new mission, and in 1933 the bank through which Jones and his associates had been receiving their monthly checks folded, and later the Chicago Gospel Tabernacle, the mainstay of the mission's support, went bankrupt. The future of the fledgling radio station was in serious doubt. On his knees in a little toolshed, Jones pleaded with God for one whole day for direction: "Are we to carry on with HCJB, or pack it in and go home?"[9]

That day was a "low spot" in Jones's life, but he left the toolshed with the assurance that God would see him through the crisis, and that night there was a buoyant enthusiasm in his voice

as he went on the air with the evening broadcast. Within days, through a financial loan from a friend and a mortgage on the transmitter, the immediate crisis was averted, and WRMF slowly climbed out of its economic peril.

One of the reasons for HCJB's survival was the growing recognition it received from the government and the people of Ecuador. From the very beginning, Larson and Jones had cooperated fully with government officials, agreeing to make their programing not only religious, but also educational and cultural as well. When gospel programs were aired they were always presented in a positive vein to avoid antagonizing the Roman Catholic Church. Patriotism was a key element of their philosophy, and the president of Ecuador had an open invitation to use the broadcasting facilities, and often did so, especially on holidays.

As word of the radio station spread, the number of receivers in Ecuador grew rapidly, and HCJB, according to Jones's biographer, "was cutting across every level of society, breaking down barriers to the gospel. Missionaries (many who had in fact strongly opposed the idea of Christian radio) were finding that where previously they were persecuted and stoned on the streets, now they could minister openly. And even when they encountered a 'Protestants Not Welcome' sign on a door, inside they could hear *La Voz de los Andes*, HCJB. Everyone seemed to be listening."[10]

The decade of the thirties was one of tremendous growth for HCJB. The first major power addition was a 1000-watt transmitter that reached far beyond the borders of Ecuador; and before the decade closed, a 10,000-watt transmitter was installed. Such an addition had seemed like a financial impossibility to Jones, who had returned to the States to raise money. A 5,000-watt transmitter was the most he had dared hope for, but only three of the ten thousand dollars needed had come in, and his year of travel was coming to an end. Then, just before sailing, he received an unusual telegram: "If you want to see me before sailing, come." It was signed "R. G. LeTourneau," a name Jones knew only as a wealthy industrialist who had a reputation for giving away the vast majority of his profits to Christian organizations. Jones's visit with LeTourneau resulted in far more than he could have hoped for. LeTourneau's initial offer to underwrite the needed seven thousand dollars for a used 5,000-watt transmitter was later changed when it was discovered that the used transmitter was defective. LeTourneau then agreed to have a new transmitter built at his Peoria plant, and instead of the proposed 5,000 watts he doubled the size to 10,000.

It was on Easter Sunday of 1940, when President Andres Cordova of Ecuador threw the switch to begin broadcasting over the new 10,000-watt transmitter that would carry the gospel further than ever before. How far was anybody's guess, but even the most optimistic observers were surprised when letters began pouring in from New Zealand, Japan, India, Germany, and Russia. That a mere 10,000 watts would broadcast over such great distances was truly amazing, but the explanation later given by radio experts was simple. Though Jones had been advised against locating near the equator, such a location was later determined to be "the very finest location

for north-south broadcasting" because the "equal distance from magnetic poles" makes it "the one place in the world freest from atmospheric disturbance."[11] And the high elevation in the mountains near Quito was an added plus. The 100-foot tower perched on a 9,600-foot mountain was almost equivalent to a 10,000-foot antenna.

As the size of HCJB grew, so did the reputation for quality programing. Jones, as many co-workers could attest to, was not easy to work for. He was a perfectionist who demanded excellence in every area of broadcasting, and some considered him "tyrannical." The live music was first class, and there were no excuses for being late to rehearsals. Even his children feared his authoritarian control and were on occasion pulled from the program when their playing was not up to his expectations. But the stringent demands of the station director turned the financially strapped operation into a professional sounding radio station that received the highest compliments even among secular critics.

Throughout the 1950s and 1960s HCJB continued to grow, increasing its power to more than 500,000 watts, but the times of blessing were accompanied by personal traumas for Jones and his family. In 1953 a head-on collision left Katherine critically ill in a coma and Clarence with such severe facial injuries that it was doubted whether he would ever play his trombone again. The recovery was slow, but by the end of the year both had returned to the ministry. Then in 1966, in another automobile accident, their only son, Dick, who with his wife and children was serving as a missionary

Clarence Jones, founder of HCJB, and his wife Katherine.

in Panama, was killed. In both instances, Jones went back to the work with even greater zeal for radio evangelism.

In 1981, with Jones living in retirement in Florida, HCJB celebrated its fiftieth anniversary. But in the half century since its founding, the World Radio Missionary Fellowship had become far more than a mere radio station. Today it operates two hospitals, mobile clinics, a printing press, and color television programs—all in addition to its twenty-four-hour-a-day radio station in Quito (broadcasting in fifteen languages) and two sister stations in Panama and Texas.

John Broger and the Far East Broadcasting Company

When R. G. LeTourneau had first met with Clarence Jones and offered him financial assistance, he strongly urged him to expand his ministry to include a station in the Philippines to reach the unevangelized millions in the Orient and Pacific Islands. But Jones declined the challenge, realizing that his ministry in South America was responsibility enough. This deep concern for reaching the Far East by radio was shared by others besides LeTourneau, but World War II shattered any dreams of undertaking such a project expeditiously. With the close of the war, however, the latent vision of three men to bring gospel radio to the Far East came to fruition. John Broger, a young United States military officer serving in the 38th Task Force Fleet in the Pacific, came home more impassioned than ever for missionary radio; and his two friends, Robert Bowman, a Los Angeles Christian radio personality, and William Roberts, a Los Angeles

377

pastor who had his own daily radio program, eagerly agreed to join him in the venture.

After weeks of intense planning and prayer, the three men decided to pool their financial resources, a total of one thousand dollars, and form a non-profit corporation. The paperwork was completed in December of 1946; and all that was left to do was to raise one hundred thousand dollars. During the first three months of publicizing their venture, some ten thousand dollars was donated, and with that encouraging beginning, it was decided that Broger should return to the Far East to lay the groundwork for their proposed ministry.

Broger's first stop in the Orient was Shanghai, a key location in his view for a transmitter that would not only reach into China but also north to Korea, across the China Sea to Japan, and south into Indo-China and the island nations. But after weeks of negotiations, Broger's hopes for obtaining a franchise from the disheveled Nationalist government dimmed. He was sent from one office to another, but no one would give him a certified franchise. The most he could obtain was a verbal commitment to consider a 500-watt station. Disappointing as the negotiations were, Broger, with the help of Chinese Christians, went ahead with his broadcasting plans and applied to the government for a franchise.

After six months of making no significant headway with Chinese officials, however, Broger sailed to Manila in the Philippines to explore the possibilities of a radio station there. Here he found the government officials far more cooperative, but there were other obstacles. Postwar inflation had skyrocketed land prices, and living costs were astronomical. To make matters worse, fund raising was progressing slowly back home, and the money that was coming in was being used to purchase and build equipment. It was a discouraging situation, but Broger resolutely continued negotiations with the government and applied for a franchise.

The application was at first denied because Broger failed to answer such vital questions as how the station would be financed, where it would be located, and how much power would be needed; but during a later interview Broger was able to explain to the officials the mission policy of depending on God for finances, and that such questions could not be answered until God provided, a response that dismayed but also seemed to impress the officials. As to power, Broger hesitantly requested ten thousand watts (twenty times what he would have been able to secure in Shanghai); but to his surprise, when the approved application was returned, that amount had been crossed out and above it was written in "Unlimited Power."

Finding property was a more difficult matter. There was nothing suitably priced under forty thousand dollars, and Broger knew his colleagues at home could never raise that much money. For weeks he checked out every lead, but nothing suitable was even close to a price range the mission could afford. "Then," wrote Broger to the home office, "God began to work." Two Christian businessmen in Manila offered him a 12½-acre plot in an ideal location, valued at fifty thousand dollars, for twenty thousand, and Broger gave them his last fifty dollars to bind the option. He then came home to raise money for the newly organized Far East Broadcasting Company before returning with staff and equipment.

Although Manila had been a disappointing second choice for the location of the first missionary radio station in the Orient, it proved to be a good choice—infinitely better than Shanghai would have been. Broger, along with most political analysts, had underestimated the strength of Mao Tse-tung's guerrilla forces. Had a franchise been granted by the Nationalist government and had Broger located the station in Shanghai, its effectiveness for spreading the gospel would have been short-lived, and by 1950 its transmitter would have been broadcasting communist propaganda.

Construction of the first FEBC transmitter began in the late fall of 1946 in an effort to meet a government-imposed deadline to begin broadcasting eighteen months later in April of 1948. The work, which involved clearing land, drilling a well, and constructing buildings, was complicated enough, but an even greater obstacle to meeting the deadline was obtaining the hard to get and very costly materials. Back in the United States, Broger and other staff members were frantically raising funds and making ready the tons of material that had to be shipped to Manila in time for the deadline. There was one delay after another, and time was running out; but finally in February of 1948, just seven weeks before the deadline, nine staff members, their families, and fifty-two cubic tons of material sailed out of San Francisco Harbor en route to Manila.

By the time Broger and company reached Manila, it was evident that the April deadline could not be met. A seven-week extension was granted, but more problems resulted in further delays and even that deadline seemed impossible to meet. Government officials refused to consider a further extension. Then, three days before the extended deadline, unexpected problems developed with the transmitter, and precious time was expended, leaving no time for the scheduled testing. On the deadline date, with high voltage wires strewn everywhere and men working in ankle deep water due to heavy rains, it was a life and death race against the clock. Broger rushed downtown to the government office building to make one last plea for an extension, but to no avail.

It was a desperate situation, as Gleason Ledyard relates: "Racing through back streets and barely missing pull-carts in the roads, Broger burned up every piece of road he could between traffic jams. Finally, just before 6:00 p.m. he raced up the road ... and came to a sliding stop in front of the transmitter building." "We'll test on the air," he shouted as he grabbed his program notes, and then "as the entire staff began singing the great hymn, 'All Hail the Power of Jesus' Name, Let Angels Prostrate Fall,' John gave the nod to Dick to throw the switch and the first of the Far East Broadcasting Company's transmitters hummed with power as it went on the air at 6:00 P.M., June 4, 1948, releasing the words of this majestic hymn to the waiting airways of the Orient."[12]

Although the early broadcasts sometimes did not even reach out to all of Manila due to a poor antenna system, there were almost immediate results from all the sacrifice that had been made. A non-Christian barber kept his radio tuned to the new station, and one of his customers, a professing atheist, was converted; and not long afterward the barber and several other customers were converted through his witness. In another instance a man who had stolen a radio was converted through the Christian programing, and as a result he returned to the owners the radio and many other items he had taken.

Excited as the missionaries were with the news of such spiritual victories, they were dissatisfied with the station's output. A larger transmitter and a tower to replace their makeshift telephone pole seemed to be financially out of the question. Word of the need spread, however, and a call came in to FEBC from a commercial broadcasting company offering to sell a three-hundred foot tower that had been purchased from war surplus. Though a comparable tower would have cost $25,000, Bowman, who was in charge in Manila at the time, embarrassingly offered all that was in the FEBC account—three hundred dollars—and the following day to his great delight the offer was accepted.

The efficiency of FEBC was largely due to the willingness of skilled technicians to volunteer their time, whether for short-term or life-term service. A much needed 6,000-watt transmitter was built on location in Manila by such dedicated men. But there were women as well who made invaluable contributions to the ministry of FEBC. Gilberta Walton, an engineer with years of broadcasting experience, served faithfully as the director of FEBC programing; and Janie Reames, a well-qualified pilot, flew her Piper Cub into remote areas, delivering receivers (nicknamed PMs for "portable missionaries") and encouraging the recipients to form listening clubs.

As station DZAS in Manila grew and as other FEBC stations were built in Okinawa and other areas of the Far East, letters began to pour in that indicated the wide listening audience FEBC had acquired. Many people who wrote expressed interest in "The Bible School of the Air," and within two years after that ministry was begun, more than twelve thousand courses had been requested. But the growing popularity of FEBC created problems. The communist governments of both Russia and China began jamming the broadcasts in order to prevent their citizens from listening. So frustrating was this jamming, especially by the Russians, that FEBC officials made the decision to drop their Russian broadcasts in favor of more broadcasts to China, where the jamming was not so effective. But the plans were dismissed when an FEBC missionary met a Russian emigrant who told of his appreciation for the broadcasts that he had heard in Russia at a friend's home: "We have been listening to you for years. You have been the only contact we have had with Christians on the outside. . . . We would go to his home in the middle of the night—two or three at a time—lest we be suspected, sit on the floor, cover our heads with a blanket, divide a set of headphones so that several could listen at one time. . . . That jamming almost drove us crazy, but you know, it was worth it all if we could hear just one word, the Name of Jesus or just one verse of Scripture."[13]

After fourteen years of service, John Broger left the ministry of FEBC on a request from the Chairman of the Joint

Chiefs of Staff that he return to military service as a consultant. With his departure, Robert Bowman became the president, and under his leadership FEBC has greatly expanded. By 1970 FEBC had twenty-one stations ranging from 1,000 to 250,000 watts, broadcasting nearly fourteen hundred program hours each week in more than forty languages. Since then more giant short-wave and medium-wave transmitters have been installed in key locations, including one in San Francisco that beams into Latin America, one on Iba in the Philippines, and one in South Korea. Yet today China and the Soviet Union remain key targeted areas; and since 1979, when China relaxed its barriers with the West, more than 10,000 letters came in during one twelve-month period from China alone—mainly from non-Christians interested in learning more about the gospel message.

Paul Freed and Trans World Radio

Of all the missionary broadcasting organizations, the largest and most geographically diverse is Trans World Radio. Founded in 1954, TWR today broadcasts over some five million watts of power with the potential of reaching eighty percent of the world's population. From Monte Carlo, Bonaire, Swaziland, Cyprus, Sri Lanka, and Guam, its giant transmitters beam out Christian programs in more than eighty different languages and dialects. How such a powerful force for evangelism originated and developed over the past decades is an exciting story of the trials and triumphs of a dedicated father-son team, Ralph and Paul Freed.

Paul Freed, the founder of TWR,

grew up in the Middle East as the son of missionaries. His father, Ralph, had been a business manager moving up in his company when he felt God's call to missions; and after studying at Nyack Missionary Training Institute he was sent with his family to Palestine to serve under the Christian and Missionary Alliance. Paul's formative years on the mission field were happy ones, though he, like many missionary children, found separation from his parents particularly painful. When he was eleven he was sent away for his schooling, which meant living with two young single women missionaries who were utterly unqualified and unprepared to handle a rebellious, homesick boy and were as unhappy as Paul was with the situation. After a time Paul returned to live with his parents, but the following year he was again sent away—this time to live with a family at a mission house outside Jerusalem where other children were also being educated. Again homesickness was overwhelming, and at the age of thirteen Paul became so desperate that one night after everyone was asleep he wrote a note explaining what he was doing and then slipped out of the house and started for home: "After cabling my father to ask him to meet me in Tiberias, Galilee, I found a public car headed north. All the way up I wondered what his reaction would be, but my heart flipped with joy when I saw his beloved face in the crowd as we pulled into the center of Tiberias."[14] Though Paul was scolded for what he had done, he was allowed to stay home with his parents on the condition that he would work hard on his studies. That was incentive enough, and during the year that followed he completed his freshman year of high school on his own and was ready to enter the sophomore class at Wheaton Academy the following year when his parents returned to the United States for furlough.

Paul's remaining two years of high school were taken in Beirut, Lebanon, and after that he returned to the United States to attend Wheaton College, where he graduated with an anthropology major. From Wheaton he went to Nyack Missionary College. Here he sat under the ministry of great preachers and missionaries, including Clarence Jones, founder of HCJB in Quito, Ecuador.

Following his training at Nyack, Paul began working with Youth for Christ under Torrey Johnson, and it was through this ministry while in Europe to attend a YFC conference that he visited Spain and became burdened for missionary work in that country. Spain had been almost entirely neglected by evangelical missions, and the task of righting that wrong seemed overwhelming. Although Paul had no experience in radio, it was that media which to him appeared to be the only hope of reaching Spain with the gospel. After returning from Europe, he left his ministry with YFC and began traveling as an evangelist, presenting the needs of Spain, but the churches he visited were unresponsive.

In 1951, Paul and his wife, Betty Jane, and another friend traveled to Spain to investigate the possibility of establishing a radio station. Although Paul had not considered any location other than Spain itself, it soon became evident that Tangier in North Africa, twenty-six miles from Spain across the Straits of Gibralter, would be the most suitable spot. There they were able to purchase, for a fraction of its value, an abandoned mission school that would serve as an ideal location for a radio station.

The Freeds returned to the United States, excited about their new venture and determined to awaken Christians to the need. To do this they produced a full-color motion picture, *Banderilla*, that dramatically presented Spanish people as they were, without an effective evangelical witness. Then with no income or pledged support, Paul and Betty Jane with their two small children began a grueling eleven-thousand-mile deputation tour across the United States and Canada, laying the groundwork for their future ministry. Although the experience was rewarding in many ways, the tiring schedule and the criticism they encountered drained their energy: "Many times we were tempted to give up. It was such a struggle ... almost more than we could stand ... just at the point where we felt strong and sure, we would be bulldozed by an avalanche of criticism."[15] The criticism came from all angles. The fact that their proposed ministry was not clearly defined and that it was not associated with an established mission disturbed some people. Others ridiculed Paul's lack of radio know-how, and still others believed there were enough missionary radio stations without starting another.

Despite the criticism and discouragement, Paul moved forward in his plans, and in February of 1952, TWR was officially founded. The following year he left for Tangier to begin building the station, financed not by enthusiastic prayer warriors, but by the sale of his own home and automobile. In Tangier he worked out an arrangement with another broadcaster to lease transmitters and antennas and broadcast under his permit. With that matter settled the next step was to secure a station director—"the best possible man." Who else but his own father, a veteran missionary who at the time was teaching at Western Canadian Bible Institute. But when he phoned his father he learned that just three days earlier he had accepted the presidency of the school. Paul was devastated. "I did not know what to say. I could not offer him anything that remotely resembled the financial security or prestige of this fine school."[16] Nevertheless, a few days later Paul received a call from his father accepting the challenge.

Although Paul had been praying that his father would come to that decision, he was overwhelmed by the sacrifice: "Father was then sixty-one, a veteran missionary who had completed a far-reaching ministry in the Middle East. God had called him and anointed him and used him. Now he was back in America, with the honor of being named president of a Bible school. It seemed exactly right, a fitting climax to his strenuous life on the mission field. But he was throwing it all out, starting all over again to help me in the brand new venture."[17]

In January of 1954, Ralph and Mildred Freed sailed for Tangier to begin their second career as missionaries, this time not supported financially by the Christian and Missionary Alliance, but going out strictly on faith in God and in their son's fund-raising ability. Starting out on a 2500-watt war surplus transmitter, Ralph soon had TWR on the air; but back in the United States progress was much slower. Paul was hitchhiking around the country, speaking wherever he could gain a hearing, but money came in slowly. Unpaid bills were piling up, creating an intolerable situation for Ralph and Mildred. "The pressure became so critical," according to Paul, "that Father took things in his own hands. A cable reached me one morning in Greensboro, just three months after Mother and Father had sailed into Tangier, 'Paul, if we don't get some real encouragement, some real help this week, I've made arrangements to give up the broadcasting business and come back.' "[18]

It was a heartbreaking message. If his parents left at this time, he would have to scuttle the whole operation. Without them at such a critical time it would be impossible to carry on. Then, on Saturday, the end of the week that his father had cabled, Paul received a visit from a pastor who knew his parents, and during that visit the pastor revealed that his church was planning to take on his parents' support. It was glorious news, and it came just in time to prevent the dismantling of the infant TWR.

That pledge of support was the turning point for TWR. More money began coming in, and individuals and churches in both the United States and Europe began to show greater interest. In 1959, after five years of broadcasting, the staff in Tangier had grown from two to twenty-five workers and "The Voice of Tangier" was being heard all over Europe, in North Africa, the Middle East, and behind the Iron Curtain. But at this very time another crisis was brewing. Almost without warning Morocco became independent and with that political change, the government announced that all of the radio stations in the country would be nationalized by the end of

1959. "It seemed black as midnight," Paul later recalled. "Father read the notification from the government to the Wednesday afternoon prayer group. It was a tremendous blow."[19]

But as crushing as the news was, the new policy did not catch the Freeds entirely without other options. In 1957 they had visited Monaco to investigate what seemed like a remote possibility of relocating there in Monte Carlo. Although they found the costs to be much greater, there were many advantages to being located on the European continent, and there was a greater opportunity to expand their broadcasting power. So in the spring of 1959 Paul and his father began seriously negotiating with officials in Monte Carlo, and in 1960, after being off the air for nine months, TWR was once again broadcasting—this time powered by ten thousand watts.

The transition from Tangier to Monte Carlo, however, was not all smooth sailing. The financial demands of the new arrangement were mind-boggling to the Freeds, who had only gradually been increasing their initial $10,000 annual budget. But the new facilities and transmitter required huge sums of money, including a half-million-dollar down payment to be paid in six $83,000 installments over the first year—a feat that, in Paul's mind, would require nothing short of a series of six miracles; and that is essentially what happened.

The first installment, needed immediately, was unexpectedly underwritten by a group of Norwegian businessmen. The second installment, according to Paul, "seemed even more impossible than the initial payment." On the day of the deadline the mission was still $13,000 short. That morning a $5,000 check came into the office, but nothing more. Paul left for the bank, $8,000 short, flinching at the thought of the heavy penalty imposed for missing a payment. Before arriving at the bank, he met a worker who had just picked up an unexpected mail delivery from the post office. In it was $5,000. Still $3,000 short, Paul went into the bank president's office; and while sitting there trying to figure out how to meet the payment, a telegram came in, wiring funds of $3,000 to the TWR account.

The third installment was another miracle story. Again on the deadline day funds were short, this time only $1,500, but the mail had all been opened and there was no more money. Much of the money had been contributed by believers in Germany, however, and a final check of the price of currency on the world money market showed a jump in the value of the German mark, bringing the total exactly $1,500 higher than it had been on the previous day when the amount had been calculated. The deadlines for the final three payments were also tension-filled times, but in each case the payments were made without penalty.

In October of 1960, thirteen months after the contract was signed with officials in Monaco, TWR in Monte Carlo was on the air. During the first year alone, some eighteen thousand letters came in from listeners, many requesting spiritual counsel. Others sent in financial contributions, and by 1965 half of TWR's support was coming from Europeans themselves.

Broadcasting into Europe and throughout the Mediterranean area required programing in as many as twenty-four different languages. That did not mean that specialists in that many languages were on staff on Monte Carlo. In order to have variety in programing, TWR produced programs in the country where they were being aired, so that various Christian leaders would have the opportunity of presenting the gospel to their own people.

To effectively produce this type of programing, competent directors were needed in each country, and TWR was fortunate to acquire such men as Horst Marquardt, who directed the German branch of the work. Following World War II, Marquardt found himself living in the Soviet dominated East Germany. An avid student of Marxism, he joined the Communist Party and later joined the staff of the East Berlin Radio Station, where he developed Communist propaganda and youth programs. After a time, though, he became disillusioned with Communism and began studying the Bible and was converted. In 1960, after becoming acquainted with Ralph Freed, he joined TWR, heading up the German work.

Dedicated and talented staff members, financial miracles, and hundreds of letters pouring into the headquarters each month all spelled success for Paul Freed and the radio station he had worked so hard for, but the physical and mental strain of the ministry took its toll, and in 1961 at the age of forty-two (after having to end a competitive tennis match because of darkness when the third set remained tied after twenty-two games), he suffered a heart attack. For one month he was flat on his back in the hospital, but even then he was planning a larger and more effective outreach for TWR.

In 1962, after several months of rest, Paul visited Puerto Rico to investigate

Paul Freed, founder of Trans World Radio.

the possibility of establishing a sister station in the Caribbean. Experts in Europe had advised him that a supplementary station was needed, preferably in the Caribbean, if TWR was to reach its target areas more effectively. In Puerto Rico Paul found that government regulations limited broadcasts to two frequencies at a time—a restriction for international radio that, in his words, "would be somewhat like having both hands and feet tied for a cross country race."

After his visit to Puerto Rico, Paul contacted Dutch officials about the possibility of building a station in the Netherlands Antilles. The officials were so enthusiastic about the project that Paul again visited the Caribbean, and within two weeks after arriving he was given permission to set up a super-power, 500,000-watt station. "Never before in the history of broadcasting," wrote Paul, "has a private

MONTE CARLO
TRANSMITTER, STUDIO

CYPRUS
TRANSMITTER

BONAIRE
TRANSMITTER,
STUDIO

SRI LANKA
TRANSMITTER,
STUDIO

GUAM
TRANSMITTER

SWAZILAND
TRANSMITTER, STUDIO

0   1000   2000 mi
0   3000 km

TRANSMITTING TOWERS OF TRANS WORLD RADIO

group of any kind been granted such a permit. It would enable us to reach multiplied thousands in the interior of many countries, thousands who would never ever hear otherwise."[20]

Bonaire, a 112-square mile island of coral rock, was chosen as the site for the new station. It was an ideal location, according to Paul: "... we discovered technically there could not be a better spot anywhere in the world—Bonaire is predominantly salt flats, with salt water on all sides, providing unbelievable conductivity, wet salt being the next best conductor to metal."[21] Another important plus for locating in Bonaire was the friendly reception by government officials who gave TWR two valuable parcels of land and agreed to pave roads, clear land, and install telephone lines free of charge. By the summer of 1964 much of the construction work was completed and TWR began broadcasting from the western hemisphere.

In the years since broadcasting began on Bonaire, four more radio stations have been added to the global ministries of TWR, and the mission staff has increased to more than four hundred. Paul's initial burden to reach Spain with the gospel has expanded into a burden to reach the whole world.

Peter Deyneka and the Slavic Gospel Association

For any radio station, programing is the lifeblood, for without effective programs, high powered antennas are of little value. The task of producing quality programs, however, is enormous, especially for mission organizations like the World Radio Missionary Fellowship, the Far East Broadcasting Company, and Trans World Radio that broadcast in dozens of languages. For that reason, most such missions depend heavily on individuals and other missions for help in programing. One such individual and mission are Peter Deyneka and the Slavic Gospel Association. Though it has no radio station of its own, the SGA views radio as a top priority and as such produces programs to be aired over missionary radio stations all over the world. Peter Deyneka, the mission's founder, has depended heavily on radio to reach his own people behind the Iron Curtain.

Peter Deyneka was sixteen years old and all alone when he stepped off the train at the Chicago Union Station in the spring of 1914 to begin his life in America. Like many Russian youths, he had emigrated to the new world for one purpose—to earn enough money to lift his family out of debt. Thus, securing employment was his first priority.

Although Peter had been brought up to reverence the Czar and the Russian Orthodox Church, in Chicago he met fellow-Russian workers who despised the Czarist land policies and who professed atheism as their philosophy. Peter began attending the Communist-inspired IWW (International Workers of the World) meetings, and soon he too was professing atheism. It was in this context that he came in contact with evangelical Christianity, first at a street meeting, later at a Billy Sunday campaign, and finally at Moody Memorial Church, where he was converted under the ministry of Paul Rader.

Following his conversion, Peter became active in Moody Memorial Church and then went on to St. Paul Bible Institute to train for Christian service, all the while exercising his gift for evangelism. After graduation, Peter worked among Russian and European immigrants in the Dakotas and Montana, though longing to return to minister to his family back in Russia. In the years following the Russian Revolution, from 1918 to 1922, Peter had not received any letters from his family but had heard much about the devastating famine that was ravishing the countryside and the cities alike. The first news from his family came when he was back in Chicago working with Paul Rader. Three brothers and two sisters had died of starvation and related diseases. The news was almost unbearable, and Peter was consumed with the urgency of reaching the remaining family members with the gospel before they, too, perished. Though he shared his faith in letters and tracts, he longed to visit, and in 1925 that opportunity came through the financial support of friends.

Peter's arrival in the little village where he had been born and raised was greeted with more sorrow than joy. His mother welcomed him in tears, telling him that his father had died only five weeks earlier, never giving up hope that he would once again be reunited with his son. The news only increased Peter's burden for his mother and brother, but they were disturbed by the change in him and were ashamed of his eagerness to evangelize neighbors and anyone else who would listen.

Peter spent the next several months in his homeland preaching to the Russian people, whom he found to be hungry for the Word of God. On one occasion when he ended a two-hour sermon, the people complained that they had come too far for such a short message. Everywhere he went people were pleading for Bibles, offering grain and in some cases cattle in exchange for a Bible. Peter was overcome by the spiritual hunger, and when he returned to the United States he brought with him a Russian evangelist and together they visited churches, raising money for Bibles for Russia.

At the very time Peter was traveling through the United States presenting the needs of the Russian people, the gospel was making great headway in his homeland. As he later observed, "The wonderful progress of the gospel in my country during the years of 1924 to 1930 amounted to a national gospel reformation. All classes of Russian people, including the clergy—all nationalities, tribes and occupations —were caught up in the sweeping revival. This was an answer to prayer—a miracle during a time after the Revolution when atheism officially controlled the government."[22] But the political atmosphere in Russia was rapidly changing, and Peter's visit there in 1930 was the last opportunity he had to freely travel and preach to his own people.

Back in the United States, Peter once again became associated with Paul Rader, this time as secretary of the Russian work for Rader's World-Wide Christian Couriers (an organization that promoted neighborhood Bible classes for the purpose of evangelism). It was an important period in Peter's life. Rader's enthusiasm for radio rubbed off on him even as it had on Clarence Jones some years earlier; and Peter, through his work with the WWCC, was seeing the need for an organization specifically aimed at evangelizing the people behind the Iron Curtain.

In 1933 Peter, whose concern for Eastern Europe had already become widely known, was invited by evangelical leaders to tour that area of the world. It was after returning from a second such tour in 1934 that he, with a group of like-minded supporters,

formed the Slavic Gospel Association—and so began a world-wide ministry to the Slavic peoples, not only in Eastern Europe but also in such countries as Argentina and Uruguay where large numbers of Eastern Europeans had immigrated. Because of the political barriers preventing the majority of Slavic peoples from freely hearing the gospel, radio soon emerged as a prime avenue for evangelism. Peter had been gratified by the response from his first radio message to the Russian people beamed by shortwave for HCJB in Quito, Ecuador, in 1941. Clarence Jones had personally arranged that historic broadcast, and from that time on the Slavic Gospel Association was inveterately tied to radio. In 1953, Peter's oldest daughter, Ruth, and her husband joined the ministry of HCJB full-time, ministering to the Russian people.

As the SGA grew, so did its involvement in radio programing, and as soon as Paul Freed had established his station in Tangier, Peter arranged for still more programing into Slavic countries. The Far East Broadcasting Company and other Christian stations were also utilized, and by the 1960s some six hundred SGA broadcasts a month were being beamed into Russia alone, including Bible Institute of the Air (later Seminary of the Air), that helped make up for the absence of Bible schools and seminaries in that country.

Although Peter Deyneka and the SGA carry on wide-ranging activities, radio has been one of their most fruitful and rewarding ministries. When Peter was able to travel in Russia he encountered hundreds of people who could not thank him enough for the programs. One lay pastor apologized

Joy Ridderhof and Gospel Recordings

Peter Deyneka, founder of the Slavic Gospel Association, with his wife.

to him for copying down the sermon outlines for his own messages because he had no other Bible study aids. Another young Russian named Boris, who worked as a radio repairman, had never known a Christian or heard the gospel until he picked up a SGA broadcast while he was repairing a radio. He began to listen regularly and was converted; and today, after three years of listening to Seminary of the Air, he has become a lay pastor.

By 1980, SGA, directed by Peter Deyneka, Jr., had more than fifty Russian radio missionaries preaching the gospel from nine stations, all in an effort to reach the Soviet people who, though lacking Bibles, study aids, and evangelical ministers, have access to some forty million shortwave radio sets. How many people, afraid of political repercussions, are secretly listening will never be known, but the opportunity to hear the gospel is available to all who want it.

As important as radio has been in world evangelism, the media has certain obvious limitations. For one thing, radio cannot reach remote tribes whose language has never been learned by a Christian able to deliver a broadcast, and even if the language were known, it would not be worth the cost to develop programing for small, isolated tribes. But if radio is impractical in reaching such people, what type of media could reach these unreached peoples? Bible translators and missionary evangelists, though limited in numbers, have done their best; but just learning the language is a slow tedious process, and then breaking it down into written form and teaching the tribal people to read involves many more years. So how could the world's most obscure tribes be given the opportunity to hear the gospel? The thought of accomplishing such a task would have been beyond comprehension if it had come all at once; but for Joy Ridderhof, who brought such a seeming impossibility to fruition, the concept developed in progressive stages. Her initial idea of using records for evangelism was for the purpose of reaching only one little tribe in Honduras—not the whole world.

It was in the early 1930s that Joy left the United States to serve as a single missionary in Honduras with the Friends Mission. Life was lonely as the only missionary in the remote mountain village that she had been assigned to, but there were occasional rewards. Here and there as she carried the gospel out to the scattered mountain dwellings, people responded and turned to Christ. But the rigors of the ministry and the tropical climate took its toll on her health, and after six years on the field she returned home to Los Angeles, severely weakened by malaria.

During the long months that followed, while Joy lay in her attic bedroom recuperating, she thought of the people she had left behind, wondering how they were progressing in their Christian faith with no missionary to guide and encourage them. "If only I could have left my voice behind," she thought over and over again to herself. Then she thought of the noisy crowded bars back in Honduras and the records that were always blaring in the background. Everyone in Honduras, it seemed, loved recorded music. That was the answer. She would send her voice back to Honduras on records, bringing the gospel through music and the spoken word.

At first Joy's idea of gospel records seemed like a far-off dream, but she began praying about such a possibility and sharing it with friends; and in 1939 her first three-and-a-half-minute record *Buenas Neuvas* (Good News) was produced. While recuperating, Joy had learned to play the guitar, and music became a part of her very first records. Soon, however, she realized the importance of finding native voices to deliver the prepared messages and the music.

As word of Joy's recordings spread, missionaries in other parts of Latin America began requesting them, and the work quickly expanded. Ann Sherwood, a college friend, joined Joy in the ministry; and when Joy's attic bedroom became overcrowded, the work was moved to larger accommodations—a stable with a dirt floor that Joy and her friends remodeled. As more requests poured in for record-

ings, volunteer workers increased; one, Herman Dyk, an experienced electronics technician, came unannounced all the way from Montana to work full-time.

The early recordings that Joy produced were taped in Los Angeles. Chinese, Mexicans, and members of various Indian tribes came to the studio to record messages in their native tongue, but Joy realized that the ministry would be limited if the speakers had to travel to Los Angeles. The solution was to go to the people themselves—a decision that marked a turning point in Gospel Recordings (incorporated originally in 1941 as Spanish Recordings). Joy and Ann made the first recording trip in 1944, spending ten months in Mexico and Central America traveling in a station wagon that had been donated to the ministry. It was a fruitful journey, one that gave them messages in thirty-five new languages and dialects.

The next trip that Joy and Ann made was in 1947 to Alaska to record messages from Indians and Eskimos. Like their trip to Latin America, their work was difficult, traveling to remote tribes and then finding a bilingual tribesman who was willing to deliver on tape the prepared message. But the months of toil were worth the effort, and Joy and Ann returned to Los Angeles with recordings in nearly twenty more tongues.

It was while they were in Alaska that Joy and Ann had been told of the tremendous need for such work in the Philippines, and thus that area of the world became their next destination. Although Joy and Ann spent less than a year in the Philippines, they recorded ninety-two languages and dialects, depending heavily on resident missionaries for help. Sometimes the process simply involved locating a missionary and a bilingual tribesman and then recording the message, but other times it was far more complicated. On occasion they trekked deep into the interior, recording languages that were entirely unknown to missionaries. To record the Palanan Negrito language, for example, they had to go through three individuals. Mrs. Maggay, a Filipino woman who understood English and was fluent in the Ibanog language, slowly recited the message to an Ibanog man who understood but could not speak Palanan Negrito, and he in turn recited the message to a Negrito man who understood Ibanog well enough to repeat the message on tape in Palanan Negrito, a process that took hours. Later the tape had to be spliced one hundred and fifty times for editing, but the message was there in a language that had never before been used to spread the gospel.

The message was simple, but, according to Phyllis Thompson, it contained the basic tenets of the gospel: "It told of the Son of the Chief of Sky, who came to earth to die on a tree tied crosswise, to bear the punishment of the sins of all people on earth, to save them from the wicked village down below, place of fire. It told that whoever believed in Yesu, Son of Chief of Sky, would himself become a child of Chief of Sky, and when death came would enter immediately into the good village above, everything pretty and happy there. It told of the Holy Spirit ... Who would come to dwell in the heart of the one who believed in Yesu."[23] Though limited by brevity and cultural barriers, Joy truly believed such a message could change lives.

By 1950, Joy and her colleagues had some three hundred and fifty languages and dialects on tape, and the recording aspect of the ministry was moving forward at a steady pace. But there were other problems—particularly relating to the use of the records in remote jungle areas. The gramophones that were available and that Gospel Recordings distributed were vulnerable to breakdowns. Much of the time the records lay idle because the "talking box" refused to talk. Joy appealed to her fellow workers and supporters to "pray until God helps ... to work out a hand-turned gramophone—cheap and motorless, one that can be operated by anyone, and that has no mechanical feature that can get out of fix."[24]

Though Joy's prayers were not immediately answered, word spread of the need, and after experimenting with various types of record players, Cardtalk, a continuous-wind cardboard player, was developed, and later small cassette tape recorders were used. The most recent innovation is the Grip, a simple cassette playback that operates without batteries.

In the early 1950s, Joy and Ann, accompanied this time by Sanna Barlow, set out on their fourth recording trip, heading for Australia, Indonesia, New Guinea, and other islands of the Pacific. In Australia they met J. Stuart Mill, who was so enthusiastic about their work that he joined the effort full-time and established an Australian branch of Gospel Recordings. After visiting tribes and taping messages in the South Pacific, Joy and her two colleagues went to Asia and on to Africa, and after five years of arduous travel they returned to Los Angeles via London, where another branch of

Gospel Recordings had been established. Back in Los Angeles they toured the new headquarters that had been secured while they were gone. Work had continued nonstop while they were away, and by 1955 over a million records had been sent out to more than a hundred different countries.

But Joy's work involved far more than statistics ranging in the millions. The ministry of Gospel Recordings resulted in the salvation of individuals and whole tribes all over the world. A man in Mexico was converted after hearing the records, and he in turn led dozens more to Christ, and elsewhere the results were equally heartwarming, as Phyllis Thompson relates: "About three hundred people in one area in India were converted, mainly through gramophone evangelism. Missionaries visiting Angola reported having met people who had been brought to the Lord through the rec-ords. An illiterate Brazilian Christian took Gospel records and went where no missionary had ever been. Five souls were won to Christ there. A man in the Philippines travelled for twelve hours to hear more about the Lord Jesus, of whom he had heard from 'a big box that talked.' Tribespeople sat through the night listening to the records that spoke their own language. Day after day letters were being received asking for more records because 'they are reaching those who might otherwise never hear.'"[25]

Today, after forty years of continuous and fruitful service with Gospel Recordings, Joy no longer serves as the director, but she continues to serve on the board and actively represent the mission. There are now fifty full-time staff members in addition to the many volunteers, and gospel messages from nearly four thousand languages and dialects have been taped for distribution.

SELECTED BIBLIOGRAPHY

Cook, Frank S. Seeds in the Wind: The Story of the Voice of the Andes, Radio Station HCJB, Quito, Ecuador. Opa Locka, Florida: World Radio Missionary Fellowship, 1976.

Freed, Paul E. Towers to Eternity. Nashville: Sceptre, 1979.

Ledyard, Gleason H. Sky Waves: The Incredible Far East Broadcasting Company Story. Chicago: Moody, 1968.

Neely, Lois. Come Up to This Mountain: The Miracle of Clarence W. Jones & HCJB. Wheaton: Tyndale, 1980.

Rohrer, Norman B. and Deyneka, Peter, Jr. Peter Dynamite: The Story of Peter Deyneka—Missionary to the Russian World. Grand Rapids: Baker, 1975.

Siedell, Barry. Gospel Radio: A 20th-Century Tool for a 20th-Century Challenge. Lincoln, Nebraska: Good News Broadcasting, 1971.

Thompson, Phyllis. Count It All Joy: The Story of Joy Ridderhof & Gospel Recordings. Wheaton: Shaw, 1978.

———. Faith by Hearing: The Story of Gospel Recordings. Kowloon, Hongkong: Rainbow, 1960.

Chapter 15

Missionary Aviation: Flying Over Jungles

Seventeen days in a dugout canoe, besieged by swarms of mosquitoes, traversing steamy jungle-lined rivers infested by poisonous snakes and alligators. Such was the travel of the jungle missionary—a twentieth-century professionally trained evangelist, severely impeded by primitive transportation. It is no wonder that the introduction of aircraft to supplement missionary work was considered a godsend to those whose lives it changed.

Prior to World War II there were a number of mission and privately owned aircraft operated by pilots with varying degrees of experience and each with a story of his own. One of the most intriguing is that of Walter Herron, an Australian missionary, who went to Bolivia in 1933 to work among the Indians. In 1938 he married, but it was a short-lived union. The following year his wife died while giving birth to their first child, Robert, who barely survived the five-day trek out of the jungle. Ironically, during that trip, Herron spotted a plane—the only one

in Bolivia—flying overhead, and at that moment he was struck by the thought that such transportation might have saved his wife.

Herron returned to Australia with hopes of developing an aviation service for himself and other missionaries in Bolivia, but soon after beginning flight lessons he was told he would never make a pilot. The final blow came when his mission board flatly rejected his proposal. But he was unable to let the matter rest. He traveled to the United States, where he enrolled in further flight training and purchased a plane. Then, in 1941 he was back in Bolivia ready to begin his jungle aviation ministry with only fifty-one hours of flying time.

For more than two decades Herron continued his aviation ministry, and in 1961 his son Robert joined him. But then in 1964, tragedy struck. On a routine flight his plane crashed over Bolivia, killing Walter and three passengers.

Herron's early experience in jungle aviation was the exception to the rule.

393

The vast majority of missionaries had no access to services such as he provided. It was not until the close of World War II that missionary aviation came into its own—not so much as a sideline, but as a specialty. The high cost of owning and operating aircraft and the expertise needed in flying over rugged terrain had convinced many mission leaders that air transportation should be left to specialists who could service large numbers of missionaries in a given area.

It was this need that led to the founding in California in 1944 of the first missionary aviation service organization, the Christian Airmen's Missionary Fellowship, later renamed Mission Aviation Fellowship. A separate but closely related aviation program was begun in Great Britain, and a few years later an Australian MAF was founded. Headed by Christian airmen who had served in the military, these organizations were dedicated to bringing the latest techniques and the best training into the field of missionary aviation; and by the 1950s, MAF was becoming recognized as an indispensable missionary service organization. Today MAF has twelve different national organizations located in key areas throughout the world. The one hundred and twenty aircraft in use are flown some thirty million seat miles each year, serving dozens of mission societies in twenty-two countries.

As important a role as MAF has played on the mission field, early on it became apparent that MAF simply could not meet the high demand for its services. Consequently, other aviation organizations were formed, the largest and most geographically dispersed being JAARS (Jungle Aviation and Radio Service), an arm of Wycliffe Bible Translators and Summer Institute of Linguistics. Other mission societies followed suit, and today New Tribes Mission, the Sudan Interior Mission, the Africa Inland Mission, and others have their own aviation services. Denominations have also entered the picture. The Seventh-Day Adventists, though resisting the widespread use of aircraft for many years, today have a large and well-equipped fleet of more than a hundred planes serving missionaries around the world. Altogether there are some fifty mission societies and denominations that now operate their own flight programs.

From the early days, missionary aviation strategy centered around the short-range use of light aircraft that were capable of landing on short airstrips or water. Some mission boards attempted to extend their aviation service to international flights for transporting missionaries to and from the field, only to realize they could never successfully compete with the safety and cost of commercial airlines. Today, helicopters, though costly to own and operate, are being used more and more in remote areas, eliminating the months of work involved in building airstrips.

Besides MAF and flight service branches of mission societies and denominations, the field of missionary aviation includes many independent missionary flyers, often referred to as "circuit riders," whose ministry depends on their own personal air travel. This type of ministry has been particularly conducive to the Arctic region, where air travel by missionaries in many areas has replaced the dog sled. Independent missionaries as well as missionaries serving under such mission boards as Arctic Missions and Eskimo Gospel Crusade, have widened their ministries considerably through the use of aircraft.

It is no exaggeration to say that missionary aviation has revolutionized Christian missions in the past several decades. The weeks and months of arduous travel have become a phenomenon of the past, and no longer do isolated missionaries in remote villages endure for months at a time without needed health services, fresh food, and mail deliveries. Today a single MAF pilot covers as much territory in six weeks as David Livingstone covered in a lifetime of African exploration, and with much less strain on his health and family relationships. Few mission leaders could have realized four decades ago what a far-reaching ministry missionary aviation could have in the awesome task of world evangelization.

Elizabeth "Betty" Greene

It is ironic that the most male-oriented and male-dominated branch of missions was begun by a woman. Though Betty Greene denies that she was the founder of MAF, it was she who did the most during the early years to get in motion the concept of missionary aviation as a specialized service. Furthermore, she was the first full-time staff worker and the first pilot to fly for the newly formed organization. Though handicapped by sexism, her qualifications and skills as a pilot were never in doubt. She served in the Air Force during the early months of World War II, flying radar missions, and later she was assigned to developmental projects that included flying B-17 bombers in high altitude equipment tests. But military service was not Betty's career objective, and before the war was over she began laying the groundwork for her life ministry as a missionary pilot.

Betty's interest in flying began as a little girl, and at the age of sixteen she began taking flight lessons. During her college years at the University of Washington she enrolled in a government civil pilot training program in preparation for her dream of one day flying as a missionary, but World War II intervened. She enlisted in the WASP (Women's Air Force Service Pilots), her primary motivation being to gain experience that would help her on the mission field. It was during the war years that Betty found time to write an article published in the Inter-Varsity HIS magazine about the need for missionary aviation and about her own plans in that direction. The article was spotted by Jim Truxton, a Navy pilot, who had discussed the same idea with two fellow pilots. He wrote to Betty and asked her to join them in forming an organization for missionary aviation.

Betty's final decision to team up with Jim Truxton was prompted by the news that WASP was being disbanded. So with her term of service over she headed for Los Angeles, where she set up headquarters for the newly formed Christian Airmen's Missionary Fellowship (later MAF), the office space being donated by Dawson Trotman, founder of the Navigators. In 1945, soon after MAF was founded, an urgent request came for assistance, and Betty was the only one available to go: "We were asked by Wycliffe Bible Translators to help them in Mexico with their jungle camp program," Betty later recalled. "I went down in

1945 to see what the situation looked like. We bought an airplane in early 1946, paid in part by the savings of one of the MAF men in the military. It was a Waco cabin plane with a 220-horse-power engine. I flew the plane down to Mexico in February of 1946—the men were still tied up with Uncle Sam."[1]

After several months of service in Mexico, Betty was asked by Cameron Townsend, founder of Wycliffe, to help out in Peru. She agreed to go, and George Wiggins, a Navy pilot, was sent to replace her. Then came the first real blow to the fledgling MAF. When Betty was "checking out" George for his new assignment, they crash-landed after clipping a small building near the runway. Neither one was hurt, but the plane was so damaged that Nate Saint, a skilled mechanic, was called down from the States to fix it. Betty went ahead with her plans to serve in Peru, where she flew a war surplus Grum-man Duck amphibian biplane that Wycliffe had acquired. Her assignment involved flying missionaries and supplies into the interior, each time crossing the towering peaks of the Andes, winning the distinction of being the first woman pilot to do so.

After a year in Peru, Betty returned to the United States, where she again worked in the MAF home office. Her next overseas assignment was in Nigeria, where for nearly two years she flew support missions over varied ter-rain from the dense Nigerian jungle to the vast Sahara Desert. Then it was back home for another stint in Los Angeles, where she involved herself in much needed public relations work in an effort to shore up the home base. After three years Betty was ready for another field assignment, and she ea-gerly accepted an invitation by the Sudan Interior Mission to help them in East Africa. There she was based in the Upper Nile, where she served mis-sionaries in the Sudan as well as in Ethiopia, Uganda, Kenya, and the Congo.

The early days of Mission Aviation Fellowship: (left to right) Grady Parrote, Selma Bauman, Peggy Truxton, Betty Greene, and Jim Truxton.

In 1960, after having returned once again to the home office, Betty left for her last overseas flight assignment, this time to Irian Jaya—an assignment that involved not only dangerous flight missions, but also a long and harrowing jungle trek. To receive flight service, each mission outpost was required to build its own airstrip. Before landings could be made, a qualified pilot had to make the overland trip to check it out. Most of Betty's previous work had been in the air, and she soon realized that she was no match for her robust female companion, Leona St. John, or for the eight Moni tribesmen carriers who were used to the daily tropical rainstorms, the frayed vine bridges, and the slippery mud embankments. "I didn't know how hard it would be," she recalls. "I suppose the carriers were perfectly aware of the trail, but for most of the way I wasn't even sure there was one. The place we were going was supposed to be thirty miles away, but I think the map meant horizontal miles, and most of ours were straight up and down."[2] The physical discomfort was quickly forgotten when the party realized that it had inadvertently come upon a tribal war—a terrifying scene of death and carnage that the two missionaries and their carriers watched in horror.

All the misery she had endured on the arduous trek was worth it when she and Leona and the carriers were greeted by the villagers and the resident missionary couple with a tumultuous celebration. Best of all, Betty found the airstrip to be suitable for landings and takeoffs, and the real celebration came the next day when an MAF co-worker landed with much-needed supplies and then flew out with Betty for her next assignment.

The rewards of Betty's ministry were abundant, but it was while she was serving in Irian Jaya that she had the opportunity of carrying out a mercy mission that she still remembers as one of the highlights of her career. She was returning from a routine mission when she received an urgent call from a station far out of her way, requesting her to come immediately to pick up a gravely ill child. With her eye on the clock, ever conscious of the sudden darkness after a tropical sunset, Betty flew to the scene and transported the little girl to a coastal hospital, thus saving her life.

Following her nearly two years in Irian Jaya, Betty retired from active flying duty and returned to headquarters to represent the mission and recruit more pilots—male pilots in particular. Despite her own success as a pilot, Betty never sought to interest other women in the field. In fact, she took a strong position against the use of female missionary pilots. When asked during an interview in 1967 if she would "encourage a girl to go into this sort of work," she answered: "MAF definitely frowns upon it, and so do I. . . . We have three reasons why we do not accept women for this work: (1) Most women are not trained in mechanics. (2) Much of the work connected with missionary aviation is heavy work. There is bulky cargo to load, in some cases impossible for a woman to handle. (3) The other is flexibility. For instance, if there is a place where it is necessary to base a pilot alone for a few days or weeks, you can't do this with a woman."[3]

Despite MAF's past policy of sex discrimination, women nevertheless continued to enter the field of missionary aviation and to serve with distinction.

Even Betty, with her indisputable qualifications and experience, was written off as a "woman driver" in the mind of Nate Saint before he discovered firsthand that she "was a pilot of such caliber that local airline and military pilots regarded her with great respect."[4] Betty's acceptance by her male counterparts in those early years no doubt had a lot to do with the fact that she willingly accepted their view that missionary aviation was a man's world and that she was an isolated exception to the rule.

Today, after more than a decade of feminist conscience raising, MAF policy has changed considerably. Women are welcomed as pilots. Recently, Gina Jordon, who has clocked some fifteen thousand hours as a pilot, left her much publicized instructing service in Canada to join MAF as a pilot in Kenya.

Nate Saint

The critical need for well-trained pilot-mechanics became evident to MAF officials in the first months of the mission's tottering existence. The first plane crash, though it claimed no lives, put the mission temporarily out of business because neither pilot on the scene had the necessary skills to repair the badly damaged plane. It was Nate Saint who was called on to go to Mexico to do the necessary repair work, and it was Nate Saint who became one of the most skilled and innovative pilot-mechanics in the history of missionary aviation. Though at one time feeling that "being a grease monkey for the Lord seemed like an inferior sort of call," he and the missionaries who depended on him came to realize the infinite value of such a ministry.

Although Nate Saint had been raised in a missionary-minded family, and though aviation had been an interest of his since childhood, missionary aviation had not caught his imagination as it had Betty Greene's. His older brother was a commercial airline pilot, and Nate envisioned a similar future for himself. To achieve his goals he enlisted in the Army Air Corps, but just before beginning his specialized training in the Air Cadet Training Program, a scar on his leg from an osteomyelitis attack as a teen-ager became inflamed —a seemingly insignificant matter, but one that changed the course of his life. "Turned twenty yesterday," he wrote in his diary. "It was a kind of rough birthday present to be told that instead of going to the airport for my first day of flying that I was going to the base for an X-ray."[5] Health-wise, Nate was found to be unfit for military flying, and though he remained with the Air Corps for two and a half more years, he began thinking seriously of focusing his life on Christian service.

It was after reading an article by Jim Truxton on the recent formation of MAF that Nate contacted the organization about the possibility of becoming involved. Jim responded immediately; and a year later, as soon as Nate was discharged from the military, he answered an urgent call from MAF (following the crash that Betty Greene and her companion were involved in) to go to Mexico to reconstruct the mission's only airplane. Nate was excited about the mission, but when he arrived and found the remains of the wing panels "in a bushel basket," he almost lost heart. Nevertheless, he set to work, and after six months of sheer frustration he finally got the plane back in the air. Considering the damage that had been done to the plane and the conditions under which he was forced to work, the accomplishment was nothing short of ingenious. What "Nate demonstrated in Mexico," writes his biographer, was "his unique ability in making repairs on a plane that would have been difficult enough in a completely equipped hanger in the States."[6]

Following his six months in Mexico, Nate returned to the States and attended Wheaton College for a year and then embarked on one of the most eventful years of his life—1948. On Valentine's Day, after a brief courtship, he was married to Marj Ferris, a graduate of the University of Southern California. The following September they left for Ecuador, Nate going to Shell Mera to establish MAF headquarters and build a house, and Marj going to Quito to await the birth of their first child. In December, while returning from a flight from Quito, Nate got "caught in tricky air currents" and crashed.[7] The plane was demolished and Nate sustained a severe back injury requiring a lengthy hospitalization and the discomfort of a body cast. Then on January 10, 1949, while Nate was hospitalized in Panama, Kathy Joan, his first child, was born.

Nate's crash, the second in MAF's very brief history, was another blow to the mission, and there was strong feeling in the home office that better training was necessary. Flight orientation was initiated for all new missionary pilots, and safety features were added to the planes. But even more significant was the seriousness with which missionary aviation came to be viewed. Jungle aviation, by its very nature, attracted daredevil adventurers, notwithstanding their commitment to

Nate Saint, missionary pilot to Ecuador, martyred by the Aucas in 1956.

God. But missionary flying was not just another exhilarating sport like mountain climbing. It was deadly serious business. Nate himself was a changed man after the crash. He admitted that he had not been as cautious as he should have been in not allowing himself the margin he needed during the takeoff. "God only knows how often I've had occasion to hate my old cocky nature. I hate it. . . . The accident is in my file under: Risks Matured and Collected."[8]

It was Nate more than anyone else who learned from his own painful experience and from a subsequent accident involving a Gospel Missionary Union pilot and passenger. Jungle flying was a highly specialized branch of aviation, and thus both the planes and the techniques had to be developed to accommodate the circumstances. The crash involving the GMU plane made him realize the need for an alternate fuel system, and he immediately began focusing his inventive genius on that problem area. After improvising with his wife's cooking oil cans and a piece of brass tubing connected by a valve to the intake manifold, he hooked up the contraption to the instrument panel and tested it out on the ground. The real test, though, was in the air: "Two thousand feet above the landing strip I pulled the mixture control to idle-cut-off. It was quite a novel experience for a fellow who had listened so long, hoping never to hear it happen. But a turn of the new little T-handle on the instrument panel brought with it a wonderful feeling as the engine wound back up to smooth full-power. For the next twenty minutes the normal fuel source was shut off tight. The engine never missed. It picked up from a slow windmill without so much as a single cough."[9]

Nate's invention (on which a patent was obtained from the U.S. government) was a breakthrough in jungle aviation and was later approved by the Civil Aeronautics Authority. "Now every MAF pilot," according to Russell Hitt, "carries the alternative fuel system—a permanent mark Nate left on missionary and other hazardous aviation."[10]

Another innovation that Nate developed was his ingenious bucket drop, a technique made famous after the fatal attempt to reach the Aucas. A bucket on the end of a spiraling line was used to give and receive gifts from this otherwise very unapproachable tribe of Indians. But the real value of the bucket drop was far more significant than making contacts with hostile Indians (which in the end proved disas-

trous anyway). The reason that Nate developed the technique was to better serve mission outposts. One day while flying over a jungle village he saw crowds of people out in an open area trying to signal a message to him. "How would you read such a crude message? About all I could do at the time was to drop a supply of aspirin, probably a feeble answer to the real need of that desperate village."[11]

From that incident Nate visualized the possibility of lowering a bucket to deliver and receive messages and materials, and while he was back in the States on furlough he began conducting tests. On his first attempt the concept proved amazingly successful. With the bucket trailing behind, he started out flying in broad circles. As he gradually began decreasing the size of the circles, the bucket and line began "bending in toward the center of the circle permitting the bucket to settle downward toward the point of a huge invisible cone" until "finally it came to rest quietly in the middle of the open field below."[12]

Nate's first opportunity to prove the value of his innovative technique was back in Ecuador soon after he returned from furlough. Word came that a jungle village was being ravaged by a "highly contagious disease." Nate flew over and lowered in his bucket a field telephone attached to 1500 feet of wire, thus establishing communication with the Wycliffe Bible translator who was on the ground and who was able to relay the symptoms to Nate flying overhead. With that information, Nate contacted a doctor and then returned to the village and lowered in the bucket the medicine the doctor had prescribed.

Although Nate had initially scorned

the idea of becoming a "grease monkey for the Lord," he loved his work as a missionary pilot and each day showed him more and more what a privilege it was to have the unique ministry of "redeeming the time" for the missionary whose work was on the ground—not only by turning days and weeks of tiring travel by foot into mere minutes and hours of air travel, but also by transporting supplies that could not feasibly be carried through the jungle. He developed a technique of dropping large quantities of canned goods and other supplies by a parachute device. "Immodest of me to say so," he wrote, "but I get a big bang out of these 'bombing runs.' I enjoy my work to the full."[13] An equally necessary but far more difficult item to transport by plane was aluminum sheeting for mission station roofs. But Nate was not deterred by the size or bulkiness of an item—especially one that was so coveted by the missionaries. So he improvised a harness sling and began transporting seven-foot lengths of aluminum to the grateful missionaries.

Developing a safer plane for jungle aviation was another matter that Nate continually wrestled with, and "converting his little single-engined monoplane to a tri-motored biplane" became his passion. To overcome the problem of "increased 'drag' . . . he fashioned a set of removable lower wing panels for the MAF plane and conducted tests as he skimmed a few feet off the ground in the simulated biplane."[14] When word of his rash experiments reached the "slide-ruling brethren"[15] who were less than enthusiastic about the concept anyway, there was anxious concern and an immediate rebuke. Nate responded by assuring the directors that he realized the seriousness of such tests and that he was "aware of what would be at stake if there were an accident," and then conceding his poor judgment he added: "I must admit I am completely defenseless, having ventured whatever confidence I may have built up with you in the past few years."[16]

It was a combination of Nate's impulsiveness and his compelling desire to hasten the evangelism of lost souls that so suddenly ended the life of this brilliant and dedicated young pilot in January of 1956, when he and his comrades were slain by the Aucas. It was through his own ingenious bucket drop that the Aucas were thought to be friendly, and through his exceptional skill as a pilot that the men were landed safely in Auca territory. But skill and technique were not enough, and missionary aviation lost one of its finest pilot-mechanic-inventors ever on that fateful day. His contribution to missionary aviation did not end with his death, for his testimony lived on and many others committed their lives to God as missionary pilots as a result of hearing his story.

Jungle Aviation and Radio Service

Ironically, it was a devastating plane crash more than anything else that prompted the founding of JAARS, an arm of Wycliffe Bible Translators. The year was 1947, and Cam Townsend, his wife, and their baby—all on their way to Mexico City—had entrusted their lives to an inexperienced Mexican pilot. On take-off from the mission outpost, the pilot turned back over the jungle before reaching sufficient altitude, and after barely missing some tall trees, the plane crashed in a ravine, shearing off a wing and landing on its side. With a broken leg, and blood soaking through his pants, Cam managed to pull himself from the wreckage and then help free his uninjured infant daughter and his wife, whose left foot, dangling by the flesh, had been almost completely severed. The pilot, too, had been badly injured, and while Cam waited for rescuers to carry his wife and the pilot back to base and then return for him, he committed himself to developing an efficient aviation support organization to service his jungle-based translators.

The urgent need for jungle aviation had troubled Cam long before the crash in Mexico. As early as 1929 he had contacted a navy pilot who had flown in South America, asking about the feasibility of establishing an aviation ministry for jungle-based missionaries. The estimated cost of such a program was high, and in 1933 when Cam presented his plan to the directors of the mission they turned it down.

During the months of slow recovery in Mexico, Cam formulated the blueprints for his Jungle Aviation and Radio Service, and he enthusiastically presented his ideas to the board when he returned to the United States. But the majority of the board members continued to balk at the idea. Their concern was linguistics and Bible translation, and it was their view that aviation should be left to MAF, even though MAF was too busy servicing other missions to meet all the needs of Wycliffe. Cam was adamant in his position: "We are in aviation (by being in the jungle) whether we like it or not"; and he was determined not to let his dream die, regardless of board opposition or costly expenditures.

Cam's rationale for an aviation program for WBT/SIL did not emerge solely as a result of his own ill-fated air crash. Other near tragedies had convinced him of the grave necessity of aviation. Two male translators were nearly drowned in river rapids, and in a similar incident a young couple and their baby were dumped into the current after their raft slammed into a log. Other Wycliffe translators had to wait for weeks to get much-needed air service or failed to receive any at all. So Cam moved ahead with his plans, despite the board's outspoken reservations. He contacted interested individuals and began raising money for the costly venture.

JAARS, like MAF, began operating with one plane, and Larry Montgomery, a Navy lieutenant, became the chief pilot. From the beginning, JAARS was strapped by a shortage of funds —sometimes so severe that the very safety JAARS had been founded to insure was in jeopardy. JAARS was described by one pilot as "a flying junkyard" with the pilots "robbing one airplane to pay another." "Everything was handled on a shoestring," according to Jamie Buckingham. "The pilots weren't even allowed to circle the base when they came in to land—it used up too much gas. If they didn't know the wind direction, they had to guess at it. They were forever moving boxes around in the dingy old hangar . . . trying to find some spare part to fix one of the always-broken airplanes."[17]

Despite the shortage of funds and spare parts, JAARS had a remarkable safety record for the millions of miles its pilots had logged over dangerous jungle areas. According to Buckingham, JAARS had "a record unmatched by any other flying organization"—

"twenty-five years of flying experience in eight countries without ever having had a fatal crash." There were air tragedies for Wycliffe during those years, however, though not ones involving JAARS. On Christmas Eve of 1971, LANSA Airlines Flight 508 went down in the Andes jungle, and among the dead were five missionaries associated with Wycliffe.

It was that devastating tragedy that led to what Buckingham refers to as a "Jungle Pentecost." "For years the Wycliffe Bible Translators in Peru—and I in particular," wrote Jerry Elder, "had been self-reliant people. We were highly trained, skilled technicians. We knew our jobs and prided ourselves that we were the best in the world. Many of our linguists had PhD degrees. Our pilots, mechanics and radio personnel were the finest on earth. We took pride in saying that we could handle any challenge that arose. If we needed to change an engine on a sandbar, we could do it. If we needed to analyze a new language, we could do it. Nothing was too hard for us." But the LANSA crash changed that self-reliant attitude into a spirit of revival. "During those days of uncertainty, when our men were combing the jungles, hoping against hope our friends were still alive, something happened in the hearts of the people on base. Love, more love than we'd ever dare express, was poured out toward the families of those lost in the jungle. And when the bodies were finally returned to the base, that love increased. It spread to others on base and flowed out into the jungle toward our Indian friends" and "leaped the boundaries of doctrinal differences."[18]

There was also a noticeable change in the attitude toward work—particularly among the pilots who had taken great pride in their outstanding safety record. "We not only considered ourselves professionals," confessed Eddie Lind, JAARS Aviation Director, "but we prided ourselves in our professionalism as well. Our motto, 'We do our best, and the Lord does the rest,' really meant we thought we could handle most emergencies. If we couldn't, we would call on God. But as the Holy Spirit began to be present in our lives, even the pilots started realizing that our best was not good enough. We were going to have to start leaning on God for everything."[19]

It was this spirit of humility and dependence on God that brought JAARS through the greatest tragedy of its history—an accident that occurred on the other side of the globe in Papua, New Guinea—a crash that killed veteran JAARS pilot Doug Hunt, the chief pilot for JAARS in New Guinea, and his six passengers, including Dr. Darlene Bee, a brilliant young linguist with a Ph.D. from Indiana University and one of Wycliffe's most respected translators. How Wycliffe, and JAARS in particular, recovered after such a loss is a story of courage in itself, but the real story of miraculous recovery is the story of a mechanic who more than anyone else was crushed beneath the burden of that tragedy.

Although it is the pilots who generally receive the glory or blame for the successes and failures that occur in flight, it is impossible to underrate the importance of the mechanic. "There is a bond," writes Buckingham, "unlike any on earth, between pilot and mechanic. Even though it is the jungle pilot upon whom all eyes are focused as he climbs into his plane and roars off over the 'green hell' on a flight into the savage past of tribes unknown, it is the mechanic who holds in his grease-stained hands not only the success of the flight, but the very life of the pilot and his passengers. One careless twist of the wrench, one tiny nut left unturned, one glance in the wrong direction while a part is being replaced—these and a thousand other factors could mean engine or structural failure at some critical moment . . . and human lives . . . are snuffed out in a fiery crash or sucked under the savage greenery of the grasping jungle."[20]

It was "one tiny nut left unturned" that broke JAARS twenty-five-year record of no fatalities—a mistake that cost seven lives and only by God's grace spared an eighth. He was an experienced JAARS mechanic, assisted by a trainee. Together they had completed a routine one-hundred-hour inspection of the twin engine Piper Aztec the day before its final flight, the flight in which Doug Hunt and his six passengers went to their deaths in a fiery crash. A subsequent inspection indicated that the explosion and resulting crash had been caused by a fine spray of gasoline escaping where a nut had not been properly tightened. The mechanic had momentarily turned his attention to another matter and had left a B-nut on the fuel-line only finger-tight, forgetting to tighten it with a wrench. For the guilt-ridden JAARS mechanic, "the funeral was a ghastly ordeal. The sight of those caskets lined up in the little opensided tropical church hit me like a blow to the stomach. I wanted nothing but to get out of there. . . . How could I face my friends? How could I face myself? I was overwhelmed with guilt. I was a failure."[21]

The overwhelming pain that the grief-stricken mechanic suffered was eased—if only so slightly—by the love and forgiveness of family members and co-workers. "Time went on and heart-healing continued. But it was a long time before I could talk about the accident. In fact, not until after I learned how God was blessing lives as a result of the book about JAARS—*Into the Glory* by Jamie Buckingham—did I realize my story could be a blessing to others. Readers seemed to find a special encouragement in the chapter about the Aztec crash and a young mechanic who thought he was a failure, but God kept him going. . . . Except for God's grace I'd be somewhere cowering in a corner in guilt-ridden despair—the eighth fatality of the Aztec crash. That would really be failure. . . . Praise God, it isn't so!"[22]

For the entire Wycliffe family, the fatal crash in 1972 was a crushing blow, but the ministry of aviation went on with even greater determination. By the end of that decade, JAARS, under the directorship of Bernie May, increased its full-time work force to over four hundred, operating some seventy planes and helicopters, risking their lives to further the cause of world evangelism.

Gleason Ledyard

If the airplane was a godsend to missionaries in jungle regions, it was perhaps even more so in Arctic regions, where nomadic bands roamed the vast ice-covered wasteland and where weather conditions prevented extensive travel by other means. The sparce population and the scattered missionaries in the Arctic regions did not generally make missionary aviation support services practicable, so frequently missionaries in that area of the world became their own pilots. One such pilot-evangelist was Gleason Ledyard, the Chairman-Director of the Eskimo Gospel Crusade, who began his ministry in the Hudson Bay region in 1946.

Missionary aviation work in the Arctic was in many ways more strenuous than in the jungle. The long flying distances with few landmarks, combined with unpredictable, rough weather made every flight a calculated risk. Emergency landings due to ice on the plane were common occurrences that meant building an igloo miles from nowhere and waiting out the storm. With temperatures reaching forty and fifty degrees below zero, the engine had to be kept warm with blow pots, and sometimes it was not until after a two- or three-day wait that the journey could be resumed. Because of the sub-zero temperatures, high altitude flying was rare, and sometimes to avoid sudden wind gusts and icing the planes were flown as low as ten feet off the ground.

The Ledyards' years in the Arctic working with the Eskimos were often filled with tension-packed days of separation, as Kathryn remained at the mission base conducting a school for Eskimo children while Gleason flew to remote areas in an effort to reach Eskimos who had never before heard the gospel. On different occasions radio contact was lost and Kathryn went for days not knowing if her husband was dead or alive. One such incident occurred not long after they began their aviation ministry in the Hudson Bay region. Gleason set off on a thousand-mile evangelistic journey with gas and food to last a month. Only hours after take-off he realized that he was off course, but he continued on, hoping to recognize something indicated on the map. By evening, it became clear to him that he was thoroughly lost somewhere in the Arctic, with no radio communication and half the gas gone. With the weather closing in fast, he landed on the edge of a lake, tied down the cruiser, and set up his little tent. Though comforted by his pocket Testament, it was an anxious time, as he later expressed: "Where was I? How would I find the right direction home? Would I have to wait until I had a strong tail wind? The sun would tell the direction but it was hidden by thick clouds. The stars would tell but the nights were too light for the stars to be seen. I would just have to wait, even if it were days."[23]

On the third day the winds died down and the overcast sky began to clear, and Gleason was able to calculate the direction from the sun. As soon as he could break camp he was airborne, and finally, after hours of flying, his hopes began to soar when he could see ahead what appeared to be Baker Lake. It was a tremendous relief when he finally was able to pinpoint his location on the map, and it was sheer joy some hours later when he landed back at the mission station.

Despite such ordeals, the rewards of reaching remote bands of Eskimos were worth the risks involved, as Gleason later related concerning one such experience: "After the spring break-up season was over, and the lakes were free of ice, God gave me a most joyful experience—the joy of teaching a band of Eskimos, for the first time the words of life.... Never before had the name of Jesus been named among them, except by the cursings of a few ungodly white men who had been in contact with them through the years. . . . Never before had I experienced such an eagerness to learn. During the time the men were not fishing or doing other necessary jobs, we would gather together in front of a tent. . . . Every word uttered would be repeated after me. If something was not clear a pause would result. I would restate my thought. As soon as they got the meaning, they would repeat it in unison."[24]

Flying to remote encampments and preaching the gospel was Gleason's primary ministry, but his skill as a pilot afforded other opportunities to serve as well. From the remote areas he frequently ferried people who needed more medical attention than he was able to give, and he transported school children to be taught by his wife in the base mission school. There were also rescue operations that required his assistance. One such mission involved a commercial pilot and five passengers who were lost somewhere on the vast bleak landscape while on their way to a mining development camp. Although they were unable to plot their location, they were in radio contact with the camp for a time after they went down. Weather conditions delayed a government search, but Gleason ventured into the wind and snow despite the danger. To him was given the privilege of finding and rescuing the shaken pilot and passengers after several days of desperate searching.

It was such rescues that won Gleason the respect of the hardened irreligious camp men. Some months after the rescue he returned and was overwhelmed by the outpouring of gratitude he received: "When we landed, it was like seeing old friends again. As soon as we announced a meeting that evening, there was much scurrying around. . . . Many of them had not had a songbook in their hands for years but they sang heartily after a little encouragement. . . . The response that came on their faces as I explained about the blood of Christ—what it can do for us, what it can mean to us, and how available it is to us—was something I had never seen before. Many men stayed around after the meeting to talk to us."[25]

Despite years of persistent evangelism in the Arctic region, the Ledyards found the work to be slow and frustrating, especially among the Eskimos. The people were outwardly friendly and receptive to their ministry, but they were reluctant to abandon their long-held pagan superstitions. Another problem they faced, common to any evangelistic work, was the false assurance of salvation that some of them had received from previous missionaries: "Christianity had been introduced to some of them before but only as a ritualistic churchianity. A heart change was practically nonexistent. In fact, one of the hardest things to combat was the false idea that being baptized, conforming to church rules and ritual, and reading the same prayers morning and night was the essence of the Christian life."[26]

Ledyard's most rewarding times were when he saw the power of the gospel break through the barriers of superstition and churchianity. On one Palm Sunday morning in an island village hundreds of miles from his mission base, revival broke out as he spoke, and nearly everyone in the village professed faith in Christ. But as significant as such occasions were, the

Ledyards were always aware of the temptation for the Eskimos to slide back into their superstition, especially when they were left alone for long periods without a resident minister. The outward signs were sometimes impressive, but would there be lasting results? "We do not keep books, nor count noses," wrote Gleason after another evangelistic tour, "but we are confident there will be some Eskimos in Heaven because of God working on that trip."[27]

If the Ledyards were unconcerned with numbers, they were even less concerned with bringing Americanized Christianity to the Eskimos. They insisted that they were not "interested in taking anything of the Christian Church"[28] to these remote people but only Christ, and it was this philosophy more than anything else that opened the way for true Christianity among these remote peoples of the Arctic wasteland.

Mark Poole

Jungle flying is generally not thought to be an advisable pursuit for an amateur without specialized training and considerable flying experience. Yet the necessity of travel over difficult jungle terrain has tempted many missionaries to entertain dreams of flying their own plane—dreams that quickly faded when the prohibitive cost of such transportation was considered. Mark Poole, a medical doctor serving in the Congo, had often entertained such dreams—not for his own convenience, but to vastly expand his medical ministry and to save precious lives—and he was one of the few who lived to see his dream fulfilled.

Poole grew up as a Texas cowboy in the 1920s, spending his high school vacations riding the range on his father's cattle ranch. After high school he attended the University of Texas and then went on to Johns Hopkins University for his medical degree. He had one goal—to serve as a medical missionary where the need was the greatest. His fellow doctors discouraged him from such an undertaking because of his own serious physical disability, a heart ailment, but Poole was determined to give his life where he could alleviate the most human suffering. He was accepted by the Board of World Missions of the Presbyterian Church, U.S., and in 1936 he and his wife began their work in equatorial Africa in an area declared by a group of medical investigators to be "the most seriously diseased area of the world."[29]

Poole's ministry was centered at Bulape in the Congo, where he established a 120-bed hospital, staffed largely by the nationals he himself trained. Though his own time was in great demand for operations and routine hospital and office work (never fewer than one hundred patients a day), he was not satisfied with the limited care he was able to offer, ever aware of the multitudes far out in the jungle. They had no medical services at all, except for the times when, in a dire emergency, he managed to come by dugout canoe, on foot, or in his battered old Plymouth. But on many occasions he arrived too late.

"Someday I'm going to get me a plane," Pool remarked to a friend in 1947, as he shared his frustration concerning his medical work. Though it may have seemed like an idle fantasy, Poole was serious. He had learned to fly years before, and flying had become

407

a passion almost as dear to him as medicine.

The dream of flying his own airplane came true in 1951, when a Presbyterian church in Florida donated a Piper Tri-Pacer to him in memory of their pastor's son, a Marine pilot. From the first day the plane arrived in the Congo, Poole's ministry took on a new expression. No longer was he tied to Bulape. He was now free to service medical outposts where no medical treatment was heretofore available. Bambuya, twenty-six miles north of Bulape, the site of a government airstrip, was the location of his first outlying clinic. Here, in a thatched roof dispensary, he installed an African assistant to handle routine medical problems. Each week Poole returned to bring supplies, treat the more serious problems, and bring any critically ill patients back to Bulape for hospitalization.

The reputation of the flying doctor quickly spread throughout the area, and other isolated tribesmen wanted similar medical service. One such tribe was the Batua, a group of primitive Pygmies who lived some seventy-five miles from Bulape. So great was their desire for medical treatment that a small party of men made the arduous journey to Bulape, carefully checked out the airstrip, and then returned home, ready to duplicate what they had seen. For weeks the Batua tribesmen worked feverishly with sticks and baskets, clearing the trees and undergrowth and smoothing the rough terrain.

Hardly was the strip ready when a medical emergency arose and a tribesman was dispatched to Bulape to fetch the *Nganga Buka* (miraculous white healer). Although Poole had heard rumors of the new airstrip being built, he doubted it would be safe for landing, but the runner was so persistent that he agreed to check it out. A close aerial survey proved to be a pleasant surprise, and Poole decided to attempt a landing: "When the Piper sliced through the trees and Dr. Poole stepped onto their airstrip, the little tribesmen ... went wild with delight. All night and the next day they danced ... and cooked antelope and wild pig ... for the celebration."[30]

As Poole continued his flying medical ministry he established more outlying dispensaries, and during the first three years alone of this expanded ministry he flew some thirty-five thousand miles, treating thousands of patients and saving hundreds of lives. But he ministered to more than the physical needs of the people. "No operation," according to George Kent, "starts without a prayer in the native language. And several times a week Mark sheds his gloves and apron and stands behind the pulpit and preaches to the people."[31]

Clair McCombs

The hazardous flying and the specialized techniques required of a missionary bush pilot have led to the development of several missionary aviation training programs. Most are connected with religious institutions (including Moody Bible Institute, Piedmont Bible College, and LeTourneau College) and offer Bible courses as well as flight instruction and maintenance training. Of all the missionary flight training schools, the Moody Flight program has made the greatest impact on missionary aviation. It is estimated that more than 50 percent of all the missionary pilots serving throughout the world today were trained through that program. One of the more recent of such programs to be developed is headed by Air Force Lieutenant Colonel Clair McCombs and is located in Lowell, Michigan, as part of Grand Rapids School of the Bible and Music.

McCombs was raised near Grand Rapids and began flying at the age of sixteen. After high school he enlisted in the Air Force and served with the allied forces for the final fifteen months of World War II. Following the war he returned home, where he met and married Joan Medler, and after their first child was born he decided to make the military his career; and so he reenlisted in the Air Force. From then on the McCombs lived in various parts of the world, including Taiwan, Panama, Germany, Vietnam, and Alaska.

From his earliest years in the Air Force, McCombs distinguished himself as a superb pilot. He received honors and awards and was recognized by his superiors as a top-notch professional. But despite the prestige and honors this brought him, he felt an emptiness in his life that award ceremonies and cocktail parties simply could not fill. Then in 1953, when he was on temporary duty with his squadron in North Africa, qualifying in air-to-air gunnery as a fighter pilot, his life changed. Sensing his need for God, he sought out an Air Force chaplain who suggested he read the Bible. It was McCombs's follow-through on that suggestion that led him to Christ.

When he returned to Germany and shared with Joan what had taken place in his life, she was confused and upset. What had happened to the man she married? What would his new-found religion do to their marriage? What would their friends and relatives say? But Joan soon realized that Clair had something in his life—a peace of mind that material wealth and military rank could never supply —and she, too, committed her life to Christ.

During the time that he was stationed in Germany in the mid 1950s, McCombs was chosen to be one of four pilots in the Air Force's most prestigious precision flying team, the *Sky Blazers.* They were known as the aerial ambassadors of Europe, and McCombs flew the slot position.

At forty-three, after twenty-two years of military service, McCombs retired. He had many potentially productive years ahead of him, and he was determined to invest them in the Lord's work. He returned to Grand Rapids, and in 1969 he enrolled at Grand Rapids School of the Bible and Music in preparation for full-time Christian service, thinking perhaps of missionary aviation or some other field of ministry.

The vision for a missionary aviation program at GRSBM had already been in the mind of President John Miles when McCombs enrolled, but his coming helped put the wheels in motion. He was asked to head up the program while he continued his course work, and thus the missionary aviation program was born. A GRSBM student-instructor, five student-trainees, and a small Cessna 150 constituted the whole operation that first year. Since that inauspicious beginning, however, the program has, under the directorship of Colonel McCombs, grown steadily, and today there are more than fifty students, six full-time in-

Clair and Joan McComb, trainers of missionary pilots and mechanics.

structors, and fifteen airplanes and two helicopters.

Besides the flight program (that includes courses in multi-engine air-craft, seaplane, and helicopter flying, as well as the preparation for private, instrument, and commercial licenses) there is a two-year maintenance program that prepares missionary pilots for the vital pre-flight checks and repair work so necessary in missionary aviation. One of the instructors, teaching in both the flight and the ground schools, is McCombs's wife, Joan, who began flying in 1970 and six years later joined her husband in the aviation program. Her expertise as a pilot and all-around aviation specialist is appreciated by all of the students, but is a particular inspiration to the young women students, who, in the tradition of Betty Greene, are preparing to serve God in the field of missionary aviation.

SELECTED BIBLIOGRAPHY

Buckingham, Jamie. Into the Glory: The Miracle-Filled Story of the Jungle Aviation and Radio Service. Plainfield, New Jersey: Logos, 1974.

Hitt, Russell T. Jungle Pilot: The Life and Witness of Nate Saint. Grand Rapids: Zondervan, 1973.

Ledyard, Gleason H. And to the Eskimos. Chicago: Moody, 1958.

Roddy, Lee. On Wings of Love: Stories From Mission Aviation Fellowship. Nashville: Nelson, 1981.

PART V

THE SHIFT
TOWARD NATIONALIZATION

PART V

The Shift
Toward Nationalization

Tremendous changes have occurred throughout the world during the decades since World War II. "The most obvious outward trait" of the period, writes Ralph Winter, "was the unprecedented 'Retreat of the West'" —a "collapse of four hundred years of European empire building in the non-Western world."[1] As the superpowers and their allies aligned against each other, the once politically insignificant countries of Africa, Asia, and South America became the much sought after "powers" of the Third World. Underdeveloped nations long ruled by colonial powers, suddenly captured world attention —often through revolutionary movements or by blatant acts of aggression by petty dictators. Oil became the world's most coveted raw material as the demand for energy expanded, and the proliferation of nuclear weapons increased. No longer was America symbolized as the peace keeper of the world. The Vietnam War, if nothing else, destroyed that image. And no longer was America held in awe by her

allies and the underdeveloped countries of the world. Superpower that she was, America learned that the way to deal with other nations was not through a position of implied superiority, but on the basis of equality.

The turbulent changes that occurred in the Third World had a decisive impact on the foreign missionary movement. During the 1960s attacks against missionaries increased, particularly in the face of leftist revolutionary movements. There were deaths among the members of almost every mission society active in troubled areas of the world.

But at the same time that missionaries were being threatened by acts of violence by their so-called enemies, they were confronting tense situations with their friends. Third World Christians were no longer willing—if, in fact, they had ever been—to submissively bow to the will of the Western missionaries. They wanted the leadership positions and control of their own affairs that in some cases had long been denied them. Most mission boards complied with the wishes of the nationals in this regard, and the exchange of authority in many instances was accomplished with remarkable ease.

In many cases the missionaries introduced the concept of national leadership before the churches were willing to accept the idea. In any case, it is true that the majority of national church bodies had to come nationally controlled prior to the landslide to political independence. Unlike traditions like the Roman Catholics and the Mormons, most Protestant missions had from the start worked toward nationalization, intentionally. Quite often (as in Kenya, for example) the leaders of the new nations were, in fact, Christian nationals whose leadership skills had been whetted by the education and responsibilities they had been given by their participation in nationally controlled church movements. It may be that the world-wide shift in national independence owes more to the mission movement than to any other force. Secular observers may miss this fact simply because, for example, they do not know that 85 percent of the schools in Africa are there because of missions. This presence and the scope' of missions is little appreciated in secular literature.

As nationals shouldered the responsibility for their own churches and local Christian ministries, they began to demonstrate a greater interest in cross-cultural evangelism. This had occurred as early as the mid-nineteenth century, particularly in such areas as the South Pacific, but it was not until a century later that this movement truly gained momentum. Thousands of missionaries from the Third World were commissioned to serve abroad, even as Westerners had been for nearly two centuries. Likewise, a number of Third World Christians emerged as internationally recognized evangelists and mission strategists.

One of the factors that has aided national leadership and participation in church ministries has been expanded Christian education. The training of national pastors and evangelists has been revolutionized in recent years through the introduction of TEE (Theological Education by Extension). Many nationals, especially married men with families were already leaders in the local church, who had been unable to enroll in Bible schools or seminaries because of the cost and the distance from their village. But through TEE, by the middle of the 1970s, some fifty thousand men and women in more than seventy countries were receiving advanced Bible training to more effectively serve in their own communities.

The same increased involvement and influence of Third World Christians in the task of world evangelism was manifested by the extent of their numbers and participation at the Lausanne Congress on World Evangelization in 1974. One third of the nearly twenty-five hundred delegates came from Third World churches, and a total of one hundred and fifty countries were represented. The Congress was a giant step toward a world-wide consensus that completing the Great Commission is not just the white man's burden. In a secondary sense, the Congress provided an opportunity for delegates from the Third World to air their grievances. Among them was Dr. Rene Padilla, who charged "that the gospel some European and North American missionaries have exported was a 'culture-Christianity,' a Christian message . . . distorted by the materialistic, consumer culture of the West."[2] Such remarks were criticized by some of the delegates, but it was a message that Christian leaders from the West needed to hear.

The Lausanne Committee on World Evangelization, which resulted from the Congress, sponsored many regional congresses in the following years, all reflecting the large number of outstanding national leaders in all parts of the world. A second world level meeting in Pattaya, Thailand, in 1980 again involved a large number of such church leaders from the non-Western world. In 1972 a Southern Baptist missionary, Luther Copeland, proposed a 1980 world level meeting of mission agency personnel, following the example of the 1910 meeting at Edinburgh. The World Consultation on Frontier Missions that resulted was smaller and more specialized than the meetings in Pattaya, but it was nevertheless the largest meeting of purely mission agency delegates ever to meet on a world level. For the first time in such a meeting Third World mission leaders (eighty-eight from fifty-seven agencies, one third of the total in both cases) rubbed shoulders as equals with Western mission delegates. In 1910, by contrast, although some Third World agencies already existed, none were invited!

The Edinburgh meeting was unique also in the respect that a simultaneous International Student Consultation on Frontier Missions was organized by younger leaders from twenty-seven countries, meeting in the plenary sessions with the agency delegates.

"Edinburgh '80" thus refers to both the International Student Consulation and the meeting of agency delegates. The leadership role of Third World mission executives can be seen in the several morning plenary addresses assigned to them.

At the same time that the strength and influence of the Third World Christians were increasing (while church attendance in the older denominations in Europe and America continued to decline), the evangelical churches in America were witnessing impressive gains. *Newsweek* magazine proclaimed 1976 to be "The Year of the Evangelicals"—a year that found both presidential contenders to be evangelical Christians. A Gallup survey that year reported that one third of all Americans professed to have been "born again," and that more than half of the Protestants questioned had sought to convert others to Christ through "witnessing."[3]

The fastest growing segment of evangelicalism in America has been in the pentecostal and charismatic wing, and this growth has been evident in overseas missionary outreach. During the decade of the 1960s the Assemblies of God and a number of other Pentecostal denominations and missions increased their missionary personnel by more than 50 percent. Partly because of this rapid growth in missionary outreach, the increase in Pentecostalism has become a world-wide phenomenon. "The explosive growth of indigenous Pentecostal churches in Chile, Brazil and South Africa has caused some to predict that the future center of Christianity will be in the southern hemisphere among non-Caucasian Pentecostals."[4] While Pentecostals have witnessed some of the greatest gains in missionary outreach, other evangelical groups have also seen impressive growth. During the decade of the 1970s the conservative evangelical missionary force increased by almost 40 percent, encompassing a total of more than thirty-two thousand missionaries. "It is well known," writes Robert T. Coote, "that the North American conservative agencies, taken as a whole, have experienced dramatic growth since the late 1960s. By 1980 they accounted for ten out of eleven North American Protestant career missionaries working overseas."[5] (Indeed, by 1983 Wycliffe Bible Translators alone was sending out twice as many missionaries as the combined total of the member denominations in the National Council of Churches.)

There is indeed reason for optimism as one looks at the overall picture of foreign missions. The Protestant missionary "movement still vibrates with life and action," wrote Herbert Kane in 1979. "Today there are more missionaries in more countries of the world than ever before in the history of the Christian church." But, as he points out, that is not the only cause for optimism. "Never before have the non-Christian people of the world been so open. . . . Some countries are now difficult to enter because of visas, resident permits, and red tape, but once in, missionaries find the people more receptive than ever before."[6]

In 1982 there were more volunteers for missionary work among the Muslims than ever before, and during that same year some ten thousand students (many influenced by Inter-Varsity's triennial Urbana Conference) spent their summer vacation in overseas missionary work. Some organiza-

tions such as Operation Mobilization, founded in 1958 and headed by George Verwer, and Youth With a Mission, also founded in the 1950s, specialize in sending young people on short-term assignments involving literature distribution and evangelistic work.

Another mission that works with short-term teams of young people is International Crusades, founded in the late 1950s by Kevin Dyer. Its work involves church planting and the teams remain in a given area for their two-year term. The teams, trained in an intensive eight-month program of Bible linguistics, and cross-cultural communication, cooperate with established mission societies once they arrive on the field, and in some cases they work with local officials in community development programs. As with most short-term mission programs, International Crusades provides a training ground for career missionaries. More than 50 percent of their force returns to the field—generally with other missions—after completing the two-year term.

As the number of short-term missionaries has increased, so has the number of nonprofessional missionaries, or "tentmakers," as they have been termed. Tentmaking "is the wave of the future," writes Herbert Kane. "Today there are millions of Americans traveling and residing overseas. If all the dedicated Christians among them could be trained and persuaded to be effective witnesses for Jesus Christ, they would add a whole new dimension to the missionary movement. The spiritual potential here is enormous."[7] Nonprofessional, tentmaker missionaries are being trained by such organizations as

Campus Crusade for Christ and the Navigators, both of which have extensive overseas ministries.

So, what is the future of Christian missions? Is the age of the traditional life-term missionary over? Will Third World missionaries, short-term evangelists, and nonprofessionals carry the burden of future missionary outreach? No, despite the new trends, the age of the pioneer missionary who spends his life in cross-cultural evangelism and church planting is not over. There are still close to 17,000 unreached people, and they constitute "a full 80 percent of the world's non-Christians," writes C. Peter Wagner, who "will initially require cross-cultural evangelism if they are going to become Christians." How will this be done? He optimistically predicts that "the number of missionaries recruited and sent out by the Third World churches will increase substantially while those sent out by the Western nations will hold their own."[8]

On a more pessimistic note, Ralph Winter fears that there may well be a retirement avalanche just ahead, in which perhaps 30,000 Western missionaries will be retiring or returning for some other reason during the next ten years, while perhaps only 5,000 more will be sent out at present rates of recruitment.

The work ahead for evangelical missions is immense, but that work should never be viewed apart from the tremendous accomplishments that have occurred in recent decades. Dr. David Barrett, in his massive study on world religions, *World Christian Encyclopedia*, points out that the widespread penetration of Christianity in all continents and among many of the world's peoples has made it the first religion in world history to become truly universal. Although he concedes that the number of nominal Christians is slightly declining proportionately to the world's population (due to a decrease in the older European and American churches), he insists that "the outreach, impact and influence of Christianity have risen spectacularly," largely as a result of the vitality of evangelical missions.[9]

In one sense, all missionaries have always been nationals from some national church somewhere. Today the major change is the shift of initiative to the non-Western world, which has been greater in the case of world Christianity than we see it in the world of the political powers. This is, for Western missions, success, not failure. Unbelievable loss of life might well have occurred in countless countries had the Christian church not led the way in the benevolent decentralization of leadership.

Chapter 16

Twentieth-Century Martyrs: "Yankee, Go Home"

The twentieth century opened with a crisis in China that took the lives of more Protestant missionaries than any other such blood bath in history, and though it would not be repeated again, it was a preview of what would follow. Few periods in church history have witnessed so many Christian martyrdoms as has the twentieth century. As independence movements emerged in developing nations, the cry was raised to throw off the shackles of foreign domination. In many instances revolutions broke out, and foreigners—particularly Americans and western Europeans—were viewed as the oppressors, with little differentiation made between the diplomat, the businessman, and the missionary. All whites were suspected of being part of an imperialist conspiracy to exploit the weaker nations of the world, a false assumption that exacted a high price on Christian missions.

It was political turbulence, then, that confronted missionaries more and more as the twentieth century progressed. No longer did the idea of martyrdom conjure up images of missionaries being boiled over a campfire for a cannibal feast, but rather images of missionaries facing hostile mobs, guerrilla warfare, and terrorist attacks. Asia, Africa, and Latin America were all torn by leftist movements during the second half of the twentieth century, and missionaries and national Christians were slain in the process. How could such killings be justified? Because missionaries and national Christians generally took the position that called for gradual rather than radical change. Moreover, they represented the views of the free world and, as such, vehemently opposed the Marxist ideology behind many of the "liberation" movements.

The persecution and martyrdom inflicted on foreign missionaries during the twentieth century was in many instances magnified in its intensity when directed toward national Christians—particularly influential pastors and evangelists whose association with foreign missionaries was seen as a threat to nationalism or independence movements. During the Boxer Rebellion, scores of dedicated Chinese evangelists were martyred for their faith—none more heroically than Chang Sen. Though blind, Chang had been one of the most effective itinerant evangelists Manchuria had ever known, but his success made him the brunt of severe persecution. At the height of the Boxer rampage he was singled out for retribution. Fearing the worst, he hid in a cave, but when word reached him that fifty Christians would be killed if his whereabouts was not disclosed he willingly came out of hiding, knowing full well the consequences. Even in death Chang had a vibrant testimony —one that made his executioners tremble. They insisted his body be cremated, fearing that he, like Christ, would rise from the dead.

Another Christian from Manchuria to endure intense suffering for his faith was Evangelist Kim, who was tortured unmercifully and arrested repeatedly for his refusal to stop preaching the gospel. During his eighth arrest he was tortured beyond what he could endure, finally agreeing to sign a document approving Shinto worship. Later he was so remorseful that he wrote to the authorities, repenting of what he had done. He was immediately returned to prison, where he remained until his death in 1943.

World War II sparked many violent attacks against missionaries—perhaps none more treacherous than the Hopevale massacre of 1943 that cost the lives of a dozen American missionaries. Hopevale was the name given to the makeshift mountain camp in a deeply wooded area on the island of Panay in the Philippines where the missionaries had fled to safety. Among them were Dr. Frederick Meyer, a graduate of Yale Medical School, and Dr. Francis Howard Rose, a graduate of the University of Chicago—both beloved and respected doctors among the Filipinos. For more than a year they hid themselves at the camp, continuing all the while to minister physically and spiritually to the people in the nearby villages. Then, in December of 1943, after they were discovered by a contingent of Japanese soldiers, they were lined up and shot with five other Americans, without even any pretense of having a presentence trial.

Following the war, except for the Soviet Union and Eastern Europe, there was a relative lull in religious persecution world-wide. The lull, though, was a temporary one. Beginning in the 1960s with the outbreak of violent independence movements in several areas of the world, the persecution and martyrdom of Christians once again hit the front-page headlines.

Despite such threats facing missionaries today, the work continues, and the Christian church in these areas torn by violent political strife continues to grow. Indeed, the church in such regions often grows faster than in areas of the world that are free from political violence. Centuries ago St. Augustine singled out Christian martyrs for special praise, and his words still hold true today: "Martyrs are holy men of God who fought or stood for truth, even unto death, so that the Word of God may be made known and falsehood and fictions be overcome. Such a sacrifice is offered to God alone, thus the martyr is received in heavenly honor. This means that God has rewarded the faith of the martyr with so much grace that death, which seems to be the enemy of life, becomes in reality an ally that helps man enter into life."[1]

Betty and John Stam and China Martyrs

During the years following the Boxer Uprising, China was anything but free from hostility toward foreigners. Missionaries were viewed with the deepest suspicion even though their work was largely humanitarian in nature. They were blamed for spreading a cholera epidemic that swept across the northern provinces in 1902, and as a result two CIM members were murdered by a mob. Another brutal attack against missionaries occurred near Hong Kong in 1905 and resulted in five deaths, including that of the greatly loved Dr. Eleanor Chestnut.

After coming to China in 1893 under the American Presbyterian Board, Dr. Chestnut built a hospital, using her own money to buy the bricks. Even before the hospital was completed she was performing surgery — in her own bathroom for want of a better place. One such operation involved the amputation of a coolie's leg. Complications arose and skin grafts were needed. Later the doctor was questioned about a leg problem from which she herself was suffering. "Oh, it's nothing," she answered, brushing off the inquiry. Later a nurse revealed that the skin graft for the "good-for-nothing coolie" had come from Dr. Chestnut's own leg while using only a local anesthetic.[2]

During the Boxer Rebellion, Dr. Chestnut remained on her post longer than most missionaries, and she returned the following year. Then in 1905 while she was busy working at the hospital with four other missionaries, a mob stormed the building. Although she got away in time to alert authorities and in fact could have escaped, she instead returned to the scene to help rescue her colleagues. It was too late. Her colleagues had been slain. But there were others who needed her help. Her final act of service to the Chinese people whom she so loved was to rip a piece of material from her own dress to bandage the forehead of a child who had been wounded during the carnage.

Despite such brutal xenophobic incidents, the early years of the twentieth century were ones of relative peace in China during which the Christian community greatly expanded. By the 1920s, though, the Chinese political scene was in chaos. Sun Yat Sen's authority was being challenged on every side. There were more than a dozen "governments" centered in various cities, and military factions ruled the countryside. In 1925 Sun Yat Sen died and the fate of foreigners in China became more tenuous than ever. The Communists, under the leadership of Mao Tse-tung, were gaining influence, and several missionaries were murdered as a result of apparent communist instigation. The situation only seemed to worsen when Chiang Kai-shek arose as an opposition leader. By 1927 his southern armies were sweeping across China, leaving thousands dead in the wake. Missionaries were ordered to leave the interior, and during 1927 alone some 50 percent of all foreign missionaries in China left, never to return again. Even the vast majority of CIM missionaries were forced to evacuate to safer areas, leaving only a skeleton crew to operate seventy stations.

It would seem that such chaotic political turmoil would have resulted in a curtailment of missionary work for the CIM, but to the contrary, "just when the general situation was at its worst in 1929, Hoste [the General Director] telegraphed to the home countries an appeal for 200 workers (the majority to be men) in the next two years." The goal was met numerically and on schedule, but "disappointingly, only eighty-four were men."[3] Despite the dangers they knew lay ahead, young women eagerly volunteered. Among them was Betty Scott, a graduate of Moody Bible Institute and the daughter of Presbyterian missionaries to China.

While at Moody, Betty had attended the CIM weekly prayer meetings, and there she became acquainted with John Stam, who also was prepared to volunteer to be one of the two hundred called for. But though Betty and John were attracted to each other and their future ambitions were pointing in the same direction, a personal desire for marriage was seen as secondary. To his father John wrote: "Betty knows that, in all fairness and love to her, I cannot ask her to enter into an engagement with years to wait. . . . The China Inland Mission has appealed for men, single men, to itinerate in sections where it would be almost impossible to take a woman, until more settled work has been commenced. . . . Some time ago I promised the Lord that, if fitted for this forward movement, I would gladly go into it, so now I cannot back down without sufficient reason, merely upon personal considerations."[4]

In the fall of 1931, Betty sailed for China while John remained at Moody

to complete his senior year. As the class speaker for his graduation ceremony, John, well aware of the depressed American economy and the political crises abroad, challenged his fellow students to go forward with the task of world evangelism: "Shall we beat a retreat, and turn back from our high calling in Christ Jesus; or dare we advance at God's command, in the face of the impossible? . . . Let us remind ourselves that the Great Commission was never qualified by clauses calling for advance only if funds were plentiful and no hardship or self-denial involved [sic]. On the contrary, we are told to expect tribulation and even persecution, but with it victory in Christ."[5]

There was reason to expect persecution. The situation in China remained grim. There were many acts of violence against missions in 1932, though none more shocking than the massacre of eleven missionaries in Sian serving under the Scandinavian Alliance Mission (now TEAM).

Following his graduation in the fall of 1932, John sailed for China, excited about his future ministry but not expecting to see Betty. Just before he arrived in China, she was forced to return to Shanghai for medical reasons, and there she and John had an unexpected but joyful reunion that resulted in their engagement. After a year of separation they were married at the home of Betty's parents in Tsinan, and during the year that followed they continued their language study while serving at the CIM mission compound in Süancheng.

In September of 1934, Betty gave birth to a baby girl, Helen Priscilla, and that fall she and John were assigned to a station in the province of Anhwei where missionaries had been evacuated two years earlier. Communist activity, they were told, had diminished, and the local magistrate personally guaranteed their safety, assuring them that there was "no danger of Communists" in the area.[6] CIM officials, anxious to reopen the station, were also convinced that the area was reasonably safe.

Unfortunately, both the Chinese and the CIM officials had seriously misjudged the situation. The Stams arrived at the end of November, and before the first week of December had passed they had been attacked in their home by communist soldiers. Though placed under heavy guard, John was permitted to send a letter to his superiors:

Tsingteh, An.
Dec. 6, 1934

China Inland Mission,
    Shanghai.

Dear Brethren,

My wife, baby and myself are today in the hands of the Communists, in the city of Tsingteh. Their demand is twenty thousand dollars for our release.

All our possessions and stores are in their hands, but we praise God for peace in our hearts and a meal tonight. God grant you wisdom in what you do, and us fortitude, courage and peace of heart. He is able—and a wonderful Friend in such a time.

Things happened so quickly this a.m. They were in the city just a few hours after the ever-persistent rumors really became alarming, so that we could not prepare to leave in time. We were just too late.

The Lord bless and guide you, and as for us, may God be glorified whether by life or by death.

In Him,
JOHN C. STAM[7]

The day after the letter was written, the Stams were forced to make a grueling march to another town. It was a mentally as well as physically anguishing time. Not only were their own lives at stake, but they could overhear their communist guards discussing plans to kill their baby girl to avoid the bother of bringing her along. Little Helen's life was spared, but no such fortune awaited John and Betty. After they arrived at their destination, they were stripped of their outer clothes and paraded through the streets and publicly ridiculed, while the communist guerrilla leaders urged the townspeople to come out in full force to view the execution.

It was not until a week after the execution that baby Helen was delivered in a rice basket to the home of another missionary family a hundred miles across the dangerous mountain terrain. A Chinese evangelist had found her abandoned in a house some thirty hours after the execution, and he accepted the responsibility of bringing her to safety.

The martyrdom of the Stams was a distressing blow to the CIM, but it, perhaps more than any incident since the death of Gracie Taylor (p. 182), did more to strengthen and unite a mission society that was being bombarded by discouragement on all sides. Many young people, inspired by the Stams' sacrifice, dedicated their lives to missions, and the year 1935 saw the greatest amount of money come into the mission since the stock market crash in 1929.

There were other missionary martyrs in China in the years that followed. Among them was John Birch, a man whose tireless work as a missionary has long been lost to the

John and Betty Stam, martyred in China in 1934.

political cause that was unfortunately named after him. He began his missionary career in Hangchow under a Baptist mission organization in 1940 when China was at war on all fronts with the Japanese invaders. Almost immediately he was recognized for his courage as he traveled about the war-torn countryside, "slipping through Japanese occupation lines and preaching in villages where missionaries had not dared to go since the war began."[8] Later he became involved in evacuating missionaries and Chinese evangelists out of the war zone, conducting a one-man rescue operation that defied all risks, bringing out as many as sixty at a time. Following the war he remained in China despite the growing threat of communist guerrillas. He continued his widespread evangelistic activity, knowing full well

the risks, and it was on one such trip north that he was ambushed and murdered by communist forces.

Another well-known name inscribed on the missionary death registry for China was Eric Liddell, the great Olympic athlete of 1924 whose story was portrayed in the award-winning film "Chariots of Fire." Liddell grew up in China, the son of missionaries, and in 1925, only a year after his momentous Olympic victory, he returned to serve as a missionary in his own right. His ministry there spanned the period of the Sino-Japanese war, and he and his family knew firsthand the hardships and dangers of missionary life. With the outbreak of World War II, the political situation in China worsened, and in 1941 Liddell decided to send his wife and two children to his wife's home in Canada until the worst of the dangers were over. Later that year, Liddell, along with six other members of the London Missionary Society, was placed under house arrest by the Japanese, and there he remained until his death early in 1945.

Though Liddell's death was not a direct result of his imprisonment, the malnutrition and lack of adequate medical care may have contributed to it. After an extended illness and what was thought to be a nervous breakdown, later complicated by a stroke, he died. The autopsy report, however, revealed that he had suffered from a massive hemorrhage on the brain caused by a tumor. His sudden death came as a shock to his family and friends and to his fans the world over, but it was also a testimony of sacrifice of a man who had so consistently put his faith in God above personal ambition and fame.

Paul Carlson and the Congo Martyrs

Not since the Boxer Rebellion of 1900 had so many missionaries been killed in a single year as in the Simba Rebellion in 1964 and 1965. The terror unleashed on innocent Congolese Christians and foreign missionaries left thousands dead and even more to suffer from physical and emotional scars that would stay with them the rest of their lives. Dr. Helen Roseveare, held captive for months and repeatedly raped and beaten, and Dr. Carl Becker, who escaped in the nick of time, were spared for further service in the Congo, but many others had their lives cut short by the very people they had come to serve. Among them was another doctor, Paul Carlson, who had served in the Congo less than two years. Most of the thirty other Protes-

tant missionaries and nearly two hundred Catholic missionaries who were slain had served considerably longer than he had and in some instances with greater distinction, but it was his story that became the most published of the Congo martyrs.

Carlson was born in California in 1928, the year before the great stock market crash, and his Christian upbringing was an important factor in his decision as a teen-ager to dedicate his life to foreign missions. Following a semester at UCLA and a short stint in the Navy, he enrolled in North Park College in Chicago for premed studies. It was while there that he met Lois, a nurse, and after their engagement in 1949, he returned to California to continue his medical course at Stanford University.

Eight years later, with a wife, two babies, and an M.D. degree, he was ready to begin his residency. It was a hectic time, and, according to Lois, "the subject of medical missions was mentioned less and less" until "eventually it disappeared completely from our discussions." Spiritually, Paul was going through a difficult period in his life, questioning "the very existence of a Triune God."[9]

Paul's repressed commitment to missions was suddenly reawakened in 1961 when he received a letter from the Christian Medical Society delineating the urgent need for medical doctors in the Congo and asking for his help. What caught Paul's attention was that it was not a request for lifetime service. In fact, a follow-up letter indicated a four-month term would be welcomed. Perhaps subconsciously hoping to fulfill his teen-age commitment in four months, Paul accepted the call, and in June of 1961 he left Lois and the two children in Michigan and flew to the Congo.

Just one year earlier—with little warning—the Congo had been granted independence from Belgium, and the political situation was highly volatile. The new premier, Patrice Lumumba, ordered Belgians to leave, and many other foreigners followed. The government was in chaos, stripped of its leaders and civil servants. Bands of soldiers and teen-age hoodlums roamed the cities and countryside. Professional and technical personnel were in short supply. It was a tense situation that provoked fear and uneasiness for even the most law-abiding citizen. It was this atmosphere that Paul encountered when he stepped off the plane in Leopoldville in 1961.

But despite the unsettled political environment, Paul's five-month term in the Ubangi Province was all that was needed to convince him of the critical need for medical missionaries. The need was greater than he ever could have imagined, and the opportunities of presenting the gospel were endless. Could he ever be happy back in the United States, where modern hospitals and Christian churches were so plentiful? "The Paul Carlson who had returned from Congo was a new person," Lois discovered. "His attitudes had changed, his ideals shone forth again, his purposes in life were well defined, his outlook on the future was confident. I knew that Paul had come back to himself and back to his God."[10]

Despite Paul's renewed commitment to medical missions, leaving the United States and returning to the Congo with his family was not an easy move. During the year following his five-month term in Africa, he joined a practice with some doctors with whom he had worked during his residency, and the security of a comfortable income was something he and Lois had never before enjoyed. "It was so easy to look to the undemanding side of life, to look forward to a comfortable existence, to expect the things that all women and families would like to have. It was easy to look forward with our medical colleagues to a better standard of living, as we Americans term it, in that we have all the comforts money can buy. We were on the verge of attaining that kind of life, and now we were faced with the decision that had to be made, that we had known would have to be made—and it had to be made by both of us."[11]

It was in the summer of 1963 that the Carlsons arrived in the Congo as full-fledged medical missionaries—this time serving under their own denomination, The Evangelical Covenant Church of America. They were assigned to Wasolo, a mission station in a remote section of the Ubangi Province where Paul had worked before and where there were only three other medical doctors in the entire province. Almost immediately Paul was consumed with routine hospital work, attending to an average of two hundred patients per day, while Lois was adjusting to the primitive style of running a household.

The first year went by quickly and relatively uneventfully, but by the beginning of their second year at Wasolo the scene began to change. Though Wasolo was often referred to as the "forgotten corner" of the Congo, it was not immune to rebel infiltration, and by August of 1964 the Simbas were threatening the government defenses in that area. Not wanting to take any unnecessary risks, Paul escorted Lois and the children across the border to the Central African Republic, and then he returned to the hospital to make final preparations before he himself would evacuate.

During the days that followed, Paul was busy handling routine cases as well as combat casualties—civilians as well as government and rebel soldiers. He crossed the river on Sunday to visit his family, promising to return the following Wednesday. But it was a visit that never took place. The Simbas moved in. Before Paul could escape he was taken into captivity, where he would endure three months of mental and physical torture before his life would be taken.

The publicity surrounding Paul Carlson's martyrdom overshadowed the heroic sacrifices made by other Christian missionaries in the Congo —particularly American missionaries who were identified as tools of American imperialism. Some, though, were killed indiscriminately by Simba guerrillas with seemingly nothing better to do. Irene Ferred and Ruth Hege, single Baptist missionaries, were attacked in their house out in the Kwilu bush by drunken teen-age rebels, and only Ruth survived to tell the story.

Hector McMillan, a Canadian, was another missionary to die at the hands of the Simbas. He, his wife Ione, and his six sons, along with several other UFM (Unevangelized Fields Mission) missionaries, were trapped at Kilometer Eight, their mission station just outside Stanleyville. Escape routes were closed, and there was no place to go. For Ione the trauma of those harrowing days was ironic. Her own call to missions had been influenced by the martyrdom of John and Betty

Stam. She felt God wanted her to go to China to help fill the void they had left behind. But China closed its doors, and Ione went to serve in the Congo instead, where she met and married Hector McMillan. Now in 1964 and six sons later, she found herself and her family in the midst of violent conflict no less terrifying than what the Stams had faced.

The attack on Kilometer Eight came suddenly. Hector was gunned down point-blank by a Simba rebel, and two of the McMillan boys were wounded. It was a day of infamy, but for Ione and the other missionaries there was no time to grieve. They had to get out as soon as possible. Al Larson, the senior UFM missionary in the area, arrived with government mercenaries soon after the attack to help evacuate the survivors. Space on the trucks was limited. There was no room for baggage, the mercenaries insisted—only room for "living" people. Hector's body would have to remain behind.

What might have been the ultimate devastation for Ione turned into a testimony of God's grace—a testimony she had been strangely prepared for by reading a biography of Adoniram Judson. Judson's mental breakdown following the death of Nancy had been exacerbated by morbid thoughts of her decaying body, and that account made a deep impression on Ione. The day before the tragedy she had vowed that she would never allow the same to happen to her: "If a member of my family is ever taken in death, by God's help I am not going to waste time and the energies He gave me worrying over a body of clay." "Why this decision just yesterday?" writes Homer Dowdy. "Why had she read so recently about Adoniram Judson's bitter experience?

Hector McMillan (with family), martyred in the Congo by the Simba rebels.

Why had someone once bought this book, perhaps put it aside, only for her to pick it up years later? Why had the great missionary struggled through this grievous vale? It was part of God's plan—God's perfect will—for her at this precise moment."[12]

Another North American missionary brutally murdered by the Simbas was Jay Tucker, a farm boy from Arkansas. Like the McMillans, Jay and his wife were married after coming to the Congo, and for twenty-five years they carried out a fruitful ministry under the auspices of the Assemblies of God. In early November of 1964, Jay was arrested by the Simbas; and some three weeks later, when the rebels realized the government troops were closing in on them, they retaliated and turned their vengeance on their captives. An Italian priest was the first to be singled out for execution. Jay Tucker was next. "In the near darkness someone swung

a bottle across the missionary's face. With a dull thump the bottle broke; blood covered the face that in agony turned to grovel in the dirt. In the glassy-eyed glee that their hemp afforded, the Simbas began to whoop as they searched for sticks to finish the job. Those finding sticks made use of them, others their rifle butts. They took turns at hitting the missionary. Starting at the neck, they worked slowly down his back, striking again each time their victim squirmed."[13]

The nearly three months of captivity for Paul Carlson had been ones of mental and physical torture. Even before his captivity, articles had surfaced in American newspapers telling of his courageous and sacrificial medical work, and after his capture more articles appeared, giving him publicity that may very well have complicated his situation in the Congo. Obviously, the Simbas did not want the world to think they were persecuting a saintly hero, so they twisted the facts; and by late October Radio Stanleyville was broadcasting reports of the upcoming trial of "Major Carlson," an American mercenary who was charged with being a spy. For more than two weeks there was no further news, but then in mid-November, the news flashed over the wires that Paul had been tried and was facing execution. Realizing his value as a hostage, the rebels postponed his execution when negotiations seemed imminent.

It was on November 24, 1964, only hours before Hector McMillan was slain at Kilometer Eight and Jay Tucker was murdered at Paulis that Paul Carlson was shot down in the streets of Stanleyville. After two days of relative peace, the hostages had awakened that morning to the sound of planes overhead and tense confusion all around them. The rescue operation had begun. Belgian paratroopers were filling the streets, and the sound of machine guns was coming closer. The prisoners were herded outside, where they fell flat on the street, hoping to avoid the cross fire. After a time the shooting stopped. It was an eerie silence and of little comfort to the exposed prisoners lying in the street. They were sitting ducks. They had to run for cover—or so they thought. In an act of desperation, Paul and several others raced to the closest building. It was a fatal mistake. The other prisoners made it, but Paul, who was behind and had difficulty scaling the veranda wall, was riddled with bullets and left to die outside the wall. In a matter of minutes, the rescue operation was over, but for Paul it was too late.

The funeral, conducted by Congolese pastors, was a moving scene.

Hundreds of Congolese Christians carrying flowers and palm branches poured into the village of Karawa where the service was held. It was their way of saying "thank you" to a man who had sacrificed all for them—a man whose life's creed was summed up in the verse on his grave marker, written in the Lingala tongue, which translated, "Greater love has no one than this, that one lay down his life for his friends."[14]

Betty Olsen and the Vietnam Martyrs

While missionaries were flooding into China during the nineteenth century, little attention was being paid to Indo-China—the three small Buddhist countries to the south: Vietnam, Laos, and Cambodia. It was not until the twentieth century that Protestant missionaries gained a permanent foothold there, and even then the work was conducted largely by one mission, the Christian and Missionary Alliance, and continued so until the missionaries were expelled in the 1970s. From the outset, Indo-China had been a very difficult area for Christian missions. In fact, there was never a time that was free from persecution. In many instances the nationals themselves were receptive to the gospel, but the ruling powers felt threatened. During the French colonial regime, evangelistic work was severely curtailed, and when the Japanese moved in during World War II, the missionaries who refused to leave were rounded up and held in internment camps.

The defeat of the Japanese in 1945 that brought an end to the war in Asia unfortunately brought no lasting peace to Indo-China. For eight years, beginning in 1946, Ho Chi Minh and his communist guerrillas fought the French colonial regime in Vietnam until the French withdrew and left the country divided along the seventeenth parallel. But still there was no real peace. When Vietnamese civilians began fleeing from the communist-controlled North to the South, pressures from the North increased. Communist guerrillas began terrorizing villagers, and the government in Saigon retaliated. Then with the introduction of the American soldiers, the conflict developed into a full-scale war, and American missionaries were in danger as never before.

Even prior to the full-scale American commitment to South Vietnam, missionaries were the brunt of guerrilla hostility. The very fact that the United States was assisting South Vietnam militarily outraged the Viet Cong and Hanoi officials, and missionaries were seen as part of a capitalist-imperialist conspiracy to control Indo-China. Missionaries were aware of such hostility, and some evacuated areas known to be heavily infiltrated with Viet Cong. Nevertheless, it came as a shock to the Christian world and to the United States State Department officials when three American missionaries were taken captive in 1962. The fact that they were serving at a leprosy hospital had given them a false sense of security. They had simply refused to believe that the guerrillas would risk the wrath of the local tribespeople by disrupting their medical work. But that is precisely what happened, and Dr. Ardel Vietti, a medical doctor from Houston, Texas; Archie Mitchell, the hospital director; and Dan Gerber, a Mennonite staff worker, were taken at gunpoint into the dense jungle, never to be heard

from again. Rumors of their whereabouts surfaced periodically, but no concrete evidence was ever obtained regarding their fate at the hands of their captors.

Left unscathed from the attack at the leprosy compound were Betty Mitchell and her children, and a nurse, Ruth Wilting, who on the very day of the attack was sewing her wedding dress for her upcoming marriage to Dan Gerber. They escaped the following morning to the nearby provincial capital of Banmethuot. Though shaken by the turn of events, the women stayed on in Banmethuot and continued in their mission duties, hoping every day for news of their loved ones.

It was in Banmethuot, six years later, that the greatest loss of missionary lives occurred. There on January 30, 1968, the day of Tet (the Vietnamese year of the monkey), the Viet Cong moved into the mission compound and carried out a bloodthirsty massacre; killing five American missionaries (including Ruth Wilting) and a four-year-old child. Less fortunate than the dead were Betty Olsen and Hank Blood, who were taken captive, along with Mike Benge, an American AID officer. For several months they suffered indescribable torture and humiliation before Betty and Hank also gave their lives as Christian martyrs.

Playing the role of a missionary heroine did not seem to fit the image of Betty Olsen. Many of those who had known her in earlier years would have doubted her usefulness on the mission field at all. Yet, in the early hours of Tet she risked her life as she nursed the critical wounds of little Carolyn Griswold (who later died) and attempted to transport her to the hospital, and in the grueling months of suffering that followed, she proved to be molded out of the stuff of which heroes are made.

Betty, a "self-possessed, trim redhead,"[15] was thirty-four years old at the time of the Banmethuot massacre. She was a registered nurse who had served for less than three years with the C&MA in Vietnam. Missionary work was not new to her. She had been raised as an MK in Africa, and some of the happiest days of her life were spent there. But her childhood days were filled with turmoil as well. Her earliest recollections were of her parents consumed in the work of the mission, often away for days at a time visiting African churches. Then, when she was eight years old she was sent away to school for eight months each year, where she spent many homesick nights crying herself to sleep. For Betty, boarding school was not a pleasant experience. She rebelled against the rules and resisted close relationships with others, fearing the hurt that would inevitably come when separations occurred. Her insecurities as a teen-ager were only exacerbated when her mother became ill and died of cancer just prior to Betty's seventeenth birthday.

Betty completed high school in the United States and then went back to Africa. She was still struggling with emotional insecurities, craving love and attention from her father, whose hectic schedule and plans for remarriage diverted his attention from her. After he remarried she returned to the United States and took nurses training at a hospital in Brooklyn before enrolling at Nyack Missionary College to prepare for a missionary career.

Betty Olsen, martyred in Vietnam following the Tet offensive.

Still, Betty found no real happiness. She desperately wanted to get married and have a family of her own, but the relationship she hoped for never developed. After graduating in 1962 she was convinced that the C&MA would not accept her as a candidate on her own merits, so she went to Africa on her own to work with her father and stepmother. It was difficult, however, for her to suppress the bitterness and rebellion she had been harboring for so long, and after a time she became so irritating to the other missionaries and so difficult to work with that she was asked to leave the field.

At the age of twenty-nine, Betty found herself in Chicago working as a nurse and thoroughly defeated in her Christian life. So depressed was she that she contemplated suicide. Then, she met a young man whose principles of Christian living would change her life. He worked actively with the youth in a Chicago-area Bible church, and he took a special interest in Betty when she shared with him the struggles she was encountering in her Christian life. He gave her scriptural principles to deal with her feelings of inadequacy and helped her cope with the overriding problem that was still plaguing her—singleness. She finally came to the point of willingness, even eagerness, to serve God as a single woman.

Out of that series of counseling sessions, Betty went on to be a productive missionary in Vietnam, and her youth counselor, Bill Gothard, went on to develop a seminar known as Institute in Basic Youth Conflicts, "based largely on the questions Betty Olsen asked."[16]

If ever sound principles of Christian living were desperately needed it was during the months that Betty endured mental and physical torment at the hands of her Viet Cong captors in the steamy insect-infested jungle. For days and weeks at a time she, along with Hank Blood and Mike Benge, was forced to march twelve to fourteen hours a day, sustained only by meager rice rations. All three suffered from dengue fever that caused high fever and chills. They pleaded for medicine, only to be ignored or, worse yet, ridiculed by their insensitive captors. Parasitic skin diseases brought on extreme discomfort; and for Betty, who remained clothed in the dress she was captured in, bloodsucking leeches by the dozens clung to her legs as she was prodded on without a moment's rest.

Awful as her ordeal was, Betty was the healthiest of the three during most of those agonizing months of the jungle death march. Mike contracted a severe case of malaria and for more than a month was delirious, floating between life and death. He survived the ordeal, but not before losing some forty pounds. It was Hank, though, who suffered the most during the early months of captivity. A middle-aged man and father of three, whose eight years in Vietnam as a Wycliffe Bible Translator had involved sedentary work, he simply could not withstand the rigors and deprivations of the debilitating marches. Besides a recurrence of kidney stones that he had suffered from some years earlier, he was tormented by painful boils and finally contracted pneumonia that was left untreated during days of drenching rain and led to his death in mid-July after more than five months of sheer agony.

By September, after nearly eight months on the jungle trails, the end seemed near for Betty and Mike, too. "Their hair turned gray. They lost their body hair, their nails stopped growing. Their teeth were loose with bleeding gums"—all signs of malnutrition.[17] Betty's legs began swelling, making it extremely difficult for her to walk, especially at the pace the guards insisted on. When she fell down she was beaten. She pleaded with her captors to go on and let her die on the jungle path, but her cries were ignored. Her final days defy description. Suffering from dysentery that caused severe diarrhea, she "became so weak she couldn't get out of her hammock" and "she had to lie in her own defecation."[18] Mike nursed her the best he could, but her condition only deteriorated. Her thirty-fifth birthday found her moaning in pain in her filthy hammock, and two days later she was dead.

Shortly after Betty died, Mike was

taken to a POW camp, where he was imprisoned with other Americans. Here he endured beatings and nearly a year in solitary confinement before he was transferred to the "Hanoi Hilton," where again he was kept in solitary for much of the time. In January of 1973, after nearly five years of captivity, he, along with most of the other POW's, was released as a condition of the American military pull-out.

The exhilaration of being released was tempered by the grueling ordeal of recounting to the families of Hank Blood and Betty Olsen the grim details of their agonizing captivity. His story, though, included more than the nightmare of the Vietnam jungle. He told how he himself put his trust in God through their selfless witness to him, and how they hid their own meager rations to share with captured native Christians whose rations were even less. In Betty, the once rebellious and bitter young woman, Mike found "the most unselfish person he had ever known." Her Christ-like love was more than he could comprehend: "She never showed any bitterness or resentment. To the end she loved the ones who mistreated her."[19]

Chet Bitterman and Latin America Martyrs

Terrorism—that dreaded political tactic of the 1970s and 1980s— periodically sent shock waves through the missionary community even as it did the diplomatic and business world. Missionaries were accused of plotting to overthrow revolutionary governments and of serving as informants for the CIA (charges that were apparently true in some instances), and they thus became targets on occasions of terrorist attacks. They were considered the avowed enemies of the leftist liberation movements around the world.

It would be inaccurate, however, to suggest that all politically related religious martyrdoms in recent decades were instigated by leftists. In Latin America and elsewhere, missionaries (particularly Roman Catholic) were sometimes associated with leftist movements, and in several instances terrorist attacks on them were instigated and carried out by right-wing government factions. Such was apparently the case in the 1980 deaths of three American nuns and a lay worker in El Salvador. Though their work involved caring for homeless children displaced by the war, they were perceived as aiding the rebel cause and were brutally murdered as a result.

In December of 1981 on the anniversary of the nuns' deaths, the Catholic church, at the prompting of its missionaries to Latin America, began a year of commemoration called the "Year of the Martyrs." Those commemorated were not only the "El Salvador Four," but also scores of other missionaries and lay workers whose lives had been lost in Latin American civil strife. Among them was Stanley Rother, a red-bearded Catholic priest from Okarche, Oklahoma, who only months before was found shot in the head in his house at a Guatemala village where he had worked among the Cakchiquel Indians for thirteen years. Though he was considered "a real low-key type," and was the "most conservative" of the Catholic priests in the area,[20] his name was, nevertheless, placed on a right-wing hit list, and as such he became the ninth priest in less than nine months to die as a result of Guatemala's political turmoil.

The most publicized Protestant to be shot by Latin American terrorists in recent years was Chet Bitterman, but he was not alone in being victimized by such a senseless outrage. In September of 1981, John Troyer was shot and killed in Guatemala. The twenty-eight-year-old Mennonite missionary from Michigan was gunned down in front of his wife and five children by a band of terrorists shouting anti-American slogans. His partner, Gary Miller, though shot in the chest, survived the ordeal. The gunmen were later identified as a leftist group calling themselves the Guerrilla Army of the Poor.

Acts of terrorism did not take mission leaders by surprise. They were well aware of this newest threat to their work, and some made policy decisions regarding their response in the event of such action. In 1975, Wycliffe members voted that the mission should not yield to terrorists' demands, recognizing that while concessions might free an individual hostage, such action would only serve to jeopardize other missionaries the world over.

It was that statement of policy, combined with the outrageous demands, that prevented Wycliffe Bible Translators and the Summer Institute of Linguistics from even considering submitting to Colombian terrorist demands early in 1981 when Chet Bitterman was kidnapped and held for forty-eight days. While government and mission officials worked feverishly to secure his release, capitulating to the terrorist demands that Wycliffe leave the country was never an option.

Chet Bitterman was new on the scene in Colombia, having arrived in the summer of 1979 with his wife Brenda who was pregnant with their second child. He was the oldest of eight children, all born and raised in Lancaster, Pennsylvania, where his father owned the Bitterman Scale Company. After high school Chet enrolled at Columbia Bible College, and in 1976 he married Brenda Gardner, the daughter of Wycliffe missionaries to Colombia. Although he was determined to become a missionary linguist before he ever met Brenda, linguistics did not come easy for him. He attended the Summer Institute of Linguistics for two summers but became discouraged by the slow progress he was making.

The Bittermans had initially hoped to serve as missionary linguists in Malaysia, but Wycliffe officials requested they go to Colombia instead. Once in Colombia they encountered obstacles as they sought to become involved in the work. They unsuccessfully attempted to begin work with three different language groups and had finally made arrangements to go to the Caryona-speaking Indians when Chet became ill and was sent to Bogota for gall bladder surgery.

It was while he was staying at the SIL residence in Bogota awaiting surgery that his kidnapping occurred. Terrorists knocked at the door at 6:30 A.M. and then burst in with revolvers and machine guns. Sylvia Riggs, a Wycliffe member, later described what happened after she was awakened by one of the hooded terrorists: "They took us all to the living room and made us lie face down on the floor while they tied our hands and feet and gagged us. There were 12 of us adults and five children.... During the course of the hour that we lay there, my hands began to hurt from the rope tied around my wrists and I began to tremble from the cold of the cement floor."[21] The paralyzing fear that gripped those seventeen helpless victims as they lay on the floor that morning of January 19 would never be forgotten, but for sixteen of them the real trauma was over by 8 A.M.

For Chet Bitterman the nightmare had only begun. Soon after the terrorists had attacked it became apparent that the individual they really wanted was Al Wheeler, the director of the Bogota SIL office. When they discovered he was not among the group, they chose Chet instead, forcing him at gunpoint into a car. Then they drove away, giving no clue as to their motives. The first real indication of why Chet was kidnapped came four days later when the terrorists, identifying themselves as the "M-19," expressed their demands in writing: "Chet Bitterman will be executed unless the Summer Institute of Linguistics (SIL) and all its members leave Colombia by 6:00 P.M. February 19."[22]

Once the demands were made known, attempts were made to negotiate, and pleas came from everywhere begging the terrorists to spare Chet's life. Garcia Herraros, a Catholic priest, wrote an open letter that was printed on the front page of a Bogota newspaper: "We want to ask the kidnappers to free this man who has dedicated his life to the extremely noble task of translating the Bible into an Indian language. We can't become insensitive or indifferent to the pain of our Protestant brothers. We esteem and respect them. We appreciate their efforts of sharing the love of Christ. We are with them in this moment of pain."[23]

When the February 19 deadline passed there was a sigh of relief. Perhaps the terrorists would realize their goals were futile. But every glimmer of hope was quickly quashed by the reality of the situation. New and conflicting deadlines were set, and rumors surfaced almost daily that the execution had already been carried out. It was a nightmare for Brenda and her fellow WBT/SIL colleagues. For Chet the ordeal may have been less traumatic than it was for his loved ones.

During the forty-eight days of his captivity, he was treated reasonably well. Though warped in their thinking, the terrorists, he realized, were human beings whom God loved. He witnessed to them, argued with them, and played chess with them. "We've even become friends," he wrote, "and we respect each other, though we view the world from opposite poles."[24] What "friendship" was established between Chet and his captors, though, did not stay his execution on March 7. He was shot once through the heart, and his body was left in a bus along a street in Bogota.

"In Columbia, South Carolina, Chet's brother learned of the news as a result of a chance look at a teletype machine. In Huntington Beach, California, Wycliffe's U.S. director Bernie May was awakened by a long-distance telephone call.... In Lancaster, Pennsylvania, Chet's parents got the word from a local newspaper reporter. And in Bogota, Columbia, the early morning stillness was jarred for Chet's wife when a nearby shopkeeper banged on the gate yelling a message that couldn't wait: 'They've found Chet's body in a bus.' "[25]

The publicity surrounding Chet Bitterman's kidnapping and death brought an outpouring of sympathy and support for the Bitterman family and for WBT/SIL. Cam Townsend reported that more than two hundred individuals had volunteered to take Chet's place. Townsend, in Colombia for the memorial service, was overwhelmed with the response. "The whole country was expressing sympathy to us. Everyone from the president to the policeman who had tears in his eyes when he called on us, was wonderful."[26]

Of the more than one hundred Wycliffe members in Colombia, none requested to leave, even though the mission offered them reassignments. They had jobs to do, and they knew their staying on would demonstrate to the world the ineffectiveness of terrorism.

For Chet's family, the news of his death was accepted with an amazing serenity. Yet there were the inevitable questions. Why had God allowed the ordeal to end the way it did? The problem with his death, Chet's father confessed, "is that we so completely misread God's intent. We fully expected Chet to lead his captors to the Lord. . . . We expected God to release Chet, perhaps in some miraculous way, so the capture of missionaries would become less attractive to revolutionary-type people. . . . God is still God. We know that, but how can we make the media people recognize it? We anticipated telling the news reporters when Chet was released, 'See what God has done?' But how is He going to do something now in a way that'll make sense to the world? . . . We've almost concluded there's very little, if anything, we can do to explain Chet's death to our unsaved friends and the media people, because the answer is to be found at the spiritual level."[27]

SELECTED BIBLIOGRAPHY

Carlson, Lois. **Monganga Paul: The Congo Ministry and Martyrdom of Paul Carlson, M.D.** *New York: Harper & Row, 1966.*

Dowdy, Homer E. **Out of the Jaws of the Lion: Christian Martyrdom in the Congo.** *New York: Harper & Row, 1965.*

Hefley, James and Marti. **By Their Blood: Christian Martyrs of the 20th Century.** *Milford, Mich.: Mott, 1979.*

———. **No Time for Tombstones: Life and Death in the Vietnamese Jungle.** *Wheaton: Tyndale, 1976.*

Lyall, Leslie. **A Passion for the Impossible: The China Inland Mission, 1865–1965.** *Chicago: Moody, 1965.*

Taylor, Mrs. Howard. **The Triumph of John and Betty Stam.** *Philadelphia: China Inland Mission, 1960.*

Chapter 17

Third World Missions: Younger Churches Reach Out

Korean Christians evangelizing their own people and reaching out to others across their borders. This is a scenario that has continued for many decades and is being repeated the world over. Missionaries no longer belong exclusively to the Western church. The day of the Western missionary is certainly not over, but the task of world evangelism is being shouldered to a greater and greater extent by Christians from Third World countries. By 1980 the Third World was sending out and supporting more than ten thousand cross-cultural missionaries, and by 1982 the count was more accurately determined to be fifteen thousand. It is estimated that by the year 2000 some 60 percent of the world's Christians will be found in Third World nations. Nationals reaching nationals has always been a key aspect of missions, but only recently have nationals from Third World countries assumed prominence in the international level of the world missionary movement.

Historically, missionaries depended heavily on nationals to conduct evangelism and pastoral work. In China, national pastors and Bible women performed invaluable service to the Christian church. Pastor Hsi, a one-time Confucian scholar and opium addict, was converted in 1879 and then worked closely with the CIM for many years. In India, Ramābai, the daughter of a Brahman scholar, became a Christian and then gave her life to evangelistic work among India's young widows and orphans. In Argentina, Juan Crisóstomo Varetto became one of Latin America's foremost Protestant leaders and an influential missionary statesman. His daughter, Agustina, taught for more than two decades at the International Seminary in Buenos Aires. And the list goes on.

In most instances nineteenth and early twentieth-century Christian nationals worked closely with the Western missionaries, often under their guidance or authority. Some nationals, however, recognizing the transitional nature of this arrangement, insisted upon independence. This was particularly true in Japan. Shimeta Niishima, a Japanese national who came to America to learn about Christianity and attend seminary, returned to his homeland in 1874 as a missionary. Though supported by the American Board, he was highly independent, and his Christian approach had an unmistakable *samurai*, rather than American, flavor. Kanzo Uchimura, another well-known Japanese Christian and Bible teacher, was a founder of the Mukyokai, a Christian "nonchurch" movement with no Western ties and "with no guide except the Bible."[1] The most vocal nineteenth-century Christian leader in Japan to speak against Western influence was Masakisa Uemura, who believed that foreigners should completely withdraw from the leadership of the Japanese church. "He was convinced that the evangelization of Japan must develop from within, through the work and witness of Japanese themselves, and that it could not be greatly promoted by help received from abroad and in the main administered by foreigners."[2] In 1904 he founded a Japanese theological seminary that was entirely independent of foreign control.

From the beginning, Western mission boards realized the necessity of strong national leadership. National churches, such as the Africa Inland Church, won their independence and began working side by side with their missionary "parent" (in this case, the Africa Inland Mission) taking over pastoral work in the areas of evangelism and education.

Today a huge unknown number of national evangelists (who reach their own people) and national missionaries (who reach people not their own) are supported by their own people. This means about 500,000 pastors and evangelists and maybe 10,000 true missionaries are supported without any foreign help. Amazingly, this may run over a half billion dollars contributed by "mission field Christians" to their own outreach. Most Americans have no conception of how large an enterprise the overseas churches really are.

On the other hand, most missions on occasion assist in the support of key national leaders whenever they do work that is not readily supported by their own people. Even so, most of the funds raised in the Western world for mission work do in fact go into the support of Western missionaries. This fact prompted a Seattle chiropractor, Dr. N. A. Jepson, in 1943 to found CNEC (Christian Nationals Evangelism Commission), an organization committed to the support of Christian nationals. The support was limited to Chinese nationals in the early years, but by 1982 the organization was assisting more than a thousand nationals in thirty-six countries.

One such national has been Anand Chaudhari, the son of a high caste Brahman priest. Following his conversion, Anand left his home in Goa to serve in Rajasthan, an area with virtually no Christian witness. After decades of tireless work he has seen thousands of Indians turn to Christianity. He founded the Rajasthan Bible Institute and began weekly radio broadcasts that are heard all over India. In 1978 he organized a team of more than thirty evangelists to spread out over India with Christian literature, and from that effort more than 60,000 people requested correspondence courses on the Bible.

Because of his own background, Anand has been able to effectively communicate with high caste Hindus. Recently he had the opportunity of leading a highborn political science professor and author to Christ—a man who initially kept his conversion a secret. How could a foreigner have understood what this man was going through? But Anand could. How well he remembered the painful ordeal of telling his own family of his conversion. Far better to them had he died. And then, soon after that visit, he received word that his family, along with hundreds of others, had been killed by an elephant stampede during a Hindu festival. It was only his Christian faith that brought him through the crisis —a gripping testimony that reaches the hearts of other Hindus.

In the Philippines, the CNEC contributes to the support of the Philippines Missionary Fellowship, a locally controlled organization that sponsors more than one hundred missionaries, many of whom have been trained at the Philippines Missionary Institute, founded in 1961. By assisting in the support of such missions, CNEC believes it is serving the cause of world missions by the most efficient means possible. Nationals living in their own country are far more cost effective than foreign missionaries, are free of language and cultural barriers, and are not barred from "closed" countries. The charge that CNEC is "spoiling" the nationals and denying their own people the privilege of supporting them is unfair, according to CNEC officials. Most of CNEC's financial aid supplements ministries already supported by nationals, as in the case of PMF that receives 80 percent of its operating budget from Filipinos.

Many mission agencies operated by nationals object to the idea of outside support and have thus refused to accept any money from the West. One such organization is the Friends Missionary Prayer Band of India. Under the leadership of Samuel Kamaleson and others, this indigenous organization has sent some four hundred missionaries into northern India.

Another Third World mission organization that merits attention is the Evangelical Missionary Association to the Nations, headed by Obed Alvarez of Peru who became the general director at the age of twenty-one. The mission had been founded more than thirty years earlier and had "limped along" until Alvarez took over in 1979. By 1983 the mission had more than one hundred missionaries and was sponsoring a school of missiology, using a test written by Alvarez himself.[3]

While most traditional mission organizations work very closely with nationals, the relationship between nationals and Western missionaries and church leaders is certainly not problem free. The need for Third World Christians to get rid of vestiges of Western culture and particularly capitalist ideology that have crept into their faith has given birth to what many view as the most disturbing theological trend today—namely Liberation Theology. One of the chief spokesman for this new movement is Gustavo Gutierrez, a Peruvian priest whose influence has been felt not only in Latin America but elsewhere throughout the Third World.

"The goal of the theology of liberation," writes Joseph Spinella, "is to free all mankind from every impediment to becoming fully human. People are urged to cooperate with God in the historic process of liberating the world. Sin, according to Gutierrez, is anything that resists or undermines this movement.... Salvation is found in commitment to love one's neighbor and to fight oppression, through revolution if necessary."[4]

While the concepts of Liberation Theology and the problems posed by syncretism in general (the combining of non-Christian religious beliefs with Christianity) present difficult issues for the missionaries and missiologists of the 1980s and beyond, the main thrust of Third World missions continues to be biblically-based evangelism. Some of the most vocal and effective missionary statesmen in the world today are from Third World nations, and the future of world evangelism is heavily dependent on their methods and ideas.

Rochunga Pudaite

One highly respected and influential Third World missionary statesmen is the internationally known Rochunga Pudaite, whose impact on Bible translation and distribution has been immense. His concern for his own Hmar tribe and for world evangelism led him on a difficult and often discouraging journey from a remote jungle village in northeast India to Wheaton, Illinois, where his mission, Bibles for the World, makes its headquarters. "His personal story," wrote entertainer Pat Boone, "is one of the most exciting and heart filling you'll ever read"—one that "could be added as an appendage to the Book of Acts."[5]

Ro Pudaite was born in Senvon, an Indian village in Manipur not far from the Burmese border. It was an area so remote from the seat of government in New Delhi that it was not even listed on the official census and had no government schools or post offices until after Ro, as a young man, brought the matter to Nehru's attention. His earliest recollections were those of a five-year-old being uprooted from the only neighborhood he had ever known to move to another village three days' journey away. The year was 1932. His mother was ill, and friends and relatives were protesting, but his father would not be swayed. God was calling him. It was not easy to leave the security he had known as the pastor of an established village church, but he felt compelled to go. Who else would bring the gospel to Phulpui, if he refused to go? Though lacking in education, Chawnga was a dynamic speaker and well-suited for pioneer evangelistic work. Within a matter of months he had a sizeable congregation and had begun traveling to surrounding villages, sharing a simple Bible message wherever he went.

Chawnga had been converted at the age of fifteen through the ministry of a Welsh missionary, Watkin Roberts, whose term in Senvon was cut short when government officials ordered him to leave. It was a keen disappointment to young Chawnga, but he quickly found a remedy to the situation. If the missionary could not come to him, he would go to the missionary. He traveled a hundred miles, far beyond the border of the Hmar tribe, where he was able to learn to read and study the Bible with his friend and spiritual father. He then returned to spend the rest of his life evangelizing his own people. In less than fifty years, 80 percent of the Hmar tribe, spread out over some four thousand square miles, were professing Christians, thanks to the dedication of Chawnga and other native evangelists and pastors.

Ro was only ten years old when his father took him aside and solemnly spoke to him about the great need for a Hmar Christian to obtain further education so that he could translate the Bible into the language of his own people. It did not take Ro long to figure out that his father had him in mind. It would mean going away to school for long periods of time to live in a strange environment. He was frightened at first, but he realized that such an opportunity was indeed rare for a Hmar youth.

The ninety-six mile journey through the jungle seemed endless, but finally after six days of arduous travel, Ro and his father arrived at the Churachandpur Mission School. It was a boarding school, and most of the boys lived in the dormitory. Such luxury, however, was beyond the means of Ro's poor family. For him, the privilege of attending the mission school meant working for his board and room—milking thirty-five cows each morning and evening, weeding the garden, and helping with household chores. There was no time for soccer and fun with the other boys, and hardly enough time for his studies. He struggled through his classes—each taught by a different native teacher in his own dialect—doubting whether he would even be able to finish the first term.

Despite all the obstacles, Ro quickly demonstrated leadership qualities and was elected president of the Junior Christian Endeavor. He accepted the position with enthusiasm; and, displaying unusual maturity for his age, he organized the group into witnessing teams to evangelize neighboring villages—following the example that had been set before him by his own father.

Though successful in his evangelistic outreach, Ro's education was plagued with difficulties, not the least of which was learning the difficult English language, so filled with inconsistencies. If ever a budding missionary translator struggled with an impossible foreign language, it was Ro. Yet he knew that without it his future ministry would be severely limited. Even though he spent long hours studying and "struggled until his brain ached," he seemed to get nowhere.

It was only through a humiliating incident that he began to conquer the language. He was asked to lead in prayer at a public prayer meeting conducted in English. "He rose, trembling. 'Our Heavenly Father . . . ,' he began, and his mind went blank. He couldn't think of a single English word. He stood there in embarrassed silence, clutching the back of the pew in front of him. He could hear his friends beginning to giggle. After six or seven minutes of tortured silence the leader said a loud 'Amen.' "[6]

Ro was so ashamed of himself that he ran straight to his dorm bed when the meeting was over. He hid under his covers and wept into his pillow, thinking only of running away before having to face his classmates. By dawn, however, after agonizing through the night with God in prayer, "a sweet calm came over him," and he was determined to win the battle. After completing his chores he went to the mission house and borrowed a copy of the *Book of Common Prayer* and another prayer book, both in English, and vowed that he would never again be at a loss for words when he was asked to pray. "Within two weeks he had memorized nearly every prayer in the books. The English language, which had been hidden to him for so long, began unfolding for him. The humiliation in prayer meeting had driven him to just the right source of victory over the barrier that could have kept him from attaining his goal."[7]

There would be more mountains for Ro to conquer as he continued his education. After high school he entered St. Paul's College in Calcutta. Though he was now in his early twenties, the competition was fierce, and Ro had never fully overcome his early educational disadvantages as a Hmar youth. When his I.A. (Immediate Arts) exam results were posted he found that he had failed—by only one point in one subject, but it jeopardized the remainder of his college education and meant retaking a year of work.

Despite the setbacks, Ro never deviated from his goal of translating the Bible for the Hmar tribe. Nothing, he vowed, would distract him from that project. During his college years he began that awesome project—allotting precious study time for that purpose. But there were distractions, not the least of which involved the very future of his own tribe. As a result of an interview that Ro had with Nehru, the tribe had been granted government recognition, and he was chosen as the tribal representative, with the hope that he would one day be elected to a seat in Parliament. It was an exhilarating time, and Ro was basking in his newly acquired recognition and popularity. On the day of the victory celebration, however, everything changed. Ro received a telegram that forced him

to reevaluate his future. The message was from a man he had never met— Watkin Roberts, the missionary who had led his father to Christ—offering to underwrite a Bible education for him in England or Scotland. It was a difficult decision, but when Ro stood up to speak, instead of giving an acceptance speech, he resigned from his newly elected position.

In Scotland, Ro not only took Bible training but also continued his translation of the Hmar New Testament and arranged with the British and Foreign Bible Society to have it published as soon as it was finished. It was there also that he met Billy Graham, who suggested he continue his education at Wheaton College. Later that year he sailed for America. Adjusting to life in America and to Wheaton College in particular was a rude cultural shock for Ro, but he quickly made friends. Among them were some influential Christian leaders, including Bob Pierce of World Vision, John D. Jess, a Christian broadcaster, and V. Raymond Edman, Wheaton College President, who saw great potential in this enthusiastic Indian tribesman.

While Ro was taking courses at Wheaton and revising his Hmar New Testament he was at the same time facing pressure from Watkin Roberts to take over the Indo-Burma Pioneer Mission he had founded years earlier. Though Ro felt indebted to Roberts, the offer was hardly an appealing one. The mission had "no assets, no capital, no board, no officials, not even a mailing list." All it had was "a group of native workers who loved the Lord and wished to serve him, and an old man on the other side of the world who wrote encouraging letters."[8] Yet, Ro found it impossible to say no to the one who had given so much of himself to the Hmar people.

In 1958, with his Hmar New Testament completed, Ro was installed as the president of the Indo-Burma Pioneer Mission. On his board of directors were several well-known Christian leaders who were eager to help him expand the outreach of the mission. Ro returned to India, and in less than a year he set up nine village schools and a Christian high school. He then returned to the United States with his new wife Mawii to continue his studies and raise funds for the mission. Back in India the first shipment of ten thousand Hmar New Testaments arrived, and within six months they were all sold out.

The decade of the 1960s was an eventful one for Ro and the mission. Receipts had risen to over two hundred thousand dollars a year and the work in India had grown rapidly. By 1970 there were some 350 national missionaries, 65 village schools, a high school, and a hospital. The future, however, was not all rosy. Communist rebels had been at work in the once tranquil Hmar tribe, and their influence among the Hmar youth was a direct threat to the tribe and to the future of Christianity. Once again, the people looked to Ro for leadership, requesting that he return to run for a seat in Parliament. He was assured of widespread support and an easy victory over the Communists.

The offer was too inviting for Ro to pass up. Despite Mawii's objections he scheduled a flight that would arrive in New Delhi two days before the filing deadline. The plane departed on schedule, but weather problems en route created extended delays, and when the plane touched down in New Delhi, it was fifteen minutes past the filing deadline. It was a keen disappointment for Ro, but he refused to let the opportunity go to waste. He plunged into crusade evangelism already planned by the Hmar church leaders, and many people turned to Christianity despite threats of persecution and family rejection. The most rewarding experience during the crusade was seeing a Muslim scholar converted—an experience that had a profound impact upon Ro.

Up until that time his burden had been for the Hmar tribe and surrounding areas, but now he began thinking in terms of the whole world. Reaching the world, though, seemed like an utter impossibility. Just sharing the gospel with everyone in India, he estimated, would require a team of a thousand missionaries a thousand years to accomplish. There had to be a better way. He began praying for a solution, and it was while praying that the answer came— perhaps in an unconventional way. The telephone advertising jingle "Let your fingers do the walking" kept running through his mind. Unable to concentrate, he stopped praying. "As he rose from his knees, his eyes caught two telephone directories on his desk. Suddenly the vision was clear. Those books listed the names and addresses of everyone in Calcutta and New Delhi wealthy enough to afford telephones—the best educated, most influential people, the very leaders he wanted to reach."[9]

Mailing New Testaments to telephone subscribers was the evangelism method Ro had been searching for. He contacted Kenneth Taylor, whose *Living Bible* had become a bestseller, and arranged to obtain all the copies

Rochunga Pudaite (with family), founder of Bibles for the World.

he needed without paying royalties. The World Home Bible League agreed to print them at cost, and with that arrangement Bibles for the World was born in 1971. The mission work to the Hmar tribe continued but only as one aspect of this new international movement.

The first page of the New Testament printed for distribution included Ro's testimony and a New Delhi address, and soon after the first mailing was sent out letters began pouring in. The first fifty thousand copies mailed out brought in more than twenty thousand responses. It was the first time many Hindus, Muslims, and Sikhs had ever seen or read the Bible, and they wanted to know more about it and to have specific questions answered.

Reaching the telephone subscribers in India alone was a monumental task, but soon Ro was looking beyond the borders to Burma, Thailand, Sri Lanka, and to the whole world's five hundred million telephone subscribers. Mailing the New Testaments and responding to inquiries led to further openings for spreading the gospel. When Ro returned to India and announced a meeting, the auditorium filled up more than an hour early, and hundreds crowded forward at the invitation to learn more about becoming a Christian. It was the beginning of one man's vision to reach the world for Christ.

Festo Kivengere

One of the most well-known Africans to take a leadership role in world evangelism has been Festo Kivengere, an Anglican bishop from Uganda. He was a product of the great East African revival and as such has brought with him a captivating spiritual vitality as he has traveled around the world preaching the gospel. It was in the 1930s, when the Western nations were struggling to pull themselves out of a paralyzing economic depression, that revival fires were being kindled in East Africa. It was the beginning of "one of the great movings of the Holy Spirit in the twentieth century." Revival spontaneously ignited among the Africans and for more than forty years continued to spread out and renew itself. It was a contagious force, according to Festo. "People who were . . . born again when they were illiterate . . . would get the verses in their heads and then go stand up and preach them without having a Bible. . . . They have won hundreds and thousands of people. . . ."[10]

Festo was converted during the early years of the revival, and his spiritual pilgrimage paralleled that continuous revival for the decades that followed. He was born in Kigezi, Uganda, and during his childhood joined with his family in worshiping the tribal gods. Then when he was about ten he was introduced to Christianity. An African evangelist came to Kigezi and preached on Christ and His love for individual human beings. It was a completely new concept to Festo—almost beyond comprehension. He wanted to learn more, and so he began reading a primer from the Gospel of Luke. He was searching for something more meaningful than the tribal gods—something "my father . . . never seemed to me to have found." His search ended a few years later when he committed his life to Christ while attending boarding school.[11]

During this time the East Africa revival was spilling over the borders of Uganda into Kenya, Tanzania, Zaire, and other neighboring countries. Festo became a part of this evangelical outreach, actively participating as a layman. He spent five years teaching school in his home village, his primary concern being the spiritual needs of his tribespeople. As time passed, however, the need to reach out beyond his own people became more and more compelling. He and his young wife Mera "felt God's call to Tanzania as missionaries."[12]

Beginning in the late 1950s, Festo's evangelistic ministry took on an international scope. After a preaching tour in Australia he served for a time as an interpreter for Billy Graham and then traveled around the world, meeting with religious leaders and speaking to crowds numbering in the thousands. His concern for Africa did not diminish, and he was an influential figure behind African Enterprise, an evangelistic team similar to the Billy Graham evangelistic team. Through this organization he helped maintain the momentum of the ongoing East Africa revival.

Festo's involvement in the revival movement was not universally well-received by his fellow churchmen in Uganda. The Anglican clergy were for the most part skeptical of what they viewed to be emotional fanaticism, and none of the top leaders were involved during the early years. They and most of the pastors "remained very dry," opposing any signs of religious "enthusiasm."[13]

During Festo's time as a missionary in Tanzania he had faced repeated insults and ridicule from established church leaders. In one instance, he later recalled, an "African pastor got up in the cathedral pulpit one Sunday when the church was packed and said, 'Now, look: I want to warn you against some strangers who have recently moved in. They talk big words about salvation, but they are wolves in sheep's skin. Be careful of them.'"[14] Festo and his co-workers refused to be deterred, however, and their persistence paid off. Some months later this same Anglican pastor "stood before his congregation . . . with tears streaming down his cheeks. He said to them, 'Months ago I told you that if any of you experienced this salvation they were talking about I would excommunicate you. I have been saved. Now you can excommunicate me if you like.'"[15]

Most of the Anglican ministers were not won over to evangelical Christianity that easily. They were satisfied with their formalism and creeds and were reluctant to have any association at all with a movement that sometimes got out of hand. "We had our excesses," Festo admitted. "All sorts of things have happened: dreams, visions in the night, conviction of sin, but no one ever put these above Christ and him crucified and moving alive among us."[16]

The task that faced Festo was that of controlling the excesses and keeping the revival on course while at the same time reaching out to the established church leaders and winning them to a warm personal faith in Christ. It was a difficult assignment, but by 1976 he could say that "more than 85 percent of the clergymen know Jesus Christ as their Saviour, as do all our bishops."[17] By that time Festo himself had been consecrated an Anglican bishop, and the church in Uganda was in the midst of a most painful period of testing and persecution.

It was in January of 1971, almost two years before Festo was called to be bishop in his own diocese of Kigezi, that Idi Amin, through a military coup, was installed as Uganda's new president. Many Ugandans were initially excited about the change, but that excitement soon began to fade. "Before three months had passed," Festo wrote, "we realized that the military had been given extraordinary powers of arrest and instant execution of anyone seeming to endanger the regime."[18]

Soon Uganda was engulfed in an atmosphere of fear and terror. Anyone, including church leaders, who spoke against the regime was seen as an enemy of the state, and even sharing one's faith with another was viewed with suspicion. It was simply not the time nor the place to be espousing Christian principles. Yet, "as danger and discomfort increased, there was a spiritual quickening. . . . There were deep repentances before God and reconciliations with the brethren. . . . All over Uganda, both village and city people were drawing their strength from God. . . ."[19]

It was during this time of turmoil in Uganda that Festo was consecrated bishop in St. Peter's Cathedral in Kampala. It was a memorable day not only for him and his family, but also for thousands of Ugandan Christians. He was replacing an Englishman, thus allowing the diocese of Kigezi to have its own African bishop. The ceremony, known as "enthronement," required special robes and liturgy and, in the words of Festo, "can make one very high and dry," but he in his humble way brought the ceremony and the adulation that accompanied it into proper perspective. He quoted his friend, Yohana Omari, the first African bishop in Tanzania. "I want to be like the little donkey our Lord chose to ride on to enter Jerusalem. They laid their robes on it and shouted, but the shouting was all for the Lord Jesus whom he was carrying."[20]

Although the political turmoil and military atrocities continued in Uganda, the years immediately following Festo's consecration as a bishop saw an expansion of the East Africa revival. His diocese alone had more confirmations in 1976, some thirty thousand, than did the entire Episcopal denomination in the United States during that same year. Churches all over Uganda were packed with people seeking security and consolation in Christ, while all around them the atmosphere was growing more tense.

Many of the acts of political terrorism during these years were directed against Christians, while Muslims were shown special favors. Clergymen were singled out for verbal as well as physical abuse. They were accused of interfering with the government and "preaching bloodshed," and their lives were in jeopardy. "Those were . . . days of fear, anxiety, torture, and death," Festo later recalled. "Several times that year, rumors reached London that I had been arrested and killed." Some months later he wrote to friends in America, telling of the situation in his beloved homeland: "I still have meetings here in Norway before my wife and I return to our 'bleeding Uganda.' I am listening to the world news right now, and it is indeed bloody. An attempt on Amin's life last week failed, leaving ten dead. Now retaliations and bloody purges have begun. Thousands have already been massacred and hundreds are in the torture chambers.

Festo Kivengere, Anglican church leader in Uganda.

So please pray that the Lord of power will deliver this bleeding country from the terror of the present regime."[21]

The government harassment of civilians was brought close to home for Festo when his daughter Charity, along with more than two hundred other university students, was physically abused in an early morning military attack on campus dormitories and then hauled away to a military prison. In the midst of the pandemonium that followed, Charity and other Christians prayed, and before long a calm settled over the frightened students. Later that day they were released and transported back to the campus, and the nightmare was over.

Not long after this scare at the university there was a rebellion in the ranks of the army that was quickly and brutally quashed. The perpetrators were immediately executed, but that was not enough. At the orders of Amin, whom *Time* magazine described as

447

"the Wild Man of Africa," thousands of soldiers and civilians were murdered. Anyone who had spoken publicly against the regime was viewed as a traitor. During this very time, Festo was asked to be the featured speaker at the consecration of another bishop. There in front of some thirty thousand people the audacious young bishop spoke his mind. He bluntly reminded government officials (many of whom were present) of their awesome responsibility before God: "Many of you have misused your authority, taking things by force, using too much force. Jesus Christ used His authority to save men and women—how are you using your authority? If you misuse the authority God gave you, God is going to judge you, because He is the one who gave it to you."[22]

Many people feared that after such a speech Festo would never be heard from again. But perhaps not to make the retaliation too obvious, the authorities bypassed Festo, whose international renown also may have influenced his temporary immunity, and instead waited more than two weeks and then arrested his immediate superior, Archbishop Janani Luwum. Prior to his arrest, Luwum was awakened at 1:30 A.M. by soldiers who proceeded to ransack his house to find evidence of his alleged subversive activities. Then about a week later he was summoned to the State House in Entebbe. Here he was formally charged with subversive activity and arms smuggling, and the government-controlled news service announced that he had been arrested. The next morning the newspaper reported that Luwum and two Christian cabinet members had been killed in a car crash that occurred when one of the cabinet members had attempted to subdue the driver.

The true account of what actually happened was a bloody horror story of torture and death—one that convinced Festo it was time for him to flee his homeland. His house was under surveillance, and rumors were rampant that he was the next on the death list. Thus, on the night of February 19, 1977, he and his wife Mera fled across the Ugandan border into Rwanda. It was a frightening journey: "As we went out into the night, the darkness was our cover.... We were lost in the mountains for two and a half hours, driving on a footpath and nearly sliding over a precipice.... Every step was a miracle of grace, especially in the last climb over the mountain. Mera had a fever from bronchitis and was coughing hard. Sometimes I wondered if we could make it. We would climb a short way, then stop to rest and pray, and climb again.... We reached the top of the mountain at dawn.... We were over the border! Exhausted and jubilant, we ... sat down ... and began to thank God."[23]

Festo's safe escape was heralded by Christians in Uganda and all over the world, and he soon became the country's most prominent exile, speaking out bluntly against the Ugandan regime. After two years in exile, during which time his country entered a bloody war to oust Amin, Festo returned to his homeland. There was a jubilant crowd on hand to welcome him at the airport, but the joy of homecoming was quickly dispelled when the reality of the devastation became evident. The eight-year reign of terror that had cost the lives of an estimated half million people (mainly Christians) had drained the country not only economically, but spiritually and morally as well. The task of rebuilding was enormous. Festo worked closely with African Enterprise, mobilizing relief work, and in the following years amidst a grievous famine he has been in the forefront of Ugandan relief efforts.

Though deeply involved in relief work, Festo's primary ministry remained spiritual. Preserving the spirit of the East Africa revival was his top priority. In 1982, nearly three years after his return, he reported "a tremendous upsurge in spiritual interest" that was occurring in Uganda. The previous year his own diocese alone had added fourteen new parishes. "The Church," according to Michael Cassidy, "is the only institution which has come out of the Amin era strengthened and fortified rather than weakened," and it has become "a key factor . . . in reconstruction and rehabilitation of the nation as a whole."[24]

Luis Palau

One of the most effective missionary-evangelists in the world today is Luis Palau, a native Argentine who has preached to an estimated three hundred million people in some forty different countries. Often referred to as the "Billy Graham of Latin America," Palau, like Graham, ministers with an evangelistic team through radio, television, and public crusades. His influence in Latin America has been enormous. In 1975, during a two-month saturation media effort, it was estimated that nearly one third of the population of that region of the world had heard the gospel through one or more of his related ministries. His goal is to see three Latin American republics become predominantly evangelical during his lifetime—a monumental task in light of the powerful Roman Catholic influence, but not unfeasible in light of the rapidly expanding Christian church that he has helped to foster.

Palau was born in Argentina in 1934 and raised by Christian parents who had been converted through the ministry of a Brethren missionary from England by the name of Charles Rogers. Because of that relationship, missions became an important part of the Palau home. From his earliest years Luis's mother read to him missionary stories and impressed upon him the crucial needs of world evangelism.

It was at a summer camp run by Anglican missionaries that Palau was converted, but during his teen-age years he turned away from the church and became involved in "foolish worldliness." Then, just before Carnival Week in 1951 he made a "clean sweep" and dedicated his life to serving the Lord. "I bought myself a new Bible, and started going to church. I went to another city and really began a new life. I broke my pipe, tore up my membership in the University Club, got rid of my car, soccer magazines, Elvis Presley records and everything. I . . . really began to study the Bible and pray on my knees for hours."[25] Every Thursday night was "gospel preaching night" at the Brethren church, and the church leaders quickly saw to it that Luis was involved. "To train us young fellows, the leaders put us up to preach. Then they would criticize our preaching and give us ideas. I don't know how the church folks stood it, but they did. It was good practice, although we never gave an invitation to receive Christ."[26]

Palau's first involvement in personal evangelism was prompted by missionaries who were specializing in children's work. With their help, he organized a class of twelve-year-old boys and experienced his first taste for soulwinning when two of them became Christians. "It was just thrilling. I got a passion to do more and more and more. It was then I thought, 'Boy, this is the greatest thing. This is what I want to do for my life work.'"[27]

Full-time evangelistic work, however, would have to wait. Financial hardships arose following the death of his father, and it fell to him to support his mother and five younger sisters. He accepted a position in a bank, and his work there consumed much of his time for the next few years. Even during this period, though, Palau was actively engaged in evangelism on a part-time basis. With two other young men, he started short daily radio programs and then purchased a tent and began holding tent meetings. "Interestingly enough," he recalls, "though I loved to preach and felt burdened to invite people to turn to Christ, my friend was considered the evangelist. People said we made a great team and that I should be the Bible teacher and he the evangelist. And that's the way it was for a while."[28]

A key element in these early evangelistic efforts was prayer. Palau and a fellow worker met for prayer every morning at 5 A.M. and on Fridays spent "the entire night in prayer." Soon Palau realized he was being caught up in ritualistic legalism: "Our times of study and prayer and work became a cycle of grim determination to stay with it, to keep on going."[29] Despite all the outward signs of spirituality, on the inside there was a "monumental emptiness." At times he was on the verge of giving up, but he vowed he would not "allow the search for" his "own victory to get in the way of offering God's love and salvation to people who had a greater need...."[30] A high point in his evangelistic work was seeing an adult converted through his preaching, but still he was plagued with "terrible ups and downs."[31]

As Palau continued his lay evangelistic ministry he realized that philosophically he was drifting further and further away from the Brethren with whom he was so closely associated. In many ways he found them too narrow—emphasizing separation to the point of refusing to cooperate with other evangelistic Christian groups. On the issue of mass evangelism he also sensed a strong difference of opinion: "The Brethren had difficulty accepting mass evangelism ... and didn't believe in giving altar calls."[32]

Palau, on the other hand, had been strongly influenced by the ministry of Billy Graham and the lives of Wesley, Whitefield, Finney, Moody, and Sunday. "My dream from all the reading and praying I had been doing was that Latin America could be reached on a large scale for Christ.... History has shown that a nation of millions cannot be converted by one-on-one evangelism, because eventually the chain breaks down and the multiplication peters out.... A nation will not be changed with timid methods."[33]

Palau's dream of becoming a great evangelist was thwarted by his continuing work at the bank, but the delay allowed him time to examine his motives. He began to envision "stadiums full" of "great crowds of people." "Was it my imagination telling me that I wanted to be a well-known preacher?" "No," Palau reasoned, "the Lord was laying on my heart what he was going to do." He accepted the "biblical sanction" that he was "ego centered," but he refused to be deterred. "I am not going to spend the rest of my life beating my breast and searching my soul," he wrote. "But I do ask the Lord, 'If I get out of hand or if I am in the way of Your greater glory, please put me down.' And I have perfect confidence that He will do it."[34]

His continued work at the bank was not the only factor that stymied Palau's dream of becoming involved in Latin American evangelism on a "massive scale." There were other problems: "I had no contacts, no money; hardly anyone outside Cordoba even knew who I was." Yet he continued preaching every opportunity he had, and his mother urged him to leave the bank and enter a full-time church planting ministry. It was not until he met a missionary representing Overseas Crusades and was asked to work with that organization that he finally left the security of his position at the bank.

Palau's initial work with Overseas Crusades was interrupted in 1960 when he was invited by Ray Stedman, a California pastor, to come to the United States for Bible training. He entered Multnomah School of the Bible in Portland, Oregon, where he acquired not only a Christian education but also an American fiancée, Pat Scofield. It was also at Multnomah that Palau's "years of searching" came to an end. The climax came during a short chapel message culminating with a challenge from Galatians 2:20. It

was a "complete release," for his "biggest spiritual struggle was finally over." "I ran back to my room in tears and fell to my knees next to my bunk. I prayed in my native Spanish, 'Lord, now I get it. . . . It's not what I'm going to do for You but rather what You're going to do through me.' "[35]

Following their schooling at Multnomah, Palau and his bride went to Detroit for missionary internship in preparation for their anticipated ministry with Overseas Crusades in Colombia. Then, before beginning their deputation work, they spent two months working with the Billy Graham crusade in Fresno, California, where Luis served as a Spanish interpreter for Graham's messages. Following their deputation ministry they went to Costa Rica, where Pat enrolled in language school, and then in 1964 it was on to Colombia as missionaries.

Though Palau realized he was "expected to be a regular missionary, training nationals in evangelism and church planting," he viewed the work as "a stepping-stone and training for crusades of the future."[36] His initial work involved local church mobilization campaigns for which OC was known. Lay people were trained in evangelism and church planting, and it was hoped that they then would become the primary catalyst for church growth. To bolster the lay evangelism, Palau, along with fellow OC missionaries, conducted street evangelism, a ministry that often met with resistance from Roman Catholic clergy and government officials. In 1965 Palau conducted his first city-wide evangelistic campaign. It was held in a tiny Presbyterian church—hardly the mass evangelism of which he had dreamed.

Following that campaign, Palau initiated a television counseling ministry from HCJB in Quito, Ecuador. It was a unique concept, offering callers personal counseling on live television, and the lines were packed. One young woman who called was a committed Marxist, deeply involved in the local Communist party. The morning after she called she met with Palau in person, and after a long and argumentative session she broke down and committed herself to Christ. Through her witness the leader of the Communist party began studying the Bible, and a planned revolution was averted.

The television work as well as the crusade ministry that Palau conducted in Colombia only heightened his desire to become a full-time evangelist reaching Latin America's masses. His eagerness as he later related, was dampened by the reservations of his superiors: "I think the men at OC were afraid that I could not handle the glory that can go along with being a successful evangelist. They weren't sure my Latin temperament was suited to the adulation that might result from it."[37]

It was 1966 when Palau was considering separating from OC and becoming an independent evangelist that he was asked by Dick Hillis, the founder and director of OC, to relocate in Mexico to serve as the field director there and to develop an evangelistic team for future crusades. Before taking this step, Palau had his first opportunity to conduct a large crusade. It was held in Bogota, Colombia, and there were some twenty thousand people in attendance and several hundred decisions.

It was not until 1968 that the Palaus arrived in Mexico, and the following year, with the help of two other OC missionaries, Luis conducted fourteen Mexican crusades. They varied in size, but the largest attracted more than thirty thousand people over a nine-day period and resulted in some two thousand decisions. It was an exhilarating time, but also a time of hardships and disappointments. Financial problems plagued the ministry, and government harassment prompted further setbacks. A big crusade planned for the baseball arena in Mexico City was canceled at the last minute by government officials.

From Mexico, Palau and his team went to El Salvador, Honduras, Paraguay, Peru, Venezuela, and other Latin American countries, holding week-long campaigns that attracted as many as one hundred thousand people. Church planting, though, remained a primary objective, and as a result the evangelical church grew wherever they went.

Through the 1970s as his crusade ministry expanded, Palau continued to serve with OC, and between 1976 and 1978 he was president of that organization. Presiding over a mission based in North America was a difficult and trying task, however, and in the fall of 1978 he resigned from the mission and set up his own organization, the Luis Palau Evangelistic Team. Though he continued to work closely with OC, he now had the independence he needed to launch a worldwide crusade ministry that took him to such unlikely places as Glasgow, Scotland, and Madison, Wisconsin. Though most at home in Latin America, Palau could no longer confine his ministry to one area. The whole world had become his mission field.

Luis Palau at Jubilee '77 with the bishop of Llandaff.

Philip Teng

The cost of foreign missionary work in China beginning with the Nestorians, and after them the Jesuits, and finally the Protestants, has been enormous. Literally thousands of Western missionaries through the centuries died prematurely through martyrdom or disease on Chinese soil. Yet when China closed its doors to Western missionaries in 1950, Christianity had still not made a major impact on that country, and it was feared that in the face of heavy persecution the faith might dwindle to nothing.

How wrong those ominous forebodings turned out to be. In the 1970s, as China began to emerge from a generation of tightly guarded isolationism, some of the first reports to reach the West indicated that the Christian church was larger and healthier than anyone could have imagined. House churches (some forty to fifty thousand) had sprung up in cities and villages all over the land. By 1980 it was estimated that there were some five million Christians in China—a fivefold increase since the missionaries had been expelled thirty years earlier. (Some estimates ran many times higher than that.)

Western missionaries had performed invaluable service in establishing the church in China, but their expulsion, forcing nationals to fill the void in church leadership, was perhaps the element needed to make Christianity a truly Chinese faith. Charges of colonialism and imperialism were no longer relevant. Christianity was standing alone without the extra baggage the missionaries had so often carried with them.

Among the Chinese outside the People's Republic of China during these years there was a corresponding growth in Christianity, and again there was capable leadership from Chinese nationals. In Hong Kong, Philip Teng, a pastor and educator, became convinced that the job of evangelization belonged to the Chinese themselves, and in the years since he has been one of the leading Christian missiologists to espouse this principle.

By the early 1950s, when the last of the missionaries were leaving China, Teng was already a well-known figure in Christian circles in Hong Kong. The son of a Presbyterian minister and a graduate of Edinburgh, he was a popular Bible teacher among Hong Kong's three hundred churches, and on weekdays his time was devoted to teaching at the Alliance Bible Seminary, Bethel Seminary, and the Evangelical Free Church Bible Institute. It was during this period, when his ministry was in such high demand, that Teng received a call from the North Point Alliance Church—a tiny congregation only five years old. Other men of his stature might have considered the call an insult, but Teng was certain of God's leading in the congregation's decision. He withdrew his name from a large church that was also considering him and accepted the call to North Point.

During the early years of his ministry there the church grew rapidly despite obvious drawbacks in the location—the sixth floor of an apartment building. Then in 1968, after ten years in that location, the congregation moved to a new seven-hundred-seat sanctuary that was soon packed for both its Sunday morning services. During this period of rapid church growth, Teng continued his teaching ministry and also traveled on evangelistic missions throughout Southeast Asia. As he traveled he became more and more conscious of the need for Asians to take up the burden of foreign missions. Then in 1961 at the

Philip Teng, Christian and Missionary Alliance leader in Hong Kong.

Third Asia Conference he was challenged by other Third World delegates who were actively involved in missions. He returned home and initiated an annual missions conference and faith-promise pledging at North Point Alliance Church and encouraged the other Hong Kong Alliance churches to follow suit. He also instituted a department of missions at the Alliance Bible Seminary, and in the twenty years that followed seventy-five foreign missionaries were sent out from the Hong Kong Alliance churches to a dozen different countries.

Although he had become one of Asia's foremost missionary statesmen, Teng was not satisfied sending others to do the work of foreign missions while he stayed home. He wanted to be in the front lines. That opportunity came in 1977 when he asked his church to release him for a year of missionary service. He placed his two youngest children in a missionary children's school in Malaysia, and he and his wife went on to Indonesia, where they ministered to hundreds of thousands of Chinese in southern Borneo.

The North Point Alliance Church had only reluctantly agreed that their pastor should serve as a foreign missionary, fearing church attendance would decline in his absence. Instead, the church grew, and when he returned his enthusiasm for the work in southern Borneo quickly spread to the other Alliance churches. They agreed to help build five new churches and a Bible school among the people to whom he had ministered, and Christians from Hong Kong went there to serve as missionaries.

Back in Hong Kong, Teng continued his pastoral and teaching ministry and took on new responsibilities as well. He accepted the presidency of the Alliance Bible Seminary and the Alliance Church Union, and he began a world-wide ministry that carried his message of missions and evangelism to five different continents. Then in 1979 he became the president of the Alliance World Fellowship, a fitting tribute to a great missionary statesman and a testimony of the Western church's growing confidence in Third World leadership.[38]

Paul Yonggi Cho

The fastest growing religious movement in the world today is the evangelical church in Korea—a church that has set a goal of launching out ten thousand cross-cultural missionaries by the end of the 1980s. "Every day in South Korea an average of ten new Protestant churches open their doors for the first time to accommodate the still-rising flood of converts."[39] An estimated one million people are converted to Christianity each year—a growth rate that would see Christians comprising half of Korea's population by the end of this century.

Protestant missionary work to Korea began in earnest in the 1880s, and almost immediately there was a receptive response—very unlike the hostility the Roman Catholics had faced barely two decades earlier. One of the reasons for this may have been the Protestants' use of the Korean term *Hananim* for God, avoiding the imported Chinese term that the Catholics used. "The choice of *Hananim*," according to Don Richardson, "could not have been more providential for Protestant missions in Korea! Preaching like houses afire in cities, towns, villages or in the countryside, Protestant missionaries began by affirming Korean belief in *Hananim*. Building upon this residual witness, Protestants masterfully disarmed the Korean people's natural antipathy toward bowing before some foreign deity."[40]

Besides permitting the Koreans to have their own term for God, the missionaries quickly established a pattern of permitting them to have their own churches. In 1890 the arrival in Seoul of John L. Nevius, a veteran Presbyterian missionary from China, paved the way for mission strategy that soon characterized Korean missions in general. The Nevius Method that called for "self-governing, self-supporting, and self-propagating" churches promoted indigenous Christianity virtually free from outside influences. Nationals quickly took leading roles in church affairs, and today, a century later, the Koreans themselves are the strength behind the church's phenomenal growth.

The two largest Protestant churches in the world today are both located in Seoul, Korea. The larger of the two is the Full Gospel Central Church, whose pastor, Paul Yonggi Cho, has seen his feeble beginnings in a ragged tent grow into a congregation of over two hundred seventy thousand. The church employs more than three hundred full-time pastors and conducts seven services each Sunday in a main auditorium and side chapels that seat some thirty thousand people. Aside from the numbers, the ministry of Cho is singularly impressive. Evangelism—world evangelism—is his all-encompassing goal, and he has effectively exported his evangelistic strategy all over the world.

Cho was born into a Buddhist family in 1936 during the long and cruel Japanese occupation of Korea. He was a sickly boy suffering from tuberculosis, and few expected him to survive to adulthood. His weak physical condition caught the attention of a young Christian girl who began visiting him, and through her faithful witness he was converted. Almost immediately he began thinking of how he could best serve God, and in the years that followed his conversion he started laying the groundwork for full-time Christian service.

In 1958, after graduating from a small Assemblies of God Bible School, Cho began a "tent church" on the outskirts of Seoul. "Assisted by his future mother-in-law, Jashel Choi . . . and later by missionary John Hurston, Pastor Cho, still ravaged by TB, ministered faith, hope, and healing to his growing

congregation of poverty-stricken people."[41] Within six years the church numbered some two thousand members, but Cho was physically and mentally exhausted. He collapsed during a church service in 1964 and was uncertain after that experience whether he could ever return to the pastorate again. How could his frail constitution endure the rigors of ministering to such a large congregation? Going back to his church and filling the traditional role as the head pastor would have been comparable, in Cho's mind, to digging his own grave. There had to be another solution.

It was during his convalescence that "God spoke to Cho through the advice of Moses' father-in-law recorded in Exodus 18:13–26."[42] From this passage he conceived the idea of dividing the church into small cell groups, each of which would be led by a competent

Paul Yonggi Cho, pastor of the world's largest church in Seoul, Korea.

lay person. The plan was not initiated without resistance from church and board members, but almost immediately rapid growth began and the responsibility of shepherding the growing flock no longer lay entirely on Cho's shoulders.

This cell-group concept allowed the Full Gospel Central Church to maintain a small-church atmosphere while at the same time enjoying the benefits a larger church can offer. Despite its size, membership was made a guarded privilege that was not given out freely. Converts were required to undergo a three-month probationary period before being received into membership. Even then membership was only granted for a twelve-month period. Each year members were reevaluated and inactive members were removed from the roles.

The growth of the Full Gospel Central Church has certainly not been the only priority of Cho. By 1982 nearly one hundred "daughter churches" had been established. In one instance Cho sent five thousand, and in another case three thousand, of his own members to initiate a new work. But Korea was only the first step in Cho's program for world evangelism. Central Church sent out its first missionaries in 1972, and in the decade that followed "more than 100 full-time, seminary-trained missionaries" were sent out to North and South America, Europe, and Asia, where Bible schools have been established to train new converts.[43]

As impressive as the one decade of missionary outreach had been, Cho set a goal of increasing the missionary force many times over each succeeding decade. Missions, he believes, is the primary aim of church growth, and

it is his church growth strategy, he further maintains, that is best suited for world evangelization.

To disseminate his strategy of church growth, Cho founded Church Growth International. In the past several years he has traveled extensively, conducting seminars for tens of thousands of pastors from forty different countries, encouraging them to put his principles into action in their own churches.

The rapid church growth that the Central Church experienced did not come without difficulties and problems. Quite naturally there has been resentment from other pastors who felt that Cho had amassed too much power. Feelings of this nature ran particularly high within his own denomination, the Korean Assemblies of God. One third of the KAG membership was made up of Central Church members alone, a factor that seemed to offbalance the influence of Cho in the denomination. It was perhaps due to this factor as much as anything that Cho, in 1981, was accused of heresy by KAG leaders and asked to resign.

The immediate issue in question related to the Korean custom of honoring the dead, an issue as old as the Chinese Rites controversy that raged in the Roman Catholic Church for more than a century after the death of Ricci (see chapter 2). The problem was settled among Catholics in 1937, when the church hierarchy dropped its long-standing opposition and permitted ceremonies for the dead. Protestants, however, continued by and large to evade the issue even though the practice is widespread. In Korea it is estimated that some 80 percent of the Christians secretly conduct services venerating the dead.

For Cho, the problem began in 1979, when one of his church members—"a troubled oldest son"—came to him, "confessing that on the first anniversary of his father's death he had followed tradition and led his wider family in lighting candles and bowing before the picture of their father."[44] He offered to drop his membership, but Cho advised him not to, insisting that he needed "the church now more than ever before."

Months after the incident occurred, Cho himself brought it to light in a sermon illustration, contending that honoring the dead was not to be lumped in the same category as worshiping the dead. For Cho's opponents such a statement provided fuel for the fire. Cho later agreed to retract his statement, but the controversy became so heated that he and his church finally withdrew from the KAG. Though wooed by Methodists and Baptists to join them, Cho was convinced that a nondenominational stance offered the church the greatest opportunity for a wide-ranging ministry.

This issue that brought so much stress personally to Cho and to his congregation illustrates his sensitivity to the particular needs of Asians, and it demonstrates the importance of Third World Christians settling their own problems. Cho is critical of the way Western missionaries have conducted evangelism in the past, although he readily understands the problems they have faced. He recognizes the difficulty they have identifying culturally and philosophically with Asians. Moreover, he believes "Western missionaries sometimes failed because they went to the upper classes. Revolutions come from common people and that is where we are winning our converts. When we have won the common people, the upper classes will listen, because they are opportunistic. . . . Now is an exciting time in Asia."[45]

Cho has not sought to exclude Western missionaries from playing a significant role in Asian evangelism, but he speaks for many Third World Christian leaders when he emphasizes the necessity of nationals reaching their own people in their own context. At the same time, the strength and vast experience of Western missions must continue to be utilized to a maximum efficiency. The future of world evangelism depends heavily on an international community of missionaries and missiologists who are able to cooperate effectively in the monumental task of reaching the world for Christ.

Another Korean, who in many respects has been more active than Paul Cho in cross-cultural missionary outreach has been David Cho, also a pastor of a large church in Seoul. Besides his duties at his two-thousand-member Presbyterian church, he actively works with the Korean International Mission and the Asia Missions Association. He is the author of *New Forces in Asian Missions* and is one of Asia's leading missiologists.

SELECTED **B**IBLIOGRAPHY

Hefley, James and Marti. **God's Tribesman: The Rochunga Pudaite Story.** *New York: Holman, 1974.*

Kivengere, Festo. **I Love Idi Amin.** *Old Tappan, N.J.: Revell, 1977.*

Palau, Luis [*as told to Jerry B. Jenkins*]. **The Luis Palau Story.** *Old Tappan, N.J.: Revell, 1980.*

Richardson, Don. **Eternity in Their Hearts.** *Ventura, Calif.: Regal, 1981.*

Chapter 18

New Methods and Strategy: Reaching Tomorrow's World

"The New Missionary." A *Time* magazine cover story in 1982 about men and women who are devoting their lives to bringing Christianity to some of the most remote and impoverished areas of the world. Who is this "new missionary"? From the perspective of *Time*, the "new missionary" is not really very different from the missionary of generations past. Both are characterized by a sacrificial devotion to carrying the gospel to the ends of the earth.

There are, however, some significant differences between the new and the old missionary. The "new missionary" represents men and women who, in many ways, are much more sophisticated and professional in their outlook than was the "old missionary." They are more concerned with methodology and principles of mission strategy, more aware of population growth and other relevant statistics, more eager to make use of the latest technology, and, as *Time* pointed out, more careful than ever to avoid any tactics that would associate them with Western imperialism. They are more likely than ever to seek to preserve colorful cultural traditions that were once viewed as unchristian.

Paralleling the development of the "new missionary" has been a significant advance in the field of missiology in recent decades that is evidenced by scholarly journals, recognized schools of mission, and an impressive task force of forward-thinking missiologists. Once a description to be given only to a handful of progressive mission board directors, today the term missiologist is associated with hundreds of professional specialists involved in developing more effective mission strategies. In 1970 the American Society of Missiology did not exist, but a decade later, eight years after its founding, it had seven hundred members.

Men such as Donald McGavran and Ralph Winter have contributed vastly to the field of missiology, as has C. Peter Wagner, who served for sixteen years as a missionary to Bolivia. Wagner has written numerous books on missions, and in the years since his active missionary career he has held a professorship in church growth, served as a member of the Lausanne Committee for World Evangelization, and authored more than a dozen books on missions and church growth.

As important as the field of missiology has become, however, it is only one aspect of the contemporary scene in world evangelism. The most striking characteristic of foreign missions is the diversity of methodology and philosophy. That aspect more than any other gives the movement a solid base as the twenty-first century approaches. The controversy that sometimes rages over methods and concepts of evangelism provides a healthy exchange of ideas and allows for a broad base of support. No one need feel excluded for lack of a compatible philosophical approach. Whether one is in favor of a straightforward evangelistic approach, a humanitarian effort, or a covert smuggling operation, the options are all available in today's very fruitful and diverse missionary enterprise.

One of the more recent developments in the field of missiology is the "hidden peoples" concept—a concept that has been widely disseminated in churches and mission agencies by men such as Ralph Winter and Don Richardson. By the time of the annual meetings of the IFMA and EFMA in the fall of 1982, there were few exceptions among the nearly two hundred mission agencies of these two largest associations of mission agencies that were not by then already talking in these terms and already making plans along these lines for expansion into new frontiers in order to reach these "hidden peoples." The concept has been widely adopted by the younger generation of mission leaders and is rapidly becoming a dominant theme in missions as the twentieth century comes to a close.

With all the diversity and the scientific and technological advances that have brought mission organizations into the modern age, the human element has changed very little. The missionaries themselves remain the *sine qua non* of world evangelism, and today as in ages past they are the greatest heroines and heroes of Christianity despite their human frailties.

R. Kenneth Strachan

Trial and error, success and failure, a visionary outlook, and a sometimes blatant inconsistency combined to make the "saturation evangelism" of Ken Strachan one of the most farsighted mission strategies of the twentieth century. His development of Evangelism-in-Depth was nothing short of a "Revolution in Evangelism," as the title of a book on the subject suggests. His concepts still stimulate controversy and claim loyal disciples today, though he died in 1965. Yet, his basic premise, "that the growth of any movement is in direct proportion to its ability to mobilize its entire membership for continuous evangelism" was not new.[1] Others had operated under the same theory, but none had developed it into such a well-defined, exhaustive missionary thrust. It was left to Ken Strachan to do that, in part as a reaction against the weaknesses he saw in his own father's evangelistic ministry.

Ken was born and raised in Latin America, the son of Susan and Harry

Strachan, co-founders of the Latin America Mission (originally called the Latin American Evangelization Campaign). Most of his early years were spent in Costa Rica, his mother being responsible for the oversight of LAM headquarters while his father conducted evangelistic tours. "A talented and untiring evangelist, Harry Strachan, as ubiquitous as the fabled Don Quixote, had moved up and down the continent in unceasing evangelistic activity, setting up, coordinating, and carrying on evangelistic campaigns in all the principal cities of Latin America. He was advance man, follow-up man, coordinator, master of ceremonies, song leader, and sometimes the evangelist himself. . . ."[2] But impressive as his individual pursuits were, he was unable to inspire others to join the ministry with equal enthusiasm. As his health declined, so did the evangelistic efforts of the mission.

That Ken could ever fill his father's shoes seemed out of the question. "Squirt" was his nickname at Wheaton College, and there was little else about him that would have pointed to a future missionary statesman. He "lacked his father's commanding pulpit presence, his singing voice, his natural authority, and his ability as a preacher and evangelist. Little wonder that he should be plagued all his life by an inferiority complex in this area of his ministry."[3]

Throughout his young adult life, Ken was plagued by spiritual battles. During his college years he frankly admitted such in a letter to his mother: "Things have not been going very well, Mother, and I hate to tell you about it, but I know you'd rather hear it from me than elsewhere. . . . I tried hard to get right with God. . . . I had a fight for several days . . . , and in the end I lost out. . . . It would not have been so bad if it were only that I had backslidden religiously, but I have lost any traces of manhood. I have no will power or self-control, I have not made myself do the things I know I should have done, and as a result, I am failing not only in Christian life but even more so than the most worldly man. . . . I feel so heartily ashamed of myself when I think of what I should have done and didn't, and yet I haven't the strength or haven't gone far enough to turn back."[4]

In 1945 Harry Strachan died, and Ken was suddenly thrust into a position of leadership that he did not relish. Immediately there were decisions to make, and the differences between father and son became readily apparent. While Ken saw the need for publicity and promotional work, he had an instinctive aversion for it. He tried to continue his father's evangelistic emphasis, but big-time evangelism was simply not his niche. He saw "inconsistencies, contradictions, and even phoniness" in things "others seemed to accept with ease." Another area that troubled him was the tightrope he was forced to walk "between the Fundamentalists and the Inclusivists, whose controversies were highly distasteful to a man of such vision for cooperation."[5]

Ken's position in the mission became that of co-director with his mother, and it was in that capacity that he served until she died in 1950. Then, as the director of the Latin America Mission, his leadership qualities blossomed. The mission expanded its radio, literature, educational, and medical services, and by

1960 the missionary force had increased to 144, an 82 percent increase since the death of his mother a decade earlier.

More important than the increased membership from North America, however, was the Latin-Americanization of the ministry. For years Ken had been concerned about the "race question" (no black versus white, per se, though he may have been alone as an evangelical mission leader to maintain membership in the NAACP). He had taken issue with his mother when she had been insensitive to employing Latins in the mission, and later when he stepped into the directorship, he took steps to bring Latins in on an equal par with North Americans. He was well aware that unless the mission opened leadership positions to Latin Americans it would risk losing the valuable services of some of the most gifted Christians available for the work.

"Latinizing" the mission did not simply mean bringing in more Latin members and allowing them opportunities for leadership. It also meant making the mission policy itself in line with Latin culture and thinking. The issue of mixed marriages, for example, was a sore point. Most of the North American missionaries had opposed such marriages—a position perceived by the Latins as one of implied superiority. Ken faced the issue squarely and insisted that such "obstacles to full fellowship be eradicated."[6] To further incorporate Latins into the mission, Spanish became the language in which all business was conducted.

Cooperating effectively with the Latin Americans came much more easily than did cooperation with fellow North American missionaries. Ken himself was eager to work with other missionaries in cooperative ventures even if they were not within the Fundamentalist camp. He quickly realized, however, that such an approach threatened to dry up contributions from zealous supporters back home. After walking the tightrope for several years, he came to the conviction that the Scriptures simply did not teach a doctrine of separation as the Fundamentalists perceived it, and LAM began to take a more cooperative approach to evangelism. By broadening the appeal in an effort to expand the evangelistic outreach, Ken and his organization lost the support of long-time friends, including the Central American Mission. Its leadership was "unhappy about the apparently ecumenical openness of Ken Strachan and his Latin America Mission colleagues. They were, in the CAM opinion, flirting with apostasy both in the Ecumenical Movement and the Roman Catholic Church."[7]

Earlier in his ministry Ken had renounced any association with groups tied to the WCC (World Council of Churches) "because of its liberalism and unscriptural basis of fellowship, the unscriptural centralization of ecclesiastical power, its dedication to other tasks and concerns than those which legitimately concern the Church of Christ" and "its virtual repudiation of the Protestant Reformation by its openly avowed wooing of the Roman Catholic Church."[8]

By the 1960s, however, his position toward both the WCC and the Roman Catholic Church had softened. The greatest threat to Latin America, he had come to believe, was communism; and to combat the evils of that system, Christians by necessity had to work

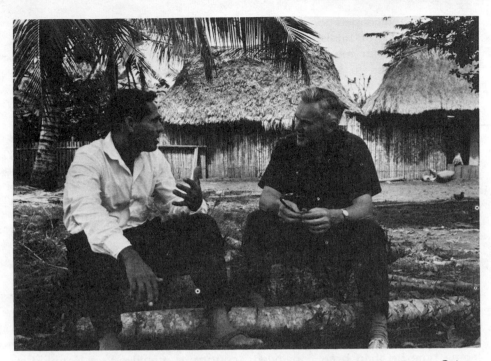

R. Kenneth Strachan of the Latin America Mission talking with Victor Landero, a Colombian leader.

together. This radical departure from traditional evangelical thinking surfaced publicly at the 1961 convention of the National Association of Evangelicals, where Ken made the statement that "Rome is changing," and "we may have to stand beside Rome against Communism."[9] Though he later qualified his optimism about the changes occurring in Catholicism, he nevertheless had created a stir that would widen the gap between him and other conservative evangelical missions and supporting churches.

Most evangelicals simply refused to acknowledge the positive changes that were occurring in Latin America through the influence of Pope John XXIII and Vatican II. "It was suddenly confusing and perplexing . . . to be offered the olive branch of friendship. A Catholicism standing with the Bible in one hand and with the other stretched out in love left us astonished. Suddenly our opponent had dropped his weapons, and was seeking peace. Was this a ruse? Could unchangeable Rome actually change? Was this a part of some sinister plot to catch us off guard? Or was the Holy Spirit truly at work, ventilating the musty corridors and putrid recesses of the ancient church?"[10] Although Ken himself did not live to steer his mission through this new era of relaxed religious tension, the Latin America Mission, under the leadership of others, continued to maintain an openness toward Catholicism, thereby isolating itself more and more from many of the other evangelical missions.

As controversial as Ken's softening toward Catholicism was, in the minds of some it was no worse than his

465

friendship and cooperation with Pentecostals. To Ken, a "ministry of reconciliation" was far more conducive to missions and to an evangelistic program than was a strict separatist position, and it was that attitude that pervaded the Evangelism-in-Depth campaigns and the total ministry of LAM.

The evangelistic crusade ministry of LAM that Ken had continued after the death of his father came to a climax in 1958 following the Billy Graham Caribbean crusade. It was an exhilarating time, and Ken and the mission had contributed immensely to its success. But despite the outward signs of immediate success, Ken had become convinced that such an approach simply would not result in the evangelization of Latin America. For some time he "had been convinced that the church, rather than the visiting evangelistic team, was ... central in God's program of evangelistic outreach."[11] Total mobilization of the church became his theme—a theme that he developed after observing and reading about the success of three rapidly expanding groups: Communists, Jehovah's Witnesses, and Pentecostals.

Ken's first experiment with Evangelism-in-Depth was a seven-month-long endeavor in Nicaragua, launched with a retreat for interested Christian workers. Following this four-day conference of seminars and Bible studies, those present fanned out across the country and began developing visitation programs and witnessing teams in local churches. This was followed by area-wide evangelistic campaigns and climaxed by a nationwide crusade in Managua. Follow-up was a key element; new believers were established in local churches and disciplined by more mature Christians. "Judged on the basis of the traditional crusade ..., this program was fabulously successful."[12] It was truly a national effort, and as a result some 2,500 people were converted.

What happened in Nicaragua was seen by many as a very encouraging new trend in missionary outreach. "The significance," wrote Arthur Glasser, "is world-wide.... In Nicaragua today we are witnessing responsible action being taken in the face of the 'population explosion' of our day about which we have all heard so much and are doing so little! Here is a well-organized effort to meet the demands of this hour.... We are being shown what can be accomplished when the total Christian strength of a country is mobilized for a united effort."[13]

Despite the praise, Ken was not fully satisfied with the Nicaraguan effort. Although nationals had undertaken the major responsibility for the extended campaign, the initiative had come from the outside, and "it could not truthfully be said that a revolution had been effected in the work and attitudes of the churches."[14]

The next Evangelism-in-Depth experiment was in Costa Rica. Here as in Nicaragua there were many decisions for Christ, but again the lasting tangible effect on the local churches was less than had been anticipated, and the local committee was left strapped with a large debt after the five-month effort was completed.

The mental and physical strain of the Costa Rican campaign and the less than stupendous results left Ken spiritually and psychologically depressed. Serious doubts arose as to whether or not the mission should move ahead with a planned Evangelism-in-Depth program for Guatemala. The mission was in deep financial straits, and the future looked dismal. Then, during a meeting in September of 1961 at Keswick Grove, New Jersey, the picture suddenly changed as Ken later recalled: "In that moment, in the slough of doubting, God spoke to one Greatheart. A promissory note was written on a piece of scratch paper and laid before the Lord. Suddenly we were brought out of the distress of mind to the perfect haven of assurance that God would provide."[15]

The Guatemalan effort went forward and the end result "was not only the biggest and the toughest but also the 'deepest' of the Evangelism-in-Depth movements to date." When the year of concentrated outreach ended, the "harvest had only begun." "The conclusion was inescapable," according to W. Dayton Roberts. "Guatemala had been shaken spiritually during 1962 as never before."[16]

The Guatemalan campaign marked the end of Ken's very active involvement with Evangelism-in-Depth. His health was declining, and in 1963 his doctors diagnosed his condition to be Hodgkin's disease—a deteriorating condition that took his life in 1965. The principles that he had developed through Evangelism-in-Depth, however, would not die. His colleagues in Latin America continued the efforts he had begun, and in nine years eight countries were reached, resulting in more than one hundred thousand conversions. As word of such successes spread, missionaries and church leaders from all over the world took notice. Invitations to conduct Evangelism-in-Depth campaigns came from as far away as Hong Kong and Japan, and LAM officials had the unique opportunity of teaching their principles to others who would carry out the actual ministry.

The West Indies Mission was one such group to institute an Evangelism-in-Depth ministry, and Allen Thompson, the field director for that mission, wrote of the impressive results: "In 1939 the West Indies Mission began work in the Dominican Republic, a country which soon proved to be almost impenetrable to the Gospel. The 27 years of difficult sowing in tears yielded 15 congregations and around 900 believers in Christ. In the year of evangelism just past, the reaping in joy has added to the WIM effort 2 churches, 8 additional preaching points, and approximately 700 new believers."[17]

Evangelism-in-Depth has changed over the years, but the basic principle of mobilizing lay people and Christian workers remains. And in the years since Ken's death the work of LAM has continued to move forward, known today as in years past for its progressive views in regard to the relationship between the mission and the national church. Instead of opting for "the most common solution . . . of two parallel but independent organizations on the same field—the association of local churches and a continuing mission structure with a coordinating committee as go-between," the mission "took a bold step in organizing each entity in Latin America under Latin leadership."[18] Some North Americans have found such a policy difficult to adjust to, but it accurately represents the farsighted mission philosophy which Ken Strachan so ably promoted.

Bob Pierce and World Vision

While Ken Strachan was seeking to reach a lost world through straightforward evangelistic strategy, Bob Pierce was making a contribution from another angle. Taking his example from the life of Jesus, he reached out in a humanitarian effort to demonstrate the reality of Christianity. In his mind, the most effective way to present Christ was through tangible acts of love and compassion: "We must first treat people's physical needs so we can then minister to their real (spiritual) needs." Next to the Lord himself, there have been few people in history who demonstrated greater compassion for suffering humanity than Bob Pierce. "Let my heart be broken with the things that break the heart of God"—the motto inscribed in his Bible succinctly summed up his outlook on life. He was humanity's friend.

Yet, with a heart that reached out to the whole world, Bob Pierce was unable to sustain the most intimate bonds of love with his own family. The love that he gave so freely to homeless orphans and ravished flood victims was given so sparingly to the ones who needed it most—his wife and daughters. His public life and his private life were separated by a great chasm, and few people knew what a troubled and frail human being he actually was. Nevertheless, God used him in a mighty way, and his imprint on the world will not soon be forgotten.

Dr. Bob, as he was affectionately called, was born in Fort Dodge, Iowa, in 1914, the youngest of seven children. When he was ten his family moved to California, and it was there that he made his home the remainder of his life. After high school he attended Pasadena Nazarene College, where he met his future wife Lorraine Johnson, the daughter of a successful evangelist.

Success did not smile on Bob during his early adult life. In college he had been president of the student body and a promising young preacher, but circumstances quickly changed. It was difficult to find work during the Depression years, and there were times during his courtship with Lorraine when he would be "aimlessly walking the streets of Santa Fe." Their marriage only seemed to aggravate the problems. Their "fantasy world" quickly faded and "the realities of married life came crashing down upon them." Bob began drifting from job to job, and Lorraine returned home to her family in Chicago. For months their only line of communication was an occasional "guarded" letter. Then, without warning, Bob wrote a tender letter, pleading for a reconciliation and ending with the words, "I love you and want you with me. But whether you come or not, I'm going on with God."[19]

What prompted Bob to write to Lorraine was in part his change in circumstances. He had given his testimony before the annual convention of the Nazarene Church. There in front of hundreds of pastors from all over the country he "confessed with tears of repentance his difficulties of the past year, proclaiming with fresh conviction his determination to serve God." The impact was electrifying. "Pastors sought him out and ... doors of ministry flew open."[20]

The years that followed found Bob and his young family barely making ends meet on the evangelistic circuit. After that he settled down for more than four years of ministry at the Los Angeles Evangelistic Center, where Bob worked alongside his father-in-law. It was not a fulfilling time for him, partly because he continually tried to compete with his successful father-in-law and ended up feeling "like a rowboat racing a windjammer." After an argument one day, he quit his position and soon after left town, and the next word Lorraine received from him came in the form of a crumpled court summons, informing her that he was suing for divorce.[21]

On the day of the court hearing, Lorraine requested to see Bob alone for a time, and through her pleading the divorce was not pursued, "but the next year and a half continued to be a time of incredible testing." While Lorraine "fought her battle in prayer," Bob "continued his lonely warfare, seemingly unable to find the key that would release him from his spiritual torment."[22] Once again, however, Bob found his way back to God, publicly repented, and returned to work for two more years at the evangelistic center.

During the time of his ministry at the evangelistic center, Bob had come to realize his special knack for dealing with youth, and in the years that followed he worked as a youth evangelist and then joined with Youth for Christ and became vice-president-at-large, serving with the well-known Torrey Johnson. It was in this capacity that Bob's future ministry came into focus. In 1947 he was asked to go to China to help conduct a series of youth campaigns. Though he was forced to leave his family in dire economic straits, he enthusiastically accepted the challenge, and perhaps for the first time he felt completely fulfilled.

The debilitating travel schedule did not discourage him. Traveling, he realized, was in his blood. And wherever he went, he saw the crying needs of humanity pleading, as it were, for him to help. Everywhere he preached there were professions of faith. It was an exhilarating time—a time in which his philosophy of Christian ministry was beginning to bud.

It was on his second trip to mainland China that Bob was challenged directly as to what his role should be in alleviating pain and suffering among the world's neediest people. While visiting a mission orphanage close to the Tibetan border his "attention was drawn to a forlorn little figure, her razor-thin body hunched resignedly at the bottom of the cold, stone steps." When he inquired as to why she was not being fed and sheltered at the orphanage, he was told that the mission was already caring for four times as many children as they could adequately handle. Bob was incensed to think that this poor hungry child was being denied the most basic necessities of life. "Why isn't something being done?" he pleaded. "What are *you* going to do about it?" the missionary retorted as she picked up the child and thrust her into his arms.[23] It was a turning point in his life. From that point on his energy was devoted to Christian humanitarianism.

Bob intended to return to China for further ministry, but with the communist takeover his attention was drawn elsewhere. In 1950 he made his first trip to Korea, where "the suffering of needy children" inspired the incorporation of World Vision International. With the Korean War ravishing the land, the initial priority was to provide food, clothing, and medicine for displaced women and children. But, "from its inception, World Vision sprouted arms of ministry in as many directions as there were needs." Within a few years the organization was providing for more than two thousand orphans, and in the years since that figure has increased more than a hundredfold.[24]

Within a few years after his worldwide ministry began, the story of Bob Pierce had become a saintly legend throughout the Far East. But his ministry was not confined to that area of the world. For nearly a decade he held the distinction of being one of the "ten most traveled men in the world," and everywhere he went he was hailed as a godsend. Back in the United States he traveled from coast to coast, awakening American Christians to the needs of the underprivileged world, raising hundreds of thousands of dollars for orphanages, hospitals, and evangelistic ministries.

It was during this rapid time of growth for World Vision that Lorraine and the girls seemed to be pushed further and further away from the top of Bob's priority list. When he did return to his family from his average of ten months of travel a year, it was almost as though he was a visitor in his own home, and conflict inevitably ensued. Though he could sympathetically relate to the world, his own family living under his own roof seemed so far away.

There were other problems that surfaced as World Vision advanced into its second decade of rapid expansion. Bob was finding it increasingly difficult to come to terms with the board of directors. In 1963 the directors voted to cancel his radio broad-

Bob Pierce of World Vision.

casts, convinced that the money would be better spent in other projects. The central issue involved was administrative style. He had been accustomed to using money as he saw fit without obtaining authorization and without having to give an account for its use. But times were changing. Government stipulations required precise accounting, and Bob deeply resented the added restrictions the board was placing on him. The conflicts continued until 1967 when they reached a boiling point and Bob resigned in a rage. "The next day World Vision presented him with legal documents of agreement, and Bob Pierce signed his life's work away."[25]

During the years immediately following his departure from World Vision, Bob's personal and professional life slowly caved in around him. In 1968 he traveled to the Orient with Lorraine on a "Good-bye Tour," sponsored as a final parting gesture by World Vision—no doubt in part to maintain their contacts in that part of the world. Near the end of that trip they received a phone call from Sharon, their oldest daughter, who urgently pleaded with her father to come home. She had faced deep personal struggles before, and Lorraine knew better than to take the situation lightly; but Bob was planning an unscheduled stop in Vietnam, and he refused to be deterred. Lorraine flew home immediately and "found Sharon weak and depressed, her wrists bound, recovering from an unsuccessful attempt to take her own life." Later that year another attempt was made, and the Pierces buried their oldest daughter at age twenty-seven.[26]

Prior to and following the time of Sharon's death, Bob was being treated for severe physical and mental exhaustion. Only slowly did he recover, and even when he seemed to be back on his feet, deep scars remained. He had become further alienated from his family, and never again would they enjoy a sustained happy relationship.

After several years of rest and recuperation, Bob began traveling again, and with World Vision support he founded Samaritan's Purse, an organization that provided assistance to missionaries in Asia. Then in 1975, after a series of medical tests, Bob's doctor broke the news that he had leukemia. It was just one more blow to a man who had been through so much, but he refused to give up. Only months later he was tirelessly coordinating a refugee assistance program in Saigon. After his work was done there he visited other trouble spots, always pouring out his heart to the suffering masses. But Dr. Bob's days

were numbered. He died in September of 1978, just days after a memorable family reunion.

In spite of the persistent conflicts and painful problems associated throughout the years with its world renowned founder, World Vision maintained a steady growth and expansion of its ministries. But while contributions and personnel continued to grow, it avoided the temptation of becoming a powerful entity in itself and continued to act as a service organization, working through other established missions and national churches. "As one travels the world," writes Richard C. Halverson, "one finds few institutions bearing the name World Vision. But there are hundreds of schools, orphanages, widows' homes, clinics, hospitals, dormitories and church buildings, built with and/or supported by funds contributed through World Vision and bearing the names of familiar overseas missionary bodies or national churches."[27]

As with most mission organizations, World Vision has benefited from the services of a number of outstanding Christians from the Third World. Among them is Dr. Samuel Kamaleson, an Indian national who ministered for many years in India under the auspices of the Methodist Church before becoming vice-president-at-large of World Vision and director of its international Pastors' Conference ministry. He also serves as the director of Bethel Agricultural Fellowship and has authored a number of books.

In 1969 Stanley Mooneyham became president of World Vision, and it was through his influence that World Vision developed into the highly efficient world relief organization that it is today, without losing that heartfelt compassion of its founder. In *What Do You Say to a Hungry World?* Mooneyham lays out the bare facts of human suffering in a forceful appeal for Christians to demonstrate through active involvement the vitality of their faith. He scolds the Church of Jesus Christ for its time-consuming involvement in the trivialities of life: "While the world goes through its greatest food crisis in history, the church shows a great capacity for diversion and not a little for self-deception." He quotes a Methodist missionary who poignantly illustrates the absurdity of modern-day institutionalized Christianity.

> The other day a Zambian dropped dead not a hundred yards from my front door. The pathologist said he'd died of hunger. In his shrunken stomach were a few leaves and what appeared to be a ball of grass. And nothing else.
>
> That same day saw the arrival of my *Methodist Recorder*, an issue whose columns were electric with indignation, consternation, fever and fret at the postponement of the final Report of the Anglican-Methodist Unity Commission....
>
> It took an ugly little man with a shrunken belly, whose total possessions, according to the police, were a pair of shorts, a ragged shirt and an empty Biro pen, to show me that this whole Union affair is the great Non-Event of recent British Church history.[28]

But Mooneyham is quick to emphasize that giving material wealth is not enough or even always the best type of assistance. He quotes a Chinese proverb illustrating the point that "how-to" knowledge is infinitely more beneficial in certain instances: "Give a man a fish and you feed him for a day; teach him to fish and he will feed himself for a lifetime." Under his leadership, World Vision has vastly expanded self-help programs in its assistance to the Third World. But as widespread and diverse as the various ministries of World Vision and other relief organizations are, the monumental task of alleviating the pain of suffering humanity has hardly begun.

So, "what do you say to a hungry world?" There's little to be said in the way of presenting Christ unless the words are backed up by deeds of Christian charity.

Brother Andrew and Open Doors

While Bob Pierce was seeking to evangelize the world through humanitarian acts of charity, others were taking a more combative approach. "God's Smuggler," the title of a popular book about him, is the description most frequently associated with Brother Andrew, an unordained Dutchman whose controversial ministry has frequently been the focus of international attention. His mission field extends from eastern Europe to the Far East and elsewhere in the world where freedom of worship is denied or seriously curtailed, and making Bibles available to the people in these countries is his major concern. Unlike other missions such as the Bible Christian Union, whose policy under the direction of W. Elwyn Davies seeks accommodation with communist regimes, Open Doors has a reputation for a confrontational approach. Defying government laws and authorities, Open Doors is guided by the philosophy that it is far better to "obey God rather than men."

In many ways the daring risks involved in smuggling Bibles across the borders of enemy countries was well suited to the young Dutch army commando whose childhood days had been filled with war games with neighborhood friends. Andrew was born into a proud Protestant family who, like most Hollanders, suffered immensely during the Nazi occupation of their land. It was after that devastating war that Andrew joined the army and soon found himself fighting to maintain Dutch rule in the tropical jungles of Indonesia. It was not a setting where heroes were easily made, but he quickly established a reputation for himself: "I became famous throughout the Dutch troops in Indonesia for my crazy bravado on the battlefield. I bought a bright yellow straw hat and wore it into combat with me. It was a dare and an invitation. 'Here I am!' it said. 'Shoot me!' Gradually I gathered around me a group of boys who were reacting as I did.... When we fought, we fought as madmen."[29]

It was inevitable that someone from the enemy camp would challenge his dare, and before the jungle madness was over, Andrew was on a hospital ship headed for home, nursing a badly wounded right ankle. That the bullet penetrated his ankle instead of his straw hat had a sobering impact on the cocky young soldier, and during his hospitalization he spent many hours reading the Bible, a book that he had never had time for before. Back in Holland in 1950, after a period of intensive Bible study, he was converted, and almost immediately he was challenged to become a missionary. To serve under the Dutch Reformed Church would have required twelve years of further schooling, so Andrew looked elsewhere for sponsorship. Through

the help of friends, he went to London to learn English, and then on to Glasgow, Scotland, to study at the WEC (Worldwide Evangelization Crusade) training school, where he graduated in 1955.

It had been Andrew's intention to serve as a foreign missionary under WEC, but that organization had no ministry behind the Iron Curtain, and it was that part of the world that had captured his attention. Just before his graduation he had come across an advertisement for a youth festival in Warsaw. It was a colorful piece of propaganda intended to lure Western youth to that beautiful city to see firsthand what socialism could offer them, but for Andrew it was an opportunity for ministry in a country that had seemingly been forgotten by the Christians in the free world.

Andrew's initial trip to Warsaw paved the way for speaking invitations back home in Holland and stirred his interest in visiting other eastern European countries. His second trip took him to Czechoslovakia, where the rigid crackdown on religion became evident immediately. What impressed him most was the scarcity of Bibles, unavailable even at the largest religious bookstore in the country. In Belgrade, Yugoslavia, Andrew discovered the same problem. While speaking at a religious meeting he challenged the people to be more diligent in prayer and Bible study. The congregation seemed dumbfounded, and then he learned that out of the entire group, only seven people, including the pastor, owned a Bible.

Andrew helped the pastor set up a system of Bible-sharing, but he left the meeting with a desire to do more. "That night," he later wrote, "I promised God that as often as I could lay my hands on a Bible, I would bring it to these children of His behind the wall that men had built. How I would buy the Bibles, how I would get them in, I didn't know. I only knew that I would bring them—here to Yugoslavia, and to Czechoslovakia, and to every other country where God opened the door long enough for me to slip through."[30]

For fifteen years Andrew, and those he could recruit to help him, smuggled Bibles behind the Iron Curtain with amazingly few arrests or detainments from communist authorities. The work remained relatively obscure until after his widely circulated book, *God's Smuggler*, was published. People from all over the world wanted to become involved, and contributions to the work dramatically increased. At the same time the book was informing the Christian world of his work it was also informing communist authorities. Andrew became a marked man, a development that brought a virtual halt to his trips across communist borders in eastern Europe.

But though he was a marked man (and by this time a husband and father), Andrew still had the impulse for risky adventure that had so hypnotized him during his commando days in Indonesia. On the very day that the Russians moved into Czechoslovakia in 1968, Andrew packed his station wagon with Bibles and headed for the border. "I didn't need a prayer meeting to tell me what to do. I figured if the Russians were coming to meet me halfway, I'd better get moving!" There was so much confusion at the border that the patrol officers waved him through without asking to see a visa or checking his vehicle. On his way to Prague he encountered two di-

visions of the Soviet army, but he managed to get through without detainment. There he was invited to preach in a church, and afterwards the people tearfully thanked him for coming. Then with a group of Czech Christians he went out into the streets and distributed tracts and Bibles. "The Czech citizens took them ... like starving men taking bread. Czech authorities were too busy coping with the Russians to worry about arresting us, and we gave away tens of thousands of tracts before we finally depleted our supply, and I headed back for Holland."[31]

During most of the decade of the 1960s, Andrew's attention was focused on the Far East, and in 1965 he made his first trip to mainland China. Once again he found Christians desperately pleading for Bibles, and once again he was moved to begin smuggling operations. Following the fall of Saigon in 1976 and the communist takeover of Laos and Cambodia, attention was turned to those countries; and more recently Open Doors has made an effort to counteract the revolutionary movements in Africa with the gospel, though a large-scale communist takeover of that continent has not materialized as Andrew had anticipated.

The most publicized and controversial Bible smuggling operation ever conducted by Open Doors occurred in the fall of 1981. "Operation Pearl," as it was dubbed, was, according to *Time* magazine, the "largest operation of its kind in the history of China." Led by an ex-Marine, it was "executed with military precision." More than two hundred tons of Bibles packed in waterproof containers were shipped from the United States to Hong Kong and from there were transported on a barge to the southeast China port city of Swatow, all at the cost of some six million dollars. There were harrowing moments when the crew feared their ploy had been discovered, but the Bibles were unloaded without incident, and not until four hours after the barge had departed did authorities storm the beach. Hundreds of the estimated twenty thousand Chinese believers who had come to help in the operation were arrested, but it is believed that well over half of the Bibles ended up in the hands of Chinese Christians for whom they were intended.[32]

As a result of this illegal operation, Chinese officials tightened restrictions on religious activities, causing an outcry against Open Doors by some Western and Chinese churchmen who feared that such efforts only served to further alienate Chinese Christians from their leaders. But with the criticism came praise. "Operation Pearl ... inspired calls from potential donors willing to finance massive new Bible-smuggling ventures to China or behind the Iron Curtain."[33]

In the face of widespread criticism, Brother Andrew emphasizes that "smuggling" is "only a small part" of the total ministry of Open Doors. Yet, as he admits, it is the "smuggling" aspect that had an adventurous appeal to many people, and it is no doubt that aspect of the ministry that draws such widespread support. Aside from the controversy the method has engendered due to its illegal tactics, Bible smuggling has provided millions of people the world over the opportunity to read the Bible for themselves—an opportunity they otherwise might never have enjoyed.

Donald McGavran

One of the world's foremost contemporary missiologists is Donald McGavran, whose focus is on a kind of "church growth" that goes far beyond traditional concepts of campaign evangelism even where they are buttressed by costly evangelistic teams and organizations. For more than a half century he has been a dynamic missionary activist, vitally involved in cross-cultural evangelism but not content with the age-old mission station approach. "His thesis is that the social sciences can be harnessed to the missionary task. Research and analysis can result in the removal of hindrances to the growth of the church. Indeed, he is the Apostle of Church Growth." So says Arthur Glasser, a leading mission strategist in his own right.[34] Church growth in itself, basically church-centric evangelism, may seem like a noncontroversial topic that everyone could agree on, but McGavran has brought a new twist to the subject that has thrust him into the very center of the fiery debate. In fact, much of the debate on mission strategy in recent decades has been focused on his ideas. "He has been lauded, and he has been blasted," according to David Allen Hubbard, "but he has not been ignored."[35]

McGavran was born in India in 1897, the son and grandson of missionaries. Despite the precedent set before him, however, foreign missions was not an automatic career choice. In fact, he initially rebelled against the thought of a lifetime of missionary barrel economics. "My father has done enough for the Lord," he reasoned. "It is time for me to strike out for myself and earn some money."[36] His student days at

Butler University were relatively uneventful. As president of his senior class and an awesome debater, he had all the earmarks of success, and a career in law was his great ambition. But that was before he surrendered his life to Christ, and the SVM caught up with him. Now his aspirations changed. After Yale Divinity School he met his wife-to-be at a SVM meeting, married, and went to India, and then began a life filled with adventure and productivity that included fending off a wounded tiger on one occasion and a wild boar on another, checking "almost single handed a cholera epidemic," climbing in the Himalayas, trekking through the jungles of remote islands in the Philippines, conducting seminars across Africa, producing a motion picture, and authoring more than a dozen books. Retirement, however, did not fit into his plans. In 1973 during his seventy-sixth year he wrote three books, taught classes, and conducted research projects with seemingly no inclination to slow down, and in the years since the hectic pace has continued.[37] In 1983 he concluded seminars in India and Japan in the same month in two separate trips.

McGavran's missionary career began in Harda, India, as the superintendent of a mission school, serving under the United Christian Missionary Society. He later served in other capacities relating to education and medical services and was also active in translation and evangelistic work. In the mid 1930s his missionary work was briefly interrupted by further graduate studies that culminated in a Ph.D. at Columbia University.

For two more decades his missionary work continued to be centered in India, at which time he was deeply involved in studying the phenomenon of mass movements, but by the mid 1950s his mission began to use him in broader activities. His practical field experience and his insatiable appetite to learn from other missionaries had made him realize the necessity of sound, well-reasoned mission theory, and he began dedicating his energies to that discipline. He had long realized that much of the work that was being carried out by missionaries was accomplishing very little toward the goal of world evangelization, and he was eager that research be done to develop new concepts of mission strategy. At that time he began teaching in the field of missions at various Christian institutions, and in 1961 he founded the Institute of Church Growth, with which his name has been associated for more than two decades.

Like Ken Strachan, McGavran studied evangelistic activities of others to discover principles and methodology that resulted in church growth. No method was sacred or beyond the scrutiny of scientific investigation. Even Strachan's Evangelism-in-Depth was put to the test. "Careful research on several Latin American republics," according to C. Peter Wagner, "could not come up with any cause and effect relationships between year-long Evangelism-in-Depth efforts and increased rates of growth in the churches."[38] For McGavran and his disciples, the actual incorporation of converts into the church—not necessarily the numbers of "decisions"— was the key factor in evaluating missionary methodology. For that reason, traditional methods of evangelism were put to the test. If crusade evangelism resulted in church growth, McGavran sought to discover why, and

Donald McGavran, author and leading mission strategist.

then he applied the principles he had discovered elsewhere.

It was through his Institute of Church Growth that missiological research developed more fully than it had anywhere or anytime in the history of the Christian church. He founded the institute at Northwest Christian College in Eugene, Oregon, beginning in 1961 with one student. In 1965 the institute was moved to Pasadena, and McGavran became the founding dean of the School of World Mission at Fuller Theological Seminary. In recent years more than one hundred seasoned missionaries (with their invaluable insights) annually have passed through the school, and some of the world's best missiologists have joined him in his research and teaching. Mission theorists have been most impressed with his modern, scientific outlook. "He was goal-oriented to the core. He dealt with principles,

not methods. Methods were accepted or rejected . . . on the basis of what he called 'fierce pragmatism.' Research became his chief tool."[39]

From his research, McGavran concluded not only that traditional methods of mass evangelism contributed little to real church growth, but that the main missionary thrust of the whole nineteenth and much of the twentieth century had been misdirected. The mission station approach that dominated missions for nearly two centuries had simply not fostered the kind of spontaneous expansion that so characterized the early church. Although missionaries had worked diligently to establish indigenous churches, Christianity continued to be focused around the mission station. "These mission station churches," writes McGavran, "are lacking in the qualities needed for growth and multiplication." The basic reason is that converts are often segregated from their former social relationships and find their only fellowship with other mission station Christians. They generally feel "immeasurably superior to their own unconverted relatives," and thus they have limited influence on them for evangelism. What results is the unintentional and misguided creation of a new tribe, a new caste, a separate society. He noted that converts in such cases tend to depend heavily on the mission station for employment and social services and sometimes "draw the easy conclusion that if more people become Christians, the resources of the mission will be spread thinner," resulting in instances where "they have actually discouraged possible converts from becoming Christian."[40]

What, then, is the answer? People

Movements, according to McGavran—movements of whole tribes or "homogeneous units" toward Christianity. Such "multi-individual" conversions, rather than individual conversions, were, in McGavran's mind, far more lasting and stable for real church growth. Such movements had occurred in the past but had "seldom been sought or desired." In India, most such movements were in fact "resisted by leaders of the church and mission where they started," in part because of the "Western preference for individual decision" over "corporate decision."[41]

No doubt the most controversial aspect of McGavran's People Movement concept, called the Homogeneous Unit Principle, became even more widely disseminated after he made a plenary session address at the Lausanne Congress in 1974. Against a current of strongly integrationist ideology, he argued that a consciousness of race should not be seen as a negative factor, but rather a positive one in the process of world evangelization. "It does no good," he insisted, "to say that tribal peoples ought not to have race prejudice. They do have it and are proud of it. It can be understood and should be made an aid to Christianization." Clearly, McGavran was not defending race prejudice. He adamantly opposed it. But he insisted that becoming free from race prejudice could not be made a prerequisite to becoming a Christian. He defined two "stages of Christianization": "discipling" and "perfecting." The first stage involves becoming a Christian, and the second, growth in the Christian life. It was only in the second stage, he believed, that real progress toward eradicating race prejudice

might be accomplished.[42]

One of McGavran's most pointed critics has been John H. Yoder, an Anabaptist theologian, who has questioned the honesty of McGavran's approach. "I would think the missionary was cheating," he charged, "if he told me after I was baptized that I had to love blacks when he had not wanted to tell me before." "If we have not said the Christian church is an integrated community initially," he asked, "what authority will we have to call for a movement toward integration later?"[43] McGavran's reply would have been that requiring love and offering nothing less than intermarriage are two different things.

Another critic of McGavran's Homogeneous Unit Principle has been Rene Padilla, a Latin America missiologist. In his view the homogeneous unit is "sub-Christian" and sinful: "The idea is that people *like* to be with those of their own race and class and we must therefore plant segregated churches, which will undoubtedly grow faster. We are told that race prejudice 'can be understood and should be made an aid to Christianization.' No amount of exegetical maneuvering can ever bring this approach in line with the explicit teaching of the New Testament regarding the unity of men in the body of Christ. . . ."[44]

Because of his prolific writing and his innovative ideas, McGavran has been in the heat of the battle over mission strategy. His critics "have accused him of stressing quantity at the expense of quality; of being so concerned with the saving of souls that he neglects the serving of human needs; of pushing for church extension and being blind to the needs of social justice; and of relying on human effort instead of the Holy Spirit."[45]

McGavran, according to Arthur Glasser, is "more widely quoted" and "more hotly debated than anyone else in the field of missions today." He "has completely upset the old, traditional and largely non-productive missionary methodology that dominated all missions . . . prior to 1955."[46] In many respects, his significance lies not so much in the correctness of his answers as in the trenchant questions he has raised, the apostolic passion with which he has unsettled the accepted answers, and in the way, more than any other person, he has lifted the study of missions from introductory courses in a few Christian schools into a widespread professional level of study the world over.

Ralph and Roberta Winter

Missions is his life. But it is not only his life, it is Roberta's, who is a full and equal partner in the work, and it is each of his four daughters who, with their husbands, all have given their lives to the same cause. If anyone could be described as a world missionary statesman—strategist, scholar, organizer, innovator, motivator, and enthusiast—it would be Ralph Winter. Although he would shun any such characterization, it would be difficult to single out anyone else who is more involved in as many facets of missions as he is. He has been referred to by some as the most innovative and visionary person in missions today.

Ralph Winter was born in Los Angeles in 1924 and, except for his years spent in school or overseas, has lived in the same house since the age of two. Although his parents were leaders in the local Presbyterian church, the strongest influence on their lives (and his) in those early days was the International Society of Christian Endeavor, which is still today the largest Christian youth movement in the world. It was this evangelical, interdenominational background that deeply influenced him in the years that followed.

Following high school, Ralph entered California Institute of Technology to pursue an engineering career. His father, who was in charge of developing the Los Angeles freeway system, had been highly successful in that field, and it seemed only natural that Ralph should follow in his footsteps. But an engineering career was not to be. After graduating from Cal Tech and serving in the Navy, he went on for further education, eventually culminating in a Ph.D. from Cornell University and a degree in theology from Princeton Theological Seminary.

Before completing his formal education, Ralph married Roberta Helm, who had just graduated from nurse's training. From the beginning it was a marriage of mutual interests and concerns. Roberta studied with Ralph as he continued his graduate education, and when they began their overseas ministry to one of the Mayan Indian groups of Guatemala their relationship continued as a partnership of equals.

After ten years as missionaries in Guatemala, Winter, at the invitation of McGavran, joined the faculty of the Fuller School of World Mission. It was a crucial opportunity that allowed him to make an indelible impression on the hundreds of seasoned missionaries who were going through his classes.

479

Leaving Fuller was not an easy decision, but after ten years, in 1976, he and Roberta gave up the security and salary of that prestigious position and set out with no financial backing to found the U. S. Center for World Mission. Together with a handful of little known missionaries, he jumped at the opportunity of buying a college campus in Pasadena. "They believed this would be the ideal base of operation to bring together men and women with the purpose of reaching the unreached. The cost: $15 million. They had $100 between them."[47]

In the years since its founding the USCWM has "faced imminent foreclosure" and "seemed destined to die at the loan desk," until "last minute funds rolled in."[48] But the focus of the battle has never been centered on mortgage payments. The focus rather has been on the estimated 17,000 distinct people groups—over two billion people—where the Christian church has not yet been planted. The USCWM is a "beehive of energy" that encompasses more than three hundred workers from sixty-four mission agencies, linking these agencies together with churches and student organizations.

The Center is essentially a cooperative "think-tank" to which mission agencies assign people to work together in the research and mobilization necessary to reach these "hidden peoples." "There's more to it than just the creative genius of its director," writes Inter-Varsity Missions specialist David Bryant. "From what I sense in many quarters, the Center's great appeal lies in the models of pioneering faith it has rallied to itself (Winter being one of them), whose zeal for the glory of God renews the faith of many

Ralph and Roberta Winter, founders of the U.S. Center for World Mission.

(including myself) in what God *can* and *will* do *through* His people for Christ's global cause." Bryant has compared the center with the town Rivendale, in Tolkien's *Lord of the Rings:* "the place where visions can be born, where fragile dreams can become reality, where battle plans can be laid for great battles ahead, and faith renewed in ultimate, inevitable success."[49]

The Center, however, is not the only brain child of Winter's "fertile mind." He was active in the founding of the William Carey Library (a publishing house specializing in books on Christian missions), the American Society of Missiology, Theological Education by Extension, Frontier Fellowship, and the William Carey International University, an international undergraduate and graduate extension program.

Part of the reason for the contagious influence for missions that the Winters exude derives from their personal lifestyle. They maintain what Ralph calls a "wartime lifestyle," not to be

480

confused with a "simple" lifestyle. "A wartime lifestyle," according to Ralph, "may be more expensive or less expensive than simple. If a man is out in a trench and he's eating K rations, he's not using up much money, but a guy who's flying a fighter plane may be using up $40,000 a month of technology. In other words, during wartime one doesn't judge according to the same model of lifestyle. What's important is getting the job done."[50]

The Winters personally demonstrate that lifestyle. While they make use of the latest computerized equipment in their offices and take advantage of expensive express mail services to facilitate urgent projects, Ralph drives a 1965 Dodge station wagon that is into its third one-hundred-thousand-mile cycle, and he is often seen wearing the same blue sport coat that he picked out of the "missionary barrel."

Through his various organizations and personal contacts Ralph has encouraged others to develop ideas and programs to promote world evangelism, and this in itself has been his most enduring contribution. Men such as Don Richardson owe him a debt of gratitude for the encouragement and enthusiastic interest he showed in their work before they had been widely recognized by others for their contributions to missions.

Don Richardson

One of the most intriguing and practical mission theorists in the West today is Don Richardson. His books *Peace Child* (which has sold nearly 300,000 copies and also became a *Reader's Digest* book-of-the-month selection) and *Lords of the Earth* (with sales of about 100,000 copies) have brought the complexity of communicating the gospel cross-culturally to lay Christians as few other books have ever done. Perhaps more than any other missionary statesman in America, he appeals to both the layperson and the scholar. His principle of Redemptive Analogy —"the application to local custom of spiritual truth"—has engendered considerable enthusiasm and debate in missiological circles ever since he first mentioned the principle in a seminar at Dallas Theological Seminary in 1973. Since that time his influence has grown through additional books and articles, conference speaking, a film of *Peace Child*, and his association with the U.S. Center for World Mission in Pasadena.

It was in a chapel service at Prairie Bible Institute in 1955 that Don, a twenty-year-old youth, answered the call to foreign missions. It was not a nebulous call to "anywhere" that he answered, but a very specific call to the headhunting tribes of Netherlands New Guinea, where savagery was a way of life. It is not surprising that others in that service listening to the seventy-one-year-old Ebenezer Vine of the Regions Beyond Missionary Union heard the same call, for Prairie Bible Institute was accustomed to seeing a large portion of its graduates go to the foreign field. Among the students who shared Don's decision that day was Carol Soderstrom, a "lovely blonde" from Cincinnati, Ohio, who would become his wife five years later.

In 1962, after completing a course with the Summer Institute of Linguistics and awaiting the birth of their first child, Don and Carol sailed for New Guinea, where they worked with other

RBMU missionaries until they were assigned to their own tribe—the Sawi, one of only a few cultures in the entire world that combined cannibalism and headhunting, and also idealized treachery! But it was not only the people that instilled fear. The land itself was awesome, as Don has so vividly portrayed: "The brooding jungle stood tall against the sky, walling in the overgrown clearing as if to create an arena for an impending contest.... The wildness of the locale seemed to taunt me. Something in the mood of the place seemed to say mockingly, 'I am not like your tame, manageable Canadian homeland. I am tangled. I am too dense to walk through. I am hot and steamy and drenched with rain. I am hip-deep mud and six-inch sago thorns. I am death adders and taipans and leeches and crocodiles. I am malaria and dysentery and filariasis and hepatitis."[51] It was a frightening place to bring a wife and a seven-month-old child, but Don never questioned his call.

If fear of treachery and disease weighed heavily on Don and Carol's subconscious thinking, fear of never coming to grips with the language was a very conscious struggle. The nineteen tenses of each verb and the very complex vocabulary was mind boggling. "In English you open your eyes, your heart, a door, a tin can or someone's understanding, all with one humdrum verb 'open.' But in Sawi you *fagadon* your eyes, *anahagkon* your heart, *tagavon* a door, *tarifan* a tin can, and *dargamon* a listener's understanding."[52] Though Don frequently felt as though his "brain circuits would get shorted," in the process, he maintained an eight- to ten-hour-day language learning schedule and soon became a proficient communicator in Sawi. He viewed the task as a "great adventure": "I often felt like a mathematician must feel as he tackles problems and breaks through into new formulas which work like magic."[53]

As Don learned the language and familiarized himself with the people, he readily became aware of the obstacles he faced in bringing them to an understanding of Christianity. The gulf that separated his own biblical Christianity from the vicious jungle treachery of the Sawi seemed almost too wide to bridge. How could they ever comprehend a loving Savior who died for them? "In their eyes Judas, not Jesus, was the hero of the Gospel. Jesus was just the dupe to be laughed at."[54] The communication barrier seemed hopeless until Don discovered a Redemptive Analogy that pointed to the Incarnate Christ far more clearly than any biblical passage alone could have. What Don discovered was the Sawi concept of the Peace Child.

The warlike nature of the Sawi was a factor that had greatly troubled Don from the earliest days of his residence among them. Despite his best efforts he could not prevent the three tribal villages in the vicinity of his work from spilling each others' blood. Don blamed himself: "I concluded . . . that Carol and I had unintentionally deprived Haenam, Kamur and Yohwi [the three villages] of the mutual isolation they needed to survive in relative peace, by drawing them together into one community. It followed that for the good of the people, we ought to leave them. It would be a bitter pill to swallow, but I knew without us, they would scatter to their deep jungle homes and be at peace."[55]

So upset were the Sawi on hearing of Don's proposed departure that they met in a special tribal session and then announced to him that the following day they were going to make peace. Encouraged by this turn of events, Don anxiously awaited the next morning. Not long after dawn, the Sawi peace ritual began. The diplomatic process, though rarely exercised, was a deeply emotional experience. Young children from each of the warring villages were to be exchanged. As long as any of those children lived the peace would continue. The decision as to whose child would be given up was a wrenching ordeal. Mothers with little children were filled with apprehension when they realized what was happening. Finally a young man grabbed his only child, and rushed toward the enemy camp, and literally gave his son to one of his enemies. A child was given in return for his, and peace was established. It was a peace based on trust—an element that had seemed to Don to be nonexistent in the Sawi culture. But in their own way the Sawi "had found a way to prove sincerity and establish peace. . . . Among the Sawi every demonstration of friendship was suspect except one. *If a man would actually give his own son to his enemies, that man could be trusted!*"[56]

It was that analogy, then, that Don used to point the Sawi to God the Father's sacrifice of his son.

The Peace Child analogy alone did not solve all the communication barriers to Christianity. Other analogies were also to be discovered, and for Don and Carol there were many more trying experiences to endure. But through their patient toil the Sawi gradually turned to Christianity. As a side benefit, they were also prepared to survive the inevitable "cultural disorientation" soon to be unleashed on them by the influx of oil, logging, and mining industries and heavy immigration from other islands of Indonesia. Don and Carol also helped the Sawi in other ways. As a nurse, Carol treated nearly 2,500 patients a month, while at the same time teaching basic hygiene and other types of preventive care. Don, with Carol's help, translated the New Testament and taught the Sawi to read. Yet, they studiously avoided any attempt to change the Sawi culture—except where it was clearly self-destructive.

By 1972, after a decade of ministry among the Sawi, much had changed. The meeting house used for Christian gatherings had been enlarged twice, and at Don's urging the villagers agreed to build a "Sawidome" that would seat at least one thousand people. It was to be a "house of peace in which former enemies" could "sit down together at the Lord's table, and a house of prayer for the tribes . . . without God's Word." The building was dedicated in the summer of 1972 and was believed to be the world's largest circular building made entirely of unmilled poles.[57]

After completing the translation of the New Testament, the Richardsons left the Sawi under the care of their own church elders and John and Esther Mills, another missionary couple. They then moved on to another tribe to help still another missionary couple analyze a language called Auyy. In 1976 (while continuing his active association with RBMU) Don began teaching at the U.S. Center of World Mission in Pasadena, where he became the Director of Tribal Peoples' Studies. Here his emphasis on "Redemptive Analogies" has found ready acceptance, and others have joined him in a similar effort to develop more effective means to communicate the gospel among tribal peoples.

In his second book, *Lords of the Earth*, Don further elaborated on the concept of Redemptive Analogies, as he related the missionary service of Stan Dale among the Yali tribe of Irian Jaya. Stan and his co-worker, Phil Masters, worked tirelessly to reach this fierce cannibalistic tribe, and by 1966 some twenty Yali tribesmen had been converted. Christianity, however, was viewed by the majority of the tribe as a threatening menace, and almost immediately two of the new converts were killed by priests of the Yali spirits called Kembu. Two years later, Stan and Phil both lost their lives in a sudden attack by Yali warriors.

"If ever a tribe needed some Christ-foreshadowing belief a missionary could appeal to," wrote Don, "it was the Yali." So, along with another missionary, he "conducted a much belated 'culture probe' to learn more about Yali customs and beliefs." Only then did he discover a Redemptive Analogy relating to Yali tradition— places of refuge consisting of circular stone walls where tribesmen could find safety from even their most

Don Richardson, missionary to Irian Jaya and author of *Peace Child*.

dreaded enemies. By building on this Yali tradition that Don discovered, missionaries were now able through the strategy of "concept fulfillment" to draw parallels between their own places of refuge and the cities of refuge among the Israelites. It then became a simple matter to communicate redemption provided through Christ as "the perfect place of refuge." Thousands of Yali tribesmen have converted to Christianity in subsequent years.[58]

Don's most brilliant piece of scholarship to date has been *Eternity in Their Hearts*, a historical work dealing with People Movements to Christianity. One of the most thought-provoking discoveries that he has made through his research is that the vast majority (some say 95 percent) of folk religions throughout the world acknowledge "one great spirit" as creator. In explaining this phenomenal discovery, Don goes directly to Acts 14:16–17, which speaks of God the creator who "has not left himself without testimony." God has in a general way revealed himself to even the most remote and primitive tribes, and Don challenges other missionaries to build on this general revelation. Through his study he has found that missionaries who have related Christianity to the people's own concept of a creator God have met with the greatest success. Missionaries who have refused to acknowledge the tribal name for God as valid have generally found less response for the gospel.

So, does Richardson imply that the end justifies the means? If a strategy works, may we use it without first checking to see if it is consistent with scriptural precedents? No, that is hardly the case with the missiological principles of Don Richardson. In fact, his heavy reliance on scriptural precedent is in part what makes him stand out so as a modern-day mis-

siologist. His principles are biblically based. They are not new. They are as old as Scripture itself. Thus, his major contribution to the field of missiology has been to rediscover the very methods and principles that the apostle Paul and others used and apply them to modern anthropological findings. For example, his belief that missionaries should seek to use an indigenous name for God has the "apostolic seal of approval." The apostle Paul apparently had no qualms at all about using the Greek term *theos* for God, even though it was the very term the pagans whom he sought to convert used. So, the evangelistic methods and principles that were relevant when the world missionary enterprise was launched from Jerusalem in the first century A.D. are still applicable today as the commission to go to "the uttermost part of the earth" is yet to be fulfilled. It is perhaps noteworthy that Don's rediscovery of these timeless methods and principles occurred in what must truly be considered the uttermost part of the world—Irian Jaya.

SELECTED BIBLIOGRAPHY

Andrew, Brother. **Battle for Africa.** *Old Tappan, N.J.: Revell, 1977.*

_____. **God's Smuggler.** *Old Tappan, N.J.: Revell, 1967.*

Dunker, Marilee Pierce. **Man of Vision, Woman of Prayer.** *Nashville: Nelson, 1980.*

Elliot, Elisabeth. **Who Shall Ascend: The Life of R. Kenneth Strachan of Costa Rica.** *New York: Harper & Row, 1968.*

Mooneyham, W. Stanley. **What Do You Say to a Hungry World?** *Waco: Word, 1975.*

Richardson, Don. **Peace Child.** *Glendale, Calif.: Regal, 1974.*

Roberts, W. Dayton. **Revolution in Evangelism: The Story of Evangelism-in-Depth in Latin America.** *Chicago: Moody, 1976.*

_____. **Strachan of Costa Rica: Missionary Insights and Strategies.** *Grand Rapids: Eerdmans, 1971.*

Tippet, A. R., ed. **God, Man and Church Growth.** *Grand Rapids: Eerdmans, 1973.*

Troutman, Charles. **Everything You Want to Know About the Mission Field, But Are Afraid You Won't Learn Until You Get There.** *Downers Grove: InterVarsity, 1976.*

Wagner, C. Peter. **Our Kind of People: The Ethical Dimensions of Church Growth in America.** *Atlanta: John Knox, 1979.*

Winter, Ralph D. and Hawthorne, Steven C., eds. Perspectives on the World Christian Movement. *Pasadena: William Carey, 1982.*

Winter, Roberta H. Once More Around Jericho: The Story of the U.S. Center for World Mission. *Pasadena, William Carey, 1978.*

Postscript

In retrospect, the most striking aspect of the Christian world mission has been the vast numbers of men and women who, against all odds, left family and homeland to endure the privations and the frustrations of cross-cultural evangelism to follow God's call. It was that nebulous and indefinable "missionary call" that impelled them to move out. If ministries in the homeland could be pursued without a "call," foreign missions could not. The stakes were too high. And it was that sense of calling, more than anything else, that was the staying power. Of course there were those who went but did not stay, and who were relegated to the role of missionary "returnee." But at least they went out, and in many cases made significant contributions. Many who remained might have been far happier staying home. Yet, they stayed on decade after decade, prodded on by their sense of calling.

Who were these who were afflicted by such a high calling? Were they men and women especially fitted for that calling? Probably not—at least no more than earnest believers in any other segment of the Christian church. The history of both mankind and of missions is a saga checkered by human shortcomings, failures, and setbacks.

After centuries of less than spectacular growth, the "Great Century" dawned, only to launch out the "father of modern missions" with an unwilling wife and another associate of questionable character. The domestic unhappiness represented by even that famous missionary was hardly an ideal example of the Christian home, and later on bitter strife between junior and senior missionaries at the Serampore mission station in India further damaged the testimony that Christianity was supposed to demonstrate.

And it was not just in India that the name of Christ was besmirched. In China, Christianity was indelibly linked to opium smuggling. In Africa, it was associated with racism and with violent outbreaks between Protestants and Catholics. In the Pacific islands there were instances of sexual immorality among the missionaries. And on virtually every mission field in the world there was a great deal of embarrassing and amateurish understanding of cultural traditions, while the Western institutionalized church was taken for granted as the only way converts could follow the Lord.

Of course modern scholars reinvestigating this generally concede that many of the failures have been incidental and, in some cases, excusable. They were only ripples on the surface of a powerful groundswell of grace that flooded the earth. But yet it is no wonder that the critics have had a heyday with Christian missions. The very humanity of the missionaries themselves provided all the fuel that was needed. Why should we be surprised that every mistake imaginable was made, plus quite a few more? Missionaries were neither the supersaints their admirers have created, nor the unlearned and zealous misfits their detractors have described. But they were somehow called by God, and their rate of success was phenomenal.

The spread of Christianity into the non-Western world, principally as a missionary achievement, is one of the great success stories of all history. After moving forward in the Reformation and gaining momentum in the awesome energy of the Evangelical Awakening, after escaping the vigorous counter forces of rationalism and secularism, and after surviving the French Revolution and Napoleonic militarism, the Christian movement suddenly expanded by leaps and bounds to become a vibrant, universal religion passionately adhered to by people from every corner of the globe. True to form, this massive extension has been a working faith. No other cause in history has ever fostered such far-reaching humanitarian efforts of good will as Christianity.

The very fact that this incredible world-wide expansion was carried out by frail and sinful human beings backed by only a minority of the saints back home, in a very real sense only enhances the glory that must be given to God alone. Nevertheless, it is difficult from a human perspective not to admire and idealize those who were willing to go—those who so willingly sacrificed their own ambitions to make whatever contribution they could to a far greater cause. There were Henry Martyns and Helen Roseveares on every field—those who relinquished what surely would have been brilliant careers in their homeland, and gave up the joys of marriage and family only to suffer pain and humiliation—all in obedience to God's call.

Far less attention has been paid to those who stayed behind and who may have been no less obedient to the Heavenly Vision. Countless individuals heard the same call and had good intentions of making the same kind of sacrifice but never went. Were they less spiritual? Were they less committed to God? Indeed, there may be only a fine line that separates those who went and those who stayed home.

It has been said that for every missionary that goes to the foreign mission field there are at least fifty individuals who at one time or another committed their lives to missions but never carried through with their commitment. Was their call to missions unrealized? In many cases it was. Their commitment was forgotten. In other instances, however, they played an indispensable role on the home front. Where would missions be today without these "stay-at-homes"? Of the one hundred thousand student volunteers who signed the "Princeton Pledge," twenty thousand actually went abroad as foreign missionaries —but how could that awesome army have endured on the front lines without the powerful backup support network at home? During those years, monetary giving to missions more than quadrupled. There was a similar support system behind the vast movement of women that poured onto the foreign mission field beginning in the late nineteenth century. For every woman who went out there were a dozen or more wholly committed female mission supporters on the home front—among them, many who had felt called to go but never went.

In recent decades another student movement has been thrust in motion largely by devoted missionary-minded "stay-at-homes." C. Stacey Woods had his plans all made to go to India in 1934, but he ended up staying in America to found and direct Inter-Varsity Christian Fellowship—a student organization vitally involved in promoting missions through its work on university campuses. Inter-Varsity is also known for its triennial Urbana Missionary Conferences—a five-day convention attracting as many as seventeen thousand students from campuses across America. Stacey's concern was global, a factor clearly evident in his formulation of the International Fellowship of Evangelical Students. Dawson Trotman, also never became a foreign missionary, but he, too, played a crucial role in missionary

outreach through his founding of the Navigators. Trotman caught a vision for missions while in Paris in 1948, and since that time the Navigators have spread out across the globe with a dynamic zeal to disciple others in the Christian faith.

Bill Bright—like Dawson—only gradually developed a vision for world missions. Campus Crusade for Christ was begun as a ministry geared primarily to reaching students, but by the 1980s it had some sixteen thousand staff members involved in evangelism in more than one hundred fifty countries and protectorates around the world. Few areas of the world have remained untouched by that organization's "Here's Life" campaigns and "Jesus" film, that has been translated into dozens of languages.

There is a growing feeling among some of today's leaders in missions that less distinction should be made between the foreign missionary and the "stay-at-home." Short term missions are being enthusiastically promoted. Such men as George Verwer of Operation Mobilization and Loren Cunningham of Youth With a Mission have dedicated their energies to getting young people committed to missions—be it short term or lifetime careers and be it home or abroad.

So, what about those who did not go overseas? How should their lives be evaluated? Are they any less a part of the Great Commission because they have stayed at home? Is their "missionary call" any less valid? How many young people have heard that "missionary call" and vowed to go, but seemingly became sidetracked along the way? Did they miss God's call? Each one must answer that question individually before God—and perhaps reevaluate the very nature of the missionary "call." Indeed, what often seems to be so plainly a geographical call to a foreign field might better be described as a call to join in completing the unfinished task—a task that can only be accomplished through whole-hearted commitment on the home front as well as in the front lines. For many who have thought they have missed their missionary call, it may be time to set aside feelings of guilt and to commit themselves more fervently than ever to the whole task of missions.

The story of those who went out is a thrilling drama—far more exciting no doubt than the story of those who stayed home. Yet, those who stayed behind also have a story that needs to be told, and sometimes it very closely resembles the story of those who went out.

One of those stories began in the 1950s in a farming community in northern Wisconsin. The setting was a summer Bible camp where missionary Delmer Smith of the Christian and Missionary Alliance was the featured speaker. There in the rustic pavilion under his moving messages a thirteen-year-old farm girl caught a vision for missions, and at the closing meeting she stood to commit her life to God as a foreign missionary.

Through her high school years that followed, foreign missions was her life's goal. Nothing, she vowed, would ever deter her.

Following her high school graduation her life was busy and eventful. Bible college, Christian liberal arts college, university, marriage, family, teaching career. One followed on another. But as the years slipped by, the prospect of embarking on an overseas missions career became less and less a reality.

Only three miles away from her childhood home another young farm girl was growing up—her cousin, Valerie Stellrecht. They attended the same schools and the same little country church. Valerie, too, felt called to foreign missions. She, too, enrolled at the St. Paul Bible College to prepare for her life's calling. And she, too, longed for marriage and family. But her sense of calling to the foreign field came first. Valerie graduated from Bible college and soon thereafter bade farewell to her family and loved ones and set out alone for Ecuador, where she continues to serve today with the Christian and Missionary Alliance.

Two young women whose lives paralleled each other's in so many respects. Two young women who felt called to foreign missions. Valerie went. I stayed home.

NOTES

Part I: Introduction

[1] Ralph D. Winter, "The Kingdom Strikes Back: The Ten Epochs of Redemptive History," in *Perspectives on the World Christian Movement*, ed. Ralph D. Winter and Steven C. Hawthorne (Pasadena: William Carey, 1981), 150.

[2] J. Herbert Kane, *A Concise History of the Christian World Mission: A Panoramic View of Missions From Pentecost to the Present* (Grand Rapids: Baker, 1978), 43.

[3] Winter, "The Kingdom Strikes Back," 148.

[4] Philip Schaff, *The Middle Ages*, vol. 5 of *History of the Christian Church* (Grand Rapids: Eerdmans, 1979), 588–89.

Chapter 1

[1] J. Herbert Kane, *A Concise History of the Christian World Mission* (Grand Rapids: Baker, 1978), 7.

[2] Stephen Neill, *A History of Christian Missions* (New York: Penguin, 1964), 24.

[3] Neill, *History of Christian Missions*, 39–40.

[4] John Foxe, *Foxe's Christian Martyrs of the World* (Chicago: Moody, n.d.), 41.

[5] Neill, *History of Christian Missions*, 45.

[6] Neill, *History of Christian Missions*, 42.

[7] Neill, *History of Christian Missions*, 43.

[8] Kenneth Scott Latourette, *The First Five Centuries*, vol. 1 of *A History of the Expansion of Christianity* (Grand Rapids: Zondervan, 1970), 80.

[9] Roland Allen, *Missionary Methods: St. Paul's or Ours?* (Chicago: Moody, 1956), 3–4.

[10] Allen, *Missionary Methods*, 6–7.

[11] F. F. Bruce, *The Spreading Flame: The Rise and Progress of Christianity From Its First Beginnings to the Conversion of the English* (Grand Rapids: Eerdmans, 1979), 174.

[12] W. H. C. Frend, *Martyrdom and Persecution in the Early Church* (Oxford: Blackwell, 1965), 241, 189.

[13] Bruce, *The Spreading Flame*, 260.

[14] Philip Schaff, *Ante-Nicene Christianity*, vol. 2 of *History of the Christian Church* (Grand Rapids: Eerdmans, 1979), 666.

[15] Elliott Wright, *Holy Company: Christian Heroes and Heroines* (New York: Macmillan, 1980), 80.

[16] Schaff, *Ante-Nicene Christianity*, 2:667.

[17] Bruce, *The Spreading Flame*, 174.

[18] Eusebius, *History of the Church* in *Eerdmans' Handbook to the History of Christianity* (Grand Rapids: Eerdmans, 1977), 81.

[19] Edith Deen, *Great Women of the Christian Faith* (New York: Harper & Row, 1959), 3.

[20] Wright, *Holy Company*, 234.

[21] Wright, *Holy Company*, 235.

[22] Deen, *Great Women*, 5.

[23] Sherwood Wirt, "God's Darling," *Moody Monthly* (February 1977): 58.

[24] Wright, *Holy Company*, 236.

[25] Deen, *Great Women*, 6.

[26] Wirt, "God's Darling," 60.

[27] Latourette, *The First Five Centuries*, 213.

[28] Neill, *A History of Christian Missions*, 55; V. Raymond Edman, *The Light in Dark Ages* (Wheaton: Van Kampen, 1949), 91.

[29] Neill, *A History of Christian Missions*, 55n.

[30] Latourette, *First Five Centuries*, 214.

[31] Philostorgius, *History of the Church* in *Eerdmans' Handbook to the History of Christianity*, 180.

[32] Edman, *Light in Dark Ages*, 93.

[33] Bruce, *The Spreading Flame*, 373.

[34] Bruce, *The Spreading Flame*, 373.

[35] Bruce, *The Spreading Flame*, 374.

[36] Bruce, *The Spreading Flame*, 376–77.

[37] J. Herbert Kane, "Saint Patrick—Evangelical Missionary to Ireland," *Eternity*, 23 no. 7 (July 1972): 34.

[38] Latourette, *First Five Centuries*, 219.

[39] Bruce, *The Spreading Flame*, 381.

[40] Edman, *Light in Dark Ages*, 145.

[41] E. H. Broadbent, *The Pilgrim Church* (London: Pickering & Inglis, 1974), 34–35.

[42] Will Durant, *The Age of Faith* in *The Story of Civilization* (New York: Simon & Schuster, 1950), 532.

[43] Latourette, *The Thousand Years of Uncertainty*, vol. 2 of *A History of the Expansion of Christianity* (Grand Rapids: Zondervan, 1970), 54.

Chapter 2

[1] Norman F. Cantor, *Medieval History: The Life and Death of a Civilization* (London: Macmillan, 1969), 130.

[2]Bruce L. Shelley, *Church History in Plain Language* (Waco: Word, 1982), 176.

[3]Stephen Neill, *A History of Christian Missions* (New York: Penguin, 1979), 67.

[4]Neill, *History of Christian Missions*, 68–69.

[5]John Stewart, *The Nestorian Missionary Enterprise: A Church on Fire* (Edinburgh: Clarke, 1923), 198, 29, 18.

[6]Neill, *History of Christian Missions*, 74; Kenneth Scott Latourette, *The Thousand Years of Uncertainty*, vol. 2 of *A History of the Expansion of Christianity* (Grand Rapids: Zondervan, 1970), 85; Christopher Dawson, *The Making of Europe* quoted in Neill, *History of Christian Missions*, 74.

[7]V. Raymond Edman, *The Light in Dark Ages* (Wheaton: Van Kampen, 1949), 192.

[8]George William Greenaway, *Saint Boniface* (London: Adam & Charles Black, 1955), 28.

[9]Philip Schaff, *Medieval Christianity*, vol. 4 of *History of the Christian Church* (Grand Rapids: Eerdmans, 1979), 94.

[10]C. H. Talbot, "St. Boniface and the German Mission," in *The Mission of the Church and the Propagation of the Faith*, ed. G. J. Cuming (Cambridge: The University Press, 1970), 49.

[11]Latourette, *Thousand Years of Uncertainty*, 95.

[12]Cantor, *Medieval History*, 186.

[13]Cantor, *Medieval History*, 187.

[14]Schaff, *Medieval Christianity*, 98.

[15]Neill, *History of Christian Missions*, 76.

[16]Latourette, *Thousand Years of Uncertainty*, 117.

[17]Schaff, *Medieval Christianity*, 114.

[18]Samuel M. Zwemer, *Raymond Lull: First Missionary to the Moslems* (New York: Funk & Wagnalls, 1902), 26.

[19]Zwemer, *Raymond Lull*, 34, 36.

[20]Zwemer, *Raymond Lull*, 52–53.

[21]Zwemer, *Raymond Lull*, 64.

[22]Zwemer, *Raymond Lull*, 63–64.

[23]Zwemer, *Raymond Lull*, 81–82.

[24]Zwemer, *Raymund Lull*, 83.

[25]Zwemer, *Raymund Lull*, 89–90.

[26]Zwemer, *Raymund Lull*, 94.

[27]Zwemer, *Raymund Lull*, 108.

[28]Zwemer, *Raymund Lull*, 110–11.

[29]Zwemer, *Raymund Lull*, 141.

[30]Zwemer, *Raymund Lull*, 135.

[31]Zwemer, *Raymund Lull*, 142–43.

[32]Neill, *History of Christian Missions*, 169.

[33]Neill, *History of Christian Missions*, 171.

[34]Latourette, *Three Centuries of Advance*, vol. 3 of *A History of the Expansion of Christianity* (Grand Rapids: Zondervan, 1978), 96.

[35]Neill, *History of Christian Missions*, 148.

[36]Will Durant, *The Reformation*, vol. 6 of *The Story of Civilization* (New York: Simon & Schuster, 1957), 914.

[37]James Brodrick, *Saint Francis Xavier* (New York: Wicklow, 1952), 204.

[38]Brodrick, *Saint Francis*, 174.

[39]Brodrick, *Saint Francis*, 145.

[40]Brodrick, *Saint Francis*, 144.

[41]Neill, *History of Christian Missions*, 150.

[42]Neill, *History of Christian Missions*, 154.

[43]Neill, *History of Christian Missions*, 156.

[44]F. A. Rouleau, "Matteo Ricci," in *The New Catholic Encyclopedia*, ed. William J. McDonald (New York: McGraw-Hill, 1967), 12:472.

[45]Vincent Cronin, *The Wise Man From the West* (New York: Dutton, 1955), 31.

[46]A. J. Broomhall, *Hudson Taylor & China's Open Century* (London: Hodder & Stoughton, 1981), 74.

[47]Broomhall, *Hudson Taylor*, 64.

[48]Rouleau, "Matteo Ricci," 471.

[49]Matthew Ricci, "The Journal of Matthew Ricci," in *Classics of Christian Missions*, ed. Francis M. DuBose (Nashville: Broadman, 1979), 172–73.

[50]Broomhall, *Hudson Taylor*, 75.

Chapter 3

[1]William J. Danker, *Profit for the Lord* (Grand Rapids: Eerdmans, 1971), 73.

[2]A. Skevington Wood, "Count von Zinzendorf," in *Eerdmans' Handbook to the History of Christianity* (Grand Rapids: Eerdmans, 1977), 477.

[3]John R. Weinlick, *Count Zinzendorf* (Nashville: Abingdon, 1956), 225.

[4]Weinlick, *Count Zinzendorf*, 200.

[5]Weinlick, *Count Zinzendorf*, 205.

[6]Louis Bobé, *Hans Egede: Colonizer and Missionary to Greenland* (Copenhagen: Rosenkilde & Bagger, 1952), 22.

[7]Bobé, *Hans Egede*, 23.

[8]Bobé, *Hans Egede*, 29.

[9]Bobé, *Hans Egede*, 82.

[10]Stephen Neill, *A History of Christian Missions* (New York: Penguin, 1964), 237.

[11]Bobé, *Hans Egede*, 155.

[12]Bobé, *Hans Egede*, 162.

[13]Bobé, *Hans Egede*, 158.

[14]Bernard Kruger, *The Pear Tree Blossoms: A History of the Moravian Mission Stations in*

South Africa, 1737–1869 (South Africa: Genedendal Printing Works, 1967), 19.

[15]Kruger, *Pear Tree Blossoms*, 31.

Chapter 4

[1]Ola Elisabeth Winslow, *John Eliot, "Apostle to the Indians"* (Boston: Houghton Mifflin, 1968), 96.

[2]Winslow, *John Eliot*, 110.

[3]Winslow, *John Eliot*, 113.

[4]Neville B. Cryer, "John Eliot," in *Five Pioneer Missionaries* (London: Banner of Truth, 1965), 212.

[5]Winslow, *John Eliot*, 179.

[6]Elisabeth D. Dodds, *Marriage to a Difficult Man: The "Uncommon Union" of Jonathan and Sarah Edwards* (Philadelphia: Westminster, 1971), 118.

[7]David Wynbeek, *David Brainerd: Beloved Yankee* (Grand Rapids: Eerdmans, 1961), 60–61.

[8]Wynbeek, *David Brainerd*, 79.

[9]Wynbeek, *David Brainerd*, 113.

[10]Jonathan Edwards, ed., *The Life and Diary of David Brainerd* (Chicago: Moody, 1949), 141, 146.

[11]R. Pierce Beaver, *Pioneers in Mission: The Early Missionary Ordination Sermons, Charges, and Instructions* (Grand Rapids: Eerdmans, 1966), 211–12.

[12]Nard Jones, *The Great Command: The Story of Marcus and Narcissa Whitman and the Oregon Country Pioneers* (Boston: Little, Brown and Company, 1959), 125.

[13]Jones, *The Great Command*, 202, 229.

[14]Jones, *The Great Command*, 219–20.

Part II: Introduction

[1]Stephen Neill, *A History of Christian Missions* (New York: Penguin, 1964), 243.

[2]Kenneth Scott Latourette, *The Great Century: North Africa and Asia*, vol. 6 of *A History of the Expansion of Christianity* (Grand Rapids: Zondervan, 1970), 445.

[3]Martin E. Marty, *A Short History of Christianity* (New York: Meridian, 1959), 318.

[4]Marty, *Short History*, 273.

[5]Harold Cook, *Highlights of Christian Missions: A History and Survey* (Chicago: Moody, 1967), 54.

[6]Latourette, *The Great Century*, 443.

[7]Neill, *History of Christian Missions*, 252.

[8]Robert Hall Glover and J. Herbert Kane, *The Progress of World-Wide Missions* (New York: Harper & Brothers, 1960), 58.

[9]A. F. Walls, "Outposts of Empire," in *Eerdmans' Handbook to the History of Christianity* (Grand Rapids: Eerdmans, 1977), 556.

[10]Ralph D. Winter, "The Kingdom Strikes Back: The Ten Epochs of Redemptive History," in *Perspectives on the World Christian Movement*, ed. Ralph D. Winter and Steven C. Hawthorne (Pasadena: William Carey, 1981), 154.

[11]Neill, *History of Christian Missions*, 259.

Chapter 5

[1]Mary Drewery, *William Carey: A Biography* (Grand Rapids: Zondervan, 1979), 25.

[2]J. Herbert Kane, *A Concise History of the Christian World Mission* (Grand Rapids: Baker, 1978), 85.

[3]Drewery, *William Carey*, 70.

[4]Drewery, *William Carey*, 89.

[5]Drewery, *William Carey*, 69, 111.

[6]Drewery, *William Carey*, 102.

[7]Drewery, *William Carey*, 115.

[8]Drewery, *William Carey*, 146.

[9]Drewery, *William Carey*, 183, 185.

[10]Drewery, *William Carey*, 173.

[11]Drewery, *William Carey*, 166.

[12]Courtney Anderson, *To the Golden Shore: The Life of Adoniram Judson* (Grand Rapids: Zondervan, 1972), 84.

[13]Anderson, *To the Golden Shore*, 181.

[14]Anderson, *To the Golden Shore*, 362.

[15]Anderson, *To the Golden Shore*, 391.

[16]Anderson, *To the Golden Shore*, 398.

[17]Anderson, *To the Golden Shore*, 478.

[18]Anderson, *To the Golden Shore*, 416.

[19]David Bentley-Taylor, *My Love Must Wait: The Story of Henry Martyn* (Downers Grove, Ill.: InterVarsity, 1975), 26.

[20]Richard T. France, "Henry Martyn" in *Five Pioneer Missionaries* (London: Banner of Truth, 1965), 255–56.

[21]Bentley-Taylor, *My Love Must Wait*, 35.

[22]William Paton, *Alexander Duff: Pioneer of Missionary Education* (New York: Doran, 1922), 150.

[23]Paton, *Alexander Duff*, 220.

[24]A. T. Pierson quoted in Robert H. Glover and J. Herbert Kane, *The Progress of World-Wide Missions* (New York: Harper, 1960), 72.

Chapter 6

[1]Jon Bonk, "'All Things to All Persons,'—The Missionary as a Racist-Imperialist, 1860–1918," *Missiology* (July 1980): 300.

[2]Bonk, "All Things to All Persons," 393–94.

[3]Cecil Northcott, *Robert Moffat: Pioneer in Africa, 1817–1870* (London: Lutterworth, 1961), 22.

[4]Northcott, *Robert Moffat*, 34.

[5]Edith Deen, *Great Women of the Christian Faith* (New York: Harper & Row, 1959), 187.

[6]J. H. Morrison, *The Missionary Heroes of Africa* (New York: Doran, 1922), 38.

[7]Deen, *Great Women*, 188.

[8]Northcott, *Robert Moffat*, 129.

[9]Geoffrey Moorhouse, *The Missionaries* (New York: Lippincott, 1973), 111.

[10]Oliver Ransford, *David Livingstone: The Dark Interior* (New York: St. Martin's, 1978), 14.

[11]Ransford, *David Livingstone*, 23.

[12]Ransford, *David Livingstone*, 38.

[13]Deen, *Great Women*, 192.

[14]Northcott, *Robert Moffat*, 189.

[15]Ransford, *David Livingstone*, 39.

[16]Deen, *Great Women*, 193–94.

[17]Deen, *Great Women*, 193–94; Ransford, *David Livingstone*, 118.

[18]Moorhouse, *The Missionaries*, 256.

[19]James and Marti Hefley, *By Their Blood: Christian Martyrs of the 20th Century* (Milford, Mich.: Mott, 1979), 343.

[20]Hefley, *By Their Blood*, 426.

[21]Stephen Neill, *A History of Christian Missions* (New York: Penguin, 1946), 378.

[22]Morrison, *Missionary Heroes*, 201.

[23]Morrison, *Missionary Heroes*, 206.

[24]Morrison, *Missionary Heroes*, 208.

[25]Morrison, *Missionary Heroes*, 215.

[26]Morrison, *Missionary Heroes*, 216.

[27]Robert H. Glover and J. Herbert Kane, *The Progress of World-Wide Missions* (New York: Harper & Row, 1960), 329.

[28]Edwin Bliss, ed., *Encyclopedia of Missions* (New York: Funk & Wagnalls, 1891), 2.

[29]Carol Christian and Gladys Plummer, *God and One Red Head: Mary Slessor of Calabar* (Grand Rapids: Zondervan, 1970), 34.

[30]W. P. Livingstone, *Mary Slessor of Calabar: Pioneer Missionary* (London: Hodder & Stoughton, 1915), 51.

[31]Christian and Plummer, *God and One Red Head*, 177.

Chapter 7

[1]A. J. Broomhall, *Hudson Taylor & China's Open Century*, Book One: *Barbarians at the Gates* (London: Hodder & Stoughton, 1981), 267.

[2]Sherwood Eddy, *Pathfinders of the World Missionary Crusade* (New York: Abingdon-Cokesbury, 1945), 34.

[3]Eddy, *Pathfinders*, 34.

[4]Marshall Broomhall, *Robert Morrison: A Master-builder* (New York: Doran, 1924), 59.

[5]Broomhall, *Robert Morrison*, 61, 131.

[6]Broomhall, *Robert Morrison*, 72.

[7]Stephen Neill, *A History of Christian Missions* (New York: Penguin, 1964), 285.

[8]J. C. Pollock, *Hudson Taylor and Maria: Pioneers in China* (Grand Rapids: Zondervan, 1976), 17.

[9]Pollock, *Hudson Taylor*, 20.

[10]Pollock, *Hudson Taylor*, 19.

[11]Pollock, *Hudson Taylor*, 29.

[12]Dr. and Mrs. Howard Taylor, *J. Hudson Taylor: God's Man in China* (Chicago: Moody, 1978), 76.

[13]Taylor, *J. Hudson Taylor*, 70.

[14]Pollock, *Hudson Taylor*, 31–32.

[15]Taylor, *J. Hudson Taylor*, 100.

[16]Pollock, *Hudson Taylor*, 49–50.

[17]Pollock, *Hudson Taylor*, 33.

[18]Pollock, *Hudson Taylor*, 81–82.

[19]Pollock, *Hudson Taylor*, 84–85.

[20]Pollock, *Hudson Taylor*, 89–91.

[21]Pollock, *Hudson Taylor*, 89–91.

[22]Pollock, *Hudson Taylor*, 95.

[23]Pollock, *Hudson Taylor*, 97–98.

[24]Pollock, *Hudson Taylor*, 140.

[25]Pollock, *Hudson Taylor*, 147.

[26]Pollock, *Hudson Taylor*, 189.

[27]Pollock, *Hudson Taylor*, 193.

[28]Pollock, *Hudson Taylor*, 196–97.

[29]Taylor, *J. Hudson Taylor*, 208.

[30]Taylor, *J. Hudson Taylor*, 272.

[31]Kenneth Scott Latourette, *The Great Century: North Africa and Asia*, vol. 6 of *A History of the Expansion of Christianity* (Grand Rapids: Zondervan, 1970), 329.

[32]Ralph D. Winter and Steven C. Hawthorne, eds. *Perspectives on the World Christian Movement* (Pasadena: William Carey, 1981), 172.

[33]Rosalind Goforth, *Goforth of China* (Grand Rapids: Zondervan, 1937), 29.

[34]Goforth, *Goforth of China*, 48.

[35]Goforth, *Goforth of China*, 54–55.

[36]Goforth, *Goforth of China*, 119.

[37]Goforth, *Goforth of China*, 157–58.

[38]Goforth, *Goforth of China*, 189.

[39]Goforth, *Goforth of China*, 187.

[40]Goforth, *Goforth of China*, 114–15.

[41]Goforth, *Goforth of China*, 162.

[42]Goforth, *Goforth of China*, 214.

Chapter 8

[1]Robert H. Glover and J. Herbert Kane, *The Progress of World-Wide Missions* (New York: Harper & Row, 1960), 433.

[2]Niel Gunson, *Messengers of Grace: Evangelical Missionaries in the South Seas, 1797–1860* (New York: Oxford, 1978), 178.

[3]Graeme Kent, *Company of Heaven: Early Missionaries in the South Seas* (New York: Nelson, 1972), 83.

[4]Glover and Kane, *The Progress*, 436.

[5]Stephen Neill, *A History of Christian Missions* (New York: Penguin, 1964), 297.

[6]Kent, *Company of Heaven*, 33.

[7]Kent, *Company of Heaven*, 35.

[8]Kent, *Company of Heaven*, 45.

[9]Gunson, *Messengers of Grace*, 202.

[10]Gunson, *Messengers of Grace*, 164–65.

[11]Gunson, *Messengers of Grace*, 153.

[12]Kent, *Company of Heaven*, 57.

[13]Kent, *Company of Heaven*, 57.

[14]Bradford Smith, *Yankees in Paradise: The New England Impact on Hawaii* (New York: Lippincott, 1956), 10.

[15]Smith, *Yankees in Paradise*, 164.

[16]Smith, *Yankees in Paradise*, 190.

[17]Smith, *Yankees in Paradise*, 191–92.

[18]Smith, *Yankees in Paradise*, 199.

[19]Smith, *Yankees in Paradise*, 205.

[20]Smith, *Yankees in Paradise*, 234.

[21]John Gutch, *Beyond the Reefs: The Life of John Williams, Missionary* (London: McDonald, 1974), 18.

[22]Gutch, *Beyond the Reefs*, 20.

[23]Gutch, *Beyond the Reefs*, 33–34.

[24]Gutch, *Beyond the Reefs*, 46.

[25]Gutch, *Beyond the Reefs*, 47.

[26]Kent, *Company of Heaven*, 79; Gutch, *Beyond the Reefs*, 87.

[27]Neill, *History of Christian Missions*, 298–99.

[28]Gutch, *Beyond the Reefs*, 109.

[29]Kent, *Company of Heaven*, 82–83.

[30]Ralph Bell, *John G. Paton: Apostle to the New Hebrides* (Butler, Ind.: Higley, 1957), 42–43.

[31]John G. Paton, *The Story of Dr. John G. Paton's Thirty Years with South Sea Cannibals* (New York: Doran, 1923), 33.

[32]Paton, *The Story*, 36.

[33]Kent, *Company of Heaven*, 118–19; Paton, *The Story*, 130.

[34]Bell, *John G. Paton*, 157.

[35]Bell, *John G. Paton*, 179.

[36]Paton, *The Story*, 180.

[37]Bell, *John G. Paton*, 237–38.

[38]James and Marti Hefley, *By Their Blood: Christian Martyrs of the 20th Century* (Milford, Mich.: Mott, 1979), 169.

[39]Kent, *Company of Heaven*, 159, 178.

[40]Neill, *History of Christian Missions*, 354.

[41]Cuthbert Lennox, *James Chalmers of New Guinea* (London: Andrew Melrose, 1902), 147–48.

[42]Delavan L. Pierson, *The Pacific Islanders: From Savages to Saints* (New York: Funk & Wagnalls, 1906), 173.

[43]Kent, *Company of Heaven*, 147.

Part III: Introduction

[1]Stephen Neill, *A History of Christian Missions* (New York: Penguin, 1964), 243.

[2]Neill, *History of Christian Missions*, 452.

[3]Neill, *History of Christian Missions*, 451.

[4]Robert D. Linder, "Introduction: The Christian Centuries," in *Eerdmans' Handbook to the History of Christianity* (Grand Rapids: Eerdmans, 1977), xxii.

[5]Linder, "Christian Centuries," xxii.

[6]Winthrop S. Hudson, *Religion in America: An Historical Account of the Development of American Religious Life* (New York: Scribner, 1973), 318.

[7]Hudson, *Religion in America*, 318.

Chapter 9

[1]R. Pierce Beaver, *American Protestant Women in World Mission* (Grand Rapids: Eerdmans, 1969), 59.

[2]Helen Barnett Montgomery, *Western Women in Eastern Lands* (New York: Macmillan, 1910), 243–44.

[3]Nancy A. Hardesty, *Great Women of Faith* (Grand Rapids: Baker, 1980), 104; Marlys Taege, *And God Gave Women Talents!* (St. Louis: Concordia, 1978), 90.

[4]Catherine Allen, *The New Lottie Moon Story* (Nashville: Broadman, 1980), 136, 140–42.

[5]J. Herbert Kane, *Life and Work on the Mission Field* (Grand Rapids: Baker, 1980), 143.

[6]Irwin Hyatt, *Our Ordered Lives Confess: Three Nineteenth-Century American Missionaries in East Shantung* (Cambridge, Mass.: Harvard University, 1976), 95.

[7]Hyatt, *Our Ordered Lives*, 96.

[8]Hyatt, *Our Ordered Lives*, 98.

[9]Hyatt, *Our Ordered Lives*, 99.

[10]Hyatt, *Our Ordered Lives*, 104–5.

[11]Hyatt, *Our Ordered Lives*, 104–5.

[12]Hyatt, *Our Ordered Lives*, 106.

[13]Hyatt, *Our Ordered Lives*, 115, 117.

[14]Hyatt, *Our Ordered Lives*, 113; Allen, *The New Lottie Moon*, 212–13.

[15]Hyatt, *Our Ordered Lives*, 114.

[16]Allen, *The New Lottie Moon*, 288.

[17]Sherwood Eddy, *Pathfinders of the World Missionary Crusade* (New York: Abingdon-Cokesbury, 1945), 125.

[18]Frank Houghton, *Amy Carmichael of Dohnavur* (London: Society for the Propagation of Christian Knowledge, 1954), 61, 73.

[19]Houghton, *Amy Carmichael*, 78.

[20]Houghton, *Amy Carmichael*, 213.

[21]Houghton, *Amy Carmichael*, 62.

[22]Evelyn Stenbock, *"Miss Terri": The Story of Maude Cary, Pioneer GMU Missionary in Morocco* (Lincoln, Neb.: Good News Broadcasting, 1970), 30.

[23]Stenbock, *"Miss Terri,"* 35–36.

[24]Stenbock, *"Miss Terri,"* 46.

[25]Isobel Kuhn, *By Searching* (Chicago: Moody, 1959), 120; Helen Roseveare, *Give Me This Mountain* (London: Inter-Varsity, 1966), 67.

[26]Stenbock, *"Miss Terri,"* 60.

[27]Stenbock, *"Miss Terri,"* 71.

[28]Stenbock, *"Miss Terri,"* 103.

[29]Stenbock, *"Miss Terri,"* 139.

[30]Henry Beets, *Johanna of Nigeria: Life and Labors of Johanna Veenstra* (Grand Rapids: Grand Rapids Printing Company, 1937), 90, 129.

[31]Johanna Veenstra, *Pioneering for Christ in the Sudan* (Grand Rapids: Smitter Book, 1926), 165.

[32]Veenstra, *Pioneering for Christ*, 210.

[33]Beets, *Johanna of Nigeria*, 205.

[34]Phyllis Thompson, *A Transparent Woman: The Compelling Story of Gladys Aylward* (Grand Rapids: Zondervan, 1971), 20.

[35]Alan Burgess, *The Small Woman* (New York: Dutton, 1957), 29.

[36]Burgess, *The Small Woman*, 166.

[37]Thompson, *A Transparent Woman*, 183.

[38]Valentin H. Rabe, "Evangelical Logistics: Mission Support and Resources to 1920" in *The Missionary Enterprise in China and America*, ed. John K. Fairbank (Cambridge, Mass.: Harvard University, 1974), 72.

[39]Alan Burgess, *Daylight Must Come: The Story of a Courageous Woman Doctor in the Congo* (New York: Dell, 1975), 135.

[40]Burgess, *Daylight Must Come*, 149.

[41]Burgess, *Daylight Must Come*, 95.

[42]"A HIS Interview with Helen Roseveare," *HIS* (January 1977): 18.

[43]Burgess, *Daylight Must Come*, 45.

[44]"A HIS Interview," 19.

Chapter 10

[1]Harold R. Cook, *Highlights of Christian Missions: A History and Survey* (Chicago: Moody, 1967), 69.

[2]James and Marti Hefley, *By Their Blood: Christian Martyrs of the 20th Century* (Milford, Mich.: Mott, 1979), 76.

[3]Sherwood Eddy, *Pathfinders of the World Missionary Crusade* (New York: Abingdon-Cokesbury, 1945), 5–6.

[4]Norman P. Grubb, *C. T. Studd: Cricketer & Pioneer* (Fort Washington, Pa.: Christian Literature Crusade, 1969), 17.

[5]J. Herbert Kane, "C. T. Studd: A Gambler for God," *Eternity* (December 1972): 39.

[6]Grubb, *C. T. Studd*, 87.

[7]Kane, "C. T. Studd," 40.

[8]Grubb, *C. T. Studd*, 121.

[9]Norman P. Brugg, *Once Caught, No Escape: My Life Story* (Fort Washington, Pa.: Christian Literature Crusade, 1969), 78.

[10]Grubb, *Once Caught*, 81.

[11]Grubb, *Once Caught*, 97.

[12]Grubb, *Once Caught*, 99, 102.

[13]Grubb, *C. T. Studd*, 205.

[14]John R. Mott, *The Larger Evangelism* (Nashville: Abindgon-Cokesbury, 1944), 11.

[15]C. Howard Hopkins, *John R. Mott, 1865–1955: A Biography* (Grand Rapids: Eerdmans, 1979), 19.

[16]Mott, *The Larger Evangelism*, 36.

[17]Hopkins, *John R. Mott*, 568.

[18]Hopkins, *John R. Mott*, 276.

[19]Quoted in Terry Hurlbert, *World Mission Today* (Wheaton: Evangelical Teacher Training Association), 29.

[20]W. Reginald Wheeler, *A Man Sent From God: A Biography of Robert E. Speer* (London: Revell, 1956), 53.

[21]Eddy, *Pathfinders*, 263.

[22]Arthur P. Johnston, *The Battle for World Evangelism* (Wheaton: Tyndale, 1978), 32.

[23]Wheeler, *A Man Sent From God*, 219.

[24]Wheeler, *A Man Sent From God*, 163.

[25]Wheeler, *A Man Sent From God*, 166.

[26]Wheeler, *A Man Sent From God*, 15.

[27]Stephen Neill, *A History of Christian Missions* (New York: Penguin, 1964), 366.

[28]J. Christy Wilson, *The Apostle to Islam: A Biography of Samuel M. Zwemer* (Grand Rapids: Baker, 1952), 23.

[29]Wilson, *The Apostle to Islam*, 47.

[30]Wilson, *The Apostle to Islam*, 43.

[31]Wilson, *The Apostle to Islam*, 234.

[32]Wilson, *The Apostle to Islam*, 81.

[33]Eddy, *Pathfinders*, 53.

[34]Eddy, *Pathfinders*, 202.

[35]Eddy, *Pathfinders*, 207.

[36]Eddy, *Pathfinders*, 206.

[37]E. Stanley Jones, *Along the Indian Road* (New York: Abingdon, 1939), 19–20.

[38]E. Stanley Jones, *The Christ of the Indian Road* (New York: Abingdon, 1925), 19–20.

[39]Jones, *The Christ*, 8.

[40]Jones, *The Christ*, 49.

[41]Chester E. Tulga, *The Case Against Modernism in Foreign Missions* (Chicago: Conservative Baptist, 1950), 44.

[42]John W. R. Stott, *Christian Mission in the Modern World* (Downers Grove, Ill.: InterVarsity, 1975), 76.

[43]Jones, *Along the Indian Road*, 183–84.

[44]Eddy, *Pathfinders*, 270; Robert H. Glover and J. Herbert Kane, *The Progress of World-Wide Missions* (New York: Harper, 1960), 185.

[45]Jones, *Along the Indian Road*, 166.

[46]Jones, *The Christ*, 212–13.

Chapter 11

[1]J. Herbert Kane, *A Concise History of the Christian World Mission* (Grand Rapids: Baker, 1978), 102.

[2]Elisabeth Elliot, *Through Gates of Splendor* (New York: Harper & Row, 1958), 176.

[3]Kane, *A Concise History*, 102.

[4]J. Herbert Kane, *Faith Mighty Faith: A Handbook of the Interdenominational Foreign Mission Association* (New York: Interdenominational Foreign Mission Association, 1956), 88.

[5]A. E. Thompson, *The Life of A. B. Simpson* (New York: Christian Alliance Publishing, 1920), 65.

[6]Thompson, *Life of A. B. Simpson*, 120.

[7]Thompson, *Life of A. B. Simpson*, 121.

[8]Thompson, *Life of A. B. Simpson*, 120.

[9]A. W. Tozer, *Wingspread: A. B. Simpson: A Study in Spiritual Altitude* (Harrisburg: Christian Publications, 1943), 87.

[10]Thompson, *Life of A. B. Simpson*, 227.

[11]Tozer, *Wingspread*, 71.

[12]Tozer, *Wingspread*, 72.

[13]J. H. Hunter, *A Flame of Fire: The Life and Work of R. V. Bingham* (Scarborough, Ontario: Sudan Interior Mission, 1961), 56.

[14]Hunter, *A Flame of Fire*, 50.

[15]Hunter, *A Flame of Fire*, 65.

[16]Hunter, *A Flame of Fire*, 67.

[17]Hunter, *A Flame of Fire*, 78.

[18]Hunter, *A Flame of Fire*, 79.

[19]Hunter, *A Flame of Fire*, 111.

[20]Hunter, *A Flame of Fire*, 149–51.

[21]Hunter, *A Flame of Fire*, 211.

[22]Raymond Davis, *Fire on the Mountains: The Story of a Miracle—The Church in Ethiopia* (Grand Rapids: Zondervan, 1975), 88.

[23]Davis, *Fire on the Mountains*, 107.

[24]Davis, *Fire on the Mountains*, 107.

[25]Davis, *Fire on the Mountains*, 115, 246–47.

[26]This is not the Sudan of the 1890s but rather a portion of that great region which became known as the Anglo-Egyptian Sudan. With independence it became known as The Republic of the Sudan or simply Sudan.

[27]Kenneth Richardson, *Garden of Miracles: The Story of the Africa Inland Mission* (London: Africa Inland Mission, 1976), 33.

[28]Richardson, *Garden of Miracles*, 70.

[29]James and Marti Hefley, *By Their Blood: Christian Martyrs of the 20th Century* (Milford, Mich.: Mott, 1979), 422–23.

[30]Mildred W. Spain, *"And in Samaria": A Story of More Than Sixty Years' Missionary Witness in Central America, 1890–1954* (Dallas: The Central American Mission, 1954), 8.

[31]"A Chain Divinely Forged," *CAM Bulletin* (Fall 1980): 5.

[32]Robert H. Glover and J. Herbert Kane, *The Progress of World-Wide Missions* (New York: Harper, 1960), 356.

[33]Harold R. Cook, *Highlights of Christian Missions: A History and Survey* (Chicago: Moody, 1967), 211–12.

[34]Cook, *Highlights of Christian Missions*, 214.

[35]Jean Dye Johnson, *God Planted Five Seeds* ((Woodworth, Wis.: New Tribes Mission, 1966), 12, 23, 26.

[36]Johnson, *God Planted Five Seeds*, 21–22.

[37]Johnson, *God Planted Five Seeds*, 43.

[38]Johnson, *God Planted Five Seeds*, 84, 73.

[39]Johnson, *God Planted Five Seeds*, 107–8.

[40]Elliot, *Through Gates of Splendor*, 152–53.

[41]Russell T. Hitt, *Jungle Pilot: The Life and Witness of Nate Saint* (Grand Rapids: Zondervan, 1973), 244.

[42]*Diary of Pete Fleming*, December 6, 1953.

[43]Elliot, *Through Gates of Splendor*, 146, 159; Hitt, *Jungle Pilot*, 241.

[44]Hitt, *Jungle Pilot*, 252.

[45]Elliot, *Through Gates of Splendor*, 104.

[46]Elliot, *Through Gates of Splendor*, 172, 176.

[47]*Diary of Pete Fleming*, December 27, 1955.

[48]Elliot, *Through Gates of Splendor*, 180.

[49]Elliot, *Through Gates of Splendor*, 196–97.

[50]James C. Hefley, "The Auca Massacre & Beyond," *Power for Living* (April 19, 1981): 5.

[51]Hitt, *Jungle Pilot*, 258.

[52]Lorry Lutz, *Born to Lose, Bound to Win: The Amazing Journey of Mother Eliza George* (Irvine, Ca.: Harvest House, 1980), *passim*.

Part IV: Introduction

[1]Winthrop S. Hudson, *Religion in America: An Historical Account of the Development of American Religious Life* (New York: Scribner, 1956), 371–72.

[2]Hudson, *Religion in America*, 382.

[3]Hudson, *Religion in America*, 383.

[4]J. Herbert Kane, *A Concise History of the Christian World Mission* (Grand Rapids: Baker, 1978), 186.

[5]Arthur J. Brown, *The Why and How of Foreign Missions* (New York: Missionary Education Movement, 1921), 127.

Chapter 12

[1]Sherwood Eddy, *Pathfinders of the World Missionary Crusade* (New York: Abingdon-Cokesbury, 1945), 225.

[2]J. Lennox Kerr, *Wilfred Grenfell: His Life and Work* (New York: Dodd, 1959), 85.

[3]Kerr, *Wilfred Grenfell*, 95.

[4]Kerr, *Wilfred Grenfell*, 181.

[5]Kerr, *Wilfred Grenfell*, 166.

[6]Kerr, *Wilfred Grenfell*, 165.

[7]Kerr, *Wilfred Grenfell*, 204.

[8]Kerr, *Wilfred Grenfell*, 166.

[9]Dorothy Clarke Wilson, *Dr. Ida: The Story of Dr. Ida Scudder of Vellore* (New York: McGraw-Hill, 1959), 5.

[10]Wilson, *Dr. Ida*, 22.

[11]Eddy, *Pathfinders*, 131.

[12]Wilson, *Dr. Ida*, 273.

[13]Wilson, *Dr. Ida*, 286.

[14]Wilson, *Dr. Ida*, 297.

[15]Wilson, *Dr. Ida*, 321.

[16]Wilson, *Dr. Ida*, 243.

[17]Clarence W. Hall, "Medicine Man on the Amazon," in *Adventures for God* (New York: Harper & Brothers, 1959), 183.

[18]William J. Peterson, *Another Hand on Mine: The Story of Dr. Carl K. Becker of Africa Inland Mission* (New York: McGraw-Hill, 1967), 40.

[19]Peterson, *Another Hand*, 54.

[20]Peterson, *Another Hand*, 89.

[21]Peterson, *Another Hand*, 127.

[22]Peterson, *Another Hand*, 154.

[23]Peterson, *Another Hand*, 227.

[24]Peterson, *Another Hand*, 144.

[25]Peterson, *Another Hand*, 127.

[26]Viggo Olsen, *Daktar: Diplomat in Bangladesh* (Chicago: Moody, 1973), 32.

[27]Olsen, *Daktar*, 32.

[28]Olsen, *Daktar*, 65–66.

[29]Olsen, *Daktar*, 67–69.

[30]Olsen, *Daktar*, 89.

[31]Olsen, *Daktar*, 79–80.

[32]Olsen, *Daktar*, 88.

[33]Olsen, *Daktar*, 350.

[34]Olsen, *Daktar*, 81.

[35]Olsen, *Daktar*, 162.

[36]Olsen, *Daktar*, 257.

[37]Olsen, *Daktar*, 12.

Chapter 13

[1]Harold K. Moulton, "Translation Work," in Stephen Neill, et al., *A Concise Dictionary of the Christian World Mission* (New York: Abingdon, 1971), 604.

[2]April 1982 Bulletin of Wycliffe Bible Translators on the death of William Cameron Townsend.

[3]James and Marti Hefley, *Uncle Cam* (Waco: Word, 1974), 26.

[4]Hefley, *Uncle Cam*, 27.

[5]Jamie Buckingham, *Into the Glory* (Plainfield, N. J.: Logos, 1974), 21.

[6]Hefley, *Uncle Cam*, 51.

[7]Hefley, *Uncle Cam*, 99.

[8]Hefley, *Uncle Cam*, 200.

[9]Hefley, *Uncle Cam*, 243.

[10]Hefley, *Uncle Cam*, 173.

[11]Clarence W. Hall, "Two Thousand Tongues to Go" in *Adventurers for God* (New York: Harper & Brothers, 1959), 119–20.

[12]Hall, "Two Thousand Tongues," 119.

[13]Hefley, *Uncle Cam*, 96.

[14]Hefley, *Uncle Cam*, 244.

[15]Hefley, *Uncle Cam*, 259.

[16]Hefley, *Uncle Cam*, 182.

[17]April 1982 Bulletin of Wycliffe Bible Translators on the death of William Cameron Townsend.

[18]Ethel E. Wallis and Mary A. Bennett, *Two Thousand Tongues to Go* (New York: Harper & Brothers, 1959), 51.

[19]Eunice V. Pike, *Ken Pike: Scholar and Christian* (Dallas: Summer Institute of Linguistics, 1981), 48.

[20]Wallis and Bennett, *Two Thousand Tongues*, 108.

[21]Pike, *Ken Pike*, 131.

[22]Pike, *Ken Pike*, 179.

[23]The Story of Marianna Slocum can be found in Helen W. Kooiman, *Cameos: Women Fashioned by God* (Wheaton: Tyndale, 1968).

[24]Ethel E. Wallis, *The Dayuma Story: Life Under Auca Spears* (New York: Harper & Row, 1960), 25.

[25]Russell T. Hitt, *Jungle Pilot: The Life and Witness of Nate Saint* (Grand Rapids: Zondervan, 1973), 120.

[26]Wallis, *The Dayuma Story*, 28.

[27]Wallis, *The Dayuma Story*, 29.

[28]Wallis, *The Dayuma Story*, 19.

[29]Wallis, *The Dayuma Story*, 92.

[30]J. H. Hunter, *Beside All Waters: The Story of Seventy-Five Years of World-Wide Ministry, The Christian and Missionary Alliance* (Harrisburg, Penn: Christian Publications, 1965), 195.

[31]Russell T. Hitt, *Cannibal Valley: The Heroic Struggle for Christ in Savage New Guinea* (New York: Harper & Row, 1962), 87.

[32]Hitt, *Cannibal Valley*, 109.

[33]Hitt, *Cannibal Valley*, 111.

[34]Hitt, *Cannibal Valley*, 111.

[35]Hitt, *Cannibal Valley*, 111.

[36]Hitt, *Cannibal Valley*, 111.

[37]Hitt, *Cannibal Valley*, 112.

[38]Shirley Horne, *An Hour to the Stone Age* (Chicago: Moody, 1973), 95.

[39]Hitt, *Cannibal Valley*, 119.

Chapter 14

[1]Barry Siedell, *Gospel Radio: A 20th-Century Tool for a 20th-Century Challenge* (Lincoln, Neb.: Good News Broadcasting, 1971), 132.

[2]Siedell, *Gospel Radio*, 134.

[3]Siedell, *Gospel Radio*, 145.

[4]Lois Neely, *Come Up to This Mountain: The Miracle of Clarence W. Jones & HCJB* (Wheaton: Tyndale, 1980), 53.

[5]Neely, *Come Up to This Mountain*, 54.

[6]Neely, *Come Up to This Mountain*, 56.

[7]Neely, *Come Up to This Mountain*, 67.

[8]Neely, *Come Up to This Mountain*, 73.

[9]Neely, *Come Up to This Mountain*, 108.

[10]Neely, *Come Up to This Mountain*, 111.

[11]Neely, *Come Up to This Mountain*, 140.

[12]Gleason H. Ledyard, *Sky Waves: The Incredible Far East Broadcasting Company Story* (Chicago: Moody, 1968), 38.

[13]Ledyard, *Sky Waves*, 107.

[14]Paul E. Freed, *Towers to Eternity* (Nashville: Sceptre Books, 1979), 38.

[15]Freed, *Towers to Eternity*, 58.

[16]Freed, *Towers to Eternity*, 63–64.

[17]Freed, *Towers to Eternity*, 65.

[18]Freed, *Towers to Eternity*, 69.

[19]Freed, *Towers to Eternity*, 90.

[20]Freed, *Towers to Eternity*, 169.

[21]Freed, *Towers to Eternity*, 173.

[22]Norman B. Rohrer and Peter Deyneka, Jr., *Peter Dynamite: The Story of Peter Deyneka— Missionary to the Russian World* (Grand Rapids: Baker, 1975), 81.

[23]Phyllis Thompson, *Faith By Hearing: The Story of Gospel Recordings* (Kowloon, Hongkong: Rainbow, 1960), 41.

[24]Thompson, *Faith By Hearing*, 45.

[25]Phyllis Thompson, *Count It All Joy: The Story of Joy Ridderhof & Gospel Recordings* (Wheaton: Shaw, 1978), 143–44.

Chapter 15

[1]Lee Roddy, *On Wings of Love: Stories From Mission Aviation Fellowship* (Nashville: Nelson, 1981), 17.

[2]Mary Wade, "On a Wing and a Prayer," *The Saturday Evening Post* (April 1980): 105.

[3]"Miss Betty Greene: First Lady of MAF," *Christian Times* (15 January 1967): 3.

[4]Russell T. Hitt, *Jungle Pilot: The Life and Witness of Nate Saint* (Grand Rapids: Zondervan, 1973), 99.

[5]Hitt, *Jungle Pilot*, 54.

[6]Hitt, *Jungle Pilot*, 100, 107.

[7]Hitt, *Jungle Pilot*, 130.

[8]Hitt, *Jungle Pilot*, 133.

[9]Hitt, *Jungle Pilot*, 143.

[10]Hitt, *Jungle Pilot*, 144.

[11]Hitt, *Jungle Pilot*, 145.

[12]Hitt, *Jungle Pilot*, 145.

[13]Hitt, *Jungle Pilot*, 203.

[14]Hitt, *Jungle Pilot*, 226.

[15]Hitt, *Jungle Pilot*, 206.

[16]Hitt, *Jungle Pilot*, 226–27.

[17]Jamie Buckingham, *Into the Glory: The Miracle-Filled Story of the Jungle Aviation and Radio Service* (Plainfield, N.J.: Logos International, 1974), 37.

[18]Buckingham, *Into the Glory*, 152–53.

[19]Buckingham, *Into the Glory*, 153.

[20]Buckingham, *Into the Glory*, 51.

[21]Craig Nimmo, "Seven Graves to Freedom," *Power for Living* (May 4, 1980): 2.

[22]Nimmo, "Seven Graves to Freedom," 3.

[23]Gleason H. Ledyard, *And to the Eskimos* (Chicago: Moody, 1958), 87.

[24]Ledyard, *Eskimos*, 91.

[25]Ledyard, *Eskimos*, 172.

[26]Ledyard, *Eskimos*, 162.

[27]Ledyard, *Eskimos*, 205.

[28]Ledyard, *Eskimos*, 237.

[29]George Kent, "Flying Doctor of the Congo," *Presbyterian Life* (9 June 1956): 20.

[30]Kent, "Flying Doctor," 21.

[31]Kent, "Flying Doctor," 36.

Part V: Introduction

[1]Ralph D. Winter, *The Twenty-five Unbelievable Years, 1945–1969* (Pasadena: William Carey, 1970), 13.

[2]John R. W. Stott, "The Bible in World Evangelism," in *Perspectives on the World Christian Movement*, ed. Ralph D. Winter and Steven C. Hawthorne (Pasadena: William Carey, 1981), 7.

[3]"Born Again," *Newsweek* (25 October 1976): 68–69.

[4]Robert Clouse, "Pentecostal Churches," in *The New International Dictionary of the Christian Church*, ed. J. D. Douglas (Grand Rapids: Zondervan, 1978), 764.

[5]Robert T. Coote, "The Uneven Growth of Conservative Evangelical Missions," *International Bulletin of Missionary Research* (July 1982): 118.

[6]J. Herbert Kane, "The Saints Keep Marching On," *Wherever* (Fall 1979): 2.

[7]J. Herbert Kane, *Understanding Christian Missions* (Grand Rapids: Baker, 1975), 405.

[8]C. Peter Wagner, "Evangelizing the World—People to People," *Decision* (March 1981): 4; C. Peter Wagner, "More People Will Be Won to Christ Than in Any Comparable Decade," *World Vision* (February 1979): 8.

[9]Richard N. Ostling, "Counting Every Soul on Earth," *Time* (3 May, 1982): 66–67.

Chapter 16

[1]Quoted in Hugh Steven, "Who Was Chet Bitterman?" *In Other Words* (April 1981): 5.

[2]James and Marti Hefley, *By Their Blood: Christian Martyrs of the 20th Century* (Milford, Mich.: Mott, 1979), 46.

[3]Leslie Lyall, *A Passion for the Impossible: The China Inland Mission, 1865–1965* (Chicago: Moody, 1965), 108–9.

[4]Mrs. Howard Taylor, *The Triumph of John and Betty Stam* (Philadelphia: China Inland Mission, 1960), 51–52.

[5]Taylor, *The Triumph*, 54–55.

[6]Taylor, *The Triumph*, 92.

[7]Taylor, *The Triumph*, 102.

[8]Hefley, *By Their Blood*, 66.

[9]Lois Carlson, *Monganga Paul: The Congo Ministry and Martyrdom of Paul Carlson, M.D.* (New York: Harper & Row, 1966), 34.

[10]Carlson, *Monganga Paul*, 50.

[11]Carlson, *Monganga Paul*, 53.

[12]Homer E. Dowdy, *Out of the Jaws of the Lion: Christian Martyrdom in the Congo* (New York: Harper & Row, 1965), 186–87.

[13]Dowdy, *Christian Martyrdom*, 193.

[14]John 15:13 (NIV).

[15]James and Marti Hefley, *No Time for Tombstones: Life and Death in the Vietnamese Jungle* (Wheaton: Tyndale, 1976), 3.

[16]Quoted in Hefley, *By Their Blood*, 126.

[17]Hefley, *No Time*, 87.

[18]Hefley, *No Time*, 91.

[19]Hefley, *By Their Blood*, 95, 131.

[20]*Time* (10 August 1981): 41.

[21]Betty Blair and Phil Landrum, "Chet Bitterman—Kidnappers' Choice," *In Other Words* (April 1981): 2.

[22]Blair and Landrum, "Chet Bitterman," 2.

[23]Blair and Landrum, "Chet Bitterman," 3.

[24]Molly Ekstrom, "Chet Bitterman: God's Special Envoy to Colombia," *In Other Words* (Summer 1981, Jubilee Edition): 19.

[25]Blair and Landrum, "Chet Bitterman," 2.

[26]Jeanne Pugh, "Death of Bible Translators Sparks Expansion of Work," *St. Petersburg Times* (4 April 1981).

[27]Harry Waterhouse, "We Gave Our Son to God," *In Other Words* (April 1981): 4.

Chapter 17

[1]Stephen Neill, *A History of Christian Missions* (New York: Penguin, 1964), 329.

[2]Neill, *History of Christian Missions*, 330.

[3]"Obed Alvarez: Peruvian Mission Leader," *Mission Frontiers* (January 1983): 8–9.

[4]Joseph Spinella, "Theology with a New Twist," *Wherever* (Spring 1982): 13.

[5]James and Marti Hefley, *God's Tribesman: The Rochunga Pudaite Story* (New York: Holman, 1974), book jacket.

[6]Hefley, *God's Tribesman*, 51.

[7]Hefley, *God's Tribesman*, 52.

[8]Hefley, *God's Tribesman*, 96.

[9]Hefley, *God's Tribesman*, 136–37.

[10]"The Revival That Was and Is: An Interview with Festo Kivengere," *Christianity Today* (21 May, 1976): 11.

[11]"The Revival," 11.

[12]"The Revival," 11.

[13]"The Revival," 12.

[14]"The Revival," 12.

[15]"The Revival, 12.

[16]"The Revival," 11.

[17]"The Revival," 12.

[18]Festo Kivengere, *I Love Idi Amin* (Old Tappan, N.J.: Revell, 1977), 18.

[19]Kivengere, *Idi Amin*, 18.

[20]Kivengere, *Idi Amin*, 23–24.

[21]Kivengere, *Idi Amin*, 37–38.

[22]Kivengere, *Idi Amin*, 44.

[23]Kivengere, *Idi Amin*, 60.

[24]"Africa's Great Awakening: An Interview with Michael Cassidy," *Eternity* (June 1981): 23.

[25]Milt Bryan, "The Luis Palau Story," *Evangelizing Today's Child* (November/ December 1976): 11.

[26]Bryan, "Luis Palau," 11.

[27]Bryan, "Luis Palau," 12.

[28]Luis Palau, as told to Jerry B. Jenkins, *The Luis Palau Story* (Old Tappan, N.J.: Revell, 1980), 77.

[29]Palau, *Luis Palau*, 79.

[30]Palau, *Luis Palau*, 82.

[31]Palau, *Luis Palau*, 85.

[32]Palau, *Luis Palau*, 87.

[33]Palau, *Luis Palau*, 88.

[34]Palau, *Luis Palau*, 89.

[35]Palau, *Luis Palau*, 135.

[36]Palau, *Luis Palau*, 151.

[37]Palau, *Luis Palau*, 161.

[38]For further information on Philip Teng, see "An Interview with Dr. Philip Teng," *Alliance Witness* (7 January 1981): 19–20.

[39]Don Richardson, *Eternity in Their Hearts* (Ventura, Calif.: Regal, 1981), 69.

[40]Richardson, *Eternity*, 68.

[41]Jamie Buckingham, "The World's Largest Pastorate," *Charisma* (June 1982): 21.

[42]Harold Hostetler, "A Church Grows in Korea . . . and Beyond," *Logos* (January/ February 1980): 13.

[43]Buckingham, "The World's Largest Pastorate," 23.

[44]Harry Genet, "Big Trouble at the World's Largest Church," *Christianity Today* (22 January 1982): 30.

[45]Hostetler, "A Church Grows in Korea," 14.

Chapter 18

[1]W. Dayton Roberts, *Revolution in Evangelism: The Story of Evangelism-in-Depth in Latin America* (Chicago: Moody, 1976), 6.

[2]Roberts, *Revolution in Evangelism*, 17–18.

[3]Roberts, *Revolution in Evangelism*, 18.

[4]Elisabeth Elliot, *Who Shall Ascend: The Life of R. Kenneth Strachan of Costa Rica* (New York: Harper & Row, 1968), 21.

[5]Elliot, *Who Shall Ascend*, 73.

[6]W. Dayton Roberts, *Strachan of Costa Rica: Missionary Insights and Strategies* (Grand Rapids: Eerdmans, 1971), 63.

[7]Roberts, *Strachan of Costa Rica*, 108.

[8]Roberts, *Strachan of Costa Rica*, 68.

[9]Roberts, *Strachan of Costa Rica*, 99.

[10]Roberts, *Strachan of Costa Rica*, 129–30.

[11]Roberts, *Strachan of Costa Rica*, 83.

[12]Roberts, *Strachan of Costa Rica*, 95.

[13]Roberts, *Strachan of Costa Rica*, 96.

[14]Roberts, *Strachan of Costa Rica*, 96.

[15]Roberts, *Revolution in Evangelism*, 60.

[16]Roberts, *Revolution in Evangelism*, 60, 64.

[17]Roberts, *Revolution in Evangelism*, 86.

[18]Charles Troutman, *Everything You Want to Know About the Mission Field, But Are Afraid You Won't Learn Until You Get There* (Downers Grove, Ill.: InterVarsity, 1976), 26.

[19]Marilee Pierce Dunker, *Man of Vision, Woman of Prayer* (Nashville: Nelson, 1980), 29–35.

[20]Dunker, *Man of Vision*, 34–35.

[21]Dunker, *Man of Vision*, 46–48.

[22]Dunker, *Man of Vision*, 48–49.

[23]Dunker, *Man of Vision*, 87–88.

[24]Dunker, *Man of Vision*, 106–7.

[25]Dunker, *Man of Vision*, 179.

[26]Dunker, *Man of Vision*, 184, 194.

[27]Richard C. Halverson, "A History of Service," *World Vision* (December 1975): 7.

[28]W. Stanley Mooneyham, *What Do You Say to a Hungry World?* (Waco: Word, 1975), 30.

[29]Brother Andrew, *God's Smuggler* (Old Tappan, N.J.: Revell, 1967), 26.

[30]Andrew, *God's Smuggler*, 108.

[31]Brother Andrew, *Battle for Africa* (Old Tappan, N.J.: Revell, 1977), 23–26.

[32]Russ Hoyle, "Risky Rendezvous at Swatow," *Time* (19 October 1981): 109; "Bible Shipment to China," *Charisma* (February 1982): 14.

[33]Hoyle, "Risky Rendezvous," 109.

[34]Arthur Glasser, "Introducing Donald McGavran," *HIS* (December 1973): 19.

[35]A. R. Tippet, ed. *God, Man and Church Growth* (Grand Rapids: Eerdmans, 1973), ix.

[36]Tippet, *Church Growth*, 18.

[37]Tippet, *Church Growth*, 18.

[38]C. Peter Wagner, "Concepts of Evangelism Have Changed Over the Years," *Evangelical Missions Quarterly* (January 1974): 43.

[39]Wagner, "Concepts of Evangelism," 44.

[40]Donald A. McGavran, "The Bridge of God," in *Perspectives on the World Christian Movement*, ed. Ralph D. Winter and Steven C. Hawthorne (Pasadena: William Carey, 1982), 282.

[41]McGavran, "The Bridge of God," 288–89.

[42]C. Peter Wagner, *Our Kind of People: The Ethical Dimensions of Church Growth in America* (Atlanta: Knox, 1979), 21, 100.

[43]Wagner, *Our Kind of People*, 100–101.

[44]Wagner, *Our Kind of People*, 23.

[45]Tippet, *Church Growth*, 35.

[46]Glasser, "Donald McGavran," 18.

[47]Gordon Aeschliman, "United States Center for World Mission," *World Christian* (March/April 1983): 20.

[48]John Maust, "Ralph Winter's Mission Center Forges Ahead; Money Still Tight," *Christianity Today* (21 January 1983): 34.

[49]David Bryant, "Concerts of Prayer: Waking Up for a New Missions Thrust," *Mission Frontiers* (March/April 1983): 8; Aeschliman, "United States Center," 22.

[50]Doris Haley, "Ralph and Roberta Winter: A Wartime Life-Style," *Family Life Today* (March 1983): 31.

[51]Don Richardson, *Peace Child* (Glendale, Calif.: Regal, 1974), 96.

[52]Richardson, *Peace Child*, 172.

[53]Richardson, *Peace Child*, 172.

[54]"How to Reach the Hidden People: An Interview with Don Richardson by Robert Walker," *Christian Life* (July 1981): 52.

[55]Richardson, *Peace Child*, 191.

[56]Richardson, *Peace Child*, 206.

[57]Richardson, *Peace Child*, 277, 283.

[58]Don Richardson, "Concept Fulfillment," in *Perspectives on the World Christian Movement*, ed. Ralph D. Winter and Steven C. Hawthorne (Pasadena: William Carey, 1982), 419–20.

GENERAL BIBLIOGRAPHY

Barker, William P. Who's Who in Church History. Old Tappan, N.J.: Revell, 1969.

Beaver, R. Pierce. American Protestant Women in World Mission. Grand Rapids: Eerdmans, 1968.

_____. Pioneers in Missions: The Early Missionary Ordination Sermons, Charges, and Instruction. Grand Rapids: Eerdmans, 1966.

Bliss, Edwin, ed. Encyclopedia of Missions. 2 vols. New York: Funk and Wagnalls, 1891.

Broadbent, E. H. The Pilgrim Church. London: Pickering & Inglis, 1978.

Coggins, Wade T. So That's What Missions Is All About. Chicago: Moody, 1975.

Coggins, Wade T. and Frizen, E. L., Jr. Evangelical Missions Tomorrow. Pasadena: William Carey, 1977.

Cook, Harold R. Highlights of Christian Missions: A History and Survey. Chicago: Moody, 1967.

Deen, Edith. Great Women of the Christian Faith. New York: Harper & Row, 1959.

Douglas, James D., ed. The New International Dictionary of the Christian Church. Grand Rapids: Zondervan, 1974.

DuBose, Francis M., ed. Classics of Christian Missions. Nashville: Broadman, 1979.

Eddy, Sherwood. Pathfinders of the World Missionary Crusade. New York: Abingdon-Cokesbury, 1945.

Glover, Robert H. and Kane, J. Herbert. The Progress of World-Wide Missions. New York: Harper & Brothers, 1960.

Harrison, Eugene Myers. Giants of the Missionary Trail. Chicago: Scripture Press, 1954.

Hefley, James and Marti. By Their Blood: Christian Martyrs of the 20th Century. Milford, Mich.: Mott, 1979.

Hulbert, Terry C. World Missions Today. Wheaton: Evangelical Teacher Training Association, 1979.

Kane, J. Herbert. A Concise History of the Christian World Mission. Grand Rapids: Baker, 1978.

_____. A Global View of Christian Missions. Grand Rapids: Baker, 1971.

_____. Life and Work on the Mission Field. Grand Rapids: Baker, 1980.

Latourette, Kenneth Scott. A History of the Expansion of Christianity. 7 vols. Grand Rapids: Zondervan, 1970.

Neill, Stephen. A History of Christian Missions. New York: Penguin, 1964.

Neill, Stephen, et al. A Concise Dictionary of the Christian World Mission. New York: Abingdon, 1971.

Thiessen, John C. A Survey of World Missions. Chicago: Moody, 1961.

Winter, Ralph D. The Twenty-five Unbelievable Years, 1945 to 1969. Pasadena: William Carey, 1970.

Winter, Ralph D. and Hawthorne, Steven C., ed. Perspectives on the World Christian Movement. Pasadena: William Carey, 1981.

Wright, Elliott. Holy Company: Christian Heroes and Heroines. New York: Macmillan, 1980.

ILLUSTRATION INDEX

GENERAL INDEX

Praise for the Clifton Chronicles

'Archer is on top form' *Daily Telegraph*

'I was touched and enthralled by this tale . . . the trademark twist, is gasp-making' *Daily Mail*

'I enjoyed the book and marvelled at both its pace and the imaginative cliffhanger ending, whetting our appetite for volume two' *Sunday Express*

'Jeffrey Archer is, first and foremost, a storyteller . . . You don't sell 250 million copies of your books (250 million!) if you can't keep an audience hooked – and that's what Archer does, book after book' Erica Wagner, Literary Editor, *The Times*

'I was reading the book . . . feverishly thumbing the pages to find out what dire machinations Hugo Barrington (a villain straight out of Victorian melodrama) would come up with next, I had to admit I was utterly hooked. It was an absurdly enjoyable read'
Anthony Horowitz, *Daily Telegraph*

'This is a cracker of a read. And quite "unputdownable". The whole thing about Jeffrey is that he has always had the knack of producing page-turners' Jerry Hayes, *Spectator*

'A rip-roaring read' *Mail on Sunday*

Praise for Jeffrey Archer's novels

'If there was a Nobel Prize for storytelling, Archer would win'
Daily Telegraph

'Probably the greatest storyteller of our age'   *Mail on Sunday*

'The man's a genius . . . the strength and excitement of the idea
carries all before it'   *Evening Standard*

'Stylish, witty and constantly entertaining'   *The Times*

'A storyteller in the class of Alexandre Dumas'
Washington Post

'Jeffrey Archer has the strange gift denied to many who think
themselves more serious novelists. He can tell a story'
Allan Massie, *Scotsman*

'Henry James's heir'   *Sunday Times*

ONLY TIME WILL TELL

JEFFREY ARCHER, whose novels and short stories include the Clifton Chronicles, *Kane and Abel* and *Cat O' Nine Tales*, is one of the world's favourite storytellers and has topped bestseller lists around the world in a career spanning four decades. His work has been sold in 97 countries and in more than 37 languages. He is the only author ever to have been a number one bestseller in fiction, short stories and non-fiction (the Prison Diaries).

Jeffrey is also an art collector, sports lover, and amateur auctioneer, conducting numerous charity auctions every year. A member of the House of Lords for over a quarter of a century, the author is married to Dame Mary Archer, and they have two sons, two grandsons and a granddaughter.

www.jeffreyarcher.com
Facebook.com/JeffreyArcherAuthor
@Jeffrey_Archer

BY JEFFREY ARCHER

THE CLIFTON CHRONICLES
Only Time Will Tell   The Sins of the Father
Best Kept Secret   Be Careful What You Wish For
Mightier than the Sword   Cometh the Hour
This Was a Man

NOVELS
Not a Penny More, Not a Penny Less
Shall We Tell the President?   Kane and Abel
The Prodigal Daughter   First Among Equals
A Matter of Honour   As the Crow Flies
Honour Among Thieves
The Fourth Estate   The Eleventh Commandment
Sons of Fortune   False Impression
The Gospel According to Judas
(*with the assistance of Professor Francis J. Moloney*)
A Prisoner of Birth   Paths of Glory   Heads You Win

SHORT STORIES
A Quiver Full of Arrows   A Twist in the Tale
Twelve Red Herrings   The Collected Short Stories
To Cut a Long Story Short   Cat O' Nine Tales
And Thereby Hangs a Tale
The New Collected Short Stories   Tell Tale

PLAYS
Beyond Reasonable Doubt   Exclusive   The Accused
Confession   Who Killed the Mayor?

PRISON DIARIES
Volume One – Belmarsh: Hell
Volume Two – Wayland: Purgatory
Volume Three – North Sea Camp: Heaven

SCREENPLAYS
Mallory: Walking Off the Map   False Impression

JEFFREY ARCHER

THE CLIFTON CHRONICLES
VOLUME ONE

ONLY TIME WILL TELL

PAN BOOKS

First published 2011 by Macmillan

This edition published 2019 by Pan Books
an imprint of Pan Macmillan
The Smithson, 6 Briset Street, London EC1M 5NR
Associated companies throughout the world
www.panmacmillan.com

ISBN 978-1-5098-4756-3

5 7 9 8 6 4

A CIP catalogue record for this book is available from the British Library.

Typeset in New Caledonia by Jouve (UK), Milton Keynes
Printed and bound by CPI Group (UK) Ltd, Croydon, CR0 4YY

Visit **www.panmacmillan.com** to read more about all our books
and to buy them. You will also find features, author interviews and
news of any author events, and you can sign up for e-newsletters
so that you're always first to hear about our new releases.

ALAN QUILTER

1927–1998

My thanks go to the following people for their
invaluable advice and research:

John Anstee, Simon Bainbridge, John Cleverdon,
Eleanor Dryden, George Havens, Alison Prince,
Mari Roberts, Susan Watt, David Watts
and Peter Watts

THE BARRINGTONS

Sir Walter Barrington   *m.*   Mary
1866–   1874–

Nicholas   Hugo *m.* Elizabeth Harvey
1894–1918   1896–   1900–

Giles   Emma   Grace
1920–   1921–   1923–

THE CLIFTONS

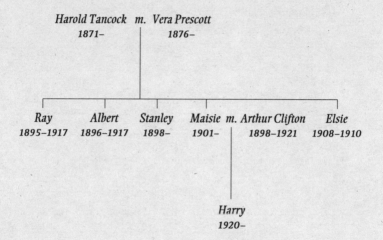

Harold Tancock m. Vera Prescott
    1871–   1876–

Ray   Albert   Stanley   Maisie m. Arthur Clifton   Elsie
1895–1917   1896–1917   1898–   1901–   1898–1921   1908–1910

Harry
1920–

MAISIE CLIFTON

1919

PRELUDE

This story would never have been written if I hadn't become pregnant. Mind you, I had always planned to lose my virginity on the works outing to Weston-super-Mare, just not to that particular man.

Arthur Clifton was born in Still House Lane, just like me; even went to the same school, Merrywood Elementary, but as I was two years younger than him he didn't know I existed. All the girls in my class had a crush on him, and not just because he captained the school football team.

Although Arthur had never shown any interest in me while I was at school, that changed soon after he'd returned from the Western Front. I'm not even sure he realized who I was when he asked me for a dance that Saturday night at the Palais but, to be fair, I had to look twice before I recognized him because he'd grown a pencil moustache and had his hair slicked back like Ronald Colman. He didn't look at another girl that night, and after we'd danced the last waltz I knew it would only be a matter of time before he asked me to marry him.

Arthur held my hand as we walked back home, and when we reached my front door he tried to kiss me. I turned away. After all, the Reverend Watts had told me often enough that I had to stay pure until the day I was married, and Miss Monday, our choir mistress, warned me that men

3

only wanted one thing, and once they'd got it, they quickly lost interest. I often wondered if Miss Monday spoke from experience.

The following Saturday, Arthur invited me to the flicks to see Lillian Gish in *Broken Blossoms*, and although I allowed him to put an arm around my shoulder, I still didn't let him kiss me. He didn't make a fuss. Truth is, Arthur was rather shy.

The next Saturday I did allow him to kiss me, but when he tried to put a hand inside my blouse, I pushed him away. In fact I didn't let him do that until he'd proposed, bought a ring and the Reverend Watts had read the banns a second time.

My brother Stan told me that I was the last known virgin on our side of the River Avon, though I suspect most of his conquests were in his mind. Still, I decided the time had come, and when better than the works outing to Weston-super-Mare with the man I was going to marry in a few weeks' time?

However, as soon as Arthur and Stan got off the charabanc, they headed straight for the nearest pub. But I'd spent the past month planning for this moment, so when I got off the coach, like a good girl guide, I was prepared.

I was walking towards the pier feeling pretty fed up when I became aware someone was following me. I looked around and was surprised when I saw who it was. He caught up with me and asked if I was on my own.

'Yes,' I said, aware that by now Arthur would be on his third pint.

When he put a hand on my bum, I should have slapped his face, but for several reasons I didn't. To start with, I thought about the advantages of having sex with someone I wasn't likely to come across again. And I have to admit I was flattered by his advances.

By the time Arthur and Stan would have been downing

their eighth pints, he'd booked us into a guest house just off the seafront. They seemed to have a special rate for visitors who had no plans to spend the night. He started kissing me even before we'd reached the first landing, and once the bedroom door was closed he quickly undid the buttons of my blouse. It obviously wasn't his first time. In fact, I'm pretty sure I wasn't the first girl he'd had on a works outing. Otherwise, how did he know about the special rates?

I must confess I hadn't expected it to be all over quite so quickly. Once he'd climbed off me, I disappeared into the bathroom, while he sat on the end of the bed and lit up a fag. Perhaps it would be better the second time, I thought. But when I came back out, he was nowhere to be seen. I have to admit I was disappointed.

I might have felt more guilty about being unfaithful to Arthur if he hadn't been sick all over me on the journey back to Bristol.

The next day I told my mum what had happened, without letting on who the bloke was. After all, she hadn't met him, and was never likely to. Mum told me to keep my mouth shut as she didn't want to have to cancel the wedding, and even if I did turn out to be pregnant, no one would be any the wiser, as Arthur and I would be married by the time anyone noticed.

HARRY CLIFTON

1920–1933

1

I was told my father was killed in the war.

Whenever I questioned my mother about his death, she didn't say any more than that he'd served with the Royal Gloucestershire Regiment and had been killed fighting on the Western Front only days before the Armistice was signed. Grandma said my dad had been a brave man, and once when we were alone in the house she showed me his medals. My grandpa rarely offered an opinion on anything, but then he was deaf as a post so he might not have heard the question in the first place.

The only other man I can remember was my uncle Stan, who used to sit at the top of the table at breakfast time. When he left of a morning I would often follow him to the city docks, where he worked. Every day I spent at the dockyard was an adventure. Cargo ships coming from distant lands and unloading their wares: rice, sugar, bananas, jute and many other things I'd never heard of. Once the holds had been emptied, the dockers would load them with salt, apples, tin, even coal (my least favourite, because it was an obvious clue to what I'd been doing all day and annoyed my mother), before they set off again to I knew not where. I always wanted to help my uncle Stan unload whatever ship had docked that morning, but he just laughed, saying, 'All in good time, my lad.' It couldn't be soon enough for me, but, without any warning, school got in the way.

I was sent to Merrywood Elementary when I was six and I thought it was a complete waste of time. What was the point of school when I could learn all I needed to at the docks? I wouldn't have bothered to go back the following day if my mother hadn't dragged me to the front gates, deposited me and returned at four o'clock that afternoon to take me home.

I didn't realize Mum had other plans for my future, which didn't include joining Uncle Stan in the shipyard.

Once Mum had dropped me off each morning, I would hang around in the yard until she was out of sight, then slope off to the docks. I made sure I was always back at the school gates when she returned to pick me up in the afternoon. On the way home, I would tell her everything I'd done at school that day. I was good at making up stories, but it wasn't long before she discovered that was all they were: stories.

One or two other boys from my school also used to hang around the docks, but I kept my distance from them. They were older and bigger, and used to thump me if I got in their way. I also had to keep an eye out for Mr Haskins, the chief ganger, because if he ever found me loitering, to use his favourite word, he would send me off with a kick up the backside and the threat: 'If I see you loiterin' round here again, my lad, I'll report you to the headmaster.'

Occasionally Haskins decided he'd seen me once too often and I'd be reported to the headmaster, who would leather me before sending me back to my classroom. My form master, Mr Holcombe, never let on if I didn't show up for his class, but then he was a bit soft. Whenever my mum found out I'd been playing truant, she couldn't hide her anger and would stop my halfpenny-a-week pocket money. But despite the occasional punch from an older boy, regular leatherings from the headmaster and the loss of my pocket money, I still couldn't resist the draw of the docks.

I made only one real friend while I 'loitered' around the dockyard. His name was Old Jack Tar. Mr Tar lived in an abandoned railway carriage at the end of the sheds. Uncle Stan told me to keep away from Old Jack because he was a stupid, dirty old tramp. He didn't look that dirty to me, certainly not as dirty as Stan, and it wasn't long before I discovered he wasn't stupid either.

After lunch with my uncle Stan, one bite of his Marmite sandwich, his discarded apple core and a swig of beer, I would be back at school in time for a game of football; the only activity I considered it worth turning up for. After all, when I left school I was going to captain Bristol City, or build a ship that would sail around the world. If Mr Holcombe kept his mouth shut and the ganger didn't report me to the headmaster, I could go for days without being found out, and as long as I avoided the coal barges and was standing by the school gate at four o'clock every afternoon, my mother would never be any the wiser.

–◄o►–

Every other Saturday, Uncle Stan would take me to watch Bristol City at Ashton Gate. On Sunday mornings, Mum used to cart me off to Holy Nativity Church, something I couldn't find a way of getting out of. Once the Reverend Watts had given the final blessing, I would run all the way to the recreation ground and join my mates for a game of football before returning home in time for dinner.

By the time I was seven it was clear to anyone who knew anything about the game of football that I was never going to get into the school team, let alone captain Bristol City. But that was when I discovered that God had given me one small gift, and it wasn't in my feet.

To begin with, I didn't notice that anyone who sat near

me in church on a Sunday morning stopped singing whenever I opened my mouth. I wouldn't have given it a second thought if Mum hadn't suggested I join the choir. I laughed scornfully; after all, everyone knew the choir was only for girls and cissies. I would have dismissed the idea out of hand if the Reverend Watts hadn't told me that choirboys were paid a penny for funerals and tuppence for weddings; my first experience of bribery. But even after I'd reluctantly agreed to take a vocal test, the devil decided to place an obstacle in my path, in the form of Miss Eleanor E. Monday.

I would never have come across Miss Monday if she hadn't been the choir mistress at Holy Nativity. Although she was only five feet three, and looked as though a gust of wind might blow her away, no one tried to take the mickey. I have a feeling that even the devil would have been frightened of Miss Monday, because the Reverend Watts certainly was.

I agreed to take a vocal test, but not before my mum had handed over a month's pocket money in advance. The following Sunday I stood in line with a group of other lads and waited to be called.

'You will always be on time for choir practice,' Miss Monday announced, fixing a gimlet eye on me. I stared back defiantly. 'You will never speak, unless spoken to.' I somehow managed to remain silent. 'And during the service, you will concentrate at all times.' I reluctantly nodded. And then, God bless her, she gave me a way out. 'But most importantly,' she declared, placing her hands on her hips, 'within twelve weeks, you will be expected to pass a reading and writing test, so that I can be sure you are able to tackle a new anthem or an unfamiliar psalm.'

I was pleased to have fallen at the first hurdle. But as I was to discover, Miss Eleanor E. Monday didn't give up easily.

'What piece have you chosen to sing, child?' she asked me when I reached the front of the line.

'I haven't chosen anything,' I told her.

She opened a hymn book, handed it to me and sat down at the piano. I smiled at the thought that I might still be able to make the second half of our Sunday morning football game. She began to play a familiar tune, and when I saw my mother glaring at me from the front row of pews, I decided I'd better go through with it, just to keep her happy.

'*All things bright and beautiful, all creatures great and small. All things wise and wonderful . . .*' A smile had appeared on Miss Monday's face long before I reached '*the Lord God made them all*'.

'What's your name, child?' she asked.

'Harry Clifton, miss.'

'Harry Clifton, you will report for choir practice on Mondays, Wednesdays and Fridays at six o'clock sharp.' Turning to the boy standing behind me, she said, 'Next!'

I promised my mum I'd be on time for the first choir practice, even though I knew it would be my last, as Miss Monday would soon realize I couldn't read or write. And it would have been my last, if it hadn't been obvious to anyone listening that my singing voice was in a different class to that of any other boy in the choir. In fact, the moment I opened my mouth, everyone fell silent, and the looks of admiration, even awe, that I had desperately sought on the football field, were happening in church. Miss Monday pretended not to notice.

After she dismissed us, I didn't go home, but ran all the way to the docks so I could ask Mr Tar what I should do about the fact that I couldn't read or write. I listened carefully to the old man's advice, and the next day I went back to school and took my place in Mr Holcombe's class.

The schoolmaster couldn't hide his surprise when he saw me sitting in the front row, and was even more surprised when I paid close attention to the morning lesson for the first time.

Mr Holcombe began by teaching me the alphabet, and within days I could write out all twenty-six letters, if not always in the correct order. My mum would have helped me when I got home in the afternoon but, like the rest of my family, she also couldn't read or write.

Uncle Stan could just about scrawl his signature, and although he could tell the difference between a packet of Wills's Star and Wild Woodbines, I was fairly sure he couldn't actually read the labels. Despite his unhelpful mutterings, I set about writing the alphabet on any piece of scrap paper I could find. Uncle Stan didn't seem to notice that the torn-up newspaper in the privy was always covered in letters.

Once I'd mastered the alphabet, Mr Holcombe introduced me to a few simple words: 'dog', 'cat', 'mum' and 'dad'. That was when I first asked him about my dad, hoping that he might be able to tell me something about him. After all, he seemed to know everything. But he seemed puzzled that I knew so little about my own dad. A week later he wrote my first four-letter word on the blackboard, 'book', and then five, 'house', and six, 'school'. By the end of the month, I could write my first sentence, 'The quick brown fox jumps over the lazy dog', which, Mr Holcombe pointed out, contained every letter in the alphabet. I checked, and he turned out to be right.

By the end of term I could spell 'anthem', 'psalm' and even 'hymn', although Mr Holcombe kept reminding me I still dropped my aitches whenever I spoke. But then we broke up for the holidays and I began to worry I would never pass Miss Monday's demanding test without Mr

Holcombe's help. And that might have been the case, if Old Jack hadn't taken his place.

◄○►

I was half an hour early for choir practice on the Friday evening when I knew I would have to pass my second test if I hoped to continue as a member of the choir. I sat silently in the stalls, hoping Miss Monday would pick on someone else before she called on me.

I had already passed the first test with what Miss Monday had described as flying colours. We had all been asked to recite *The Lord's Prayer*. This was not a problem for me, because for as long as I could remember my mum knelt by my bed each night and repeated the familiar words before tucking me up. However, Miss Monday's next test was to prove far more demanding.

By this time, the end of our second month, we were expected to read a psalm out loud, in front of the rest of the choir. I chose Psalm 121, which I also knew off by heart, having sung it so often in the past. *I will lift up mine eyes unto the hills, from whence cometh my help.* I could only hope that my help cometh from the Lord. Although I was able to turn to the correct page in the psalm book, as I could now count from one to a hundred, I feared Miss Monday would realize that I was unable to follow every verse line by line. If she did, she didn't let on, because I remained in the choir stalls for another month while two other miscreants – her word, not that I knew what it meant until I asked Mr Holcombe the next day – were dispatched back to the congregation.

When the time came for me to take the third and final test, I was ready for it. Miss Monday asked those of us who remained to write out the Ten Commandments in the correct order without referring to the Book of Exodus.

The choir mistress turned a blind eye to the fact that I placed theft ahead of murder, couldn't spell 'adultery', and certainly didn't know what it meant. Only after two other miscreants were summarily dismissed for lesser offences did I realize just how exceptional my voice must be.

On the first Sunday of Advent, Miss Monday announced that she had selected three new trebles – or 'little angels', as the Reverend Watts was wont to describe us – to join her choir, the remainder having been rejected for committing such unforgivable sins as chattering during the sermon, sucking a gobstopper and, in the case of two boys, being caught playing conkers during the *Nunc Dimittis*.

The following Sunday, I dressed up in a long blue cassock with a ruffled white collar. I alone was allowed to wear a bronze medallion of the Virgin Mother around my neck, to show that I had been selected as the treble soloist. I would have proudly worn the medallion all the way back home, even to school the next morning, to show off to the rest of the lads, if only Miss Monday hadn't retrieved it at the end of each service.

On Sundays I was transported into another world, but I feared this state of delirium could not last for ever.

2

WHEN UNCLE STAN rose in the morning, he somehow managed to wake the entire household. No one complained, as he was the breadwinner in the family, and in any case he was cheaper and more reliable than an alarm clock.

The first noise Harry would hear was the bedroom door slamming. This would be followed by his uncle tramping along the creaky wooden landing, down the stairs and out of the house. Then another door would slam as he disappeared into the privy. If anyone was still asleep, the rush of water as Uncle Stan pulled the chain, followed by two more slammed doors before he returned to the bedroom, served to remind them that Stan expected his breakfast to be on the table by the time he walked into the kitchen. He only had a wash and a shave on Saturday evenings before going off to the Palais or the Odeon. He took a bath four times a year on quarter-day. No one was going to accuse Stan of wasting his hard-earned cash on soap.

Maisie, Harry's mum, would be next up, leaping out of bed moments after the first slammed door. There would be a bowl of porridge on the stove by the time Stan came out of the privy. Grandma followed shortly afterwards, and would join her daughter in the kitchen before Stan had taken his place at the head of the table. Harry had to be down within five minutes of the first slammed door if he hoped to get any breakfast. The last to arrive in the kitchen would be Grandpa, who was so deaf he often managed to sleep through Stan's early morning ritual. This daily routine in the Clifton household never varied. When you've only got one outside privy, one sink and one towel, order becomes a necessity.

By the time Harry was splashing his face with a trickle of cold water, his mother would be serving breakfast in the kitchen: two thickly sliced pieces of bread covered in lard for Stan, and four thin slices for the rest of the family, which she would toast if there was any coal left in the sack dumped outside the front door every Monday. Once Stan had finished his porridge, Harry would be allowed to lick the bowl.

A large brown pot of tea was always brewing on the hearth, which Grandma would pour into a variety of mugs through a silver-plated Victorian tea strainer she had inherited from her mother. While the other members of the family enjoyed a mug of unsweetened tea – sugar was only for high days and holidays – Stan would open his first bottle of beer, which he usually gulped down in one draught. He would then rise from the table and burp loudly before picking up his lunch box, which Grandma had prepared while he was having his breakfast: two Marmite sandwiches, a sausage, an apple, two more bottles of beer and a packet of five coffin nails. Once Stan had left for the docks, everyone began to talk at once.

Grandma always wanted to know who had visited the tea shop where her daughter worked as a waitress: what they ate, what they were wearing, where they sat; details of meals that were cooked on a stove in a room lit by electric light bulbs that didn't leave any candle wax, not to mention customers who sometimes left a thruppenny-bit tip, which Maisie had to split with the cook.

Maisie was more concerned to find out what Harry had done at school the previous day. She demanded a daily report, which didn't seem to interest Grandma, perhaps because she'd never been to school. Come to think of it, she'd never been to a tea shop either.

Grandpa rarely commented, because after four years of loading and unloading an artillery field gun, morning, noon and night, he was so deaf he had to satisfy himself with watching their lips move and nodding from time to time. This could give outsiders the impression he was stupid, which the rest of the family knew to their cost he wasn't.

The family's morning routine only varied at weekends. On Saturdays, Harry would follow his uncle out of the kitchen, always remaining a pace behind him as he walked to the docks. On Sunday, Harry's mum would accompany the boy to Holy Nativity Church, where, from the third row of the pews, she would bask in the glory of the choir's treble soloist.

But today was Saturday. During the twenty-minute walk to the docks, Harry never opened his mouth unless his uncle spoke. Whenever he did, it invariably turned out to be the same conversation they'd had the previous Saturday.

'When are you goin' to leave school and do a day's work, young'un?' was always Uncle Stan's opening salvo.

'Not allowed to leave until I'm fourteen,' Harry reminded him. 'It's the law.'

'A bloody stupid law, if you ask me. I'd packed up school and was workin' on the docks by the time I were twelve,' Stan would announce as if Harry had never heard this profound observation before. Harry didn't bother to respond, as he already knew what his uncle's next sentence would be. 'And what's more I'd signed up to join Kitchener's army before my seventeenth birthday.'

'Tell me about the war, Uncle Stan,' said Harry, aware that this would keep him occupied for several hundred yards.

'Me and your dad joined the Royal Gloucestershire Regiment on the same day,' Stan said, touching his cloth cap as if saluting a distant memory. 'After twelve weeks' basic training at Taunton Barracks, we was shipped off to Wipers to fight the Boche. Once we got there, we spent most of our time cooped up in rat-infested trenches waiting to be told by some toffee-nosed officer that when the bugle sounded, we was going over the top, bayonets fixed, rifles firing as we advanced towards the enemy lines.' This would be followed by a long pause, after which Stan would add, 'I was one of the lucky ones. Got back to Blighty all ship-shape and Bristol fashion.' Harry could have predicted his next sentence word for word, but remained silent. 'You just don't know how lucky you are, my lad. I lost two brothers, your uncle Ray and your uncle Bert, and your father not only lost a brother, but his father, your other grandad, what you never met. A proper man, who could down a pint of beer faster than any docker I've ever come across.'

If Stan had looked down, he would have seen the boy mouthing his words, but today, to Harry's surprise, Uncle Stan added a sentence he'd never uttered before. 'And your dad would still be alive today, if only management had listened to me.'

Harry was suddenly alert. His dad's death had always been the subject of whispered conversations and hushed tones. But Uncle Stan clammed up, as if he realized he'd gone too far. Maybe next week, thought Harry, catching his uncle up and keeping in step with him as if they were two soldiers on a parade ground.

'So who are City playin' this afternoon?' asked Stan, back on script.

'Charlton Athletic,' Harry replied.

'They're a load of old cobblers.'

'They trounced us last season,' Harry reminded his uncle.

'Bloody lucky, if you ask me,' said Stan, and didn't open his mouth again. When they reached the entrance to the dockyard, Stan clocked in before heading off to the pen where he was working with a gang of other dockers, none of whom could afford to be a minute late. Unemployment was at an all-time high and too many young men were standing outside the gates waiting to take their place.

Harry didn't follow his uncle, because he knew that if Mr Haskins caught him hanging around the sheds he would get a clip round the ear, followed by a boot up the backside from his uncle for annoying the ganger. Instead, he set off in the opposite direction.

Harry's first port of call every Saturday morning was Old Jack Tar, who lived in the railway carriage at the other end of the dockyard. He had never told Stan about his regular visits because his uncle had warned him to avoid the old man at all costs.

'Probably hasn't had a bath in years,' said a man who washed once a quarter, and then only after Harry's mother complained about the smell.

But curiosity had long ago got the better of Harry, and one morning he'd crept up to the railway carriage on his hands and knees, lifted himself up and peeped through a window. The old man was sitting in first class, reading a book.

Old Jack turned to face him and said, 'Come on in, lad.' Harry jumped down, and didn't stop running until he reached his front door.

The following Saturday, Harry once again crawled up to the carriage and peered inside. Old Jack seemed to be fast asleep, but then Harry heard him say, 'Why don't you come in, my boy? I'm not going to bite you.'

Harry turned the heavy brass handle and tentatively pulled open the carriage door, but he didn't step inside. He just stared at the man seated in the centre of the carriage. It was hard to tell how old he was because his face was covered in a well-groomed salt-and-pepper beard, which made him look like the sailor on the Players Please packet. But he looked at Harry with a warmth in his eyes that Uncle Stan had never managed.

'Are you Old Jack Tar?' Harry ventured.

'That's what they call me,' the old man replied.

'And is this where you live?' Harry asked, glancing around the carriage, his eyes settling on a stack of old newspapers piled high on the opposite seat.

'Yes,' he replied. 'It's been my home for these past twenty years. Why don't you close the door and take a seat, young man?'

Harry gave the offer some thought before he jumped back out of the carriage and once again ran away.

The following Saturday, Harry did close the door, but he kept hold of the handle, ready to bolt if the old man as much as twitched a muscle. They stared at each other for some time before Old Jack asked, 'What's your name?'

'Harry.'

'And where do you go to school?'

'I don't go to school.'

'Then what are you hoping to do with your life, young man?'

'Join my uncle on the docks, of course,' Harry replied.

'Why would you want to do that?' said the old man.

'Why not?' Harry bristled. 'Don't you think I'm good enough?'

'You're far too good,' replied Old Jack. 'When I was your age,' he continued, 'I wanted to join the army, and nothing my old man could say or do would dissuade me.' For the next hour Harry stood, mesmerized, while Old Jack Tar reminisced about the docks, the city of Bristol, and lands beyond the sea that he couldn't have been taught about in geography lessons.

The following Saturday, and for more Saturdays than he would remember, Harry continued to visit Old Jack Tar. But he never once told his uncle or his mother, for fear they would stop him going to see his first real friend.

◄O►

When Harry knocked on the door of the railway carriage that Saturday morning, Old Jack had clearly been waiting for him, because his usual Cox's Orange Pippin had been placed on the seat opposite. Harry picked it up, took a bite and sat down.

'Thank you, Mr Tar,' Harry said as he wiped some juice from his chin. He never asked where the apples came from; it just added to the mystery of the great man.

How different he was from Uncle Stan, who repeated the little he knew again and again, whereas Old Jack introduced Harry to new words, new experiences, even new worlds every week. He often wondered why Mr Tar wasn't a schoolmaster – he seemed to know even more than Miss Monday, and almost as much as Mr Holcombe. Harry was convinced that Mr Holcombe knew everything, because he never failed to answer any question Harry put to him. Old Jack smiled across at him, but didn't speak until Harry had finished his apple and thrown the core out of the window.

'What have you learnt at school this week,' the old man asked, 'that you didn't know a week ago?'

'Mr Holcombe told me there are other countries beyond the sea that are part of the British Empire, and they are all reigned over by the King.'

'He's quite right,' said Old Jack. 'Can you name any of those countries?'

'Australia. Canada. India.' He hesitated. 'And America.'

'No, not America,' said Old Jack. 'That used to be the case, but it isn't any more, thanks to a weak Prime Minister and a sick King.'

'Who was the King, and who was the Prime Minister?' demanded Harry angrily.

'King George III was on the throne in 1776,' said Old Jack, 'but to be fair, he was a sick man, while Lord North, his Prime Minister, simply ignored what was taking place in the colonies, and, sadly, in the end our own kith and kin took up arms against us.'

'But we must have beaten them?' said Harry.

'No, we didn't,' said Old Jack. 'Not only did they have right on their side – not that that's a prerequisite for victory—'

'What does prerequisite mean?'

'Required as a pre-condition,' said Old Jack, who then continued as if he hadn't been interrupted. 'But they were also led by a brilliant general.'

'What was his name?'

'George Washington.'

'You told me last week that Washington was the capital of America. Was he named after the city?'

'No, the city was named after him. It was built on an area of marshland known as Columbia, through which the Potomac River flows.'

'Is Bristol named after a man too?'

'No,' chuckled Old Jack, amused by how quickly Harry's inquisitive mind could switch from subject to subject. 'Bristol was originally called Brigstowe, which means the site of a bridge.'

'So when did it become Bristol?'

'Historians differ in their opinions,' said Old Jack, 'although Bristol Castle was built by Robert of Gloucester in 1109, when he saw the opportunity to trade wool with the Irish. After that, the city developed into a trading port. Since then it's been a centre of shipbuilding for hundreds of years, and grew even more quickly when the navy needed to expand in 1914.'

'My dad fought in the Great War,' said Harry with pride. 'Did you?'

For the first time, Old Jack hesitated before answering one of Harry's questions. He just sat there, not saying a word. 'I'm sorry, Mr Tar,' said Harry. 'I didn't mean to pry.'

'No, no,' said Old Jack. 'It's just that I haven't been asked that question for some years.' Without another word, he opened his hand to reveal a sixpence.

Harry took the little silver coin and bit it, something he'd seen his uncle do. 'Thank you,' he said before pocketing it.

'Go and buy yourself some fish and chips from the dockside café, but don't tell your uncle, because he'll only ask where you got the money.'

In truth, Harry had never told his uncle anything about Old Jack. He'd once heard Stan tell his mum, 'The loony ought to be locked up.' He'd asked Miss Monday what a loony was, because he couldn't find the word in the dictionary, and when she told him, he realized for the first time just how stupid his Uncle Stan must be.

'Not necessarily stupid,' Miss Monday counselled, 'simply ill-informed and therefore prejudiced. I have no doubt, Harry,' she added, 'that you'll meet many more such men during your lifetime, some of them in far more exalted positions than your uncle.'

3

MAISIE WAITED UNTIL she heard the front door slam and was confident that Stan was on his way to work before she announced, 'I've been offered a job as a waitress at the Royal Hotel.'

No one seated round the table responded, as conversations at breakfast were supposed to follow a regular pattern and not take anyone by surprise. Harry had a dozen questions he wanted to ask but waited for his grandma to speak first. She simply busied herself with pouring another cup of tea, as if she hadn't heard her daughter in the first place.

'Will someone please say something?' said Maisie.

'I didn't even realize you were looking for another job,' ventured Harry.

'I wasn't,' said Maisie. 'But last week a Mr Frampton, the manager of the Royal, dropped into Tilly's for coffee. He came back several times, and then he offered me a job!'

'I thought you were happy at the tea shop,' said Grandma, finally joining in. 'After all, Miss Tilly pays well, and the hours suit.'

'I am happy,' said Harry's mum, 'but Mr Frampton's offering me five pounds a week, and half of all the tips. I could be bringing home as much as six pounds

on a Friday.' Grandma sat there with her mouth wide
open.

'Will you have to work nights?' asked Harry, once
he'd finished licking Stan's porridge bowl.

'No, I won't,' Maisie said, ruffling her son's hair, 'and
what's more I'll get one day off a fortnight.'

'Are your clothes posh enough for a grand hotel like
the Royal?' asked Grandma.

'I'll be supplied with a uniform, and a fresh white
apron every morning. The hotel even has its own
laundry.'

'I don't doubt it,' said Grandma, 'but I can think of
one problem we're all going to have to learn to live
with.'

'And what's that, Mum?' asked Maisie.

'You could end up earnin' more than Stan, and he's
not going to like that, not one little bit.'

'Then he'll just have to learn to live with it, won't
he?' said Grandpa, offering an opinion for the first time
in weeks.

◄○►

The extra money was going to come in useful, especially
after what had happened at the Holy Nativity. Maisie
had been about to leave the church after the service
when Miss Monday walked purposefully down the aisle
towards her.

'Can I have a private word with you, Mrs Clifton?'
she asked, before turning and walking back down the
aisle towards the vestry. Maisie chased after her like a
child in the Pied Piper's wake. She feared the worst.
What had Harry been up to this time?

Maisie followed the choir mistress into the vestry
and felt her legs give way when she saw the Reverend

Watts, Mr Holcombe and another gentleman standing there. As Miss Monday closed the door quietly behind her, Maisie began to shake uncontrollably.

The Reverend Watts placed an arm around her shoulder. 'There's nothing for you to worry about, my dear,' he assured her. 'On the contrary, I hope you will feel we are the bearers of glad tidings,' he added, offering her a seat. Maisie sat down, but still couldn't stop shaking.

Once everyone was seated, Miss Monday took over. 'We wanted to talk to you about Harry, Mrs Clifton,' she began. Maisie pursed her lips; what could the boy possibly have done to bring three such important people together?

'I'll not beat about the bush,' the choir mistress continued. 'The music master at St Bede's has approached me and asked if Harry would consider entering his name for one of their choral scholarships.'

'But he's very happy at Holy Nativity,' said Maisie. 'In any case, where is St Bede's Church? I've never even heard of it.'

'St Bede's is not a church,' said Miss Monday. 'It's a choir school that supplies choristers for St Mary Redcliffe, which was famously described by Queen Elizabeth as the fairest and godliest church in all the land.'

'So would he have to leave his school, as well as the church?' asked Maisie in disbelief.

'Try to look upon it as an opportunity that might change his whole life, Mrs Clifton,' said Mr Holcombe, speaking for the first time.

'But wouldn't he have to mix with posh, clever boys?'

'I doubt if there will be many children at St Bede's cleverer than Harry,' said Mr Holcombe. 'He's the brightest lad I've ever taught. Although we get the occasional boy into the grammar school, none of our pupils has ever been offered the chance of a place at St Bede's before.'

'There's something else you need to know before you make up your mind,' said the Reverend Watts. Maisié looked even more anxious. 'Harry would have to leave home during term time, because St Bede's is a boarding school.'

'Then it's out of the question,' said Maisie. 'I couldn't afford it.'

'That shouldn't prove a problem,' said Miss Monday. 'If Harry is offered a scholarship, the school would not only waive any fees, but also award him a bursary of ten pounds a term.'

'But is this one of those schools where the fathers wear suits and ties, and the mothers don't work?' asked Maisie.

'It's worse than that,' said Miss Monday, trying to make light of it. 'The masters wear long black gowns and mortarboards on their heads.'

'Still,' said the Reverend Watts joining in, 'at least there would be no more leatherings for Harry. They're far more refined at St Bede's. They just cane the boys.'

Only Maisie didn't laugh. 'But why would he want to leave home?' she asked. 'He's settled at Merrywood Elementary, and he won't want to give up being senior chorister at Holy Nativity.'

'I must confess that my loss would be even greater than his,' said Miss Monday. 'But then, I'm sure our Lord would not want me to stand in the way of such a gifted child, simply because of my own selfish desires,' she added quietly.

'Even if I agree,' said Maisie, playing her last card, 'that doesn't mean Harry will.'

'I had a word with the boy last week,' admitted Mr

Holcombe. 'Of course he was apprehensive about such a challenge, but if I recall, his exact words were "I'd like to have a go, sir, but only if you think I'm good enough." But,' he added before Maisie could respond, 'he also made it clear that he wouldn't even consider the idea unless his mother agreed.'

—◦—

Harry was both terrified and excited by the thought of taking the entrance exam, but just as anxious about failing and letting so many people down as he was about succeeding and having to leave home.

During the following term, he never once missed a lesson at Merrywood, and when he returned home each evening, he went straight up to the bedroom he shared with Uncle Stan, where, with the aid of a candle, he studied for hours that until then he hadn't realized existed. There were even occasions when his mother found Harry sound asleep on the floor, open books scattered around him.

Every Saturday morning he continued to visit Old Jack, who seemed to know a great deal about St Bede's, and continued to teach Harry about so many other things, almost as if he knew where Mr Holcombe had left off.

On Saturday afternoons, much to the disgust of Uncle Stan, Harry no longer accompanied him to Ashton Gate to watch Bristol City, but returned to Merrywood, where Mr Holcombe gave him extra lessons. It would be years before Harry worked out that Mr Holcombe was also forgoing his regular visits to support the Robins, in order to teach him.

As the day of the examination drew nearer, Harry became even more frightened of failure than of the possibility of success.

On the appointed day, Mr Holcombe accompanied his star pupil to the Colston Hall, where the two-hour examination would take place. He left Harry at the entrance to the building, with the words, 'Don't forget to read each question twice before you even pick up your pen,' a piece of advice he'd repeated several times during the past week. Harry smiled nervously, and shook hands with Mr Holcombe as if they were old friends.

He entered the examination hall to find about sixty other boys standing around in small groups, chattering. It was clear to Harry that many of them already knew each other, while he didn't know anyone. Despite this, one or two of them stopped talking and glanced at him as he made his way to the front of the hall trying to look confident.

'Abbott, Barrington, Cabot, Clifton, Deakins, Fry . . .'

Harry took his place at a desk in the front row, and just moments before the clock struck ten, several masters in long black gowns and mortarboards swept in and placed examination papers on the desks in front of each candidate.

'Gentlemen,' said a master standing at the front of the hall, who had not taken part in the distribution of the papers, 'my name is Mr Frobisher, and I am your invigilator. You have two hours in which to answer one hundred questions. Good luck.'

A clock he couldn't see struck ten. All around him, pens dipped into inkwells and began to scratch furiously across paper, but Harry simply folded his arms, leant on the desk and read each question slowly. He was among the last to pick up his pen.

Harry couldn't know that Mr Holcombe was pacing up and down on the pavement outside, feeling far more nervous than his pupil. Or that his mother was glancing up at the clock in the foyer of the Royal Hotel every few minutes as she served morning coffee. Or that Miss Monday was kneeling in silent prayer before the altar at Holy Nativity.

Moments after the clock had struck twelve, the examination papers were gathered up and the boys were allowed to leave the hall, some laughing, some frowning, others thoughtful.

When Mr Holcombe first saw Harry, his heart sank. 'Was it that bad?' he asked.

Harry didn't reply until he was certain no other boy could overhear his words. 'Not at all what I expected,' he said.

'What do you mean?' asked Mr Holcombe anxiously.

'The questions were far too easy,' replied Harry.

Mr Holcombe felt that he had never been paid a greater compliment in his life.

◄○►

'Two suits, madam, grey. One blazer, navy. Five shirts, white. Five stiff collars, white. Six pairs of calf-length socks, grey. Six sets of undergarments, white. And one St Bede's tie.' The shop assistant checked the list carefully. 'I think that covers everything. Oh, no, the boy will also need a school cap.' He reached under the counter, opened a drawer and removed a red and black cap which he placed on Harry's head. 'A perfect fit,' he pronounced. Maisie smiled at her son with considerable pride. Harry looked every inch a St Bede's boy. 'That will be three pounds, ten shillings and six pence, madam.'

Maisie tried not to look too dismayed. 'Is it possible to purchase any of these items second-hand?' she whispered.

'No, madam, this is not a second-hand shop,' said the assistant, who had already decided that this customer would not be allowed to open an account.

Maisie opened her purse, handed over four pound notes and waited for the change. She was relieved that St Bede's had paid the first term's bursary in advance, especially as she still needed to buy two pairs of leather shoes, black with laces, two pairs of gym shoes, white with laces, and one pair of slippers, bedroom.

The assistant coughed. 'The boy will also need two pairs of pyjamas and a dressing gown.'

'Yes, of course,' said Maisie, hoping she had enough money left in her purse to cover the cost.

'And am I to understand that the boy is a choral scholar?' asked the assistant, looking more closely at his list.

'Yes, he is,' Maisie replied proudly.

'Then he'll also require one cassock, red, two surplices, white, and a St Bede's medallion.' Maisie wanted to run out of the shop. 'Those items will be supplied by the school when he attends his first choir practice,' the assistant added before handing over her change. 'Will you be requiring anything else, madam?'

'No, thank you,' said Harry, who picked up the two bags, grabbed his mother by the arm and led her quickly out of T.C. Marsh, Tailors of Distinction.

—<o>—

Harry spent the Saturday morning before he was due to report to St Bede's with Old Jack.

'Are you nervous about going to a new school?' asked Old Jack.

'No, I'm not,' said Harry defiantly. Old Jack smiled. 'I'm terrified,' he admitted.

'So is every new bug, as you'll be called. Try to treat

the whole thing as if you're starting out on an adventure to a new world, where everyone begins as equals.'

'But the moment they hear me speak, they'll realize I'm not their equal.'

'Possibly, but the moment they hear you sing, they'll realize they're not *your* equal.'

'Most of them will have come from rich families, with servants.'

'That will only be a consolation for the more stupid ones,' said Old Jack.

'And some of them will have brothers at the school, and even fathers and grandfathers who were there before them.'

'Your father was a fine man,' said Old Jack, 'and none of them will have a better mother, of that I can assure you.'

'You knew my father?' said Harry, unable to mask his surprise.

'Knew would be an exaggeration,' said Old Jack, 'but I observed him from afar, as I have many others who have worked at the docks. He was a decent, courageous, God-fearing man.'

'But do you know how he died?' asked Harry, looking Old Jack in the eye, hoping he would at last get an honest reply to the question that had troubled him for so long.

'What have you been told?' asked Old Jack cautiously.

'That he was killed in the Great War. But as I was born in 1920, even I can work out that that can't be possible.'

Old Jack didn't speak for some time. Harry remained on the edge of his seat.

'He was certainly badly wounded in the war, but you're right, that was not the cause of his death.'

'Then how did he die?' asked Harry.

'If I knew, I'd tell you,' replied Old Jack. 'But there were so many rumours flying around at the time that I wasn't sure who to believe. However, there are several men, and three in particular, who undoubtedly know the truth about what happened that night.'

'My uncle Stan must be one of them,' said Harry, 'but who are the other two?'

Old Jack hesitated, before he replied, 'Phil Haskins and Mr Hugo.'

'Mr Haskins? The ganger?' said Harry. 'He wouldn't give me the time of day. And who's Mr Hugo?'

'Hugo Barrington, the son of Sir Walter Barrington.'

'The family who own the shipping line?'

'The same,' replied Old Jack, fearing he'd gone too far.

'And are they also decent, courageous, God-fearing men?'

'Sir Walter is among the finest men I've ever known.'

'But what about his son, Mr Hugo?'

'Not cut from the same cloth, I fear,' said Old Jack, without further explanation.

4

THE SMARTLY DRESSED BOY sat next to his mother
on the back seat of the tram.

'This is our stop,' she said when the tram came to a
halt. They got off, and began to walk slowly up the hill
towards the school, going a little slower with each step.

Harry held on to his mother with one hand, while
he clutched a battered suitcase with the other. Neither
of them spoke as they watched several hansom cabs, as
well as the occasional chauffeur-driven car, pull up
outside the front gates of the school.

Fathers were shaking hands with their sons, while
fur-draped mothers embraced their offspring before
giving them a peck on the cheek, like a bird finally
having to acknowledge her fledglings were about to fly
the nest.

Harry didn't want his mother to kiss him in front of
the other boys, so he let go of her hand when they were
still fifty yards from the gate. Maisie, sensing his discomfort, bent down and kissed him quickly on the forehead.
'Good luck, Harry. Make us all proud of you.'

'Goodbye, Mum,' he said, fighting back the tears.

Maisie turned and began to walk back down the hill,
tears flooding down her own cheeks.

Harry walked on, recalling his uncle's description of

going over the top at Ypres before charging towards the enemy lines. *Never look back, or you're a dead man.* Harry wanted to look back, but he knew if he did, he would not stop running until he was safely on the tram. He gritted his teeth and kept on walking.

'Did you have a good hols, old chap?' one of the boys was asking a friend.

'Topping,' the other replied. 'The pater took me to Lord's for the Varsity match.'

Was Lord's a church, Harry wondered, and if so, what sort of match could possibly take place in a church? He marched resolutely on through the school gates, coming to a halt when he recognized a man standing by the front door of the school holding a clipboard.

'And who are you, young man?' he asked, giving Harry a welcoming smile.

'Harry Clifton, sir,' he replied, removing his cap just as Mr Holcombe had instructed him to do whenever a master or a lady spoke to him.

'Clifton,' he said, running a finger down a long list of names. 'Ah, yes.' He placed a tick by Harry's name. 'First generation, choral scholar. Many congratulations, and welcome to St Bede's. I'm Mr Frobisher, your housemaster, and this is Frobisher House. If you leave your suitcase in the hall, a prefect will accompany you to the refectory where I'll be addressing all the new boys before supper.'

Harry had never had supper before. 'Tea' was always the last meal in the Clifton household, before being sent to bed the moment it was dark. Electricity hadn't yet reached Still House Lane, and there was rarely enough money over to spend on candles.

'Thank you, sir,' said Harry, before making his way through the front door and into a large, highly polished wood-panelled hall. He put his case down and stared up at a painting of an old man with grey hair and bushy white sideburns, dressed in a long black gown with a red hood draped around his shoulders.

'What's your name?' barked a voice from behind him.

'Clifton, sir,' said Harry, turning to see a tall boy wearing long trousers.

'You don't call me sir, Clifton. You call me Fisher. I'm a prefect, not a master.'

'Sorry, sir,' said Harry.

'Leave your case over there and follow me.'

Harry placed his second-hand, battered suitcase next to a row of leather trunks. His was the only one that didn't have a set of initials stamped on it. He followed the prefect down a long corridor that was lined with photographs of old school teams and display cabinets filled with silver cups, to remind the next generation of past glories. When they reached the refectory, Fisher said, 'You can sit anywhere you like, Clifton. Just be sure to stop talking the moment Mr Frobisher enters the refectory.'

Harry hesitated for some time before deciding which of the four long tables he would sit at. A number of boys were already milling around in clusters, talking quietly. Harry walked slowly to the far corner of the room and took a place at the end of the table. He looked up to see several boys pouring into the hall, looking just as perplexed as he felt. One of them came and sat next to Harry, while another sat opposite him. They continued chatting to each other as if he wasn't there.

Without warning, a bell rang and everyone stopped talking as Mr Frobisher entered the refectory. He took his place behind a lectern Harry hadn't noticed and tugged at the lapels of his gown.

'Welcome,' he began, doffing his mortarboard to the

assembled gathering, 'on this, the first day of your first term at St Bede's. In a few moments' time you will experience your first school meal, and I can promise you that it doesn't get any better.' One or two of the boys laughed nervously. 'Once you have finished supper, you will be taken up to your dormitories, where you will unpack. At eight o'clock, you will hear another bell. Actually it's the same bell, just being rung at a different time.' Harry smiled, although most of the boys hadn't caught Mr Frobisher's little joke.

'Thirty minutes later, the same bell will ring again, and you will then go to bed, but not before you've washed and brushed your teeth. You will then have thirty minutes to read before lights out, after which you will go to sleep. Any child caught talking after lights out will be punished by the duty prefect. You will not hear another bell,' continued Mr Frobisher, 'until six thirty tomorrow morning, when you will rise, wash and dress in time to report back to the refectory before seven. Any child who is late will forgo his breakfast.

'Morning assembly will be held at eight o'clock in the great hall, where the headmaster will address us. This will be followed by your first lesson at eight thirty. There will be three sixty-minute lessons during the morning, with ten-minute breaks between them, giving you time to change classrooms. This will be followed by lunch at twelve.

'In the afternoon there will only be two more lessons before games, when you will play football.' Harry smiled for a second time. 'This is compulsory for everyone who is not a member of the choir.' Harry frowned. No one had told him that choristers didn't get to play football. 'After games or choir practice, you will return to Frobisher House for supper, which will be followed by an hour of prep before you retire to bed, when once again you can read until lights out – but only if the book has been approved by Matron,' added Mr Frobisher. 'This must all sound very bemusing to you' – Harry made a mental note to look up the word in the dictionary Mr Holcombe had presented him with. Mr Frobisher once again tugged at the lapels of his gown before continuing. 'But don't worry, you'll soon get used to our traditions at St Bede's. That's all I'm going to say for the moment. I'll now leave you to enjoy your supper. Goodnight, boys.'

'Goodnight, sir,' some boys had the courage to reply as Mr Frobisher left the room.

Harry didn't move a muscle as several women in pinafores marched up and down the tables placing bowls of soup in front of each boy. He watched attentively as the boy opposite him picked up a strangely shaped spoon, dipped it into his soup and pushed it away from him before putting it to his mouth. Harry attempted to imitate the motion, but only ended up spilling several drops of soup on the table, and when he did manage to transfer what was left into his mouth, most of it dribbled down his chin. He wiped his mouth with his sleeve. This didn't attract much attention, but when he slurped loudly with each mouthful, several of the boys stopped eating and stared at him. Embarrassed, Harry placed the spoon back on the table and left his soup to go cold.

The second course was a fishcake, and Harry didn't move until he'd seen which fork the boy opposite him picked up. He was surprised to notice that the boy placed his knife and fork on the plate between each mouthful, while Harry clung on to his as firmly as if they were pitchforks.

A conversation struck up between the boy opposite him and the boy next to him, on the subject of riding to hounds. Harry didn't join in, partly because the nearest he'd been to sitting on a horse was a halfpenny ride on a donkey one afternoon on an outing to Weston-super-Mare.

Once the plates had been whisked away, they were replaced with puddings, or what his mum called treats, because he didn't get them often. Yet another spoon, yet another taste, yet another mistake. Harry didn't realize that a banana wasn't like an apple, so to the astonishment of all those around him, he tried to eat the skin. For the rest of the boys, their first lesson might well be tomorrow at 8.30 a.m., but Harry's was already taking place.

After supper had been cleared away, Fisher returned and, as duty prefect, led his charges up a wide wooden staircase to the dormitories on the first floor. Harry entered a room with thirty beds neatly lined up in three rows of ten. Each had a pillow, two sheets and two blankets. Harry had never had two of anything.

'This is the new bugs' dorm,' said Fisher with disdain. 'It's where you'll remain until you're civilized. You'll find your names in alphabetical order, at the foot of each bed.'

Harry was surprised to find his suitcase on the bed and wondered who'd put it there. The boy next to him was already unpacking.

'I'm Deakins,' he said, pushing his spectacles further up his nose so he could take a closer look at Harry.

'I'm Harry. I sat next to you during exams last summer. I couldn't believe you answered all the questions in just over an hour.'

Deakins blushed.

'That's why he's a scholar,' said the boy on the other side of Harry.

Harry swung around. 'Are you a scholar, too?' he asked.

'Good heavens, no,' said the boy as he continued to unpack. 'The only reason they let me into St Bede's was because my father and grandfather were here before me. I'm the third generation to go to the school. Was your father here by any chance?'

'No,' said Harry and Deakins in unison.

'Stop chattering!' shouted Fisher, 'and get on with unpacking your cases.'

Harry opened his suitcase and began taking his clothes out and placing them neatly in the two drawers next to his bed. His mother had put a bar of Fry's Five Boys chocolate in between his shirts. He hid it under the pillow.

A bell sounded. 'Time to get undressed!' declared Fisher. Harry had never undressed in front of another boy, let alone a room full of them. He faced the wall, took off his clothes slowly and quickly pulled on his pyjamas. Once he'd tied the cord of his dressing gown, he followed the other boys into the washroom. Once again, he watched carefully as they washed their faces with flannels before brushing their teeth. He didn't have a flannel or a toothbrush. The boy from the next bed rummaged around in his wash bag and handed him a brand new toothbrush and a tube of toothpaste. Harry didn't want to take them until the boy said, 'My mother always packs two of everything.'

'Thank you,' said Harry. Although he cleaned his teeth quickly, he was still among the last to return to the dormitory. He climbed into bed, two clean sheets, two blankets and a soft pillow. He had just looked across to see that Deakins was reading *Kennedy's Latin Primer* when the other boy said, 'This pillow is brick hard.'

'Would you like to swap with me?' Harry asked.

'I think you'll find they're all the same,' the boy said with a grin, 'but thanks.'

43

Harry took his bar of chocolate from under the pillow and broke it into three pieces. He handed one piece to Deakins, and another to the boy who'd given him the toothbrush and toothpaste.

'I see your mater's far more sensible than mine,' he said after taking a bite. Another bell. 'By the way, my name's Giles Barrington. What's yours?'

'Clifton. Harry Clifton.'

Harry didn't sleep for more than a few minutes at a time, and it wasn't just because his bed was so comfortable. Could it be possible that Giles was related to one of the three men who knew the truth about how his father had died? And if so, was he cut from the same cloth as his father, or his grandfather?

Suddenly Harry felt very lonely. He unscrewed the top of the toothpaste Barrington had given him and began to suck it until he fell asleep.

◄o►

When the now-familiar bell rang at 6.30 next morning, Harry climbed slowly out of bed, feeling sick. He followed Deakins into the washroom, to find Giles was testing the water. 'Do you think this place has ever heard of hot water?' he asked.

Harry was just about to reply when the prefect hollered, 'No talking in the washroom!'

'He's worse than a Prussian general,' said Barrington, clicking his heels. Harry burst out laughing.

'Who was that?' asked Fisher, glaring at the two boys.

'Me,' said Harry immediately.

'Name?'

'Clifton.'

'Open your mouth again, Clifton, and I'll slipper you.'

Harry had no idea what being slippered meant, but he had a feeling it wouldn't be pleasant. Once he'd brushed his teeth, he walked quickly back into the dorm and dressed without another word. Once he'd done up his tie – something else he hadn't quite mastered – he caught up with Barrington and Deakins as they made their way down the stairs to the refectory.

Nobody said a word, as they weren't sure if they were allowed to talk while they were on the staircase. When they sat down for breakfast in the refectory, Harry slipped in between his two new friends, and watched as bowls of porridge were placed in front of each boy. He was relieved to find there was only one spoon in front of him, so he couldn't make a mistake this time.

Harry gulped down his porridge so quickly it was as if he was afraid Uncle Stan would appear and snatch it away from him. He was the first to finish, and without a moment's thought he put his spoon down on the table, picked up his bowl and began to lick it. Several other boys stared at him in disbelief, some pointed, while others sniggered. He turned a bright shade of crimson and put the bowl back down. He would have burst into tears, if Barrington hadn't picked up his own bowl and begun licking it.

5

THE REVEREND SAMUEL OAKSHOTT MA (Oxon) stood, feet apart, at the centre of the stage. He peered benignly down on his flock, for that was certainly how the headmaster of St Bede's viewed the pupils.

Harry, seated in the front row, stared up at the frightening figure who towered above him. Dr Oakshott was well over six feet tall, and had a head of thick, greying hair and long bushy sideburns that made him look even more forbidding. His deep blue eyes pierced right through you and he never seemed to blink, while the criss-cross of lines on his forehead hinted at great wisdom. He cleared his throat before addressing the boys.

'Fellow Bedeans,' he began. 'We are once again gathered together at the beginning of a new school year, no doubt prepared to face whatever challenges should confront us. For the senior boys,' he turned his attention to the back of the hall, 'you don't have a moment to lose if you hope to be offered a place at the school of your first choice. Never settle for second best.

'For the middle school,' his eyes moved to the centre of the hall, 'this will be a time when we discover which of you is destined for greater things. When you return next year, will you be a prefect, a monitor, a house captain or a captain of sport? Or will you simply be among the also-rans?' Several boys bowed their heads.

'Our next duty is to welcome the new boys, and do everything in our power to make them feel at home. They are being handed the baton for the first time as they begin life's long race. Should the pace prove to be too demanding, one or two of you may fall by the wayside,' he warned, staring down at the front three rows. 'St Bede's is not a school for the faint-hearted. So be sure never to forget the words of the great Cecil Rhodes: *If you are lucky enough to have been born an Englishman, you have drawn first prize in the lottery of life.*'

The assembled gathering burst into spontaneous applause as the headmaster left the stage, followed by a crocodile of masters whom he led down the centre aisle, out of the great hall and into the morning sunshine.

Harry, his spirits raised, was determined not to let the headmaster down. He followed the senior boys out of the hall, but the moment he stepped out into the quad, his exuberance was dampened. A posse of older boys were hanging around in one corner, hands in pockets to indicate they were prefects.

'There he is,' said one of them, pointing at Harry.

'So that's what a street urchin looks like,' said another.

A third, whom Harry recognized as Fisher, the prefect who had been on duty the previous night, added, 'He's an animal, and it's nothing less than our duty to see that he's returned to his natural habitat as quickly as possible.'

Giles Barrington ran after Harry. 'If you ignore them,' he said, 'they'll soon get bored and start picking on someone else.' Harry wasn't convinced, and ran ahead to the classroom where he waited for Barrington and Deakins to join him.

A moment later, Mr Frobisher entered the room. Harry's first thought was, does he also think I'm a street urchin, unworthy of a place at St Bede's?

'Good morning, boys,' said Mr Frobisher.

'Good morning, sir,' replied the boys as their form master took his place in front of the blackboard. 'Your first lesson this morning,' he said, 'will be history. As I am keen to get to know you, we will start with a simple test to discover how much you have already learnt, or perhaps how little. How many wives did Henry the Eighth have?'

Several hands shot up. 'Abbott,' he said, looking at a chart on his desk and pointing to a boy in the front row.

'Six, sir,' came back the immediate reply.

'Good, but can anyone name them?' Not quite as many hands were raised. 'Clifton?'

'Catherine of Aragon, Anne Boleyn, Jane Seymour, then another Anne I think,' he said before coming to a halt.

'Anne of Cleves. Can anyone name the missing two?' Only one hand remained in the air. 'Deakins,' said Frobisher after checking his chart.

'Catherine Howard and Catherine Parr. Anne of Cleves and Catherine Parr both outlived Henry.'

'Very good, Deakins. Now, let's turn the clock forward a couple of centuries. Who commanded our fleet at the Battle of Trafalgar?' Every hand in the room shot up. 'Matthews,' he said, nodding at a particularly insistent hand.

'Nelson, sir.'

'Correct. And who was Prime Minister at the time?'

'The Duke of Wellington, sir,' said Matthews, not sounding quite as confident.

'No,' said Mr Frobisher, 'it wasn't Wellington, although he was a contemporary of Nelson's.' He looked around the class, but only Clifton's and Deakins's hands were still raised. 'Deakins.'

'Pitt the Younger, 1783 to 1801, and 1804 to 1806.'

'Correct, Deakins. And when was the Iron Duke Prime Minister?'

'1828 to 1830, and again in 1834,' said Deakins.

'And can anyone tell me what his most famous victory was?'

Barrington's hand shot up for the first time. 'Waterloo, sir!' he shouted before Mr Frobisher had time to select anyone else.

'Yes, Barrington. And whom did Wellington defeat at Waterloo?'

Barrington remained silent.

'Napoleon,' whispered Harry.

'Napoleon, sir,' said Barrington confidently.

'Correct, Clifton,' said Frobisher, smiling. 'And was Napoleon also a Duke?'

'No, sir,' said Deakins, after no one else had attempted to answer the question. 'He founded the first French Empire, and appointed himself Emperor.'

Mr Frobisher was not surprised by Deakins's response, as he was an open scholar, but he was impressed by Clifton's knowledge. After all, he was a choral scholar, and over the years he had learnt that gifted choristers, like talented sportsmen, rarely excel outside their own field. Clifton was already proving an exception to that rule. Mr Frobisher would have liked to know who had taught the boy.

When the bell rang for the end of class, Mr Frobisher announced, 'Your next lesson will be geography with Mr Henderson, and he is not a master who likes to be kept waiting. I recommend that during the break you find out where his classroom is, and are seated in your places long before he enters the room.'

Harry stuck close to Giles, who seemed to know where everything was. As they strolled across the quad together, Harry became aware that some of the boys lowered their voices when they passed, and one or two even turned to stare at him.

Thanks to countless Saturday mornings spent with Old Jack, Harry held his own in the geography lesson, but in maths, the final class of the morning, no one came close to Deakins, and even the master had to keep his wits about him.

When the three of them sat down for lunch, Harry could feel a hundred eyes watching his every move. He pretended not to notice, and simply copied everything Giles did. 'It's nice to know there's something I can teach you,' Giles said as he peeled an apple with his knife.

Harry enjoyed his first chemistry lesson later that afternoon, especially when the master allowed him to light a Bunsen burner. But he didn't excel at nature studies, the final lesson of the day, because Harry was the only boy whose home didn't have a garden.

When the final bell sounded, the rest of the class went off for games, while Harry reported to the chapel for his first choir practice. Once again, he noticed everyone was staring at him, but this time it was for all the right reasons.

But no sooner had he walked out of the chapel than he was subjected to the same sotto voce jibes from boys who were making their way back from the playing fields.

'Isn't that our little street urchin?' said one.

'Pity he doesn't have a toothbrush,' said another.

'Sleeps down at the docks at night, I'm told,' said a third.

Deakins and Barrington were nowhere to be seen as

Harry hurried back to his house, avoiding any gatherings of boys on the way.

During supper, the gawping eyes were less obvious, but only because Giles had made it clear to everyone within earshot that Harry was his friend. But Giles was unable to help when they all went up to the dormitory after prep and found Fisher standing by the door, clearly waiting for Harry.

As the boys began to undress, Fisher announced in a loud voice, 'I'm sorry about the smell, gentlemen, but one of your form comes from a house without a bath.' One or two of the boys sniggered, hoping to ingratiate themselves with Fisher. Harry ignored him. 'Not only does this guttersnipe not have a bath, he doesn't even have a father.'

'My father was a good man who fought for his country in the war,' said Harry proudly.

'What makes you think I was talking about you, Clifton?' said Fisher. 'Unless of course you're also the boy whose mother works –' he paused – 'as a hotel waitress.'

'An hotel,' said Harry, correcting him.

Fisher grabbed a slipper. 'Don't you ever answer me back, Clifton,' he said angrily. 'Bend down and touch the end of your bed.' Harry obeyed, and Fisher administered six strokes with such ferocity that Giles had to turn away. Harry crept into bed, fighting to hold back the tears.

Before Fisher switched off the light, he added, 'I'll look forward to seeing you all again tomorrow night, when I will continue with my bedtime tale of the Cliftons of Still House Lane. Wait until you hear about Uncle Stan.'

The following night, Harry learnt for the first time

that his uncle had spent eighteen months in prison for burglary. This revelation was worse than being slippered. He crept into bed wondering if his father could still be alive but in jail, and that was the real reason no one at home ever talked about him.

Harry hardly slept for a third night running, and no amount of success in the classroom, or admiration in the chapel, could stop him continually thinking about the next inevitable encounter with Fisher. The slightest excuse, a drop of water spilt on the washroom floor, a pillow that wasn't straight, a sock that had fallen around his ankle, would ensure that Harry could expect six of the best from the duty prefect; a punishment that would be administered in front of the rest of the dorm, but not before Fisher had added another episode from the Clifton Chronicles. By the fifth night, Harry had had enough, and even Giles and Deakins could no longer console him.

During prep on Friday evening, while the other boys were turning the pages of their *Kennedy's Latin Primer*, Harry ignored Caesar and the Gauls and went over a plan that would ensure Fisher never bothered him again. By the time he climbed into bed that night, after Fisher had discovered a Fry's wrapper by his bed and slippered him once again, Harry's plan was in place. He lay awake long after lights out, and didn't stir until he was certain every boy was asleep.

Harry had no idea what time it was when he slipped out of bed. He dressed without making a sound, then crept between the beds until he reached the far side of the room. He pushed the window open, and the rush of cold air caused the boy in the nearest bed to turn over. Harry climbed out on to the fire escape and slowly closed the window before making his way down to the ground. He walked around the edge of the lawn, taking advantage of any shadows to avoid a full moon that seemed to beam down on him like a searchlight.

Harry was horrified to discover that the school gates were locked. He crept along the wall, searching for the slightest crack or indentation that would allow him to climb over the top and escape to freedom. At last he spotted a missing brick and was able to lever himself up until he was straddling the wall. He lowered himself down the other side, clinging on by the tips of his fingers, said a silent prayer, then let go. He landed on the ground in a heap, but didn't seem to have broken anything.

Once he'd recovered, he began to run down the road, slowly at first, but then he speeded up and didn't stop running until he reached the docks. The night shift was just coming off duty and Harry was relieved to find his uncle was not among them.

After the last docker had disappeared out of sight, he walked slowly along the quayside, past a line of moored ships that stretched as far as the eye could see. He noticed that one of the funnels proudly displayed the letter B, and thought about his friend who would be fast asleep. Would he ever . . . his thoughts were interrupted when he came to a halt outside Old Jack's railway carriage.

He wondered if the old man was also fast asleep. His question was answered when a voice said, 'Don't just stand there, Harry, come inside before you freeze to death.' Harry opened the carriage door to find Old Jack striking a match and trying to light a candle. Harry slumped into the seat opposite him. 'Have you run away?' asked Old Jack.

Harry was so taken aback by his direct question that he didn't answer immediately. 'Yes, I have,' he finally spluttered.

'And no doubt you've come to tell me why you've made this momentous decision.'

'I didn't make the decision,' said Harry. 'It was made for me.'

'By whom?'

'His name is Fisher.'

'A master or a boy?'

'My dormitory prefect,' said Harry, wincing. He then told Old Jack everything that had happened during his first week at St Bede's.

Once again, the old man took him by surprise. When Harry came to the end of his story, Jack said, 'I blame myself.'

'Why?' asked Harry. 'You couldn't have done more to help me.'

'Yes I could,' said Old Jack. 'I should have prepared you for a brand of snobbery that no other nation on earth can emulate. I should have spent more time on the significance of the old school tie, and less on geography and history. I had rather hoped things just might have changed after the war to end all wars, but they clearly haven't at St Bede's.' He fell into a thoughtful silence before finally asking, 'So what are you going to do next, my boy?'

'Run away to sea. I'll take any boat that will have me,' said Harry, trying to sound enthusiastic.

'What a good idea,' said Old Jack. 'Why not play straight into Fisher's hands?'

'What do you mean?'

'Just that nothing will please Fisher more than to be able to tell his friends that the street urchin had no guts, but then, what do you expect from the son of a docker whose mother is a waitress?'

'But Fisher's right. I'm not in his class.'

'No, Harry, the problem is that Fisher already real-izes he's not in your class, and never will be.'

'Are you saying I should go back to that horrible place?' said Harry.

'In the end, only you can make that decision,' said Old Jack, 'but if you run away every time you come up against the Fishers of this world, you'll end up like me, one of life's also-rans, to quote the headmaster.'

'But you're a great man,' said Harry.

'I might have been,' said Old Jack, 'if I hadn't run away the moment I came across my Fisher. But I settled for the easy way out, and only thought about myself.'

'But who else is there to think about?'

'Your mother for a start,' said Old Jack. 'Don't forget all the sacrifices she made to give you a better start in life than she ever dreamed was possible. And then there's Mr Holcombe, who when he discovers you've run away will only blame himself. And don't forget Miss Monday, who called in favours, twisted arms and spent countless hours to make sure you were good enough to win that choral scholarship. And when you come to weigh up the pros and cons, Harry, I suggest you place Fisher on one side of the scales and Barrington and Deakins on the other, because I suspect that Fisher will quickly fade into insignificance, while Barrington and Deakins will surely turn out to be close friends for the rest of your life. If you run away, they will be forced to listen to Fisher continually reminding them that you weren't the person they thought you were.'

Harry remained silent for some time. Finally, he rose slowly to his feet. 'Thank you, sir,' he said. Without another word he opened the carriage door and let himself out.

He walked slowly down the quayside, once again

staring up at the vast cargo ships, all of which would soon be departing for distant ports. He kept on walking until he reached the dockyard gates, where he broke into a run and headed back towards the city. By the time he reached the school gates they were already open, and the clock on the great hall was about to chime eight times.

Despite the telephone call, Mr Frobisher would have to walk across to the headmaster's house and report that one of his boys was missing. As he looked out of his study window, he caught a glimpse of Harry nipping in and out between the trees as he made his way cautiously towards the house. Harry tentatively opened the front door as the final chime rang out, and came face to face with his housemaster.

'Better hurry, Clifton,' Mr Frobisher said, 'or you'll miss breakfast.'

'Yes, sir,' said Harry, and ran down the corridor. He reached the dining room just before the doors were closed and slipped into place between Barrington and Deakins.

'For a moment I thought I'd be the only one licking my bowl this morning,' said Barrington. Harry burst out laughing.

He didn't come across Fisher that day, and was surprised to find that another prefect had replaced him on dorm duty that night. Harry slept for the first time that week.

6

THE ROLLS-ROYCE drove through the gates of the Manor House and up a long driveway lined with tall oaks, standing like sentinels. Harry had counted six gardeners even before he set eyes on the house.

During their time at St Bede's, Harry had picked up a little about how Giles lived when he returned home for the holidays, but nothing had prepared him for this. When he saw the house for the first time, his mouth opened, and stayed open.

'Early eighteenth century would be my guess,' said Deakins.

'Not bad,' said Giles, '1722, built by Vanbrugh. But I'll bet you can't tell me who designed the garden. I'll give you a clue: it's later than the house.'

'I've only ever heard of one landscape gardener,' said Harry, still staring at the house. 'Capability Brown.'

'That's exactly why we chose him,' said Giles, 'simply so that my friends would have heard of the fellow two hundred years later.'

Harry and Deakins laughed as the car came to a halt in front of a three-storey mansion built from golden Cotswold stone. Giles jumped out before the chauffeur had a chance to open the back door. He ran up the steps with his two friends following less certainly in his wake.

The front door was opened long before Giles reached the top step, and a tall man, elegantly dressed in a long black coat, pinstripe trousers and a black tie, gave a slight bow as the young master shot past him. 'Happy birthday, Mr Giles,' he said.

'Thank you, Jenkins. Come on, chaps!' shouted Giles as he disappeared into the house. The butler held open the door to allow Harry and Deakins to follow.

As soon as Harry stepped into the hall, he found himself transfixed by the portrait of an old man who appeared to be staring directly down at him. Giles had inherited the man's beak-like nose, fierce blue eyes and square jaw. Harry looked around at the other portraits that adorned the walls. The only oil paintings he'd seen before were in books: the *Mona Lisa*, the *Laughing Cavalier* and *Night Watch*. He was looking at a land-scape by an artist called Constable when a woman swept into the hall wearing what Harry could only have described as a ball gown.

'Happy birthday, my darling,' she said.

'Thank you, Mater,' said Giles, as she bent down to kiss him. It was the first time Harry had ever seen his friend look embarrassed. 'These are my two best friends, Harry and Deakins.' As Harry shook hands with a woman who wasn't much taller than he was, she gave him such a warm smile that he immediately felt at ease.

'Why don't we all go through to the drawing room,' she suggested, 'and have some tea?' She led the boys across the hall and into a large room that overlooked the front lawn.

When Harry entered, he didn't want to sit down but to look at the paintings that hung on every wall. How-ever, Mrs Barrington was already ushering him towards the sofa. He sank down into the plush cushions and couldn't stop himself staring out of the bay window on to a finely cut lawn that was large enough to play a game of cricket on. Beyond the lawn, Harry could see a lake where contented mallards swam aimlessly around, clearly not worried about where their next meal would be coming from. Deakins sat himself down on the sofa next to Harry.

Neither of them spoke as another man, this one dressed in a short black jacket, entered the room, followed by a young woman in a smart blue uniform, not unlike the one his mother wore at the hotel. The maid carried a large silver tray which she placed on an oval table in front of Mrs Barrington.

'Indian or China?' Mrs Barrington asked, looking at Harry.

Harry wasn't sure what she meant.

'We'll all have Indian, thank you, Mother,' said Giles.

Harry thought Giles must have taught him everything there was to know about etiquette as practised in polite society, but Mrs Barrington had suddenly raised the bar to a new level.

Once the under-butler had poured three cups of tea, the maid placed them in front of the boys, along with a side plate. Harry stared at a mountain of sandwiches, not daring to touch. Giles took one and put it on his plate. His mother frowned. 'How many times have I told you, Giles, always to wait until your guests decide what they would like before you help yourself?'

Harry wanted to tell Mrs Barrington that Giles always took the lead, just so that he would know what to do and, more important, what not to do. Deakins selected a sandwich and put it on his plate. Harry did the same. Giles waited patiently until Deakins had picked up his sandwich and taken a bite.

'I do hope you like smoked salmon,' said Mrs Barrington.

'Spiffing,' said Giles, before his friends had a chance to admit that they had never tasted smoked salmon before. 'We only get fish paste sandwiches at school,' he added.

'So, tell me how you're all getting on at school,' said Mrs Barrington.

'Room for improvement, is how I think the Frob describes my efforts,' said Giles, as he took another sandwich. 'But Deakins is top of everything.'

'Except for English,' said Deakins, speaking for the first time, 'Harry pipped me in that subject by a couple of per cent.'

'And did you pip anyone in anything, Giles?' asked his mother.

'He came second in maths, Mrs Barrington,' said Harry, coming to Giles's rescue. 'He has a natural gift for figures.'

'Just like his grandfather,' said Mrs Barrington.

'That's a nice picture of you above the fireplace, Mrs Barrington,' said Deakins.

She smiled. 'It's not me, Deakins, it's my dear mother.' Deakins bowed his head before Mrs Barrington quickly added, 'But what a charming compliment. She was considered a great beauty in her day.'

'Who painted it?' asked Harry, coming to Deakins's rescue.

'László,' replied Mrs Barrington. 'Why do you ask?'

'Because I was wondering if the portrait of the gentleman in the hall might be by the same artist.'

'How very observant of you, Harry,' said Mrs Barrington. 'The painting you saw in the hall is of my father, and was indeed also painted by László.'

'What does your father do?' asked Harry.

'Harry never stops asking questions,' said Giles. 'One just has to get used to it.'

Mrs Barrington smiled. 'He imports wines to this country, in particular, sherries from Spain.'

'Just like Harvey's,' said Deakins, his mouth full of cucumber sandwich.

'Just like Harvey's,' repeated Mrs Barrington. Giles grinned. 'Do have another sandwich, Harry,' said Mrs Barrington, noticing that his eyes were fixed on the plate.

'Thank you,' said Harry, unable to choose between smoked salmon, cucumber, or egg and tomato. He settled for salmon, wondering what it would taste like.

'And how about you, Deakins?'

'Thank you, Mrs Barrington,' he said, and took another cucumber sandwich.

'I can't go on calling you Deakins,' said Giles's mother. 'It makes you sound like one of the servants. Do tell me your Christian name.'

Deakins bowed his head again. 'I prefer to be called Deakins,' he said.

'It's Al,' said Giles.

'Such a nice name,' said Mrs Barrington, 'although I expect your mother calls you Alan.'

'No she doesn't,' said Deakins, his head still bowed. The other two boys looked surprised by this revelation, but said nothing. 'My name's Algernon,' he finally spluttered.

Giles burst out laughing.

Mrs Barrington paid no attention to her son's outburst. 'Your mother must be an admirer of Oscar Wilde,' she said.

'Yes, she is,' said Deakins. 'But I wish she'd called me Jack, or even Ernest.'

'I wouldn't let it worry you,' said Mrs Barrington. 'After all, Giles suffers from a similar indignity.'

'Mother, you promised you wouldn't—'

'You must get him to tell you his middle name,' she said, ignoring the protest. When Giles didn't respond, Harry and Deakins looked at Mrs Barrington hopefully. 'Marmaduke,' she declared with a sigh. 'Like his father and grandfather before him.'

'If either of you tell anyone about this when we get back to school,' Giles said, looking at his two friends, 'I swear I'll kill you, and I mean, kill you.' Both boys laughed.

'Do you have a middle name, Harry?' asked Mrs Barrington.

Harry was about to reply when the drawing-room door flew open and a man who couldn't have been mistaken for a servant strode into the room carrying a large parcel. Harry looked up at a man who could only have been Mr Hugo. Giles leapt up and ran towards his father, who handed him the parcel and said, 'Happy birthday, my boy.'

'Thank you, Papa,' said Giles, and immediately began to untie the ribbon.

'Before you open your present, Giles,' said his mother, 'perhaps you should first introduce your guests to Papa.'

'Sorry, Papa. These are my two best friends, Deakins and Harry,' said Giles, placing the gift on the table. Harry noticed that Giles's father had the same athletic build and restless energy he'd assumed was uniquely his son's.

'Pleased to meet you, Deakins,' said Mr Barrington, shaking him by the hand. He then turned to Harry. 'Good afternoon, Clifton,' he added, before sitting down in the empty chair next to his wife. Harry was puzzled that Mr Barrington didn't shake hands with him. And how did he know his name was Clifton?

Once the under-butler had served Mr Barrington

with a cup of tea, Giles removed the wrapping from his present and let out a yelp of delight when he saw the Roberts radio. He pushed the plug into a wall socket and began to tune the radio to different stations. The boys applauded and laughed with each new sound that was emitted from the large wooden box.

'Giles tells me that he came second in mathematics this term,' said Mrs Barrington, turning to her husband.

'Which doesn't make up for him being bottom in almost every other subject,' he retorted. Giles tried not to look embarrassed, as he continued to search for another station on his radio.

'But you should have seen the goal he scored against Avonhurst,' said Harry. 'We're all expecting him to captain the eleven next year.'

'Goals aren't going to get him into Eton,' said Mr Barrington, not looking at Harry. 'It's time the boy buckled down and worked harder.'

No one spoke for some time, until Mrs Barrington broke the silence. 'Are you the Clifton who sings in the choir at St Mary Redcliffe?' she asked.

'Harry's the treble soloist,' said Giles. 'In fact, he's a choral scholar.'

Harry became aware that Giles's father was now staring at him.

'I thought I recognized you,' said Mrs Barrington. 'Giles's grandfather and I attended a performance of the Messiah at St Mary's, when the choir of St Bede's joined forces with Bristol Grammar School. Your *I Know That My Redeemer Liveth* was quite magnificent, Harry.'

'Thank you, Mrs Barrington,' said Harry, blushing.

'Are you hoping to go on to Bristol Grammar School after you leave St Bede's, Clifton?' asked Mr Barrington.

Clifton again, thought Harry. 'Only if I win a scholarship, sir,' he replied.

'But why is that important?' asked Mrs Barrington. 'Surely you will be offered a place, like any other boy?'

'Because my mother wouldn't be able to afford the fees, Mrs Barrington. She's a waitress at the Royal Hotel.'

'But wouldn't your father—'

'He's dead,' said Harry. 'He was killed in the war.' He watched carefully to see how Mr Barrington would react, but like a good poker player he gave nothing away.

'I'm sorry,' said Mrs Barrington. 'I didn't realize.'

The door opened behind Harry and the under-butler entered, carrying a two-tier birthday cake on a silver tray which he placed on the centre of the table. After Giles had succeeded in blowing out all twelve candles with one puff, everyone applauded.

'And when's your birthday, Clifton?' asked Mr Barrington.

'It was last month, sir,' Harry replied.

Mr Barrington looked away.

The under-butler removed the candles before handing the young master a large cake knife. Giles cut deep into the cake and placed five uneven slices on the tea plates the maid had laid out on the table.

Deakins devoured the lumps of icing that had fallen on to his plate before taking a bite of the cake. Harry followed Mrs Barrington's lead. He picked up the small silver fork by the side of his plate, using it to remove a tiny piece of his cake before placing it back on the plate.

Only Mr Barrington didn't touch his cake. Suddenly, without warning, he rose from his place and left without another word.

Giles's mother made no attempt to conceal her surprise at her husband's behaviour, but she said nothing. Harry never took his eyes off Mr Hugo as he left the room, while Deakins, having finished his cake, turned his attention back to the smoked salmon sand-wiches, clearly oblivious to what was going on around him.

Once the door was closed, Mrs Barrington continued to chat as if nothing unusual had happened. 'I'm sure you'll win a scholarship to Bristol Grammar, Harry, especially considering everything Giles has told me about you. You're obviously a very clever boy, as well as a gifted singer.'

'Giles does have a tendency to exaggerate, Mrs Barrington,' said Harry. 'I can assure you only Deakins is certain of winning a scholarship.'

'But doesn't BGS offer grants for music scholars?' she asked.

'Not for trebles,' said Harry. 'They won't take the risk.'

'I'm not sure I understand,' said Mrs Barrington. 'Nothing can take away the years of choral training you've been put through.'

'True, but sadly no one can predict what will happen when your voice breaks. Some trebles end up as basses or baritones, and the really lucky ones become tenors, but there's no way of telling in advance.'

'Why not?' asked Deakins, taking an interest for the first time.

'There are plenty of treble soloists who can't even get a place in their local choir once their voice has broken. Ask Master Ernest Lough. Every household in England has heard him sing *Oh, for the wings of a dove*, but after his voice broke no one ever heard from him again.'

'You're just going to have to work harder,' said Deakins between mouthfuls. 'Don't forget the grammar school awards twelve scholarships every year, and I can only win one of them,' he added matter-of-factly.

'But that's the problem,' said Harry. 'If I'm going to

work any harder, I'll have to give up the choir, and without my bursary, I'd have to leave St Bede's, so . . .'

'You're between a rock and a hard place,' said Deakins.

Harry had never heard the expression before and decided to ask Deakins later what it meant.

'Well, one thing's for certain,' said Mrs Barrington, 'Giles isn't likely to win a scholarship to any school.'

'Maybe not,' said Harry. 'But Bristol Grammar isn't likely to turn down a left-handed batsman of his calibre.'

'Then we'll have to hope that Eton feels the same way,' said Mrs Barrington, 'because that's where his father wants him to go.'

'I don't want to go to Eton,' said Giles, putting down his fork. 'I want to go to BGS and be with my friends.'

'I'm sure you'll make a lot of new friends at Eton,' said his mother. 'And it would be a great disappointment to your father if you didn't follow in his footsteps.'

The under-butler coughed. Mrs Barrington looked out of the window to see a car drawing up at the bottom of the steps. 'I think the time has come for you all to return to school,' she said. 'I certainly don't want to be responsible for anyone being late for prep.'

Harry looked longingly at the large plate of sandwiches and the half-finished birthday cake but reluctantly rose from his place and began to walk towards the door. He glanced back once and could have sworn he saw Deakins put a sandwich in his pocket. He took one last look out of the window and was surprised to notice, for the first time, a gangly young girl with long pigtails who was curled up in the corner reading a book.

'That's my frightful sister, Emma,' said Giles. 'She never stops reading. Just ignore her.' Harry smiled at Emma, but she didn't look up. Deakins didn't give her a second look.

Mrs Barrington accompanied the three boys to the front door, where she shook hands with Harry and Deakins. 'I do hope you'll both come again soon,' she said. 'You're such a good influence on Giles.'

'Thank you very much for having us to tea, Mrs Barrington,' Harry said. Deakins just nodded. Both boys looked away when she hugged her son and gave him a kiss.

As the chauffeur drove down the long driveway towards the gates, Harry looked out of the back window at the house. He didn't notice Emma staring out of the window at the disappearing car.

7

THE SCHOOL TUCK SHOP was open between four and six every Tuesday and Thursday afternoon.

Harry rarely visited the 'Emporium', as it was known by the boys, since he only had two shillings' pocket money a term, and he knew his mother wouldn't appreciate any little extras appearing on his end-of-term account. However, on Deakins's birthday, Harry made an exception to this rule, as he intended to purchase a one-penny bar of fudge for his friend.

Despite Harry's rare visits to the tuck shop, a bar of Fry's Five Boys chocolate could be found on his desk every Tuesday and Thursday evening. Although there was a school rule that no boy could spend more than sixpence a week in the tuck shop, Giles would also leave a packet of Liquorice Allsorts for Deakins, making it clear to his friends that he expected nothing in return.

When Harry arrived at the tuck shop that Tuesday, he joined a long queue of boys waiting to be served. His mouth watered as he stared at the neatly stacked rows of chocolate, fudge, jelly babies, liquorice and, the latest craze, Smiths potato crisps. He'd considered buying a packet for himself, but after a recent introduction to Mr Wilkins Micawber, he had been left in no doubt about the value of sixpence.

As Harry ogled the Emporium's treasures, he heard Giles's voice and noticed that he was a few places ahead of him in the queue. He was just about to hail his friend when he saw Giles remove a bar of chocolate from a shelf and slip it into his trouser pocket. A few moments later, a packet of chewing gum followed. When Giles reached the front of the queue, he placed on the counter a box of Liquorice Allsorts, 2d, and a bag of crisps, 1d, which Mr Swivals, the master in charge of the shop, entered neatly in his ledger against the name of Barrington. The two other items remained in Giles's pocket, unaccounted for.

Harry was horrified, and before Giles could turn round, he slipped out of the shop, not wanting his friend to spot him. Harry walked slowly around the school block, trying to work out why Giles would want to steal anything, when he could so obviously afford to pay. He assumed there had to be some simple explanation, although he couldn't imagine what it might be.

Harry went up to his study just before prep, to find the pilfered bar of chocolate on his desk, and Deakins tucking into a box of Liquorice Allsorts. He found it difficult to concentrate on the causes of the Industrial Revolution while he tried to decide what, if anything, he should do about his discovery.

By the end of prep, he'd made his decision. He placed the unopened bar of chocolate in the top drawer of his desk, having decided he would return it to the tuck shop on Thursday, without telling Giles.

Harry didn't sleep that night, and after breakfast he took Deakins to one side and explained why he hadn't been able to give him a birthday present. Deakins couldn't hide his disbelief.

'My dad's been having the same problem in his shop,' said Deakins. 'It's called shoplifting. The *Daily Mail* is blaming it on the Depression.'

'I don't think Giles's family will have been affected much by the Depression,' said Harry with some feeling.

Deakins nodded thoughtfully. 'Perhaps you should tell the Frob?'

'Sneak on my best friend?' said Harry. 'Never.'

'But if Giles is caught he could be expelled,' said Deakins. 'The least you can do is warn him you've found out what he's up to.'

'I'll think about it,' said Harry. 'But in the meantime I'm going to return anything Giles gives me to the tuck shop without letting him know.'

Deakins leant over. 'Could you take my stuff back as well?' he whispered. 'I never go to the tuck shop, so I wouldn't know what to do.'

Harry agreed to take on the responsibility, and after that he went to the tuck shop twice a week and placed Giles's unwanted gifts back on the shelves. He had concluded that Deakins was right and that he would have to confront his friend before he was caught, but decided to put it off until the end of term.

◄○►

'Good shot, Barrington,' said Mr Frobisher as the ball crossed the boundary. A ripple of applause broke out around the ground. 'Mark my words, headmaster, Barrington will play for Eton against Harrow at Lord's.'

'Not if Giles has anything to do with it,' Harry whispered to Deakins.

'What are you doing for the summer hols, Harry?' asked Deakins, seemingly oblivious to all that was going on around him.

'I don't have any plans to visit Tuscany this year, if that's what you're asking,' Harry replied with a grin.

'I don't think Giles really wants to go either,' said

Deakins. 'After all, the Italians have never understood cricket.'

'Well, I'd be happy to change places with him,' said Harry. 'It doesn't bother me that Michelangelo, Da Vinci and Caravaggio were never introduced to the finer subtleties of leg break bowling, not to mention all that pasta he'll be expected to wade through.'

'So where are you going?' asked Deakins.

'A week on the Riviera of the West,' said Harry with bravado. 'The grand pier at Weston-super-Mare is usually the high spot, followed by fish and chips at Coffins café. Care to join me?'

'Can't spare the time,' said Deakins, who clearly thought Harry was being serious.

'And why's that?' asked Harry, playing along.

'Too much work to do.'

'You intend to go on working during the holidays?' asked Harry in disbelief.

'Work *is* a holiday for me,' said Deakins. 'I enjoy it every bit as much as Giles does his cricket, and you do your singing.'

'But where do you work?'

'In the municipal library, clot. They have everything I need.'

'Can I join you?' asked Harry, sounding just as serious. 'I need all the help I can get if I'm to have any chance of winning a scholarship to BGS.'

'Only if you agree to remain silent at all times,' said Deakins. Harry would have laughed, but he knew his friend didn't consider work a laughing matter.

'But I desperately need some help with my Latin grammar,' said Harry. 'I still don't understand the consecutive clause, let alone subjunctives, and if I don't manage a pass mark in the Latin paper, it's curtains, even if I do well in every other subject.'

'I'd be willing to help you with your Latin,' said Deakins, 'if you do me a favour in return.'

'Name it,' said Harry, 'though I can't believe you're hoping to perform a solo at this year's carol service.'

'Good shot, Barrington,' said Mr Frobisher again. Harry joined in the applause. 'That's his third half-century this season, headmaster,' added Mr Frobisher.

'Don't be frivolous, Harry,' said Deakins. 'The truth is, my dad needs someone to take over the morning paper round during the summer holidays, and I've suggested you. The pay is a shilling a week, and as long as you can report to the shop by six o'clock every morning, the position's yours.'

'Six o'clock?' said Harry scornfully. 'When you've got an uncle who wakes up the whole house at five, that's the least of your problems.'

'Then you'd be willing to take on the job?'

'Yes of course,' said Harry. 'But why don't you want it? A bob a week is not to be sniffed at.'

'Don't remind me,' said Deakins, 'but I can't ride a bicycle.'

'Oh hell,' said Harry. 'I don't even have a bicycle.'

'I didn't say I didn't *have* a bicycle,' sighed Deakins, 'I said I couldn't ride one.'

'Clifton,' said Mr Frobisher as the cricketers walked off the ground for tea, 'I'd like to see you in my study after prep.'

◄o►

Harry had always liked Mr Frobisher, who was one of the few masters who treated him as an equal. He also didn't appear to have any favourites, while some of the other beaks left him in no doubt that a docker's son should never have been allowed to enter the hallowed portals of St Bede's however good his voice was.

When the bell rang at the end of prep, Harry put down his pen and walked across the corridor to Mr Frobisher's study. He had no idea why his housemaster wanted to see him, and hadn't given the matter a great deal of thought.

Harry knocked on the study door.

'Come,' said the voice of a man who never wasted words. Harry opened the door and was surprised not to be greeted with the usual Frob smile.

Mr Frobisher stared up at Harry as he came to a halt in front of his desk. 'It has been brought to my attention, Clifton, that you have been stealing from the tuck shop.' Harry's mind went blank as he tried to think of a response that wouldn't condemn Giles. 'You were seen by a prefect, removing goods from the shelves,' continued Frobisher in the same uncompromising tone, 'and then slipping out of the shop before you reached the front of the queue.'

Harry wanted to say, 'Not removing, sir, returning,' but all he managed was, 'I have never taken anything from the tuck shop, sir.' Despite the fact that he was telling the truth, he could still feel his cheeks reddening.

'Then how do you explain your twice weekly visits to the Emporium, when there isn't a single entry against your name in Mr Swivals's ledger?'

Mr Frobisher waited patiently, but Harry knew if he told the truth, Giles would surely be expelled.

'And this bar of chocolate and packet of Liquorice Allsorts were found in the top drawer of your desk, not long after the tuck shop had closed.'

Harry looked down at the sweets, but still said nothing.

'I'm waiting for an explanation, Clifton,' said Mr Frobisher. After another long pause, he added, 'I am of course aware that you have far less pocket money than any other boy in your class, but that is no excuse for stealing.'

'I have never stolen anything in my life,' said Harry.

It was Mr Frobisher's turn to look dismayed. He rose from behind his desk. 'If that is the case, Clifton – and I want to believe you – you will report back to me after choir practice with a full explanation of how you came to be in possession of tuck you clearly didn't pay for. Should you fail to satisfy me, we will both be paying a visit to the headmaster, and I have no doubt what his recommendation will be.'

Harry left the room. The moment he closed the door behind him, he felt sick. He made his way back to his study, hoping Giles wouldn't be there. When he opened the door, the first thing he saw was another bar of chocolate on his desk.

Giles looked up. 'Are you feeling all right?' he asked when he saw Harry's flushed face. Harry didn't reply. He placed the bar of chocolate in a drawer and left for choir practice without saying a word to either of his friends. Giles's eyes never left him, and once the door was closed, he turned to Deakins and asked casually, 'What's his problem?' Deakins went on writing as if he hadn't heard the question. 'Didn't you hear me, cloth ears?' said Giles. 'Why's Harry in a sulk?'

'All I know is that he had an appointment to see the Frob.'

'Why?' asked Giles, sounding more interested.

'I've no idea,' said Deakins, who didn't stop writing.

Giles stood up and strolled across the room to Deakins's side. 'What aren't you telling me?' he demanded, grabbing him by the ear.

Deakins dropped his pen, nervously touched the bridge of his glasses and pushed them further up his

nose, before he eventually squeaked, 'He's in some sort
of trouble.'

'What sort of trouble?' asked Giles, twisting the ear.

'I think he might even be expelled,' whimpered
Deakins.

Giles let go of his ear and burst out laughing. 'Harry,
expelled?' he scoffed. 'The Pope's more likely to be
defrocked.' He would have returned to his desk if he
hadn't noticed beads of sweat appearing on Deakins's
forehead. 'What for?' he asked more quietly.

'The Frob thinks he's been stealing from the tuck
shop,' said Deakins.

If Deakins had looked up, he would have seen that
Giles had turned ashen white. A moment later, he heard
the door close. He picked up his pen and tried to
concentrate, but for the first time in his life, he didn't
finish his prep.

◄○►

When Harry came out of choir practice an hour later,
he spotted Fisher leaning on the wall, unable to mask a
smile. That was when he realized who must have
reported him. He ignored Fisher and strolled back to
his house as if he didn't have a care in the world,
whereas in fact he felt like a man mounting the gallows,
knowing that unless he ditched his closest friend, a stay
of execution would not be possible. He hesitated before
knocking on his housemaster's door.

The 'Come' was far gentler than it had been earlier
that afternoon, but when Harry entered the room he
was greeted with the same uncompromising stare. He
bowed his head.

'I owe you a sincere apology, Clifton,' said Frobisher,
rising from behind his desk. 'I now realize that you were
not the culprit.'

Harry's heart was still beating fast, but his anxiety was now for Giles. 'Thank you, sir,' he said, his head still bowed. He had so many questions he would have liked to ask the Frob, but he knew none of them would be answered.

Mr Frobisher stepped out from behind his desk and shook hands with Harry, something he'd never done before. 'You'd better hurry, Clifton, if you hope to get any supper.'

When Harry came out of the Frob's study, he walked slowly towards the dining room. Fisher was standing by the door, a surprised look on his face. Harry walked straight past him and took his place on the end of the bench next to Deakins. The seat opposite him was empty.

8

GILES DIDN'T SHOW UP for supper, and his bed wasn't slept in that night. If St Bede's hadn't lost their annual fixture against Avonhurst by thirty-one runs, Harry suspected that not many boys or even masters would have noticed he was missing.

But, unfortunately for Giles, it was a home match, so everyone had an opinion on why the school's opening batsman had not taken his guard at the crease, not least Fisher, who was telling anyone who cared to listen that the wrong man had been rusticated.

◄○►

Harry hadn't been looking forward to the holidays; not just because he wondered if he'd ever see Giles again, but also because it meant returning to No. 27 Still House Lane and once again having to share a room with his uncle Stan, who more often than not returned home drunk.

After spending the evening going over old exam papers, Harry would climb into bed around ten. He quickly fell asleep, only to be woken sometime after midnight by his uncle, who was often so drunk he couldn't find his own bed. The sound of Stan trying to pee into a chamberpot, and not always hitting the target, was something that would remain etched in Harry's mind for the rest of his life.

Once Stan had collapsed on to his bed – he rarely bothered to get undressed – Harry would try to fall asleep a second time, often to be woken a few minutes later by loud drunken snores. He longed to be back at St Bede's, sharing a dormitory with twenty-nine other boys.

Harry still hoped that in an unguarded moment Stan might let slip some more details about his father's death, but most of the time he was too incoherent to answer even the simplest question. On one of the rare occasions when he was sober enough to speak, he told Harry to bugger off and warned him that if he raised the subject again, he'd thrash him.

The only good thing about sharing a room with Stan was that there was never any chance of his being late for his paper round.

Harry's days at Still House Lane fell into a well-ordered routine: up at five, one slice of toast for break-fast – he no longer licked his uncle's bowl – report to Mr Deakins at the newsagent's by six, stack the papers in the correct order, then deliver them. The whole exercise took about two hours, allowing him to be back home in time for a cup of tea with Mum before she went off to work. At around eight thirty Harry would set off for the library, where he would meet up with Deakins, who was always sitting on the top step waiting for someone to open the doors.

In the afternoon, Harry would report for choir prac-tice at St Mary Redcliffe, as part of his obligation to St Bede's. He never considered it an obligation because he enjoyed singing so much. In fact, he'd more than once whispered, 'Please God, when my voice breaks, let me be a tenor, and I'll never ask for anything else.'

After he returned home for tea in the evening, Harry

would work at the kitchen table for a couple of hours before going to bed, dreading his uncle's return every bit as much as he had Fisher's in his first week at St Bede's. At least Fisher had departed for Colston's Grammar School, so Harry assumed their paths would never cross again.

◄O►

Harry was looking forward to his final year at St Bede's, although he wasn't in any doubt just how much his life would change if he and his two friends ended up going their separate ways: Giles to he knew not where, Deakins to Bristol Grammar, while if he failed to win a scholarship to BGS, he might well have to return to Merrywood Elementary, and then, at the age of fourteen, leave school and look for a job. He tried not to think about the consequences of failure, despite Stan never missing an opportunity to remind him he could always find work at the docks.

'The boy should never have been allowed to go to that stuck-up school in the first place,' he regularly told Maisie once she'd placed his bowl of porridge in front of him. 'It's given him ideas above his station,' he added, as if Harry wasn't there. A view that Harry felt Fisher would have happily agreed with, but then he'd long ago come to the conclusion that Uncle Stan and Fisher had a lot in common.

'But surely Harry should be given the chance to better himself?' countered Maisie.

'Why?' said Stan. 'If the docks was good enough for me and his old man, why aren't they good enough for him?' he demanded with a finality that brooked no argument.

'Perhaps the boy's cleverer than both of us,' suggested Maisie.

This silenced Stan for a moment, but after another spoonful of porridge, he declared, 'Depends on what you mean by clever. After all, there's clever and then there's clever.' He took another spoonful, but added nothing more to this profound observation.

Harry would cut his slice of toast into four pieces as he listened to his uncle play the same record again and again every morning. He never spoke up for himself, as clearly Stan had already made up his mind on the subject of Harry's future and nothing was going to budge him. What Stan didn't realize was that his constant jibes only inspired Harry to work even harder.

'Can't hang around here all day,' would be Stan's final comment, especially if he felt he was losing the argument. 'Some of us have a job to do,' he added as he rose from the table. No one bothered to argue. 'And another thing,' he said as he opened the kitchen door. 'None of you've noticed the boy's gone soft. He doesn't even lick my porridge bowl no longer. God knows what they've been teachin' him at that school.' The door slammed behind him.

'Take no notice of your uncle,' said Harry's mother. 'He's just jealous. He doesn't like the fact that we're all so proud of you. And even he'll have to change his tune when you win that scholarship, just like your friend Deakins.'

'But that's the problem, Mum,' said Harry. 'I'm not like Deakins, and I'm beginning to wonder if it's all worth it.'

The rest of the family stared at Harry in silent disbelief, until Grandpa piped up for the first time in days. 'I wish I'd been given the chance to go to Bristol Grammar School.'

'Why's that, Grandpa?' shouted Harry.

'Because if I had, we wouldn't have had to live with your uncle Stan all these years.'

—◁◦▷—

Harry enjoyed his morning paper round, and not just because it got him out of the house. As the weeks went by, he came to know several of Mr Deakins's regulars, some of whom had heard him sing at St Mary's and would wave when he delivered their paper, while others offered him a cup of tea, even an apple. Mr Deakins had warned him that there were two dogs he should avoid on the round; within a fortnight, both of them were wagging their tails when he got off his bicycle.

Harry was delighted to discover that Mr Holcombe was one of Mr Deakins's regular customers, and they often had a word when he dropped off his copy of *The Times* each morning. His first teacher left Harry in no doubt that he didn't want to see him back at Merrywood, and added that if he needed any extra tuition, he was free most evenings.

When Harry returned to the newsagent's after his round, Mr Deakins would always slip a penny bar of Fry's chocolate into his satchel before sending him on his way. It reminded him of Giles. He often wondered what had become of his friend. Neither he nor Deakins had heard from Giles since the day Mr Frobisher had asked to see Harry after prep. Then, before he left the shop to go home, he always paused in front of the display cabinet to admire a watch he knew he'd never be able to afford. He didn't even bother to ask Mr Deakins how much it cost.

There were only two regular breaks in Harry's weekly routine. He would always try to spend Saturday morning with Old Jack, taking with him copies of all the previous week's *Times*, and on Sunday evenings, once he'd fulfilled his duties at St Mary's, he would rush across the city so he could be at Holy Nativity in time for Evensong.

A frail Miss Monday would beam with pride during the treble solo. She only hoped she would live long enough to see Harry go up to Cambridge. She had plans to tell him about the choir at King's College, but not until he'd won a place at Bristol Grammar.

⟨○⟩

'Is Mr Frobisher going to make you a prefect?' asked Old Jack, even before Harry had sunk into his usual seat on the opposite side of the carriage.

'I've no idea,' replied Harry. 'Mind you, the Frob always says,' he added, tugging his lapels, '*Clifton, in life you get what you deserve, no more and certainly no less.*'

Old Jack chuckled, and just stopped himself saying, 'Not a bad imitation of the Frob.' He satisfied himself with, 'Then my bet is you're about to become a prefect.'

'I'd rather win a scholarship to BGS,' said Harry, suddenly sounding older than his years.

'And what about your friends, Barrington and Deakins?' Old Jack asked, trying to lighten the mood. 'Are they also destined for higher things?'

'They'll never make Deakins a prefect,' said Harry. 'He can't even take care of himself, let alone anyone else. In any case, he's hoping to be the library monitor, and as no one else wants the job, Mr Frobisher shouldn't lose too much sleep over that appointment.'

'And Barrington?'

'I'm not sure he'll be coming back next term,' said Harry wistfully. 'Even if he does, I'm fairly certain they won't make him a prefect.'

'Don't underestimate his father,' said Old Jack. 'That

man will undoubtedly have found a way to ensure that his son returns on the first day of term. And I wouldn't put money on his not being a prefect.'

'Let's hope you're right,' said Harry.

'And if I am, I presume he will then follow his father to Eton?'

'Not if he has any say in it. Giles would prefer to go to BGS with Deakins and me.'

'If he doesn't get into Eton, they're unlikely to offer him a place at the grammar school. Their entrance exam is one of the hardest in the country.'

'He told me he's got a plan.'

'It had better be a good one, if he hopes to fool his father as well as the examiners.'

Harry didn't comment.

'How's your mother?' asked Old Jack, changing the subject, as it was clear that the boy didn't want to go any further down that path.

'She's just been promoted. She's now in charge of all the waitresses in the Palm Court room, and reports directly to Mr Frampton, the hotel manager.'

'You must be very proud of her,' said Old Jack.

'Yes, I am, sir, and what's more, I'm going to prove it.'

'What do you have in mind?'

Harry let him in to his secret. The old man listened attentively, and nodded his approval from time to time. He could see one small problem, but it wasn't insurmountable.

⬦

When Harry returned to the shop having completed his last paper round before going back to school, Mr Deakins gave him a shilling bonus. 'You're the best paper boy I've ever had,' he said.

'Thank you, sir,' said Harry, pocketing the money. 'Mr Deakins, can I ask you a question?'

'Yes, of course, Harry.'

Harry walked over to the cabinet, where two watches were displayed side by side on the top shelf. 'How much is that one?' he asked, pointing to the Ingersoll.

Mr Deakins smiled. He'd been waiting for Harry to ask that question for some weeks, and had his answer well prepared. 'Six shillings,' he said.

Harry couldn't believe it. He'd been sure that such a magnificent object would cost more than double that. But despite his having put aside half his earnings each week, even with Mr Deakins's bonus, he was still a shilling short.

'You do realize, Harry, that it's a lady's watch?' said Mr Deakins.

'Yes, I do, sir,' said Harry. 'I was hoping to give it to my mother.'

'Then you can have it for five shillings.'

Harry couldn't believe his luck.

'Thank you, sir,' he said as he handed over four shillings, one sixpence, one thruppence and three pennies, leaving him with empty pockets.

Mr Deakins took the watch out of the display cabinet, discreetly removed the sixteen-shilling price tag and then placed it in a smart box.

Harry left the shop whistling. Mr Deakins smiled and placed the ten-shilling note in the till, delighted that he'd fulfilled his part of the bargain.

9

THE BELL WENT.

'Time to get undressed,' said the duty prefect in the new boys' dorm on the first evening of term. They all looked so small and helpless, Harry thought. One or two of them were clearly fighting back tears, while others were looking around, uncertain what they should do next. One boy was facing the wall, shaking. Harry walked quickly across to him.

'What's your name?' Harry asked gently.

'Stevenson.'

'Well, I'm Clifton. Welcome to St Bede's.'

'And I'm Tewkesbury,' said a boy standing on the other side of Stevenson's bed.

'Welcome to St Bede's, Tewkesbury.'

'Thank you, Clifton. Actually, my father and grand-father were here, before they went on to Eton.'

'I don't doubt it,' said Harry. 'And I'll bet they captained Eton against Harrow at Lord's,' he added, immediately regretting his words.

'No, my father was a wet bob,' said Tewkesbury unperturbed, 'not a dry bob.'

'A wet bob?' said Harry.

'He captained Oxford against Cambridge in the boat race.'

Stevenson burst into tears.

'What's the matter?' asked Harry, sitting down on the bed beside him.

'My dad's a tram driver.'

Everyone else stopped unpacking and stared at Stevenson.

'Is that right?' said Harry. 'Then I'd better let you into a secret,' he added, loud enough to be sure that every boy in the dormitory could hear his words. 'I'm the son of a dock worker. I wouldn't be surprised to discover that you're the new choral scholar.'

'No,' said Stevenson, 'I'm an open scholar.'

'Many congratulations,' said Harry, shaking him by the hand. 'You follow in a long and noble tradition.'

'Thank you. But I have a problem,' the boy whispered.

'And what's that, Stevenson?'

'I don't have any toothpaste.'

'Don't worry about that, old chap,' said Tewkesbury, 'my mother always packs a spare one.'

Harry smiled as the bell rang again. 'Everyone into bed,' he said firmly as he walked across the dormitory towards the door.

He heard a voice whisper, 'Thank you for the toothpaste.'

'Think nothing of it, old chap.'

'Now,' said Harry as he flicked off the light, 'I don't want to hear another word from any of you until the bell goes at six thirty tomorrow morning.' He waited for a few moments before he heard someone whispering. 'I meant it – not another word.' He smiled as he walked down the staircase to join Deakins and Barrington in the senior prefects' study.

Harry had been surprised by two things when he arrived back at St Bede's on the first day of term. No sooner had he walked through the front door than Mr Frobisher took him to one side.

'Congratulations, Clifton,' he said softly. 'It won't be announced until assembly tomorrow morning, but you're to be the new school captain.'

'It should have been Giles,' said Harry without thinking.

'Barrington will be captain of games, and—'

Harry had leapt in the air the moment he heard the news that his friend would be returning to St Bede's. Old Jack had been right when he said Mr Hugo would find a way to make sure his son was back for the first day of term.

When Giles walked into the front hall a few moments later, the two boys shook hands, and Harry never once referred to the subject that must have been on both their minds.

'What are the new bugs like?' Giles asked as Harry entered the study.

'One of them reminds me of you,' said Harry.

'Tewkesbury, no doubt.'

'You know him?'

'No, but Papa was at Eton at the same time as his father.'

'I told him I was the son of a docker,' said Harry as he slumped into the only comfortable chair in the room.

'Did you now?' said Giles. 'And did he tell you he's the son of a cabinet minister?'

Harry said nothing.

'Are there any others I should keep an eye out for?' asked Giles.

'Stevenson,' said Harry. 'He's a cross between Deakins and me.'

'Then we'd better lock the fire-escape door before he makes a dash for it.'

Harry often thought about where he might be now if Old Jack hadn't talked him into returning to St Bede's that night.

'What's our first lesson tomorrow?' asked Harry, checking his timetable.

'Latin,' said Deakins. 'Which is why I'm guiding Giles through the first Punic war.'

'264 to 241 BC,' said Giles.

'I bet you're enjoying that,' said Harry.

'Yes, I am,' said Giles, 'and I just can't wait for the sequel, the second Punic war.'

'218 to 201 BC,' said Harry.

'It always amazes me how the Greeks and Romans seemed to know exactly when Christ would be born,' said Giles.

'Ho, ho, ho,' said Harry.

Deakins didn't laugh, but said, 'And finally, we will have to consider the third Punic War, 149 to 146 BC.'

'Do we really need to know about all three of them?' said Giles.

◄○►

St Mary Redcliffe was packed with town and gown who'd come to celebrate an Advent service of eight readings and eight carols. The choir made their entrance through the nave, and advanced slowly down the aisle singing *O Come All Ye Faithful*, then took their places in the choir stalls.

The headmaster read the first lesson. This was followed by *O Little Town of Bethlehem*. The service sheet indicated that the soloist for the third verse would be Master Harry Clifton.

How silently, how silently, the wondrous gift is given, while God . . . Harry's mother sat proudly in the third row, while the old lady sitting next to her wanted to tell everyone in the congregation that they were listening to her grandson. The man seated on the other side of Maisie couldn't hear a word, but you would never have known that from the contented smile on his face. Uncle Stan was nowhere to be seen.

The captain of games read the second lesson, and when Giles returned to his place, Harry noticed that he was seated next to a distinguished-looking man with a head of silver hair, who he assumed must be Sir Walter Barrington. Giles had once told him that his grandfather lived in an even larger house than his, but Harry didn't think that could be possible. On the other side of Giles sat his mother and father. Mrs Barrington smiled across at him, but Mr Barrington didn't once look in his direction.

When the organ struck up the prelude for *We Three Kings*, the congregation rose and sang lustily. The next lesson was read by Mr Frobisher, after which came what Miss Monday anticipated would be the highlight of the service. The thousand-strong congregation didn't stir while Harry sang *Silent Night* with a clarity and confidence that caused even the headmaster to smile.

The library monitor read the next lesson. Harry had already coached him through St Mark's words several times. Deakins had tried to get out of the chore, as he described it to Giles, but Mr Frobisher had insisted; the fourth lesson was always read by the librarian. Deakins wasn't Giles, but he wasn't bad. Harry winked at him as he shuffled back to his seat next to his parents.

The choir then rose to sing *In Dulci Jubilo* while the congregation remained seated. Harry considered the carol to be among the most demanding in their repertoire, because of its unconventional harmonies.

Mr Holcombe closed his eyes so that he could hear the senior choral scholar more clearly. Harry was singing

Now let all hearts be singing when he thought he heard a slight, almost imperceptible, crack in the voice. He assumed Harry must have a cold. Miss Monday knew better. She'd heard those early signs so many times before. She prayed that she was mistaken, but knew her prayer would not be answered. Harry would get through the rest of the service with only a handful of people realizing what had happened, and he would even be able to carry on for a few more weeks, possibly months, but by Easter another child would be singing *Rejoice that the Lord has arisen.*

An old man who'd turned up only moments after the service had begun was among those who weren't in any doubt what had happened. Old Jack left just before the bishop gave his final blessing. He knew Harry wouldn't be able to visit him until the following Saturday, which would give him enough time to work out how to answer the inevitable question.

◄○►

'Might I have a private word with you, Clifton?' said Mr Frobisher as the bell sounded for the end of prep. 'Perhaps you'd join me in my study.' Harry would never forget the last time he'd heard those words.

When Harry closed the study door, his housemaster beckoned him towards a seat by the fire, something he had never done before. 'I just wanted to assure you, Harry' – another first – 'that the fact you are no longer able to sing in the choir will not affect your bursary. We at St Bede's are well aware that the contribution you have made to school life stretches far beyond the chapel.'

'Thank you, sir,' said Harry.

'However, we must now consider your future. The

music master tells me that it will be some time before your voice fully recovers, which I'm afraid means that we must be realistic about your chances of being offered a choral scholarship to Bristol Grammar School.'

'There is no chance,' said Harry calmly.

'I have to agree with you,' said Frobisher. 'I'm relieved to find you understand the situation. But,' he continued, 'I would be happy to enter your name for an open scholarship to BGS. However,' he added before Harry had time to respond, 'in the circumstances, you might consider that you'd have a better chance of being offered a bursary at, say, Colston's School, or King's College Gloucester, both of which have far less demanding entrance examinations.'

'No, thank you, sir,' said Harry. 'My first choice remains Bristol Grammar.' He'd said the same thing to Old Jack just as firmly the previous Saturday, when his mentor had mumbled something about not burning your boats.

'So be it,' said Mr Frobisher, who had not expected any other response, but had still felt it was nothing less than his duty to come up with an alternative. 'Now, let's turn this setback to our advantage.'

'How do you suggest I do that, sir?'

'Well, now that you've been released from daily choir practice, you will have more time to prepare for your entrance exam.'

'Yes, sir, but I still have my responsibilities as—'

'And I will do everything in my power to ensure that your duties as school captain are less onerous in future.'

'Thank you, sir.'

'By the way, Harry,' said Frobisher as he rose from his chair, 'I've just read your essay on Jane Austen, and I was fascinated by your suggestion that if Miss Austen had been able to go to university, she might never have written a novel, and even if she had, her work probably wouldn't have been so insightful.'

'Sometimes it's an advantage to be disadvantaged,' said Harry.

'That doesn't sound like Jane Austen,' said Mr Frobisher.

'It isn't,' replied Harry. 'But it was said by someone else who didn't go to university,' he added without explanation.

◄○►

Maisie glanced at her new watch and smiled. 'I'll have to leave now, Harry, if I'm not going to be late for work.'

'Of course, Mum,' said Harry, leaping up from the table. 'I'll walk with you to the tram stop.'

'Harry, have you thought about what you'll do if you don't win that scholarship?' said his mother, finally asking a question she'd been avoiding for weeks.

'Constantly,' said Harry as he opened the door for her. 'But I won't be given much choice in the matter. I'll just have to go back to Merrywood, and when I turn fourteen I'll leave and look for a job.'

10

'DO YOU FEEL READY to face the examiners, my boy?' asked Old Jack.

'As ready as I'm ever likely to be,' replied Harry. 'By the way, I took your advice, and checked over the examination papers for the past ten years. You were right, there's a definite pattern, with some of the same questions coming up at regular intervals.'

'Good. And how's your Latin coming on? We can't afford to fail that, however well we do in your other papers.'

Harry smiled when Old Jack said 'we'. 'Thanks to Deakins I managed 69 per cent in mocks last week, even if I did have Hannibal crossing the Andes.'

'Only about six thousand miles out,' chuckled Old Jack. 'So what do you think will be your biggest problem?'

'The forty boys from St Bede's who are also taking the exam, not to mention the two hundred and fifty from other schools.'

'Forget them,' said Old Jack. 'If you do what you're capable of, they won't be a problem.'

Harry remained silent.

93

'So, how's your voice coming along?' asked Old Jack, who always changed the subject whenever Harry fell silent.

'Nothing new to report,' said Harry. 'It could be weeks before I know if I'm a tenor, a baritone or a bass, and even then, there's no guarantee I'll be any good. One thing's for certain, BGS aren't going to offer me a choral scholarship while I'm like a horse with a broken leg.'

'Snap out of it,' said Old Jack. 'It's not that bad.'

'It's worse,' said Harry. 'If I was a horse, they'd shoot me and put me out of my misery.'

Old Jack laughed. 'So when are the exams?' he asked, even though he knew the answer.

'Thursday week. We start with general knowledge at nine o'clock, and there are five other papers during the day, ending with English at four.'

'It's good that you finish with your favourite subject,' said Jack.

'Let's hope so,' said Harry. 'But pray there's a question on Dickens, because there hasn't been one for the past three years, which is why I've been reading his books after lights out.'

'Wellington wrote in his memoirs,' said Old Jack, 'that the worst moment of any campaign is waiting for the sun to rise on the morning of battle.'

'I agree with the Iron Duke, which means I won't be getting much sleep for the next couple of weeks.'

'All the more reason not to come and see me next Saturday, Harry. You ought to be making better use of your time. In any case, if I remember correctly, it's your birthday.'

'How did you know that?'

'I confess that I didn't read it on the court page of

The Times. But as it fell on the same day last year, I took a gamble and bought a small gift for you.' He picked up a parcel wrapped in a page from one of last week's newspapers, and handed it to Harry.

'Thank you, sir,' said Harry as he untied the string. He removed the newspaper, opened the small dark blue box and stared in disbelief at the man's Ingersoll watch he'd last seen in the display cabinet at Mr Deakins's shop.

'Thank you,' Harry repeated as he strapped the watch on his wrist. He couldn't take his eyes off it for some time, and could only wonder how Old Jack could possibly afford six shillings.

◄◦►

Harry was wide awake long before the sun rose on the morning of the exams. He skipped breakfast in favour of going over some old general knowledge papers, checking capitals against countries from Germany to Brazil, dates of prime ministers from Walpole to Lloyd George, and of monarchs from King Alfred to George V. An hour later he felt ready to face the examiner.

Once again, he was seated in the front row, between Barrington and Deakins. Was this the last time, he wondered. When the clock on the tower struck ten, several masters marched down the rows of desks handing out the general knowledge paper to forty nervous boys. Well, thirty-nine nervous boys, and Deakins.

Harry read through the questions slowly. When he reached number 100, he allowed a smile to cross his face. He picked up his pen, dipped the nib in the inkwell and began to write. Forty minutes later he was back at question 100. He glanced at his watch; he still had another ten minutes in which to double-check his answers. He stopped for a moment at question 34 and reconsidered his original answer. Was it Oliver Cromwell or Thomas Cromwell who was sent to the Tower of London for treason? He recalled the fate of Cardinal Wolsey, and selected the man who'd taken his place as Lord Chancellor.

When the clock began to strike again, Harry had reached question 92. He quickly looked over his last eight answers before his paper was snatched away, the ink still drying on his final answer, Charles Lindbergh.

During the twenty-minute break, Harry, Giles and Deakins walked slowly around the cricket field where Giles had scored a century only a week before.

'Amo, amas, amat,' said Deakins as he painstakingly took them through their conjugations without once referring to *Kennedy's Latin Primer*.

'Amamus, amatis, amant,' repeated Harry as they made their way back towards the examination hall.

When Harry handed in his Latin paper an hour later, he felt confident he'd scored more than the required 60 per cent, and even Giles looked pleased with himself. As the three of them strolled across to the refectory, Harry put an arm around Deakins's shoulder and said, 'Thanks, old chum.'

After Harry had read through the geography paper later that morning, he silently thanked his secret weapon. Old Jack had passed on so much knowledge over the years without ever making him feel that he'd been in a classroom.

Harry didn't pick up a knife or fork during lunch. Giles managed half a pork pie, while Deakins didn't stop eating.

History was the first paper that afternoon, and didn't cause him any anxiety. Henry VIII, Elizabeth, Raleigh, Drake, Napoleon, Nelson and Wellington all marched on to the battlefield, and Harry marched them back off again.

The mathematics paper was far easier than he had expected, and Giles even thought he might have scored another century.

During the final break, Harry returned to his study and glanced over an essay he'd written on *David Copperfield*, confident that he would excel in his favourite subject. He walked slowly back to the examination hall, repeating Mr Holcombe's favourite word again and again. Concentrate.

He stared down at the final paper of the day, to find that this year belonged to Thomas Hardy and Lewis Carroll. He'd read *The Mayor of Casterbridge* and *Alice's Adventures in Wonderland*, but the Mad Hatter, Michael Henchard and the Cheshire Cat were not as familiar to him as Peggotty, Dr Chillip and Barkis. His pen scratched slowly across the page, and when the clock chimed on the hour, he wasn't sure if he'd done enough. He walked out of the hall and into the afternoon sunshine, feeling a little depressed, although it was clear from the looks on the faces of his rivals that no one thought it had been an easy paper. That made him wonder if he was still in with a chance.

–◦–

There followed what Mr Holcombe had often described as the worst part of any exam, those days of endless waiting before the results were formally posted on the school notice board; a time when boys end up doing something they will later regret, almost as if they want to be rusticated rather than learn their fate. One boy was caught drinking cider behind the bicycle shed, another smoking a Woodbine in the lavatory, while a third was seen leaving the local cinema after lights out.

Giles was out for a duck the following Saturday, his first of the season. While Deakins returned to the library, Harry went on long walks, going over every answer in his head again and again. It didn't improve matters.

On Sunday afternoon, Giles had a long net; on Monday, Deakins reluctantly handed over his responsibilities to the new library monitor, and on Tuesday Harry read *Far from the Madding Crowd* and cursed out loud. On Wednesday night, Giles and Harry talked into the small hours, while Deakins slept soundly.

◄o►

Long before the clock on the tower struck ten that Thursday morning, forty boys were already roaming around the quad, hands in pockets, heads bowed as they waited for the headmaster to make his appearance. Although every one of them knew that Dr Oakshott wouldn't be a minute early or a minute late, by five to ten most eyes were staring across the quad waiting for the door of the headmaster's house to open. The rest were looking up at the clock on the great hall, willing the minute hand to move a little faster.

As the first chime sounded, the Reverend Samuel Oakshott opened his front door and stepped out on to the path. He was carrying a sheet of paper in one hand and four tin-tacks in the other. Not a man who left anything to chance. When he reached the end of the path, he opened the little wicket gate and walked across the quad at his usual pace, oblivious to all around him. The boys quickly stood aside, creating a corridor so the headmaster's progress would not be impeded. He came to a halt in front of the notice board as the tenth chime rang out. He posted the exam results on the board, and departed without a word.

Forty boys rushed forward, forming a scrum around the notice board. No one was surprised that Deakins headed the list, with 92 per cent, and had been awarded the Peloquin Scholarship to Bristol Grammar School. Giles leapt in the air, making no attempt to disguise his relief when he saw 64 per cent by his name.

They both turned to look for their friend. Harry was standing alone, far from the madding crowd.

MAISIE CLIFTON

1920–1936

11

When Arthur and me got married, the occasion couldn't have been described as pushing the boat out, but then, neither the Tancocks nor the Cliftons ever did have two brass farthings to rub together. The biggest expense turned out to be the choir, half a crown, and worth every penny. I'd always wanted to be a member of Miss Monday's choir, and although she told me my voice was good enough, I wasn't considered on account of the fact I couldn't read or write.

The reception, if you could call it that, was held at Arthur's parents' terraced house in Still House Lane: a barrel of beer, some peanut butter sandwiches and a dozen pork pies. My brother Stan even brought his own fish and chips. And to top it all, we had to leave early to catch the last bus to Weston-super-Mare for our honeymoon. Arthur booked us into a seafront guest house on the Friday evening, and as it rained for most of the weekend, we rarely left the bedroom.

It felt strange that the second time I had sex was also in Weston-super-Mare. I was shocked when I saw Arthur naked for the first time. A deep red, roughly stitched scar stretched tight across his stomach. Damn the Germans. He never said he'd been wounded during the war.

I wasn't surprised that Arthur became aroused the

moment I pulled off my slip, but I must admit I'd expected him to take his boots off before we made love.

We checked out of the guest house on Sunday afternoon and caught the last bus back to Bristol, as Arthur had to report to the dockyard by six o'clock on Monday morning.

After the wedding, Arthur moved into our house – just until we could afford a place of our own, he told my father, which usually meant until one of our parents passed away. In any case, both our families had lived on Still House Lane for as long as anyone could remember.

Arthur was delighted when I told him I was in the family way, because he wanted at least six babies. My worry was whether the first would be his, but, as only my mum and I knew the truth, there was no reason for Arthur to be suspicious.

Eight months later I gave birth to a boy, and thank God there was nothing to suggest that he wasn't Arthur's. We christened him Harold, which pleased my father, because it meant his name would survive for another generation.

From then on, I took it for granted that, like Mum and Gran, I would be stuck at home having a baby every other year. After all, Arthur came from a family of eight, and I was the fourth of five. But Harry turned out to be my only child.

◄○►

Arthur usually came straight home after work of an evening so he could spend some time with the baby before I put him to bed. When he didn't turn up that Friday night, I assumed he'd gone off to the pub with my brother. But when Stan staggered in just after midnight, blind drunk and flashing a wad of fivers, Arthur was nowhere to be seen. In fact, Stan gave me one of the fivers, which made me wonder if he'd robbed a bank. But when I asked him where Arthur was, he clammed up.

I didn't go to bed that night, just sat on the bottom step

of the stairs waiting for my husband to come home. Arthur had never stayed out all night from the day we was married.

Although Stan had sobered up by the time he came down to the kitchen the following morning, he didn't say a word during breakfast. When I asked him again where Arthur was, he claimed he hadn't seen him since they'd clocked off work the previous evening. It's not difficult to tell when Stan's lying, because he won't look you in the eye. I was about to press him further when I heard a loud banging on the front door. My first thought was that it must be Arthur, so I rushed to answer it.

When I opened the door, two policemen burst into the house, ran into the kitchen, grabbed Stan, handcuffed him and told him he was being arrested for burglary. Now I knew where the wad of fivers had come from.

'I didn't steal anything,' protested Stan. 'Mr Barrington gave me the money.'

'A likely story, Tancock,' said the first copper.

'But it's the God's honest truth, officer,' he was saying as they dragged him off to the nick. This time I knew Stan wasn't lying.

I left Harry with my mum and ran all the way to the dockyard, hoping to find that Arthur had reported for the morning shift and would be able to tell me why Stan had been arrested. I tried not to think about the possibility that Arthur might also be locked up.

The man on the gate told me he hadn't seen Arthur all morning. But after he checked the rota, he looked puzzled, because Arthur hadn't clocked off the night before. All he had to say was, 'Don't blame me. I wasn't on the gate last night.'

It was only later that I wondered why he'd used the word 'blame'.

I went into the dockyard and asked some of Arthur's mates, but they all parroted the same line. 'Haven't seen him since he clocked off last night.' Then they quickly walked away. I was about to go off to the nick to see if Arthur had been arrested as well, when I saw an old man going past, head bowed.

I chased after him, quite expecting him to tell me to bugger off or claim he didn't know what I was talking about. But when I approached, he stopped, took off his cap and said, 'Good morning.' I was surprised by his good manners, which gave me the confidence to ask him if he'd seen Arthur that morning.

'No,' he replied. 'I last saw him yesterday afternoon when he was on the late shift with your brother. Perhaps you should ask him.'

'I can't,' I said. 'He's been arrested and taken off to the nick.'

'What have they charged him with?' asked Old Jack, looking puzzled.

'I don't know,' I replied.

Old Jack shook his head. 'I can't help you, Mrs Clifton,' he said. 'But there are at least two people who know the whole story.' He nodded towards the large red-brick building that Arthur always called 'management'.

I shivered when I saw a policeman coming out of the front door of the building, and when I looked back, Old Jack had disappeared.

I thought about going into 'management', or Barrington House, to give it its proper name, but decided against it. After all, what would I say if I came face to face with Arthur's boss? In the end I began to walk aimlessly back home, trying to make sense of things.

―◁◦▷―

I watched Hugo Barrington when he gave his evidence. The same self-confidence, the same arrogance, the same half-truths spouted convincingly to the jury, just as he'd whispered them to me in the privacy of the bedroom. When he stepped down from the witness box, I knew Stan didn't have a snowball's chance in hell of getting off.

In the judge's summing-up, he described my brother as a common thief, who had taken advantage of his position to rob his employer. He ended by saying he had no choice but to send him down for three years.

I had sat through every day of the trial, hoping to pick up some snippet of information that might give me a clue as to what had happened to Arthur that day. But by the time the judge finally declared, 'Court adjourned,' I was none the wiser, although I was in no doubt that my brother wasn't telling the whole story. It would be some time before I found out why.

The only other person who attended the court every day was Old Jack Tar, but we didn't speak. In fact, I might never have seen him again if it hadn't been for Harry.

-◄o►-

It was some time before I was able to accept that Arthur would never be coming home.

Stan had only been away for a few days before I discovered the true meaning of the words 'eke out'. With one of the two breadwinners in the family banged up, and the other God knows where, we soon found ourselves quite literally on the bread-line. Luckily there was an unwritten code that operated in Still House Lane: if someone was 'away on holiday', the neighbours did whatever they could to help support his family.

The Reverend Watts dropped in regularly, and even returned some of the coins we'd put in his collection plate over the years. Miss Monday appeared irregularly and dispensed far more than good advice, always leaving with an empty basket. But nothing could compensate me for the loss of a husband, an innocent brother locked up in jail, and a son who no longer had a father.

Harry had recently taken his first step, but I was already fearful of hearing his first word. Would he even remember who used to sit at the head of the table, and ask why he was no longer there? It was Grandpa who came up with a solution as to what we should say if Harry started to ask questions. We all made a pact to stick to the same story; after all, Harry was hardly likely to come across Old Jack.

But at that time the Tancock family's most pressing problem was how to keep the wolf from our door, or, more important, the rent collector and the bailiff. Once I'd spent Stan's five pounds, pawned my mum's silver-plated tea strainer, my engagement ring and finally my wedding ring, I feared it couldn't be long before we were evicted.

But that was delayed for a few weeks by another knock on the door. This time it wasn't the police, but a man called Mr Sparks, who told me he was Arthur's trade union representative, and that he'd come to see if I'd had any compensation from the company.

Once I'd settled Mr Sparks down in the kitchen and poured him a cup of tea, I told him, 'Not a brass farthing. They say he left without giving notice, so they aren't responsible for his actions. And I still don't know what really happened that day.'

'Neither do I,' said Mr Sparks. 'They've all clammed up, not just the management, but the workers as well. I can't get a word out of them. "More than my life's worth," one of them told me. But your husband's subs were fully paid up,' he added, 'so you're entitled to union compensation.'

I just stood there, with no idea what he was going on about.

Mr Sparks took a document out of his briefcase, placed it on the kitchen table and turned to the back page.

'Sign here,' he said placing a forefinger on the dotted line.

After I had put an X where he was pointing, he took an envelope out of his pocket. 'I'm sorry it's so little,' he said as he handed it to me.

I didn't open the envelope until he had finished his cup of tea and left.

Seven pounds, nine shillings and sixpence turned out to be the value they'd put on Arthur's life. I sat alone at the kitchen table, and I think that was the moment I knew I'd never see my husband again.

That afternoon I went back to the pawn shop and redeemed my wedding ring from Mr Cohen; it was the least I could do in memory of Arthur. The following morning I cleared the rent arrears, as well as the slate at the butcher, the baker and yes, the candlestick maker. There was just enough left over to buy some second-hand clothes from the church jumble sale, mostly for Harry.

But it was less than a month before the chalk was once again scratching across the slate at the butcher, the baker and the candlestick maker, and it wasn't long after that I had to return to the pawn shop and hand my wedding ring back to Mr Cohen.

When the rent collector came knocking on the door of number 27 and never received a reply, I suppose none of the family should have been surprised that the next caller would be the bailiff. That was when I decided the time had come for me to look for a job.

12

MAISIE'S ATTEMPTS to find a job didn't turn out to be easy, not least because the government had recently issued a directive to all employers advising them to take on men who had served in the armed forces before considering any other candidates. This was in keeping with Lloyd George's promise that Britain's soldiers would return home to a land fit for heroes.

Although women over thirty had been given the vote at the last election after their sterling service in munitions factories during the war, they were pushed to the back of the queue when it came to peacetime jobs. Maisie decided that her best chance of finding employment was to apply for jobs men wouldn't consider, either because they felt they were too demeaning, or the pay was derisory. With that in mind, Maisie stood in line outside W.D. & H.O. Wills, the city's largest employer. When she reached the front of the queue, she asked the supervisor, 'Is it true you're looking for packers in the cigarette factory?'

'Yes, but you're too young, luv,' he told her.

'I'm twenty-two.'

'You're too young,' he repeated. 'Come back in two or three years' time.'

Maisie was back at Still House Lane in time to share

a bowl of chicken broth and a slice of last week's bread with Harry and her mum.

The next day, she joined an even longer queue outside Harvey's, the wine merchants. When she reached the front, three hours later, she was told by a man wearing a starched white collar and a thin black tie that they were only taking on applicants with experience.

'So how do I get experience?' Maisie asked, trying not to sound desperate.

'By joining our apprentice scheme.'

'Then I'll join,' she told the starched collar.

'How old are you?'

'Twenty-two.'

'You're too old.'

Maisie repeated every word of the sixty-second interview to her mother over a thinner bowl of broth from the same pot along with a crust of bread from the same loaf.

'You could always try the docks,' her mother suggested.

'What do you have in mind, Mum? Should I sign up to be a stevedore?'

Maisie's mum didn't laugh, but then Maisie couldn't remember the last time she had. 'They've always got work for cleaners,' she said. 'And God knows that lot owe you.'

Maisie was up and dressed long before the sun had risen the following morning and, as there wasn't enough breakfast to go round, she set out hungry on the long walk to the docks.

When she arrived, Maisie told the man on the gate she was looking for a cleaning job.

'Report to Mrs Nettles,' he said, nodding in the direction of the large red-brick building she'd so nearly entered once before. 'She's in charge of hirin' and firin' cleaners.' He clearly didn't remember her from her previous visit.

Maisie walked uneasily towards the building, but came to a halt a few paces before she reached the front door. She stood and watched as a succession of smartly dressed men wearing hats and coats and carrying umbrellas made their way through the double doors.

Maisie remained rooted to the spot, shivering in the cold morning air as she tried to find enough courage to follow them inside. She was just about to turn away when she spotted an older woman in overalls entering another door, at the side of the building. Maisie chased after her.

'What do you want?' asked the woman suspiciously once Maisie had caught up with her.

'I'm lookin' for a job.'

'Good,' she said. 'We could do with some young 'uns. Report to Mrs Nettles,' she added, pointing towards a narrow door that might have been mistaken for a broom cupboard. Maisie walked boldly up to it and knocked.

'Come on in,' said a tired voice.

Maisie opened the door to find a woman of about her mother's age sitting on the only chair, surrounded by buckets, mops and several large bars of soap.

'I was told to report to you if I was lookin' for a job.'

'You was told right. That's if you're willing to work all the hours God gives, for damn all pay.'

'What are the hours, and what's the pay?' asked Maisie.

'You start at three in the morning, and you have to be off the premises by seven, before their nibs turns up, when they expect to find their offices spick and span. Or you can start at seven of an evening and work through till midnight, whichever suits you. Pay's the same whatever you decide, sixpence an hour.'

'I'll do both shifts,' said Maisie.

'Good,' the woman said, selecting a bucket and mop. 'I'll see you back here at seven this evenin'', when I'll show you the ropes. My name's Vera Nettles. What's yours?'

'Maisie Clifton.'

Mrs Nettles dropped the bucket on the floor and propped the mop back up against the wall. She walked across to the door and opened it. 'There's no work for you here, Mrs Clifton,' she said.

◄○►

Over the next month, Maisie tried to get a job in a shoe shop, but the manager didn't feel he could employ someone with holes in her shoes; a milliner's, where the interview was terminated the moment they discovered she couldn't add up; and a flower shop, which wouldn't consider taking on anyone who didn't have their own garden. Grandpa's allotment didn't count. In desperation, she applied for a job as a barmaid in a local pub, but the landlord said, 'Sorry, luv, but your tits aren't big enough.'

The following Sunday at Holy Nativity, Maisie knelt and asked God to give her a helping hand.

That hand turned out to be Miss Monday's, who told Maisie she had a friend who owned a tea shop on Broad Street and was looking for a waitress.

'But I don't have any experience,' said Maisie.

'That may well prove to be an advantage,' said Miss Monday. 'Miss Tilly is most particular, and prefers to train her staff in her own way.'

'Perhaps she'll think I'm too old, or too young.'

'You are neither too old nor too young,' said Miss Monday. 'And be assured, I wouldn't recommend you if I didn't think you were up to it. But I must warn you,

Maisie, that Miss Tilly is a stickler for time-keeping. Be at the tea shop before eight o'clock tomorrow. If you're late, that will not only be the first impression you make, but also the last.'

Maisie was standing outside Tilly's Tea Shop at six o'clock the following morning, and didn't budge for the next two hours. At five minutes to eight a plump, middle-aged, smartly dressed woman, with her hair arranged in a neat bun and a pair of half-moon spectacles propped on the end of her nose, turned the 'closed' sign on the door to 'open', to allow a frozen Maisie to step inside.

'You've got the job, Mrs Clifton,' were her new boss's first words.

--o--

Harry was left in the care of his grandmother whenever Maisie went to work. Although she was only paid nine pence an hour, she was allowed to keep half her tips, so that at the end of a good week she could take home as much as three pounds. There was also an unexpected bonus. Once the 'open' sign had been turned back to 'closed' at six o'clock in the evening, Miss Tilly would allow Maisie to take home any food that was left over. The word 'stale' was never allowed to cross a customer's lips.

After six months, Miss Tilly was so pleased with Maisie's progress that she put her in charge of her own station of eight tables, and after another six months, several regulars would insist that Maisie served them. Miss Tilly solved the problem by increasing Maisie's allocation of tables to twelve, and raising her pay to a shilling an hour. With two pay packets coming in each week, Maisie was once again able to wear both her engagement ring and her wedding ring, and the silver-plated tea strainer was back in its place.

—◄o►—

If Maisie was honest about it, Stan being released from prison for good behaviour after only eighteen months turned out to be a bit of a mixed blessing.

Harry, now aged three and a half, had to move back into his mother's room, and Maisie tried not to think about just how peaceful it had been while Stan was away.

Maisie was surprised when Stan got his old job back at the docks as if nothing had happened. This only convinced her that he knew far more about Arthur's disappearance than he let on, however much she pressed him. On one occasion when she became a little too persistent, he belted her one. Although, the following morning, Miss Tilly pretended not to notice the black eye, one or two of the customers did, so Maisie never raised the subject with her brother again. But whenever Harry asked him about his father, Stan stuck to the family line and said, 'Your old man was killed in the war. I was standin' by his side when the bullet hit him.'

—◄o►—

Maisie spent as much of her spare time with Harry as she could. She assumed that once he was old enough to attend Merrywood Elementary School, her life would become a lot easier. But taking Harry to school in the morning meant the added expense of a tram ride to make sure she was not late for work. She would then take a break in the afternoon so she could pick him up from school. Once Maisie had given him his tea, she would leave him in the care of his grandma and return to work.

Harry had only been at school for a few days when Maisie noticed some cane marks on his backside while she was giving him his weekly bath.

'Who did that?' she demanded.

'The headmaster.'

'Why?'

'Can't tell you, Mum.'

When Maisie saw six new red stripes even before the previous ones had faded, she questioned Harry again, but still he didn't let on. The third time the marks appeared, she put on her coat and set off for Merrywood Elementary with the intention of giving his teacher a piece of her mind.

Mr Holcombe wasn't at all what Maisie had expected. To start with, he couldn't have been much older than she was, and he stood up when she entered the room – not at all like the teachers she remembered from her days at Merrywood.

'Why is my son being caned by the headmaster?' she demanded, even before Mr Holcombe had a chance to offer her a seat.

'Because he keeps playing truant, Mrs Clifton. He disappears soon after morning assembly, and gets back in time for football in the afternoon.'

'So where is he spending the day?'

'At the docks would be my guess,' said Mr Holcombe. 'Perhaps you might be able to tell me why.'

'Because his uncle works there, and he's always telling Harry that school is a waste of time because sooner or later he'll end up joining him at Barrington's.'

'I hope not,' said Mr Holcombe.

'Why do you say that?' asked Maisie. 'It was good enough for his father.'

'That may well be, but it won't be good enough for Harry.'

'What do you mean?' Maisie asked indignantly.

'Harry is bright, Mrs Clifton. Very bright. If only I could persuade him to attend class more regularly, there's no saying what he might achieve.'

Maisie suddenly wondered if she would ever find out which of the two men was Harry's father.

'Some clever children don't discover how bright they are until after they've left school,' continued Mr Holcombe, 'and then spend the rest of their lives regretting the wasted years. I want to make sure Harry does not fall into that category.'

'What would you like me to do?' asked Maisie, finally sitting down.

'Encourage him to stay at school, and not slope off to the docks every day. Tell him how proud you'd be if he did well in class, and not only on the football field – which, just in case you didn't realize, Mrs Clifton, isn't his forte.'

'His forte?'

'I do apologize. But even Harry must have worked out by now that he's never going to make the school XI, let alone play for Bristol City.'

'I'll do anything I can to help,' promised Maisie.

'Thank you, Mrs Clifton,' said Mr Holcombe as Maisie rose to leave. 'If you felt able to encourage him, I've no doubt it will be far more effective in the long term than the headmaster's cane.'

From that day, Maisie began to take a far greater interest in what Harry got up to at school. She enjoyed listening to his stories about Mr Holcombe and what he'd taught him that day, and as the stripes didn't reappear, she assumed he must have stopped playing truant. And then one night just before going to bed, she checked on the sleeping child and found that the stripes were back, redder and deeper than before. She didn't need to go and see Mr Holcombe, because he called in at the tea shop the following day.

'He managed to come to my class for a whole month,' said Mr Holcombe, 'and then he disappeared again.'

'But I don't know what more I can do,' said Maisie helplessly. 'I've already stopped his pocket money, and told him not to expect another penny from me unless he stays at school. The truth is, his uncle Stan has far more influence over him than I do.'

'More's the pity,' said Mr Holcombe. 'But I may have found a solution to our problem, Mrs Clifton. However, it has no chance of succeeding without your full cooperation.'

◄o►

Maisie assumed that although she was only twenty-six, she would never marry again. After all, widows with a child in tow were not much of a catch when there were so many single women available. The fact that she always wore her engagement and wedding rings probably cut down the number of propositions she received at the tea shop, although one or two still tried it on. She didn't include dear old Mr Craddick, who just liked to hold her hand.

Mr Atkins was one of Miss Tilly's regulars, and he liked to sit at one of the tables where Maisie was serving. He dropped in most mornings, always ordering a black coffee and a piece of fruit cake. To Maisie's surprise, after he'd paid his bill one morning, he invited her to the cinema.

'Greta Garbo in *Flesh and the Devil*,' he said, trying to make it sound more tempting.

This wasn't the first time one of the customers had

asked Maisie out, but it was the first time someone young and good-looking had shown any interest.

In the past, her stock response had succeeded in putting off the most persistent of suitors. 'How kind of you, Mr Atkins, but I like to spend any spare time I have with my son.'

'Surely you could make an exception for just one evening?' he said, not giving up quite as easily as the others.

Maisie glanced quickly at his left hand: no sign of a wedding ring, or, even more damning, a pale circle revealing that one had been removed.

She heard herself saying, 'How kind of you, Mr Atkins,' and agreed to meet him on Thursday evening, after she'd put Harry to bed.

'Call me Eddie,' he said, leaving a sixpenny tip.

Maisie was impressed when Eddie turned up in a Flatnose Morris to drive her to the cinema. And to her surprise, all he got up to while they sat together in the back row was to watch the film. She wouldn't have complained if he had put an arm around her shoulder. In fact, she was considering how far she would let him go on their first date.

After the curtain came down, the organ lit up and they all rose to sing the National Anthem.

'Care for a drink?' asked Eddie as they made their way out of the cinema.

'I ought to be getting home before the trams pack up for the night.'

'You don't have to worry about the last tram, Maisie, when you're with Eddie Atkins.'

'All right then, just a quick one,' she said as he guided her across the road to the Red Bull.

'So what do you do, Eddie?' Maisie asked as he

placed a half pint of orange squash on the table in front of her.

'I'm in the entertainment business,' he said, without going into any detail. Instead, he switched the subject back to Maisie. 'I don't have to ask what you do.'

After a second orange juice, he looked at his watch and said, 'I've got an early start tomorrow, so I'd better get you home.'

On the way back to Still House Lane, Maisie chatted about Harry, and how she was hoping he would join the choir at Holy Nativity. Eddie seemed genuinely interested, and when he brought the car to a halt outside No. 27, she waited for him to kiss her. But he just jumped out, opened the car door for her and accompanied Maisie to her front door.

Maisie sat at the kitchen table and told her mother everything that had happened, or not happened, that night. All Grandma had to say was, 'What's his game?'

13

WHEN MAISIE SAW Mr Holcombe walk into Holy Nativity accompanied by a smartly dressed man, she assumed that Harry must be in trouble again. She was surprised, because there hadn't been any red marks for over a year.

She braced herself as Mr Holcombe headed towards her, but the moment he saw Maisie he simply gave her a shy smile before he and his companion slipped into the third pew on the other side of the aisle.

From time to time, Maisie glanced across to look at them, but she didn't recognize the other man, who was considerably older than Mr Holcombe. She wondered if he might be the headmaster of Merrywood Elementary.

When the choir rose to sing the first anthem, Miss Monday glanced in the direction of the two men, before nodding to the organist to show that she was ready.

Maisie felt that Harry excelled himself that morning, but she was surprised when a few minutes later he rose to sing a second solo, and even more surprised when he performed a third. Everyone knew that Miss Monday never did anything unless there was a reason, but it still wasn't clear to Maisie what that reason might be.

After the Reverend Watts had blessed his flock at the end of the service, Maisie remained in her place and waited for Harry to appear, hoping he'd be able to tell her why he'd been asked to sing three solos. As she chatted anxiously to her mother, her eyes never left Mr Holcombe, who was introducing the older man to Miss Monday and the Reverend Watts.

A moment later, the Reverend Watts led the two men into the vestry. Miss Monday marched down the aisle towards Maisie, a resolute look on her face, which every parishioner knew meant she was on a mission. 'Can I have a private word with you, Mrs Clifton?' she asked.

She didn't give Maisie a chance to reply, but simply turned and walked back down the aisle towards the vestry.

◄○►

Eddie Atkins hadn't shown his face in Tilly's for over a month, but then one morning he reappeared and took his usual seat at one of Maisie's tables. When she came over to serve him, he gave her a huge smile, as if he'd never been away.

'Good morning, Mr Atkins,' Maisie said as she opened her notepad. 'What can I get for you?'

'My usual,' said Eddie.

'It's been so long, Mr Atkins,' said Maisie. 'You'll have to remind me.'

'I'm sorry I haven't been in touch, Maisie,' said Eddie, 'but I had to go to America at rather short notice, and I only got back last night.'

She wanted to believe him. Maisie had already admitted to her mother that she was a little disappointed she hadn't heard from Eddie after he'd taken her to the cinema. She'd enjoyed his company and felt the evening had gone rather well.

Another man had started visiting the tea shop regularly, and like Eddie he would only sit at one of Maisie's tables. Although she couldn't help noticing that he was showing considerable interest in her, she didn't give him any encouragement, because not only was he middle-aged but he was also wearing a wedding ring. He had a detached air about him, like a solicitor who is studying a client, and whenever he spoke to her he sounded a little pompous. Maisie could hear her mother asking, 'What's his game?' But perhaps she'd misunderstood his intentions, because he never once tried to strike up a conversation with her.

Even Maisie couldn't resist a grin when, a week later, both of her suitors dropped in for a coffee on the same morning, and both asked if they could meet up with her later.

Eddie was first, and he got straight to the point. 'Why don't I pick you up after work this evening, Maisie? There's something I'm rather keen to show you.'

Maisie wanted to tell him she already had a date, just to make him realize she wasn't available whenever it suited him, but when she returned to his table a few minutes later with his bill, she found herself saying, 'I'll see you after work then, Eddie.'

She still had a smile on her face when the other customer said, 'I wonder if I might have a word with you, Mrs Clifton?'

Maisie wondered how he knew her name.

'Wouldn't you prefer to speak to the manageress, Mr . . . ?'

'Frampton,' he replied. 'No, thank you, it's you I was hoping to speak to. Might I suggest we meet at the Royal Hotel during your afternoon break? It shouldn't take more than fifteen minutes of your time.'

'Talk about buses never turning up when you need one,' Maisie said to Miss Tilly, 'and then two arrive at once.' Miss Tilly told Maisie she thought she recognized Mr Frampton, but couldn't place him.

When Maisie presented Mr Frampton with his bill, she emphasized that she could only spare fifteen minutes because she had to be on time to pick up her son from school at four o'clock. He nodded as if that was something else he was aware of.

◄○►

Was it really in Harry's best interests to apply for a scholarship to St Bede's?

Maisie wasn't sure who to discuss the problem with. Stan was bound to be against the idea, and wasn't likely to consider the other side of the argument. Miss Tilly was too close a friend of Miss Monday's to give a dispassionate view, and the Reverend Watts had already advised her to seek the Lord's guidance, which hadn't proved particularly reliable in the past. Mr Frobisher had seemed such a nice man, but he'd made it clear that only she could make the final decision. Mr Holcombe hadn't left her in any doubt how he felt.

Maisie didn't give Mr Frampton another thought until she'd finished serving her last customer. She then exchanged a pinafore for her old coat.

Miss Tilly watched through the window as Maisie set off in the direction of the Royal Hotel. She felt a little anxious, but wasn't sure why.

Although Maisie had never been in the Royal before, she knew it had the reputation of being one of the best-run hotels in the West Country, and the chance to see it from the inside was one of the reasons she'd agreed to see Mr Frampton.

She stood on the opposite pavement and watched as customers pushed their way through the revolving doors. She'd never seen anything quite like them, and only when she felt confident she'd got the hang of how they worked did she cross the road and step inside. She pushed a little too hard and found herself propelled into the foyer more quickly than she'd anticipated.

Maisie looked around and spotted Mr Frampton sitting alone in a quiet alcove in the corner of the foyer. She walked across to join him. He immediately rose from his place, shook hands with her, and waited until she had taken the seat opposite him.

'Can I order you a coffee, Mrs Clifton?' he asked, and before she could reply he added, 'I should warn you, it's not in the same class as Tilly's.'

'No, thank you, Mr Frampton,' said Maisie, whose only interest was to find out why he wanted to see her.

Mr Frampton took his time lighting a cigarette, then inhaled deeply. 'Mrs Clifton,' he began as he placed the cigarette on the ashtray, 'you cannot have failed to notice that I have recently become a regular customer at Tilly's.' Maisie nodded. 'I have to confess that my only reason for visiting the café was you.' Maisie had her well-prepared 'amorous suitor' line ready for just as soon as he stopped talking. 'In all the years I've been in the hotel trade,' he continued, 'I've never seen anyone do their job more efficiently than you. I only wish that every waitress in this hotel was of your calibre.'

'I've been well trained,' said Maisie.

'So have the other four waitresses in that tea shop, but none of them has your flair.'

'I'm flattered, Mr Frampton. But why are you telling—'

'I am the general manager of this hotel,' he said, 'and I'd like you to take charge of our coffee room, which is known as the Palm Court. As you can see –' he waved a hand expansively – 'we have about a hundred covers, but less than a third of the places are regularly occupied. That's not exactly a worthwhile return on the company's investment. No doubt that would change if you were to take over. I believe I can make it worth your while.'

Maisie didn't interrupt him.

'I can't see why your hours should differ greatly from those of your current employment. I'd be willing to pay you five pounds a week, and all the tips earned by the waitresses in the Palm Court would be split fifty-fifty with you. If you were able to build up the clientele, that could prove very remunerative. And then I—'

'But I couldn't think of leaving Miss Tilly,' interrupted Maisie. 'She's been so good to me over the past six years.'

'I fully appreciate your feelings, Mrs Clifton. Indeed, I would have been disappointed if that had not been your immediate response. Loyalty is a trait I greatly admire. However, you must not only consider your own future, but also your son's, should he take up the offer of a choral scholarship to St Bede's.'

Maisie was speechless.

◄○►

When Maisie finished work that evening, she found Eddie sitting in his car outside the tea shop waiting for her. She noticed that he didn't jump out to open the passenger door this time.

'So, where are you taking me?' she asked as she climbed in beside him.

'It's a surprise,' said Eddie as he pressed the starter, 'but I don't think you'll be disappointed.'

He pushed the gear lever into first, and headed towards a part of the city that Maisie hadn't visited before. A few minutes later, he drove into a side alley and came to a halt outside a large oak door below a neon sign that announced in glowing red letters, EDDIE'S NIGHTCLUB.

'This is yours?' asked Maisie.

'Every square inch,' said Eddie proudly. 'Come inside and see for yourself.' He leapt out of the car, opened the front door and led Maisie inside. 'This used to be a granary,' he explained as he took her down a narrow wooden staircase. 'But now that ships can no longer sail this far up the river, the company's had to move, so I was able to pick up their lease for a very reasonable price.'

Maisie entered a large, dimly lit room. It was some time before her eyes had adjusted well enough to take it all in. There were half a dozen men sitting on high leather stools drinking at the bar, and almost as many waitresses fluttering around them. The wall behind the bar consisted of a vast mirror, giving the impression the room was far larger than it actually was. At the centre was a dance floor, surrounded by plush velvet ban-quettes that would just about seat two people. At the far end was a small stage with a piano, double bass, a set of drums and several music stands.

Eddie took a seat at the bar. Looking around the room he said, 'This is why I've been spending so much time in America. Speakeasies like this are springing up all over New York and Chicago, and they're making a fortune.' He lit a cigar. 'And I promise you, there won't be anything else like this in Bristol, that's for sure.'

'That's for sure,' Maisie repeated as she joined him at the bar, but didn't attempt to climb up on to one of the high stools.

'What's your poison, doll?' said Eddie, in what he imagined to be an American accent.

'I don't drink,' Maisie reminded him.

'That's one of the reasons I chose you.'

'Chose me?'

'Sure. You'd be the ideal person to take charge of the cocktail waitresses. Not only would I pay you six pounds a week, but if the place takes off, the tips alone would be more than you could ever hope to earn at Tilly's.'

'And would I be expected to dress like that?' asked Maisie, pointing to one of the waitresses who was wearing an off-the-shoulder red blouse and a tight-fitting black skirt that barely covered her knees. It amused Maisie that they were the same colours as the St Bede's uniform.

'Why not? You're a great-lookin' broad, and the punters will pay good money to be served by someone like you. You'll get the odd proposition, of course, but I feel sure you can handle that.'

'What's the point of a dance floor if it's a men-only club?'

'Another idea I picked up from the States,' said Eddie. 'If you want to dance with one of the cocktail waitresses, it'll cost you.'

'And what else does that cost include?'

'That's up to them,' said Eddie with a shrug of the shoulders. 'So long as it doesn't take place on the premises, nothing to do with me,' he added, laughing a little too loudly. Maisie didn't laugh. 'So what do you think?' he asked.

'I think I'd better be getting home,' said Maisie. 'I didn't have time to let Harry know I'd be late.'

'Whatever you say, honey,' said Eddie. He draped an arm around her shoulder and led her out of the bar and back up the stairs.

As he drove her to Still House Lane, he told Maisie about his plans for the future. 'I've already got my eye on a second site,' he said excitedly, 'so the sky's the limit.'

'The sky's the limit,' Maisie repeated, as they drew up outside No. 27.

Maisie jumped out of the car and walked quickly to the front door.

'So will you need a few days to think it over?' said Eddie, chasing after her.

'No, thank you, Eddie,' said Maisie without hesitation. 'I've already made up my mind,' she added, taking a key out of her handbag.

Eddie grinned and put an arm around her. 'I didn't think it would be a difficult decision for you to make.'

Maisie removed the arm, smiled sweetly and said, 'It's kind of you to consider me, honey, but I think I'll stick to serving coffee.' She opened her front door before adding, 'But thanks for asking.'

'Anything you say, doll, but if you change your mind, my door is always open.'

Maisie closed the door behind her.

14

MAISIE FINALLY SETTLED ON the one person she felt she could seek advice from. She decided to turn up at the docks unannounced and hope he'd be around when she knocked on his door.

She didn't tell either Stan or Harry who she was visiting. One of them would try to stop her, while the other would feel she'd betrayed a confidence.

Maisie waited until her day off, and once she had dropped Harry at school, she took a tram to the dockyard. She had chosen her time carefully: late morning, when he was still likely to be in his office, while Stan would be fully occupied loading or unloading cargo at the other end of the dock.

Maisie told the man on the gate that she'd come to apply for a job as a cleaner. He pointed indifferently towards the red-brick building and still didn't remember her.

As she walked towards Barrington House, Maisie looked up at the windows on the fifth floor and wondered which office was his. She recalled her encounter with Mrs Nettles, and the way she had been shown the door the moment she mentioned her name. Now Maisie not only had a job she enjoyed and where she was respected, but she'd had two other offers in the past few days. She didn't give Mrs Nettles another thought as she walked straight past the building and continued along the quayside.

Maisie didn't slacken her pace until she could see his home. She found it hard to believe that anyone could possibly live in a railway carriage, and began to wonder if she'd made a dreadful mistake. Had Harry's stories of a dining room, a bedroom and even a library, been exaggerated? 'You can't stop now you've come this far, Maisie Clifton,' she told herself, and knocked boldly on the carriage door.

'Come in, Mrs Clifton,' said a gentle voice.

Maisie opened the door to find an old man sitting in a comfortable seat, with books and other possessions scattered around him. She was surprised how clean the carriage was, and realized that, despite Stan's claims, it was she, and not Old Jack, who lived in third class. Stan had perpetuated a myth that had been ignored when viewed through the eyes of an unprejudiced child.

Old Jack immediately rose from his place and beckoned her towards the seat opposite. 'You'll have come to see me about young Harry, no doubt.'

'Yes, Mr Tar,' she replied.

'Let me guess,' he said. 'You can't make up your mind whether he should go to St Bede's, or remain at Merrywood Elementary.'

'How could you possibly know that?' asked Maisie.

'Because I've been considering the same problem for the past month,' said Old Jack.

'So what do you think he should do?'

'I think that despite the many difficulties he will undoubtedly face at St Bede's, if he doesn't take this opportunity, he could well spend the rest of his life regretting it.'

'Perhaps he won't win a scholarship and the decision will be taken out of our hands.'

'The decision was taken out of our hands,' said Old Jack, 'the moment Mr Frobisher heard young Harry sing. But I have a feeling that wasn't the only reason you came to see me.'

Maisie was beginning to understand why Harry admired this man so much. 'You're quite right, Mr Tar, I need your advice on another matter.'

'Your son calls me Jack, except when he's cross with me, then he calls me Old Jack.'

Maisie smiled. 'I've been worried that even if he did win a scholarship, I wasn't earning enough for Harry to have all the little extras that the other boys at a school like St Bede's take for granted. But fortunately I've just been offered another job, which would mean more money.'

'And you're worried about how Miss Tilly will react when you tell her you're thinking of leaving?'

'You know Miss Tilly?'

'No, but Harry has spoken of her many times. She's clearly from the same mould as Miss Monday, and let me assure you, that's a limited edition. There's no need for you to concern yourself.'

'I don't understand,' said Maisie.

'Allow me to explain,' said Old Jack. 'Miss Monday has already invested a great deal of her time and expertise in making sure that Harry not only wins a scholarship to St Bede's but, far more important, goes on to prove himself worthy of it. My bet is that she will have discussed every possible eventuality with her closest friend, who just happens to be Miss Tilly. So when you tell her about the new job, you may well find it doesn't come as a complete surprise.'

'Thank you, Jack,' said Maisie. 'How lucky Harry is to have you as a friend. The father he never knew,' she said softly.

'That is the nicest compliment I've received for a good many years,' said Old Jack. 'I'm only sorry that he lost his father in such tragic circumstances.'

'Do you know how my husband died?'

'Yes, I do,' replied Old Jack. Aware that he should never had raised the subject, he quickly added, 'But only because Harry told me.'

'What did he tell you?' asked Maisie anxiously.

'That his father was killed in the war.'

'But you know that's not true,' said Maisie.

'Yes, I do,' said Old Jack. 'And I suspect Harry also knows his father couldn't have died in the war.'

'Then why doesn't he say so?'

'He probably thinks there's something you don't want to tell him.'

'But I don't know the truth myself,' admitted Maisie.

Old Jack didn't comment.

Maisie walked slowly home; one question answered, another still unresolved. Even so, she wasn't in any doubt that Old Jack could be added to the list of people who knew the truth about what had happened to her husband.

Old Jack turned out to be right about Miss Tilly, because when Maisie told her about Mr Frampton's offer, she couldn't have been more supportive and understanding.

'We'll all miss you,' she said, 'and frankly the Royal is lucky to have you.'

'How can I begin to thank you for all you've done for me over the years?' said Maisie.

'It's Harry who should be thanking you,' said Miss

Tilly, 'and I suspect it will only be a matter of time before he realizes that.'

—◁○▷—

Maisie started her new job a month later, and it didn't take her long to discover why the Palm Court was never more than a third full.

The waitresses regarded their work simply as a job, unlike Miss Tilly, who considered it to be a vocation. They never bothered to remember the customers' names, or their favourite tables. Worse, the coffee was often cold by the time it was served, and the cakes were left to go stale until someone bought them. Maisie wasn't surprised they didn't get any tips; they didn't deserve them.

After another month, she began to realize just how much Miss Tilly had taught her.

After three months, Maisie had replaced five of the seven waitresses, without having to recruit anyone from Tilly's. She had also ordered smart new uniforms for all her staff, along with new plates, cups and saucers and, even more important, changed her coffee supplier and her cake-maker. That was something she was willing to steal from Miss Tilly.

'You're costing me a lot of money, Maisie,' said Mr Frampton when another stack of bills landed on his desk. 'Try not to forget what I said about return on investment.'

'Give me another six months, Mr Frampton, and you'll see the results.'

Although Maisie worked night and day, she always found time to drop Harry off at school in the morning and pick him up in the afternoon. But she warned Mr Frampton that there would be one day when she wouldn't be on time for work.

When she told him why, he gave her the whole day off.

◄○►

Just before they left the house, Maisie checked herself in the mirror. She was dressed in her Sunday best but not going to church. She smiled down at her son, who looked so smart in his new red and black school uniform. Even so, she felt a little self-conscious as they waited at the tram stop.

'Two to Park Street,' she told the clippie when the No. 11 pulled away. She was unable to hide her pride when she noticed him taking a closer look at Harry. It only convinced Maisie that she had made the right decision.

When they reached their stop, Harry refused to let his mum carry his suitcase. Maisie held on to his hand as they walked slowly up the hill towards the school, not sure which one of them was more nervous. She couldn't take her eyes off the hansom cabs and chauffeur-driven cars that were dropping off other boys for their first day of term. She only hoped that Harry would be able to find at least one friend among them. After all, some of the nannies were better dressed than she was.

Harry began to slow down as they got nearer the school gates. Maisie could sense his discomfort – or was it just fear of the unknown?

'I'll leave you now,' she said, and bent down to kiss him. 'Good luck, Harry. Make us all proud of you.'

'Goodbye, Mum.'

As she watched him walk away, Maisie noticed that someone else appeared to be taking an interest in Harry Clifton.

135

15

MAISIE WOULD NEVER FORGET the first time she had to turn away a customer.

'I'm sure there will be a table available in a few minutes, sir.'

She prided herself on the fact that once a customer had paid the bill, her staff could clear the table, replace the cloth and have it re-laid and ready for the next guest within five minutes.

The Palm Court quickly became so popular that Maisie had to keep a couple of tables permanently reserved, just in case one of her regulars turned up unexpectedly.

She was a little embarrassed that some of her old customers from Tilly's had begun to migrate to the Palm Court, not least dear old Mr Craddick, who remembered Harry from his paper round. She considered it an even greater compliment when Miss Tilly herself began to drop in for a morning coffee.

'Just checking on the opposition,' she said. 'By the way, Maisie, this coffee is superb.'

'So it should be,' Maisie replied. 'It's yours.'

Eddie Atkins also came in from time to time, and if the size of his cigars, not to mention his waistline, was anything to go by, the sky must still have been the limit.

Although he was friendly, he never asked Maisie out, but he did regularly remind her that his door was always open.

Not that Maisie didn't have a string of admirers she occasionally allowed to take her out in the evening, maybe to dinner at a fashionable restaurant, sometimes a visit to the Old Vic or the cinema, especially if a Greta Garbo film was playing. But when they parted at the end of the evening, she allowed none of them more than a peck on the cheek before returning home. At least, not until she met Patrick Casey, who proved that the charm of the Irish was not just a cliché.

When Patrick first walked into the Palm Court, hers wasn't the only head that turned to take a closer look. He was a shade over six foot, with wavy dark hair and the build of an athlete. That would have been enough for most women, but it was the smile that captivated Maisie, as, she suspected, it had many others.

Patrick told her he was in finance, but then Eddie had said he was in the entertainment business. His work brought him to Bristol once or twice a month, when Maisie would allow him to take her to dinner, the theatre or the cinema, and occasionally she even broke her golden rule, and didn't take the last tram back to Still House Lane.

She wouldn't have been surprised to discover that Patrick had a wife and half a dozen offspring back at home in Cork, although he swore, hand on heart, that he was a bachelor.

―◦―

Whenever Mr Holcombe dropped into the Palm Court, Maisie would guide him to a table in the far corner of the room that was partly obscured by a large pillar and was shunned by her regulars. But its privacy allowed her to bring him up to date on how Harry was getting on.

Today, he seemed more interested in the future than the past, and asked, 'Have you decided what Harry will do once he leaves St Bede's?'

'I haven't given it much thought,' Maisie admitted. 'After all, it's not for some time.'

'It's soon enough,' said Mr Holcombe, 'and I can't believe you'll want him to return to Merrywood Elementary.'

'No, I don't,' said Maisie firmly, 'but what choice is there?'

'Harry says he'd like to go to Bristol Grammar School, but if he fails to win a scholarship, he's worried that you won't be able to afford the fees.'

'That won't be a problem,' Maisie assured him. 'With my present pay, combined with the tips, no one need know his mother is a waitress.'

'Some waitress,' said Mr Holcombe, looking around the packed room. 'I'm only surprised you haven't opened your own place.'

Maisie laughed, and didn't give it another thought until she had an unexpected visit from Miss Tilly.

◄o►

Maisie attended Matins at St Mary Redcliffe every Sunday so she could hear her son sing. Miss Monday had warned her that it wouldn't be much longer before Harry's voice broke, and she mustn't assume that a few weeks later he'd be singing tenor solos.

Maisie tried to concentrate on the canon's sermon that Sunday morning but found her mind drifting. She glanced across the aisle to see Mr and Mrs Barrington sitting with their son Giles and two young girls who she assumed must be their daughters, but whose names she didn't know. Maisie had been surprised when Harry told her that Giles Barrington was his closest friend. Nothing more than a coincidence of the alphabet had put them together in the first place, he'd said. She hoped it would never become necessary for her to tell him that Giles might be more than just a good friend.

◄○►

Maisie often wished she could do more to help Harry with his efforts to win a scholarship to Bristol Grammar School. Although Miss Tilly had taught her how to read a menu, add and subtract, and even write a few simple words, just the thought of what Harry must be putting himself through filled her with trepidation.

Miss Monday boosted Maisie's confidence by continually reminding her that Harry would never have got this far if she hadn't been willing to make so many sacrifices. 'And in any case,' she added, 'you're every bit as clever as Harry, you just haven't been given the same opportunities.'

Mr Holcombe kept her informed on what he described as 'the timing', and, as the date of the examination drew nearer, Maisie became just as nervous as the candidate. She realized the truth of one of Old Jack's remarks, that often the onlooker suffers even more than the participant.

The Palm Court room was now packed every day, but it didn't stop Maisie from initiating even more changes in a decade the press were describing as the 'frivolous thirties'.

In the morning, she had started offering her customers a variety of biscuits to go with their coffee, and in the afternoon, her tea menu was proving just as popular, especially after Harry told her that Mrs Barrington had given him the choice of Indian or China tea.

However, Mr Frampton vetoed the suggestion that smoked salmon sandwiches should appear on the menu.

Every Sunday, Maisie would kneel on her little cushion; her one prayer was to the point. 'Please God make sure Harry wins a scholarship. If he does, I'll never ask you for anything again.'

With a week to go to the exams, Maisie found she couldn't sleep, and lay awake wondering how Harry was coping. So many customers wanted to pass on their best wishes to him, some because they had heard him singing in the church choir, others because he'd delivered their morning papers, or simply because their own children had been, were, or would at some time in the future be going though the same experience. It seemed to Maisie that half of Bristol was taking the exam.

On the morning of the examination, Maisie placed several regulars at the wrong table, gave Mr Craddick coffee instead of his usual hot chocolate, and even presented two customers with someone else's bill. No one complained.

Harry told her he thought he'd done quite well, but he couldn't be certain if he'd done well enough. He mentioned someone called Thomas Hardy, but Maisie wasn't sure if he was a friend or one of the masters.

When the long-case clock in the Palm Court room struck ten on that Thursday morning, Maisie knew the headmaster would be posting the exam results on the school notice board. But it was another twenty-two minutes before Mr Holcombe walked into the room and headed straight for his usual table behind the pillar. Maisie could not tell how Harry had done from the expression on the schoolmaster's face. She quickly crossed the room to join him and, for the first time in four years, sat down in the seat opposite a customer, although 'collapsed' might be a more accurate description.

'Harry has passed with distinction,' said Mr Holcombe, 'but I'm afraid he just missed out on a scholarship.'

'What does that mean?' Maisie asked, trying to stop her hands from trembling.

'The top twelve candidates had marks of 80 per cent or above, and were all awarded open scholarships. In fact, Harry's friend Deakins came top, with 92 per cent. Harry achieved a very commendable 78 per cent, and came seventeenth out of three hundred. Mr Frobisher told me his English paper let him down.'

'He should have read Hardy instead of Dickens,' said a woman who'd never read a book.

'Harry will still be offered a place at BGS,' said Mr Holcombe, 'but he won't receive the annual hundred pounds a year scholar's grant.'

Maisie rose from her place. 'Then I'll just have to work three shifts instead of two, won't I? Because he's not going back to Merrywood Elementary, Mr Holcombe, I can tell you that.'

<o>

Over the next few days, Maisie was surprised by how many regulars offered their congratulations on Harry's magnificent achievement. She also discovered that one or two of her customers had children who had failed to pass the exam, in one case by a single percentage point. They would have to settle for their second choice. It made Maisie all the more determined that nothing would stop Harry reporting to Bristol Grammar School on the first day of term.

One strange thing she noticed during the next week was that her tips doubled. Dear old Mr Craddick slipped her a five-pound note, saying, 'For Harry. May he prove worthy of his mother.'

When the thin white envelope dropped through the letterbox in Still House Lane, an event in itself, Harry opened the letter and read it to his mother. 'Clifton, H.' had been offered a place in the A stream for the Michaelmas term starting on September 15th. When he came to the last paragraph, which asked Mrs Clifton to write and confirm whether the candidate wished to accept or reject the offer, he looked nervously at her.

'You must write back straight away, accepting the offer!' she said.

Harry threw his arms around her and whispered, 'I only wish my father was alive.'

Perhaps he is, thought Maisie.

—◦—

A few days later, a second letter landed on the doormat. This one detailed a long list of items that had to be purchased before the first day of term. Maisie noticed that Harry seemed to require two of everything, in some cases three or more, and in one case, six: socks, grey calf length, plus garters.

'Pity you can't borrow a pair of my suspenders,' she said. Harry blushed.

A third letter invited new pupils to select three extra-curricular activities from a list ranging from the car club to the Officer Training Corps – some of which involved an added charge of five pounds per activity. Harry chose the choir, for which there was no extra charge, as well as the theatre club and the Arts Appreciation Society. The latter included a proviso that any visits to galleries outside Bristol would incur an extra cost.

Maisie wished there were a few more Mr Craddicks around, but she never allowed Harry to suspect there was any reason for concern, even though Mr Holcombe reminded her that her boy would be at Bristol Grammar School for the next five years. The first member of the family not to leave school before the age of fourteen, she told him.

Maisie braced herself for another visit to T.C. Marsh, Tailors of Distinction.

By the time Harry was fully kitted out and ready for the first day of term, Maisie had once again begun to walk to and from work, saving five pence a week on tram fares, or as she told her mother, 'A pound a year, enough to pay for a new suit for Harry.'

—◇—

Parents, Maisie had learnt over the years, may be considered an unfortunate necessity by their offspring, but more often than not they are also an embarrassment.

On her first speech day at St Bede's, Maisie had been the only mother not wearing a hat. After that, she had bought one from a second-hand shop and, however out of fashion it would become, it was going to have to last until Harry left Bristol Grammar School.

Harry had agreed that she should accompany him to school on the first day of term, but Maisie had already decided that he was old enough to catch a tram home in the evening. Her main anxiety was not about how Harry would get to and from school, but what to do with him in the evenings, now he was a day boy and would no longer be sleeping at school during term. She had no doubt that if he went back to sharing a room with his uncle Stan, it could only end in tears. She tried to put the problem out of her mind as she prepared for Harry's first day in his new school.

Hat in place, best, and only, overcoat recently cleaned, sensible black shoes with the only pair of silk stockings she possessed, Maisie felt ready to face the other parents. When she came down the stairs, Harry was already waiting for her by the door. He looked so smart in his new uniform of claret and black that she would have liked to parade him up and down Still House Lane so the neighbours would know that someone from the street was going to Bristol Grammar School.

As they had on his first day at St Bede's, they caught the tram, but Harry asked Maisie if they could get off one stop before University Road. She was no longer allowed to hold his hand, although she did straighten his cap and tie more than once.

When Maisie first saw the noisy gathering of young men crowded around the school gates, she said, 'I'd better be off or I'll be late for work,' which puzzled Harry, because he knew Mr Frampton had given her the day off.

She gave her son a quick hug, but kept a wary eye on him as he made his way up the hill. The first person to greet him was Giles Barrington. Maisie was surprised to see him, as Harry had told her he would probably be going to Eton. They shook hands like a couple of grown men who had just closed an important deal.

Maisie could see Mr and Mrs Barrington standing at the back of the crowd. Was he making sure he avoided her? A few minutes later, Mr and Mrs Deakins joined them, accompanied by the Peloquin Memorial scholar. More handshakes, left-handed in Mr Deakins's case.

As the parents began to take leave of their children, Maisie watched Mr Barrington as he shook hands first with his son and then with Deakins, but turned away when Harry offered his hand. Mrs Barrington looked embarrassed, and Maisie wondered if she might later ask why Hugo had ignored Giles's closest friend. If she did, Maisie felt certain he would not tell her the real reason. Maisie feared it couldn't be long before Harry asked why Mr Barrington always snubbed him. As long as only three people knew the truth, she couldn't think of any reason why Harry would ever find out.

16

MISS TILLY HAD BECOME such a regular at the Palm Court that she even had her own table.

She would usually arrive around four o'clock, and order a cup of tea (Earl Grey) and a cucumber sandwich. She always declined to take anything from the large assortment of cream cakes, jam tarts and chocolate éclairs, but would occasionally allow herself a buttered scone. When she popped by just before five one evening, unusually late for her, Maisie was relieved that her usual table was free.

'I wonder if I might sit somewhere a little more discreet today, Maisie. I need to have a quiet word with you.'

'Of course, Miss Tilly,' said Maisie, and led her to Mr Holcombe's preferred table behind the pillar at the far end of the room. 'I'm off in ten minutes,' Maisie told her. 'I'll join you then.'

When her deputy Susan arrived to take over, Maisie explained that she would be joining Miss Tilly for a few minutes, but didn't expect to be served.

'Is the old duck unhappy about something?' Susan asked.

'That old duck taught me everything I know,' said Maisie with a grin.

When five o'clock struck, Maisie walked across the

room and took the seat opposite Miss Tilly. She rarely sat down with a customer, and on the few occasions she did, she had never felt at ease.

'Would you care for some tea, Maisie?'

'No, thank you, Miss Tilly.'

'I quite understand. I'll try not to keep you too long, but before I tell you my real purpose for wanting to see you, may I ask how Harry is getting on?'

'I wish he'd stop growing,' said Maisie. 'I seem to be letting down his trousers every few weeks. At this rate his long trousers will be short trousers before the end of the year.'

Miss Tilly laughed. 'What about his work?'

'His end-of-term report said – ' Maisie paused, trying to recall the exact words – '"A most satisfactory start. Very promising." He came top in English.'

'Somewhat ironic,' said Miss Tilly. 'If I remember correctly, that was the subject that let him down in the entrance exam.'

Maisie nodded, and tried not to think about the financial consequences of Harry not having read enough Thomas Hardy.

'You must be very proud of him,' said Miss Tilly. 'And when I went to St Mary's on Sunday, I was delighted to see that he's back in the choir.'

'Yes, but he now has to be satisfied with a place in the back row with the other baritones. His days as a soloist are over. But he's joined the theatre club, and because there are no girls at BGS, he's playing Ursula in the school play.'

'*Much Ado About Nothing*,' said Miss Tilly. 'Still, I mustn't waste any more of your time, so I'll come to the reason I wanted to see you.' She took a sip of tea, as if she wanted to compose herself before she spoke again, and then it all came out in a rush.

'I'll be sixty next month, my dear, and for some time I have been considering retiring.'

It had never crossed Maisie's mind that Miss Tilly wouldn't go on for ever.

'Miss Monday and I have been thinking about moving down to Cornwall. We have our eye on a little cottage by the sea.'

You mustn't leave Bristol, Maisie wanted to say. I love you both, and if you go, who will I turn to for advice?

'Matters came to a head last month,' continued Miss Tilly, 'when a local businessman made me an offer for the tea shop. It seems he wants to add it to his growing empire. And although I don't care for the idea of Tilly's being part of a chain, his offer was far too tempting to turn down out of hand.' Maisie only had one question, but she didn't interrupt while Miss Tilly was in full flow. 'Since then, I've been giving the matter a great deal of thought, and I decided that if you were able to come up with the same amount he has offered, I would rather you took over the business than I hand it over to a stranger.'

'How much did he offer?'

'Five hundred pounds.'

Maisie sighed. 'I'm flattered you even thought of me,' she said at last, 'but the truth is, I don't have five hundred pennies to my name, let alone five hundred pounds.'

'I was afraid you might say that,' said Miss Tilly. 'But if you could find a backer, I feel sure they would consider the business a good investment. After all, I made a profit of one hundred and twelve pounds and ten shillings last year, which didn't include my salary. I would have let you have it for less than five hundred pounds, but we've found a delightful little cottage in St

Mawes, and the owners won't consider a penny less than three hundred. Miss Monday and I could just about survive on our savings for a year or two, but as neither of us has a pension to fall back on, the extra two hundred pounds will make all the difference.'

Maisie was just about to tell Miss Tilly how sorry she was but it was out of the question, when Patrick Casey strolled into the room and sat down at his usual table.

◄○►

It wasn't until after they'd made love that Maisie told Patrick about Miss Tilly's offer. He sat up in bed, lit a cigarette and inhaled deeply.

'Raising that amount of capital shouldn't prove too difficult. After all, it's hardly Brunel trying to raise the money to build Clifton Suspension Bridge.'

'No, but it is Mrs Clifton trying to raise five hundred pounds when she hasn't got two halfpennies to rub together.'

'True, but you'd be able to show a cash flow and a proven income stream, not to mention the tea shop's goodwill. Mind you, I'll need to look at the books for the past five years and make sure you've been told the whole story.'

'Miss Tilly would never try to deceive anyone.'

'You'll also have to check that there isn't a rent review due in the near future,' Patrick said, ignoring her protestations, 'and double-check that her accountant hasn't come up with penalty clauses the moment you start making a profit.'

'Miss Tilly wouldn't do something like that,' said Maisie.

'You're so trusting, Maisie. What you have to re-member is, this won't be in the hands of Miss Tilly, but a lawyer who feels he's got to earn his fee, and an accountant looking for a pay-day in case you don't retain him.'

'You've clearly never met Miss Tilly.'

'Your faith in the old lady is touching, Maisie, but my job is to protect people like you, and a hundred and twelve pounds ten shillings profit a year wouldn't be enough for you to live on, remembering you'll be expected to make regular repayments to your investor.'

'Miss Tilly assured me that the profit didn't include her salary.'

'That might well be the case, but you don't know what that salary is. You'll need at least another two hundred and fifty pounds a year if you're to survive, otherwise not only will you be out of pocket, but Harry will be out of the grammar school.'

'I can't wait for you to meet Miss Tilly.'

'And what about tips? At the Royal you get 50 per cent of all the tips, which comes to at least another two hundred pounds a year, which at the moment isn't taxed, although I've no doubt some future government will catch on to that.'

'Perhaps I should tell Miss Tilly that it's too great a risk. After all, as you keep reminding me, I have a guaranteed income at the Royal, with no risks attached.'

'True, but if Miss Tilly is half as good as you say she is, this could be an opportunity that might not arise again.'

'Make your mind up, Patrick,' said Maisie, trying not to sound exasperated.

'I will, the moment I've seen the books.'

'You will, the moment you meet Miss Tilly,' Maisie said, 'because then you'll understand the real meaning of goodwill.'

'I can't wait to meet this paragon of virtue.'

'Does that mean you'll represent me?'

'Yes,' he said, stubbing out his cigarette.

'And how much will you be charging this penniless widow, Mr Casey?'

'Turn the light out.'

-◄○►-

'Are you sure this is a risk worth taking,' asked Mr Frampton, 'when you have so much to lose?'

'My financial adviser thinks so,' replied Maisie. 'He's assured me that not only do all the figures add up, but once I've paid off the loan, I should be showing a profit within five years.'

'But those are the years Harry will be at Bristol Grammar.'

'I'm well aware of that, Mr Frampton, but Mr Casey has secured a substantial salary for me as part of the bargain, and after I've split the tips with my staff, I should be earning roughly the same amount I'm currently taking home. More important, in five years' time I'll own a real asset, and from then on, all the profits will be mine,' she said, trying to recall Patrick's exact words.

'It's clear to me that you've made up your mind,' said Mr Frampton. 'But let me warn you, Maisie, there's a great deal of difference between being an employee, when you know you'll be taking home a wage packet every week, and being an employer, when it will be your responsibility to put your money into several wage packets every Friday night. Frankly, Maisie, you are the best at what you do, but are you really sure you want to switch from being a player to joining the management?'

'Mr Casey will be there to advise me.'

'Casey's a capable fellow, I'll give you that, but he also has to look after more important clients right across the country. It will be you who has to run the business from day to day. If anything were to go wrong, he won't always be around to hold your hand.'

'But I may not be given an opportunity like this again in my lifetime.' Another of Patrick's pronouncements.

'So be it, Maisie,' said Frampton. 'And don't be in any doubt how much we'll all miss you at the Royal. The only reason you're not irreplaceable is because you trained your deputy so well.'

'Susan won't let you down, Mr Frampton.'

'I'm sure she won't. But she'll never be Maisie Clifton. Let me be the first to wish you every success in your new venture, and if things don't work out as planned, there will always be a job for you here at the Royal.'

Mr Frampton rose from behind his desk and shook hands with Maisie, just as he'd done six years before.

17

A MONTH LATER, Maisie signed six documents in the presence of Mr Prendergast, the manager of the National Provincial Bank on Corn Street. But not until Patrick had taken her through each page, line by line, now happy to admit how wrong he'd been to doubt Miss Tilly. If everyone behaved as honourably as she did, he told her, he'd be out of a job.

Maisie handed Miss Tilly a cheque for £500 on March 19th, 1934, receiving a huge hug and a tea shop in return. A week later, Miss Tilly and Miss Monday left for Cornwall.

When Maisie opened her doors for business the following day, she retained the name 'Tilly's'. Patrick had advised her never to underestimate the goodwill of Tilly's name above the door ('founded in 1898') and that she should not even think of changing it until Miss Tilly was of blessed memory and perhaps not even then. 'Regulars don't like change, especially sudden ones, so don't rush them into anything.'

Maisie did, however, spot a few changes that could be made without offending any of the regulars. She felt a new set of tablecloths wouldn't go amiss, and the chairs and even the tables were beginning to look, well, quaint. And hadn't Miss Tilly noticed the carpet was wearing a bit thin?

'Pace yourself,' Patrick warned her on one of his monthly visits. 'Remember that it's far easier to spend money than to earn it, and don't be surprised if a few of the old biddies disappear and you don't make quite as much as you'd anticipated in the first few months.'

Patrick turned out to be right. The number of covers dropped in the first month, and then again in the second, proving just how popular Miss Tilly had been. Had they fallen again in the third, Patrick would have been advising Maisie about cash flow and overdraft limits, but it bottomed – another of Patrick's expressions – and even began to climb the following month, though not sharply.

◄○►

At the end of her first year, Maisie had broken even, but she hadn't made enough to pay back any of the bank's loan.

'Don't fret, my dear,' Miss Tilly told her on one of her rare visits to Bristol. 'It was years before I made a profit.' Maisie didn't have years.

The second year began well, with some of her regulars from the Palm Court returning to their old stamping ground. Eddie Atkins had put on so much weight, and his cigars were so much larger, that Maisie could only assume the entertainment business was thriving. Mr Craddick appeared at eleven o'clock every morning, dressed in a raincoat, umbrella in hand, whatever the weather. Mr Holcombe dropped in from time to time, always wanting updates on how Harry was getting on, and she never allowed him to pay the bill. Patrick's first stop whenever he returned to Bristol was always Tilly's.

During her second year, Maisie had to replace one supplier who didn't seem to know the difference between fresh and stale, and one waitress who wasn't convinced that the customer was always right. Several young women applied for the job, as it was becoming more acceptable for women to go to work. Maisie settled on a young lady called Karen, who had a mop of curly fair hair, big blue eyes and what the fashion magazines were describing as an hourglass figure. Maisie had a feeling that Karen might attract some new customers who were a little younger than most of her regulars.

Selecting a new cake supplier proved a more difficult task. And although several companies tendered for the contract, Maisie was very demanding. However, when Bob Burrows of Burrows' Bakery (founded 1935) turned up on her doorstep and told her that Tilly's would be his first customer, she put him on a month's trial.

Bob turned out to be hard-working and reliable, and even more important, his goods were always so fresh and tempting that her customers would often say, 'Well, perhaps just one more.' His cream buns and fruit scones were particularly popular, but it was his chocolate brownies, the new fad, that seemed to disappear from the cakestand long before midday. Although Maisie regularly pressed him, Bob kept telling her that he just couldn't make any more.

One morning, after Bob had dropped off his wares, Maisie thought he looked a little forlorn, so she sat him down and poured him a cup of coffee. He confessed to her that he was suffering from the same cash-flow problems she'd experienced in her first year. But he was confident things would soon look up as he'd recently been taken on by two new shops, although he stressed how much he owed to Maisie for giving him his first break.

As the weeks passed, these morning coffee breaks became something of a ritual. Even so, Maisie couldn't have been more surprised when Bob asked her out on a date, as she considered theirs to be a professional relationship. He had bought tickets for *Glamorous Night*, a new musical that was playing at the Hippodrome, which Maisie had hoped Patrick might take her to. She thanked Bob, but said she didn't want to spoil their relationship. She would have liked to add that there were already two men in her life, a fifteen-year-old who was worrying about his acne, and an Irishman who only visited Bristol once a month and didn't seem to realize she was in love with him.

Bob didn't take no for an answer, and a month later Maisie was even more embarrassed when he presented her with a marcasite brooch. She kissed him on the cheek, and wondered how he'd found out it was her birthday. That evening she placed the brooch in a drawer, and might have forgotten all about it if other gifts hadn't followed at regular intervals.

Patrick seemed amused by his rival's persistence, and over dinner one night he reminded Maisie that she was a good-looking woman with prospects.

Maisie didn't laugh. 'It's got to stop,' she said.

'Then why don't you find another supplier?'

'Because good ones are a lot harder to find than lovers. In any case, Bob's reliable, his cakes are the best in town and his prices are lower than any of his competitors.'

'And he's in love with you,' said Patrick.

'Don't tease, Patrick. It's got to stop.'

'I'll tell you something far more important that's got to stop,' said Patrick, bending down and opening his briefcase.

'May I remind you,' said Maisie, 'that we're meant

to be having a romantic candlelit dinner together, not talking business.'

'I'm afraid this can't wait,' he said, placing a sheaf of papers on the table. 'These are your accounts for the past three months, and they don't make happy reading.'

'But I thought you said things have been looking up.'

'So they have. You've even managed to keep your outgoings within the limit recommended by the bank, but, inexplicably, your income has dropped during the same period.'

'How's that possible?' said Maisie. 'We did a record number of covers last month.'

'That's why I decided to check carefully through all your bills and receipts for the past month. They just don't add up. I've come to the sad conclusion, Maisie, that one of your waitresses must have her hand in the till. It's common enough in the catering trade; it usually turns out to be the barman or the head waiter but once it starts, there's no way of stopping it until you find the person responsible and sack them. If you don't identify the culprit fairly soon, you're going to have another year without showing a profit, and you won't be able to pay back one penny of the bank loan, let alone start reducing your overdraft.'

'What do you advise?'

'You'll have to keep a closer eye on all your staff in future, until one of them gives herself away.'

'How will I know which one it is?'

'There are several signs to look out for,' said Patrick. 'Someone who's living beyond their means, perhaps wearing a new coat or an expensive piece of jewellery, or taking a holiday they wouldn't normally be able to afford. She'll probably tell you she's got a new boyfriend, but—'

'Oh, hell,' said Maisie. 'I think I know who it might be.'

'Who?'

'Karen. She's only been with me a few months, and recently she's been going up to London on her weekends off. Last Monday she turned up at work wearing a new scarf and a pair of leather gloves that made me feel quite envious.'

'Don't jump to any conclusions,' said Patrick, 'but keep a close eye on her. Either she's pocketing the tips or she's got her hands in the till, or both. And one thing I can promise you, it won't stop. In most cases the thief becomes more and more confident until they're finally caught. You need to stop it, and stop it quickly, before she puts you out of business.'

◄○►

Maisie hated having to spy on her staff. After all, she'd chosen most of the younger ones herself, while the older ones had been at Tilly's for years.

She kept an especially close eye on Karen, but there weren't any obvious signs that she was stealing. But then, as Patrick had warned her, thieves are more cunning than honest people, and there was no way Maisie could keep an eye on her all the time.

And then the problem solved itself. Karen handed in her notice, announcing that she was engaged and would be joining her fiancé in London at the end of the month. Maisie thought her engagement ring was quite exquisite, although she could only wonder who'd paid for it. But she dismissed the thought, relieved she would now have one less problem to worry about.

But when Patrick returned to Bristol a few weeks later, he warned Maisie that her monthly income had dropped again, so it couldn't have been Karen.

'Is it time to call in the police?' Maisie asked.

'Not yet. The last thing you need are any false accusations or rumours that will only cause ill-feeling among your staff. The police may well flush out the thief, but before they do you could lose some of your best staff, who won't like being under suspicion. And you can also be sure that some of the customers will find out, and you don't need that.'

'How much longer can I afford to go on like this?'

'Let's give it another month. If we haven't found out who it is by then, you'll have to call in the police.' He gave her a huge smile. 'Now let's stop talking business and try to remember that we're meant to be celebrating your birthday.'

'That was two months ago,' she said. 'And if it hadn't been for Bob, you wouldn't even have known.'

Patrick opened his briefcase once again, but this time he produced a royal blue box with Swan's familiar logo on it. He passed it across to Maisie, who took her time opening it, to find a pair of black leather gloves and a woollen scarf in the traditional Burberry pattern.

'So you're the one who's been robbing me blind,' said Maisie as she threw her arms around him.

Patrick didn't respond.

'What's the matter?' asked Maisie.

'I have another piece of news.' Maisie looked into his eyes, and wondered what else could possibly be going wrong at Tilly's. 'I've been promoted. I'm to be the new deputy manager of our head office in Dublin. I'll be tied to my desk most of the time, so somebody else will be taking my place over here. I will still be able to visit you, but not that often.'

Maisie lay in his arms and cried all night. She had thought she wouldn't want to get married again, until the man she loved was no longer available.

She turned up late for work the following morning to find Bob waiting on the doorstep. Once she'd opened the front door, he began to unload the morning delivery from his van.

'I'll be with you in a moment,' said Maisie as she disappeared into the staff washroom.

She'd said her last goodbyes to Patrick as he boarded a train at Temple Meads, when she'd burst into tears again. She must have looked a sight and didn't want the regulars to think anything was wrong. 'Never bring your personal problems to work,' Miss Tilly had often reminded her staff. 'The customers have enough problems of their own without having to worry about yours.'

Maisie looked in the mirror: her make-up was a mess. 'Damn,' she said out loud when she realized she'd left her handbag on the counter. As she walked back into the shop to retrieve it, she suddenly felt sick. Bob was standing with his back to her, one hand in the till. She watched as he stuffed a handful of notes and coins into a trouser pocket, closed the till quietly and then went back to his van to pick up another tray of cakes.

Maisie knew exactly what Patrick would have advised. She walked into the café and stood by the till as Bob strolled back through the door. He was not carrying a tray, but a small red leather box. He gave her a huge smile and fell on one knee.

'You will leave the premises right now, Bob Burrows,' Maisie said, in a tone that surprised even her. 'If I ever see you anywhere near my tea shop again, I will call the police.'

She expected a stream of explanations or expletives, but Bob simply stood up, put the money he'd stolen back on the counter and left without a word. Maisie collapsed on to the nearest chair just as the first member of staff arrived.

'Good morning, Mrs Clifton. Nice weather for the time of year.'

18

WHENEVER A THIN BROWN envelope dropped through the letterbox at No. 27, Maisie assumed it was from Bristol Grammar School, and would probably be another bill for Harry's tuition fees, plus any 'extras', as the Bristol Municipal Charities liked to describe them.

She always called into the bank on the way home to deposit the day's takings in the business account and her share of the tips in a separate account, described as 'Harry's', hoping that at the end of each quarter she would have enough to cover the next bill from BGS.

Maisie ripped open the envelope, and, although she couldn't read every word of the letter, recognized the signature and, above it, the figures £37 10s. It was going to be a close-run thing, but after Mr Holcombe had read Harry's latest report to her, she had to agree with him: it was proving to be a good investment.

'Mind you,' Mr Holcombe had warned her, 'the outgoings aren't going to be any less when the time comes for him to leave school.'

'Why not?' Maisie asked. 'He shouldn't find it hard to get a job after all that education, and then he can start paying his own bills.'

Mr Holcombe shook his head sadly, as if one of his less attentive pupils had failed to grasp a point. 'I'm rather hoping that when he leaves Bristol, he'll want to go up to Oxford and read English.'

'And how long will that take?' asked Maisie.

'Three, possibly four years.'

'He should have read an awful lot of English by then.'

'Certainly enough to get a job.'

Maisie laughed. 'Perhaps he'll end up a schoolmaster like you.'

'He's not like me,' said Mr Holcombe. 'If I had to guess, he'll end up as a writer.'

'Can you make a living as a writer?'

'Certainly, if you're successful. But if that doesn't work out, you could be right – he might end up a schoolmaster like me.'

'I'd like that,' Maisie said, missing the irony.

She placed the envelope in her bag. When she called into the bank after work that afternoon, she would have to make sure there was at least £37 10s in Harry's account before she could consider writing out a cheque for the full amount. Only the bank makes money when you're overdrawn, Patrick had told her. The school had occasionally given her two or three weeks' grace in the past, but Patrick had explained that, like the tea shop, they would also have to balance their books at the end of each term.

Maisie didn't have long to wait for her tram, and once she had taken her seat, her thoughts returned to Patrick. She would never admit to anyone, even her mother, how much she missed him.

Her thoughts were interrupted by a fire engine overtaking the tram. Some of the passengers stared out of the window to follow its progress. Once it was out of sight, Maisie turned her attention to Tilly's. Since she'd sacked Bob Burrows, the bank manager had reported that the tea shop had begun to make a steady profit each month, and might even break Miss Tilly's record of £112 10s by the end of the year, which would allow Maisie to start paying back some of the £500 loan. There might even be enough left over to buy a new pair of shoes for Harry.

Maisie got off the tram at the end of Victoria Street. As she made her way across Bedminster Bridge, she checked her watch, his first present, and once again thought about her son. Seven thirty-two: she would have more than enough time to open the tea shop and be ready to serve her first customer by eight. It always pleased her to find a little queue waiting on the pavement as she turned the 'closed' sign to 'open'.

Just before she reached the High Street, another fire engine shot past, and she could now see a plume of black smoke rising high into the sky. But it wasn't until she turned into Broad Street that her heart began to beat faster. The three fire engines and a police car were parked in a semi-circle outside Tilly's.

Maisie began to run.

'No, no, it can't be Tilly's,' she shouted, and then she spotted several members of her staff standing in a group on the other side of the road. One of them was crying. Maisie was only a few yards from where the front door used to be when a policeman stepped in her path and prevented her from going any further.

'But I'm the owner!' she protested as she stared in disbelief at the smoking embers of what had once been the most popular tea shop in the city. Her eyes watered and she began to cough as the thick black smoke enveloped her. She stared at the charred remains of the once gleaming counter, while a layer of ash covered the floor where the chairs and tables with their spotless white tablecloths had stood when she'd locked up the previous evening.

'I'm very sorry, madam,' said the policeman, 'but for your own safety I must ask you to join your staff on the other side of the road.'

Maisie turned her back on Tilly's and reluctantly began to cross the road. Before she reached the other side, she saw him standing on the edge of the crowd. The moment their eyes met, he turned and walked away.

◄○►

Detective Inspector Blakemore opened his notebook and looked across the table at the suspect.

'Can you tell me where you were at around three o'clock this morning, Mrs Clifton?'

'I was at home in bed,' Maisie replied.

'Is there anyone who can verify that?'

'If by that, Detective Inspector, you mean was anyone in bed with me at the time, the answer is no. Why do you ask?'

The policeman made a note, which gave him a little more time to think. Then he said, 'I'm trying to find out if anyone else was involved.'

'Involved in what?' asked Maisie.

'Arson,' he replied, watching her carefully.

'But who would want to burn down Tilly's?' Maisie demanded.

'I was rather hoping you might be able to assist me on that point,' said Blakemore. He paused, hoping Mrs Clifton would add something that she would later regret. But she said nothing.

Detective Inspector Blakemore couldn't make up his mind if Mrs Clifton was a very cool customer, or simply naive. He knew one person who would be able to answer that question.

◄o►

Mr Frampton rose from behind his desk, shook hands with Maisie and motioned her towards a chair.

'I was so sorry to hear about the fire at Tilly's,' he said. 'Thank God no one was hurt.' Maisie hadn't been thanking God a lot lately. 'I do hope the building and contents were comprehensively insured,' he added.

'Oh, yes,' said Maisie. 'Thanks to Mr Casey it was well covered, but unfortunately the insurance company is refusing to pay out a penny until the police can confirm that I was not involved.'

'I can't believe the police think you're a suspect,' said Frampton.

'With my financial problems,' said Maisie, 'who can blame them?'

'It will only be a matter of time before they work out that's a ridiculous suggestion.'

'I don't have any time,' said Maisie. 'Which is why I've come to see you. I've got to find a job, and when we last met in this room, I recall you saying that if I ever wanted to come back to the Royal . . .'

'And I meant it,' interrupted Mr Frampton. 'But I can't give you your old position back, because Susan's doing an excellent job, and I've recently taken on three of Tilly's staff, so I don't have any vacancies in the Palm Court. The only position I have available at the moment is hardly worthy—'

'I'll consider anything, Mr Frampton,' said Maisie, 'and I mean anything.'

'Some of our customers have been telling us that they would like something to eat after the hotel restaurant has closed for the night,' said Mr Frampton.

'I've been considering introducing a limited service of coffee and sandwiches after ten o'clock, which would be available until the breakfast room opens at six a.m. I could only offer you three pounds a week to begin with, although of course all the tips would be yours. Naturally I'd understand if you felt—'

'I'll take it.'

'When would you be able to start?'

'Tonight.'

◄○►

When the next brown envelope landed on the mat at No. 27, Maisie stuffed it in her bag, unopened, and wondered how long it would be before she received a second, perhaps a third, and then finally a thick white envelope containing a letter not from the bursar, but the headmaster, requesting that Mrs Clifton withdraw her son from the school at the end of term. She dreaded the moment when Harry would have to read that letter to her.

In September Harry was expecting to enter the sixth form, and he couldn't hide the excitement in his eyes whenever he talked about 'going up' to Oxford and reading English at the feet of Alan Quilter, one of the most prominent scholars of the day. Maisie couldn't bear the thought of having to tell him that would no longer be possible.

Her first few nights at the Royal had been very quiet, and things didn't get much busier during the following month. She hated being idle, and when the cleaning staff arrived at five in the morning they would often discover there was nothing for them to do in the Palm Court room. Even on her busiest night Maisie didn't have more than half a dozen customers, and several of those had been turfed out of the hotel bar just after midnight and seemed more interested in propositioning her than in ordering coffee and a ham sandwich.

Most of her customers were commercial travellers who only booked in for one night, so her chances of building up a regular clientele didn't look promising, and the tips were certainly not going to take care of the brown envelope that remained unopened in her handbag.

Maisie knew that if Harry was to remain at Bristol Grammar School and have the slightest chance of going up to Oxford, there was only one person she could turn to for help. She would beg if necessary.

19

'WHAT MAKES YOU THINK Mr Hugo would be willing to help?' asked Old Jack, leaning back in his seat. 'He's never shown any sign of caring about Harry in the past. On the contrary . . .'

'Because if there's one person on earth who ought to feel some responsibility for Harry's future, it's that man.' Maisie immediately regretted her words.

Old Jack was silent for a moment before he asked, 'Is there something you're not telling me, Maisie?'

'No,' she replied, a little too quickly. She hated lying, especially to Old Jack, but she was determined that this was one secret she would take to her grave.

'Have you given any thought to when and where you will confront Mr Hugo?'

'I know exactly what I'm going to do. He rarely leaves his office before six in the evening, and by then most of the other staff in the building have already left for the night. I know his office is on the fifth floor, I know it's the third door on the left. I know—'

'But do you know about Miss Potts?' interrupted Old Jack. 'Even if you did manage to get past reception and somehow made it to the fifth floor unnoticed, there's no way of avoiding her.'

'Miss Potts? I've never heard of her.'

'She's been Mr Hugo's private secretary for the past fifteen years. I can tell you from personal experience, you don't need a guard dog if you've got Miss Potts as a secretary.'

'Then I'll just have to wait until she goes home.'

'Miss Potts never goes home before the boss, and she's always behind her desk thirty minutes before he arrives in the morning.'

'But I'll have even less chance of getting into the Manor House,' said Maisie, 'where they have a guard dog too. He's called Jenkins.'

'Then you'll have to find a time and place when Mr Hugo will be on his own, can't escape and can't rely on Miss Potts or Jenkins to come to his rescue.'

'Is there such a time and place?' asked Maisie.

'Oh yes,' said Old Jack. 'But you'll have to get your timing right.'

◄◦►

Maisie waited until it was dark before she slipped out of Old Jack's railway carriage. She tiptoed across the gravel path, eased open the back door, climbed in, and shut it behind her. Resigned to a long wait, she settled herself down on the comfortable leather seat. She had a clear view of the building through a side window. Maisie waited patiently for each light to go out. Old Jack had warned her that his would be among the last.

She used the time to go over the questions she planned to ask him. Questions she'd rehearsed for several days before trying them out on Old Jack that afternoon. He'd made several suggestions, which she'd happily agreed to.

Just after six, a Rolls-Royce drew up and parked outside the front of the building. A chauffeur got out and stationed himself alongside. A few moments later

Sir Walter Barrington, the chairman of the company, marched out of the front door, climbed into the back of the car and was whisked away.

More and more lights went out, until finally only one was still aglow, like a single star on the top of a Christmas tree. Suddenly Maisie heard feet crunching across the gravel. She slipped off the seat and crouched down on the floor. She could hear two men, deep in conversation, heading towards her. Her plan didn't include two men, and she was about to leap out of the other side and try to disappear into the night when they came to a halt.

'. . . But despite that,' said a voice she recognized, 'I'd be obliged if my involvement could remain strictly between the two of us.'

'Of course, sir, you can rely on me,' said another voice she'd heard before, although she couldn't remember where.

'Let's keep in touch, old fellow,' said the first voice. 'I have no doubt I'll be calling on the bank's services again.'

Maisie heard one set of footsteps moving away. She froze when the car door opened.

He got in, took his place behind the wheel and pulled the door closed. Doesn't have a chauffeur, prefers to drive the Bugatti himself, fancies himself behind the wheel – all priceless pieces of information supplied by Old Jack.

He switched on the ignition and the vehicle shuddered into life. He revved the engine several times before crunching the gear lever into first. The man on the gate saluted as Mr Barrington drove out on to the main road and headed towards the city, just as he did every night, on his way back to the Manor House.

'Don't let him know you're in the back until he's

reached the city centre,' Old Jack had advised. 'He won't risk stopping there, because he'll be afraid someone might see you together and recognize him. But once he reaches the outskirts of the city, he won't hesitate to chuck you out. You'll have ten to fifteen minutes at most.'

'That's all I'll need,' Maisie had told him.

Maisie waited until he'd driven past the cathedral and across College Green, which was always busy at that time of night. But just as she was about to sit up and tap him on the shoulder, the car began to slow down and then came to a halt. The door opened, he got out, the door closed. Maisie peered between the front seats and was horrified to see that he had parked outside the Royal Hotel.

A dozen thoughts flashed through her mind. Should she jump out before it was too late? Why was he visiting the Royal? Was it a coincidence that it was on her day off? How long did he plan to be there? She decided to stay put, fearing she would be spotted if she got out in such a public place. Besides, this could well be her last chance to confront him face to face before the bill had to be paid.

The answer to one of her questions turned out to be twenty minutes, but long before he got back into the driver's seat and drove off, Maisie was in a cold sweat. She had no idea her heart could beat that fast. She waited until he had gone about half a mile before she sat up and tapped him on the shoulder.

He looked shocked as he turned round, which was followed by a look of recognition, and then realization. 'What do you want?' he demanded, recovering slightly.

'I have a feeling you know exactly what I want,' said Maisie. 'My only interest is Harry, and making sure his school fees are paid for the next two years.'

'Give me one good reason why I should pay your son's school fees.'

'Because he's your son,' Maisie replied calmly.

'And what makes you so sure of that?'

'I watched you when you first saw him at St Bede's,' said Maisie, 'and every Sunday at St Mary's when he sang in the choir. I saw the look in your eyes then, and I saw it again when you refused to shake hands with him on the first day of term.'

'That's not proof,' said Barrington, sounding a little more confident. 'It's nothing more than a woman's intuition.'

'Then perhaps the time has come to let another woman know what you get up to on a works outing.'

'What makes you think she'd believe you?'

'Nothing more than a woman's intuition,' said Maisie. This silenced him, and gave her the confidence to continue. 'Mrs Barrington might also be interested to know why you went to so much trouble to have my brother arrested the day after Arthur disappeared.'

'A coincidence, nothing more.'

'And is it also just a coincidence that my husband has never been seen since?'

'I had nothing to do with Clifton's death!' shouted Barrington as he swerved across the road, narrowly missing an oncoming vehicle.

Maisie sat bolt upright, stunned by what she'd heard. 'So it was you who was responsible for my husband's death.'

'You have no proof of that,' he said defiantly.

'I don't need any more proof. But in spite of all the damage you've done to my family over the years, I'll still give you an easy way out. You take care of Harry's education while he's still at Bristol Grammar School, and I won't bother you again.'

It was some time before Barrington responded. He eventually said, 'I'll need a few days to work out the best way to handle the payments.'

'The company's charitable trust could easily take care of such a small amount,' said Maisie. 'After all, your father is chairman of the governors.'

This time he didn't have a ready response. Was he wondering how she'd come across that piece of information? He wasn't the first person to underestimate Old Jack. Maisie opened her handbag, pulled out the thin brown envelope and placed it on the seat beside him.

The car swung into an unlit alley. Barrington jumped out and opened the back door. Maisie stepped out, feeling that the confrontation couldn't have gone much better. As her feet touched the ground, he grabbed her by the shoulders and shook her violently.

'Now you listen to me, Maisie Clifton, and listen carefully,' he said, a look of fury in his eyes. 'If you ever threaten me again, I'll not only see that your brother is sacked, but I'll make sure he never works in this city again. And if you're ever foolish enough to even hint to my wife that I'm that boy's father, I'll have you arrested, and it won't be a prison you'll end up in, but a mental asylum.'

He let go of her, clenched a fist and then punched her full in the face. She collapsed on to the ground and curled up into a ball, expecting him to kick her again and again. When nothing happened, she looked up to see him standing over her. He was tearing the thin brown envelope into little pieces and scattering them like confetti over a bride.

Without another word, he jumped back into the car and sped away.

When the white envelope came through the letterbox, Maisie knew she was beaten. She would have to tell Harry the truth when he got back from school that afternoon. But first she had to drop into the bank, deposit her meagre tips from the previous evening, and tell Mr Prendergast there would be no more bills from BGS, as her son would be leaving at the end of term.

She decided to walk to the bank and save a penny on the tram fare. On the way, she thought about all the people she'd let down. Would Miss Tilly and Miss Monday ever forgive her? Several of her staff, particularly some of the older ones, hadn't been able to find another job. Then there were her parents, who had always watched over Harry so that she could go to work; Old Jack, who couldn't have done more to help her son; and most of all, Harry himself, who in the words of Mr Holcombe, was about to be crowned with the laurels of victory.

When she reached the bank, she joined the longest queue, as she was in no hurry to be served.

'Good morning, Mrs Clifton,' said the teller cheerfully when she eventually reached the front of the line.

'Good morning,' Maisie replied before placing four shillings and sixpence on the counter.

The teller checked the amount carefully, then placed the coins in different trays below the counter. He next wrote out a slip to confirm the sum Mrs Clifton had deposited, and handed it to her. Maisie stood to one side to allow the next customer to take her place while she put the slip in her bag.

'Mrs Clifton,' said the teller.

'Yes?' she said, looking back up.

'The manager was hoping to have a word with you.'

'I quite understand,' she said. Maisie didn't need him to tell her there wasn't enough money in her account to cover the latest invoice from the school. In fact, it would be a relief to let Mr Prendergast know there would be no further bills for extra-curricular activities.

The young man led her silently across the banking hall and down a long corridor. When he reached the manager's office, he knocked gently on the door, opened it and said, 'Mrs Clifton, sir.'

'Ah, yes,' said Mr Prendergast. 'I do need to have a word with you, Mrs Clifton. Please come in.' Where had she heard that voice before?

'Mrs Clifton,' he continued once she was seated, 'I am sorry to have to inform you that we have been unable to honour your most recent cheque for thirty-seven pounds ten shillings, made payable to Bristol Municipal Charities. Were you to present it again, I fear there are still insufficient funds in your account to cover the full amount. Unless, of course, you anticipate depositing any further funds in the near future?'

'No,' said Maisie, taking the white envelope from her bag and placing it on the desk in front of him. 'Perhaps you would be kind enough to let the BMC know that, given time, I will pay off any other expenses that have arisen during Harry's last term.'

'I'm very sorry, Mrs Clifton,' said Mr Prendergast. 'I only wish I could help in some way.' He picked up the white envelope. 'May I open this?' he asked.

'Yes, of course,' said Maisie, who until that moment had tried to avoid finding out just how much she still owed the school.

Mr Prendergast picked up a thin silver paperknife from his desk and slit open the envelope. He extracted a cheque from the Bristol and West of England Insurance Company to the value of six hundred pounds, made payable to Mrs Maisie Clifton.

HUGO BARRINGTON

1921–1936

20

I wouldn't even have remembered her name, if she hadn't later accused me of killing her husband.

It all began when my father insisted I accompany the workers on their annual outing to Weston-super-Mare. 'Good for their morale to see the chairman's son taking an interest,' he said.

I wasn't convinced, and quite frankly considered the whole exercise a waste of time, but once my father has made up his mind about anything, there is no point arguing. And it would have been a waste of time if Maisie – such a common name – hadn't come along for the ride. Even I was surprised to find how eager she was to jump into bed with the boss's son. I assumed that once we were back in Bristol, I'd never hear from her again. Perhaps I wouldn't have, if she hadn't married Arthur Clifton.

◄○►

I was sitting at my desk going over the tender for the *Maple Leaf*, checking and rechecking the figures, hoping to find some way the company might save a little money, but however hard I tried, the bottom line didn't make good reading. It didn't help that it had been my decision to tender for the contract.

My opposite number at Myson had driven a hard bargain, and after several delays I hadn't budgeted for, we were running five months behind schedule, with penalty clauses that would be triggered should we fail to complete the build by December 15th. What had originally looked like a dream contract that would show a handsome profit, was turning into a nightmare, where we would wake up on December 15th with heavy losses.

My father had been against Barrington's taking on the contract in the first place and had made his views clear. 'We should stick to what we're good at,' he repeated from the chair at every board meeting. 'For the past hundred years, Barrington's Shipping Line has transported goods to and from the far corners of the earth, leaving our rivals in Belfast, Liverpool and Newcastle to build ships.'

I knew I wouldn't be able to sway him, so I spent my time trying to persuade the younger members of the board that we had missed out on several opportunities in recent years, while others had snapped up lucrative contracts that could easily have come our way. I finally convinced them, by a slim majority, to dip a toe in the water and sign up with Myson to build them a cargo vessel to add to their fast-growing fleet.

'If we do a good job and deliver the *Maple Leaf* on time,' I told the board, 'more contracts are sure to follow.'

'Let's hope we don't live to regret it,' was my father's only comment after he'd lost the vote at the board meeting.

I was already regretting it. Although the Barrington Line was predicting record profits for 1921, it was beginning to look as if its new subsidiary, Barrington Shipbuilding, would be the only red entry on the annual balance sheet. Some members of the board were already distancing themselves from the decision, while reminding everyone that they had voted with my father.

I had only recently been appointed managing director of the company and I could just imagine what was being said behind my back. 'Chip off the old block' clearly wasn't on anyone's lips. One director had already resigned and couldn't have made his views more clear when he departed, warning my father, 'The boy lacks judgement. Be careful he doesn't end up bankrupting the company.'

But I hadn't given up. I remained convinced that as long as we finished the job on time, we could still break even, and possibly make a small profit. So much depended on what happened during the next few weeks. I'd already given the order to work round the clock in three eight-hour shifts, and promised the workforce handsome bonuses if they managed to complete the contract on time. After all, there were enough men hanging around outside the gates, desperate for work.

◄○►

I was just about to tell my secretary I was going home, when he burst into my office unannounced.

He was a short, squat man, with heavy shoulders and bulging muscles, the build of a stevedore. My first thought was to wonder how he had managed to get past Miss Potts, who followed in his wake looking unusually flustered. 'I couldn't stop him,' she said, stating the obvious. 'Shall I call the watchman?'

I looked into the man's eyes and said, 'No.'

Miss Potts remained by the door while we sized each other up, like a mongoose and a snake, each wondering who would strike first. Then the man reluctantly removed his cap and started jabbering. It was some time before I could understand what he was saying.

'My best mate's goin' to die! Arthur Clifton's goin' to die unless you do somethin' about it.'

I told him to calm down and explain what the problem was, when my works manager came charging into the room.

'I'm sorry you've been troubled by Tancock, sir,' he said

once he'd caught his breath, 'but I can assure you it's all under control. Nothin' for you to worry about.'

'What is all under control?' I asked.

'Tancock here claims that his mate Clifton was workin' inside the hull when the shift changed, and the new shift somehow managed to seal him inside.'

'Come and see for yourself!' shouted Tancock. 'You can hear him tappin'!'

'Could that be possible, Haskins?' I asked.

'Anything's possible, sir, but it's more likely Clifton's buggered off for the day and is already in the pub.'

'Then why hasn't he signed off at the gate?' demanded Tancock.

'Nothing unusual in that, sir,' said Haskins, not looking at him. 'Signin' on's what matters, not signin' off.'

'If you don't come and see for yourself,' said Tancock, 'you'll go to your grave with his blood on your hands.' This outburst silenced even Haskins.

'Miss Potts, I'm going down to number one dock,' I said. 'I shouldn't be too long.'

The squat little man ran out of my office without another word.

'Haskins, join me in my car,' I said. 'We can discuss what ought to be done on the way.'

'Nothin' needs to be done, sir,' he insisted. 'It's all stuff and nonsense.'

It wasn't until we were alone in the car that I put it bluntly to my ganger. 'Is there any chance that Clifton really might be sealed up in the hull?'

'No chance, sir,' said Haskins firmly. 'I'm only sorry to be wastin' your time.'

'But the man seems pretty certain,' I said.

'Like he's always certain about what'll win the three thirty at Chepstow.'

I didn't laugh.

'Clifton's shift ended at six,' Haskins continued, taking on a more serious tone. 'He must've known that the welders would be moving in and would expect to finish the job before the next shift reported for duty at two in the mornin'.'

'What was Clifton doing down in the hull in the first place?'

'Making the final checks before the welders got to work.'

'Is it possible he didn't realize his shift had ended?'

'You can hear the end-of-shift horn in the middle of Bristol,' said Haskins as we drove past Tancock, who was running like a man possessed.

'Even if you were deep inside the hull?'

'I suppose it's just possible he might not have heard it if he was in the double bottom, but I've never come across a docker who didn't know what time his shift ends.'

'As long as he has a watch,' I said, looking to see if Haskins was wearing one. He wasn't. 'If Clifton really is still down there, do we have the equipment to get him out?'

'We've got enough acetylene torches to burn through the hull and remove a complete section. Problem is, it'd take hours, and if Clifton's down there, there wouldn't be much chance of him still bein' alive by the time we reached him. On top of that, it would take the men another fortnight, perhaps longer, to replace the whole section. And as you keep remindin' me, guv, you've got everyone on bonuses to save time, not waste it.'

The night shift was well into its second hour by the time I brought my car to a halt by the side of the ship. There must have been over a hundred men on board, working flat out, hammering, welding and sealing in the rivets. As I climbed the gangway, I could see Tancock running towards the ship. When he caught up with me a few moments later he had to bend double, his hands on his thighs, while he recovered.

'So, what do you expect me to do, Tancock?' I asked once he'd caught his breath.

'Stop them all workin', guv, just for a few minutes, then you'll hear him tappin'.'

I nodded my approval.

Haskins shrugged his shoulders, clearly unable to believe I would even consider giving such an order. It took him several minutes to get everyone to down tools and for the workers to fall silent. Every man on the ship, as well as the dockside, stood still and listened intently, but other than the occasional squawk from a passing gull or a smoker's cough, I heard nothing.

'Like I said, sir, it's been a waste of everyone's time,' said Haskins. 'By now Clifton will be suppin' his third pint at the Pig and Whistle.'

Someone dropped a hammer, and the sound echoed around the docks. Then for a moment, just a moment, I thought I heard a different sound, regular and soft.

'That's him!' shouted Tancock.

And then, as suddenly as it had started, the noise stopped.

'Did anyone else hear anything?' I shouted.

'I didn't hear nothin',' said Haskins, looking around at the men, almost daring them to defy him.

Some of them stared back at him, while one or two picked up their hammers menacingly, as if they were waiting for someone to lead them over the top.

I felt like a captain who was being given one last chance to quell a mutiny. Either way I couldn't win. If I told the men to go back to work, the rumours would spread until every man in the dockyard believed I was personally responsible for Clifton's death. It would be weeks, months, possibly even years before I could recover my authority. But if I gave the order to break open the hull, any hope of making a profit on the contract would be scuppered, and with it my chances of ever becoming chairman of the board. I just stood there, hoping the continued silence would convince the men that

Tancock was wrong. As each second of silence passed, my confidence grew.

'It seems no one heard nothin', sir,' Haskins said a few moments later. 'Can I have your permission to put the men back to work?'

They didn't move a muscle, just continued to glare defiantly at me. Haskins stared back at them, and one or two eventually lowered their eyes.

I turned to the ganger and gave the order to get back to work. In the moment's silence that followed, I could have sworn I heard a tap. I glanced at Tancock, but then the sound was drowned out by a thousand other noises as the men went resentfully back to work.

'Tancock, why don't you bugger off down the pub and see if your mate's there,' said Haskins. 'And when you find him, give him a tickin' off for wastin' everybody's time.'

'And if he isn't,' I said, 'call by his house and ask his wife if she's seen him.' I realized my mistake the moment I'd spoken, and quickly added, 'That is, assuming he has a wife.'

'Yes, guv, he does,' said Tancock. 'She's my sister.'

'If you still can't find him, report back to me.'

'It'll be too late by then,' said Tancock as he turned and walked off, his shoulders slumped.

'I'll be in my office should you need me, Haskins,' I said, before walking down the gangway. I drove back to Barrington House, hoping never to see Tancock again.

I returned to my desk, but was unable to concentrate on the letters Miss Potts had left for me to sign. I could still hear that tapping in my head, repeating itself again and again, like a popular melody that plays continually in your mind and even stops you from sleeping. I knew that if Clifton didn't report for work the next morning, I would never be rid of it.

During the next hour, I began to feel more confident that

Tancock must have found his mate and would now be regretting making such a fool of himself.

It was one of the rare occasions when Miss Potts left the office before me, and I was just locking the top drawer of my desk before going home, when I heard footsteps running up the stairs. It could only be one man.

I looked up, and the man I'd hoped never to see again was standing in the doorway, pent-up fury blazing in his eyes.

'You killed my best mate, you bastard,' he said, shaking a fist. 'You may as well have murdered him with your bare hands!'

'Now, steady on, Tancock, old chap,' I said. 'For all we know, Clifton may still be alive.'

'He's gone to his grave just so you could finish your bloody job on time. No man will ever sail on that ship once they find out the truth.'

'Men die in shipbuilding accidents every day,' I said lamely.

Tancock took a pace towards me. He was so angry that for a moment I thought he was going to hit me, but he just stood there, feet apart, fists clenched, glaring at me. 'When I've told the police what I know, you'll have to admit you could've saved his life with a single word. But because you were only interested in how much money you would make, I'm going to make sure that no man on these docks will ever work for you again.'

I knew if the police did become involved, half of Bristol would think Clifton was still inside that hull and the union would demand it was opened up. If that happened, I wasn't in any doubt what they'd find.

I rose slowly from my chair and walked across to the safe on the far side of the room. I entered the code, turned the key, pulled open the door and extracted a thick white envelope before returning to my desk. I picked up a silver letter opener, slit open the envelope and took out a five-pound note. I even wondered whether Tancock had ever seen one before. I placed it on the blotting pad in front of him and watched his piggy eyes grow larger by the second.

'Nothing is going to bring back your friend,' I said, placing a second note on top of the first. His eyes never left the money. 'And anyway, who knows, he might just have done a bunk for a few days. That wouldn't be considered unusual in his line of work.' I placed a third note on top of the second. 'And when he comes back, your mates will never let you forget it.' A fourth note was followed by a fifth. 'And you wouldn't want to be charged with wasting the police's time, would you? That's a serious offence for which you can go to jail.' Two more notes. 'And of course you'd also lose your job.' He looked up at me, his anger visibly turning to fear. Three more notes. 'I could hardly be expected to employ a man who was accusing me of murder.' I placed the last two notes on top of the pile. The envelope was empty.

Tancock turned away. I took out my wallet and added one more five-pound note, three pounds and ten shillings to the pile: £68 10s in all. His eyes returned to the notes. 'There's plenty more where that came from,' I said, hoping I sounded convincing.

Tancock walked slowly towards my desk and, without looking at me, gathered up the notes, stuffed them into his pocket and left without a word.

I went to the window and watched as he walked out of the building and headed slowly for the dock gate.

I left the safe wide open, scattered some of its contents on the floor, dropped the empty envelope on my desk and left my office without locking up. I was the last person to leave the building.

21

'DETECTIVE INSPECTOR BLAKEMORE, sir,' said Miss Potts, then stood aside to allow the policeman to enter the managing director's office.

Hugo Barrington studied the inspector carefully as he entered the room. He couldn't have been much more than the regulation minimum height of five feet nine inches, and he was a few pounds overweight, but still looked fit. He was carrying a raincoat that had probably been bought when he was still a constable, and wore a brown felt hat of a more recent vintage, indicating that he hadn't been an inspector all that long.

The two men shook hands, and once he was seated, Blakemore took a notebook and pen out of an inside jacket pocket. 'As you know, sir, I am following up enquiries concerning an alleged theft that took place on these premises last night.' Barrington didn't like the word 'alleged'. 'Could I begin by asking when you first discovered that the money was missing?'

'Yes, of course, inspector,' said Barrington, trying to sound as helpful as possible. 'I arrived at the docks around seven o'clock this morning and drove straight to the sheds to check how the night shift had got on.'

'Is that something you do every morning?'

'No, only from time to time,' said Hugo, puzzled by the question.

'And how long did you spend there?'

'Twenty, perhaps thirty minutes. Then I came up to my office.'

'So you would have been in your office at around seven twenty, seven thirty at the latest.'

'Yes, that sounds about right.'

'And was your secretary already here by then?'

'Yes, she was. I rarely manage to get in before her. She's a formidable lady,' he added with a smile.

'Quite,' said the detective inspector. 'So it was Miss Potts who told you the safe had been broken into?'

'Yes. She said that when she came in this morning, she'd found the safe door open and some of its contents scattered on the floor, so she immediately rang the police.'

'She didn't ring you first, sir?'

'No, inspector. I would have been in my car on the way to work at that time.'

'So, you say your secretary arrived before you this morning. And did you leave before her last night, sir?'

'I don't recall,' said Barrington. 'But it would be most unusual for me to leave after her.'

'Yes, Miss Potts has confirmed that,' said the detective inspector. 'But she also said – ' he glanced down at his notebook – '"I left before Mr Barrington last night, as a problem had arisen which needed his attention."' Blakemore looked up. 'Are you able to tell me what that problem was, sir?'

'When you run a company as large as this,' said Hugo, 'problems arise all the time.'

'So you don't remember what particular problem arose yesterday evening?'

'No, inspector, I do not.'

'When you arrived in your office this morning and found the safe door open, what was the first thing you did?'

'I checked to see what was missing.'

'And what did you discover?'

'All my cash had been taken.'

'How can you be sure it had *all* been taken?'

'Because I found this open envelope on my desk,' Hugo said, handing it over.

'And how much should there have been in the envelope, sir?'

'Sixty-eight pounds and ten shillings.'

'You seem very certain of that.'

'Yes, I am,' said Hugo. 'Why should that surprise you?'

'It's simply that Miss Potts told me there was only sixty pounds in the safe, all in five-pound notes. Perhaps you could tell me, sir, where the other eight pounds and ten shillings came from?'

Hugo didn't answer immediately. 'I do sometimes keep a little loose change in my desk drawer, inspector,' he said finally.

'That's quite a large sum to describe as "a little loose change". However, allow me to return to the safe for a moment. When you entered your office this morning, the first thing you noticed was that the safe door was open.'

'That is correct, inspector.'

'Do you have a key for the safe?'

'Yes, of course.'

'Are you the only person who knows the code and is in possession of a key, sir?'

'No, Miss Potts also has access to the safe.'

'Can you confirm that the safe was locked when you went home last night?'

'Yes, it always is.'

'Then we must assume that the burglary was carried out by a professional.'

'What makes you say that, inspector?' asked Barrington.

'But if he was a professional,' said Blakemore, ignoring the question, 'what puzzles me is why he left the safe door open.'

'I'm not sure I'm following you, inspector.'

'I'll explain, sir. Professional burglars tend to leave everything just as they found it, so that their crime won't be found out immediately. It allows them more time to dispose of the stolen goods.'

'More time,' repeated Hugo.

'A professional would have closed the safe door and taken the envelope with him, making it more likely that it would be some time before you discovered anything was missing. In my experience, some people don't open their safes for days, even weeks. Only an amateur would have left your office in such disarray.'

'Then perhaps it was an amateur?'

'Then how did he manage to open the safe, sir?'

'Maybe he somehow got hold of Miss Potts's key?'

'And the code as well? But Miss Potts assures me that she takes her safe key home every night, as I understand you do, sir.' Hugo said nothing. 'May I be allowed to look inside the safe?'

'Yes, of course.'

'What is that?' asked the inspector, pointing to a tin box on the bottom shelf of the safe.

'It's my coin collection, inspector. A hobby of mine.'

'Would you be kind enough to open it, sir?'

'Is that really necessary?' asked Hugo impatiently.

'Yes, I'm afraid it is, sir.'

Hugo reluctantly opened the box, to reveal a hoard of gold coins he had collected over many years.

'Now, here's another mystery,' said the inspector. 'Our thief takes sixty pounds from the safe, and eight pounds ten shillings from your desk drawer, but leaves behind a box of gold coins that must be worth considerably more. And then there's the problem of the envelope.'

'The envelope?' said Hugo.

'Yes, sir, the envelope you say contained the money.'

'But I found it on my desk this morning.'

'I don't doubt that, sir, but you will notice that it has been slit neatly open.'

'Probably with my letter opener,' said Hugo, holding it up triumphantly.

'Quite possibly, sir, but in my experience, burglars have a tendency to rip open envelopes, not slit them neatly with a letter opener as if they already knew what was inside.'

'But Miss Potts told me that you'd found the thief,' said Hugo, trying not to sound exasperated.

'No, sir. We have found the money, but I'm not convinced that we've found the guilty party.'

'But you found some of the money in his possession?'

'Yes, we did, sir.'

'Then what more do you want?'

'To be certain we've got the right man.'

'And who is the man you've charged?'

'I didn't say I'd charged him, sir,' said the inspector as he turned a page in his notebook. 'A Mr Stanley Tancock, who turns out to be one of your stevedores. Name ring a bell, sir?'

'Can't say it does,' said Hugo. 'But if he works in the yard, he would certainly have known where my office was.'

'I am in no doubt, sir, that Tancock knew where your office was, because he says he came to see you around seven yesterday evening to tell you that his brother-in-law, a Mr Arthur Clifton, was trapped in the hull of a ship being built in the yard, and if you didn't give the order to get him out, he would die.'

'Ah, yes, I remember now. I did go over to the yard yesterday afternoon as my ganger will confirm, but it turned out to be a false alarm and a waste of everyone's time. Clearly he just wanted to find out where the safe was, so he could come back later and rob me.'

'He admits that he came back to your office a second time,' said Blakemore, turning another page of his notes, 'when he claims you offered him sixty-eight pounds and ten shillings if he would keep his mouth shut about Clifton.'

'I've never heard such an outrageous suggestion.'

'Then let us consider the alternative for a moment, sir. Let us suppose that Tancock did come back to your office with the intention of robbing you some time between seven o'clock and seven thirty yesterday evening. Having somehow managed to get into the building unobserved he reaches the fifth floor, makes his way to your office, and with either your key or Miss Potts's unlocks the safe, enters the code, removes the envelope, slits it neatly open and takes out the money, but doesn't bother with a box of gold coins. He leaves the safe door open, spreads some of its contents on the floor and places the neatly opened envelope on your desk, and then, like the Scarlet Pimpernel, disappears into thin air.'

'It needn't have been between seven and seven thirty in the evening,' said Hugo defiantly. 'It could have been any time before eight this morning.'

'I think not, sir,' said Blakemore. 'You see, Tancock has an alibi between eight and eleven o'clock last night.'

'No doubt this so-called "alibi" is some mate of his,' said Barrington.

'Thirty-one of them, at the last count,' said the detective inspector. 'It seems that having stolen your money, he turned up at the Pig and Whistle public house at around eight o'clock, and not only were the drinks on him, but he also cleared his slate. He paid the landlord with a new five-pound note, which I have in my possession.'

The detective removed his wallet, took out the note and placed it on Barrington's desk.

'The landlord also added that Tancock left the pub at around eleven, and was so drunk that two of his friends had to accompany him to his home in Still House Lane, where we found him this morning. I am bound to say, sir, that if it was Tancock who robbed you, we have a master criminal on our hands and I'd be proud to be the man who puts him behind bars. Which I suspect is exactly what you had in mind, sir,' he added, looking directly at Barrington, 'when you *gave* him the money.'

'And why on earth would I do that?' said Hugo, trying to keep his voice even.

'Because if Stanley Tancock was arrested and sent to jail, no one would take his story about Arthur Clifton seriously. Incidentally, Clifton hasn't been seen since yesterday afternoon. So I shall be recommending to my superiors that the hull be opened up without further delay so that we can discover if it was a false alarm and Tancock was wasting everyone's time.'

◄○►

Hugo Barrington checked in the mirror and straightened his bow tie. He hadn't told his father about the Arthur Clifton incident or the visit from Detective Inspector Blakemore. The less the old man knew the better. All he'd said was that some money had been stolen from his office and one of the stevedores had been arrested.

Once he'd put on his dinner jacket, Hugo sat on the end of the bed and waited for his wife to finish dressing. He hated being late, but he knew that no amount of badgering would make Elizabeth move any faster. He'd checked on Giles and his baby sister Emma, who were both fast asleep.

Hugo had wanted two sons, an heir and a spare. Emma was an inconvenience, which meant he'd have to try again. His father had been a second child and lost his older brother fighting the Boers in South Africa. Hugo's older brother had been killed at Ypres, along with half his regiment. So, in time, Hugo could expect to succeed his father as chairman of the company and, when his father died, to inherit the title and the family fortune.

So he and Elizabeth would have to try again. Not that making love to his wife was a pleasure any more. In fact, he couldn't remember if it ever had been. Recently he'd been looking for distractions elsewhere.

'Yours is a marriage made in heaven,' his mother used to say. His father was more practical. He had felt that bringing together his elder son and the only daughter of Lord Harvey was more of a merger than a marriage. When Hugo's brother was killed on the Western Front, his fiancée was passed on to Hugo. No longer a merger, more of a takeover. Hugo wasn't surprised to discover on his wedding night that Elizabeth was a virgin; his second virgin, in fact.

Elizabeth finally emerged from the dressing room, apologizing, as she always did, for keeping him waiting. The journey from the Manor House to Barrington Hall was only a couple of miles, and all the land in between the two houses belonged to the family. By the time Hugo and Elizabeth entered his parents' drawing room at a few minutes past eight, Lord Harvey was already on his second sherry. Hugo glanced around the room at the other guests. There was only one couple he didn't recognize.

His father immediately took him across and introduced him to Colonel Danvers, the recently appointed chief constable of the county. Hugo decided not to mention his meeting that morning with Detective Inspector Blakemore to the colonel, but just before they sat down for dinner, he took his father on one side to bring him up to date on the theft, never once mentioning the name of Arthur Clifton.

Over a dinner of game soup, succulent lamb and green beans, followed by crème brûlée, the conversation ranged from the Prince of Wales's visit to Cardiff and his less than helpful remarks about sympathizing with the mine workers, to Lloyd George's latest import tariffs and the effect they would have on the shipping industry, and George Bernard Shaw's *Heartbreak House*, which had recently opened to mixed reviews at the Old Vic Theatre, before returning to the Prince of Wales and the vexed question of how to find him a suitable wife.

When the servants had cleared the table after dessert, the ladies retired to the drawing room to enjoy coffee, while the butler offered the gentlemen brandy or port.

'Shipped by me and imported by you,' said Sir Walter, raising a glass to Lord Harvey while the butler circled the table offering cigars to the guests. Once Lord Harvey's Romeo y Julieta had been lit to his satisfaction, he turned to his son-in-law and said, 'Your father tells me that some blighter broke into your office and stole a large amount of cash.'

'Yes, that's correct,' Hugo replied. 'But I'm pleased to say they've caught the thief. Sadly he turned out to be one of our stevedores.'

'Is that right, Danvers?' asked Sir Walter. 'You've caught the man?'

'I did hear something about it,' responded the chief constable, 'but I wasn't told that anybody had been charged yet.'

'Why not?' demanded Lord Harvey.

'Because the man is saying that I *gave* him the money,' Hugo interjected. 'In fact, when the detective inspector questioned me this morning, I began to wonder which one of us was the criminal, and which the injured party.'

'I'm sorry to hear you feel that way,' said Colonel Danvers. 'May I ask who the officer in charge of the investigation was?'

'Detective Inspector Blakemore,' said Hugo, before adding, 'I got the impression he might have a grudge against our family.'

'When you employ as many people as we do,' said Sir Walter, placing his glass back on the table, 'there's bound to be the odd person who bears a grudge.'

'I must admit,' said Danvers, 'that Blakemore's not known for his tact. But I'll look into the matter, and if I feel he's overstepped the mark I'll assign someone else to the case.'

22

SCHOOLDAYS ARE THE happiest days of your life, claimed R.C. Sherriff, but that had not been Hugo Barrington's experience. Although he had a feeling that Giles would, as his father put it, 'make a better fist of things'.

Hugo tried to forget what had happened on his first day at school, some twenty-four years ago. He'd been driven to St Bede's in a hansom carriage, accompanied by his father, mother and elder brother Nicholas, who had just been appointed school captain. Hugo had burst into tears when another new bug had innocently asked, 'Is it true your grandfather was a docker?' Sir Walter was proud his father had 'pulled himself up by his bootstraps', but with eight-year-olds, first impressions stick. 'Grandpa was a docker! Grandpa was a docker! Cry baby! Cry baby!' chanted the rest of the dorm.

Today his son Giles would be driven to St Bede's in Sir Walter Barrington's Rolls-Royce. Hugo had wanted to take his son to school in his own car, but his father wouldn't hear of it. 'Three generations of Barringtons have been educated at St Bede's and Eton. My heir must arrive in style.'

Hugo didn't point out to his father that Giles hadn't, as yet, been offered a place at Eton, and that it was even possible the boy might have ideas of his own as to where he would like to be educated. 'Heaven forbid,' he could hear his father saying. 'Ideas smack of rebellion and rebellions must be put down.'

Giles hadn't spoken since they'd left the house, although his mother hadn't stopped fussing over her only son for the past hour. Emma had started to sob when she was told she couldn't accompany them, while Grace – another girl; he wouldn't bother to try again – just clung on to Nanny's hand and waved from the top step as they drove away.

Hugo had other things than the family's female line on his mind as the car manoeuvred its way slowly through the country lanes towards the city. Was he about to see Harry Clifton for the first time? Would he recognize him as the other son he'd wanted but would never have, or would he be left in no doubt the moment he saw the boy that he couldn't be his kinsman?

Hugo would have to be careful to avoid Clifton's mother. Would he even recognize her? He'd recently discovered that she was working as a waitress in the Palm Court room at the Royal Hotel, which he used to frequent whenever he had business meetings in the city. Now he would have to confine himself to the occasional visit in the evening, and then only if he was certain she'd left for the day.

Maisie's brother, Stan Tancock, had been released from prison after serving eighteen months of his three-year sentence. Hugo never did find out what had happened to Detective Inspector Blakemore but he never saw the man again following his father's dinner party. A young detective sergeant gave evidence at Tancock's trial, and he clearly wasn't in any doubt who the guilty party was.

Once Tancock was safely behind bars, speculation

about what had happened to Arthur Clifton quickly dried up. In a business where death is commonplace, Arthur Clifton became just another statistic. However, when Lady Harvey launched the *Maple Leaf* six months later, Hugo couldn't help thinking that *Davy Jones's Locker* would have been a more appropriate name for the vessel.

When the final figures were presented to the board, Barrington's ended up showing a loss of £13,712 on the project. Hugo didn't suggest that they tender for any more shipbuilding contracts in the future, and Sir Walter never referred to the subject again. In the years that followed, Barrington's returned to its traditional business as a shipping line, and continued to go from strength to strength.

After Stan had been carted off to the local prison, Hugo had assumed that would be the last he heard of him. But shortly before Tancock was due to be released, the deputy governor of HMP Bristol rang Miss Potts and asked for an appointment. When they met, the deputy governor pleaded with Barrington to give Tancock his old job back, otherwise he would have little hope of ever being employed again. At first, Hugo was delighted to hear this piece of news, but after giving the matter some thought, changed his mind and dispatched Phil Haskins, his chief ganger, to visit Tancock in prison and tell him he could have his job back on one condition: he was never to mention the name of Arthur Clifton again. If he did, he could collect his cards and look for work elsewhere. Tancock had accepted the offer gratefully, and as the years passed it became clear that he had kept his side of the bargain.

The Rolls-Royce drew up outside the front gate of St Bede's and the chauffeur leapt out to open the back door. Several pairs of eyes turned to look in their direction, some with admiration, others with envy.

Giles clearly didn't enjoy the attention and quickly walked away, disowning the chauffeur as well as his parents. His mother chased after him, bent down and pulled his socks up, before giving his fingernails one last inspection. Hugo spent his time looking into the faces of countless children, wondering if he would instantly recognize someone he'd never seen before.

And then he saw a boy walking up the hill, unaccompanied by a mother or father. He looked past the boy to see a woman watching him, a woman he could never forget. Both of them must have been wondering if he had one son or two reporting for their first day at St Bede's.

◄○►

When Giles caught chicken pox and had to spend a few days in the sanatorium, his father realized this might be his chance to prove that Harry Clifton wasn't his son. He didn't tell Elizabeth he was going to visit Giles while he was in the san, as he didn't want her around when he asked Matron a seemingly innocuous question.

Once he'd dealt with the morning post, Hugo told Miss Potts that he would be popping into St Bede's to see his son and she shouldn't expect him back for at least a couple of hours. He drove into the city and parked outside Frobisher House. He remembered only too well where the san was, as he'd had to visit it regularly when he was at St Bede's.

Giles was sitting up in bed having his temperature taken when his father strode into the room. The boy's face lit up the moment he saw him.

Matron was standing by the bed, checking her

patient's temperature. 'Down to ninety-nine. We'll have you back in time for the first lesson on Monday morning, young man,' she declared as she shook the thermometer. 'I'll leave you now, Mr Barrington, so you can spend a little time with your son.'

'Thank you, Matron,' said Hugo. 'I wonder if I might have a word with you before I leave?'

'Of course, Mr Barrington. You'll find me in my office.'

'You don't look too bad to me, Giles,' said Hugo once Matron had left the room.

'I'm fine, Papa. In fact, I was rather hoping Matron would let me out on Saturday morning so I can play football.'

'I'll have a word with her before I go.'

'Thank you, Papa.'

'So, how's the work coming along?'

'Not bad,' said Giles. 'But that's only because I share a study with the two brightest boys in my class.'

'And who are they?' asked his father, dreading the reply.

'There's Deakins, he's the cleverest boy in the school. In fact, the other boys won't even talk to him because they think he's a swot. But my best friend is Harry Clifton. He's very clever too, but not as clever as Deakins. You've probably heard him singing in the choir. I know you'll like him.'

'But isn't Clifton the son of a stevedore?' Hugo said.

'Yes, and just like Grandpa he doesn't hide the fact. But how did you know that, Papa?'

'I think Clifton used to work for the company,' Hugo said, immediately regretting his words.

'It must have been before your time, Papa,' said Giles, 'because his father was killed in the war.'

'Who told you that?' said Hugo.

'Harry's mother. She's a waitress at the Royal Hotel. We went to tea there on his birthday.'

Hugo would have liked to have asked when Clifton's birthday was, but feared it might be one question too many. Instead, he said, 'Your mother sends her love. I think she and Emma plan to visit you later this week.'

'Yuk. That's all I need,' said Giles. 'Chicken pox and a visit from my dreadful sister.'

'She's not that bad,' said his father, laughing.

'She's worse,' said Giles. 'And Grace doesn't look as if she's going to be any better. Do they have to come on holiday with us, Papa?'

'Yes, of course they do.'

'I was wondering if Harry Clifton could join us in Tuscany this summer. He's never been abroad.'

'No,' said Hugo a little too firmly. 'Holidays are strictly for the family, not to be shared with strangers.'

'But he's not a stranger,' said Giles. 'He's my best friend.'

'No,' Hugo repeated, 'and that's an end of the matter.' Giles looked disappointed. 'So what would you like for your birthday, my boy?' Hugo asked, quickly changing the subject.

'The latest radio,' said Giles without hesitation. 'It's called a Roberts Reliable.'

'Are you allowed to have radios at school?'

'Yes,' said Giles, 'but you can only play them at weekends. If you're caught listening after lights out or during the week, they get confiscated.'

'I'll see what I can do. Will you be coming home on your birthday?'

'Yes, but only for tea. I have to be back at school in time for prep.'

'Then I'll try and drop in,' said Hugo. 'I'll be off now. I want a word with Matron before I leave.'

'Don't forget to ask her if she'll let me out on Saturday morning,' Giles reminded him as his father left the room to carry out the real purpose of his visit.

'I'm so glad you were able to drop by, Mr Barrington. It will perk Giles up no end,' said Matron as he walked into her office. 'But as you can see, he's almost fully recovered.'

'Yes, and he's hoping you'll let him out on Saturday morning so he can play in a football match.'

'I'm sure that will be possible,' said Matron. 'But you said there was something else you wanted to talk about?'

'Yes, Matron. As you know, Giles is colour-blind. I just wanted to ask if it was causing him any difficulties.'

'Not that I'm aware of,' said Matron. 'If it is, it certainly doesn't stop him hitting a red ball across a green field until it reaches a white boundary.'

Barrington laughed before he delivered his next well-prepared line. 'When I was at St Bede's, I used to be teased because I was the only boy who suffered from colour-blindness.'

'Let me assure you,' said Matron, 'no one teases Giles. And in any case, his best friend is also colour-blind.'

◄○►

Hugo drove back to his office thinking that something had to be done before the situation got out of control. He decided to have another word with Colonel Danvers.

Once he was back behind his desk, he told Miss Potts he didn't want to be disturbed. He waited until she'd closed the door before he picked up the telephone. A few moments later the chief constable was on the line.

'It's Hugo Barrington, Colonel.'

'How are you, my boy?' asked the chief constable.

'I'm well, sir. I was wondering if you could advise me on a private matter.'

'Fire away, old fellow.'

'I'm looking for a new head of security, and I wondered if you might be able to point me in the right direction.'

'As a matter of fact I do know a man who might fit the bill, but I'm not sure if he's still available. I'll find out and give you a call back.'

The chief constable was as good as his word, and phoned back the following morning. 'The man I had in mind has a part-time job at the moment, but he's looking for something more permanent.'

'What can you tell me about him?' asked Hugo.

'He was being groomed for higher things in the force, but he had to leave when he was badly injured trying to apprehend a robber during a raid on the Midland Bank. You probably remember the story. It even hit the national press. In my opinion, he'd be the ideal candidate to head your security team, and frankly you'd be lucky to get him. If you're still interested, I could drop you a line with his details.'

◄○►

Barrington rang Derek Mitchell from his home, as he didn't want Miss Potts to find out what he was up to. He agreed to meet the former policeman at the Royal Hotel at six o'clock on Monday evening, after Mrs Clifton would have left for the day and the Palm Court would be empty.

Hugo arrived a few minutes early and headed straight for a table at the far end of the room that he wouldn't normally have considered. He took a seat behind the pillar, where he knew his meeting with

Mitchell would not be seen or overheard. While he waited, he went over a list of questions in his mind that needed answering if he was going to put his trust in a complete stranger.

At three minutes to six, a tall, well-built man of military bearing pushed his way through the revolving doors. His dark navy blazer, grey flannels, short hair and highly polished shoes all suggested a life of discipline.

Hugo stood and raised a hand as if he was summoning a waiter. Mitchell walked slowly across the room, making no attempt to disguise a slight limp, an injury which, according to Danvers, was the reason Mitchell had been invalided out of the police service.

Hugo recalled the last occasion he'd come face to face with a police officer, but this time he would be asking the questions.

'Good evening, sir.'

'Good evening, Mitchell,' said Hugo as they shook hands. Once Mitchell had sat down, Hugo took a closer look at his broken nose and cauliflower ears, and also recalled from Colonel Danvers's notes that he used to play in the second row for Bristol.

'Let me say from the outset, Mitchell,' said Hugo, not wasting any time, 'that what I want to discuss with you is of a highly confidential nature, and must be kept strictly between the two of us.' Mitchell nodded. 'It is so confidential, in fact, that even Colonel Danvers has no idea of the real reason I needed to see you, as I am certainly not looking for someone to head up my security operation.'

Mitchell's face remained inscrutable as he waited to hear what Hugo had in mind.

'I am looking for someone to act as a private detective. His sole purpose will be to report to me each month on the activities of a woman who lives in this city, and in fact works in this hotel.'

'I understand, sir.'

'I want to know everything she gets up to, whether professional or personal, however insignificant it might seem. She must never, I repeat, never, become aware of your interest in her. So before I reveal her name, do you consider yourself capable of carrying out such an assignment?'

'These things are never easy,' said Mitchell, 'but they're not impossible. As a young detective sergeant, I worked on an undercover operation which resulted in a particularly loathsome individual ending up behind bars for sixteen years. If he were to walk into this hotel now, I'm confident he wouldn't recognize me.'

Hugo smiled for the first time. 'Before I go any further,' he continued, 'I need to know if you would be willing to take on such an assignment?'

'That would depend on several things, sir.'

'Such as?'

'Would it be a full-time position, because I currently have a night security job, working for a bank.'

'Hand in your notice tomorrow,' said Hugo. 'I don't want you to be working for anyone else.'

'And what are the hours?'

'At your discretion.'

'And my salary?'

'I will pay you eight pounds a week, a month in advance, and will also cover any legitimate expenses.'

Mitchell nodded. 'May I suggest you make any payments in cash, sir, so that nothing can be traced back to you?'

'That seems sensible,' said Hugo, who'd already made that decision.

'And would you want the monthly reports to be in writing, or in person?'

'In person. I want as little committed to paper as possible.'

'Then we should always meet at a different location and never on the same day of the week. That way it would be unlikely that anyone would come across us more than once.'

'I have no problem with that,' said Hugo.

'When would you want me to start, sir?'

'You started half an hour ago,' said Barrington. He removed a slip of paper and an envelope containing £32 from an inside pocket and handed them to Mitchell.

Mitchell studied the name and address written on the piece of paper for a few moments before handing it back to his new boss. 'I'll also need your private number, sir, and details of when and where you can be contacted.'

'At my office any evening between five and six,' said Hugo. 'You must never contact me at home unless it's an emergency,' he added as he took out a pen.

'Just tell me the numbers, sir, don't write them down.'

23

'WERE YOU THINKING OF attending Master Giles's birthday party?' asked Miss Potts.

Hugo looked at his diary. *Giles, 12th birthday, 3 p.m., Manor House* was written in bold letters at the top of the page.

'Do I have time to pick up a present on the way home?'

Miss Potts left the room, and returned a moment later carrying a large parcel wrapped in shiny red paper and tied with a ribbon.

'What's inside?' asked Hugo.

'The latest Roberts radio; the one he asked for when you visited him in the san last month.'

'Thank you, Miss Potts,' said Hugo. He checked his watch. 'I'd better leave now if I'm going to be in time to see him cut the cake.'

Miss Potts placed a thick file in his briefcase and before he could ask, she said, 'Your background notes for tomorrow morning's board meeting. You can go over them after Master Giles has returned to St Bede's. That way there will be no need for you to come back this evening.'

'Thank you, Miss Potts,' said Hugo. 'You think of everything.'

As he drove through the city on his way home, Hugo couldn't help noticing how many more cars there seemed to be on the highway than there had been a year ago. Pedestrians were becoming more wary of casually crossing the road since the government had increased the speed limit to 30 miles per hour. A horse reared up as Hugo shot past a hansom cab. He wondered how much longer they could hope to survive now that the city council had authorized its first taxi cab.

Once he had driven out of the city, Hugo sped up, not wanting to be late for his son's party. How quickly the boy was growing. He was already taller than his mother. Would he end up taller than his father?

When Giles left St Bede's and took up his place at Eton in a year's time, Hugo felt confident that his friendship with the Clifton boy would soon be forgotten, although he realized there were other difficulties that needed to be addressed before then.

He slowed down as he passed through the gates of his estate. He always enjoyed the long drive through the avenue of oaks up to the Manor House. Jenkins was standing on the top step as Hugo got out of the car. He held open the front door and said, 'Mrs Barrington is in the drawing room sir, with Master Giles and two of his school friends.'

As he walked into the hall, Emma came running down the stairs and threw her arms around her father.

'What's in the parcel?' she demanded.

'A birthday present for your brother.'

'Yes, but what is it?'

'You'll have to wait and see, young lady,' said her father with a smile before he handed his briefcase to the butler. 'Would you put that in my study, Jenkins,' he said as Emma grabbed him by the hand and began to tug him towards the drawing room.

Hugo's smile evaporated the moment he opened the door and saw who was sitting on the sofa.

Giles leapt up and ran towards his father, who handed him the parcel and said, 'Happy birthday, my boy.'

'Thank you, Papa,' he said, before introducing his friends.

Hugo shook Deakins's hand, but when Harry offered his, he just said, 'Good afternoon, Clifton,' and sat down in his favourite chair.

Hugo watched with interest as Giles undid the ribbon on his parcel and they both saw the present for the first time. Even his son's unbridled delight with his new radio didn't bring a smile to Hugo's lips. He had a question that he needed to ask Clifton, but it mustn't appear as if the boy's reply was of any significance.

He remained silent while the three boys took turns tuning into the two stations and listening intently to the strange voices and music that came out of the speaker. This was regularly followed by laughter or applause.

Mrs Barrington chatted to Harry about a recent concert of the *Messiah* she'd attended, adding how much she'd enjoyed his rendition of *I Know That My Redeemer Liveth*.

'Thank you, Mrs Barrington,' said Harry.

'Are you hoping to go on to Bristol Grammar School after you leave St Bede's, Clifton?' asked Hugo, spotting an opening.

'Only if I win a scholarship, sir,' he replied.

'But why is that important?' asked Mrs Barrington. 'Surely you will be offered a place, like any other boy?'

'Because my mother wouldn't be able to afford the fees, Mrs Barrington. She's a waitress at the Royal Hotel.'

'But wouldn't your father—'

'He's dead,' said Harry. 'He was killed in the war.'

'I'm sorry,' said Mrs Barrington. 'I didn't realize.'

At that moment the door opened and the under-butler entered the room carrying a large cake on a silver tray. After Giles had succeeded in blowing out all twelve candles with one puff, everyone applauded.

'And when's your birthday, Clifton?' asked Hugo.

'It was last month, sir,' Harry replied.

After Giles had cut the cake, Hugo stood up and left the room without another word.

He went straight to his study, but found he couldn't concentrate on his papers for the next day's board meeting. Clifton's reply meant he would have to seek advice from a lawyer who specialized in the law of heredity.

After an hour or so he heard voices in the hall, then the front door closing and the sound of a car driving away. A few minutes later there was a knock on his study door, and Elizabeth walked in.

'What made you leave us so abruptly?' she asked. 'And why didn't you come and say goodbye, when you must have known Giles and his guests were leaving?'

'I have a very tricky board meeting tomorrow morning,' he said without looking up.

'That's no reason not to say goodbye to your son, especially on his birthday.'

'I've got a lot on my mind,' he said, still looking down at his notes.

'Surely nothing is so important that you need to be rude to guests. You were more offhand with Harry Clifton than you would be with one of the servants.'

Hugo looked up for the first time. 'That's possibly because I consider Clifton inferior to our servants.' Elizabeth looked shocked. 'Did you know that his father was a dock labourer and his mother is a waitress? I'm not sure that's the sort of boy Giles should be mixing with.'

'Giles clearly thinks otherwise, and whatever his background, Harry's a charming boy. I can't understand why you're so against him. You didn't treat Deakins that way, and his father's a newsagent.'

'He's also an open scholar.'

'And Harry is the school's prize choral scholar, as every church-going citizen in Bristol knows. Next time you come across him, I hope you'll be a little more civil.' Without another word, Elizabeth left the room, closing the door firmly behind her.

—◦—

Sir Walter Barrington remained in his place at the head of the boardroom table as his son entered the room.

'I'm becoming increasingly concerned about the government's proposed legislation on import tariffs,' said Hugo as he took a seat on the right of his father, 'and the effect it might have on our balance sheet.'

'That's why we have a lawyer on the board,' said Sir Walter, 'so that he can advise us on such matters.'

'But I've calculated that it could cost us twenty thousand pounds a year if it becomes law. Don't you think we ought to seek a second opinion?'

'I suppose I could have a word with Sir James Amhurst when I'm next in London.'

'I'm travelling up to London on Tuesday for the Association of British Ship Owners' annual dinner,' said Hugo. 'As he's the industry's legal adviser, perhaps I should have a word with him.'

'Only if you're convinced it's necessary,' said Sir Walter. 'And don't forget that Amhurst charges by the hour, even at dinner.'

—◦—

The Association of British Ship Owners' dinner was held at the Grosvenor House, and was attended by over a thousand members and their guests.

Hugo had earlier phoned the association's secretary and asked if he could be seated next to Sir James Amhurst. The secretary raised an eyebrow, but agreed to rearrange the guests on the top table. After all, old Joshua Barrington had been a founder member of the association.

After the Bishop of Newcastle had said grace, Hugo made no attempt to interrupt the eminent silk while he was deep in conversation with the man on his right. However, when the lawyer finally turned his attention to the stranger they'd put on his left, Hugo didn't waste any time in getting to the point.

'My father, Sir Walter Barrington,' he began, capturing his quarry's attention, 'is rather concerned about the import tariff bill that is going through the House of Commons, and the effects it might have on the industry. He wonders if he could consult you on the subject when he's next in London.'

'By all means, dear boy,' said Sir James. 'Just ask his secretary to give my clerk a call and I'll make sure I'm free when he's next in town.'

'Thank you, sir,' said Hugo. 'On a lighter note, I wondered if you'd ever read anything by Agatha Christie?'

'Can't say I have,' said Sir James. 'Is she any good?'

'I'm much enjoying her latest book, *Where There's a Will*,' said Hugo, 'but I'm not sure if the plot would stand up in a court of law.'

'What's the lady suggesting?' asked Amhurst as a sliver of over-cooked beef served on a cold plate was placed in front of him.

'According to Miss Christie, the eldest son of an

hereditary knight automatically inherits his father's title, even if the child is illegitimate.'

'Ah, now that is indeed an interesting legal conundrum,' said Sir James. 'In fact, the Law Lords have quite recently reviewed such a case. Benson *v*. Carstairs, if I remember correctly. It's often referred to by the press as "the bastard's amendment".'

'And what conclusion did their lordships come to?' asked Hugo, trying not to sound too interested.

'If no loophole could be found in the original will, they came out in favour of the first born, even if the young man in question was illegitimate.' Another answer Hugo hadn't wanted to hear. 'However,' Sir James continued, 'their lordships decided to cover their backsides, and added a codicil that each case should be treated on its own merits, and then only after it had been reviewed by the Garter King of Arms. Typical of the Law Lords,' he added before picking up his knife and fork and attacking the beef. 'Too frightened to set a precedent, but quite happy to pass the buck.'

When Sir James returned his attention to the man on his right, Hugo thought about the implications of Harry Clifton discovering that he might have the right to inherit not only the Barrington shipping line, but also the family estate. Having to admit he had sired an illegitimate son would be bad enough, but the idea of Harry Clifton inheriting the family title after his death and becoming Sir Harry did not bear thinking about. He would be willing to do anything in his power to make sure that wouldn't be the outcome.

24

HUGO BARRINGTON was having breakfast when he read the letter from the headmaster of St Bede's, outlining the details of an appeal the school was launching to raise a thousand pounds to build a new cricket pavilion for the First XI. He opened his cheque book and had written the figures '100' when he was distracted by the sound of a car coming to a halt on the gravel outside.

Hugo walked across to the window to see who could possibly be visiting him so early on a Saturday morning. He was puzzled when he saw his son step out of the back of a taxi carrying a suitcase, as he'd been looking forward to watching him open the batting for the school that afternoon in the final match of the season against Avonhurst.

Jenkins appeared just in time to open the front door as Giles reached the top step. 'Good morning, Master Giles,' he said, as if he'd been expecting him.

Hugo walked quickly out of the breakfast room to find his son standing in the hall, head bowed, suitcase by his side. 'What are you doing at home?' he asked. 'Isn't there another week to go before the end of term?'

'I've been rusticated,' said Giles simply.

'Rusticated?' repeated his father. 'And what have you done to merit that, may I ask?'

Giles looked up at Jenkins, who stood silently by the front door. 'I'll take Master Giles's suitcase up to his bedroom,' the butler said, before picking up the bag and proceeding slowly up the stairs.

'Follow me,' said Hugo once the butler was out of sight.

Neither of them spoke again until Hugo had closed the study door behind him. 'What have you done to cause the school to take such a drastic measure?' demanded his father as he sank back into his chair.

'I was caught stealing from the tuck shop,' said Giles, who had been left standing in the middle of the room.

'Is there some simple explanation? A misunderstanding, perhaps?'

'No, there isn't, sir,' said Giles, fighting back tears.

'Do you have anything to say in your defence?'

'No, sir.' Giles hesitated. 'Except . . .'

'Except what?'

'I always gave the sweets away, Papa. I never kept them for myself.'

'To Clifton, no doubt.'

'And to Deakins as well,' said Giles.

'Was it Clifton who put you up to it in the first place?'

'No, it was not,' responded Giles firmly. 'In fact, once he found out what I'd been up to, Harry always took the sweets I gave him and Deakins back to the tuck shop. He even took the blame when Mr Frobisher accused him of stealing them.'

A long silence followed before his father said, 'So you've been rusticated, not actually expelled?'

Giles nodded.

'Do you think they will allow you to go back next term?'

'I doubt it,' said Giles.

'What makes you so sure of that?'

'Because I've never seen the headmaster so angry.'

'Not half as angry as your mother will be when she finds out.'

'Please don't tell her, Papa,' pleaded Giles, bursting into tears.

'And how do you expect me to explain to her why you're home a week early and might not even be returning to St Bede's next term?'

Giles made no attempt to respond, but continued to sob quietly.

'And Heaven knows what your grandparents will say,' his father added, 'when I have to tell them why you won't be going to Eton after all.'

Another long silence followed.

'Go to your room, and don't even think about coming back down until I say so.'

'Yes, sir,' said Giles. He turned to leave.

'And whatever you do, don't discuss this with anyone, especially not in front of the servants.'

'Yes, Papa,' said Giles, who ran out of the room, nearly colliding with Jenkins as he shot past him on the stairs.

Hugo leant forward in his chair, trying to think if there might be some way to turn the situation around before he had to face an inevitable call from the headmaster. He placed his elbows on the desk and his head in his hands, but it was some time before his eyes focused on the cheque.

A smile crossed his lips as he added an extra nought before signing it.

25

MITCHELL WAS SEATED in the far corner of the waiting room, reading the *Bristol Evening Post* when Hugo walked across and sat down beside him. It was so draughty that Hugo kept his hands in his pockets.

'The subject,' said Mitchell, still looking at his newspaper, 'is trying to raise five hundred pounds for a business venture.'

'What sort of business venture could she possibly be interested in?'

'Tilly's tea shop,' replied Mitchell. 'It seems the subject worked there before she moved to the Palm Court room at the Royal. Miss Tilly has recently had an offer of five hundred pounds for the business from a Mr Edward Atkins. Miss Tilly doesn't care for Atkins and has made it clear to the subject that if she were able to raise the same amount, she would prefer her to take over the business.'

'Where could she possibly hope to get hold of that much money?'

'Perhaps from someone who wished to have financial control over her, which might at a later date prove advantageous?'

Hugo remained silent. Mitchell's eyes never left his paper.

'Has she approached anyone to try and raise the money?' Hugo eventually asked.

'She's currently taking advice from a Mr Patrick Casey, who represents Dillon and Co., a finance company based in Dublin. They specialize in raising loans for private clients.'

'How do I get in touch with Casey?'

'I wouldn't advise that,' said Mitchell.

'Why not?'

'He visits Bristol about once a month, and always stays at the Royal.'

'We wouldn't have to meet at the Royal.'

'He has struck up a close personal relationship with the subject. Whenever he's in town he takes her to dinner or the theatre, and recently she's been seen returning with him to the hotel, where they spend the night together in room 371.'

'Fascinating,' said Hugo. 'Anything else?'

'It may also interest you to know that the subject banks with the National Provincial, 49 Corn Street. The manager is a Mr Prendergast. Her current account is showing a balance of twelve pounds and nine shillings.'

Hugo would like to have asked how Mitchell had come across that particular piece of information, but satisfied himself with saying, 'Excellent. The moment you come up with anything else, however insignificant, ring me.' He took a bulky envelope from his overcoat pocket and slipped it across to Mitchell.

'The train now arriving at platform nine is the seven twenty-two from Taunton.'

Mitchell pocketed the envelope, folded his newspaper and walked out of the waiting room. He'd never once looked at his employer.

◄○►

Hugo had been unable to hide his anger when he discovered the real reason Giles had failed to be offered a place at Eton. He'd phoned the headmaster, who refused to take his calls, his prospective housemaster, who sympathized but offered no hope of redemption, and even the provost, who said he'd call back, but didn't. Although Elizabeth and the girls had no idea what had caused Hugo to so regularly lose his temper of late, and for no apparent reason, they continued to bear the brunt of Giles's misdemeanours with equanimity.

Hugo reluctantly accompanied Giles to Bristol Grammar School on his first day of term, although he wouldn't allow either Emma or Grace to join them, despite Emma bursting into tears and sulking.

When Hugo brought the car to a halt in College Street, the first person he saw standing outside the school gates was Harry Clifton. Even before he pulled on the brake, Giles had leapt out and run across to greet his friend.

Hugo avoided mingling with the other parents, whom Elizabeth seemed quite happy to chat to, and when he inadvertently came across Clifton, he made a point of not shaking hands with him.

On the journey back to the Manor House, Elizabeth asked her husband why he treated Giles's best friend with such disdain. Hugo reminded his wife that their son should have gone to Eton, where he would have mixed with other gentlemen and not with the sons of local tradesmen and, in Clifton's case, far worse. Elizabeth retreated into the comparative safety of silence, as she had so often done recently.

26

'LOCAL TEA SHOP burnt to the ground! Arson suspected!' hollered the paperboy standing on the corner of the Broad.

Hugo threw on the brakes, leapt out of his car and handed the lad a ha'penny. He began reading the front page as he walked back to his car.

> Tilly's Tea Shop, a Bristol landmark, much
> frequented by local citizens, was razed to the
> ground in the early hours of the morning.
> Police have arrested a local man in his early
> thirties and charged him with arson. Miss Tilly,
> who now lives in Cornwall . . .

Hugo smiled when he saw the photograph of Maisie Clifton and her staff standing on the pavement, grimly surveying the burnt-out remains of Tilly's. The gods were clearly on his side.

He climbed back into his car, placed the newspaper on the passenger seat and continued on his journey to Bristol Zoo. He would need to make an early appointment to see Mr Prendergast.

Mitchell had advised him that if he hoped to keep the fact that he was the subject's backer confidential, any meetings with Prendergast should be held in Barrington's offices, and preferably after Miss Potts had gone home for the night. Hugo didn't attempt to explain to Mitchell that he wasn't sure if Miss Potts did go home at night. He was looking forward to the meeting with Prendergast, when he would administer the last rites, but there was someone else he needed to see before he could do that.

◄○►

Mitchell was feeding Rosie when he arrived.

Hugo walked slowly across, leant on the railing and pretended to take an interest in the Indian elephant that Bristol Zoo had recently acquired from the United Provinces, and was already attracting a large number of visitors. Mitchell tossed up a lump of bread, which Rosie caught in her trunk and transferred to her mouth in one fluid movement.

'The subject has returned to work at the Royal Hotel,' said Mitchell as if he was addressing the elephant. 'She's doing the late shift in the Palm Court from ten at night until six the following morning. She's paid three pounds a week, plus whatever she can make in tips, which, as there are so few customers at that time of night, doesn't add up to much.' He threw another crust at the elephant, and continued, 'A Bob Burrows has been arrested and charged with arson. Burrows was her patisserie supplier before the subject sacked him. He's made a full confession, even admitting that he had planned to propose to the subject and had purchased an engagement ring, but she'd spurned him; or at least that's his story.'

A smile crossed Hugo's lips. 'And who's in charge of the case?' he asked.

'A Detective Inspector Blakemore,' said Mitchell. Hugo's smile was replaced by a frown. 'Although Blakemore initially thought the subject might be an accomplice of Burrows,' continued Mitchell, 'he has since informed the Bristol and West of England Insurance Company that she is no longer a suspect.'

'That's a pity,' said Hugo, the frown still in place.

'Not necessarily,' said Mitchell. 'The insurance company will be issuing Mrs Clifton with a cheque for six hundred pounds in full and final settlement of her claim.' Hugo smiled.

'I wonder if she's told her son,' said Hugo, almost to himself.

If Mitchell heard the comment, he ignored it. 'The only other piece of information that might be of some interest to you,' he continued, 'is that Mr Patrick Casey booked into the Royal Hotel on Friday night, and took the subject to the Plimsoll Line for dinner. They returned to the hotel afterwards, when she accompanied him to his room, No. 371, and didn't leave until just after seven o'clock the following morning.'

A long silence followed, always the sign that Mitchell had come to the end of his monthly report. Hugo removed an envelope from an inside pocket and slipped it to Mitchell, who didn't acknowledge the transaction as he threw his last piece of bread to a contented Rosie.

◄○►

'Mr Prendergast to see you,' said Miss Potts, standing aside to allow the banker to enter the managing director's office.

'It's good of you to come all this way,' said Hugo. 'I'm sure you'll appreciate why I didn't want to discuss such a highly confidential matter at the bank.'

'I quite understand,' said Prendergast, who had opened his Gladstone bag and extracted a thick file even before he'd sat down. He passed a single sheet of paper across the desk to Mr Barrington.

Hugo checked the bottom line, before settling back in his chair.

'Just to recap, if I may,' said Prendergast. 'You put up a capital sum of five hundred pounds, which allowed Mrs Clifton to purchase the business known as Tilly's, a tea shop on Broad Street. The agreed contract was for the full amount, plus compound interest at five per cent per annum, to be paid back to the principal within a period of five years.

'Although Tilly's managed to declare a small trading profit in Mrs Clifton's first year and again in her second, there was never a large enough surplus for her either to pay the interest or to return any part of the capital sum, so at the time of the fire, Mrs Clifton owed you £572 16 shillings. To this sum I must add bank charges of £20, making a grand total of £592 16 shillings. This, of course, will be well covered by the insurance payout, which means that while your investment is secure, Mrs Clifton will be left with virtually nothing.'

'How unfortunate,' said Hugo. 'May I ask why the final sum doesn't appear to include any charge for services rendered by Mr Casey?' he added after studying the figures more closely.

'Because Mr Casey has informed the bank that he will not be submitting any bills for his services.'

Hugo frowned. 'At least that is one piece of good news for the poor woman.'

'Indeed. None the less, I fear she will no longer be able to cover her son's fees at Bristol Grammar School for next term.'

'How sad,' said Hugo. 'So will the boy have to be removed?'

'I'm sorry to say that's the inevitable conclusion,' said Mr Prendergast. 'It is a great shame, because she dotes on the child, and I believe she would sacrifice almost anything to keep him there.'

'A great shame,' repeated Hugo as he closed the file and rose from his chair. 'I won't keep you any longer, Mr Prendergast,' he added. 'I have an appointment in the city in about half an hour. Perhaps I can give you a lift?'

'That is most kind of you, Mr Barrington, but it won't be necessary. I drove myself over here.'

'What do you drive?' Hugo asked as he picked up his briefcase and headed towards the door.

'A Morris Oxford,' said Prendergast, quickly stuffing some papers back into his Gladstone bag and following Hugo out of the office.

'The people's car,' said Hugo. 'I'm told that, like you, Mr Prendergast, it's very reliable.' Both men laughed as they walked down the stairs together. 'Sad business, Mrs Clifton,' said Hugo as they stepped out of the building. 'But then, I'm not altogether sure I approve of women getting involved in business. It's not the natural way of things.'

'I quite agree,' said Prendergast, as the two men came to a halt by Barrington's car. 'Mind you,' he added, 'you could not have done more for the poor woman.'

'It's kind of you to say so, Prendergast,' said Hugo. 'But despite that, I'd be obliged if my involvement could remain strictly between the two of us.'

'Of course, sir,' said Prendergast as the two men shook hands, 'you can rely on me.'

'Let's keep in touch, old fellow,' said Hugo as he climbed into his car. 'I have no doubt I'll be calling on the bank's services again.' Prendergast smiled.

As Hugo drove towards the city, his thoughts

returned to Maisie Clifton. He had dealt her a blow from which she was unlikely to recover, but he now intended to deliver the knock-out punch.

He drove into Bristol wondering where she was at that moment. Probably sitting her son down to explain to him why he would have to leave BGS at the end of the summer term. Had she even for one fleeting moment imagined that Harry might be able to continue his studies as if nothing had happened? Hugo decided that he wouldn't raise the subject with Giles until the boy told him the sad news that his friend Harry would not be returning to BGS to join him in the sixth form.

Even the thought of his own son having to go to Bristol Grammar School still made him pulse with anger, but he had never let Elizabeth or his father know the real reason Giles had failed to get a place at Eton.

Once he'd driven past the cathedral, he continued across College Green before turning into the entrance of the Royal Hotel. He was a few minutes early for his appointment, but he was confident the manager would not keep him waiting. He pushed his way through the revolving doors and strolled across the lobby, not needing to be told where Mr Frampton's office was.

The manager's secretary leapt up the moment Hugo entered the room. 'I'll let Mr Frampton know you're here,' she said, almost running into the adjoining office. The manager appeared a moment later.

'What a pleasure to see you, Mr Barrington,' he said, ushering him into his office. 'I do hope you and Mrs Barrington are both well.' Hugo nodded and took a seat opposite the hotel manager, but didn't shake hands.

'When you asked to see me, I took the liberty of checking over the arrangements for your company's annual dinner,' said Frampton. 'Just over three hundred guests will be attending, I understand?'

'I have no interest how many guests are attending,' said Hugo. 'That isn't the reason I came to see you, Frampton. I wish to discuss a private matter that I find most distasteful.'

'I'm very sorry to hear that,' said Frampton, sitting bolt upright.

'One of our non-executive directors was staying at the hotel on Thursday night, and the following day he made a most serious allegation that I feel it is my duty to bring to your attention.'

'Yes, of course,' said Frampton, rubbing his sweating palms on his trousers. 'The last thing we would want to do is annoy one of our most valued customers.'

'I'm glad to hear it,' said Hugo. 'The gentleman in question checked into the hotel after the restaurant had closed and went into the Palm Court in the hope of being provided with some light refreshment.'

'A service I myself instituted,' said Frampton, allowing himself a strained smile.

'He gave his order to a young lady who appeared to be in charge,' continued Hugo, ignoring the comment.

'Yes, that would be our Mrs Clifton.'

'I've no idea who it was,' said Hugo. 'However, as she was serving him with a cup of coffee and some sandwiches, another gentleman entered the Palm Court, made an order and asked if it could be sent up to his room. The only thing my friend recalls about the man was that he had a slight Irish accent. My friend then signed his bill and retired for the night. He rose early the following morning, as he wished to have breakfast and go over his papers before the board meeting. When he came out of his room he observed the same woman, still dressed in her hotel uniform, leaving room 371. She then walked to the end of the corridor, climbed through the window and out on to the fire escape.'

'I'm absolutely appalled, sir. I . . .'

'The board member concerned has requested that whenever he comes to Bristol in the future, he should be booked into another hotel. Now, I don't wish to appear prudish, Frampton, but the Royal has always been somewhere I've been happy to bring my wife and children.'

'Be assured, Mr Barrington, the person concerned will be dismissed immediately, and not supplied with a reference. May I add how grateful I am that you have brought this matter to my attention.'

Hugo rose from his place. 'Of course, I wouldn't want any reference made to me or the company should you feel it necessary to dismiss the lady in question.'

'You can be assured of my discretion,' said Frampton.

Hugo smiled for the first time. 'On a happier note, may I say how much we're all looking forward to the annual dinner, which no doubt will be up to your usual high standard. Next year we'll be celebrating the company's centenary, so I feel sure my father will want to push the boat out.' Both men laughed a little too loudly.

'You can rely on us, Mr Barrington,' said Frampton as he followed his client out of the office.

'And one more thing, Frampton,' said Hugo, as they walked across the foyer. 'I'd rather you didn't say anything to Sir Walter about this. My father can be a little old-fashioned when it comes to such matters, so I think it's best kept between ourselves.'

'I couldn't agree more, Mr Barrington,' said Frampton. 'You can be assured I shall deal with the matter personally.'

As Hugo pushed his way back through the revolving doors, he couldn't help wondering just how many hours Mitchell must have spent at the Royal before he was

able to supply him with such a priceless piece of information.

He jumped back into his car, switched on the engine
and continued on his journey home. He was still thinking about Maisie Clifton when he felt a tap on his
shoulder. He experienced a moment of blind panic as
he turned around and saw who was sitting on the back
seat. He even wondered if somehow she'd found out
about his meeting with Frampton.

'What do you want?' he demanded, not slowing down
for fear that someone might see them together.

As he listened to her demands, he could only wonder
how she was so well informed. Once she'd finished, he
readily agreed to her terms, knowing that it would be
the easiest way of getting her out of the car.

Mrs Clifton placed a thin brown envelope on the
passenger seat next to him. 'I'll wait to hear from you,'
she said.

Hugo put the envelope in an inside pocket. He only
slowed down when he came to an unlit alley, but didn't
stop until he was certain no one else could see them.
He leapt out of the car and opened the back door. When
he saw the look on her face, it was clear she felt she'd
more than achieved her purpose.

Hugo allowed her a moment of triumph, before he
grabbed her by the shoulders and shook her as if he was
trying to remove an obstinate apple from a tree. Once
he'd left her in no doubt what would happen if she ever
bothered him again, he punched her in the face with all
his strength. She collapsed to the ground curled up into
a ball, and didn't stop shaking. Hugo thought about
kicking her in the stomach but didn't want to risk being
witnessed by a passer-by. He drove away without giving
her another thought.

OLD JACK TAR

1925–1936

27

On a balmy Thursday afternoon in the Northern Transvaal, I killed eleven men, and a grateful nation awarded me the Victoria Cross for service above and beyond the call of duty. I haven't had a peaceful night's sleep since.

If I'd killed one Englishman in my homeland, a judge would have sentenced me to hang by the neck until I was dead. Instead, I have been sentenced to life imprisonment, because I still see the faces of those eleven wretched young men every day, like an image on a coin that never fades. I've often considered suicide, but that would be the coward's way out.

In the citation, gazetted in *The Times*, it was stated that my actions had been responsible for saving the lives of two officers, five non-commissioned officers and seventeen private soldiers of the Royal Gloucesters. One of those officers, Lieutenant Walter Barrington, has made it possible for me to serve my sentence with some dignity.

Within weeks of the action I was shipped back to England, and a few months later I was honourably discharged following what would now be described as a mental breakdown. After six months in an army hospital, I was released back into the world. I changed my name, avoided my home town of Wells in Somerset, and set off for Bristol. Unlike the prodigal son, I refused to travel a few miles into the next county where I would have been able to enjoy the tranquillity of my father's home.

During the day, I would roam the streets of Bristol, rummaging around in dustbins for scraps, while at night my bedroom was a park, my resting place a bench, my blanket a newspaper, my morning call the first bird to announce a new dawn. When it was too cold or wet, I retreated to the waiting room of a local railway station, where I slept below the bench and rose before the first train shunted in the next morning. As the nights became longer, I signed up as a non-paying guest of the Salvation Army on Little George Street, where kind ladies supplied me with thick bread and thin soup before I fell asleep on a horse-hair mattress below a single blanket. Luxury.

As the years passed I hoped that my former companions-in-arms and brother officers would assume I was dead. I had no desire for them to find out that this was the prison I'd chosen to carry out my life sentence in. And it might have stayed thus, had a Rolls-Royce not screeched to a halt in the middle of the road. The back door swung open and out leapt a man I hadn't seen for years.

'Captain Tarrant!' he cried as he advanced towards me. I looked away, hoping he'd think he'd made a mistake. But I remembered only too well that Walter Barrington was not a man who suffered from self-doubt. He grabbed me by the shoulders and stared at me for some time before he said, 'How can this be possible, old fellow?'

The more I tried to convince him I did not need his help, the more determined he became to be my saviour. I finally gave in, but not before he had agreed to my terms and conditions.

At first he begged me to join him and his wife at the Manor House, but I'd survived too long without a roof over my head to regard such comfort as anything other than a burden. He even offered me a seat on the board of the shipping company that bore his name.

'What use could I possibly be to you?' I asked.

'Your very presence, Jack, would be an inspiration to us all.'

I thanked him, but explained that I had not yet completed my sentence for the murder of eleven men. Still he didn't give in.

I finally agreed to take the job of night watchman at the docks, with three pounds a week pay and accommodation provided: an abandoned Pullman railway carriage now became my prison cell. I suppose I might have continued my life sentence until the day I died, had I not come into contact with Master Harry Clifton.

Harry would claim, years later, that I had shaped his whole life. In truth, it was he who saved mine.

The first time I came across young Harry, he couldn't have been more than four or five. 'Come on in, lad,' I called to him when I spotted him crawling towards the carriage on his hands and knees. But he immediately leapt up and ran away.

The following Saturday he got as far as looking in through the window. I tried again. 'Why don't you come in, my boy? I'm not going to bite you,' I said, trying to reassure him. This time he took up my offer and opened the door, but after exchanging a few words, he ran away again. Was I that frightening a figure?

The next Saturday, he not only opened the door, but stood, feet apart, in the doorway, staring at me defiantly. We chatted for over an hour, about everything from Bristol City FC to why snakes shed their skins and who built Clifton Suspension Bridge, before he said, 'I'll have to be off now, Mr Tar, my mum's expecting me home for tea.' This time he walked away, but looked back several times.

After that, Harry came to visit me every Saturday until he went to Merrywood Elementary School, when he started turning up most mornings. It took me some time to convince the boy that he should stay at school and learn to read and write. Frankly I wouldn't have managed even that without the help of Miss Monday, Mr Holcombe and Harry's spirited mother. It took a formidable team to get Harry Clifton to realize his potential, and I knew we had succeeded when once again he could only find the time to visit me on Saturday mornings because he was preparing to enter for a choral scholarship to St Bede's.

Once Harry had started at his new school, I didn't expect to see him again until the Christmas holidays. But to my surprise, I found him standing outside my door just before eleven o'clock on the first Friday night of term.

He told me he'd left St Bede's because a prefect was bullying him – damned if I can recall the cad's name – and he was going to run away to sea. If he had, I suspect the boy would have ended up an admiral. But happily he listened to my advice and was back at school in time for breakfast the following morning.

Because he always used to come to the docks with Stan Tancock, it was some time before I realized Harry was Arthur Clifton's boy. He once asked me if I'd known his father, and I told him yes, and that he was a good and decent man with a fine war record. He then asked me if I knew how he died. I said I didn't. The only time I ever lied to the boy. It was not for me to ignore the wishes of his mother.

─◁○▷─

I was standing on the dockside when the shift changed. No one ever gave me a second glance, almost as if I wasn't there, and I knew that some of them thought I wasn't *all* there. I did nothing to dispel this, as it allowed me to serve my sentence in anonymity.

Arthur Clifton had been a good ganger, one of the best, and he took his job seriously, unlike his best mate, Stan Tancock, whose first port of call on the way home was always the Pig and Whistle. That was on the nights he managed to get home.

I watched Clifton as he disappeared inside the hull of the *Maple Leaf* to make some final checks before the welders moved in to seal the double bottom. It was the raucous sound of the shift horn that must have distracted everyone; one shift coming off, another coming on, and the welders needed to get started promptly if they were going to finish the job by the end of their shift and earn their bonus. No one gave a second thought to whether Clifton had climbed back out of the double bottom, myself included.

We all assumed that he must have heard the blast on the horn and was among the hundreds of dockers trooping through the gates, making their way home. Unlike his brother-in-law, Clifton rarely stopped for a pint at the Pig and Whistle, preferring to go straight to Still House Lane and be with his wife and child. In those days, I didn't know his wife or child, and perhaps I never would have if Arthur Clifton had returned home that night.

The second shift was working flat out when I heard Tancock shouting at the top of his voice. I saw him pointing to the ship's hull. But Haskins, the chief ganger, simply brushed him aside as if he were a tiresome wasp.

Once Tancock realized he was getting nowhere with Haskins, he charged down the gangway and began to run along the quayside in the direction of Barrington House. When Haskins realized where Tancock was headed, he chased after him and had nearly caught up with him by the time he barged through the swing doors into the shipping line's headquarters.

To my surprise, a few minutes later Tancock came running back out of the building, and I was even more surprised when Haskins and the managing director followed close behind. I couldn't imagine what would have convinced Mr Hugo to leave his office after such a brief conversation with Stan Tancock.

I found out the reason soon enough, because the moment Mr Hugo arrived on the dock, he gave orders for the entire shift to lay down their tools, stop working and remain silent, as if it were Remembrance Sunday. And indeed, a minute later, Haskins ordered them all back to work.

That was when it first occurred to me that Arthur Clifton might still be inside the double bottom. But surely no man could be so callous as to walk away if he'd thought, even for a moment, that someone might be trapped alive in a steel grave of their own making.

When the welders went back to work, Mr Hugo spoke to Tancock again before Tancock trooped off through the dock-yard gates and out of sight. I looked back to see if Haskins was pursuing him again, but he was clearly more interested in pushing his men to their limits to recover lost time, like a galley master driving his slaves. A moment later, Mr Hugo walked down the gangway, climbed back into his car and drove off to Barrington House.

The next time I looked out of my carriage window I saw Tancock running back through the gates and once again charging towards Barrington House. This time he didn't reappear for at least half an hour, and when he did, he was no longer red-cheeked and pulsating with rage, but appeared far calmer. I decided he must have found Clifton and was simply letting Mr Hugo know.

I looked up at Mr Hugo's office and saw him standing by the window watching Tancock as he left the yard. He didn't move away from the window until he was out of sight. A few minutes later Mr Hugo came out of the building, walked across to his car and drove away.

I wouldn't have given the matter another thought if Arthur Clifton had clocked in for the morning shift, but he didn't, nor did he ever again.

The following morning, a Detective Inspector Blakemore paid me a visit in my carriage. You can often judge the character of a person by the way he treats his fellow men. Blakemore was one of those rare people who could see beyond his nose.

'You say that you saw Stanley Tancock leaving Barrington House between seven and seven thirty yesterday evening?'

'Yes, I did,' I told him.

'Did he appear to be in a hurry, or anxious, or attempting to slip away unnoticed?'

'On the contrary,' I said. 'I remember thinking at the time he looked remarkably carefree given the circumstances.'

'Given the circumstances?' repeated Blakemore.

'Only an hour or so earlier, he'd been protesting that his mate Arthur Clifton was trapped in the double bottom of the *Maple Leaf*, and they were doing nothing to help him.'

Blakemore wrote down my words in his notebook.

'Do you have any idea where Tancock went after that?'

'No,' I replied. 'When I last saw him he was walking out of the gates with an arm around one of his mates.'

'Thank you, sir,' said the detective inspector. 'That's been most helpful.' It had been a long time since anyone had called me sir. 'Would you be willing, at your own convenience, to come down to the station and make a written statement?'

'I'd prefer not to, inspector,' I told him, 'for personal reasons. But I'd be quite happy to write out a statement that you could collect at any time that suits you.'

'That's good of you, sir.'

The detective inspector opened his briefcase, dug out a

police statement sheet and handed it to me. He then raised his hat and said, 'Thank you, sir, I'll be in touch.' But I never saw him again.

Six weeks later, Stan Tancock was sentenced to three years' imprisonment for theft, with Mr Hugo acting as the prosecution's principal witness. I attended every day of the trial, and there wasn't any doubt in my mind which one of them was the guilty party.

28

'TRY NOT TO FORGET that you saved my life.'

'I've spent the last twenty-six years trying to forget,' Old Jack reminded him.

'But you were also responsible for saving the lives of twenty-four of your fellow West Countrymen. You remain a hero in this city and you seem to be totally unaware of the fact. So I'm bound to ask, Jack, how much longer you intend to go on torturing yourself?'

'Until I can no longer see the eleven men I killed as clearly as I can see you now.'

'But you were doing no more than your duty,' protested Sir Walter.

'That's how I saw it at the time,' admitted Jack.

'So what changed?'

'If I could answer that question,' replied Jack, 'we wouldn't be having this conversation.'

'But you're still capable of doing so much for your fellow men. Take that young friend of yours, for example. You tell me he keeps playing truant, but if he was to discover that you are Captain Jack Tarrant of the Royal Gloucestershire Regiment, winner of the Victoria Cross, don't you think he might listen to you with even more respect?'

'He might also run away again,' replied Jack. 'In any case, I have other plans for young Harry Clifton.'

'Clifton, Clifton . . .' said Sir Walter. 'Why is that name familiar?'

'Harry's father was trapped in the double bottom of the *Maple Leaf*, and no one came to his—'

'That's not what I heard,' said Sir Walter, his tone changing. 'I was told that Clifton left his wife because she was, not to put too fine a point on it, a loose woman.'

'Then you were misled,' said Jack, 'because I can tell you that Mrs Clifton is a delightful and intelligent woman, and any man who was lucky enough to be married to her would never want to leave her.'

Sir Walter looked genuinely shocked, and it was some time before he spoke again. 'Surely you don't believe that cock and bull story about Clifton being trapped in the double bottom?' he asked quietly.

'I'm afraid I do, Walter. You see, I witnessed the whole episode.'

'Then why didn't you say something about it at the time?'

'I did. When I was interviewed by Detective Inspector Blakemore the following day, I told him everything I'd seen, and at his request I made a written statement.'

'Then why wasn't your statement produced in evidence at Tancock's trial?' asked Sir Walter.

'Because I never saw Blakemore again. And when I turned up at the police station, I was told he was no longer in charge of the case and his replacement refused to see me.'

'I had Blakemore taken off the case,' said Sir Walter. 'The damn man was as good as accusing Hugo of giving the money to Tancock, so there wouldn't be an investigation into the Clifton affair.' Old Jack remained silent.

'Let's not talk of this any more,' said Sir Walter. 'I know my son is far from perfect, but I refuse to believe—'

'Or perhaps you don't want to believe,' said Old Jack. 'Jack, whose side are you on?'

'On the side of justice. As you used to be when we first met.'

'And I still am,' said Sir Walter. But he fell silent for some time before adding, 'I want you to make me a promise, Jack. If you ever find out anything about Hugo that you believe would harm the family's reputation, you won't hesitate to tell me.'

'You have my word on it.'

'And you have my word, old friend, that I would not hesitate to hand Hugo over to the police if I thought for one moment that he had broken the law.'

'Let's hope nothing else arises that would make that necessary,' said Old Jack.

'I agree, old friend. Let's talk of more palatable things. Is there anything you are in need of at the moment? I could still . . .'

'Do you have any old clothes that are surplus to requirements?'

Sir Walter raised an eyebrow. 'Dare I ask?'

'No, you daren't,' said Old Jack. 'But I have to visit a particular gentleman, and I'll need to be appropriately dressed.'

◄○►

Old Jack had grown so thin over the years that Sir Walter's clothes hung off him like flax on a distaff, and, like Sir Andrew Aguecheek, he was several inches taller than his old friend, so he had to let down the turn-ups on the trousers and even then they barely reached his ankles. But he felt that the tweed suit, checked shirt and striped tie would serve its purpose for this particular meeting.

As Jack walked out of the dockyard for the first time in years, a few familiar faces turned to give the smartly dressed stranger a second look.

When the school bell rang at four o'clock, Old Jack stepped back into the shadows while the noisy, boisterous nippers poured out through the gates of Merrywood Elementary as if they were escaping from prison.

Mrs Clifton had been waiting there for the past ten minutes, and when Harry saw his mum, he reluctantly allowed her to take him by the hand. A damn finelooking woman, Old Jack thought as he watched the two of them walking away, Harry, as always, jumping up and down, endlessly chattering, displaying as much energy as Stephenson's *Rocket*.

Old Jack waited until they were out of sight before he crossed the road and walked into the school yard. If he'd been dressed in his old clothes, he would have been stopped by someone in authority long before he reached the front door. He looked up and down the corridor, and spotted a master coming towards him.

'I'm sorry to trouble you,' said Old Jack, 'but I'm looking for Mr Holcombe.'

'Third door on the left, old fellow,' the man said, pointing down the corridor.

When Old Jack came to a halt outside Mr Holcombe's classroom he gave a gentle tap on the door.

'Come in.'

Old Jack opened the door to find a young man, his long black gown covered in chalk dust, seated at a table in front of rows of empty desks, marking exercise books. 'I'm sorry to disturb you,' said Old Jack, 'I'm looking for Mr Holcombe.'

'Then you need look no further,' said the schoolmaster, putting down his pen.

'My name is Tar,' he said as he stepped forward, 'but my friends call me Jack.'

Holcombe's face lit up. 'I do believe you're the man Harry Clifton goes off to visit most mornings.'

'I fear I am,' admitted Old Jack. 'I apologize.'

'No need,' said Holcombe. 'I only wish I had the same influence over him that you do.'

'That's why I came to see you, Mr Holcombe. I'm convinced that Harry's an exceptional child and should be given every chance to make the best of his talents.'

'I couldn't agree with you more,' said Holcombe. 'And I suspect he has one talent even you don't know about.'

'And what might that be?'

'He has the voice of an angel.'

'Harry's no angel,' said Old Jack with a grin.

'I quite agree, but it may turn out to be our best chance of breaking down his defences.'

'What do you have in mind?' asked Old Jack.

'There's a possibility he might just be tempted to join the choir at Holy Nativity. So if you were able to convince him to come to school more often, I know I can teach him to read and write.'

'Why's that so important for a church choir?'

'It's compulsory at Holy Nativity, and Miss Monday, the choir mistress, refuses to make any exceptions to the rule.'

'Then I'll just have to make sure the boy attends your lessons, won't I?' said Old Jack.

'You could do more than that. On the days he doesn't come to school, you could teach him yourself.'

'But I'm not qualified to teach anyone.'

'Harry Clifton is not impressed by qualifications, and we both know that he listens to you. Perhaps we could work as a team.'

'But if Harry were to find out what we were up to, neither of us would ever see him again.'

'How well you know him,' said the schoolmaster with a sigh. 'We'll just have to make sure he doesn't find out.'

'That may prove something of a challenge,' said Old Jack, 'but I'm willing to give it a try.'

'Thank you, sir,' said Mr Holcombe. The schoolmaster paused before adding, 'I wonder if I might be allowed to shake hands with you.' Old Jack looked surprised as the schoolmaster thrust out his hand. Old Jack shook it warmly. 'And may I say it has been an honour to meet you, Captain Tarrant.'

Old Jack looked horrified. 'How could you possibly . . .'

'My father has a picture of you that still hangs on the wall in our front room.'

'But why?' asked Old Jack.

'You saved his life, sir.'

◄o►

Harry's visits to Old Jack became less frequent during the next few weeks, until the only time they met was on a Saturday morning. Old Jack knew that Mr Holcombe must have succeeded in his plan when Harry asked him if he would come to Holy Nativity the following Sunday to hear him sing.

On Sunday morning, Old Jack rose early, used Sir Walter's private cloakroom on the fifth floor of Barrington House to have a shower, a recent invention, and even trimmed his beard, before putting on the other suit Sir Walter had given him.

Arriving at Holy Nativity just before the service

began, he slipped into the back row and took a seat at the end of the pew. He spotted Mrs Clifton in the third row, sitting between what could only have been her mother and father. As for Miss Monday, he could have picked her out in a congregation of a thousand.

Mr Holcombe had not been exaggerating about the quality of Harry's voice. It was as good as anything he could remember from his days at Wells Cathedral. As soon as the boy opened his mouth to sing *Lead Me, Lord*, Old Jack was left in no doubt that his protégé had an exceptional gift.

Once the Reverend Watts had given his final blessing, Old Jack slipped back out of the church and quickly made his way to the docks. He would have to wait until the following Saturday before he could tell the boy how much he'd enjoyed his singing.

As he walked back, Old Jack recalled Sir Walter's reproach. 'You could do so much more for Harry if you would only give up this self-denial.' He thought carefully about Sir Walter's words but he wasn't yet ready to remove the shackles of guilt. He did, however, know a man who could change Harry's life, a man who had been with him on that dreadful day, a man he hadn't spoken to for more than twenty-five years. A man who taught at a school that supplied St Mary Redcliffe with choristers. Unfortunately Merrywood Elementary was not a natural recruiting ground for its annual choral scholarship, so the man would have to be guided in the right direction.

Old Jack's only fear was that Lieutenant Frobisher might not remember him.

29

OLD JACK WAITED until Hugo had left Barrington House, but it was another half an hour before the lights finally went out in Miss Potts's room.

Jack stepped out of the railway carriage and began to walk slowly towards Barrington House, aware that he had only half an hour before the cleaning ladies came on duty. He slipped into the unlit building and climbed the stairs to the fifth floor; after twenty-five years of Sir Walter turning a blind eye, like a cat he could find his way to the door marked 'Managing Director' in the dark.

He sat down at Hugo's desk. He switched on the light; if anyone noticed it was on, they would simply assume Miss Potts was working late. He thumbed through the telephone directory until he came to the 'St's: Andrew's, Bartholomew's, Beatrice's, Bede's.

He picked up a telephone for the first time in his life, not quite sure what to do next. A voice came on the line. 'Number please?'

'TEM 8612,' said Jack, his forefinger resting just below the number.

'Thank you, sir.' As he waited, Old Jack became more nervous by the minute. What would he say if someone else came on the line? He'd just put the phone down. He took a piece of paper out of his pocket, unfolded it and laid it out on the desk in front of him. Next, he heard a ringing tone, followed by a click, then a man's voice. 'Frobisher House.'

'Is that Noel Frobisher?' he asked, recalling the tradition that each house at St Bede's was named after the housemaster of the day. He looked down at his script; each line had been carefully prepared and endlessly rehearsed.

'Speaking,' said Frobisher, clearly surprised to hear a voice he didn't recognize addressing him by his Christian name. A long silence followed. 'Is there anyone there?' Frobisher asked, sounding a little irritated.

'Yes, it's Captain Jack Tarrant.'

There was an even longer silence, before Frobisher eventually said, 'Good evening, sir.'

'Forgive me for calling at this late hour, old fellow, but I need to seek your advice.'

'Not at all, sir. It's a great privilege to speak to you after all these years.'

'Kind of you to say so,' said Old Jack. 'I'll try not to waste too much of your time, but I need to know if St Bede's still supplies St Mary Redcliffe with trebles for its choir?'

'We do indeed, sir. Despite so many changes in this modern world, that's one tradition that remains constant.'

'And in my day,' said Old Jack, 'the school awarded a choral scholarship each year to a treble who showed exceptional talent.'

'We still do, sir. In fact, we will be considering applications for the position in the next few weeks.'

'From any school in the county?'

'Yes, from any school that can produce a treble of outstanding quality. But they must also have a solid academic grounding.'

'Well, if that's the case,' said Old Jack, 'I would like to submit a candidate for your consideration.'

'Of course, sir. Which school is the boy attending at the moment?'

'Merrywood Elementary.'

Another long silence followed. 'I have to admit that it would be the first time we've had an applicant from that particular school. Do you by any chance know the name of its music master?'

'It doesn't have a music master,' said Old Jack, 'but you should get in touch with the boy's teacher, Mr Holcombe, who will introduce you to his choir mistress.'

'May I ask the boy's name?' said Frobisher.

'Harry Clifton. If you want to hear him sing, I recommend you attend Matins at Holy Nativity Church this Sunday.'

'Will you be there, sir?'

'No,' said Old Jack.

'How do I get in touch with you once I've heard the boy sing?' asked Frobisher.

'You don't,' said Old Jack firmly, and put the phone down. As he folded up his script and placed it back in his pocket, he could have sworn he heard footsteps crunching across the gravel outside. He quickly switched off the light, slipped out of Mr Hugo's office and into the corridor.

He heard a door open, and voices on the stairs. The last thing he needed was to be found on the fifth floor, which was strictly out of bounds to anyone other than the company's executives and Miss Potts. He wouldn't want to embarrass Sir Walter.

He began to walk quickly down the stairs. He'd reached the third floor when he saw Mrs Nettles heading towards him, a mop in one hand, a bucket in the other, a woman he didn't recognize by her side.

'Good evening, Mrs Nettles,' said Old Jack. 'And what a fine evening it is to be doing my rounds.'

'Evenin', Old Jack,' she replied as she ambled past him. Once he had turned the corner, he stopped and listened attentively. 'That's Old Jack,' he heard Mrs Nettles say. 'The so-called night watchman. He's completely crackers, but quite harmless. So if you come across him, just ignore him . . .' Old Jack chuckled as her voice faded with each step she took.

As he strolled back towards the railway carriage, he wondered how long it would be before Harry came to seek his advice on whether he should enter his name for a choral scholarship to St Bede's.

30

HARRY KNOCKED ON the carriage door, strolled in and took the seat opposite Old Jack in first class.

During term time at St Bede's, Harry had only been able to see Old Jack regularly on Saturday mornings. Jack had returned the compliment by attending Matins at St Mary Redcliffe, where from the back pew he enjoyed watching Mr Frobisher and Mr Holcombe beam with pride at his protégé.

In the school holidays, Old Jack could never be sure exactly when Harry was going to turn up because he treated the railway carriage like a second home. Whenever he returned to St Bede's at the beginning of a new term, Old Jack missed the boy's company. He was touched when Mrs Clifton described him as the father Harry never had. In truth, Harry was the son he'd always wanted.

'Finished your paper round early?' said Old Jack, rubbing his eyes and blinking, when Harry strolled into the carriage that Saturday morning.

'No, you just dozed off, old man,' said Harry, passing him a copy of the previous day's *Times*.

'And you're getting cheekier by the day, young man,' Old Jack said with a grin. 'So, how's the paper round working out?'

'Good. I think I'm going to be able to save enough money to buy my mum a watch.'

'A sensible present, considering your mother's new job. But can you afford it?'

'I've already saved four shillings,' said Harry. 'I reckon I'll have about six by the end of the holidays.'

'Have you chosen the watch you want?'

'Yes. It's in Mr Deakins's display cabinet, but it won't be there for much longer,' said Harry, grinning.

Deakins. A name Old Jack could never forget. 'How much is it?' he asked.

'No idea,' said Harry. 'I'm not going to ask Mr Deakins until the day before I go back to school.'

Old Jack wasn't sure how to tell the boy that six shillings wasn't going to be enough to buy a watch, so he changed the subject. 'I hope the paper round isn't stopping you from studying. I'm sure I don't have to remind you that the exams are getting closer by the day.'

'You're worse than the Frob,' said Harry, 'but you'll be pleased to learn that I'm spending two hours every morning in the library with Deakins, and another two most afternoons.'

'*Most* afternoons?'

'Well, Giles and I do occasionally go to the flicks, and as Gloucestershire are playing Yorkshire at the county ground next week, it will be a chance to see Herbert Sutcliffe batting.'

'You'll miss Giles when he goes to Eton,' said Old Jack.

'He's still working on his father to let him join me and Deakins at BGS.'

'Deakins and me,' said Old Jack. 'And be warned, if Mr Hugo has made up his mind, it will take more than Giles to shift him.'

'Mr Barrington doesn't like me,' said Harry, taking Old Jack by surprise.

'What makes you say that?'

'He treats me differently from the other boys at St Bede's. It's as if I'm not good enough to be a friend of his son.'

'You're going to have to face that problem all your life, Harry,' said Old Jack. 'The English are the biggest snobs on earth, and most of the time without reason. The lesser the talent, the bigger the snob, in my experience. It's the only way the so-called upper classes can hope to survive. Be warned, my boy, they don't care for upstarts like you who barge into their club without an invitation.'

'But you don't treat me like that,' said Harry.

'That's because I'm not upper class,' said Old Jack, laughing.

'Perhaps not, but my mum says you're first class,' said Harry, 'so that's what I want to be.'

It didn't help that Old Jack couldn't tell Harry the real reason Mr Hugo was always so off-hand. He sometimes wished he hadn't been in the wrong place at the wrong time, and witnessed what had really happened the day the boy's father died.

'Have you fallen asleep again, old man?' said Harry. 'Because I can't hang around chatting to you all day. I promised my mum I'd meet her at Clarks in the Broad because she wants to buy me a new pair of shoes. Not that I can see what's wrong with the pair I've got.'

'Special lady, your mum,' said Old Jack.

'That's why I'm buying her a watch,' said Harry.

◄○►

The bell above the door rang as he entered the shop. Old Jack hoped that enough time had passed to ensure that Private Deakins wouldn't remember him.

'Good morning, sir. How can I help you?'

Old Jack couldn't fail to recognize Mr Deakins immediately. He smiled and walked across to the display cabinet and studied the two watches on the top shelf. 'I just need to know the price of this Ingersoll.'

'The lady's or the gentleman's model, sir?' asked Mr Deakins, coming out from behind the counter.

'The lady's,' said Old Jack.

Deakins unlocked the cabinet with his one hand, deftly removed the watch from its stand, checked the label and said, 'Sixteen shillings, sir.'

'Good,' said Old Jack, and placed a ten-bob note on the counter. Mr Deakins looked even more puzzled. 'When Harry Clifton asks you how much the watch is, Mr Deakins, please tell him it's six shillings, because that's how much he will have saved by the time he stops working for you, and I know he's hoping to buy it as a present for his mother.'

'You must be Old Jack,' said Deakins. 'He'll be so touched that you . . .'

'But you won't ever tell him,' said Old Jack, looking Mr Deakins in the eye. 'I want him to believe that the price of the watch is six shillings.'

'I understand,' said Mr Deakins, placing the watch back on the stand.

'And how much is the man's watch?'

'One pound.'

'Would you allow me to put down another ten bob as a deposit, and then give you half a crown a week for the next month until I've paid off the full amount?'

'That is quite acceptable, sir. But wouldn't you like to try it on first?'

'No, thank you,' said Old Jack. 'It's not for me. I'm going to give it to Harry when he wins a scholarship to Bristol Grammar School.'

'I had the same thought,' said Mr Deakins, 'should my son Algy be fortunate enough to win one.'

'Then you'd better order another one pretty quickly,' said Old Jack, 'because Harry tells me your son's a racing certainty.'

Mr Deakins laughed, and took a closer look at Old Jack. 'Have we met before, sir?'

'I don't think so,' said Old Jack, and left the shop without another word.

31

IF MUHAMMAD WON'T COME to the mountain ...
Old Jack smiled to himself as he rose to greet Mr
Holcombe and offered him a seat.

'Would you care to join me in the buffet car for a
cup of tea?' Old Jack asked. 'Mrs Clifton was kind
enough to supply me with a quite excellent packet of
Earl Grey.'

'No, thank you sir,' said Holcombe, 'I've only just
had breakfast.'

'So, the boy just missed out on a scholarship,' said
Old Jack, assuming that was what the schoolmaster had
come to see him about.

'Failed is how Harry looks upon it,' said Holcombe,
'despite coming seventeenth out of three hundred, and
being offered a place in the school's A stream this
September.'

'But will he be able to accept the offer? It will place
an extra financial burden on his mother.'

'As long as there are no unexpected bombshells, she
should be able to get Harry through the next five years.'

'Even so, Harry won't be able to afford the little
extras most of the other boys will take for granted.'

'Possibly, but I have managed to cover some of his
sundry expenses from the school's list, so he'll be able

to consider at least two of the three extra-curricular activities he's keen to sign up for.'

'Let me guess,' said Old Jack. 'The choir, the theatre club and . . . ?'

'Art appreciation,' said Holcombe. 'Miss Monday and Miss Tilly are taking responsibility for any trips the choir might make, I'm covering the theatre club and . . .'

'So I get art appreciation,' said Old Jack. 'His new passion. I can still hold my own with Harry when it comes to Rembrandt and Vermeer, even this new chap, Matisse. Now he's trying to get me interested in a Spaniard called Picasso, but I can't see it myself.'

'I've never heard of him,' admitted Holcombe.

'And I doubt if you ever will,' said Old Jack, 'but don't tell Harry I said so.' He picked up a small tin box, opened it, and took out three notes and almost all the coins he possessed.

'No, no,' said Holcombe, 'that isn't the reason I came to see you. In fact, I plan to visit Mr Craddick later this afternoon, and I'm confident he'll—'

'I think you'll find that I take precedence over Mr Craddick,' said Old Jack, handing across the money.

'That's very generous of you.'

'Money well spent,' said Old Jack, 'even if it is the widow's mite. At least my father would approve,' he added as an afterthought.

'Your father?' repeated Holcombe.

'He's the resident canon at Wells Cathedral.'

'I had no idea,' said Holcombe. 'So at least you're able to visit him from time to time.'

'Sadly not. I fear I am a modern prodigal son,' said Old Jack. Not wishing to go any further down that road, he said, 'So tell me, young man, why did you want to see me?'

'I can't remember the last occasion anyone called me "young man".'

'Just be grateful that anyone still does,' said Old Jack.

Holcombe laughed. 'I've got a couple of tickets for the school play, *Julius Caesar*. As Harry is performing, I thought you might like to join me for the opening night.'

'I knew he was auditioning,' said Old Jack. 'What part did he get?'

'He's playing Cinna,' said Holcombe.

'Then we'll know him by his gait.'

Holcombe bowed low. 'Does that mean you'll join me?'

'I fear not,' said Old Jack, raising a hand. 'It's extremely kind of you to think of me, Holcombe, but I'm not yet ready for a live performance, even as just a member of the audience.'

◄○►

Old Jack was disappointed to miss Harry's performance in the school play and had to be satisfied with being told the boy's version of how he had performed. The following year, when Holcombe suggested that perhaps Old Jack should attend because Harry's roles were getting bigger, he nearly gave in, but it wasn't until Harry played Puck, a year later, that he finally allowed the dream a reality.

Although he was still fearful of large crowds, Old Jack had decided that he would slip into the back of the school hall, where no one would see him or, even worse, recognize him.

It was while he was trimming his beard in the fifth-floor washroom of Barrington House that he noticed the screaming headline in a copy of the local rag that someone had left behind. *Tilly's tea shop burnt to the ground. Arson suspected.* When he saw the photograph below it, he felt sick; Mrs Clifton was standing on the pavement surrounded by her staff, surveying the burnt-out remains of the shop. *Turn to page 11 for full story.* Old Jack obeyed the instruction, but there was no page 11.

He quickly left the washroom, hoping to find the missing page on Miss Potts's desk. He wasn't surprised to find that her desk was clear and her wastepaper basket had been emptied. He tentatively opened the door to the managing director's office, looked inside and spotted the missing page laid out on Mr Hugo's desk. He sat down in the high-backed leather chair and began to read.

Jack's immediate reaction once he'd finished was to wonder if Harry would have to leave school.

The report noted that unless the insurance company paid the full amount on her premium, Mrs Clifton would be facing bankruptcy. The reporter went on to say that a spokesman for the Bristol and West of England had made it clear that the company wouldn't be paying out a brass farthing until the police had eliminated all suspects from their enquiries. What else could possibly go wrong for the poor woman, Old Jack wondered.

The reporter had been careful not to refer to Maisie by name, but Old Jack wasn't in any doubt why her photograph was so prominently displayed on the front page. He continued to read the article. When he discovered that Detective Inspector Blakemore was in charge of the case, he felt a little more hopeful. It wouldn't take that particular gentleman long to work out that Mrs Clifton built things up; she didn't burn them down.

As Old Jack placed the newspaper back on Mr Hugo's desk, he noticed a letter for the first time. He would have ignored it, none of his business, if he hadn't seen the name 'Mrs Clifton' in the first paragraph.

He began to read the letter, and found it hard to believe it was Hugo Barrington who had put up the five hundred pounds that had made it possible for Mrs Clifton to purchase Tilly's. Why would he want to help Maisie, he wondered. Was it possible he felt some remorse about the death of her husband? Or did he feel ashamed that he had sent an innocent man to prison for a crime he had not committed? Certainly he had given Tancock his old job back the moment he was released. Old Jack began to wonder if he should perhaps give Hugo the benefit of the doubt. He recalled Sir Walter's words: 'He's not all bad, you know.'

He read the letter once again. It was from Mr Prendergast, the manager of the National Provincial Bank, who wrote that he had been pressing the insurance company to fulfil its contractual obligations and recompense Mrs Clifton for the full value of the policy, which was £600. Mrs Clifton, Prendergast pointed out, was the innocent party, and Detective Inspector Blakemore had recently informed the bank that she no longer played any part in his enquiries.

In the final paragraph of his letter, Prendergast suggested that he and Barrington should meet in the near future to resolve the matter, so that Mrs Clifton could receive the full amount she was entitled to. Old Jack looked up when the little clock on the desk chimed seven times.

He switched off the light, ran into the corridor and down the stairs. He didn't want to be late for Harry's performance.

32

WHEN OLD JACK got home later that night, he picked up a copy of *The Times* Harry had left for him earlier in the week. He never bothered with the personal ads on the front page as he didn't need a new bowler hat, a pair of suspenders or a first edition of *Wuthering Heights*.

He turned the page to find a photo of King Edward VIII, enjoying a yachting holiday in the Mediterranean. Standing by his side was an American woman called Mrs Simpson. The report was couched in ambiguous terms, but even the Thunderer was finding it hard to support the young King in his desire to marry a divorced woman. It made Old Jack sad, because he admired Edward, especially after his visit to the Welsh miners when he had so clearly been affected by their plight. But as his old nanny used to say, there'll be tears before bedtime.

Old Jack then spent some considerable time reading a report on the Tariff Reform Bill, which had just passed its second reading in the House, despite the firebrand Winston Churchill declaring that it was neither 'fish nor fowl', and no one would benefit from it, including the government, when it came to an election. He couldn't wait to hear Sir Walter's unexpurgated views on that particular subject.

He turned a page to learn that the British Broadcasting Corporation had made its first television broadcast from Alexandra Palace. This was a concept he couldn't begin to comprehend. How could a picture be beamed into your home? He didn't even have a radio, and had absolutely no desire to own a television.

He moved on to the sports pages, to find a photograph of an elegantly dressed Fred Perry under the headline, *Three times Wimbledon champion tipped to win the American Open*. The tennis correspondent went on to suggest that some of the foreign competitors might be wearing shorts at Forest Hills, something else Jack couldn't come to terms with.

As he did whenever he read *The Times*, Old Jack saved the obituaries till last. He'd reached that age when men younger than himself were dying, and not just in wars.

When he turned the page, the colour drained from his face, and he experienced an overwhelming sadness. He took his time reading the obituary of the Reverend Thomas Alexander Tarrant, Resident Canon of Wells Cathedral, described in the headline as a godly man. When Old Jack had finished reading his father's obituary, he felt ashamed.

◄○►

'Seven pounds four shillings?' repeated Old Jack. 'But I thought you got a cheque for six hundred pounds from the Bristol and West of England Insurance Company, "in full and final settlement", if I recall the exact words.'

'I did,' said Maisie, 'but by the time I'd paid back the original loan, the compound interest on that loan, as well as bank charges, I ended up with seven pounds and four shillings.'

'I'm so naive,' said Old Jack. 'And to think that for a

moment, just a moment, I actually thought Barrington was trying to be helpful.'

'You're not half as naive as me,' said Maisie. 'Because if I had thought, even for one moment, that man was involved, I would never have taken a penny of his money, and because I did, I've lost everything. Even my job at the hotel.'

'But why?' asked Old Jack. 'Mr Frampton always said you were irreplaceable.'

'Well, it seems I'm not any more. When I asked him why he'd sacked me, he refused to give a reason, other than to say he'd received a complaint about me from an "unimpeachable source". It can't be a coincidence that I was sacked the day after that "unimpeachable source" dropped into the Royal Hotel for a chat with the manager.'

'Did you see Barrington going into the hotel?' asked Old Jack.

'No, I didn't, but I saw him coming out. Don't forget, I was hiding in the back of his car, waiting for him.'

'Of course,' said Old Jack. 'So what happened when you confronted him about Harry?'

'While we were in the car,' said Maisie, 'he virtually admitted to being responsible for Arthur's death.'

'He finally came clean after all these years?' said Old Jack in disbelief.

'Not exactly,' said Maisie. 'More a slip of the tongue, but when I left the envelope with the invoice for next term's fees on the front seat of his car, he put it in his pocket and said he'd see what he could do to help.'

'And you fell for it?'

'Hook, line and sinker,' admitted Maisie, 'because when he stopped the car he even got out to open the back door for me. But the moment I stepped out, he knocked me to the ground, tore up the bill and drove off.'

'Is that how you got the black eye?'

Maisie nodded. 'And he also warned me he'd have me committed to a mental asylum if I even thought about contacting his wife.'

'That's nothing more than a bluff,' said Old Jack, 'because even he couldn't get away with that.'

'You may be right,' said Maisie, 'but it's not a risk I'm willing to take.'

'And if you did tell Mrs Barrington that her husband was responsible for Arthur's death,' said Old Jack, 'all he'd have to do is let her know you're Stan Tancock's sister, and she'd dismiss it out of hand.'

'Possibly,' said Maisie. 'But she wouldn't dismiss it out of hand if I told her her husband might be Harry's father . . .'

Old Jack was stunned into silence as he tried to take in the implications of Maisie's words. 'I'm not only naive,' he eventually managed, 'but I'm also bone stupid. Hugo Barrington won't care if his wife does or doesn't believe he was involved in your husband's death. His greatest fear is Harry ever finding out that he might be his father . . .'

'But I would never tell Harry,' said Maisie. 'The last thing I'd want is for him to spend the rest of his life wondering who his father is.'

'That is precisely what Barrington is banking on. And now he's broken you, he'll be hell-bent on destroying Harry.'

'But why?' asked Maisie. 'Harry's never done him any harm.'

'Of course he hasn't, but if Harry were able to prove that he is Hugo Barrington's eldest son, he might just be in line to inherit not only the title, but everything that goes with it, and at the same time, Giles would end up with nothing.'

It was Maisie's turn to be speechless.

'So, now we've discovered the real reason Barrington is so keen to have Harry thrown out of the grammar school, perhaps the time has come for me to pay a visit to Sir Walter, and tell him some unpalatable truths about his son.'

'No, please don't do that,' begged Maisie.

'Why not? It might be our one chance of keeping Harry at BGS.'

'Possibly, but it would also guarantee that my brother Stan would get the sack, and God knows what else Barrington is capable of.'

Old Jack didn't reply for some time. Then he said, 'If you won't allow me to tell Sir Walter the truth, I'll have to start crawling around in the sewer that Hugo Barrington currently occupies.'

33

'YOU WANT WHAT?' asked Miss Potts, not sure she'd heard him correctly.

'A private meeting with Mr Hugo,' said Old Jack.

'And am I permitted to enquire what the purpose of this meeting might be?' she said, making no attempt to hide the sarcasm in her voice.

'His son's future.'

'Wait here for a moment. I'll see if Mr Barrington is willing to see you.'

Miss Potts knocked gently on the managing director's door and disappeared inside. She returned a moment later with a surprised look on her face.

'Mr Barrington will see you now,' she said, holding open the door.

Old Jack couldn't resist a smile as he strolled past her. Hugo Barrington looked up from behind his desk. He didn't offer the old man a seat, and made no attempt to shake hands with him.

'What possible interest can you have in Giles's future?' asked Barrington.

'None,' admitted Old Jack. 'It's your other son whose future I'm interested in.'

'What the hell are you talking about?' said Barrington, a little too loudly.

'If you didn't know who I was talking about, you wouldn't have agreed to see me,' replied Old Jack contemptuously.

The colour drained from Barrington's face. Old Jack even wondered if he was going to faint. 'What do you want from me?' he finally said.

'All your life you've been a trader,' said Old Jack. 'I am in possession of something you'll want to trade.'

'And what could that possibly be?'

'The day after Arthur Clifton mysteriously disappeared and Stan Tancock was arrested for a crime he didn't commit, I was asked by Detective Inspector Blakemore to make a statement of everything I'd witnessed that evening. Because you had Blakemore taken off the case, that statement remains in my possession. I have a feeling it would make very interesting reading if it were to fall into the wrong hands.'

'I think you'll find that's blackmail,' said Barrington, spitting out the words, 'for which you can go to prison for a very long time.'

'Some might consider it nothing more than a matter of civic duty for such a document to enter the public domain.'

'And who do you imagine would be interested in the ravings of an old man? Certainly not the press, once my lawyers have explained the libel laws to them. And as the police closed the file some years ago, I can't see the chief constable going to the trouble and expense of reopening it on the word of an old man who might be considered at best eccentric and at worst mad. So I'm bound to ask, who else do you have in mind to share your preposterous allegations with?'

'Your father,' said Old Jack, bluffing, but then Barrington didn't know about his promise to Maisie.

Barrington slumped back in his chair, only too aware of the influence Old Jack had with his father, even if he had never understood why. 'How much do you expect me to pay for this document?'

'Three hundred pounds.'

'That's daylight robbery!'

'It's no more and no less than the amount required to cover the fees and any little extras that will allow Harry Clifton to remain at Bristol Grammar School for the next two years.'

'Why don't I just pay his fees at the beginning of each term, as I do for my own son?'

'Because you would stop paying one of your sons' fees the moment you got your hands on my statement.'

'You'll have to take cash,' said Barrington, taking a key from his pocket.

'No, thank you,' said Old Jack. 'I remember only too well what happened to Stan Tancock after you'd handed him your thirty pieces of silver. And I have no desire to spend the next three years in prison for a crime I didn't commit.'

'Then I'll have to call the bank if I'm to write out a cheque for such a large amount.'

'Be my guest,' said Old Jack, gesturing towards the phone on Barrington's desk.

Barrington hesitated for a moment before picking up the handset. He waited for a voice to come on the line. 'TEM 3731,' he said.

Another wait, before another voice said, 'Yes?'

'Is that you, Prendergast?'

'No, sir,' said the voice.

'Good, you're just the man I need to speak to,' Barrington replied. 'I'll be sending a Mr Tar around to see you in the next hour, with a cheque for three hundred pounds made payable to Bristol Municipal Charities. Would you see that it's processed immediately, and make sure you phone me straight back.'

'If you want me to ring you back, just say "Yes, that's right," and I'll call in a couple of minutes,' the voice said.

'Yes, that's right,' said Barrington, and put the phone down.

He opened the drawer of his desk, took out a cheque book and wrote the words *Pay Bristol Municipal Charities* and, on a separate line, *Three hundred pounds*. He then signed the cheque and passed it to Old Jack, who studied it carefully and nodded.

'I'll just put it in an envelope,' said Barrington. He pressed the buzzer under his desk. Old Jack glanced at Miss Potts as she entered the room.

'Yes, sir?'

'Mr Tar is leaving to go to the bank,' said Barrington, placing the cheque in the envelope. He sealed it and addressed it to Mr Prendergast, adding the word PRIVATE in bold letters, then handed it to Old Jack.

'Thank you,' said Jack. 'I'll deliver the document to you personally as soon as I get back.'

Barrington nodded, just as the phone on his desk began to ring. He waited for Old Jack to leave the room before he picked it up.

Old Jack decided to take the tram into Bristol, feeling that the expense was justified on such a special occasion. When he walked into the bank twenty minutes later, he told the young man on the reception that he had a letter for Mr Prendergast. The receptionist didn't seem particularly impressed, until Old Jack added, 'It's from Mr Hugo Barrington.'

The young man immediately deserted his post, led Old Jack across the banking hall and down a long corridor to the manager's office. He knocked on the door, opened it and announced, 'This gentleman has a letter from Mr Barrington, sir.'

Mr Prendergast leapt up from behind his desk, shook hands with the old man and ushered him to a seat on the other side of the desk. Old Jack handed the envelope to Prendergast, with the words, 'Mr Barrington asked me to give this to you personally.'

'Yes, of course,' said Prendergast, who immediately recognized the familiar hand of one of his most valued customers. He slit open the envelope and extracted a cheque. He looked at it for a moment, before saying, 'There must be some mistake.'

'There's no mistake,' said Old Jack. 'Mr Barrington would like the full amount to be paid to Bristol Municipal Charities at your earliest convenience, as he instructed you over the phone only half an hour ago.'

'But I haven't spoken to Mr Barrington this morning,' said Prendergast, passing the cheque back to Old Jack.

Old Jack stared in disbelief at a blank cheque. It only took him a few moments to realize that Barrington must have switched the cheques when Miss Potts entered the room. The true genius of his action was to address the envelope to Mr Prendergast and mark it private, thus ensuring it wouldn't be opened until it had been handed to the manager. But the one mystery Jack couldn't fathom was: who had been on the other end of the phone?

Old Jack hurried out of the office without saying another word to Prendergast. He crossed the banking hall and ran out into the street. He only had to wait a few minutes for a tram to the docks. He couldn't have been away for much more than an hour by the time he walked back through the gates and into the dockyard.

A man he didn't recognize was striding towards him. He had a military air about him and Old Jack wondered if the limp had been caused by an injury he'd suffered in the Great War.

Old Jack hurried past him and on down the quayside. He was relieved to see that the carriage door was closed, and when he opened it he was even more pleased to find that everything was just as he'd left it. He sank to his knees and lifted the corner of the carpet, but the police statement was no longer there. Detective Inspector Blakemore would have described the theft as the work of a professional.

34

OLD JACK TOOK his place in the fifth row of the congregation, hoping no one would recognize him. The cathedral was so packed that people who had been unable to find a seat in the side chapels stood in the aisles and were crammed in at the back.

The Bishop of Bath and Wells brought tears to Old Jack's eyes when he talked about his father's unquestioning faith in God, and how, since the premature death of his wife, the canon had devoted himself to serving the community, 'The proof of which,' proclaimed the Bishop, raising his arms to acknowledge the vast congregation, 'can be seen by the number of those present, who have come to honour him from so many walks of life, and to pay their respects.

'And although the man knew no vanity, he could not hide a certain pride in his only son, Jack, whose selfless courage, bravery and willingness to sacrifice his own life in South Africa during the Boer War saved so many of his comrades, and led to him being awarded the Victoria Cross.' He paused, looked down into the fifth row and said, 'And how delighted I am to see him in the congregation today.'

Several people began looking around for a man they had never seen before. Jack bowed his head in shame.

At the end of the service, many members of the congregation came up to tell Captain Tarrant how much they had admired his father. The words 'dedication', 'selflessness', 'generosity' and 'love' fell from everyone's lips.

Jack felt proud of being his father's son, while at the same time ashamed that he had excluded him from his life, in the same way as he had the rest of his fellow men.

As he was leaving, he thought he recognized an elderly gentleman standing by the great gates, clearly waiting to speak to him. The man stepped forward and raised his hat. 'Captain Tarrant?' he enquired with a voice that suggested authority.

Jack returned the compliment. 'Yes, sir?'

'My name is Edwin Trent. I had the privilege of being your father's solicitor, and, I'd like to think, one of his oldest and closest friends.'

Jack shook him warmly by the hand. 'I remember you well, sir. You taught me a love of Trollope and an appreciation of the finer points of spin bowling.'

'It's kind of you to remember,' Trent chuckled. 'I wonder if I might accompany you on your way back to the station?'

'Of course, sir.'

'As you know,' said Trent as they began walking towards the town, 'your father was resident canon of this cathedral for the past nine years. You'll also know that he cared nothing for worldly goods, and shared even the little he had with those less fortunate than himself. If he were to be canonized, he would surely be the patron saint of vagabonds.'

Old Jack smiled. He recalled going to school one morning without breakfast because three tramps were sleeping in the hallway and, to quote his mother, they had eaten them out of house and home.

'So when his will comes to be read,' continued Trent, 'it will show that just as he entered this world with nothing, he has also left it with nothing – other than a thousand friends, that is, which he would have considered a veritable fortune. Before he died, he entrusted me with one small task should you attend his funeral, namely that of handing you the last letter he ever wrote.' He extracted an envelope from an inside pocket of his overcoat and handed it to Old Jack, raised his hat once more and said, 'I have carried out his request, and am proud to have met his son once again.'

'I am obliged, sir. I only wish that I hadn't made it necessary for him to have to write in the first place.' Jack raised his hat and the two men parted.

Old Jack decided that he would not read his father's letter until he was on the train, and had begun the journey back to Bristol. As the engine shunted out of the station, billowing clouds of grey smoke, Jack settled back in a third-class compartment. As a child, he remembered asking his father why he always travelled third class, to which he had replied, 'Because there isn't a fourth class.' It was ironic that, for the past thirty years, Jack had been living in first class.

He took his time unsealing the envelope, and even after he had extracted the letter, he left it folded while he continued to think about his father. No son could have asked for a better mentor or friend. When he looked back on his life, all his actions, judgements and decisions were nothing more than pale imitations of his father's.

When he finally unfolded the letter, another flood of memories came rushing back the moment he saw the familiar bold, copperplate hand in jet-black ink. He began to read.

The Close
Wells Cathedral
Wells, Somerset

26th August, 1936

My beloved son,

If you were kind enough to attend my funeral, you must now be reading this letter. Allow me to begin by thanking you for being among the congregation.

Old Jack raised his head and looked out at the passing countryside. He felt guilty once again for treating his father in such an inconsiderate and thoughtless manner, and now it was too late to ask for his forgiveness. His eyes returned to the letter.

When you were awarded the Victoria Cross, I was the proudest father in England, and your citation still hangs above my desk to this very day. But then, as the years passed, my happiness turned to sorrow, and I asked our Lord what I had done that I should be so punished by losing not only your dear mother, but also you, my only child.

I accept that you must have had some noble purpose for turning your head and your heart against this world, but I wish you had shared your reason for so doing with me. But, should you read this letter, perhaps you might grant me one last wish.

Old Jack removed the handkerchief from his top pocket and wiped his eyes before he was able to continue reading.

God gave you the remarkable gift of leadership and the ability to inspire your fellow men, so I beg you not to go to your grave knowing that when the time comes for you to face your maker, you will, as in the parable Matthew 25, v14–30, have to confess that you buried the one talent He gave you.

Rather, use that gift for the benefit of your fellow men, so that when your time comes, as it surely must, and those same men attend your funeral, the Victoria Cross will not be the only thing they remember when they hear the name Jack Tarrant.

Your loving father

'Are you all right, my luv?' asked a lady who had moved from the other side of the carriage to sit next to Old Jack.

'Yes, thank you,' he said, the tears streaming down his face. 'It's just that I was released from prison today.'

GILES BARRINGTON

1936–1938

35

I was thrilled when I saw Harry walk through the school gates on the first day of term. I'd spent the summer hols at our villa in Tuscany, so I wasn't in Bristol when Tilly's was burnt to the ground and didn't find out about it until I returned to England the weekend before term began. I had wanted Harry to join us in Italy, but my father wouldn't hear of it.

I've never met anyone who didn't like Harry, with the exception of my father, who won't even allow his name to be mentioned in the house. I once asked Mama if she could explain why he felt so strongly, but she didn't seem to know any more than I did.

I didn't press the point with my old man, as I've never exactly covered myself in glory in his eyes. I nearly got myself expelled from my prep school for stealing – heaven knows how he managed to fix that – and after that I let him down by failing to get into Eton. I told Papa when I came out of the exam that I couldn't have tried harder, which was the truth. Well, half the truth. I would have got away with it if my co-conspirator had only kept his mouth shut. At least it taught me a simple lesson: if you make a deal with a fool, don't be surprised when they act foolishly.

My co-conspirator was the Earl of Bridport's son, Percy. He was facing an even greater dilemma than I was, because seven generations of Bridports had been educated at Eton, and it was looking as if young Percy was going to ruin that rather fine batting average.

Eton has been known to bend the rules when it comes to members of the aristocracy and will occasionally allow a stupid boy to darken its doors, which is why I selected Percy for my little subterfuge in the first place. It was after I overheard the Frob saying to another beak, 'If Bridport was any brighter, he'd be a half-wit,' that I knew I didn't need to look any further for my accomplice.

Percy was as desperate to be offered a place at Eton as I was to be rejected, so I saw this as no more than an opportunity for both of us to achieve our purpose.

I didn't discuss my plan with Harry or Deakins. Harry would undoubtedly have disapproved, he's such a morally upright fellow, and Deakins wouldn't have been able to understand why anyone would want to fail an exam.

On the day before the examination was due to take place my father drove me to Eton in his swish new Bugatti, which could do a hundred miles an hour, and once we hit the A4 he proved it. We spent the night at the Swann Arms, the same hotel in which he had stayed over twenty years before when he took the entrance exam. Over dinner, Papa didn't leave me in any doubt how keen he was that I should go to Eton and I nearly had a change of heart at the last moment, but I had given my word to Percy Bridport, and felt I couldn't let him down.

Percy and I had shaken hands on the deal back at St Bede's, agreeing that when we entered the examination hall, we would give the recorder the other's name. I rather enjoyed being addressed as 'my lord' by all and sundry, even if it was only for a few hours.

The examination papers were not as demanding as the ones I'd sat a fortnight earlier for Bristol Grammar, and I felt I'd done more than enough to ensure that Percy would be returning to Eton in September. However, they were difficult enough for me to feel confident that his lordship would not let me down.

Once we'd handed in our papers and reverted to our true personas, I went off to tea with my pa, in Windsor. When he asked me how it had gone, I told him I'd done the best I possibly could. He seemed satisfied by this, and even began to relax, which only made me feel more guilty. I didn't enjoy the journey back to Bristol, and felt even worse when I got home and my mother asked me the same question.

Ten days later, I received an *I'm sorry to have to inform you* letter from Eton. I had only managed 32 per cent. Percy scored 56 per cent and was offered a place for the Michaelmas term, which delighted his father and was met with incredulity by the Frob.

Everything would have worked out just fine, if Percy hadn't told a friend how he'd managed to get into Eton. The friend told another friend, who told another friend, who told Percy's father. The Earl of Bridport MC, being an honourable man, immediately informed the headmaster of Eton. This resulted in Percy being expelled before he'd even set foot in the place. If it hadn't been for a personal intervention by the Frob, I might have suffered the same fate at Bristol Grammar.

My father tried to convince the headmaster of Eton that it was simply a clerical error, and that, as I'd actually scored 56 per cent in the exam, I should be reinstated in Bridport's place. This piece of logic was rejected by return of post, as Eton wasn't in need of a new cricket pavilion. I duly reported to Bristol Grammar School on the first day of term.

◄○►

During my first year, I restored my reputation somewhat by scoring three centuries for the Colts and ended the season being awarded my colours. Harry played Ursula in *Much Ado*

About Nothing, and Deakins was Deakins, so no one was surprised when he won the First Form prize.

During my second year, I became more aware of the financial constraints Harry's mother must be experiencing when I noticed that he was wearing his shoes with the laces undone, and he admitted they were pinching because they were so tight.

So when Tilly's was burnt to the ground only weeks before we were expected to enter the sixth form, I was not altogether surprised to learn that Harry thought he might not be able to stay on at the school. I thought about asking my father if he might be able to help, but Mama told me I would be wasting my time. That's why I was so delighted when I saw him walking through the school gates on the first day of term.

He told me that his mother had begun a new job at the Royal Hotel, working nights, and it was proving to be far more lucrative than she had originally thought possible.

During the next summer hols I would, once again, have liked to invite Harry to join the family in Tuscany, but I knew my father would not consider the idea. But as the Arts Appreciation Society, of which Harry was now secretary, was planning a trip to Rome, we agreed to meet up there, even if it did mean I would have to visit the Villa Borghese.

—◇—

Although we were living in a little bubble of our own down in the West Country, it would have been impossible not to be aware of what was taking place on the continent.

The rise of the Nazis in Germany, and the Fascists in Italy, didn't seem to be affecting the average Englishman, who was still enjoying a pint of cider and a cheese sandwich at his local on a Saturday, before watching, or in my case playing, cricket on the village green in the afternoon. For years this blissful state of affairs had been able to continue because another war with Germany didn't bear thinking about. Our fathers had fought in the war to end all wars, but now the unmentionable seemed to be on everyone's lips.

Harry told me in no uncertain terms that if war was declared, he wouldn't be going to university but would join up immediately, just as his father and uncle had done some twenty years before. My father had 'missed out', as he put it, because unfortunately he was colour-blind, and those in authority thought he'd serve the war effort better by remaining at his post, playing an important role in the docks. Though I've never been quite sure exactly what that important role was.

◄о►

In our final year at BGS, both Harry and I decided to enter our names for Oxford; Deakins had already been offered an open scholarship to Balliol College. I wanted to go to the House, but was informed most politely by the entrance tutor that Christ Church rarely took grammar school boys, so I settled for Brasenose, which had once been described by Bertie Wooster as a college 'where brains are neither here nor there'.

As Brasenose was also the college with the most cricket blues, and I had scored three centuries in my final year as captain of BGS, one of them at Lord's for a Public Schools XI, I felt I must be in with a chance. In fact, my form master, Dr Paget, told me that when I went for my interview they would probably throw a cricket ball at me as I entered the room. If I caught it, I would be offered a place. If I caught it one-handed, a scholarship. This turned out to be apocryphal. However, I'm bound to admit that during drinks with the college principal, he asked me more questions about Hutton than Horace.

There were other highs and lows during my last two years at school: Jesse Owens winning four gold medals at the Olympic Games in Berlin, right under Hitler's nose, was a definite high, while the abdication of Edward VIII because he wished to marry an American divorcee was an undoubted low.

The nation seemed to be divided on whether the King should have abdicated, as were Harry and I. I failed to understand how a man born to be King could be willing to sacrifice the throne to marry a divorced woman. Harry was far more sympathetic to the King's plight, saying that we couldn't begin to understand what the poor man was going through until we fell in love ourselves. I dismissed this as codswallop, until that trip to Rome that was to change both our lives.

36

IF GILES IMAGINED he'd worked hard during his final days at St Bede's, in those last two years at Bristol Grammar School both he and Harry became acquainted with hours only Deakins was familiar with.

Dr Paget, their sixth-form master, told them in no uncertain terms that if they hoped to be offered a place at Oxford or Cambridge, they would have to forget any other activities, as they would need to spend every waking moment preparing for the entrance exams.

Giles was hoping to captain the school's First XI in his final year, while Harry was keen to land the lead in the school play. Dr Paget raised an eyebrow when he heard this, even though *Romeo and Juliet* was the set text for Oxford that year. 'Just be sure you don't sign up for anything else,' he said firmly.

Harry reluctantly resigned from the choir, which gave him two more free evenings a week to study. However, there was one activity no pupil could exempt himself from: every Tuesday and Thursday, at four o'clock, all the boys had to be standing to attention on the parade ground, fully kitted out and ready for inspection as members of the Officer Training Corps.

'Can't allow the Hitler Youth to imagine that if

Germany is foolish enough to declare war on us a second time, we won't be ready for them,' bellowed the RSM.

Every time ex-Regimental Sergeant Major Roberts delivered these words, it sent a shiver through the ranks of schoolboys, who realized as each day passed that it was becoming more and more likely they would be serving on the front line as junior officers in some foreign field, rather than going up to university as under-graduates.

Harry took the RSM's words to heart and was quickly promoted to cadet officer. Giles took them less seriously, knowing that if he was called up, he could, like his father, take the easy way out and remind them of his colour-blindness to avoid coming face to face with the enemy.

Deakins showed little interest in the whole process, declaring with a certainty that brooked no argument, 'You don't need to know how to strip a Bren gun when you're in the intelligence corps.'

By the time the long summer nights began to draw to a close, they were all ready for a holiday before they would return for their final year, at the end of which they would have to face the examiners once again. Within a week of term ending, all three of them had left for their summer break: Giles to join his family at their villa in Tuscany, Harry to Rome with the school's Arts Appreciation Society, while Deakins entombed himself in Bristol Central library, avoiding contact with any other human beings, despite the fact that he'd already been offered a place at Oxford.

◄o►

Over the years, Giles had come to accept that if he wanted to see Harry during the holidays, he had to make sure his father didn't find out what he was up to, otherwise the best-laid schemes of mice and . . . But in order to achieve this, he often had to get his sister Emma to join in the subterfuge, and she never failed to extract her pound of flesh before agreeing to become his accomplice.

'If you take the lead over dinner tonight, I'll follow up,' said Giles once he'd outlined his latest scheme to her.

'Sounds like the natural order of things,' said Emma scornfully.

After the first course had been served, Emma innocently asked her mother if she could possibly take her to the Villa Borghese the following day, as it had been recommended as a must by her art mistress. She was well aware that Mama had already made other plans.

'I'm so sorry, darling,' she said, 'but your father and I are going to lunch with the Hendersons in Arezzo tomorrow. You're most welcome to join us.'

'There's nothing to stop Giles taking you into Rome,' interjected his father from the other end of the table.

'Do I have to?' said Giles, who had just been about to make the same suggestion.

'Yes, you do,' replied his father firmly.

'But what's the point, Pa? By the time we get there, we'll have to turn round and come back. It's hardly worth it.'

'Not if you were to spend the night at the Plaza Hotel. I'll call them first thing in the morning, and book a couple of rooms.'

'Are you sure they're grown up enough for that?' asked Mrs Barrington, sounding a little anxious.

'Giles will be eighteen in a few weeks. It's time he grew up and took some responsibility.' Giles bowed his head as if he had given in meekly.

The following morning, a taxi drove him and Emma

to the local station just in time to catch the early morning train to Rome.

'Be sure to take care of your sister,' were his father's last words before they left the villa.

'I will,' promised Giles as the car drove off.

Several men rose to offer Emma their seat as she entered the carriage, while Giles was left standing for the entire journey. On arrival in Rome, they took a taxi to the Via del Corso, and once they'd booked into their hotel they continued on to the Villa Borghese. Giles was struck by how many young men not much older than himself were in uniform, while almost every pillar and lamp-post they passed displayed a poster of Mussolini.

Once the taxi had dropped them off, they made their way up through the gardens, passing more men in uniform and even more posters of 'Il Duce' before they finally reached the palatial Villa Borghese.

Harry had written to tell Giles they would be setting out on their official tour at ten o'clock. He checked his watch – a few minutes past eleven, with luck the tour would be nearly over. He bought two tickets, handed one to Emma, bounded up the steps to the galleria and went in search of the school party. Emma took her time admiring the Bernini statues that dominated the first four rooms, but then she wasn't in a hurry. Giles went from gallery to gallery until he spotted a group of young men dressed in dark claret jackets and black flannel trousers, who were crowded around a small portrait of an elderly man dressed in a cream silk cassock with a white mitre on his head.

'There they are,' he said, but Emma was nowhere to be seen. Not giving his sister another thought, he headed over to the attentive group. The moment he saw her, he quite forgot the reason he had come to Rome.

'Caravaggio was commissioned to paint this portrait of Pope Paul V in 1605,' she said, with a slight accent. 'You will notice that it was not finished, and that is because the artist had to flee from Rome.'

'Why, miss?' demanded a young boy in the front row, who was clearly determined to take Deakins's place at some time in the future.

'Because he became involved in a drunken brawl, during which he ended up killing a man.'

'Did they arrest him?' asked the same boy.

'No,' said the tour guide, 'Caravaggio always managed to move on to the next city before the forces of justice could catch up with him, but in the end the Holy Father decided to grant him a pardon.'

'Why?' demanded the same boy.

'Because he wanted Caravaggio to carry out several more commissions for him. Some of them are among the seventeen works that can still be seen in Rome today.'

At that moment, Harry spotted Giles gazing in awe in the direction of the painting. He left the group and walked across to join him. 'How long have you been standing there?' he asked.

'Long enough to fall in love,' said Giles, his eyes still fixed on the tour guide.

Harry laughed when he realized it wasn't the painting Giles was staring at, but the elegant, self-assured young woman who was addressing the boys. 'I think she's a bit out of your age group,' said Harry, 'and I suspect even your price range.'

'I'm willing to take that risk,' said Giles as the guide led her little group into the next room. Giles followed obediently and positioned himself so he had a clear view of her, while the rest of the group studied a statue of

Paolina Borghese by Canova, 'arguably the greatest sculptor of all time', she said. Giles wasn't going to disagree with her.

'Well, that brings us to the end of our tour,' she announced. 'But if you have any more questions I will be here for a few more minutes, so don't hesitate to ask.'

Giles didn't hesitate.

Harry watched in amusement as his friend strode up to the young Italian woman and began chatting to her as if they were old friends. Even the little boy from the front row didn't dare to interrupt him. Giles rejoined Harry a few minutes later, a large grin plastered across his face.

'She's agreed to have dinner with me tonight.'

'I don't believe you,' said Harry.

'But a problem has arisen,' he added, ignoring his friend's Doubting Thomas look.

'More than one, I suspect.'

'. . . which can be overcome with your assistance.'

'You need a chaperone to accompany you,' suggested Harry, 'just in case things get out of hand.'

'No, you ass. I want you to take care of my sister while Caterina introduces me to Rome's night-life.'

'Not a hope,' said Harry. 'I didn't come all the way to Rome just to act as your babysitter.'

'But you're my best friend,' pleaded Giles. 'If you won't help me, who else can I turn to?'

'Why don't you try Paolina Borghese? I doubt if she has any plans for tonight.'

'All you have to do is take her out for dinner, and make sure she's in bed by ten.'

'Forgive me for mentioning it, Giles, but I thought you'd come to Rome to have dinner with me?'

'I'll give you a thousand lira if you take her off my

hands. And we can still have breakfast at my hotel in the morning.'

'I'm not that easily bribed.'

'And,' said Giles, playing his trump card, 'I'll also give you my recording of Caruso singing *La Bohème*.'

Harry turned to find a young girl standing by his side.

'By the way,' said Giles, 'this is my sister, Emma.'

'Hello,' said Harry. Turning back to Giles, he said, 'You've got yourself a deal.'

—◦—

Harry joined Giles for breakfast at the Palace Hotel the following morning, when his friend greeted him with the same immodest smile he always wore just after he'd scored a century.

'So, how was Caterina?' Harry asked, not wanting to hear his reply.

'Beyond my wildest dreams.'

Harry was about to question him more closely when a waiter appeared by his side. '*Cappuccino, per favore.*' Then he asked, 'So how far did she let you go?'

'All the way,' said Giles.

Harry's mouth fell open, but no words came out. 'Did you . . .'

'Did I what?'

'Did you . . .' Harry tried again.

'Yes?'

'See her naked?'

'Yes, of course.'

'The whole body?'

'Naturally,' said Giles as a cup of coffee was placed in front of Harry.

'The bottom half as well as the top?'

'Everything,' said Giles. 'And I mean everything.'

'Did you touch her breasts?'

'I licked her nipples actually,' said Giles, taking a sip of coffee.

'You did what?'

'You heard me,' said Giles.

'But did you, I mean, did you . . .'

'Yes, I did.'

'How many times?'

'I lost count,' said Giles. 'She was insatiable. Seven, perhaps eight. She just wouldn't let me get to sleep. I'd still be there now if she hadn't had to be at the Vatican museum at ten this morning to lecture the next bunch of brats.'

'But what if she gets pregnant?' said Harry.

'Don't be so naive, Harry. Try to remember she's an Italian.' After another sip of coffee, he asked, 'So, how did my sister behave herself?'

'The food was excellent, and you owe me your Caruso recording.'

'That bad? Well, we can't all be winners.'

Neither of them had noticed Emma enter the room until she was standing by their side. Harry leapt up and offered her his seat. 'Sorry to leave you,' he said, 'but I have to be at the Vatican museum by ten.'

'Give Caterina my love!' shouted Giles as Harry almost ran out of the breakfast room.

Giles waited until Harry was out of sight before he asked his sister, 'So, how did last night go?'

'Could have been worse,' she said, picking up a croissant. 'A bit serious, isn't he?'

'You should meet Deakins.'

Emma laughed. 'Well, at least the food was good. But don't forget, I now own your gramophone.'

37

GILES LATER DESCRIBED IT as the most memorable night of his life – for all the wrong reasons.

The annual play is one of the major events in the Bristol Grammar School calendar, not least because the city boasts a fine theatre tradition, and 1937 was to prove a vintage year.

The school, like so many others in the country, performed one of Shakespeare's set texts for the year. The choice had been between *Romeo and Juliet* and *A Midsummer Night's Dream*. Dr Paget chose the tragedy rather than the comedy, not least because he had a Romeo and he didn't have a Bottom.

For the first time in the school's history, the young ladies of Red Maids' on the other side of the city were invited to audition for the girls' parts, but not before several discussions had taken place with Miss Webb, the headmistress, who had insisted on a set of ground rules that would have impressed a mother superior.

The play was to be performed on three consecutive evenings in the last week of term. As always, the Saturday night was sold out first, because former pupils and the parents of the cast wished to attend the closing night.

Giles was standing anxiously in the foyer checking

his watch every few moments as he waited impatiently for his parents and younger sister to arrive. He hoped that Harry would give another fine performance, and his father would finally come round to accepting him.

The critic from the *Bristol Evening World* had described Harry's performance as 'mature beyond his years', but he had saved the highest praise for Juliet, reporting that he had not seen the death scene performed more movingly even at Stratford.

Giles shook hands with Mr Frobisher as he walked into the foyer. His old housemaster introduced his guest, a Mr Holcombe, before they went through to the great hall to take their seats.

A murmur rippled around the audience when Captain Tarrant walked down the centre aisle and took his place in the front row. His recent appointment as a governor of the school had been met with universal approval. As he leant across to have a word with the chairman of the governors, he spotted Maisie Clifton sitting just a few rows behind. He gave her a warm smile, but didn't recognize the man she was sitting with. The next surprise came when he studied the cast list.

The headmaster and Mrs Barton were among the last members of the audience to enter the great hall. They took their places in the front row alongside Sir Walter Barrington and Captain Tarrant.

Giles was becoming more nervous with each passing minute. He was beginning to wonder if his parents would turn up before the curtain rose.

'I'm so sorry, Giles,' said his mother when they finally appeared. 'It's my fault, I lost track of time,' she added as she and Grace hurried into the hall. His father followed a yard behind and raised his eyebrows when he saw his son. Giles didn't hand him a programme as he wanted it to be a surprise, although he had shared the news with his mother who, like him, hoped her husband would finally treat Harry as if he were a friend of the family, and not an outsider.

The curtain rose only moments after the Barringtons had taken their seats, and a hush of anticipation descended on the packed audience.

When Harry made his first entrance, Giles glanced in his father's direction. As there didn't appear to be any immediate reaction, he began to relax for the first time that evening. But this happy state of affairs only lasted until the ballroom scene, when Romeo, and Hugo, saw Juliet for the first time.

Some people in the seats near the Barringtons became irritated by a restless man who was spoiling their enjoyment of the play with his loud whispering and demands to see a programme. They became even more annoyed after Romeo said, 'Is she not Capulet's daughter?' at which point Hugo Barrington stood up and barged along the row, not caring whose feet he trod on. He then marched down the centre aisle, pushed his way through the swing doors and disappeared into the night. It was some time before Romeo fully regained his composure.

Sir Walter tried to give the impression he hadn't noticed what was going on behind him, and although Captain Tarrant frowned, his eyes never left the stage. Had he turned round, he would have seen Mrs Clifton was ignoring Barrington's unscripted exit as she concentrated on every word the two young lovers had to say.

During the interval, Giles went in search of his father but couldn't find him. He checked the car park, but there was no sign of the Bugatti. When he returned to the foyer, he saw his grandfather bending down and whispering in his mother's ear.

'Has Hugo gone completely mad?' asked Sir Walter.

'No, he's sane enough,' said Elizabeth, making no attempt to hide her anger.

'Then what in heaven's name does he think he's up to?'

'I have no idea.'

'Could it possibly have something to do with the Clifton boy?'

She would have replied if Jack Tarrant hadn't walked across to join them.

'Your daughter has a remarkable talent, Elizabeth,' he said after kissing her hand, 'as well as the advantage of inheriting your beauty.'

'And you're an old flatterer, Jack,' she said, before adding, 'I don't think you've met my son, Giles.'

'Good evening, sir,' said Giles. 'It's a great honour to meet you. May I congratulate you on your recent appointment.'

'Thank you, young man,' said Tarrant. 'And how do you feel about your friend's performance?'

'Remarkable, but did you know—'

'Good evening, Mrs Barrington.'

'Good evening, headmaster.'

'I must be joining a long queue of those who wish to add their . . .'

Giles watched as Captain Tarrant slipped away to join Harry's mother, and wondered how they knew each other.

'How lovely to see you, Captain Tarrant.'

'And you, Mrs Clifton, and how glamorous you're looking tonight. If Cary Grant had known that such beauty existed in Bristol, he would never have deserted us for Hollywood.' He then lowered his voice. 'Did you have any idea that Emma Barrington was playing Juliet?'

'No, Harry didn't mention it to me,' said Maisie. 'But then, why should he?'

'Let's hope that the affection they are displaying for one another on stage is nothing more than good acting, because if it's how they really feel about each other, we may have an even bigger problem on our hands.' He looked around to make sure no one was eavesdropping on their conversation. 'I presume you still haven't said anything to Harry?'

'Not a word,' said Maisie. 'And from Barrington's ill-mannered behaviour it seems he was also taken by surprise.'

'Good evening, Captain Tarrant,' said Miss Monday, touching Jack's arm. Miss Tilly was by her side. 'How good of you to come all the way down from London to see your protégé.'

'My dear Miss Monday,' said Tarrant, 'Harry's every bit as much your protégé and he'll be so pleased that you travelled all the way up from Cornwall to see his performance.' Miss Monday beamed, as a bell sounded to indicate the audience should return to their seats.

Once everyone had settled back in their places, the curtain rose for the second half, although one seat in the sixth row remained conspicuously empty. The death scene brought tears to the eyes of some who had never shed a tear in public, while Miss Monday hadn't wept that much since Harry's voice had broken.

The moment the final curtain fell, the audience rose as one. Harry and Emma were greeted by a storm of applause as they walked to the front of the stage, holding hands, and grown men, who rarely showed their feelings, cheered.

When they turned to bow to each other, Mrs Barrington smiled, and blushed. 'Good heavens, they weren't acting,' she said, loud enough for Giles to hear. The same thought had also crossed the minds of Maisie Clifton and Jack Tarrant long before the actors took their final bow.

Mrs Barrington, Giles and Grace went backstage to find Romeo and Juliet still holding hands as people queued up to lavish praise on them.

'You were great,' said Giles, slapping his friend on the back.

'I was all right,' said Harry, 'but Emma was magnificent.'

'So when did all this happen?' he whispered.

'It began in Rome,' admitted Harry with an impish grin.

'And to think I sacrificed my Caruso recording, not to mention my gramophone, to bring you two together.'

'As well as paying for our first dinner date.'

'Where's Papa?' asked Emma, looking around.

Grace was about to tell her sister what had happened when Captain Tarrant appeared.

'Congratulations, my boy,' he said. 'You were quite splendid.'

'Thank you sir,' said Harry, 'but I don't think you've met the real star of the show.'

'No, but let me assure you, young lady, if I was forty years younger, I'd see off any of my rivals.'

'You don't have any rivals for my affection,' said Emma. 'Harry never stops telling me how much you've done for him.'

'That's a two-way street,' said Jack as Harry spotted his mother and threw his arms around her.

'I'm so proud of you,' said Maisie.

'Thank you, Mum. But let me introduce you to Emma Barrington,' he said, placing an arm around Emma's waist.

'Now I know why your son is so good-looking,' said

Emma as she shook Harry's mother by the hand. 'May I introduce my mother,' she added.

It was a meeting Maisie had thought about for many years, but this was not a scenario that had ever crossed her mind. She was apprehensive as she shook hands with Elizabeth Barrington, but was greeted with such a friendly smile that it quickly became clear she was unaware of any possible connection between them.

'And this is Mr Atkins,' said Maisie, introducing the man who had been sitting beside her during the performance.

Harry had never come across Mr Atkins before. Looking at his mother's fur coat, he wondered if Atkins was the reason he now had three pairs of shoes.

He was about to speak to Mr Atkins, when he was interrupted by Dr Paget, who was keen to introduce him to Professor Henry Wyld. Harry recognized the name at once.

'I hear that you're hoping to come up to Oxford to read English,' said Wyld.

'Only if I can be taught by you, sir.'

'I see that Romeo's charm has not been left behind on the stage.'

'And this is Emma Barrington, sir.'

Oxford's Merton Professor of English Language and Literature gave a slight bow. 'You were quite magnificent, young lady.'

'Thank you, sir,' said Emma. 'I am also hoping to be taught by you,' she added. 'I've applied to Somerville for next year.'

Jack Tarrant glanced at Mrs Clifton, and couldn't miss the unmasked horror in her eyes.

'Grandfather,' said Giles as the chairman of the governors joined them. 'I don't think you know my friend, Harry Clifton.'

Sir Walter shook Harry warmly by the hand, before throwing his arms around his granddaughter. 'You two made an old man proud,' he said.

It was becoming painfully clear to Jack and Maisie that the two 'star-crossed lovers' had no idea of the problems they had set in motion.

◄○►

Sir Walter ordered his chauffeur to drive Mrs Barrington and the children back to the Manor House. Despite Emma's triumph, her mother made no attempt to hide her feelings as the car made its way towards Chew Valley. As they drove through the gates and up to the house, Giles noticed that some lights were still on in the drawing room.

Once the chauffeur had dropped them off, Elizabeth told Giles, Emma and Grace to go to bed, in a tone of voice none of them had heard for many years, while she headed for the drawing room. Giles and Emma reluctantly climbed the wide staircase but sat down on the top step the moment their mother was out of sight, while Grace obediently went to her room. Giles even wondered if his mother had left the door open on purpose.

When Elizabeth entered the room, her husband didn't bother to stand up. She noticed a half empty bottle of whisky and a tumbler on the table by his side.

'No doubt you have some explanation for your unforgivable behaviour?'

'I don't have to explain anything I do to you.'

'Emma somehow managed to rise above your appalling behaviour tonight.'

Barrington poured himself another tumbler of whisky and took a gulp. 'I have arranged for Emma to be removed from Red Maids immediately. Next term she will be enrolled at a school far enough away to ensure she never sees that boy again.'

On the stairs, Emma burst into tears. Giles wrapped an arm around her.

'What can Harry Clifton possibly have done to make you behave in such a shameful way?'

'It's none of your business.'

'Of course it's my business,' said Elizabeth, trying to remain calm. 'We are discussing our daughter and your son's closest friend. If Emma has fallen in love with Harry, and I suspect she has, I can't think of a nicer or more decent young man for her to lose her heart to.'

'Harry Clifton is the son of a whore. That's why her husband left her. And I repeat, Emma will never be allowed to come in contact with the little bastard again.'

'I'm going to bed before I lose my temper,' said Elizabeth. 'Don't even think of joining me in your present state.'

'I wasn't thinking of joining you in any state,' said Barrington, pouring himself another whisky. 'You haven't given me any pleasure in the bedroom for as long as I can remember.'

Emma leapt up and ran to her room, locking the door behind her. Giles didn't move.

'You are obviously drunk,' said Elizabeth. 'We'll discuss this in the morning, when you're sober.'

'There will be nothing to discuss in the morning,' slurred Barrington as his wife left the room. A moment later his head fell back on the cushion and he began to snore.

—◁◦▷—

When Jenkins pulled back the shutters in the drawing room just before eight the following morning he showed no surprise when he found his master slumped in an armchair, sound asleep and still wearing his dinner jacket.

The morning sunlight caused Barrington to stir. He blinked, and peered at the butler before he checked his watch.

'There will be a car coming to pick up Miss Emma in about an hour's time, Jenkins, so be sure she's packed and ready.'

'Miss Emma is not here, sir.'

'What? Then where is she?' demanded Barrington as he tried to stand up, but wobbled unsteadily for a moment before falling back into the chair.

'I have no idea, sir. She and Mrs Barrington left the house just after midnight.'

38

'WHERE DO YOU THINK they've gone?' asked Harry, once Giles had described what happened after he had arrived back at the Manor House.

'I've no idea,' said Giles. 'I was asleep when they left the house. All I could get out of Jenkins was that a taxi had taken them to the station just after midnight.'

'And you say your father was drunk when you returned home last night?'

'As a skunk, and he hadn't sobered up by the time I came down for breakfast this morning. He was shouting and screaming at anyone who crossed his path. He even tried to blame me for everything. That was when I decided to go and stay with my grandparents.'

'Do you think your grandfather might know where they are?'

'I don't think so, although he didn't seem that surprised when I told him what had happened. Grandma said I could stay with them for as long as I wanted to.'

'They can't be in Bristol,' said Harry, 'if the taxi took them to the station.'

'They could be anywhere by now,' said Giles.

Neither of them spoke again for some time, until Harry suggested, 'Your villa in Tuscany perhaps?'

'Unlikely,' said Giles. 'That's the first place Papa would think of, so they wouldn't be safe there for long.'

'So it has to be somewhere your father would think twice about before going after them.' Both boys fell silent again, until Harry said, 'I can think of someone who might know where they are.'

'And who's that?'

'Old Jack,' said Harry, who still couldn't quite bring himself to call him Captain Tarrant. 'I know he's become a friend of your mother's, and she certainly trusts him.'

'Do you know where he might be at the moment?'

'Anyone who reads *The Times* knows that,' said Harry scornfully.

Giles punched his friend on the arm. 'So where is he, clever clogs?'

'He'll be at his office in London. Soho Square, if I remember correctly.'

'I've always wanted an excuse to spend a day in London,' said Giles. 'It's just a pity I've left all my money back at the house.'

'Not a problem,' said Harry. 'I'm flush. That Atkins fellow gave me a fiver, although he did say I was to spend it on books.'

'Don't worry,' said Giles, 'I can think of an alternative plan.'

'Like what?' asked Harry, looking hopeful.

'We can just sit around and wait for Emma to write to you.'

It was Harry's turn to punch his friend. 'OK,' he said. 'But we'd better get going before anyone finds out what we're up to.'

◄○►

'I'm not in the habit of travelling third class,' said Giles as the train pulled out of Temple Meads.

'Well, you'd better get used to it while I'm paying,' said Harry.

'So tell me, Harry, what's your friend Captain Tarrant up to? I know the government has appointed him Director of the Citizens Displacement Unit, which sounds pretty impressive, but I'm not sure what he actually does.'

'What it says,' said Harry. 'He's responsible for finding accommodation for refugees, in particular those families who are escaping the tyranny of Nazi Germany. He says he's carrying on his father's work.'

'Class act, your friend Captain Tarrant.'

'You don't know the half of it,' said Harry.

'Tickets, please.'

The two boys spent most of the journey trying to work out where Emma and Mrs Barrington could possibly be, but by the time the train pulled into Paddington Station, they still hadn't come to any firm conclusions.

They took the tube to Leicester Square, emerged into the sunlight and went in search of Soho Square. As they made their way through the West End, Giles became so distracted by the bright neon lights and shop windows full of goods he'd never seen before that Harry occasionally had to remind him why they'd actually come to London.

When they reached Soho Square, neither of them could have missed the steady flow of bedraggled men, women and children, heads bowed, shuffling in and out of a vast building on the far side of the square.

The two young men dressed in blazers, grey flannels and ties looked strangely incongruous as they entered the building and followed the arrows directing them to the third floor. Several of the refugees stood to one side to allow them to pass, assuming they must be there on official business.

Giles and Harry joined the long queue outside the director's office, and might have been there for the rest of the day if a secretary had not come out and spotted them. She walked straight up to Harry and asked if he had come to see Captain Tarrant.

'Yes,' said Harry. 'He's an old friend.'

'I know,' said the woman. 'I recognized you immediately.'

'How?' asked Harry.

'He has a photograph of you on his desk,' she said. 'Follow me. Captain Tarrant will be delighted to see you.'

Old Jack's face lit up when the two boys – he should stop thinking of them as boys, they were now young men – walked into his office. 'It's good to see you both,' he said, jumping up from behind his desk to greet them. 'So who are you running away from this time?' he added with a smile.

'My father,' said Giles quietly.

Old Jack crossed the room, closed the door and sat the two young men down on an uncomfortable sofa. He drew up a chair and listened carefully as they told him everything that had happened since they'd seen him at the play the previous evening.

'I saw your father leave the theatre, of course,' said Old Jack, 'but it would never have crossed my mind he could treat your mother and sister quite so appallingly.'

'Do you have any idea where they might be, sir?' asked Giles.

'No. But if I had to guess, I'd say they were staying with your grandfather.'

'No, sir, I spent the morning with Grandpa, and even he doesn't know where they are.'

'I didn't say which grandfather,' said Jack.

'Lord Harvey?' said Harry.

'That would be my bet,' said Jack. 'They'd feel safe with him, and confident that Barrington would think twice before going after them.'

'But Grandpa has at least three homes that I'm aware of,' said Giles. 'So I wouldn't know where to begin looking.'

'How stupid of me,' said Harry. 'I know exactly where he is.'

'You do?' said Giles. 'Where?'

'At his country estate in Scotland.'

'You sound very certain,' said Jack.

'Only because last week he dropped Emma a line to explain why he wouldn't be able to attend the school play. It seems he always spends December and January in Scotland. But I'm damned if I can remember the address.'

'Mulgelrie Castle, near Mulgelrie, Highlands,' said Giles.

'Most impressive,' said Jack.

'Not really, sir. It's just years of Mama making me write thank-you letters to all my relations on Boxing Day. But as I've never been to Scotland, I haven't got a clue where it is.'

Old Jack got up and removed a large atlas from the bookshelf behind his desk. He looked up Mulgelrie in the index, flicked over several pages and then laid it on the desk in front of him. Running a finger from London to Scotland, he said, 'You'll have to take the overnight sleeper to Edinburgh, and then change to a local train for Mulgelrie.'

'I don't think we've got enough money left for that,' said Harry, checking his wallet.

'Then I'll have to issue you both with rail warrants, won't I?' said Jack. He opened his desk drawer, pulled out a large buff-coloured pad and tore off two forms.

He filled them in, signed and stamped them. 'After all,' he added, 'you are clearly stateless refugees in search of a home.'

'Thank you, sir,' said Giles.

'One last word of advice,' said Old Jack as he rose from behind his desk. 'Hugo Barrington is not a man who likes to be crossed, and while I'm fairly confident he won't do anything to annoy Lord Harvey, that doesn't necessarily apply to you, Harry. So be on your guard until you're safely inside Mulgelrie Castle. Should you at any time come across a man with a limp,' he added, 'be wary of him. He works for Giles's father. He's clever and resourceful, but more important, he has no allegiance to anyone except his paymaster.'

39

GILES AND HARRY were directed to another third-class carriage, but they were both so tired that despite the frequent opening and closing of carriage doors during the night, the clattering of the wheels over points and the regular blast of the train's whistle, they slept soundly.

Giles woke with a start as the train pulled into Newcastle a few minutes before six. He looked out of the window to be greeted by a dull grey day and the sight of lines of soldiers waiting to board the train. A sergeant saluted a second lieutenant who didn't look much older than Giles and asked, 'Permission to board the train, sir?' The young man returned his salute and replied in a softer voice, 'Carry on, sergeant,' and the soldiers began to file on to the train.

The ever-present threat of war, and the question of whether he and Harry would be in uniform before they had the chance to go up to Oxford, was never far from Giles's mind. His uncle Nicholas, whom he'd never met, an officer just like the young man on the platform, had led a platoon of soldiers and been cut down at Ypres. Giles wondered what would be the names of the battlefields that would be commemorated with poppies every year if there was to be another Great War to end all wars.

His thoughts were interrupted when he noticed a passing reflection in the carriage window. He swung round, but the figure was no longer there. Had Captain Tarrant's warning caused him to overreact, or was it just a coincidence?

Giles looked across at Harry, who was still sound asleep, but then he probably hadn't slept for the past two nights. As the train shunted into Berwick-on-Tweed, Giles noticed the same man walking past their compartment. Just a glance, and he was gone; no longer a coincidence. Was he checking to see which station they got off at?

Harry finally woke, blinked and stretched his arms. 'I'm starving,' he said.

Giles leant over and whispered, 'I think there's someone on this train who's following us.'

'What makes you say that?' asked Harry, suddenly wide awake.

'I've seen the same man pass our carriage once too often.'

'Tickets please!'

Giles and Harry handed their warrants to the ticket collector. 'How long does this train stop at each station?' he asked once the man had clipped them.

'Now, that all depends on whether we're runnin' on time or not,' he replied a little wearily, 'but never less than four minutes is the company regulation.'

'What is the next station?' asked Giles.

'Dunbar. We should be there in about thirty minutes. But you've both got warrants for Mulgelrie,' he added before moving on to the next compartment.

'What was all that about?' asked Harry.

'I'm trying to find out if we're being followed,' said Giles, 'and the next part of my plan will involve you.'

'What role will I be playing this time?' said Harry, sitting on the edge of his seat.

'Certainly not Romeo,' said Giles. 'When the train stops at Dunbar, I want you to get off while I watch if anyone follows you. Once you're on the platform, walk quickly towards the ticket barrier, then turn back, go into the waiting room and buy a cup of tea. Don't forget you've only got four minutes to be back on board before the train sets off again. And whatever you do, don't look back, or he'll know we're on to him.'

'But if there is someone following us, surely he'll be more interested in you than me?'

'I don't think so,' said Giles, 'and certainly not if Captain Tarrant is right, because I have a feeling your friend knows more than he's willing to admit.'

'That doesn't exactly fill me with confidence,' said Harry.

Half an hour later, the train shuddered to a halt in Dunbar. Harry opened the carriage door, stepped out on to the platform and headed for the exit.

Giles caught no more than a glimpse of the man as he hurried after Harry.

'Got you,' Giles said, then leant back and closed his eyes, confident that once the man realized Harry had only got off to buy a cup of tea, he would look in his direction just to make sure he hadn't also left the carriage.

Giles opened his eyes again when Harry returned to the compartment holding a bar of chocolate.

'Well,' said Harry, 'did you spot anyone?'

'Sure did,' said Giles. 'In fact, he's just getting back on the train.'

'What does he look like?' asked Harry, trying not to sound anxious.

'I only caught a glimpse of him,' said Giles, 'but I'd say he's around forty, a little over six foot, smartly dressed, with very short hair. The one thing you can't miss is his limp.'

'So now we know what we're up against, Sherlock, what next?'

'First, Watson, it's important to remember that we have several things going for us.'

'I can't think of one,' said Harry.

'Well, for a start, we know we're being followed, but he doesn't know we know. We also know where we're going, which he clearly doesn't. We're also fit, and less than half his age. And with that limp, he won't be able to move all that quickly.'

'You're rather good at this,' said Harry.

'I do have a built-in advantage,' said Giles. 'I am my father's son.'

<o>

By the time the train pulled into Edinburgh Waverley, Giles had gone over his plan with Harry a dozen times. They stepped out of the carriage and walked slowly down the platform towards the barrier.

'Don't even think about looking back,' said Giles as he produced his rail warrant, then headed towards a line of taxis.

'The Royal Hotel,' said Giles to the cabbie. 'And can you let me know if another taxi follows us?' he added before joining Harry in the back.

'Right you are,' said the cabbie, as he eased off the rank and joined the traffic.

'How do you know there's a Royal Hotel in Edinburgh?' asked Harry.

'There's a Royal Hotel in every city,' said Giles.

A few minutes later the cabbie said, 'I cannae be sure, but the next cab off the rank isn't far behind us.'

'Good,' said Giles. 'How much is the fare to the Royal?'

'Two shillings, sir.'

'I'll give you four if you can lose him.'

The driver immediately put his foot down on the accelerator, causing both of his passengers to be thrown back into their seats. Giles recovered quickly and looked through the back window to see the taxi behind them had also speeded up. They had gained sixty or seventy yards, but Giles realized that advantage wouldn't last for long.

'Cabbie, take the next turning on the left and then slow down for a moment. After we jump out, I want you to continue on to the Royal and don't stop until you reach the hotel.' An outstretched arm appeared. Harry placed two florins into the palm.

'When I jump out,' said Giles, 'just follow me, and then do exactly as I do.' Harry nodded.

The taxi swung round the corner and slowed down for a moment just as Giles opened the door. He leapt out on to the pavement, toppled over, quickly picked himself up, then dashed into the nearest shop, throwing himself on the floor. Harry followed only seconds later, slammed the door behind him and was lying by his friend's side just as the second cab shot around the corner.

'Can I help you, sir?' asked a sales assistant, hands on hips, looking down at the two young men lying prostrate on the ground.

'You already have,' said Giles, rising to his feet and giving her a warm smile. He brushed himself down, said 'Thank you,' and left the shop without another word.

When Harry stood up, he came face to face with a slim-waisted mannequin wearing only a corset. He turned bright red, ran out of the shop and joined Giles on the pavement.

'I don't expect the man with the limp will be booking into the Royal for the night,' said Giles, 'so we'd better get moving.'

'Agreed,' said Harry as Giles flagged down another cab. 'Waverley station,' he said before climbing into the back.

'Where did you learn how to do all that?' asked Harry in admiration, as they headed back in the direction of the station.

'You know, Harry, you should read a little less Joseph Conrad and a little more John Buchan if you want to know how to travel in Scotland while being pursued by a fiendish foe.'

The journey to Mulgelrie was considerably slower and far less exciting than the one to Edinburgh had been, and there was certainly no sign of any man with a limp. When the engine finally dragged its four carriages and two passengers into the little station, the sun had already disappeared behind the highest mountain. The station master was standing by the exit waiting to check their tickets when they got off the last train that day.

'Any hope of getting a taxi?' Giles asked as they handed over their warrants.

'No, sir,' replied the station master. 'Jock goes home for tea around six o'clock, and he'll nae be back for another hour.'

Giles thought twice about explaining the logic of Jock's actions to the station master, before he asked, 'Then perhaps you'd be kind enough to tell us how we can get to Mulgelrie Castle.'

'You'll have to walk,' said the station master helpfully.

'And which direction might it be?' asked Giles, trying not to sound exasperated.

'It's about three miles up yonder,' the man said, pointing up the hill. 'You cannae miss it.'

'Up yonder' turned out to be the only accurate piece of information the station master had offered, because after the two of them had been walking for over an hour, it was pitch black and there was still no sign of any castle.

Giles was beginning to wonder if they were going to have to spend their first night in the Highlands sleeping in a field with only a flock of sheep to keep them company, when Harry shouted, 'There it is!'

Giles stared through the misty gloom and although he still couldn't quite make out the outline of a castle, his spirits were lifted by flickering lights coming from several windows. They trudged on until they reached a massive pair of wrought-iron gates which had not been locked. As they made their way up the long driveway Giles could hear barking, but he couldn't see any dogs. After about another mile they came to a bridge spanning a moat, and on the far side, a heavy oak door that didn't look as if it welcomed strangers.

'Leave the talking to me,' said Giles as they staggered across the bridge and came to a halt outside the door.

Giles banged three times with the side of his fist, and within moments the door was pulled open to reveal a giant of a man dressed in a kilt with a dark lovat jacket, white shirt and white bow tie.

The head steward looked down on the weary, bedraggled objects that stood in front of him. 'Good evening, Mr Giles,' he said, although Giles had never set eyes on the man before. 'His lordship has been expecting you for some time, and wondered if you would care to join him for dinner?'

40

```
GILES AND HARRY CLIFTON ON THEIR WAY

TO MULGELRIE -(STOP)- SHOULD ARRIVE

AROUND SIX -(STOP)-
```

LORD HARVEY handed the telegram to Giles and chuckled. 'Sent by our mutual friend, Captain Tarrant. He only turned out to be wrong about what time you'd arrive.'

'We had to walk all the way from the station,' protested Giles between mouthfuls.

'Yes, I did consider sending the car to meet you off the last train,' said Lord Harvey, 'but there's nothing like a bracing Highland walk to work up a good appetite.'

Harry smiled. He'd hardly spoken since they'd come down for dinner, and as Emma had been placed at the far end of the table he had to satisfy himself with the occasional wistful gaze, wondering if they'd ever be left alone together.

The first course was a thick Highland broth, which Harry finished a little too quickly, but when Giles was served a second helping, he also allowed his bowl to be refilled. Harry would have asked for a third helping if everyone else hadn't continued making polite conversation while they waited for him and Giles to finish so that the main course could be served.

'There's no need for either of you to be anxious about anyone wondering where you are,' said Lord Harvey, 'because I've already sent telegrams to Sir Walter and to Mrs Clifton, to assure them you are both safe and well. I didn't bother to get in touch with your father, Giles,' he added without further comment. Giles glanced across the table to see his mother purse her lips.

Moments later the dining room doors swung open and several liveried servants entered and whisked away the soup bowls. Three more servants followed, carrying silver salvers on which rested what looked to Harry like six small chickens.

'I do hope you like grouse, Mr Clifton,' said Lord Harvey, the first person ever to call him Mr, as a bird was placed in front of him. 'I shot these myself.'

Harry couldn't think of an appropriate response. He watched as Giles picked up his knife and fork and began to slice tiny pieces off the bird, bringing back memories of their first meal together at St Bede's. By the time the plates were cleared, Harry had only managed about three morsels and wondered how old he would have to be before he could say, 'No, thank you, I'd prefer another bowl of soup.'

Things improved a little when a large plate of different fruits, some of which Harry had never seen before, was placed in the centre of the table. He would have liked to ask his host their names and the countries they originated from, but memories of his first banana came to mind, when he had definitely slipped. He satisfied himself with following Giles's lead, watching carefully to see which had to be peeled, which had to be cut and which you could simply take a bite out of.

When he'd finished, a servant appeared and placed a bowl of water by the side of his plate. He was just about to pick it up and drink it, when he saw Lady Harvey place her fingers in hers and moments later a servant passed her a linen napkin so she could dry her hands. Harry dipped his fingers in the water and, like magic, a napkin immediately appeared.

After dinner, the ladies retired to the drawing room. Harry wanted to join them so he could at last catch up with Emma and tell her everything that had happened since she'd poisoned herself. But no sooner had she left the room than Lord Harvey sat back down, a sign for the under-butler to offer his lordship a cigar while another servant poured him a large glass of Cognac.

Once he'd taken a sip, he nodded and glasses were placed in front of Giles and Harry. The butler closed the humidor, before filling their glasses with brandy.

'Well,' said Lord Harvey after two or three luxuriant puffs. 'Am I to understand that you are both hoping to go up to Oxford?'

'Harry's a safe bet,' said Giles. 'But I'll need to score a couple of centuries during the summer, and preferably one at Lord's if the examiners are going to overlook my more obvious deficiencies.'

'Giles is being modest, sir,' said Harry. 'He has just as good a chance of being offered a place as I do. After all, he's not only the captain of cricket, he's also school captain.'

'Well, if you are successful, I can assure you that you'll experience three of the happiest years of your life. That's assuming Herr Hitler isn't foolish enough to insist on a replay of the last war in the vain hope that he'll be able to reverse the result.'

The three of them raised their glasses and Harry took his first sip of brandy. He didn't like the taste and was wondering if it would be thought discourteous if he didn't finish it, when Lord Harvey came to his rescue.

'Perhaps it's time for us to join the ladies,' he said, draining his glass. He put his cigar in an ashtray, rose from his place and marched out of the dining room, not waiting for a second opinion. The two young men followed him across the hall and into the drawing room.

Lord Harvey took the seat next to Elizabeth, while Giles winked at Harry and went across to join his grandmother. Harry sat next to Emma on the sofa.

'How gallant of you to come all this way, Harry,' she said, touching his hand.

'I'm so sorry about what happened after the play. I only hope I wasn't responsible for causing the problem in the first place.'

'How could you possibly be responsible, Harry? You've never done anything that could have caused my father to speak to Mama that way.'

'But it's no secret that your father doesn't think we should be together, even on stage.'

'Let's talk about it tomorrow morning,' Emma whispered. 'We can go for a long walk in the hills and be on our own, with only the Highland cattle to overhear us.'

'I'll look forward to that,' said Harry. He would have liked to hold her hand, but there were too many eyes continually glancing in their direction.

'You two young men must be very tired after such an exhausting journey,' said Lady Harvey. 'Why don't you both go off to bed, and we'll see you at breakfast in the morning.'

Harry didn't want to go to bed; he wanted to stay with Emma and try to find out if she'd discovered why her father was so opposed to them being together. But Giles rose immediately, kissed his grandmother and mother on the cheek and said goodnight, leaving Harry with no choice but to join him. He leaned across and kissed Emma on the cheek, thanked his host for a wonderful evening and followed Giles out of the room.

As they walked down the hall, Harry paused to admire a painting of a bowl of fruit by an artist called Peploe when Emma came dashing out of the drawing room, threw her arms around his neck and kissed him gently on the lips.

Giles continued up the stairs as if he hadn't noticed, while Harry kept his eyes on the drawing-room door. Emma broke away when she heard it opening behind her.

'Good night, good night, parting is such sweet sorrow,' she whispered.

'That I shall say good night till it be morrow,' Harry replied.

◄○►

'Where are you two off to?' asked Elizabeth Barrington as she came out of the breakfast room.

'We're going to climb Crag Cowen,' said Emma. 'Don't wait up, because you may never see us again.'

Her mother laughed. 'Then make sure you wrap up well, because even the sheep catch cold in the Highlands.' She waited until Harry had closed the door behind them before she added, 'Giles, your grandfather wishes to see us in his study at ten o'clock.' It sounded to Giles more like a command than a request.

'Yes, Mother,' he said, before looking through the window and watching Harry and Emma walking down the path towards Crag Cowen. They'd only gone a few yards before Emma took Harry's hand. Giles smiled as they turned the corner and disappeared behind a row of pines.

When the clock in the hall began to strike, Giles had to walk quickly along the corridor to make sure he reached his grandfather's study before the tenth chime. His grandparents and his mother stopped talking the moment he entered the room. They had clearly been waiting for him.

'Have a seat, dear boy,' said his grandfather.

'Thank you, sir,' Giles replied, and sat down on a chair between his mother and his grandmother.

'I suppose this would best be described as a council of war,' said Lord Harvey, looking up from his high-backed leather chair as if he was addressing a board meeting. 'I'll try to bring everyone up to date before we decide what the best course of action should be.' Giles was flattered that his grandfather now considered him to be a full member of the family board.

'I telephoned Walter last night. He was just as appalled by Hugo's conduct at the play as I was when Elizabeth told me about it, although I had to fill him in on what happened when she returned to the Manor House.' Giles's mother bowed her head, but didn't interrupt. 'I went on to tell him that I'd had a long talk with my daughter, and that we felt there were only two possible courses of action.'

Giles sat back in his chair, but didn't relax.

'I left Walter in no doubt that if Elizabeth were even to consider returning to the Manor House, it would be necessary for Hugo to make several concessions. First, he must apologize unequivocally for his appalling behaviour.'

Giles's grandmother nodded in agreement.

'Second, he will never again, and I repeated, never again, suggest that Emma should be taken out of her school, and he will in future fully support her efforts to gain a place at Oxford. God knows it's hard enough for a young man to make the grade nowadays, but it's damn nigh impossible for a woman.

'My third and most important demand, and on this I was quite adamant, is that he explain to us all why he continues to treat Harry Clifton so appallingly. I suspect it might have something to do with Harry's uncle stealing from Hugo. The sins of the father are one thing, but an uncle ... I refuse to accept, as he has so often claimed to Elizabeth, that he considers Clifton unworthy to mix with his children simply because his father was a docker and his mother is a waitress. Perhaps Hugo has forgotten that my grandfather was a jobbing clerk in a firm of wine merchants, while his own grandfather left school at the age of twelve and started out as a docker like young Clifton's father, and just in case anyone has forgotten, I'm the first Lord Harvey in this family, and you don't get much more nouveau than that.'

Giles wanted to cheer.

'Now, none of us can have failed to notice,' continued Lord Harvey, 'how Emma and Harry feel about each other, which is hardly surprising as they are two exceptional young people. If, in the fullness of time, their relationship blossoms, no one would be more delighted than Victoria and I. On that subject, Walter was in full agreement with me.'

Giles smiled. He liked the idea of Harry becoming a member of the family, even though he didn't believe his father would ever accept it.

'I told Walter,' continued his grandfather, 'that if Hugo felt unable to abide by these terms, Elizabeth would be left with no choice but to institute divorce proceedings immediately. I would also have to resign from the board of Barrington's, and make public my reasons for doing so.'

Giles was saddened by this, as he knew there had never been a divorce in either family.

'Walter kindly agreed to get back to me in the next few days, after he's had a chance to talk things over with his son, but he did tell me that Hugo has already promised to stop drinking, and that he appears to be genuinely contrite. Let me finish by reminding you that this is a family matter and should not in any circumstances be discussed with outsiders. We must hope that this proves to be nothing more than an unfortunate incident that will soon be forgotten.'

◄◦►

The following morning, Giles's father telephoned and asked to speak to him. He apologized profusely, saying how sorry he was to have blamed Giles for something that was entirely his own fault. He begged Giles to do everything in his power to convince his mother and Emma to return to Gloucestershire so they could all spend Christmas together at the Manor House. He also hoped that, as his father-in-law had suggested, the incident would be quickly forgotten. He made no mention of Harry Clifton.

41

ONCE THEY'D DISEMBARKED from the train at Temple Meads, Giles and his mother waited in the car while Emma said goodbye to Harry.

'They've just spent the last nine days together,' said Giles. 'Have they forgotten that they'll be seeing each other again tomorrow?'

'And probably the next day,' said Giles's mother. 'But try not to forget, unlikely though it might seem, that it could even happen to you one day.'

Emma eventually joined them, but when they drove off she continued to look out of the back window and didn't stop waving until Harry was out of sight.

Giles was keen to get home and finally discover what it was that Harry could have done to make his father treat him so cruelly over the years. Surely it couldn't be worse than stealing from the tuck shop or deliberately failing your exams. He'd considered a dozen possibilities but none of them made any sense. Now, at last, he hoped he was going to find out the truth. He glanced across at his mother. Although she rarely displayed her emotions, she was clearly becoming more and more agitated as they approached Chew Valley.

Giles's father was standing on the top step waiting to greet them when the car drew up outside the house; no sign of Jenkins. He apologized immediately to Elizabeth and then the children, before telling them how much he'd missed them.

'Tea is set up in the drawing room,' he said. 'Please join me there as soon as you're ready.'

Giles was the first back downstairs and he sat uneasily in a chair opposite his father. While they waited for his mother and Emma to join them, his father confined himself to asking Giles how he'd enjoyed Scotland, and to explain that Nanny had taken Grace into Bristol to buy her school uniform. At no time did he mention Harry. When Giles's mother and sister entered the room a few minutes later, his father immediately stood up. Once they were seated, he poured them all a cup of tea. He clearly didn't want any servants to overhear what he was about to reveal.

Once everyone had settled, Giles's father sat on the edge of his seat and began to speak softly.

'Let me begin by saying to all three of you how unacceptable my behaviour was on the night of what everyone has described as Emma's great triumph. That your father was not there for the curtain call was bad enough, Emma,' he said, looking directly at his daughter, 'but the way I treated your mother when you returned home that night was quite unforgivable, and I realize it may take some time before such a deep wound can be healed.'

Hugo Barrington placed his head in his hands and Giles noticed that he was trembling. He eventually steadied himself.

'You have all, for different reasons, asked to know why I have treated Harry Clifton so badly over the years. It is true that I cannot bear to be in his presence, but the fault is entirely of my own making. When you learn the reason, you might begin to understand, and possibly even sympathize.'

Giles glanced at his mother, who was sitting stiffly in her chair. There was no way of telling how she felt.

'Many years ago,' continued Barrington, 'when I first became managing director of the company, I convinced the board that we should branch out into shipbuilding, despite my father's reservations. I signed a contract with a Canadian company to build a merchant ship called the *Maple Leaf*. That not only turned out to be a financial disaster for the company, but a personal catastrophe for me, from which I have never fully recovered and doubt if I ever will. Allow me to explain.

'One afternoon a docker burst into my office insisting that his work mate was trapped inside the hull of the *Maple Leaf* and if I didn't give the order to break it open, his life would be lost. Naturally I went down to the dock immediately and the ganger assured me there was absolutely no truth in the story. However, I insisted the men down tools so that we could listen for any sound coming from inside the hull. I waited for some considerable time, but as there was no sound, I gave the order for them to return to work, as we were already several weeks behind schedule.

'I assumed the docker in question would sign on for his usual shift the following day. But not only did he not turn up, he was never seen again. The possibility of his death has been on my conscience ever since.' He paused, raised his head and said, 'That man's name was Arthur Clifton, and Harry is his only son.'

Emma began to sob.

'I want you to imagine, if you possibly can, what I go through whenever I see that young man, and how he would feel were he ever to find out that I might have been responsible for his father's death. That Harry Clifton has become Giles's closest friend, and fallen in love with my daughter, is the stuff of a Greek tragedy.'

Once again, he buried his head in his hands and didn't speak for some time. When he finally looked up, he said, 'If you wish to ask me any questions, I will do my best to answer them.'

Giles waited for his mother to speak first. 'Were you responsible for sending an innocent man to jail for a crime he did not commit?' Elizabeth asked quietly.

'No, my dear,' said Barrington. 'I hope you know me well enough to realize I am not capable of such a thing. Stan Tancock was a common thief, who broke into my office and robbed me. Because he was Arthur Clifton's brother-in-law, and for no other reason, I gave him back his job the day he was released from prison.' Elizabeth smiled for the first time.

'Father, I wonder if I might be allowed to ask a question,' said Giles.

'Yes, of course.'

'Did you have Harry and me followed when we travelled up to Scotland?'

'Yes, I did, Giles. I was desperate to find out where your mother and Emma were so I could apologize to them for my disgraceful behaviour. Please try to forgive me.'

Everyone turned their attention to Emma, who hadn't yet spoken. When she did, her words took them all by surprise. 'You'll have to tell Harry everything you've told us,' she whispered, 'and if he is willing to forgive you, you must then welcome him into our family.'

'I would be delighted to welcome him into the family, my darling, although it would be understandable if he never wanted to speak to me again. But I cannot tell him the truth about what happened to his father.'

'Why not?' demanded Emma.

'Because Harry's mother has made it clear that she

does not want him ever to find out how his father died, as he has been brought up to believe he was a brave man who was killed in the war. Up until this moment, I have kept my promise never to reveal to anyone what took place on that dreadful day.'

Elizabeth Barrington rose, walked across to her husband and kissed him gently. Barrington broke down and sobbed. A moment later Giles joined his parents and placed an arm around his father's shoulders.

Emma didn't move.

42

'HAS YOUR MOTHER always been that good-looking?' said Giles. 'Or am I just getting older?'

'I've no idea,' said Harry. 'All I can say is that *your* mother always looks so elegant.'

'Much as I love the dear creature, she looks positively prehistoric compared to yours,' said Giles as Elizabeth Barrington, parasol in one hand and handbag in the other, bore down upon them.

Giles, like every other boy, had been dreading what outfit his mother might turn up in. As for the selection of hats, it was worse than Ascot, with every mother and daughter trying to outdo each other.

Harry looked more carefully at his mother, who was chatting to Dr Paget. He had to admit that she was attracting more attention than most of the other mothers, which he found a little embarrassing. But he was pleased that she no longer appeared to be burdened by financial worries, and assumed the man standing on her right had something to do with that.

However grateful he was to Mr Atkins, he didn't care for the idea of him becoming his stepfather. Mr Barrington may in the past have been over-zealous about his daughter, but Harry could not deny that he felt just as protective when it came to his mother.

She had recently told him that Mr Frampton was so pleased with her work at the hotel that he had promoted her to night supervisor and given her another pay rise. And certainly Harry no longer had to wait for his trousers to be too short before they were replaced. But even he had been surprised when she hadn't commented about the cost of his travelling to Rome with the Arts Appreciation Society.

'How nice to see you, Harry, on your day of triumph,' said Mrs Barrington. 'Two prizes, if I remember correctly. I'm only sorry that Emma can't be with us to share in your glory, but as Miss Webb pointed out, her gels cannot be expected to take the morning off for someone else's speech day, even if her brother is the school captain.'

Mr Barrington came across to join them, and Giles watched his father carefully as he shook hands with Harry. There was still a distinct lack of warmth on his father's part, although no one could deny that he was making every effort to conceal it.

'So, when are you expecting to hear from Oxford, Harry?' asked Barrington.

'Some time next week, sir.'

'I'm confident they'll offer you a place, although I suspect it will be a close-run thing for Giles.'

'Don't forget he's also had his moment of glory,' said Harry.

'I don't recall that,' said Mrs Barrington.

'I think Harry's referring to the century I scored at Lord's, Mama.'

'Admirable though that might be, for the life of me I can't see how it will help you get into Oxford,' said his father.

'Normally I would agree with you, Papa,' said Giles, 'were it not for the fact that the Professor of History was sitting next to the President of the MCC at the time.'

The laughter that followed was drowned out by the sound of bells. The boys began to move rapidly in the direction of the great hall, with their parents following dutifully a few paces behind them.

Giles and Harry took their places among the prefects and prize-winners in the front three rows.

'Do you recall our first day at St Bede's?' said Harry, 'when we all sat in the front row, quite terrified of Dr Oakshott?'

'I was never terrified of the Shot,' said Giles.

'No, of course you weren't,' said Harry.

'But I do remember when we came down for breakfast on the first morning that you licked your porridge bowl.'

'And I remember you swore you'd never mention it again,' whispered Harry.

'And I promise I never will again,' replied Giles not whispering. 'What was the name of that frightful bully who slippered you on our first night?'

'Fisher,' said Harry. 'And it was the second night.'

'Wonder what he's up to now?'

'He's probably running a Nazi youth camp.'

'Then that's a good enough reason to go to war,' said Giles as everyone in the hall rose to welcome the chairman of the governors and his board.

The crocodile of smartly dressed men made their way slowly down the aisle and up on to the stage. The last person to take his seat was Mr Barton, the headmaster, but not before he'd ushered the guest of honour into the centre chair in the front row.

Once everyone had settled, the headmaster rose to welcome the parents and guests, before delivering the school's annual report. He began by describing 1938 as a vintage year, and for the next twenty minutes he elaborated on this claim, giving details of the school's academic and sporting achievements. He ended by inviting the Right Honourable Winston Churchill MP, Chancellor of Bristol University and Member of Parliament for Epping, to address the school and present the prizes.

Mr Churchill rose slowly from his place and stared down at the audience for some time before he began.

'Some guests of honour begin their speeches by telling their audience that they never won any prizes when they were at school, in fact they were always bottom of the class. I cannot make such a claim: although I certainly never won a prize, at least I was never bottom of the class – I was second to bottom.' The boys roared and cheered, while the masters smiled. Only Deakins remained unmoved.

The moment the laughter had subsided, Churchill scowled. 'Our nation today faces another of those great moments in history, when the British people may once again be asked to decide the fate of the free world. Many of you present in this great hall . . .' He lowered his voice and concentrated his attention on the rows of boys seated in front of him, not once looking in the direction of their parents.

'Those of us who lived through the Great War will never forget the tragic loss of life our nation suffered, and the effect it has had on an entire generation. Of the twenty boys in my class at Harrow who went on to serve in the front line, only three of them lived long enough to cast a vote. I only hope that whoever delivers this speech in twenty years' time will not need to refer to that barbaric and unnecessary waste of life as the *First* World War. With that single hope, I wish you all long, happy and successful lives.'

Giles was among the first to rise and give the guest

of honour a standing ovation as he returned to his seat. He felt that if Britain were left with no choice but to go to war, this was the one man who should take over from Neville Chamberlain and become Prime Minister. When everyone had resumed their places some minutes later, the headmaster invited Mr Churchill to present the prizes.

Giles and Harry cheered when Mr Barton not only announced that Deakins was scholar of the year but added, 'This morning I received a telegram from the Master of Balliol College, Oxford, to say that Deakins has been awarded the senior classics scholarship. I might add,' continued Mr Barton, 'that he is the first boy to achieve this distinction in the school's four-hundred-year history.'

Giles and Harry were on their feet immediately, as a gangly, six-foot-two-inch boy with pebble glasses, wearing a suit that hung on him as if it had never left its coathanger, made his way slowly up on to the stage. Mr Deakins wanted to leap up and take a photograph of his son being presented with his prize by Mr Churchill, but didn't do so, for fear it might be frowned upon.

Harry received a warm reception when he was awarded the English prize, as well as the school reading prize. The headmaster added, 'None of us will ever forget his performance as Romeo. Let us all hope that Harry will be among those who receive a telegram next week offering them a place at Oxford.'

When Mr Churchill presented Harry with his prize, he whispered, 'I never went to university. I only wish I had. Let's hope you receive that telegram, Clifton. Good luck.'

'Thank you, sir,' said Harry.

But the biggest cheer of the day was reserved for Giles Barrington when he went up to receive the headmaster's prize for captain of the school and captain of cricket. To the guest of honour's surprise, the chairman of the governors leapt up from his place and shook hands with Giles before he reached Mr Churchill.

'My grandson, sir,' Sir Walter explained with considerable pride.

Churchill smiled, gripped Giles by the hand and, looking up at him, said, 'Be sure you serve your country with the same distinction with which you have clearly served your school.'

That was the moment when Giles knew exactly what he would do if Britain went to war.

Once the ceremony was over, the boys, parents and masters rose as one to sing *Carmen Bristoliense*.

Sit clarior, sit dignior, quotquot labuntur menses:
Sit primus nobis hic decor, Sumus Bristolienses.

Once the last chorus had rung out, the headmaster led the guest of honour and his staff off the stage, out of the great hall and into the afternoon sunshine. Moments later, everyone else poured out on to the lawn to join them for tea. Three boys in particular were surrounded by well-wishers, as well as by a bevy of sisters who thought Giles was 'just cute'.

'This is the proudest day of my life,' said Harry's mother as she embraced him.

'I know how you feel, Mrs Clifton,' said Old Jack, shaking Harry by the hand. 'I only wish Miss Monday had lived long enough to see you today, because I don't doubt it would have also been the happiest day of her life.'

Mr Holcombe stood to one side and waited patiently to add his congratulations. Harry introduced him to Captain Tarrant, unaware that they were old friends.

When the band had stopped playing, and the captains and the kings had departed, Giles, Harry and Deakins sat alone on the grass and reminisced about things past, no longer schoolboys.

43

A TELEGRAM WAS DELIVERED to Harry's study by a junior boy on Thursday afternoon. Giles and Deakins waited patiently for him to open it, but instead he handed the little brown envelope to Giles.

'Passing the buck again,' said Giles as he ripped it open. He couldn't hide his surprise when he read the contents.

'You failed,' said Giles, sounding shocked. Harry collapsed back into his chair. 'To win a scholarship. However,' Giles added, reading the telegram aloud, '*We are delighted to offer you an exhibition to Brasenose College, Oxford. Many congratulations. Details to follow in the next few days. W.T.S. Stallybrass, Principal.* Not bad, but you're clearly not in Deakins's class.'

'And which class are you in?' said Harry, immediately regretting his words.

'One scholar, one exhibitionist—'

'Exhibitioner,' corrected Deakins.

'And one commoner,' said Giles, ignoring his friend. 'Has a nice ring about it.'

Eleven other telegrams were delivered to successful applicants from Bristol Grammar School that day, but none was addressed to Giles Barrington.

'You should let your mother know,' said Giles as they

walked into the hall for supper. 'She probably hasn't slept all week worrying about it.'

Harry looked at his watch. 'It's too late, she'll already have left for work. I won't be able to tell her until tomorrow morning.'

'Why don't we go and surprise her at the hotel?' said Giles.

'I can't do that. She'd think it unprofessional to interrupt her while she's at work, and I don't feel I can make an exception, even for this,' he said, waving the telegram triumphantly.

'But don't you think she has a right to know?' said Giles. 'After all, she's sacrificed everything to make it possible for you. Frankly, if they offered me a place at Oxford, I'd interrupt Mama even if she was addressing the Mothers' Union. Don't you agree, Deakins?'

Deakins removed his glasses and began to polish them with a handkerchief, always a sign that he was deep in thought. 'I'd ask Paget's opinion, and if he raises no objection—'

'Good idea,' said Giles. 'Let's go and see the Page.'

'Are you coming, Deakins?' asked Harry, but then noticed that Deakins's glasses had been returned to the end of his nose, a sign that he had been transported to another world.

'Many congratulations,' said Dr Paget once he'd read the telegram. 'And well deserved, if I may say so.'

'Thank you, sir,' said Harry. 'I wondered if it would be possible for me to go to the Royal Hotel so I can tell my mother the news?'

'I can't see any reason why not, Clifton.'

'Can I trot along with him?' asked Giles innocently.

Paget hesitated. 'Yes, you can, Barrington. But don't even think about having a drink or smoking while you're in the hotel.'

'Not even one glass of champagne, sir?'

'No, Barrington, not even a glass of cider,' said Paget firmly.

As the two young men strolled out of the school gates, they passed a lamp lighter who was standing on his bicycle, stretching up to light a street lamp. They chatted about the summer hols, when Harry would be joining Giles's family in Tuscany for the first time, and agreed they would have to be back in time to see the Australians when they played against Gloucestershire at the county ground. They discussed the possibility, or, according to Harry, the probability, of war being declared now that everyone had been issued with a gas mask. But neither of them touched on another subject that was on both of their minds: would Giles be joining Harry and Deakins at Oxford in September?

As they approached the hotel, Harry had second thoughts about interrupting his mother while she was at work, but Giles had already barged through the revolving doors and was standing in the foyer waiting for him.

'It will only take a couple of minutes,' said Giles when Harry joined him. 'Just tell her the good news and we can go straight back to school.' Harry nodded.

Giles asked the doorman where the Palm Court was, and he directed them to a raised area at the far end of the foyer. After climbing the half dozen steps, Giles walked up to the desk and, keeping his voice low, asked the receptionist, 'Can we have a quick word with Mrs Clifton?'

'Mrs Clifton?' asked the girl. 'Has she made a reservation?' She ran her finger down a list of bookings.

'No, she works here,' said Giles.

'Oh, I'm new here,' said the girl, 'but I'll just ask one of the waitresses. They're bound to know.'

'Thank you.'

Harry remained on the bottom step, his eyes searching the room for his mother.

'Hattie,' the receptionist asked a passing waitress, 'does a Mrs Clifton work here?'

'Not any longer she doesn't,' came back the immediate reply. 'She left a couple of years ago. Haven't heard a dicky-bird from her since.'

'There must be some mistake,' said Harry, bounding up the steps to join his friend.

'Do you have any idea where we might find her?' asked Giles, keeping his voice low.

'No,' said Hattie. 'But you could have a word with Doug, the night porter. He's been here for ever.'

'Thank you,' said Giles and, turning to Harry, added, 'There's bound to be a simple explanation, but if you'd prefer to leave it . . .'

'No, let's find out if Doug knows where she is.'

Giles walked slowly across to the porter's desk, giving Harry enough time to change his mind, but he didn't say a word. 'Are you Doug?' he asked a man dressed in a faded blue frockcoat with buttons that no longer shone.

'I am, sir,' he replied. 'How can I help you?'

'We're looking for Mrs Clifton.'

'Maisie don't work here any longer, sir. She must have left at least a couple of years back.'

'Do you know where she is working now?'

'I've no idea, sir.'

Giles took out his purse, extracted half a crown and placed it on the counter. The porter eyed it for some time before he spoke again. 'It's just possible you'll find her at Eddie's Nightclub.'

'Eddie Atkins?' enquired Harry.

'I believe that's correct, sir.'

'Well, that explains it,' said Harry. 'And where is Eddie's Nightclub?'

'Welsh Back, sir,' replied the porter as he pocketed the half a crown.

Harry left the hotel without another word and jumped into the back of a waiting cab. Giles got in beside him. 'Don't you think we should get back to school?' said Giles, looking at his watch. 'You can always tell your mother in the morning.'

Harry shook his head. 'It was you who said you'd interrupt your mother even if she was addressing the Mothers' Union,' Harry reminded him. 'Eddie's Nightclub, Welsh Back, please, cabbie,' he said firmly.

Harry didn't speak during the short journey. When the cab turned into a dark alley and came to a halt outside Eddie's, he got out and walked towards the entrance.

Harry banged firmly on the door. A shutter slid open and a pair of eyes stared at the two young men. 'The entrance fee is five shillings each,' said a voice behind the eyes. Giles pushed a ten-shilling note through the hole. The door swung open immediately.

The two of them made their way down a dimly lit staircase to the basement. Giles saw her first and quickly turned to leave, but it was too late. Harry was staring, transfixed, at a row of girls seated on stools at the bar, some chatting to men, others on their own. One of them, wearing a white see-through blouse, a short black leather skirt and black stockings, approached them and said, 'Can I help you, gents?'

Harry ignored her. His eyes had settled on a woman at the far end of the bar who was listening intently to an older man who had his hand on her thigh. The girl looked to see who he was staring at. 'I must say, you know class when you see it,' she said. 'Mind you, Maisie can be choosy, and I have to warn you, she doesn't come cheap.'

Harry turned and bolted back up the steps, pulled open the door and ran out on to the street, with Giles chasing after him. Once Harry was on the pavement, he fell to his knees and was violently sick. Giles knelt and put his arm around his friend, trying to comfort him.

A man who had been standing in the shadows on the other side of the road limped away.

EMMA BARRINGTON

1932–1939

44

I'll never forget the first time I saw him.

He came to tea at the Manor House to celebrate my brother's twelfth birthday. He was so quiet and reserved that I wondered how he could possibly be Giles's best friend. The other one, Deakins, was really strange. He never stopped eating and hardly said a word all afternoon.

And then Harry spoke, a soft, gentle voice that made you want to listen. The birthday party had apparently been going swimmingly until my father burst into the room, and then he hardly spoke again. I'd never known my father to be so off-hand with anyone, and I couldn't understand why he should behave in that way towards a complete stranger. But even more inexplicable was Papa's reaction when he asked Harry when his birthday was. How could such an innocuous question bring on such an extreme reaction? A moment later my father got up and left the room, without even saying goodbye to Giles and his guests. I could see that Mama was embarrassed by his behaviour, although she poured another cup of tea and pretended not to notice.

A few minutes later, my brother and his two friends left to go back to school. He turned and smiled at me before leaving, but just like my mother, I pretended not to notice. But when the front door closed I stood by the drawing-room window and watched as the car disappeared down the driveway and out of sight. I thought I saw him looking out of the back window, but I couldn't be sure.

After they had left, Mama went straight to my father's study and I could hear raised voices, which had recently become more and more common. When she came back out, she smiled at me as if nothing unusual had happened.

'What's the name of Giles's best friend?' I asked.

'Harry Clifton,' she replied.

◄○►

The next time I saw Harry Clifton was at the Advent carol service at St Mary Redcliffe. He sang *O Little Town of Bethlehem*, and my best friend, Jessica Braithwaite, accused me of swooning as if he was the new Bing Crosby. I didn't bother to deny it. I saw him chatting to Giles after the service and I would have liked to congratulate him, but Papa seemed to be in a hurry to get home. As we left, I saw his nanny giving him a huge hug.

I was also at St Mary Redcliffe the evening his voice broke, but at the time I didn't understand why so many heads were turning and some members of the congregation began to whisper among themselves. All I know is that I never heard him sing again.

When Giles was driven to the grammar school on his first day, I begged my mother to let me go along, but only because I wanted to meet Harry. But my father wouldn't hear of it, and despite my bursting into controlled tears, they still left me standing on the top step with my younger sister Grace. I knew Papa was cross about Giles not being offered a place at Eton, something I still don't understand, because a lot of boys more stupid than my brother passed the exam. Mama didn't seem to mind which school Giles went to, whereas I was delighted he was going to Bristol Grammar, because it meant I'd have a better chance of seeing Harry again.

In fact I must have seen him at least a dozen times during the next three years, but he was never able to recall any of those occasions, until we met up in Rome.

The family were all staying at our villa in Tuscany that summer when Giles took me to one side and said he needed to ask my advice. He only ever did that when he wanted something. But this time it turned out to be something I wanted just as much as he did.

'So what are you expecting me to do this time?' I asked.

'I need an excuse to go into Rome tomorrow,' he said, 'because I'm meant to be meeting up with Harry.'

'Harry who?' I said, feigning indifference.

'Harry Clifton, stupid. He's on a school trip to Rome and I promised to get away and spend the day with him.' He didn't need to spell out that Papa wouldn't have approved. 'All you have to do,' he continued, 'is ask Mama if she could take you to Rome for the day.'

'But she'll need to know why I want to go into Rome.'

'Tell her you've always wanted to visit the Villa Borghese.'

'Why the Villa Borghese?'

'Because that's where Harry will be at ten o'clock tomorrow morning.'

'But what happens if Mama agrees to take me? Then you'll be stymied.'

'She won't. They're having lunch with the Hendersons in Arezzo tomorrow, so I'll volunteer to be your chaperone.'

'And what do I get in exchange?' I demanded, as I didn't want Giles to know how keen I was to see Harry.

'My gramophone,' he said.

'For keeps, or just to borrow?'

Giles didn't speak for some time. 'For ever,' he said reluctantly.

'Hand it over now,' I said, 'or you can forget it.' To my surprise he did.

I was even more amazed when, the next day, my mother fell for his little ploy. Giles didn't even have to offer to act as my chaperone; Papa insisted that he accompany me. My deceitful brother made a show of protesting, but finally gave in.

I rose early the following morning and spent some considerable time thinking about what I should wear. It would have to be fairly conservative if my mother wasn't to become suspicious, but on the other hand I wanted to make sure Harry noticed me.

While we were on the train to Rome, I disappeared into the lavatory and put on a pair of mother's silk stockings and just a touch of lipstick, not enough for Giles to notice.

Once we'd checked into our hotel, Giles wanted to leave immediately for the Villa Borghese. So did I.

As we walked through the gardens and up towards the villa, a soldier turned to look at me. It was the first time that had happened, and I could feel my cheeks reddening.

No sooner had we entered the gallery than Giles went off in search of Harry. I hung back, pretending to take a great deal of interest in the paintings and statues. I needed to make an entrance.

When I eventually caught up with them, I found Harry chatting to my brother, although Giles wasn't even pretending to listen to him as he was clearly besotted by the tour guide. If he'd asked me, I could have told him he didn't have a chance. But older brothers rarely listen to their sisters when it comes to women; I would have advised him to comment on her shoes, which made me quite envious. Men think the Italians are only famous for designing cars. One exception to this rule is Captain Tarrant, who knows exactly how to treat a lady. My brother could learn a lot from him. Giles simply regarded me as his gauche little sister, not that he would have known what the word gauche meant.

I picked my moment, then strolled across and waited

for Giles to introduce us. Imagine my surprise when Harry invited me to join him for dinner that night. My only thought was that I hadn't packed a suitable evening dress. Over dinner, I discovered that my brother had paid Harry a thousand lira to take me off his hands, but he had refused until Giles also agreed to part with his Caruso recording. I told Harry he'd got the records and I'd got the gramophone. He didn't catch on.

As we crossed the road on the way back to the hotel, he held my hand for the first time, and when we reached the other side, I didn't let go. I could tell it was the first time Harry had held a girl's hand, because he was so nervous he was sweating.

I tried to make it easy for him to kiss me when we got back to my hotel, but he just shook hands and said good night as if we were old chums. I hinted that perhaps we might bump into each other again once we were back in Bristol. This time he responded more positively, and even suggested the most romantic location for our next date: the city's central library. He explained that it was somewhere Giles would never come across us. I happily agreed.

It was just after ten when Harry left and I went up to my room. A few minutes later I heard Giles unlocking his bedroom door. I had to smile. His evening with Caterina can't have been worth a Caruso recording and a gramophone.

When the family returned to Chew Valley a couple of weeks later, there were three letters waiting for me on the hall table, each with the same handwriting on the envelope. If my father noticed, he said nothing.

During the next month, Harry and I spent many happy hours together in the city library without anyone becoming suspicious, not least because he'd discovered a room where no one was likely to find us, even Deakins.

Once term began and we weren't able to see each other

as often, I quickly became aware just how much I missed Harry. We wrote every other day, and tried to grab a few hours together at the weekends. And that's how it might have continued, had it not been for the unwitting intervention of Dr Paget.

Over coffee at Carwardine's one Saturday morning, Harry, who had become quite bold, told me that his English master had persuaded Miss Webb to allow her girls to take part in the Bristol Grammar School play that year. By the time the auditions were held three weeks later, I knew the part of Juliet by heart. Poor innocent Dr Paget couldn't believe his luck.

Rehearsals meant not only that the two of us could be together for three afternoons a week, but that we were allowed to play the parts of young lovers. By the time the curtain went up on the first night, we were no longer acting.

The first two performances went so well that I couldn't wait for my parents to attend the closing night, although I didn't tell my father I was playing Juliet as I wanted it to be a surprise. It wasn't long after my first entrance that I became distracted by someone noisily leaving the auditorium. But Dr Paget had told us on several occasions never to look into the audience, it broke the spell, so I had no idea who had left so publicly. I prayed it wasn't my father, but when he didn't come backstage after the performance I realized my prayer had not been answered. What made it worse was my certainty that his little outburst was aimed at Harry, although I still didn't know why.

When we returned home that night, Giles and I sat on the stairs and listened to my parents having another row. But it was different this time, because I'd never heard my father be so unkind to Mama. When I could bear it no longer, I went to my room and locked myself in.

I was lying on my bed, thinking about Harry, when I

heard a gentle knock on the door. When I opened it, my mother made no attempt to hide the fact that she'd been crying, and told me to pack a small suitcase because we would be leaving shortly. A taxi drove us to the station and we arrived just in time to catch the milk train to London. During the journey, I wrote to Harry to let him know what had happened and where he could get in touch with me. I posted the letter in a box on King's Cross station before we boarded another train for Edinburgh.

Imagine my surprise when the following evening Harry and my brother turned up at Mulgelrie Castle, just in time for dinner. We spent an unexpected and glorious nine days in Scotland together. I didn't ever want to return to Chew Valley, even though my father had rung and apologized unreservedly for the way he'd behaved on the night of the play.

But I knew that eventually we would have to go home. I promised Harry on one of our long morning walks that I would try to find out the reason for my father's continued hostility towards him.

When we arrived back at the Manor House, Papa could not have been more conciliatory. He tried to explain why he had treated Harry so badly over the years, and my mother and Giles seemed to accept his explanation. But I wasn't convinced he had told us the whole story.

What made things even more difficult for me was that he forbade me to tell Harry the truth about how his father had died, as his mother was adamant that it should remain a family secret. I had a feeling that Mrs Clifton knew the real reason my father didn't approve of Harry and me being together, although I would have liked to tell them both that nothing and no one could keep us apart. However, it all came to a head in a way I could never have predicted.

I was just as impatient as Harry to find out if he'd been

offered a place at Oxford, and we arranged to meet outside the library on the morning after he received the telegram letting him know the result.

I was a few minutes late that Friday morning, and when I saw him sitting on the top step, head in hands, I knew he must have failed.

45

HARRY LEAPT UP and threw his arms around Emma the moment he saw her. He continued to cling to her, something he'd never done in public before, which confirmed her belief that it could only be bad news.

Without a word passing between them, he took her by the hand, led her into the building, down a circular wooden staircase and along a narrow brick corridor until he came to a door marked 'Antiquities'. He peered inside to make sure that no one else had discovered their hiding place.

The two of them sat opposite each other at a small table where they had spent so many hours studying during the past year. Harry was trembling, and not because of the chill in the windowless room that was lined on all sides by shelves of leather-bound books covered in dust, some of which looked as if they hadn't been opened for years. In time they would become antiquities in their own right.

It was some time before Harry spoke.

'Do you think there is anything I could say or do that would stop you loving me?'

'No, my darling,' said Emma, 'absolutely nothing.'

'I've found out why your father has been so determined to keep us apart.'

'I already know,' said Emma, bowing her head slightly, 'and I promise you it makes no difference.'

'How can you possibly know?' said Harry.

'My father told us the day we returned from Scotland, but he swore us to secrecy.'

'He told you my mother was a prostitute?'

Emma was stunned. It was some time before she recovered enough to speak. 'No, he did not,' she said vehemently. 'How could you say anything so cruel?'

'Because it's the truth,' said Harry. 'My mother hasn't been working at the Royal Hotel for the past two years, as I thought, but at a nightclub called Eddie's.'

'That doesn't make her a prostitute,' said Emma.

'The man sitting at the bar with a glass of whisky in one hand and the other on her thigh wasn't hoping for stimulating conversation.'

Emma leant across the table and touched Harry gently on the cheek. 'I'm so sorry, my darling,' she said, 'but it makes no difference to how I feel about you, and it never will.'

Harry managed a weak smile, but Emma remained silent, knowing it could only be a few moments before he asked her the inevitable question.

'If that wasn't the secret your father asked you to keep,' he said, suddenly serious again, 'what did he tell you?'

It was Emma's turn to hold her head in her hands, aware that he'd left her with no choice but to tell him the truth. Like her mother, she was no good at dissembling.

'What did he tell you?' Harry repeated, more emphatically.

Emma held on to the edge of the table as she tried to steady herself. Finally she summoned up the strength to look at Harry. Although he was only a few feet away, he could not have been more distant. 'I need to ask you the same question you asked me,' said Emma. 'Is there anything I could say or do that would stop you loving me?'

Harry leant across and took her hand. 'Of course not,' he said.

'Your father wasn't killed in the war,' she said softly. 'And my father was probably responsible for his death.' She gripped his hand firmly before revealing everything her father had told them the day they returned from Scotland.

When she'd finished, Harry looked dazed and was unable to speak. He tried to stand up but his legs gave way beneath him, like a boxer who'd taken one punch too many, and he fell back into his chair.

'I've known for some time that my father couldn't have died in the war,' Harry said quietly, 'but what I still don't understand is why my mother didn't simply tell me the truth.'

'And now you do know the truth,' said Emma, trying to hold back the tears, 'I would understand if you wanted to break off our relationship after what my father has put your family through.'

'It's not your fault,' said Harry, 'but I'll never forgive him.' He paused before adding, 'And I won't be able to face him once he finds out the truth about my mother.'

'He need never find out,' said Emma, taking him by the hand again. 'It will always be a secret between us.'

'That's not possible any longer,' said Harry.

'Why not?'

'Because Giles saw the man who followed us to Edinburgh standing in a doorway opposite Eddie's Nightclub.'

'Then it's my father who's prostituted himself,' said Emma, 'because not only did he lie to us yet again, but he's already gone back on his word.'

'How?'

'He promised Giles that man would never follow him again.'

'That man wasn't interested in Giles,' said Harry. 'I think he was following my mother.'

'But why?'

'Because if he was able to prove how my mother earned her living, he must have hoped it would convince you to give me up.'

'How little he knows his own daughter,' said Emma, 'because I'm now even more determined that nothing will keep us apart. And he certainly can't stop me admiring your mother even more than I did before.'

'How can you say that?' said Harry.

'She works as a waitress to support her family, ends up owning Tilly's, and when it's burnt to the ground she's accused of arson, but holds her head high, knowing she is innocent. She finds herself another job at the Royal Hotel, and when she's sacked, she still refuses to give up. She receives a cheque for six hundred pounds, and for a moment believes all her problems are solved, only to discover she's in fact penniless just at the time when she needs money to make sure you can stay at school. In desperation, she then turns to . . .'

'But I wouldn't have wanted her to . . .'

'She would have known that, Harry, but she still felt it was a sacrifice worth making.'

Another long silence followed. 'Oh my God,' said Harry. 'How can I ever have thought badly of her.' He looked up at Emma. 'I need you to do something for me.'

'Anything.'

'Can you go and see my mother? Use any excuse, but try to find out if she saw me in that dreadful place last night.'

'How will I know, if she isn't willing to admit it?'

'You'll know,' said Harry quietly.

'But if your mother did see you, she's bound to ask me what you were doing there.'

'I was looking for her.'

'But why?'

'To tell her that I've been offered a place at Oxford.'

—◦—

Emma slipped into a pew at the back of Holy Nativity and waited for the service to end. She could see Mrs Clifton sitting in the third row, next to an old lady. Harry had seemed a little less tense when they'd met again earlier that morning. He'd been very clear what he needed to find out, and she promised not to stray beyond her remit. They had rehearsed every possible scenario several times, until she was word perfect.

After the elderly priest had given the final blessing, Emma stepped out into the centre of the aisle and waited, so Mrs Clifton couldn't possibly miss her. When Maisie saw Emma, she couldn't hide a look of surprise, but it was quickly replaced by a welcoming smile. She walked quickly towards her and introduced the old lady who was with her. 'Mum, this is Emma Barrington, she's a friend of Harry's.'

The old lady gave Emma a toothy grin. 'There's a great deal of difference between being his friend and being his girlfriend. Which are you?' she demanded.

Mrs Clifton laughed, but it was clear to Emma that she was just as interested to hear her reply.

'I'm his girlfriend,' said Emma proudly.

The old lady delivered another toothy grin, but Maisie didn't smile.

'Well, that's all right then, isn't it?' Harry's grandmother said, before adding, 'I can't stand around here all day chatting, I've got dinner to make.' She began to walk away, but then turned back and asked, 'Would you like to join us for dinner, young lady?'

This was a question that Harry had anticipated, and for which he'd even scripted a reply. 'That's very kind of you,' said Emma, 'but my parents will be expecting me.'

'Quite right too,' said the old lady. 'You should always respect your parents' wishes. I'll see you later, Maisie.'

'May I walk with you, Mrs Clifton?' asked Emma as they stepped out of the church.

'Yes, of course, my dear.'

'Harry asked me to come and see you, because he knew you'd want to know that he's been offered a place at Oxford.'

'Oh, that's wonderful news,' said Maisie, throwing her arms around Emma. She suddenly released her, and asked, 'But why didn't he come and tell me himself?'

Another scripted reply. 'He's stuck in detention,' said Emma, hoping she didn't sound over-rehearsed, 'writing out passages from Shelley. I'm afraid my brother's to blame. You see, after he heard the good news, he smuggled a bottle of champagne into school, and they were caught celebrating in his study last night.'

'Is that so wicked?' asked Maisie, grinning.

'Dr Paget seemed to think so. Harry's dreadfully sorry.'

Maisie laughed so uproariously that Emma had no doubt she'd no idea her son had visited the club last night. She would have liked to ask one more question that still puzzled her, but Harry couldn't have been more emphatic: 'If my mother doesn't want me to know how my father died, so be it.'

'I'm sorry you can't stay to lunch,' said Maisie, 'because there was something I wanted to tell you. Perhaps another time.'

46

HARRY SPENT THE FOLLOWING week waiting for another bombshell to drop. When it did, he cheered out loud.

Giles received a telegram on the last day of term telling him he'd been offered a place at Brasenose College, Oxford, to read History.

'By the skin of his teeth,' was the expression Dr Paget used when he informed the headmaster.

Two months later, one scholar, one exhibitioner and one commoner arrived in the ancient university city, by different modes of transport, to begin their three-year undergraduate courses.

Harry signed up for the dramatic society and the officer training corps, Giles for the union and the cricket club, while Deakins settled himself down in the bowels of the Bodleian library, and, like a mole, was rarely seen above ground. But then, he had already decided that Oxford was where he was going to spend the rest of his life.

Harry couldn't be so sure how he would be spending the rest of his life, while the Prime Minister continued to fly back and forth to Germany, finally returning to Heston airport with a smile on his face, waving a piece of paper and telling people what they wanted to hear.

Harry wasn't in any doubt that Britain was on the brink of war. When Emma asked him why he was so convinced, he replied, 'Haven't you noticed that Herr Hitler never bothers to visit us? We are always the importunate suitor, and in the end we will be spurned.' Emma ignored his opinion, but then, like Mr Chamberlain, she didn't want to believe he might be right.

Emma wrote to Harry twice a week, sometimes three times, despite the fact that she was working flat out preparing for her own entrance exams to Oxford.

<o>

When Harry returned to Bristol for the Christmas vacation, the two of them spent as much time together as possible, although Harry made sure he kept out of the way of Mr Barrington.

Emma turned down the chance to spend her holiday with the rest of the family in Tuscany, not hiding the fact from her father that she'd rather be with Harry.

As her entrance exam drew nearer, the number of hours Emma spent in the Antiquities room would have impressed even Deakins, but then Harry was coming to the conclusion that she was about to impress the examiners just as much as his reclusive friend had done the year before. Whenever he suggested this to Emma, she would remind him that there were twenty male students at Oxford for every female.

'You could always go to Cambridge,' Giles foolishly suggested.

'Where they're even more prehistoric,' Emma responded. 'They still don't award degrees to women.'

Emma's greatest fear was not that she wouldn't be offered a place at Oxford, but that by the time she took it up, war would have been declared, and Harry would have signed up and departed for some foreign field that was not forever England. All her life she had been continually reminded of the Great War by the number of women who still wore black every day, in memory of their husbands, lovers, brothers and sons who had never returned from the Front, in what nobody was any longer calling the war to end all wars.

She had pleaded with Harry not to volunteer if war was declared, but at least to wait until he was called up. But after Hitler had marched into Czechoslovakia and annexed the Sudetenland, Harry never wavered in his belief that war with Germany was inevitable, and that the moment it was declared, he would be in uniform the following day.

When Harry invited Emma to join him for the Commem Ball at the end of his first year, she resolved not to discuss the possibility of war. She also made another decision.

—◄o►—

Emma travelled up to Oxford on the morning of the ball and checked into the Randolph Hotel. She spent the rest of the day being shown around Somerville, the Ashmolean and the Bodleian by Harry, who was confident she would be joining him as an undergraduate in a few months' time.

Emma returned to the hotel, giving herself plenty of time to prepare for the ball. Harry had arranged to pick her up at eight.

He strolled through the front door of the hotel a few minutes before the appointed hour. He was dressed in a fashionable midnight blue dinner jacket which his mother had given him for his nineteenth birthday. He called Emma's room from the front desk to tell her he was downstairs and would wait for her in the foyer.

'I'll be straight down,' she promised.

As the minutes passed, Harry began to pace around the foyer, wondering what Emma meant by 'straight down'. But Giles had often told him that she'd learnt how to tell the time from her mother.

And then he saw her, standing at the top of the staircase. He didn't move as she walked slowly down, her strapless turquoise silk dress emphasizing her graceful figure. Every other young man in the foyer looked as if he'd be happy to change places with Harry.

'Wow,' he said as she reached the bottom step. 'Who needs Vivien Leigh? By the way, I love the shoes.' Emma felt the first part of her plan was falling into place.

They walked out of the hotel and strolled arm in arm towards Radcliffe Square. As they entered the gates of Harry's college, the sun began to dip behind the Bodleian. No one entering Brasenose that evening would have thought that Britain was only a few weeks away from a war in which over half the young men who danced the night away would never graduate.

But nothing could have been further from the thoughts of the gay young couples dancing to the music of Cole Porter and Jerome Kern. While several hundred undergraduates and their guests consumed crates of champagne and ate their way through a mountain of smoked salmon, Harry rarely let Emma out of his sight, fearful that some ungallant soul might attempt to steal her away.

Giles drank a little too much champagne, ate far too many oysters and didn't dance with the same girl twice the entire evening.

At two o'clock in the morning, the Billy Cotton Dance Band struck up the last waltz. Harry and Emma clung to each other as they swayed to the rhythm of the orchestra.

When the conductor finally raised his baton for the National Anthem, Emma couldn't help noticing that all the young men around her, whatever state of inebriation they were in, stood rigidly to attention as they sang 'God Save the King'.

Harry and Emma walked slowly back to the Randolph chatting about nothing of any consequence, just not wanting the evening to end.

'Well, at least you'll be back in a fortnight's time to sit your entrance exam,' said Harry as they climbed the steps to the hotel, 'so it won't be too long before I see you again.'

'True,' said Emma, 'but there'll be no time for any distractions until I've completed the last paper. Once that's out of the way, we can spend the rest of the weekend together.'

Harry was about to kiss her goodnight, when she whispered, 'Would you like to come up to my room? I've got a present for you. I wouldn't want you to think I'd forgotten your birthday.'

Harry looked surprised, as did the hall porter when the young couple walked up the staircase together hand in hand. When they reached Emma's room, she fumbled nervously with the key before finally pushing open the door.

'I'll just be a moment,' she said as she disappeared into the bathroom.

Harry sat down in the only chair in the room and tried to think of what he'd most like for his birthday. When the bathroom door opened, Emma was framed in the half light. The elegant strapless gown had been replaced by a hotel towel.

Harry could hear his heart beating as she walked slowly towards him.

'I think you're a little overdressed, my darling,' Emma said, as she slipped off his jacket and let it fall to the floor. Next she undid his bow tie before unbuttoning his shirt, and both joined the jacket. Two shoes and two socks followed, before she slowly pulled down his trousers. She was about to remove the one remaining obstacle in her path, when he gathered her up in his arms and carried her across the bedroom.

As he dumped her unceremoniously on to the bed, the towel fell to the floor. Emma had often imagined this moment since they'd returned from Rome, and assumed that her first attempts at making love would be awkward and clumsy. But Harry was gentle and considerate, although he was clearly every bit as nervous as she was. After they'd made love, she lay in his arms, not wanting to fall asleep.

'Did you like your birthday present?' she asked.

'Yes I did,' said Harry. 'But I hope it's not going to be another year before I can unwrap the next one. That reminds me, I've got a present for you too.'

'But it's not my birthday.'

'It's not a birthday present.'

He jumped out of bed, picked his trousers up off the floor and rummaged around in the pockets until he came across a small leather box. He returned to the bedside, fell to one knee and said, 'Emma, my darling, will you marry me?'

'You look quite ridiculous down there,' said Emma, frowning. 'Get back into bed before you freeze to death.'

'Not until you've answered my question.'

'Don't be silly, Harry. I decided that we were going

to be married the day you came to the Manor House for Giles's twelfth birthday.'

Harry burst out laughing as he placed the ring on the third finger of her left hand.

'I'm sorry it's such a small diamond,' he said.

'It's as big as the Ritz,' she said as he climbed back into bed. 'And as you seem to have everything so well organized,' she teased, 'what date have you chosen for our wedding?'

'Saturday, July the twenty-ninth, at three o'clock.'

'Why then?'

'It's the last day of term, and in any case, we can't book the university church after I've gone down.'

Emma sat up, grabbed the pencil and pad from the bedside table and started to write.

'What are you doing?' asked Harry.

'I'm working on the guest list. If we've only got seven weeks . . .'

'That can wait,' said Harry, taking her back in his arms. 'I feel another birthday coming on.'

◄◦►

'She's too young to be thinking about marriage,' said Emma's father, as if she wasn't in the room.

'She's the same age I was when you proposed to me,' Elizabeth reminded him.

'But you weren't about to sit the most important exam of your life, just weeks before the wedding.'

'That's exactly why I've taken over all the arrangements,' said Elizabeth. 'That way Emma won't have any distractions until her exams are over.'

'Surely it would be better to put the wedding off for a few months. After all, what's the hurry?'

'What a good idea, Daddy,' said Emma, speaking for

the first time. 'Perhaps we could also ask Herr Hitler if he'd be kind enough to put off the war for a few months, because your daughter wants to get married.'

'And what does Mrs Clifton think about all of this?' her father asked, ignoring his daughter's comment.

'Why should she be anything other than delighted by the news?' Elizabeth asked him. He didn't respond.

◄○►

An announcement of the forthcoming marriage between Emma Grace Barrington and Harold Arthur Clifton was published in *The Times* ten days later. The first banns were read from the pulpit of St Mary's by the Reverend Styler on the following Sunday and over three hundred invitations were sent out during the next week. No one was surprised when Harry asked Giles to be his best man, with Captain Tarrant and Deakins as the principal ushers.

But Harry was shocked when he received a letter from Old Jack, declining his kind invitation because he couldn't leave his post in the current circumstances. Harry wrote back, begging him to reconsider and at least attend the wedding, even if he felt unable to take on the task of being an usher. Old Jack's reply left Harry even more confused: 'I feel my presence might turn out to be an embarrassment.'

'What is he talking about?' said Harry. 'Surely he knows that we'd all be honoured if he came.'

'He's almost as bad as my father,' said Emma. 'He's refusing to give me away, and says he's not even sure he'll come.'

'But you told me he'd promised to be more supportive in the future.'

'Yes, but that all changed the moment he heard we were engaged.'

'I can't pretend that my mother sounded all that enthusiastic when I told her the news either,' Harry admitted.

◄○►

Emma didn't see Harry again until she returned to Oxford to sit her exams, and even then not until she'd completed the final paper. When she came out of the examination hall, her fiancé was waiting on the top step, a bottle of champagne in one hand and two glasses in the other.

'So, how do you think you got on?' he asked as he filled her glass.

'I don't know,' sighed Emma, as dozens of other girls poured out of the examination hall. 'I didn't realize what I was up against until I saw that lot.'

'Well, at least you've got something to distract you while you wait for the results.'

'Just three weeks to go,' Emma reminded him. 'That's more than enough time for you to change your mind.'

'If you don't win a scholarship, I may have to reconsider my position. After all, I can't be seen associating with a commoner.'

'And if I do win a scholarship, I may have to reconsider my position and look for another scholar.'

'Deakins is still available,' said Harry as he topped up her glass.

'It will be too late by then,' said Emma.

'Why?'

'Because the results are due to be announced on the morning of our wedding.'

Emma and Harry spent most of the weekend locked away in her little hotel room, endlessly going over the wedding arrangements when they weren't making love. By Sunday night, Emma had come to one conclusion.

'Mama has been quite magnificent,' she said, 'which is more than I can say for my father.'

'Do you think he'll even turn up?'

'Oh yes. Mama's talked him into coming, but he's still refusing to give me away. What's the latest on Old Jack?'

'He hasn't even replied to my last letter,' said Harry.

47

'HAVE YOU PUT ON a little weight, darling?' asked Emma's mother as she tried to fasten the last clasp on the back of her daughter's wedding dress.

'I don't think so,' replied Emma, looking at herself critically in the full-length mirror.

'Stunning,' was Elizabeth's verdict as she stood back to admire the bride's outfit.

They had travelled to London several times to have the dress fitted by Madame Renée, the proprietor of a small, fashionable boutique in Mayfair, thought to be patronized by Queen Mary and Queen Elizabeth. Madame Renée had personally supervised each fitting, and the Victorian embroidered lace around the neck and hem, something old, blended quite naturally with the silk bodice and empire bell skirt that was proving so fashionable that year, something new. The little cream tear-drop hat, Madame Renée had assured them, was what women of fashion would be wearing next year. The only comment Emma's father made on the subject came when he saw the bill.

Elizabeth Barrington glanced at her watch. Nineteen minutes to three. 'No need to rush,' she told Emma when there was a knock on the door. She was sure she'd hung the Do Not Disturb sign on the doorknob and told the chauffeur not to expect them before three. At the rehearsal the previous day, the journey from the hotel to the church had taken seven minutes. Elizabeth intended Emma to be fashionably late. 'Keep them waiting for a few minutes, but don't give them any cause for concern.' A second knock.

'I'll get it,' Elizabeth said, and went to the door. A young porter in a smart red uniform handed her a telegram, the eleventh that day. She was about to close the door when he said, 'I was told to inform you, madam, that this one is important.'

Elizabeth's first thought was to wonder who could possibly have cancelled at the last moment. She only hoped it wouldn't mean reorganizing the top table at the reception. She tore open the telegram and read the contents.

'Who's it from?' asked Emma, adjusting the angle of her hat by another inch and wondering if it was perhaps a little too risqué.

Elizabeth handed her the telegram. Once Emma had read it, she burst into tears.

'Many congratulations, darling,' said her mother, taking a handkerchief out of her handbag and beginning to dry her daughter's tears. 'I'd hug you, but I don't want to crease your dress.'

Once Elizabeth was satisfied that Emma was ready, she spent a moment checking her own outfit in the mirror. Madame Renée had pronounced, 'You mustn't outdo your daughter on her big day, but at the same time, you can't afford to go unnoticed.' Elizabeth particularly liked the Norman Hartnell hat, even if it was not what the young were calling 'chic'.

'Time to leave,' she declared after one more look at her watch. Emma smiled as she glanced at the going-away outfit she would change into once the reception was over, when she and Harry would travel up to Scotland for their honeymoon. Lord Harvey had offered them Mulgelrie Castle for a fortnight, with the promise that no other member of the family would be allowed within ten miles of the estate during that time and, perhaps more important, Harry could ask for three portions of Highland broth every night, without a suggestion of grouse to follow.

Emma followed her mother out of the suite and along the corridor. By the time she reached the top of the staircase, she felt sure her legs were about to give way. As she descended the stairs, other guests stood aside so that nothing would impede her progress.

A porter held open the front door of the hotel for her, while Sir Walter's chauffeur stood by the back door of the Rolls so the bride could join her grandfather. As Emma sat down beside him, carefully arranging her dress, Sir Walter placed his monocle in his right eye and declared, 'You look quite beautiful, young lady. Harry is indeed a most fortunate man.'

'Thank you, Grandpa,' she said, kissing him on the cheek. She glanced out of the rear window to see her mother climbing into a second Rolls-Royce, and a moment later the two cars moved off to join the afternoon traffic as they began their sedate journey to the university church of St Mary's.

'Is Daddy at the church?' asked Emma, trying not to sound anxious.

'Among the first to arrive,' said her grandfather. 'I do believe he's already regretting allowing me the privilege of giving you away.'

'And Harry?'

'Never seen him so nervous. But Giles seems to have everything under control, which must be a first. I know he's spent the last month preparing his best man's speech.'

'We're both lucky to have the same best friend,' said Emma. 'You know, Grandpa, I once read that every bride has second thoughts on the morning of her wedding.'

'That's natural enough, my dear.'

'But I've never had a second thought about Harry,' said Emma, as they came to a halt outside the university church. 'I know we'll spend the rest of our lives together.'

She waited for her grandfather to step out of the car before she gathered up her dress and joined him on the pavement.

Her mother rushed forward to check Emma's outfit one last time before she would allow her to enter the church. Elizabeth handed her a small bouquet of pale pink roses as the two bridesmaids, Emma's younger sister Grace and her school friend Jessica, gathered up the end of the train.

'You next, Grace,' said her mother, bending down to unruffle her bridesmaid's dress.

'I hope not,' said Grace, loud enough for her mother to hear.

Elizabeth stepped back and nodded. Two sidesmen pulled open the heavy doors, the sign for the organist to strike up Wagner's *Wedding March*, and the congregation to rise and welcome the bride.

As Emma stepped into the church, she was taken by surprise to see how many people had travelled to Oxford to share in her happiness. She walked slowly down the aisle on her grandfather's arm, the guests turning to smile at her as she made her way towards the altar.

She noticed Mr Frobisher sitting next to Mr Holcombe

on the right-hand side of the aisle. Miss Tilly, who was wearing quite a daring hat, must have come all the way from Cornwall, while Dr Paget gave her the warmest of smiles. But nothing compared with the smile that appeared on her own face when she spotted Captain Tarrant, head bowed, wearing a morning suit that didn't quite fit. Harry would be so pleased he had decided to come after all. In the front row sat Mrs Clifton, who had clearly spent some time selecting her outfit because she looked so fashionable. A smile crossed Emma's lips, but she was surprised and disappointed that her future mother-in-law didn't turn to look at her as she passed.

And then she saw Harry, standing on the altar steps next to her brother as they waited for the bride. Emma continued up the aisle on the arm of one grandfather, while the other stood bolt upright in the front row, next to her father, who she thought looked a little melancholy. Perhaps he really was regretting his decision not to give her away.

Sir Walter stood to one side as Emma climbed the four steps to join her future husband. She leaned over and whispered, 'I nearly had a change of heart.' Harry tried not to grin as he waited for the punch line. 'After all, scholars of this university cannot be seen to marry beneath themselves.'

'I'm so proud of you, my darling,' he said. 'Many congratulations.'

Giles bowed low in genuine respect, and Chinese whispers broke out among the congregation as the news spread from row to row.

The music stopped, and the college chaplain raised his hands and said, '*Dearly beloved, we are gathered together here in the sight of God, and in the face of this congregation, to join together this Man and this Woman, in holy matrimony . . .*'

Emma suddenly felt nervous. She had learnt all the responses by heart but now she couldn't recall one of them.

'*First it was ordained for the procreation of children . . .*'

Emma tried to concentrate on the chaplain's words, but she couldn't wait to escape and be alone with Harry. Perhaps they should have gone up to Scotland the night before and eloped at Gretna Green; so much more convenient for Mulgelrie Castle, she'd pointed out to Harry.

'*Into which holy estate these two persons present come now to be joined. Therefore if any man can show any just cause why they may not lawfully be joined together, let him now speak, or else hereafter for ever hold his peace . . .*'

The chaplain paused, to allow a diplomatic period of time to pass before he pronounced the words, *I require and charge you both*, when a clear voice declared, 'I object!'

Emma and Harry both swung round to see who could possibly have uttered two such damning words.

The chaplain looked up in disbelief, wondering for a moment if he had misheard, but all over the church, heads were turning as the congregation tried to discover who had made the unexpected intervention. The chaplain had never experienced such a turn of events before, and tried desperately to recall what he was expected to do in the circumstances.

Emma buried her head in Harry's shoulder, while he searched among the chattering congregation, trying to find out who it was who had caused such consternation. He assumed it must be Emma's father, but when he looked down at the front row he saw Hugo Barrington, white as a sheet, was also trying to see who had brought the ceremony to a premature halt.

The Reverend Styler had to raise his voice to be heard above the growing clamour. 'Would the gentleman who has objected to this marriage taking place please make himself known.'

A tall, upright figure stepped out into the aisle. Every eye remained fixed on Captain Jack Tarrant as he made his way up to the altar before coming to a halt in front of the chaplain. Emma clung on to Harry, fearful he was about to be prised away from her.

'Am I to understand, sir,' said the chaplain, 'that you feel this marriage should not be allowed to proceed?'

'That is correct, sir,' said Old Jack quietly.

'Then I must ask you, the bride and groom and the members of their immediate family to join me in the vestry.' Raising his voice, he added, 'The congregation should remain in their places until I have considered the objection, and made my decision known.'

Those who had been bidden were led by the chaplain into the vestry, followed by Harry and Emma. Not one of them spoke, although the congregation continued to whisper noisily among themselves.

Once the two families had crammed themselves into the tiny vestry, the Reverend Styler closed the door.

'Captain Tarrant,' he began, 'I must tell you that I alone am vested by law with the authority to decide whether this marriage should continue. Naturally I shall not come to any decision until I have heard your objections.'

The only person in that overcrowded room who appeared calm was Old Jack. 'Thank you, chaplain,' he began. 'Firstly, I must apologize to you all, and in particular to Emma and Harry, for my intervention. I have spent the past few weeks wrestling with my conscience before coming to this unhappy decision. I could have taken the easy way out and simply found some excuse for not attending this ceremony today. I have remained silent until now in the hope that in time any objection would prove irrelevant. But sadly that has not proved to be the case, for Harry and Emma's love for each other has in fact grown over the years, and not diminished, which is why it has become impossible for me to remain silent any longer.'

Everyone was so gripped by Old Jack's words that only Elizabeth Barrington noticed her husband slip quietly out of the back door of the vestry.

'Thank you, Captain Tarrant,' said the Reverend Styler. 'While I accept your intervention in good faith, I need to know what specific charges you bring against these two young people.'

'I bring no charge against Harry or Emma, both of whom I love and admire, and believe to be as much in the dark as the rest of you. No, my charge is against Hugo Barrington, who has known for many years that there is a possibility that he is the father of both of these unfortunate children.'

A gasp went around the room as everyone tried to grasp the enormity of this statement. The chaplain said nothing until he was able to regain their attention. 'Is there anyone present who can verify or refute Captain Tarrant's claim?'

'This can't possibly be true,' said Emma, still clinging on to Harry. 'There must be some mistake. Surely my father can't . . .'

That was the moment everyone became aware that the father of the bride was no longer among them. The chaplain turned his attention to Mrs Clifton, who was quietly sobbing.

'I can't deny Captain Tarrant's fears,' she said haltingly. It was some time before she continued. 'I confess I did have a relationship with Mr Barrington on one occasion.' She paused again. 'Only once, but, unfortunately, it was just a few weeks before I married my husband – ' she raised her head slowly – 'so I have no way of knowing who Harry's father is.'

'I should point out to you all,' said Old Jack, 'that Hugo Barrington threatened Mrs Clifton on more than one occasion, should she ever reveal his dreadful secret.'

'Mrs Clifton, may I be allowed to ask you a question?' said Sir Walter gently.

Maisie nodded, although her head remained bowed.

'Did your late husband suffer from colour-blindness?'

'Not that I'm aware of,' she said, barely loudly enough to be heard.

Sir Walter turned to Harry. 'But I believe you do, my boy?'

'Yes I do, sir,' said Harry without hesitation. 'Why is that of any importance?'

'Because I am also colour-blind,' said Sir Walter. 'As are my son and grandson. It is a hereditary trait that has troubled our family for several generations.'

Harry took Emma in his arms. 'I swear to you, my darling, I didn't know anything about this.'

'Of course you didn't,' said Elizabeth Barrington, speaking for the first time. 'The only man who knew was my husband, and he didn't have the courage to come forward and admit it. If he had, none of this need ever have happened. Father,' she said, turning to Lord Harvey, 'can I ask you to explain to our guests why the ceremony will not be continuing.'

Lord Harvey nodded. 'Leave it to me, old gal,' he said, touching her gently on the arm. 'But what are you going to do?'

'I'm going take my daughter as far away from this place as possible.'

'I don't want to go as far away as possible,' Emma said, 'unless it's with Harry.'

'I fear your father has left us with no choice,' said Elizabeth, taking her gently by the arm. But Emma continued to cling on to Harry until he whispered, 'I'm afraid your mother's right, my darling. But one thing your father will never be able to do is stop me loving you, and if it takes the rest of my life, I'll prove he's not my father.'

'Perhaps you'd prefer to leave by the rear entrance, Mrs Barrington,' suggested the chaplain. Emma reluctantly released Harry and allowed her mother to take her away.

The chaplain led them out of the vestry and down a narrow corridor to a door that he was surprised to find unlocked. 'May God go with you, my children,' he said before letting them out.

Elizabeth accompanied her daughter around the outside of the church to the waiting Rolls-Royces. She ignored those members of the congregation who had strayed outside for some fresh air or to smoke a cigarette and now made no attempt to conceal their curiosity when they spotted the two women climbing unceremoniously into the back of the limousine.

Elizabeth had opened the door of the first Rolls and bundled her daughter into the back seat before the chauffeur spotted them. He had stationed himself by the great door as he hadn't expected the bride and groom to appear for at least another half an hour, when a peal of bells would announce the marriage of Mr and Mrs Harry Clifton to the world. The moment the chauffeur heard the door slam, he stubbed out his cigarette, ran across to the car and jumped behind the wheel.

'Take us back to the hotel,' Elizabeth said.

Neither of them spoke again until they had reached

the safety of their room. Emma lay sobbing on the bed while Elizabeth stroked her hair, the way she had when she was a child.

'What am I going to do?' cried Emma. 'I can't suddenly stop loving Harry.'

'I'm sure you never will,' said her mother, 'but fate has decreed that you cannot be together until it can be proved who Harry's father is.' She continued to stroke her daughter's hair, and thought she might even have fallen asleep, until Emma quietly added, 'What will I tell my child when they ask who their father is?'

HARRY CLIFTON

1939–1940

48

The thing I remember most after Emma and her mother had left the church was how calm everyone appeared to be. No hysterics, no one fainted, there weren't even any raised voices. A visitor might have been forgiven for not realizing how many people's lives had just been irreparably damaged, even ruined. How very British, stiff upper lip and all that; no one willing to admit that their personal life had been shattered in the space of a single hour. Well, I have to admit, mine had.

I had stood in numbed silence as the different actors played out their roles. Old Jack had done no more or less than what he considered his duty, though the pallor of his skin and the deeply etched lines on his face suggested otherwise. He could have taken the easy way out and simply declined our invitation to the wedding, but Victoria Cross winners don't walk away.

Elizabeth Barrington was cast from that metal which, when put to the test, proved she was the equal of any man: a veritable Portia, who sadly hadn't married a Brutus.

As I looked around the vestry waiting for the chaplain to return, I felt saddest for Sir Walter, who had walked his granddaughter down the aisle, and had not gained a grandson, but rather lost a son, who, as Old Jack had warned me so many years ago, 'was not cut from the same cloth' as his father.

My dear mother was fearful to respond when I tried to take her in my arms and reassure her of my love. She clearly believed she alone was to blame for everything that had taken place that day.

And Giles, he became a man when his father crept out of the vestry to hide under some slimy stone, leaving the responsibility for his actions to others. In time, many of those present would become aware that what had taken place that day was every bit as devastating for Giles as for Emma.

Finally, Lord Harvey. He was an example to us all of how to behave in a crisis. Once the chaplain had returned and explained the legal implications of consanguinity to us, we agreed among ourselves that Lord Harvey should address the waiting congregation on behalf of both families.

'I would like Harry to stand on my right,' he said, 'as I wish everyone present to be left in no doubt, as my daughter Elizabeth made abundantly clear, that no blame rests on his shoulders.

'Mrs Clifton,' he said, turning to my mother, 'I hope you will be kind enough to stand on my left. Your courage in adversity has been an example to us all, and to one of us in particular.

'I hope that Captain Tarrant will stand by Harry's side: only a fool blames the messenger. Giles should take his place beside him. Sir Walter, perhaps you would stand next to Mrs Clifton, while the rest of the family take their places behind us. Let me make it clear to you all,' he continued, 'that I only have one purpose in this tragic business, namely to ensure that everyone gathered in this church today will be in no doubt of our resolve in this matter, so that no one will ever say we were a divided house.'

Without another word, he led his small flock out of the vestry.

When the chattering congregation saw us filing back into the church, Lord Harvey didn't need to call for silence. Each one of us took our allocated place on the altar steps as if we were about to pose for a family photograph that would later find its way into a wedding album.

'Friends, if I may be so bold,' began Lord Harvey, 'I have been asked to let you know on behalf of our two families that sadly the marriage between my granddaughter, Emma Barrington, and Mr Harry Clifton will not be taking place today, or for that matter on any other day.' Those last four words had a finality about them that was chilling when you were the only person present who still clung on to a vestige of hope that this might one day be resolved. 'I must apologize to you all,' he continued, 'if you have been inconvenienced in any way for that was surely not our purpose. May I conclude by thanking you for your presence here today, and wish you all a safe journey home.'

I wasn't sure what would happen next, but one or two members of the congregation rose from their places and began to make their way slowly out of the church; within moments the trickle turned into a steady stream, until finally those of us standing on the altar steps were the only ones remaining.

Lord Harvey thanked the chaplain, and warmly shook hands with me before accompanying his wife down the aisle and out of the church.

My mother turned to me and tried to speak, but was overcome by her emotions. Old Jack came to our rescue, taking her gently by the arm and leading her away, while Sir Walter took Grace and Jessica under his wing. Not a day mothers or bridesmaids would want to recall for the rest of their lives.

Giles and I were the last to leave. He had entered the church as my best man, and now he left it wondering if he was my half-brother. Some people stand by you in your darkest hour, while others walk away; only a select few march towards you and become even closer friends.

Once we had bidden farewell to the Reverend Styler, who seemed unable to find the words to express how sorry he felt, Giles and I trudged wearily across the cobbled stones of the quad and back to our college. Not a word passed between us as we climbed the wooden staircase to my rooms and sank into old leather chairs and young maudlin silence.

We sat alone as day turned slowly into night. Sparse conversation that had no sequence, no meaning, no logic. When the first long shadows appeared, those heralds of darkness that so often loosen the tongue, Giles asked me a question I hadn't thought about for years.

'Do you remember the first time you and Deakins visited the Manor House?'

'How could I forget? It was your twelfth birthday, and your father refused to shake hands with me.'

'Have you ever wondered why?'

'I think we found out the reason today,' I said, trying not to sound too insensitive.

'No, we didn't,' said Giles quietly. 'What we found out today was the possibility that Emma might be your half-sister. I now realize the reason my father kept his affair with your mother secret for so many years was because he was far more worried you might find out you were his son.'

'I don't understand the difference,' I said, staring at him.

'Then it's important for you to recall the only question my father asked on that occasion.'

'He asked when my birthday was.'

'That's right, and when he discovered you were a few

weeks older than me, he left the room without another word. And later, when we had to leave to go back to school, he didn't come out of his study to say goodbye, even though it was my birthday. It wasn't until today that I realized the significance of his actions.'

'How can that minor incident still be of any significance after all these years?' I asked.

'Because that was the moment my father realized you might be his first born, and that when he dies it could be you, not me, who inherits the family title, the business, and all his worldly goods.'

'But surely your father can leave his possessions to whomever he pleases, and that certainly wouldn't be me.'

'I wish it was that simple,' said Giles, 'but as my grandpa so regularly reminds me, his father, Sir Joshua Barrington, was knighted by Queen Victoria in 1877 for services to the shipping industry. In his will, he stated that all his titles, deeds and possessions were to be left to the first-born surviving son, in perpetuity.'

'But I have no interest in claiming what clearly is not mine,' I said, trying to reassure him.

'I'm sure you don't,' said Giles, 'but you may have no choice in the matter, because in the fullness of time, the law will require you to take your place as head of the Barrington family.'

—<o>—

Giles left me just after midnight to drive to Gloucestershire. He promised to find out if Emma was willing to see me, as we'd parted without even saying goodbye, and said he would return to Oxford the moment he had any news.

I didn't sleep that night. So many thoughts were racing through my mind, and for a moment, just a moment, I even contemplated suicide. But I didn't need Old Jack to remind me that that was the coward's way out.

I didn't leave my rooms for the next three days. I didn't respond to gentle knocks on the door. I didn't answer the telephone when it rang. I didn't open the letters that were pushed under the door. It may have been inconsiderate of me not to respond to those who had only kindness in their hearts, but sometimes an abundance of sympathy can be more overwhelming than solitude.

Giles returned to Oxford on the fourth day. He didn't need to speak for me to realize his news wasn't going to give me succour. It turned out to be far worse than I had even anticipated. Emma and her mother had left for Mulgelrie Castle, where we had meant to be spending our honeymoon, with no relations to be allowed within ten miles. Mrs Barrington had instructed her solicitors to begin divorce proceedings, but they were unable to serve any papers on her husband as no one had seen him since he'd crept unnoticed out of the vestry. Lord Harvey and Old Jack had both resigned from the board of Barrington's, but out of respect for Sir Walter neither had made their reasons for doing so public – not that that would stop the rumour-mongers having a field day. My mother had left Eddie's Nightclub and taken a job as a waitress in the dining room of the Grand Hotel.

'What about Emma?' I said. 'Did you ask her . . .'

'I didn't have a chance to speak to her,' said Giles. 'They'd left for Scotland before I arrived. But she'd left a letter for you on the hall table.' I could feel my heart beating faster as he handed me an envelope bearing her familiar handwriting. 'If you feel like a little supper later, I'll be in my rooms.'

'Thank you,' I said, inadequately.

I sat in my chair by the window overlooking Cobb's quad, not wanting to open a letter that I knew wouldn't offer me a glimmer of hope. I finally tore open the envelope and extracted three pages written in Emma's neat hand. Even then, it was some time before I could read her words.

> The Manor House
> Chew Valley
> Gloucestershire

July 29th, 1939

My Darling Harry,

It's the middle of the night, and I am sitting in my bedroom writing to the only man I will ever love.

Deep hatred for my father, whom I can never forgive, has been replaced by a sudden calm, so I must write these words before bitter recrimination returns to remind me of just how much that treacherous man has denied us both.

I only wish we'd been allowed to part as lovers, and not as strangers in a crowded room, the fates having decided we should never say the words 'until death do us part', although I am certain I will go to my grave only having loved one man.

I will never be satisfied with just the memory of your love, for while there is the slightest hope that Arthur Clifton was your father, be assured, my darling, that I will remain constant.

Mama is convinced that given enough time, the memory of you, like the evening sun, will fade, and then finally disappear, before heralding a new dawn. Does she not recall telling me on the day of my wedding that our love for each other was so pure, so simple and so rare, that it would unquestionably withstand the test of time, which Mama confessed she could only envy, as she had never experienced such happiness.

But until I can be your wife, my darling, I am

*resolved that we must remain apart, unless, and until
such time, it can be shown that we can be legally
bound. No other man can hope to take your place and,
if necessary, I will remain single, rather than settle for
some counterfeit.*

*I wonder if the day will dawn when I do not reach
out, expecting to find you by my side, and if it will ever
be possible to fall asleep without whispering your name.*

*I would happily sacrifice the rest of my life to spend
another year like the one we have just shared together,
and no law made by God or man can change that. I still
pray that the day will come when we can be joined
together in the sight of that same God and those same
men, but until then, my darling, I will always be your
loving wife in all but name,*

Emma

49

WHEN HARRY FINALLY summoned up the strength to
open the countless letters that littered the floor, he came
across one from Old Jack's secretary in London.

> Soho Square
> London
>
> Wednesday, August 2nd, 1939
>
> Dear Mr Clifton,
>
> You may not receive this letter until you've returned
> from your honeymoon in Scotland, but I wondered
> if Captain Tarrant stayed on in Oxford after the
> wedding. He didn't return to the office on Monday
> morning, and he hasn't been seen since, so I
> wondered if you had any idea where I might contact
> him.
>
> I look forward to hearing from you.
> Yours sincerely,
>
> Phyllis Watson

Old Jack had clearly forgotten to let Miss Watson
know he was going down to Bristol to spend a few days

with Sir Walter, to make it clear that, although he had caused the wedding to be abandoned and had resigned from the board of Barrington's, he remained a close friend of the chairman's. As there wasn't a second letter from Miss Watson among his pile of unopened mail, Harry assumed that Old Jack must have returned to Soho Square and be back behind his desk.

Harry spent the morning answering every one of the letters he'd left unopened; so many kind people offering sympathy – it wasn't their fault they reminded him of his unhappiness. Suddenly Harry decided he had to be as far away from Oxford as possible. He picked up the phone and told the operator he wanted to make a long-distance call to London. Half an hour later, she called back to tell him the number was continually engaged. Next, he tried Sir Walter at Barrington Hall, but the number just rang and rang. Frustrated by his failure to contact either of them, Harry decided to follow one of Old Jack's maxims: *Get off your backside and do something positive.*

He grabbed the suitcase he had packed for his honeymoon in Scotland, walked across to the lodge and told the porter he was going up to London and wouldn't be returning until the first day of term. 'Should Giles Barrington ask where I am,' he added, 'please tell him I've gone to work for Old Jack.'

'Old Jack,' repeated the porter, writing the name down on a slip of paper.

On the train journey to Paddington, Harry read in *The Times* about the latest communiqués that were bouncing back and forth between the Foreign Office in London and the Reich Ministry in Berlin. He was beginning to think that Mr Chamberlain was the only person who still believed in the possibility of peace in our time. *The Times* was predicting that Britain would be at war within days and that the Prime Minister couldn't hope to survive in office if the Germans defied his ultimatum and marched into Poland.

The Thunderer went on to suggest that in that eventuality, a coalition government would have to be formed, led by the Foreign Secretary, Lord Halifax (a safe pair of hands), and not Winston Churchill (unpredictable and irascible). Despite the paper's obvious distaste for Churchill, Harry didn't believe that Britain needed a 'safe pair of hands' at this particular moment in history, but someone who was not frightened to bully a bully.

When Harry stepped off the train at Paddington, he was met by a wave of different coloured uniforms coming at him from every direction. He'd already decided which service he would join the moment war was declared. A morbid thought crossed his mind as he boarded a bus for Piccadilly Circus: if he was killed while serving his country, it would solve all the Barrington family's problems – except one.

When the bus reached Piccadilly, Harry jumped off and began to weave his way through the clowns that made up the West End circus, through theatre land and on past exclusive restaurants and overpriced nightclubs, which appeared determined to ignore any suggestion of war. The queue of displaced immigrants trooping in and out of the building in Soho Square appeared even longer and more bedraggled than on Harry's first visit. Once again, as he climbed the stairs to the third floor, several of the refugees stood aside, assuming he must be a member of staff. He hoped he would be within the hour.

When he reached the third floor, he headed straight for Miss Watson's office. He found her filling in forms, issuing rail warrants, arranging accommodation and handing out small amounts of cash to desperate people. Her face lit up when she saw Harry. 'Do tell me Captain Tarrant's with you,' were her first words.

'No, he isn't,' said Harry. 'I assumed he'd returned to London, which is why I'm here. I was wondering if you might be able to use an extra pair of hands.'

'That's very kind of you, Harry,' she said, 'but the most useful thing you could do for me right now is to find Captain Tarrant. This place is bursting at the seams without him.'

'The last I heard he was staying with Sir Walter Barrington at his home in Gloucester,' said Harry, 'but that was at least a fortnight ago.'

'We haven't set eyes on him since the day he went to Oxford for your wedding,' said Miss Watson as she tried to comfort two more immigrants who couldn't speak a word of English.

'Has anyone phoned his flat to see if he's there?' asked Harry.

'He doesn't have a phone,' said Miss Watson, 'and I've hardly been to my own home for the past two weeks,' she added, nodding in the direction of a queue that stretched as far as the eye could see.

'Why don't I start there, and report back to you?'

'Would you?' said Miss Watson as two little girls began sobbing. 'Don't cry, everything's going to be all right,' she reassured the children as she knelt and placed an arm round them.

'Where does he live?' asked Harry.

'Number twenty-three, Prince Edward Mansions, Lambeth Walk. Take the number eleven bus to Lambeth, then you'll have to ask for directions. And thank you, Harry.'

Harry turned and headed towards the stairs. Something wasn't right, he thought. Old Jack would never have deserted his post without giving Miss Watson a reason.

'I forgot to ask,' Miss Watson shouted after him, 'how was your honeymoon?'

Harry felt he was far enough away not to have heard her.

Back at Piccadilly Circus he boarded a double-decker bus overcrowded with soldiers. It drove down Whitehall, which was full of officers, and on through Parliament Square, where a vast crowd of onlookers was waiting for any snippets of information that might come out of the House of Commons. The bus continued its journey across Lambeth Bridge, and Harry got off when it reached Albert Embankment.

A paperboy who was shouting *'Britain Awaits Hitler's Response'* told Harry to take the second on the left, then the third on the right, and added for good measure, 'I thought everyone knew where Lambeth Walk was.'

Harry began to run like a man being pursued and he didn't stop until he came to a block of flats that was so dilapidated he could only wonder which Prince Edward it had been named after. He pushed open a door that wouldn't survive much longer on those hinges and walked quickly up a flight of stairs, stepping nimbly between piles of rubbish that hadn't been cleared for days.

When he reached the second floor, he stopped outside No. 23 and knocked firmly on the door, but there was no reply. He knocked again, louder, but still no one responded. He ran back down the stairs in search of someone who worked in the building, and when he reached the basement he found an old man slumped in an even older chair, smoking a roll-up and flicking through the pages of the *Daily Mirror*.

'Have you seen Captain Tarrant recently?' Harry asked sharply.

'Not for the past couple of weeks, sir,' said the man, leaping to his feet and almost standing to attention when he heard Harry's accent.

'Do you have a master key that will open his flat?' asked Harry.

'I do, sir, but I'm not allowed to use it except in emergencies.'

'I can assure you this is an emergency,' said Harry, who turned and bounded back up the stairs, not waiting for his reply.

The man followed, if not quite as quickly. Once he'd caught up, he opened the door. Harry moved quickly from room to room, but there was no sign of Old Jack. The last door he came to was closed. He knocked quietly, fearing the worst. When there was no reply, he cautiously went in, to find a neatly made bed and no sign of anyone. He must still be with Sir Walter, was Harry's first thought.

He thanked the porter, walked back down the stairs and out on to the street as he tried to gather his thoughts. He hailed a passing taxi, not wanting to waste any more time on buses in a city that did not know him.

'Paddington Station. I'm in a hurry.'

'Everyone seems to be in a hurry today,' said the cabbie as he moved off.

Twenty minutes later Harry was standing on platform 6, but it was another fifty minutes before the train would depart for Temple Meads. He used the time to grab a sandwich and a cup of tea – 'Only got cheese, sir' – and to phone Miss Watson to let her know that Old Jack hadn't been back to his flat. If it was possible, she sounded even more harassed than when he had left her. 'I'm on my way to Bristol,' he told her. 'I'll ring you as soon as I catch up with him.'

As the train made its way out of the capital, through

the smog-filled back streets of the city and into the clean air of the countryside, Harry decided he had no choice but to go straight to Sir Walter's office at the dockyard, even if it meant running into Hugo Barrington. Finding Old Jack surely outweighed any other consideration.

Once the train shunted into Temple Meads, Harry knew the two buses he needed to catch without having to ask the paperboy who was standing on the corner bellowing 'Britain Awaits Hitler's Response' at the top of his voice. Same headline, but this time a Bristolian accent. Thirty minutes later, Harry was at the dockyard gates.

'Can I help you?' asked a guard who didn't recognize him.

'I have an appointment with Sir Walter,' said Harry, hoping this would not be questioned.

'Of course, sir. Do you know the way to his office?'

'Yes, thank you,' said Harry. He started walking slowly towards a building he'd never entered before. He began to think about what he would do if he came face to face with Hugo Barrington before he reached Sir Walter's office.

He was pleased to see the chairman's Rolls-Royce parked in its usual place, and even more relieved that there was no sign of Hugo Barrington's Bugatti. He was just about to enter Barrington House when he glanced at the railway carriage in the distance. Was it just possible? He changed direction and walked towards the Pullman *wagon lit*, as Old Jack was wont to describe it after a second glass of whisky.

When Harry reached the carriage he knocked gently on the glass pane as if it were a grand home. A butler did not appear, so he opened the door and climbed in. He walked along the corridor to first class, and there he was, sitting in his usual seat.

It was the first time Harry had ever seen Old Jack wearing his Victoria Cross.

Harry took the seat opposite his friend and recalled the first time he'd sat there. He must have been about five and his feet hadn't reached the ground. Then he thought of the time he'd run away from St Bede's, and the shrewd old gentleman had persuaded him to be back in time for breakfast. He recalled when Old Jack had come to hear him sing a solo in the church, the time his voice had broken. Old Jack had dismissed this as a minor setback. Then there was the day he learnt he'd failed to win a scholarship to Bristol Grammar School, a major setback. Despite his failure, Old Jack had presented him with the Ingersoll watch he was still wearing today. It must have cost him every penny he possessed. In Harry's last year at school, Old Jack had travelled down from London to see him playing Romeo, and Harry had introduced him to Emma for the first time. And he would never forget his final speech day, when Jack had sat on stage as a governor of his old school and watched Harry being awarded the English prize.

And now, Harry would never be able to thank him for so many acts of friendship over the years that couldn't be repaid. He stared at a man he'd loved and had assumed would never die. As they sat there together in first class, the sun went down on his young life.

50

HARRY WATCHED AS the stretcher was placed in the ambulance. A heart attack, the doctor had said, before the ambulance drove away.

Harry didn't need to go and tell Sir Walter that Old Jack was dead, because when he woke the following morning, the chairman of Barrington's was sitting by his side.

'He told me he no longer had any reason to live,' were Sir Walter's first words. 'We have both lost a close and dear friend.'

Harry's response took Sir Walter by surprise. 'What will you do with this carriage, now that Old Jack is no longer around?'

'No one will be allowed anywhere near it, as long as I'm chairman,' said Sir Walter. 'It harbours too many personal memories for me.'

'Me too,' said Harry. 'I spent more time here when I was a boy than I did in my own home.'

'Or in the classroom for that matter,' said Sir Walter with a wry smile. 'I used to watch you from my office window. I thought what an impressive child you must be if Old Jack was willing to spend so much time with you.'

Harry smiled when he remembered how Old Jack

had come up with a reason why he should go back to school and learn to read and write.

'What will you do now, Harry? Return to Oxford and continue with your studies?'

'No, sir. I fear that we'll be at war by . . .'

'By the end of the month would be my guess,' said Sir Walter.

'Then I'll leave Oxford immediately and join the navy. I've already told my college supervisor, Mr Bainbridge, that that's what I plan to do. He assured me I can return and continue with my studies as soon as the war is over.'

'Typical of Oxford,' said Sir Walter, 'they always take the long view. So will you go to Dartmouth and train as a naval officer?'

'No, sir, I've been around ships all my life. In any case, Old Jack started out as a private soldier and managed to work his way up through the ranks, so why shouldn't I?'

'Why not indeed?' said Sir Walter. 'In fact, that was one of the reasons he was always considered to be a class above the rest of us who served with him.'

'I had no idea you'd served together.'

'Oh yes, I served with Captain Tarrant in South Africa,' said Sir Walter. 'I was one of the twenty-four men whose lives he saved on the day he was awarded the Victoria Cross.'

'That explains so much that I've never really understood,' said Harry. He then surprised Sir Walter a second time. 'Do I know any of the others, sir?'

'The Frob,' said Sir Walter. 'But in those days he was Lieutenant Frobisher. Corporal Holcombe, Mr Holcombe's father. And young Private Deakins.'

'Deakins's father?' said Harry.

'Yes. Sprogg, as we used to call him. A fine young soldier. He never said much, but he turned out to be very brave. Lost an arm on that dreadful day.'

The two men fell silent, each lost in his own thoughts of Old Jack, before Sir Walter asked, 'So if you're not going to Dartmouth, my boy, may I ask how you plan to win the war single-handed?'

'I'll serve on any ship that will take me, sir, as long as they're willing to go in search of His Britannic Majesty's enemies.'

'Then it's possible I may be able to help.'

'That's kind of you, sir, but I want to join a war ship, not a passenger liner or a cargo vessel.'

Sir Walter smiled again. 'And so you will, dear boy. Don't forget, I'm kept informed about every ship that comes in and out of these docks and I know most of their captains. Come to think of it, I knew most of their fathers when they were captains. Why don't we go up to my office and see what ships are due in and out of the port in the next few days, and, more important, find out if any of them might be willing to take you on?'

'That's very decent of you, sir, but would it be all right if I visited my mother first? I might not have the chance to see her again for some time.'

'Only right and proper, my boy,' said Sir Walter. 'And once you've been to see your mother, why don't you drop into my office later this afternoon? That should give me enough time to check on the latest shipping lists.'

'Thank you, sir. I'll return as soon as I've told my mother what I plan to do.'

'When you come back, just tell the man on the gate you've got an appointment with the chairman, then you shouldn't have any trouble getting past security.'

'Thank you, sir,' said Harry, masking a smile.

'And do pass on my kindest regards to your dear mother. A remarkable woman.'

Harry was reminded why Sir Walter was Old Jack's closest friend.

◄○►

Harry walked into the Grand Hotel, a magnificent Victorian building in the centre of the city, and asked the doorman the way to the dining room. He walked across the lobby and was surprised to find a small queue at the maître d's desk, waiting to be allocated tables. He joined the back of the queue, recalling how his mother had always disapproved of him dropping in to see her at Tilly's or the Royal Hotel during working hours.

While Harry waited, he looked around the dining room, which was full of chattering people, none of whom looked as if they were anticipating a food shortage, or thinking of enlisting in the armed forces should the country go to war. Food was being whisked in and out of the swing doors on heavily laden silver trays, while a man in a chef's outfit was wheeling a trolley from table to table, slicing off slivers of beef, while another followed in his wake carrying a gravy boat.

Harry could see no sign of his mother. He was even beginning to wonder if Giles had only told him what he wanted to hear, when suddenly she burst through the swing doors, three plates balanced on her arms. She placed them in front of her customers so deftly they hardly noticed she was there, then returned to the kitchen. She was back a moment later, carrying three vegetable dishes. By the time Harry had reached the front of the queue he'd been reminded of who had given him his boundless energy, uncritical enthusiasm and a spirit that didn't contemplate defeat. How would he ever be able to repay this remarkable woman for all the sacrifices she had made—

'I'm sorry to have kept you waiting, sir,' said the maître d', interrupting his thoughts, 'but I don't have a table available at the moment. If you'd care to come back in about twenty minutes?'

Harry didn't tell him he didn't actually want a table, and not just because his mother was one of the wait-resses, but because he wouldn't have been able to afford anything on the menu other than perhaps the gravy.

'I'll come back later,' he said, trying to sound disap-pointed. About ten years later, he thought, by which time he suspected his mother would probably be the maître d'. He left the hotel with a smile on his face and took a bus back to the docks.

He was ushered straight through to Sir Walter's office by his secretary and found the chairman leaning on his desk, peering down at the port schedules, timetables and ocean charts that covered every inch of its surface.

'Have a seat, dear boy,' said Sir Walter, before fixing his monocle in his right eye and looking sternly at Harry. 'I've had a little time to think about our conversation this morning,' he continued, sounding very serious, 'and before we go any further, I need to be convinced that you're making the right decision.'

'I'm absolutely certain,' said Harry without hesita-tion.

'That may be, but I'm equally certain that Jack would have advised you to return to Oxford and wait until you were called up.'

'He may well have done so, sir, but he wouldn't have taken his own advice.'

'How well you knew him,' said Sir Walter. 'Indeed,

that's exactly what I expected you to say. Let me tell you what I've come up with so far,' he continued, returning his attention to the papers that covered his desk. 'The good news is that the Royal Navy battleship HMS *Resolution* is due to dock at Bristol in about a month's time, when it will refuel before awaiting further orders.'

'A month?' said Harry, making no attempt to hide his frustration.

'Patience, boy,' said Sir Walter. 'The reason I chose the *Resolution* is because the captain is an old friend, and I'm confident I can get you on board as a deckhand, as long as the other part of my plan works out.'

'But would the captain of the *Resolution* consider taking on someone with no seafaring experience?'

'Probably not, but if everything else falls into place, by the time you board the *Resolution* you will be an old sea dog.'

Recalling one of Old Jack's favourite homilies, *I find I don't learn a lot while I'm talking*, Harry decided to stop interrupting and start listening.

'Now,' Sir Walter continued, 'I've identified three ships that are due to leave Bristol in the next twenty-four hours and are expected to return within three to four weeks, which will give you more than enough time to sign up as a deckhand on the *Resolution*.'

Harry wanted to interrupt, but didn't.

'Let's begin with my first choice. The *Devonian* is bound for Cuba, with a manifest of cotton dresses, potatoes and Raleigh Lenton bicycles, and is due to return to Bristol in four weeks' time with a cargo of tobacco, sugar and bananas.

'The second ship on my shortlist is the SS *Kansas Star*, a passenger vessel that will be sailing to New York on the first tide tomorrow. It has been requisitioned by the United States government to transport American nationals back home before Britain finds itself at war with Germany.

'The third is an empty oil tanker, the SS *Princess Beatrice*, which is on its way back to Amsterdam to refuel and will return to Bristol with a full load before the end of the month. All three skippers are painfully aware that they need to be safely back in port as quickly as possible, because if war is declared, the two merchant vessels will be considered fair game by the Germans, while only the *Kansas Star* will be safe from the German U-boats skulking around the Atlantic just waiting for the order to sink anything flying a red or blue ensign.'

'What crew are these ships in need of?' asked Harry. 'I'm not exactly over-qualified.'

Sir Walter searched around his desk again, before extracting another sheet of paper. 'The *Princess Beatrice* is short of a deckhand, the *Kansas Star* is looking for someone to work in the kitchens, which usually means as a washer-upper or a waiter, while the *Devonian* needs a fourth officer.'

'So that one can be removed from the shortlist.'

'Funnily enough,' said Sir Walter, 'that's the position I consider you best qualified for. The *Devonian* has a crew of thirty-seven, and rarely goes to sea with a trainee officer, so no one would expect you to be anything other than a novice.'

'But why would the captain consider me?'

'Because I told him you were my grandson.'

51

HARRY WALKED ALONG the dock towards the *Devonian*. The small suitcase he was carrying made him feel
like a schoolboy on his first day of term. What would the
headmaster be like? Would he sleep in a bed next to a
Giles or a Deakins? Would he come across an Old Jack?
Would there be a Fisher on board?

Although Sir Walter had offered to accompany him
and introduce him to the captain, Harry had felt that
would not be the best way to endear himself to his new
shipmates.

He stopped for a moment and looked closely at the
ancient vessel on which he would be spending the next
month. Sir Walter had told him that the *Devonian* had
been built in 1913, when the oceans were still dominated by sail and a motorized cargo vessel would have
been thought the latest thing. But now, twenty-six years
later, it wouldn't be too long before she was decommis-
sioned and taken to that area of the docks where old
ships are broken up and their parts sold for scrap.

Sir Walter had also hinted that as Captain Havens
only had one more year to serve before he retired, the
owners might decide to scrap him at the same time as
his ship.

The *Devonian*'s Articles of Agreement showed a

crew of thirty-seven, but as on so many cargo ships, that number wasn't quite accurate: a cook and a washer-up picked up in Hong Kong didn't appear on the payroll, nor did the occasional deckhand or two who was fleeing the law and had no desire to return to his homeland.

Harry made his way slowly up the gangway. Once he'd stepped on deck, he didn't move until he'd received permission to board. After all his years of hanging around the docks, he was well aware of ship's protocol. He looked up at the bridge and assumed the man he saw giving orders must be Captain Havens. Sir Walter had told him the senior officer on a cargo vessel was in fact a master mariner but should always be addressed on board as captain. Captain Havens was a shade under six foot, and looked nearer fifty than sixty. He was stockily built, with a weathered, tanned face and a dark neatly trimmed beard that, as he was going bald, made him look like George V.

When he spotted Harry waiting at the top of the gangway, the captain gave a crisp order to the officer standing next to him on the bridge, before making his way down on to the deck.

'I'm Captain Havens,' he said briskly. 'You must be Harry Clifton.' He shook Harry warmly by the hand. 'Welcome aboard the *Devonian*. You come highly recommended.'

'I should point out, sir,' began Harry, 'that this is my first—'

'I'm aware of that,' said Havens, lowering his voice, 'but I'd keep it to yourself if you don't want your time on board to be a living hell. And whatever you do, don't mention you were at Oxford, because most of this lot,' he said, indicating the seamen working on the deck, 'will think it's just the name of another ship. Follow me. I'll show you the fourth officer's quarters.'

Harry followed in the captain's wake, aware that a dozen suspicious eyes were watching his every move.

'There are two other officers on my ship,' said the captain once Harry had caught up with him. 'Jim Patterson, the senior engineer, spends most of his life down below in the boiler room, so you'll only see him at mealtimes, and sometimes not even then. He's served with me for the past fourteen years, and frankly I doubt if this old lady would still make it halfway across the Channel, let alone the Atlantic, if he wasn't down there to coax her along. My third officer, Tom Bradshaw, is on the bridge. He's only been with me for three years, so he's not yet earned his ticket. He keeps himself to himself, but whoever trained him knew what they were doing, because he's a damn fine officer.'

Havens began to disappear down a narrow stairwell that led to the deck below. 'That's my cabin,' he said as he continued down the corridor, 'and that's Mr Patterson's.' He came to a halt in front of what appeared to be a broom cupboard. 'This is your cabin.' He pushed the door open but it only moved a few inches before it banged against a narrow wooden bed. 'I won't come in as there isn't room for both of us. You'll find some clothes on the bed. Once you've changed, join me on the bridge. We'll be setting sail within the hour. Leaving the harbour will probably be the most interesting part of the voyage until we dock in Cuba.'

Harry squeezed through the half-open door and had to close it behind him to allow enough room to change his clothes. He checked the gear that had been left, neatly folded, on his bunk: two thick blue sweaters, two white shirts, two pairs of blue trousers, three pairs of blue woollen socks and a pair of canvas shoes with thick rubber soles. It really was like being back at school. Every item had one thing in common: they all looked as if they'd been worn by several other people before Harry. He quickly changed into his seaman's gear, then unpacked his suitcase.

As there was only one drawer, Harry placed the little suitcase, full of his civilian clothes, under the bed – the only thing in the cabin that fitted perfectly. He opened the door, squeezed back into the corridor and went in search of the stairwell. Once he'd located it, he emerged back on deck. Several more pairs of suspicious eyes followed his progress.

'Mr Clifton,' said the captain as Harry stepped on to the bridge for the first time, 'this is Tom Bradshaw, the third officer, who will be taking the ship out of the harbour as soon as we've been given clearance by the port authority. By the way, Mr Bradshaw,' said Havens, 'one of our tasks on this voyage will be to teach this young pup everything we know, so that when we return to Bristol in a month's time the crew of HMS *Resolution* will mistake him for an old sea dog.'

If Mr Bradshaw commented, his words were drowned by two long blasts on a siren, a sound Harry had heard many times over the years, indicating that the two tug boats were in place and waiting to escort the *Devonian* out of the harbour. The captain pressed some tobacco into his well-worn briar pipe, while Mr Bradshaw acknowledged the signal with two blasts of the ship's horn, to confirm that the *Devonian* was ready to depart.

'Prepare to cast off, Mr Bradshaw,' said Captain Havens, striking a match.

Mr Bradshaw removed the cover from a brass voice-pipe Harry hadn't noticed until that moment. 'All engines slow ahead, Mr Patterson. The tug boats are in place and ready to escort us out of harbour,' he added, revealing a slight American accent.

'All engines slow ahead, Mr Bradshaw,' came back a voice from the boiler room.

Harry looked down over the side of the bridge and watched as the crew carried out their allotted tasks. Four men, two at the bow and two at the stern, were unwinding thick ropes from the capstans on the dock. Another two were hauling up the gangway. 'Keep your eye on the pilot,' said the captain between puffs on his pipe. 'It's his responsibility to guide us out of the harbour and safely into the Channel. Once he's done that, Mr Bradshaw will take over. If you turn out to be any good, Mr Clifton, you may be allowed to take his place in about a year's time, but not until I've retired and Mr Bradshaw has taken over command.' As Bradshaw didn't give even the flicker of a smile, Harry remained silent and continued to watch everything going on around him. 'No one is allowed to take my girl out at night,' continued Captain Havens, 'unless I'm sure he won't take any liberties with her.' Again, Bradshaw didn't smile, but then he may have heard the comment before.

Harry found himself fascinated by how smoothly the whole operation was carried out. The *Devonian* eased away from the quayside and, with the help of the two tug boats, nosed her way slowly out of the docks, along the River Avon and under the suspension bridge.

'Do you know who built that bridge, Mr Clifton?' the captain asked, taking his pipe out of his mouth.

'Isambard Kingdom Brunel, sir,' said Harry.

'And why did he never live to see it opened?'

'Because the local council ran out of money, and he died before the bridge was completed.'

The captain scowled. 'Next you'll be telling me it's named after you,' he said, putting his pipe back in his mouth. He didn't speak again until the tug boats had reached Barry Island, when they gave two more long blasts, released their lines and headed back to port.

The *Devonian* may have been an old lady, but it soon became clear to Harry that Captain Havens and his crew knew exactly how to handle her.

'Take over, Mr Bradshaw,' said the captain, as another pair of eyes appeared on the bridge, their owner carrying two mugs of hot tea. 'There will be three officers on the bridge during this crossing, Lu, so be sure that Mr Clifton also gets a mug of tea.' The Chinaman nodded and disappeared below deck.

Once the harbour lights had disappeared over the horizon, the waves became larger and larger, causing the ship to roll from side to side. Havens and Bradshaw stood, feet apart, appearing to be glued to the deck, while Harry found himself regularly having to cling on to something to make sure he didn't fall over. When the Chinaman reappeared with a third mug of tea, Harry chose not to mention to the captain that it was cold, and that his mother usually added a lump of sugar.

Just as Harry was beginning to feel a little more confident, almost enjoying the experience, the captain said, 'Not much more you can do tonight, Mr Clifton. Why don't you go below and try to catch some shut-eye. Be back on the bridge by seven twenty to take over the breakfast watch.' Harry was about to protest, when a smile appeared on Mr Bradshaw's face for the first time.

'Goodnight, sir,' said Harry before making his way down the steps and on to the deck. He wobbled slowly towards the narrow stairwell, feeling with every step he took that he was being watched by even more eyes. One voice said, loud enough for him to hear, 'He must be a passenger.'

'No, he's an officer,' said a second voice.

'What's the difference?' Several men laughed.

Once he was back in his cabin, he undressed and climbed on to the thin wooden bunk. He tried to find a comfortable position without falling out or rolling into the wall as the ship swayed from side to side as well as lurching up and down. He didn't even have a wash basin to be sick in, or a porthole to be sick out of.

As he lay awake, his thoughts turned to Emma. He wondered if she was still in Scotland or had returned to the Manor House, or perhaps she'd already taken up residence at Oxford. Would Giles be wondering where he was, or had Sir Walter told him he'd gone to sea and would be joining the *Resolution* the moment he landed back in Bristol? And would his mother be wondering where he could be? Perhaps he should have broken her golden rule and interrupted her at work. Finally, he thought about Old Jack, and suddenly felt guilty when he realized he wouldn't be back in time for his funeral.

What Harry couldn't know was that his own funeral would take place before Old Jack's.

52

HARRY WAS WOKEN BY the sound of four bells. He leapt up, hitting his head on the ceiling, threw on his clothes, squeezed into the corridor, shot up the stairwell, ran across the deck and bounded up the steps on to the bridge.

'Sorry I'm late, sir, I must have overslept.'

'You don't have to call me sir when we're on our own,' said Bradshaw, 'the name's Tom. And as a matter of fact, you're over an hour early. The skipper obviously forgot to tell you it's seven bells for the breakfast watch, and four for the six o'clock watch. But as you're here, why don't you take over the wheel while I take a leak.' The shock for Harry was to realize that Bradshaw wasn't joking. 'Just be sure the arrow on the compass is always pointing sou'-sou'-west, then you can't go far wrong,' he added, his American accent sounding more pronounced.

Harry took the wheel with both hands and stared intently at the little black arrow as he tried to keep the ship ploughing through the waves in a straight line. When he looked back at the wake, he saw that the neat straight line Bradshaw had achieved with such apparent ease had been replaced by the sort of curves more associated with Mae West. Although Bradshaw was only away for a few minutes, Harry had rarely been more pleased to see anyone when he returned.

Bradshaw took over and the uninterrupted straight line quickly reappeared, although he only had one hand on the wheel.

'Remember, you're handling a lady,' said Bradshaw. 'You don't cling on to her, but gently caress her. If you can manage that, she'll stay on the straight and narrow. Now try again, while I plot our seven bells position on the daily chart.'

When one bell rang twenty-five minutes later and the captain appeared on the bridge to relieve Bradshaw, Harry's line in the ocean may not have been entirely straight, but at least it no longer appeared as if the ship was being steered by a drunken sailor.

◄○►

At breakfast, Harry was introduced to a man who could only have been first engineer.

Jim Patterson's ghostly complexion made him look as if he'd spent most of his life below decks, and his paunch suggested he spent the rest of the time eating. Unlike Bradshaw, he never stopped talking, and it quickly became clear to Harry that he and the skipper were old friends.

The Chinaman appeared, carrying three plates that could have been cleaner. Harry avoided the greasy bacon and fried tomatoes in favour of a piece of burnt toast and an apple.

'Why don't you spend the rest of the morning finding your way around the ship, Mr Clifton,' suggested the captain after the plates had been cleared away. 'You could even join Mr Patterson in the engine room and see how many minutes you survive down there.' Patterson burst out laughing, grabbed the last two pieces of toast and said, 'If you think these are burnt, wait until you've spent a few minutes with me.'

—◦—

Like a cat that has been left alone in a new house, Harry began stalking around the outside of the deck as he tried to become familiar with his new kingdom.

He knew the ship was 475 feet long with a 56-foot beam and its top speed was fifteen knots, but he'd had no idea there would be so many nooks and crannies that undoubtedly served some purpose which, given time, he would learn. Harry also noticed there wasn't any part of the deck the captain couldn't keep a watchful eye on from the bridge, so there was no chance of escape for an idle seaman.

Harry took the stairwell down to the middle deck. The aft section consisted of the officers' quarters, amidships was the galley, and forward was a large open area of slung hammocks. How anyone could possibly sleep in one of those was beyond him. Then he noticed half a dozen sailors, who must have come off the dog watch, swaying gently from side to side with the rhythm of the ship and sleeping contentedly.

A narrow steel stairwell led down to the lower deck, where the wooden crates that held the 144 Raleigh bicycles, a thousand cotton dresses and two tons of potatoes were all safely secured, and wouldn't be opened until after the ship docked in Cuba.

Finally, he descended a narrow ladder that led to the boiler room, and Mr Patterson's domain. He heaved open the heavy metal hatch and, like Shadrach, Meshach and Abednego, marched boldly into the fiery furnace. He stood and watched as half a dozen squat, muscle-bound men, their vests soiled with black dust, sweat pouring down their backs, shovelled coal into two gaping mouths that needed to be fed more than four meals a day.

As Captain Havens had predicted, it was only a few minutes before Harry had to stagger back into the corridor, sweating and gasping for breath. It was some time before he recovered enough to make his way back up on to the deck, where he fell on his knees and gulped in the fresh air. He could only wonder how those men could survive in such conditions and be expected to carry out three two-hour shifts a day, seven days a week.

Once Harry had recovered, he made his way back up to the bridge, armed with a hundred questions, from which star in the Plough points to the North Star, to how many nautical miles the ship could average per day, to how many tons of coal were required for ... The captain happily answered them all, without once appearing exasperated by the young fourth officer's unquenchable thirst for knowledge. In fact, Captain Havens remarked to Mr Bradshaw during Harry's break that what impressed him most about the lad was that he never asked the same question twice.

◄O►

During the next few days, Harry learnt how to check the compass against the dotted line on the chart, how to gauge wind direction by watching seagulls, and how to take the ship through the trough of a wave and still maintain a constant course. By the end of the first week, he was allowed to take over the wheel whenever an officer took a meal break. By night, the captain taught him the names of the stars, which, he pointed out, were every bit as reliable as a compass, but he confessed his knowledge was limited to the northern hemisphere as the *Devonian* had never crossed the equator in all her twenty-six years on the high seas.

After ten days at sea, the captain was almost hoping for a storm, not only to stop the endless questions but also to see if there was anything that could throw this young man off his stride. Jim Patterson had already warned him that Mr Clifton had survived for an hour in the boiler room that morning and was determined to complete a full shift before they docked in Cuba.

'At least you're spared his endless questions down there,' remarked the captain.

'This week,' responded the chief engineer.

Captain Havens wondered if a time would come when he learnt something from his fourth officer. It happened on the twelfth day of the voyage, just after Harry had completed his first two-hour shift in the boiler room.

'Did you know that Mr Patterson collects stamps, sir?' Harry asked.

'Yes, I did,' replied the captain confidently.

'And that his collection now numbers over four thousand, including an unperforated Penny Black and a South African triangular Cape of Good Hope?'

'Yes, I did,' repeated the captain.

'And that the collection is now worth more than his home in Mablethorpe?'

'It's only a cottage, damn it,' said the captain, trying to hold his own, and before Harry could ask his next question, he added, 'I'd be more interested if you could find out as much about Tom Bradshaw as you seem to have wormed out of my chief engineer. Because frankly, Harry, I know more about you after twelve days than I do about my third officer after three years, and until now, I'd never thought of Americans as being a reserved race.'

The more Harry thought about the captain's observation, the more he realized just how little he too knew about Tom, despite having spent many hours with him on the bridge. He had no idea if the man had any brothers or sisters, what his father did for a living, where his parents lived, or whether he even had a girlfriend. And only his accent gave away the fact that he was an American, because Harry didn't know which town, or even state, he hailed from.

Seven bells rang. 'Would you take over the wheel, Mr Clifton,' said the captain, 'while I join Mr Patterson and Mr Bradshaw for dinner? Don't hesitate to let me know if you spot anything,' he added as he left the bridge, 'especially if it's bigger than we are.'

'Aye aye, sir,' said Harry, delighted to be left in charge, even if it was only for forty minutes, although those forty minutes were being extended each day.

◄○►

It was when Harry asked him how many more days it would be before they reached Cuba that Captain Havens realized the precocious youth was already bored. He was beginning to feel some sympathy for the captain of HMS *Resolution*, who had no idea what he was letting himself in for.

Harry had recently been taking over the wheel after dinner so that the other officers could enjoy a few hands of gin rummy before returning to the bridge. And whenever the Chinaman took up Harry's mug of tea now, it was always piping hot, with the requested one lump of sugar.

Mr Patterson was heard to remark to the captain one evening that should Mr Clifton decide to take over the ship before they got back to Bristol, he wasn't sure who he'd side with.

'Are you thinking of inciting a mutiny, Jim?' asked Havens as he poured his chief engineer another tot of rum.

'No, but I must warn you, skipper, that the young turk has already reorganized the shifts in the boiler room. So I know whose side my lads would be on.'

'Then the least we can do,' said Havens, pouring himself a glass of rum, 'is order the flag officer to send a message to the *Resolution*, warning them what they'll be up against.'

'But we don't have a flag officer,' said Patterson.

'Then we'll have to clap the lad in irons,' said the captain.

'Good idea, skipper. It's just a shame we don't have any irons.'

'More's the pity. Remind me to pick some up as soon as we get back to Bristol.'

'But you seem to have forgotten Clifton's leaving us to join the *Resolution* the moment we dock,' Patterson said.

The captain swallowed a mouthful of rum before repeating, 'More's the pity.'

53

HARRY REPORTED TO the bridge a few minutes before seven bells to relieve Mr Bradshaw, so he could go below and join the captain for dinner.

The length of time Tom left him in charge of the bridge was becoming longer and longer with each watch, but Harry never complained, because he enjoyed the illusion that for an hour a day the ship was under his command.

He checked the arrow on the compass and steered the course that had been set by the captain. He had even been entrusted with entering their position on the chart and writing up the daily log before he came off duty.

As Harry stood alone on the bridge, a full moon, a calm sea, and a thousand miles of ocean ahead of him, his thoughts drifted back to England. He wondered what Emma was doing at that moment.

Emma was sitting in her room at Somerville College, Oxford, tuning her radio to the Home Service so she could hear Mr Neville Chamberlain address the nation.

'This is the BBC in London. You will now hear a statement from the Prime Minister.'

'I am speaking to you from the Cabinet room, Ten Downing Street. This morning the British Ambassador

*in Berlin handed the German government a final note,
stating that unless we heard from them by eleven o'clock,
that they were prepared at once to withdraw their troops
from Poland, a state of war would exist between us. I
have to tell you now, that no such undertaking has been
received, and that consequently, this country is at war
with Germany.'*

But as the *Devonian's* radio was unable to pick up
the BBC, everyone on board went about their business
as if it was a normal day.

Harry was still thinking about Emma when the first
one shot past the bow. He wasn't sure what he should
do. He was loath to disturb the captain during dinner
for fear of being reprimanded for wasting his time.
Harry was wide awake when he saw the second one, and
this time he had no doubt what it was. Harry watched
as the long, slender, shiny object slithered below the
surface towards the bow of the ship. He instinctively
swung the wheel to starboard but the ship veered to
port. It wasn't quite what he'd intended, but the mistake
gave him enough time to raise the alarm because the
object shot past the bow, missing the ship by several
yards.

This time he didn't hesitate and jammed the palm
of his hand on the klaxon, which immediately emitted
a loud blast. Moments later Mr Bradshaw appeared on
deck and began racing towards the bridge, closely followed by the captain, pulling on his jacket.

One by one, the rest of the crew came rushing out
of the bowels of the ship and headed straight for their
stations, assuming it must be an unscheduled fire drill.

'What's the problem, Mr Clifton?' asked Captain
Havens calmly as he stepped on to the bridge.

'I think I saw a torpedo, sir, but as I've never seen
one before, I can't be sure.'

'Could it have been a dolphin enjoying our leftovers?' suggested the captain.

'No, sir, it wasn't a dolphin.'

'I've never seen a torpedo either,' Havens admitted as he took over the wheel. 'Which direction was it coming from?'

'Nor'-nor'-east.'

'Mr Bradshaw,' said the captain, 'all crew to emergency stations and prepare to lower the lifeboats on my command.'

'Aye aye, sir,' said Bradshaw, who slid down the railings on to the deck and immediately began to organize the crew.

'Mr Clifton, keep your eyes peeled and tell me the moment you spot anything.'

Harry grabbed the binoculars and began a slow sweep of the ocean. At the same time, the captain bellowed down the voicepipe, 'All engines reverse, Mr Patterson, all engines reverse, and stand by for further orders.'

'Aye aye, sir,' said a startled chief engineer, who hadn't heard that order since 1918.

'Another one,' said Harry. 'Nor'-nor'-east, coming directly towards us.'

'I see it,' said the captain. He swung the wheel to the left and the torpedo missed them by only a few feet. He knew he was unlikely to pull off that trick again.

'You were right, Mr Clifton. That wasn't a dolphin,' said Havens matter-of-factly. Under his breath he added, 'We must be at war. The enemy has torpedoes, and all I've got is a hundred and forty-four Raleigh bicycles, a few sacks of potatoes and some cotton dresses.' Harry kept his eyes peeled.

The captain remained so calm that Harry felt almost

no sense of danger. 'Number four coming directly at us, sir,' he said. 'Nor'-nor'-east again.'

Havens gamely tried to manoeuvre the old lady one more time, but she didn't respond quickly enough to his unwelcome advances and the torpedo ripped into the ship's bow. A few minutes later Mr Patterson reported that a fire had broken out below the waterline and that his men were finding it impossible to douse the flames with the ship's primitive foam hoses. The captain didn't need to be told that he was facing a hopeless task.

'Mr Bradshaw, prepare to abandon ship. All crew to stand by the lifeboats and await further orders.'

'Aye aye, sir,' shouted Bradshaw from the deck.

Havens bellowed down the voicepipe. 'Mr Patterson, get yourself and your men out of there immediately, and I mean immediately, and report to the lifeboats.'

'We're on our way, skipper.'

'Another one, sir,' said Harry. 'Nor'-nor'-west, heading towards the starboard side, amidships.'

The captain swung the wheel once again, but he knew this time he would not be able to ride the punch. Seconds later, the torpedo ripped into the ship, which began to list to one side.

'Abandon ship!' shouted Havens, reaching for the tannoy. 'Abandon ship!' he repeated several times, before he turned to Harry who was still scanning the sea through his binoculars.

'Make your way to the nearest lifeboat, Mr Clifton, and sharpish. There's no point in anyone remaining on the bridge.'

'Aye aye, sir,' said Harry.

'Captain,' came a voice from the engine room, 'number four hold is jammed. I'm trapped below deck along with five of my men.'

'We're on our way, Mr Patterson. We'll have you out of there in no time. Change of plan, Mr Clifton. Follow me.' The captain shot down the stairs, his feet barely touching the steps, with Harry just inches behind him.

'Mr Bradshaw,' shouted the captain as he dodged in and out of the oil-fed, lapping flames, which had reached the upper deck, 'get the men into the lifeboats sharpish and abandon ship.'

'Aye aye, sir,' said Bradshaw, who was clinging on to the ship's railings.

'I need an oar. And make sure you have one lifeboat on standby ready to take Mr Patterson and his men from the boiler room.'

Bradshaw grabbed an oar from one of the lifeboats and, with the help of another seaman, managed to pass it to the captain. Harry and the skipper took one end each and stumbled along the deck towards number four hold. Harry was puzzled what use an oar could possibly be against torpedoes, but this wasn't the time to be asking questions.

The captain charged on, past the Chinaman, who was on his knees, head bowed, praying to his God.

'Get yourself into the lifeboat, now, you stupid bugger!' shouted Havens. Mr Lu rose unsteadily to his feet, but didn't move. As Harry staggered past, he shoved the man in the direction of the third officer, causing Mr Lu to topple forwards and almost fall into Mr Bradshaw's arms.

When the captain reached the hatch above number four hold, he wedged the thin end of the oar into an arched hook, jumped up and threw all his weight on to the blade. Harry quickly joined him and together they managed to lever up the massive iron plate until there was a gap of about a foot.

'You pull the men out, Mr Clifton, while I try to

keep the hatch open,' said Havens, as two hands appeared through the gap.

Harry let go of the oar, fell to his knees and crawled towards the open hatch. As he grabbed the man's shoulders, a wave of water swept over him and into the hold. He yanked the seaman out and shouted at him to report straight to the lifeboats. The second man was more agile and managed to pull himself out without Harry's assistance, while the third was in such a blind panic that he shot through the hole and banged his head on the hatch lid before staggering off after his shipmates. The next two followed in quick succession and scrambled on their hands and knees in the direction of the last remaining lifeboat. Harry waited for the chief engineer to appear, but there was no sign of him. The ship lurched further over and Harry had to cling to the deck to stop himself falling head-first into the hold.

He peered down into the darkness and spotted an outstretched hand. He put his head through the hole and leaned down as far as he could without falling in, but couldn't quite reach the second officer's fingers. Mr Patterson tried several times to jump up, but with each attempt his efforts were hampered as more water poured in on top of him. Captain Havens could see what the problem was but couldn't come to their assistance, because if he let go of the oar the hatch lid would come crashing down on Harry.

Patterson, who was now up to his knees in water, shouted, 'For God's sake you two, get yourselves into the lifeboats before it's too late!'

'Not a chance,' said the captain. 'Mr Clifton, get yourself down there and push the bastard up, then you can follow.'

Harry didn't hesitate. He lowered himself backwards, feet first, into the hold, gripping on to the ledge with his fingertips. Finally he let go and dropped into the darkness. The sloshing, oily, freezing water broke his fall and once he'd regained his balance he gripped the sides, lowered himself down into the water and said, 'Climb on to my shoulders, sir, and you should be able to reach.'

The chief engineer obeyed the fourth officer, but when he stretched up, he was still a few inches short of the deck. Harry used every ounce of strength in his body to push Patterson further up until he was able to reach the rim of the hatch and cling on by the tips of his fingers. Water was now pouring into the hold, as the ship listed further and further over. Harry placed a hand under each of Mr Patterson's buttocks and began to press like a weightlifter until the chief engineer's head appeared above the deck.

'Good to see you, Jim,' grunted the captain, as he continued to place every ounce of his weight on to the oar.

'You too, Arnold,' replied the chief engineer, as he pulled himself slowly out of the hold.

It was at that moment the last torpedo hit the sinking ship. The oar snapped in half and the iron hatch lid came crashing down on the chief engineer. Like the axe of a medieval executioner, with one slice it cleanly severed his head and slammed shut. Patterson's body fell back into the hold, landing in the water next to Harry.

Harry thanked God he couldn't see Mr Patterson in the darkness that now surrounded him. At least the water had stopped flooding in, even if it meant there was now no escape.

As the *Devonian* began to keel over, Harry assumed the captain must also have been killed or he surely would have been banging on the hatch trying to find some way of getting him out. As he slumped down into the water, Harry thought how ironic it was that he should go to his grave like his father, entombed in the hollow bottom of a ship. He clung to the side of the hold in one final effort to cheat death. As he waited for the water to rise inch by inch above his shoulders, his neck, his head, myriad faces flashed before him. Strange thoughts take over when you know you only have a few moments left to live.

At least his death would solve problems for so many people he loved. Emma would be released from her pledge to forsake all others for the rest of her days. Sir Walter would no longer have to worry about the implications of his father's will. In time, Giles would inherit the family title and all his father's worldly goods. Even Hugo Barrington might survive now that it would no longer be necessary for him to prove he wasn't Harry's father. Only his dear mother . . .

Suddenly there was an almighty explosion. The *Devonian* split in two and seconds later both halves reared up like a startled horse, before the broken ship unceremoniously sank to the bottom of the ocean.

The captain of the U-boat watched through his periscope until the *Devonian* had disappeared below the waves, leaving in its wake a thousand brightly coloured cotton dresses and countless bodies bobbing up and down in the sea, surrounded by potatoes.

54

'CAN YOU TELL ME your name?' Harry looked up at the nurse but couldn't move his lips. 'Can you hear me?' she asked. Another American accent.

Harry managed a faint nod, and she smiled. He heard a door opening and although he couldn't see who had entered the sick bay, the nurse left him immediately, so it had to be someone in authority. Even if he couldn't see them, he could hear what they were saying. It made him feel like an eavesdropper.

'Good evening, Nurse Craven,' said an older man's voice.

'Good evening, Dr Wallace,' she replied.

'How are our two patients?'

'One's showing definite signs of improvement. The other's still unconscious.'

So at least two of us survived, thought Harry. He wanted to cheer but, although his lips moved, no words came out.

'And we still have no idea who they are?'

'No, but Captain Parker came in earlier to see how they were, and when I showed him what was left of their uniforms, he wasn't in much doubt they were both officers.'

Harry's heart leapt at the thought that Captain

Havens might have survived. He heard the doctor walk over to the other bed but he couldn't turn his head to see who was lying there. A few moments later, he heard, 'Poor devil, I'll be surprised if he survives the night.'

Then you obviously don't know Captain Havens, Harry wanted to tell him, because you won't kill him off that easily.

The doctor returned to Harry's bedside and began to examine him. Harry could just make out a middle-aged man with a serious, thoughtful face. Once Dr Wallace had finished his examination, he turned away and whispered to the nurse, 'I feel a lot more hopeful about this one, although the odds are still no better than fifty-fifty after what he's been through. Keep fighting, young man,' he said, turning to face Harry, though he couldn't be sure if the patient could hear him. 'We're going to do everything in our power to keep you alive.' Harry wanted to thank him, but all he could manage was another slight nod, before the doctor walked away. 'If either of them should die during the night,' he heard the doctor whisper to the nurse, 'are you familiar with the correct procedure?'

'Yes, doctor. The captain is to be informed immediately, and the body is to be taken down to the morgue.' Harry wanted to ask how many of his shipmates were already there.

'And I'd also like to be kept informed,' added Wallace, 'even if I've turned in for the night.'

'Of course, doctor. Can I ask what the captain has decided to do with those poor devils who were already dead when we pulled them out of the water?'

'He's given an order that as they were all sailors, they are to be buried at sea, at first light tomorrow morning.'

'Why so early?'

'He doesn't want the passengers to realize just how many lives were lost last night,' the doctor added as he walked away. Harry heard a door open. 'Goodnight, nurse.'

'Goodnight, doctor,' the nurse replied, and the door closed.

Nurse Craven walked back and sat down by Harry's bedside. 'I don't give a damn about the odds,' she said. 'You're going to live.'

Harry looked up at a nurse who was hidden behind her starched white uniform and white cap, but even so, he couldn't miss the burning conviction in her eyes.

◄○►

When Harry next woke, the room was in darkness apart from a glimmer of light in the far corner, probably from another room. His first thought was of Captain Havens, fighting for his life in the next bed. He prayed that he would survive and they'd be able to return to England together, when the captain would retire and Harry could sign up with any Royal Navy vessel Sir Walter could get him on.

His thoughts turned to Emma once again, and how his death would have solved so many problems for the Barrington family, that would now return to haunt them.

Harry heard the door open again and someone with an unfamiliar step walked into the sick bay. Although he couldn't see who it was, the sound of their shoes suggested two things: it was a man, and he knew where he was going. Another door opened on the far side of the room and the light became brighter.

'Hi, Kristin,' said a man's voice.

'Hello, Richard,' came back the nurse's reply. 'You're late,' she said, teasing, not angry.

'Sorry, honey. All the officers had to remain on the

bridge until the search for survivors was finally abandoned.'

The door closed, and the light softened once more. Harry had no way of knowing how much time had passed before the door opened again – half an hour, an hour perhaps – and he heard their voices.

'Your tie's not straight,' said the nurse.

'That won't do,' the man replied. 'Someone might figure out what we've been up to.' She laughed as he began walking towards the door. Suddenly he stopped. 'Who are these two?'

'Mr A and Mr B. The only survivors from last night's rescue operation.'

I'm Mr C, Harry wanted to tell her as they walked towards his bed. Harry closed his eyes; he didn't want them to think he'd been listening to their conversation. She took his pulse.

'I think Mr B is getting stronger by the hour. You know, I can't bear the thought of not saving at least one of them.' She left Harry and walked over to the other bed.

Harry opened his eyes and turned his head slightly to see a tall young man in a smart white dress uniform with gold epaulettes. Without warning, Nurse Craven began to sob. The young man placed an arm gently around her shoulder and tried to comfort her. No, no, Harry wanted to shout, Captain Havens can't die. We're going back to England together.

'What's the procedure in these circumstances?' asked the young officer, sounding rather formal.

'I have to inform the captain immediately, and then wake Dr Wallace. Once all the papers have been signed and clearance has been authorized, the body will be taken down to the morgue and prepared for tomorrow's burial service.'

No, no, no, Harry shouted, but neither of them heard him.

'I pray to whatever God,' continued the nurse, 'that America doesn't become involved in this war.'

'That's never going to happen, honey,' said the young officer. 'Roosevelt's far too canny to get himself involved in another European war.'

'That's what the politicians said last time,' Kristin reminded him.

'Hey, what's brought this on?' He sounded concerned.

'Mr A was about the same age as you,' she said. 'Perhaps he also had a fiancée back home.'

Harry realized that it wasn't Captain Havens in the next bed, but Tom Bradshaw. That was when he made the decision.

<o>

When Harry woke again, he could hear voices coming from the next room. Moments later, Dr Wallace and Nurse Craven walked into the sick bay.

'It must have been heart-wrenching,' said the nurse.

'It wasn't at all pleasant,' admitted the doctor. 'Somehow it was made worse because they all went to their graves nameless, although I had to agree with the captain, that's the way a sailor would have wanted to be buried.'

'Any news from the other ship?' asked the nurse.

'Yes, they've done a little better than us. Eleven dead, but three survivors: a Chinaman and two Englishmen.'

Harry wondered if it was possible that one of the Englishmen might be Captain Havens.

The doctor bent down and unbuttoned Harry's pyjama top. He placed a cold stethoscope on several parts of his chest and listened carefully. Then the nurse placed a thermometer in Harry's mouth.

'His temperature is well down, doctor,' said the nurse after she had checked the vein of mercury.

'Excellent. You might try giving him some thin soup.'

'Yes, of course. Will you need my help with any of the passengers?'

'No, thank you, nurse, your most important job is to make sure this one survives. I'll see you in a couple of hours.'

Once the door had closed, the nurse returned to Harry's bedside. She sat down and smiled. 'Can you see me?' she asked. Harry nodded. 'Can you tell me your name?'

'Tom Bradshaw,' he replied.

55

'Tom,' said Dr Wallace once he'd completed his examination of Harry, 'I wonder if you can tell me the name of your fellow officer who died last night. I'd like to write to his mother, or his wife if he had one.'

'His name was Harry Clifton,' said Harry, his voice barely audible. 'He wasn't married, but I know his mother quite well. I'd planned to write to her myself.'

'That's good of you,' said Wallace, 'but I'd still like to send her a letter. Do you have her address?'

'Yes, I do,' said Harry. 'But it might be kinder if she heard from me first, and not from a complete stranger,' he suggested.

'If you think so,' said Wallace, not sounding at all sure.

'Yes, I do,' said Harry, a little more firmly this time. 'You can always post my letter when the *Kansas Star* returns to Bristol. That's assuming the captain is still planning to sail back to England, now we're at war with Germany.'

'*We* are not at war with Germany,' said Wallace.

'No, of course we're not,' said Harry, quickly correcting himself. 'And let's hope it never comes to that.'

'Agreed,' said Wallace, 'but that won't stop the *Kansas Star* making the return journey. There are still hundreds of Americans stranded in England, with no other way of getting home.'

'Isn't that a bit of a risk?' asked Harry. 'Especially considering what we've just been through.'

'No, I don't think so,' said Wallace. 'The last thing the Germans will want to do is sink an American passenger ship, which would be sure to drag us into the conflict. I suggest you get some sleep, Tom, because I'm hoping that tomorrow the nurse will be able to take you for a turn around the deck. Only one lap to begin with,' he emphasized.

Harry closed his eyes but made no attempt to sleep as he began to think about the decision he'd made, and how many lives it would affect. By taking Tom Bradshaw's identity, he had allowed himself a little breathing space to consider his future. Once they learnt that Harry Clifton had been killed at sea, Sir Walter and the rest of the Barrington family would be released from any obligations they might have felt bound by, and Emma would be free to begin a new life. A decision he felt Old Jack would have approved of, although the full implications hadn't yet sunk in.

However, the resurrection of Tom Bradshaw would undoubtedly create its own problems, and he would have to remain constantly on his guard. It didn't help that he knew almost nothing about Bradshaw, so that whenever Nurse Craven asked him about his past, he either had to make something up or change the subject.

Bradshaw had proved very adept at deflecting any questions he didn't wish to answer, and had clearly been a loner. He hadn't set foot in his own country for at least three years, possibly more, so his family would have no way of knowing of his imminent return. As soon as the *Kansas Star* arrived in New York, Harry planned to sail back to England on the first available ship.

His greatest dilemma was how to prevent his mother from being put through any unnecessary suffering by thinking she'd lost her only son. Dr Wallace had gone some way to solving that particular problem when he promised to post a letter to Maisie the moment he arrived back in England. But Harry still had to write that letter.

He had spent hours going over the text in his mind, so that by the time he'd recovered enough to commit his thoughts to paper, he almost knew the script by heart.

New York,
September 8th, 1939

My dearest mother,

I have done everything in my power to make sure you receive this letter before anyone can tell you I was killed at sea.

As the date on this letter shows, I did not die when the Devonian *was sunk on September 4th. In fact, I was plucked out of the sea by an American ship and am very much alive. However, an opportunity arose for me to assume another man's identity, and I did so, in the hope it would release both you and the Barrington family from the many problems I seem to have unwittingly caused over the years.*

It is important that you realize my love for Emma has in no way diminished; far from it. But I do not feel I have the right to expect her to spend the rest of her life clinging on to the vain hope that at some time in the future I might be able to prove that Arthur Clifton and not Hugo Barrington was

*my father. This way, she can at least consider a
future with someone else. I envy that man.*

*I plan to return to England in the near future.
Should you receive any communication from a Tom
Bradshaw, it will be from me.*

*I will be in touch with you the moment I set foot
in England, but in the meantime, I must beg you to
keep my secret as steadfastly as you kept your own
for so many years.*

Your loving son,

Harry

He read the letter several times before placing it in
an envelope marked 'Strictly private and confidential'.
He addressed it to Mrs Arthur Clifton, 27 Still House
Lane, Bristol.

The following morning, he handed the letter over to
Dr Wallace.

◄o►

'Do you think you're ready to try a short walk around
the deck?' asked Kristin.

'Sure am,' Harry replied, trying out one of the
expressions he'd heard her boyfriend use, although he
still found it unnatural to add the word 'honey'.

During those long hours he'd spent in bed, Harry
had listened carefully to Dr Wallace, and whenever he
was alone, he tried to imitate his accent, which he'd
heard Kristin describe to Richard as east coast. Harry
was thankful for the hours he'd spent with Dr Paget
learning voice skills that he'd assumed would only be of
use on stage. He was on stage. However, he still had the
problem of how to deal with Kristin's innocent curiosity
about his family background and upbringing.

He was assisted by a novel by Horatio Alger and another by Thornton Wilder, the only two books that had been left behind in the sick bay. From these he was able to conjure up a fictional family who hailed from Bridgeport, Connecticut. They consisted of a father who was a small-town bank manager with Connecticut Trust and Savings, a mother who was a dutiful home-maker and had once come second in the town's annual beauty pageant, and an older sister, Sally, who was happily married to Jake, who ran the local hardware store. He smiled to himself when he recalled Dr Paget's remark that, with his imagination, he was more likely to end up a writer than an actor.

Harry placed his feet tentatively on the floor and, with Kristin's help, pulled himself slowly up. Once he'd put on a dressing gown, he took her by the arm and made his way unsteadily towards the door, up a flight of steps and out on to the deck.

'How long is it since you've been home?' asked Kristin as they began their slow progress around the deck.

Harry always tried to stick to the little he actually knew about Bradshaw, adding a few snippets from the life of his fictitious family. 'Just over three years,' he said. 'My family never complain, because they knew I wanted to go to sea from an early age.'

'But how did you come to be serving on a British ship?'

Damn good question, thought Harry. He only wished he knew the answer. He stumbled, to give himself a little more time to come up with a convincing reply. Kristin bent down to assist him.

'I'm fine,' he said, once he'd taken Kristin's arm again. Then he began to sneeze repeatedly.

'Perhaps it's time to take you back to the ward,' suggested Kristin. 'We can't afford to have you catching a cold. We can always try again tomorrow.'

'Whatever you say,' said Harry, relieved she didn't ask any more questions.

After she'd tucked him up like a mother putting a young child to bed, he quickly fell into a deep sleep.

—◁◦▷—

Harry managed eleven laps of the deck the day before the *Kansas Star* sailed into New York Harbour. Although he couldn't admit it to anyone, he was quite excited about the prospect of seeing America for the first time.

'Will you be going straight back to Bridgeport once we've docked?' asked Kristin during his final lap. 'Or are you planning to stay in New York?'

'Haven't given it a lot of thought,' said Harry, who had in fact given it a great deal of thought. 'I suppose it will depend on what time we dock,' he added, as he tried to anticipate her next question.

'It's just that, if you'd like to spend the night at Richard's apartment on the East-side, that would be swell.'

'Oh, I wouldn't want to put him to any trouble.'

Kristin laughed. 'You know, Tom, there are times when you sound more like an Englishman than an American.'

'I guess after all those years serving on British ships you're bound to eventually get corrupted by the limeys.'

'Is that also the reason you felt unable to share your problem with us?' Harry came to a sudden halt: a stumble or a sneeze wasn't going to rescue him this time. 'If you'd been just a little more frank in the first place, we'd have been happy to sort out the problem.

But, given the circumstances, we had no choice but to inform Captain Parker and leave him to decide what should be done.'

Harry collapsed into the nearest deckchair, but as Kristin made no attempt to come to his rescue, he knew he was beaten. 'It's far more complicated than you realize,' he began. 'But I can explain why I didn't want to involve anyone else.'

'No need to,' said Kristin. 'The captain's already come to our rescue. But he did want to ask how you intended to deal with the bigger problem.'

Harry bowed his head. 'I'm willing to answer any questions the captain might have,' he said, feeling almost a sense of relief that he'd been found out.

'Like the rest of us, he wanted to know how you're going to get off the ship when you don't have any clothes, or a dime to your name?'

Harry smiled. 'I figured New Yorkers might consider a *Kansas Star* dressing gown to be pretty nifty.'

'Frankly, not too many New Yorkers would notice even if you did walk down Fifth Avenue in a robe,' said Kristin. 'And the ones that did would probably think it was the latest fashion. But just in case they don't, Richard's come up with a couple of white shirts and a sports jacket. Pity he's so much taller than you, otherwise he'd have been able to supply a pair of pants as well. Dr Wallace can spare a pair of brown wingtips, a pair of socks and a tie. That still leaves us with the problem of the pants, but the captain has a pair of Bermuda shorts that no longer fit him.' Harry burst out laughing. 'We hope you won't be offended, Tom, but we also held a little collection among the crew,' she added, passing him a thick envelope. 'I think you'll find there's more than enough to get you to Connecticut.'

'How do I begin to thank you?' said Harry.

'No need to, Tom. We're all so pleased you survived. I only wish we could have saved your friend Harry Clifton as well. Still, you'll be glad to hear that Captain Parker has instructed Dr Wallace to deliver your letter to his mother personally.'

56

HARRY WAS AMONG the first on deck that morning, some two hours before the *Kansas Star* was due to sail into New York Harbour. It was another forty minutes before the sun joined him, by which time he'd worked out exactly how he was going to spend his first day in America.

He had already said farewell to Dr Wallace, after trying, inadequately, to thank him for all he'd done. Wallace assured him that he would post his letter to Mrs Clifton just as soon as he arrived in Bristol, and had reluctantly accepted that it might not be wise to visit her, after Harry had hinted that she was of a nervous disposition.

Harry was touched when Captain Parker called into the sick bay to deliver a pair of Bermuda shorts and wish him luck. After he had returned to the bridge, Kristin said firmly, 'It's time for you to go to bed, Tom. You'll need all your strength if you're going to travel to Connecticut tomorrow.' Tom Bradshaw would have liked to spend a day or two with Richard and Kristin in Manhattan, but Harry Clifton couldn't afford to waste any time now that Britain had declared war on Germany.

'When you wake up in the morning,' continued Kristin, 'try to get up on to the passenger deck before first light, then you can watch the sun rising as we sail into New York. I know you'll have seen it many times before, Tom, but it never fails to excite me.'

'Me too,' said Harry.

'And once we've docked,' continued Kristin, 'why don't you wait for Richard and me to come off duty and then we can disembark together?'

◄o►

Dressed in Richard's sports jacket and shirt, a little too large, the captain's Bermuda shorts, a little too long, and the doctor's shoes and socks, a little too tight, Harry couldn't wait to go ashore.

The ship's purser had telegraphed ahead to advise the New York Immigration Department that they had an extra passenger on board, an American citizen called Tom Bradshaw. The NYID had telegraphed back to say that Mr Bradshaw should make himself known to one of the immigration officials and they would take it from there.

Once Richard had dropped him off at Grand Central, Harry planned to hang around in the station for a little while before heading back to the docks, where he intended to report straight to the union office and find out which ships were due to sail for England. It didn't matter which port they were heading for, as long as it wasn't Bristol.

Once he had identified a suitable vessel, he would sign up for any job on offer. He didn't care if he worked on the bridge or in the boiler room, scrubbed the decks or peeled potatoes, just as long as he got back to England. If there turned out to be no jobs available, he would book the cheapest passage home. He'd already checked the contents of the bulky white envelope Kristin had given him and there was more than enough to pay

445

for a berth that couldn't be smaller than the broom cupboard he'd slept in on the *Devonian*.

It saddened Harry that when he returned to England he wouldn't be able to contact any of his old friends, and he'd have to be cautious even when he got in touch with his mother. But the moment he stepped ashore, his only purpose would be to join one of His Majesty's war ships and enlist in the fight against the King's enemies, even though he knew that whenever that ship returned to port he would have to remain on board, like a criminal on the run.

Harry's thoughts were interrupted by a lady. He gazed in admiration when he first saw the Statue of Liberty looming up in front of him through the early-morning mist. He had seen photographs of the iconic landmark but they had not given a true sense of her size as she towered above the *Kansas Star*, welcoming visitors, immigrants and her fellow countrymen to the United States.

As the ship continued on its way towards the harbour, Harry leant over the railings and looked towards Manhattan, disappointed that the skyscrapers didn't appear to be any taller than some of the buildings he remembered in Bristol. But then, as each minute passed, they grew and grew until they appeared to soar up into the heavens and he had to shade his eyes from the sun as he stared up at them.

A New York Port Authority tug boat came out to join them and guided the *Kansas Star* safely to its berth on number seven dock. When Harry saw the cheering crowds, he began to feel apprehensive for the first time, even though the young man who was sailing into New York that morning was far older than the fourth officer who'd left Bristol only three weeks earlier.

'Smile, Tom.'

Harry turned to see Richard looking down into a Kodak Brownie Box camera. He was peering at an upside-down image of Tom, with the Manhattan skyline as a backdrop.

'You'll be one passenger I sure won't forget in a hurry,' said Kristin, as she walked across to join him so that Richard could take a second photograph of them together. She had exchanged her nurse's uniform for a smart polka-dot dress, white belt and white shoes.

'Nor me you,' said Harry, hoping that neither of them could sense how nervous he was.

'Time for us to go ashore,' said Richard, closing the shutter of his camera.

The three of them took the wide staircase down to the lower deck, where several passengers were already streaming off the ship to be reunited with relieved relatives and anxious friends. As they made their way down the gangway, Harry's spirits were lifted by how many of the ship's passengers and crew wanted to shake him by the hand and wish him luck.

Once they'd stepped on to the dockside, Harry, Richard and Kristin headed towards immigration, where they joined one of four long queues. Harry's eyes darted about in every direction, and he wanted to ask so many questions, but any one of them would have revealed that this was the first time he'd set foot in America.

The first thing that struck him was the patchwork quilt of different colours that made up the American people. He'd only ever seen one black man in Bristol, and remembered stopping to stare at him. Old Jack had told him it was both rude and inconsiderate, adding, 'How would you feel if everyone stopped to stare at you just because you were white?' But it was the noise, the bustle and the sheer pace of everything around him that most caught Harry's imagination and made Bristol seem as if it were languishing in a bygone age.

He was already beginning to wish that he'd accepted Richard's offer to stay with him overnight and perhaps spend a few days in a city he was finding so exciting even before he'd left the dockside.

'Why don't I go through first?' said Richard, as they reached the head of the queue. 'Then I can pick up my car and meet you both outside the terminal.'

'Good idea,' said Kristin.

'Next!' shouted an immigration officer.

Richard walked up to the desk and handed over his passport to the official, who glanced briefly at the photo before stamping it. 'Welcome home, Lieutenant Tibbet.'

'Next!'

Harry stepped forward, uncomfortably aware that he had no passport, no identification and someone else's name.

'My name's Tom Bradshaw,' he said with a confidence he didn't feel. 'I think the purser of the SS *Kansas Star* telegraphed ahead to warn that I would be coming ashore.'

The immigration officer looked closely at Harry, then picked up a sheet of paper and began to study a long list of names. Finally he put a tick by one before turning round and nodding. For the first time, Harry noticed two men standing on the other side of the barrier, wearing identical grey suits and grey hats. One of them gave him a smile.

The immigration officer stamped a piece of paper and handed it to Harry. 'Welcome back, Mr Bradshaw. It's been a long time.'

'Sure has,' said Harry.

'Next!'

'I'll wait for you,' said Harry as Kristin made her way to the desk.

'I'll only be a moment,' she promised.

Harry passed through the barrier and entered the United States of America for the first time.

The two men in grey suits stepped forward. One of them said, 'Good morning, sir. Are you Mr Thomas Bradshaw?'

'That's me,' said Harry.

The words were hardly out of his mouth before the other man grabbed him and pinned his arms behind his back, while the first man handcuffed him. It all happened so quickly that Harry didn't even have time to protest.

He remained outwardly calm, as he had already considered the possibility that someone might work out that he wasn't Tom Bradshaw, but in fact an Englishman called Harry Clifton. Even so, he had assumed that the worst they could do was serve him with a deportation order and have him shipped back to Britain. And as that was exactly what he'd planned to do anyway, he didn't put up a fight.

Harry spotted two cars waiting by the sidewalk. The first was a black police car, with its back door being held open by another unsmiling man in a grey suit. The second was a red sports car, with Richard sitting on the bonnet, smiling.

The moment Richard saw that Tom had been hand-cuffed and was being led away, he leapt up and began to run towards him. At the same time, one of the police officers began to read Mr Bradshaw his rights, while the other continued to grip Harry firmly by the elbow.

'What the hell do you think you're doing?' demanded Richard, the moment he'd caught up with them.

Neither officer made any attempt to answer his question, as they marched Tom towards the waiting car.

Richard matched them stride for stride, and was amazed by how calm Tom appeared to be, almost as if he wasn't surprised to have been arrested. Despite this, he was determined to assist his friend, even though the two officers continued to ignore him. Just as they reached the police car, Richard leapt in front of the two detectives and blocked their path.

'What are you charging Mr Bradshaw with?' he said firmly.

The senior detective came to a halt, looked Richard in the eye, and said, 'First degree murder.'

The story continues in

THE SINS OF THE FATHER

VOLUME TWO
OF THE CLIFTON CHRONICLES

Engrossing and memorable, *The Sins of the Father* takes us to New York in 1939 where our hero Harry Clifton is in desperate need of help.

Only days before Britain declares war on Germany, Harry joins the Merchant Navy, unable to face long-held family secrets and the fact he will never be able to marry his true love Emma Barrington. But when his ship is sunk mid-Atlantic, Harry takes the opportunity to assume the identity of one his deceased rescuers and begin a new life.

Landing in America, he quickly discovers he has made a mistake and without any way to prove his true identity, Harry is now chained to a past that could be far worse than the one he had hoped to escape . . .

Brimming with intrigue, Jeffrey Archer takes readers into a world they will never want to leave as the Clifton Chronicles continues its powerful journey with family loyalties stretched to their limits and fates decided.

THE COMPLETE
CLIFTON CHRONICLES